Objects as History in Twentieth-Century German Art

The publisher gratefully acknowledges the generous support of the Richard and Harriett Gold Endowment Fund in Arts and Humanities of the University of California Press Foundation.

The publisher also gratefully acknowledges the generous support of the Art History Program Fund of the School of Art and Design, The College of Liberal Arts, and the Office of the Vice Chancellor for Research and Graduate Dean, Southern Illinois University Carbondale.

Objects as History in Twentieth-Century German Art

Beckmann to Beuys

Peter Chametzky

University of California Press Berkeley Los Angeles London

University of California Press, one of the most distinguished university presses in the United States, enriches lives around the world by advancing scholarship in the humanities, social sciences, and natural sciences. Its activities are supported by the UC Press Foundation and by philanthropic contributions from individuals and institutions. For more information, visit www.ucpress.edu.

University of California Press
Berkeley and Los Angeles, California

University of California Press, Ltd.
London, England

Library of Congress Cataloging-in-Publication Data

Chametzky, Peter.
Objects as history in twentieth-century German art : Beckmann to Beuys / Peter Chametzky.
p. cm.
Includes bibliographical references and index.
ISBN 978-0-520-26042-9 (cloth : alk. paper)
1. Art and history—Germany. 2. Art, German—20th century. I. Title.
N72.H58C47 2010
709.430904—dc22 2010024453

Manufactured in the United States of America

19 18 17 16 15 14 13 12 11 10
10 9 8 7 6 5 4 3 2 1
The paper used in this publication meets the minimum requirements of ANSI/NISO Z39.48-1992 (R 1997) (*Permanence of Paper*).

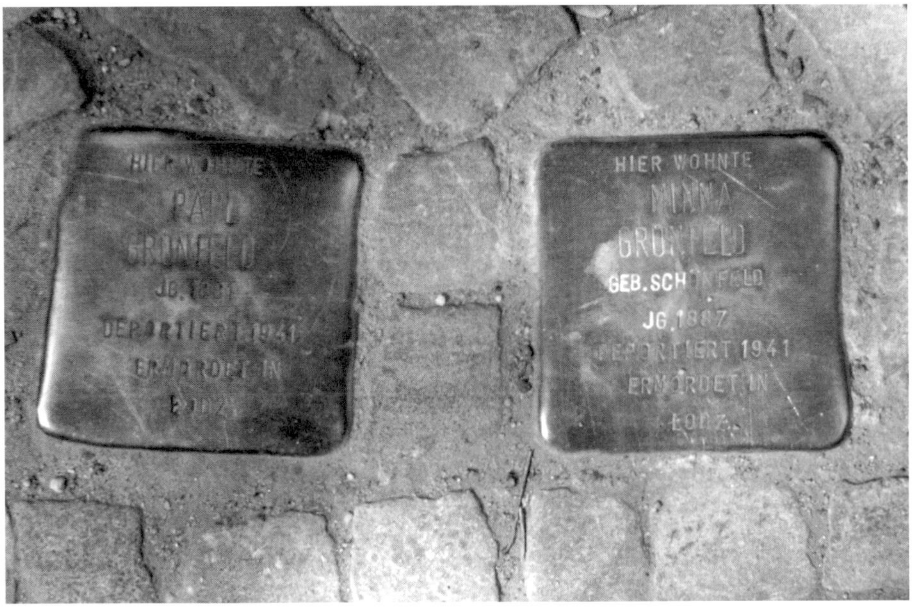

The same old plod of sluggish blood,
and self-indulgences, and dreams of gulls.
A small, echt deutsch disease on cobblestone
and sidewalk brick with moss

—FROM ANNE HALLEY, "HOMEOPATHIC"

ABOVE: Gunter Demnig, *Stolpersteine* (Stumbling blocks) for Minna and Paul Grünfeld, Landauer Straße 3, Berlin, 2005. Photo: Author.

For my family

Contents

Acknowledgments

My work on this book's subject matter extends back two decades and more, to my days as a graduate student at the City Uiversity of New York Graduate Center and my dissertation on Willi Baumeister. Rose-Carol Washton Long was a model thesis advisor and mentor then, and she has been a most supportive colleague and friend since. That dissertation also benefited from the perspicacious readings of Rosemarie Bletter, Rosalind Krauss, and Linda Nochlin.

I was fortunate to be hired by the School of Art and Design at Southern Illinois University in 1998, for which I particularly thank the search committee chair, Dennis Taylor, and Robert Paulson, then director of the school. My research was supported from 2000 to 2002 by a Southern Illinois University Carbondale (SIUC) ORDA special research grant and a summer research grant, enabling me to hire two energetic and capable graduate research assistants, Kristi Weaver and Katy Patterson. The art history endowment of the School of Art and Design (SoAD)—for which I thank our anonymous lead donor—has been of tremendous help in subventing research expenses. I completed a first draft of this book during a year's sabbatical in Berlin in 2005–6, for which I thank my former dean, Shirley Clay Scott, and Harris Deller, former SoAD director. In Berlin my research was facilitated by a grant from the German Academic Exchange Service. Affiliation with the Institute of Art History of the Free University (Freie Universität, FU) and access to its library was critical, for which I thank Thomas Gaehtgens and Martin Schieder. The library's director, Wolfgang Beyrodt, and his staff were extremely accommodating, as were the staffs of the Kunstbibliothek, the Staatsbibliothek, and the FU's main library. Christoph Zuschlag and Andreas Hüneke of the Forschungsstelle Entartete Kunst at the FU provided fruitful collaboration. Other Berliners to whom I owe thanks include Ralf Burmeister and Wolfgang Erler of the Hannah-Höch-Archiv; Hannelore John, Antje Keller-Hanack, Michael Kresja, Anita Metelka, and Anke Matelowski of the archives of the Akademie der Künste; Annette Groschke of the Deutsche Kinemathek, Film Archive; Monika Flacke, Deutsches Historisches Museum; and, at the Staatliche Museen, Gerda Berger, Herr Beisert, Jörn Grabowski, and especially Angela Schneider, who arranged for my private study of Höch's *Cut with the*

Kitchen Knife Dada and generously joined me in study and discussion of it. Thanks, too, to Helena Pereña, Max Beckmann Archiv, Munich; Timothy Shipe, International Dada Archive, University of Iowa; Randall Bytwerk, German Propaganda Archive; Dietmar Elger, Gerhard Richter Archive; Robert Rameil, Geschichtsverein Meerbusch; Stephan Arntz, Ron Mannheim, Barbara Strieder, Joseph Beuys Museum and Archive, Schloss Moyland; Klaus Pohl, Hessisches Landesmuseum; Carmen Prokopiak, Friedrich Wilhelm Murnau Stiftung; and Volker Schubert, Sächsisches Staatsarchiv. Felicitas Baumeister and the late Krista Gutbrod Baumeister have long provided researchers open access to a beautifully organized and accessible archive of their father's work, from which I have benefited tremendously. Hadwig Goez of the Willi Baumeister Archiv at the Kunstmuseum Stuttgart ably extends their legacy of most congenial professionalism.

Colleagues in the School of Art and Design's art history program since 1998, including Anna Brzyski, Marian Bleecke, Carlee Bradbury, Sandra Charlson, John Decker, Elina Gertsman, Jo Nast, Linda Phipps, Angela Reinoehl, Stacey Sloboda, and especially my colleague for the entire period, Carma Gorman, have been a pleasure to work with, as have been many other colleagues, including Najjar Abdul-Musawwir, Joel Feldman, Ed Shay, and Kay Pick Zivkovich. Staff at the school have been tremendously helpful, especially Connie Christy, LouAnn Elwell, Don Hausman, Mike Harrell, and Eric Peterson—my guru in things digital. My thanks also to Megan Lotts, Julie Mosbo, Tammy Winter, and especially Greg Wendt of SIUC's Morris Library. Earlier I mentioned my former director, Harris Deller, but I mention him here again for all his support over the years, as well as my current dean, Alan Vaux, and vice chancellor John Koropchak.

Special thanks go to Maria Makela and Maud Lavin for reading and commenting on my chapters on Berlin Dada, and to Maria for her skillful editing of an earlier version of my Beckmann chapter for the anthology she coedited with Rose-Carol Washton Long, *Of 'Truths Impossible to Put In Words': Max Beckmann Contextualized* (2009). Other colleagues and friends I thank for their support, advice, shelter, and sustenance include Mathew Affron, Kerstin Barndt, Timothy Benson, Miriam Bratu Hansen, Martha Buskirk, Barbara Buenger, Jay Clarke, Ina Conzen, Harry Cooper, Dennis Crockett, Stephanie D'Alessandro, Jula Dech, Peter Dreher, James van Dyck, Sabine Eckmann, David Ehrenpreis, Janet Fuller, Françoise Forster-Hahn, Christian Fuhrmeister, Ulrike Gauss, Curt Germundsen, Sander Gilman, Cordula Grewe, Jochen Gutbrod, Kai Gutschow, Mona Hadler, Amy Hamlin, Ulla Haselstein, Reinhold Heller, Klaus Herding, Robert Hobbs, Kathrin Hoffmann-Curtius, Keith Holz, Paul Jaskot, Ralph Jentsch, David Johnson, Ursula Junk, Kathy Kageff, Abdallah Kahil, Charlotte Klonk, Karen Koehler, Lutz Koepnick, Yvonne Korshak, Juliet Koss, Jessica Levin Martinez, Therese Lichtenstein, Sarah Lowe, Christopher Lyon, Gregory Maertz, Nancy Malloy, Steven Mansbach, Barbara McCloskey, Jordana Mendelson, Claudia Mesch, Johannes von Moltke, Marsha Morton, Eric Mumford, Peter Nisbet, Ulrike Ottinger, Sylvia Parker, Jay Prosser, Beatrice Rehl, Dorothy Rowe, Bettina Schaske, Jochen Schindler, Rebecca Schneider, Frieder Schnock, Frederic Schwarz, Lisa Shoemaker, Sherwin Simmons, Kassy Simonds,

Joann Skrypzak, Werner Sollors, Buzz Spector, Renata Stih, Jelena Stojanovic, Despina Stratigakos, Adrian Sudhalter, Katharina Sykora, Ekwueme Michael Thelwell, James Throgmorton, Monika Wagner, Michael White, Jonathan Wiesen, Catherine Wilkins, Natasha Zaretsky, Paul and Ruth Zaslansky, and Rolf Zimmermann.

The work of gathering photographs and permissions was aided and abetted by Sylvia Bandi, Catherine Belloy, Klaus Bilger, Antje Birthälmer, Cécile Brunner, Yvonne Crevier, Bodo von Dewitz, Maurice Dorren, Claudia Drautzburg, Stephan Erfurt, Gerhard Finckh, Andreas Fischer, Anna Fischer, Marina Fröhling, Christian Fuhrmeister (big thanks!), Joseph Gräf, Sabine Gruber, Philipp Gutbrod, Kirsten Hamann, Kiowa Hammons, Anne Hebebrand, Sylvia Iburg, Andreas Kaernbach, Namrata Kanchan, Margot Klütsch, Albert Knoll, Claudia Koelle, Lauri Kramer, Anna-Dorte Krause, Chris Linnane, Rose Lord, Markus Lüpertz, Aimee Marshall, Shlomo Mayer, Andrea Mihalovic-Lee, Didari Mikeladze, Heike Moritz, Evelyn Bertram Neunzig, Gabriele Prager, Kate Ralston, Courtney Richter, Laura Rosenstock, Kathi Rumlow, Elke Schneider, Tricia Smith, Inga Schube, Christian Tagger, Wolfgang Theis, Rainer Waeger, Kevin Wallace, Marc Wellmann, and Dagmar Wolff. Maggie Fleming of Artists Rights Society, New York, has been especially helpful in clearing rights for some fifty artworks. A succession of diligent and intelligent SIUC student workers have helped in many ways, among them Lisa Furby, Aleta Lanier, Lauren McKeen, Loren Malloy, Serena Perrone, Catherine Shotick, and Nancy Weichert.

My editor at University of California Press, Stephanie Fay, contracted a manuscript and skillfully guided me through the process of turning it into a book. I thank her especially for her careful and critical reading of the text, and her assistant, Eric Schmidt, for handling technical questions and procedures with aplomb. Two anonymous outside readers and one for the press's faculty committee offered support and solid suggestions for improvement. The final text benefited greatly from the expert editing of Sue Heinemann and copyediting of Juliane Brand. I thank them all for their good work, and assume sole responsibility for any errors that might remain.

My family has been a constant source of inspiration and pleasure. Thanks to my brothers, Matthew and Robert, for leading the way. The imprint of my wife, the brilliant film scholar and art historian Susan Felleman, is everywhere in this book and in my life, to its and my benefit. Our children, Benjamin and Hallie, make the work (and play!) that goes into a project such as this both more worthwhile and less *langweilig*. My in-laws, Philip Felleman and the late Joan Sharaf Felleman, have been consistently supportive. My father, Jules Chametzky, has been my role model as a scholar and a man. My mother and familial connection to the German twentieth century, Anne Halley Chametzky, who understood and expressed the power of objects much better than I ever will, did not live to see *Objects as History* itself become an object. Lines from one of her poems provide the book's epigraph, and every word I've written has been inflected by her experience and example.

INTRODUCTION Art Objects as History

In this book I study works of German art as representatives, rather than representations, of twentieth-century history. The case studies I have chosen demonstrate how artworks have both been involved in and encouraged their viewers to engage with modern and contemporary history. Some engagements have been public, some private. They have involved paintings, sculptures, photomontages, and postcards that were mailed, rediscovered later, and then publicly displayed in art museums. Not confined to a discrete historical period or artistic movement, *Objects as History* offers a synthesizing view of art's role as it lends visual and material form to processes and events, ruptures and continuities in twentieth-century German history.

Art historians have developed refined techniques to describe artistic styles and analyze how they represent ideas. In *Stilfragen* (Questions of style) of 1893 and *Spätrömische Kunstindustrie* (Late Roman art industry) of 1902, the Vienna School art historian Alois Riegl developed the concept of *Kunstwollen,* a period's "will to form," and argued that artistic styles derive neither from technical procedures nor from advances or declines in artistic skill. Artworks driven into being by a *Kunstwollen* were the appropriate expressions—indeed, the only possible ones—of the worldview of the culture that created them. More recently, in *Painting and Experience in Fifteenth-Century Italy* (1992), Michael Baxandall, in contrast to the psychosocial and metaphysical speculations of the Vienna School, has supported his concept of the "period eye" with concrete social information and analysis. For Baxandall, fifteenth-century Italian Renaissance works, regardless of their subject matter, are both products and evidence of their makers' and their audience's visual understanding of the world. Perspective, for example, was not only a pictorial convention employed to depict compellingly realistic religious narratives; it was also a means to display and train the ability to measure volumes, a crucial secular competency in a mercantile culture in which the gauging of wine barrels and grain sacks was not yet standardized.

I shall analyze how the interconnecting social, political, and personal connotations that artworks evoke—not only in their style but also by their imagery, their materiality, and, especially, their histories as objects—coalesce to produce meaning, as generated in discourse about specific artworks at particular times and in particular places. I study how the receptions of artworks have been influenced by their structures, formats, materials, and style, as well as by their status as extant, lost, overlooked, or rediscovered objects. So, in addition to reception history, with its emphasis on social context, I engage in what the German art historian and theorist Wolfgang Kemp has termed "reception aesthetics," analyzing how the artwork itself, as image and as object, influences its reception. In doing so, I also pay attention to points of contact and contrast between artworks and other, newer ways of representing history, especially cinema. In my analysis, twentieth-century artworks and artists alike become actors in a turbulent historical drama—objects in, of, and as history—in which their roles shift over time in response to their changing contexts of creation, presentation, and interpretation.

German artists of the past century often intended a social and historical role for their art. And their public, which included politicians and government officials, readily perceived that role. Germany's political systems of the twentieth century actively supported, and sometimes suppressed, art that explored contemporary history. But the media depicting, narrating, and dramatizing contemporary history—including photography, film, television, video, and digital images—reached a wider public than painting, sculpture, and other object-based art forms could. The depictions and dramatizations in new media created expectations among the viewers of art, and this in turn affected how the presence (or absence) of material art objects, and of the artists who created them and the stories told about them, encouraged and challenged spectators to confront recent history. In a culture in which historical narratives are conveyed by immaterial images, objects constitute the tangible, touchable, smellable material residue of history itself.

The art historian Hans Belting traces historical themes in German modern art and its interpretation to the constant "reinventing of ourselves as a nation."[1] German national unity dates only from 1871. Since then, Germany's borders, political system, and self-conception have changed often. The political scientist Mary Fulbrook has argued that complex and evolving social, cultural, and political constructions therefore constitute modern German national identity.[2] Artistic identity is more mutable still than national identity. Artworks, artists, and ideas have moved across even fixed and fortified political borders.[3] Modern and postmodern art have been primarily international phenomena, undermining any notion that an essentially German variety of it might express German identity, or the identity of individual artists as Germans.

George Grosz, Hannah Höch, and the other Berlin Dadaists, for instance, would have been loath to define themselves as Germans, or to be defined as German artists. Even so, denials that art expresses "Germanness" must derive from a sense of what German art might be. For example, when the French critic Michel Seuphor claimed in 1931 that Willi Baumeister's work of the 1920s had "no trace of the Germanic spirit" and was closer to that of Fernand Léger than to that of other German artists, he explained and justified his statement by explaining that "Léger's painting is more violent, more

Germanic than that of Baumeister, which is more nuanced, more French!"[4] Art, as Belting argues, helps to define national traditions, as well as to provide personal, often oppositional, alternatives to them.

The historical objects I study here are grounded in Germany's shifting modern and postmodern political and artistic terrain, whether they were created there, existed there, or fled or disappeared. This has governed their interpretation and meaning. I argue that every artwork's meaning is contingent on where it is located and interpreted, physically and historically. In the famous closing line of his 1967 essay "Art and Objecthood" the art historian and theorist Michael Fried denied the social-historical contingency of the modernist artwork and reinvested it with a timeless, quasi-religious aura: "Presentness is grace."[5] According to this view the severing of the modern, autonomous artwork from its context isolates it and its viewer in a blissful state of purely optical apprehension and comprehension, providing a refuge from the mundane mortal world we, along with those art objects he termed "literalist" (i.e., minimalist), obdurately inhabit. Fried, writing in response to minimalist sculpture and, in disapproving of it, providing one of the best analyses of its phenomenology, insisted that modernist artworks—his example was the constructed sculptures of Anthony Caro—"defeat" the "theatricality" of minimalism's simple, inexpressive objects. Unlike the modernist artwork, minimalist objects depend for completion on the viewer's subjective vantage point and the creation of a "situation," what the minimalist Robert Morris called a "strong gestalt."[6] For Fried, though, works such as Caro's succeeded by creating utterly consistent and completely internal relations of part-to-part and part-to-whole, transcending temporally specific objecthood and achieving "continuous and entire presentness, amounting, as it were, to the perpetual creation of itself, that one experiences as a kind of *instantaneousness*."[7] A more accurate title might have been "Art *or* Objecthood," as Fried presented these as mutually exclusive material and ontological conditions.

In contrast to Fried's "presentness is grace," I argue throughout this book that presentness is *place:* the artwork, whether modern or postmodern, is always embedded in a context. Social, political, and discursive contexts—even in the museum—are either always overdetermined and shift around the artwork, or the artwork moves through them, effectively changing its meaning. This in no way compromises the work's "quality," negates its status as art, or transforms it into theater, as Fried would have it. The imagery, style, and format of an artwork, the prestige of its creator, and sometimes chance endow certain artworks with potent emblematic significance in relation to their audience and history, corresponding to what the literary theorist Stephen Greenblatt has termed an artwork's "resonance": the ability to evoke the "complex, dynamic cultural forces from which it has emerged."[8] Resonance is not intrinsic to the artwork. It occurs within the viewer, the result of a complex of interactions between the object, its context of display, and the viewer's knowledge and feelings. Artworks engender resonance through their presence as objects in the presence of the viewer: their presentness in time and place.

When Max Beckmann's first triptych, *Departure,* arrived in America, where it would stay, in 1938, it was said to be about the artist's flight from Nazi Germany, and the work itself came to represent the exile of modern art in the New World (plate 2). After Hannah Höch showed her photomontage *Cut with the Kitchen Knife Dada through Germany's Last Weimar Beer-Belly Cultural Epoch (Schnitt mit dem Küchenmesser durch die letzte Weimarer Bierbauchkulturepoche Deutschlands),* in the First International Dada Fair in Berlin in 1920, it was not seen again in public until the 1960s (plate 3 and fig. 9). Like the artist, the work survived Nazi Germany but remained unseen and unmentioned for reasons that included sexism and the artist's own reticence about showing it. Since its reemergence and purchase by Berlin's National Gallery in 1961, *Cut with the Kitchen Knife Dada* has resonated with enough viewers to become the best-known representative of Berlin Dada's critique of contemporary German society, of Höch's feminist perspective on it, and of women artists' historically marginal status in modern art.

In 1933 the new National Socialist (NS, or Nazi) government dismissed Willi Baumeister from his professorship. By 1937 his works had been removed from public collections and put on display in traveling exhibitions meant to demonstrate the "degeneracy" of modern art. In the early 1940s he responded by creating an extraordinary series of underground works critiquing Nazi art (plate 5 and figs. 39, 40, and 51). They were executed on reproductions of works by the most powerful artists of the time, including Arno Breker, whose sculptures of muscular nude males embodied—literally, figuratively, publicly—Nazi Germany's antimodernist art policies and the imaginary idealized "Aryan" warriors who would enforce its ruthless will to power (figs. 65, 70, and 71). With the fall of the Nazi state, Breker's figures largely disappeared from public view, emerging only rarely; on the occasions when they were shown, especially since the 1980s, they invariably incited debate and controversy. Baumeister's anti-Nazi doodles and collages, seen only by the artist's friends in Nazi Germany, and neglected in the postwar period, became objects of a broader public discussion only in 1989. At the end of the twentieth century and in the early twenty-first, interpretations of the transgressive appropriation and alteration of mass media images propagating Nazi aesthetics and ideology in his works correspond to contemporary critiques of the role of art in consolidating political power and enforcing gendered identities.

Since 1989 controversies over what is "German" art have focused on the status of artists active in the German Democratic Republic (GDR, or East Germany), especially that of the founders of the Leipzig School of representational painters—Werner Tübke, Bernard Heisig, and Walter Mattheuer—who rebelled against naturalistic Socialist Realism, incorporating influences from Picasso, Expressionism, Surrealism, and medievalism into their work, yet enjoyed official patronage and academic positions from the mid-1960s on. Are these artists to be accorded status as creative artists and, especially, as representatives of German art in equal measure with their West German counterparts? And what about those who fled the East to the West, such as A. R. Penck, who was forbidden from exhibiting in the East between 1970 and his defection in 1980, or the earlier émigré Georg Baselitz, who famously averred shortly after 1989 that by that date there were no "real" artists left in the East. The answers to this question would go to the core of what one perceives as particularly "German," and of what makes a "real" artist. I would argue that the way GDR artists and their works negotiated obedience and defiance, and their collective goals and individual expression, expresses a characteristic twentieth-century German artistic dialectic.

Art produced in NS Germany and in the GDR have received considerable scholarly and popular attention in recent years. I would like to address just one aspect of that attention, which I believe confirms a central thesis of this book: in the twentieth century the function of narrating history passed from painting and sculpture to other media, despite the fact that historical narrative did not vanish as a visual artistic genre, and indeed flourished especially among artists in NS Germany and in the GDR. The GDR artist Werner Tübke, for instance, was responsible for creating, between 1983 and 1987, a 14 × 123-meter mural, located in Bad Frankenhausen, depicting the sixteenth-century peasant uprisings that Friedrich Engels wrote about. The painting's spectacularly anachronistic revival of the nineteenth-century panorama format and meticulously illusionistic painting has had little influence in providing a narrative account of its putative subject. It has, instead, been called the "the high point of history painting in the GDR" for its role in serving as propaganda for that state. It was designed to affect popular conceptions of the GDR and of the GDR's origins among the German working class, rather than of sixteenth century history.[9] Whatever fascination the work still possesses today is connected not to its internal narrative but to its status as an artifact of the GDR and its history. Its creation by a team of students from the New Leipzig school of representational painters, which has since become prominent in the post-unification German and international art worlds (e.g., Neo Rauch), lends it added interest as an object of GDR art history. Tübke's earlier 1965–67 series of paintings, *Reminiscences of JD Schulze,* were inspired by the Frankfurt Auschwitz Trials of 1963–65 and reflected ambiguously on the memories and guilt of jurists from the Nazi period who resumed careers in postwar Germany. The art critic Eduard Beaucamp concludes that in the GDR these works, redolent of Otto Dix and Surrealism, initially "met with official rejection but also found admirers and defenders who saw in it a hidden critic of the GDR system."[10] First in post-NS, and now in post-GDR Germany, the most important debates about works such as Arno Breker's and Tübke's have been not about the histories narrated in them but about their status as artworks and as material representatives of their own historical periods.

The artists whose works I study in detail—Beckmann, George Grosz, Höch, Baumeister, Breker, Joseph Beuys, and, in the conclusion, Gerhard Richter—are all significant figures in German twentieth-century art, and in modern and postmodern art generally. Their dates of birth range from 1884 (Beckmann) to 1932 (Richter). All lived through the Nazi period and survived it to pursue their art in the postwar period. They, their works, and the interpretations of those works were deeply affected by the war and the reconstruction that followed. Beckmann and Grosz (born in 1893) went into exile from Nazism and became influential teachers and figures in the United States. Höch and Baumeister, both born in 1889, stayed in Germany as "inner emigrants," a term applied to artists and intellectuals who continued their work privately, without bowing to Nazi ideology. Both became more prominent after the war than they had been before, as links to the pre-Nazi avant-garde. Breker (born in 1900), active as a modernist sculptor in Paris from 1927 to 1933, had returned to Nazi Germany and risen to become the textbook example of a Nazi artist. He too was active in the postwar period, receiving many private and some public commissions. But the history to which he was linked was that of Nazism itself, including debates about the function of art and the role of artists in Nazi Germany, the fate of works created in service to that state, and the feasibility of artists such as Breker continuing "denazified" careers.

Joseph Beuys (born in 1921) flew in the German Air Force, and the story of his near-death experience when shot down in 1944 informed his work, his self-presentation, and the interpretation of both. Not single-handedly, but certainly centrally, from the later 1950s through the 1970s, Beuys reoriented German sculpture's gaze downward, away from Breker's towering stone and bronze neo-Neoclassical monuments toward everyday materials and poignantly visible processes. Beuys's work and career also assert the desire of postmodern artists for greater control over the display of their work, public image, and historical legacy. Gerhard Richter exemplifies this desire. His work has been deeply involved in and affected by German history, especially Nazism, the Cold War, and the East-West German divide, with the artist's self-conceived and constructed career providing a continuous, unifying narrative that transcends these historical fissures.

The oldest artist I study here, Max Beckmann, was also the first to die, in 1950, while walking in New York's Central Park. Baumeister died at his easel, at home in Stuttgart, in 1955; Grosz, having returned to Berlin in the late 1950s, collapsed and died after an overindulgent night out in 1959. Hannah Höch lived and worked through the 1950s, 1960s, and most of the 1970s in her garden home in Heiligensee, a Berlin suburb, and she died there, amid her flowers, in 1978. Joseph Beuys's weakened heart gave out in 1986, and Arno Breker endured until 1991. Gerhard Richter continues today as one of the world's most prominent living painters.

These artists' lives and works span the twentieth century in Germany, from the end of the Wilhelmine Empire through two World Wars, the Weimar Republic, the Nazi dictatorship, the Holocaust, the Cold War division of the country, and the unification that commenced in 1989 and led to the founding of the current Berlin Republic. In addition to these epochal events and processes I also attend to the lived existence of each artist as subject. Although I am not much concerned with biography as a motivation for particular works, I am interested in art-work—the work of making art—as a motivation for the artist's life. I am also concerned with how the works the artist created and the history they enacted have affected the narrative of the artist's life as a mission: *Departure* as the mythic overture to Max Beckmann's exile in America; Arno Breker's devotion to sculpting supposedly perfect physical specimens interpreted as the artist's living "a life for the beautiful"; Gerhard Richter's continuing production in various genres and styles as the expression of his craftsman-like "daily practice of painting." Like the artworks I study, these artists serve as telling representatives of twentieth-century history.

1 *Titanic* Sinks, *Departure* Arrives

Max Beckmann's Melodramatic Role in the Fall of History Painting and Rise of the Historical Object

Paintings as Objects and Actors

At the end of his 1938 speech "On My Painting," Max Beckmann recounts a waking dream in which he encountered Henri Rousseau and William Blake. Blake waved to Beckmann and greeted him "like a super-terrestrial patriarch. 'Have confidence in objects,' he said. 'Do not let yourself be intimidated by the horror of the world.' "[1] Beckmann's spectral Blake provided him with a mystical credo for trust not only in objective (or representational) painting but also in paintings themselves as objects embodying the artist's defiance of "the horror of the world."

In this chapter I shall test Beckmann's trust by analyzing the reception histories of his paintings *The Sinking of the Titanic* (1912–13, plate 1) and *Departure* (1932–33, plate 2). *Titanic* is a large canvas depicting a contemporary historical subject, a specific and unique event; *Departure* is an allegorical triptych that came to be interpreted as itself becoming a part of contemporary history, an object that embodied the condition of exile. Both paintings had to contend with the startlingly accelerated pace of contemporary history's visual representation by other media. By the summer of 1912, as Beckmann began working in his Berlin studio on his depiction of the April 1912 sinking of the *Titanic,* the *second* dramatic silent film turning the disaster into a moving, melodramatic narrative, Mime Misu's *In Nacht und Eis* (In night and ice; fig. 1), had already been shot and edited in Berlin, where it premiered in August. In a context saturated with photography and, increasingly, with motion pictures that could more effectively convey narrative content, Beckmann's *Titanic* failed to convince its immediate audience.

By 1913, when Beckmann's *Titanic* was first shown to the Berlin public, this painterly tour de force already seemed outdated. Even if it did not convince its contemporary audience, Beckmann's Realist approach rewards analysis today. His bravura handling of paint to convey nature's daunting power is impressive. Muscular men battle powerful waves rendered with equally muscular brushstrokes. Women and children huddle together in open boats. Yet despite such active elements, the image as a whole lacks drama. Beckmann's *Titanic* serves neither as a compelling representation nor as a tell-

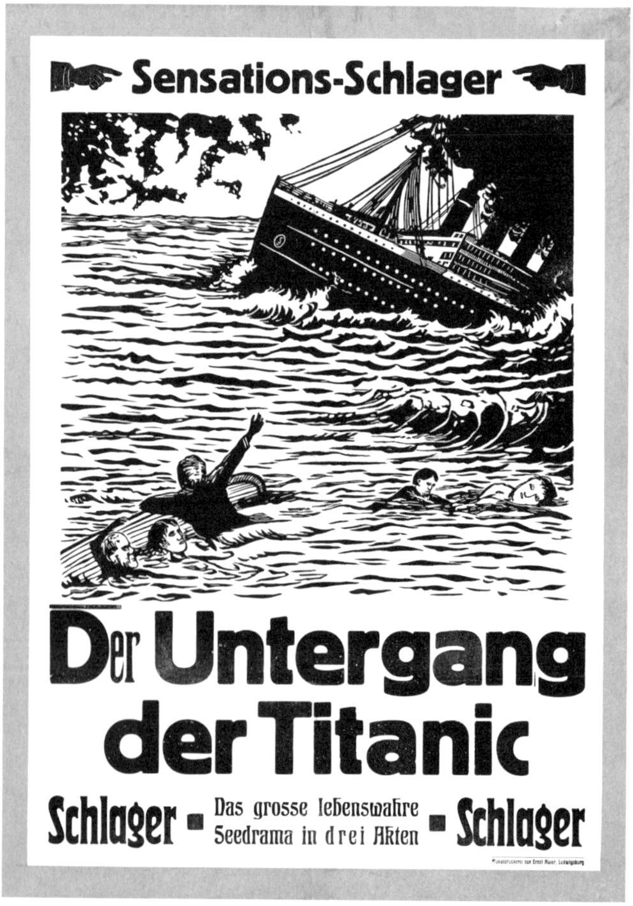

FIGURE 1. Poster advertising Mime Misu, *In Nacht und Eis* (referred to as *Der Untergang der Titanic*), 1912. Collection Deutsche Kinemathek, Berlin. Photo: Deutsche Kinemathek, Berlin.

ing representative of its subject matter. *Titanic*'s failure as history painting, especially in comparison with *Departure*'s later success, suggests certain ways that paintings and other traditional artworks have successfully engaged and thematized history in the modern and postmodern worlds. Whereas the function of depicting and dramatizing contemporary history—what Beckmann referred to as "the horror of the world"—has passed to other media, art objects can become focal points for the public perception of historical events, processes, or ideas. They do so most effectively, and affectively, I believe, when they are seen physically or metaphorically to embody and enact some aspect of that history, as was the case with *Departure*. *Titanic*'s failure demonstrates that modern artworks require more than technical proficiency and imposing scale to bring history to life.

Interpreters often connect the object to its creator's life and see it as an emanation of that individual's subjectivity as it has been shaped by history; the art object is therefore interpreted as a remnant of the artist's attempt to negotiate his or her times. No such connection could be found between Beckmann the Realist "reporter," heroic only in his painterly efforts, and his painting *Titanic*. In *Departure*, object and artist became historical surrogates, akin to characters in a dramatic, historical film. Characters such as those of *In Nacht und Eis* personalize the experience of cataclysmic historical events, encouraging spectators to identify with their melodramatic stories and engage with history through them. Beckmann himself seems to have liked this tendency and to have wanted to be such a character. He was an avid film fan and is reported to have joked, after being impressed by William Dieterle's 1939 version of *The Hunchback of Notre Dame*, that he'd like Charles Laughton to star in "The Beckmann Film."[2]

In Beckmann's oeuvre the confluence of object, history, and imagery, and the conception of these as expressing the artist's personal experience, occurred with the arrival of *Departure* in New York in 1938 and its permanent installation at the Museum of Modern Art in 1942. After leaving Germany in 1937, on the day after the opening in Munich of the Nazi's "Degenerate Art" exhibition, in which his works were well represented, Beckmann lived in exile, mainly in Amsterdam and briefly in 1938–39 in Paris, before accepting a position as Philip Guston's replacement at Washington University in St. Louis in 1947–48 while Guston was on leave. In St. Louis, Perry Rathbone, the director of the City Museum of Art, and the department store magnate Morton May supported his work and collected it. Thanks to them, the Saint Louis Art Museum has the finest Beckmann collection in America—probably the finest in the world. The collection includes *Titanic*, which generally hangs outside the main Beckmann gallery, presented as a singular work serving as a prelude to the artist's more mature achievements, from the museum's Christian-themed and expressionistically styled *Christ and the Woman Taken in Adultery* (1917) to the kinkily erotic, monumental masked figure of Columbine in *Carnival Mask, Green, Violet and Pink* (1950).

Departure remains in the collection of the Museum of Modern Art (MoMA). Although *Descent from the Cross* (1917) and *Family Picture* (1920) are also often on view there, *Departure* has, from its acquisition in 1942 to the present, been presented as the major Beckmann work in the collection and as the artist's definitive statement.[3] When *Departure* arrived in New York, MoMA's curators offered it as evidence of the movement from Europe to New York of major modernist artworks and artists, indeed of modernism itself. Along with an even more famous European émigré, Picasso's *Guernica*, Beckmann's large triptych helped turn the focus of MoMA's galleries from the sequence of prewar European "isms" to the "big pictures" of the New York School.[4] In 1947 the MoMA curator James Thrall Soby gave *Departure* a speaking part in this narrative, declaring that it could "look Picasso's *Guernica* in the face, without apology or stammer."[5]

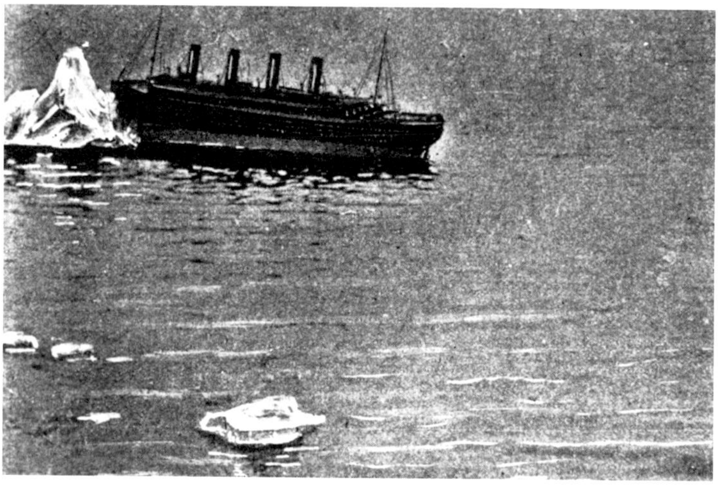

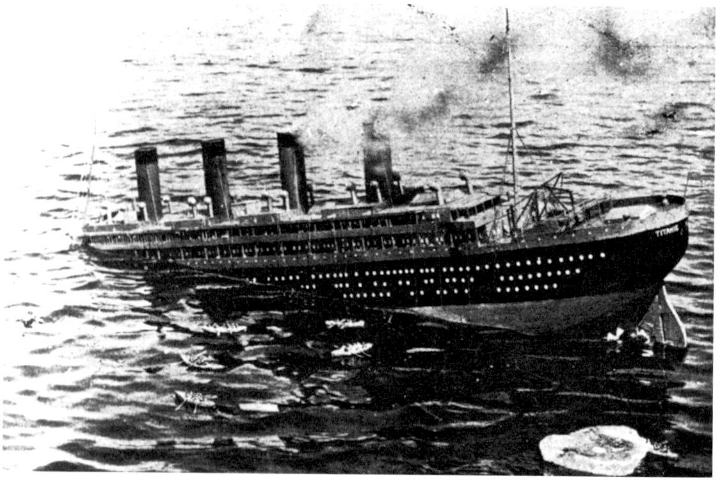

FIGURE 2. Mime Misu, *In Nacht und Eis,* 1912, film still. Photo: Deutsche Kinemathek, Berlin. FIGURE 3. Mime Misu, *In Nacht und Eis,* 1912, film still. Photo: Deutsche Kinemathek, Berlin.

Titanic Sinks

On April 14, 1912, at 10:25 P.M. EST, the White Star liner *Titanic,* on its maiden voyage across the North Atlantic to New York City, struck an iceberg. The last signals from it were received at 12:27 A.M., and two hours later the unsinkable ship had sunk, about a thousand miles short of its destination.[6] Two months later an expatriate Romanian filmmaker named Mime Rosescu, working under the stage name Mime Misu, set to work in the Continental-Kunstfilm studios at Chaussee Street 123 in Berlin on a narrative film version of this event.[7] Misu's film, *In Nacht und Eis,* premiered in Berlin on August 17, 1912, the second in a long series of dramatizations of this quintessentially modern and instantly historical disaster.[8] By the time Misu's film premiered, people were already familiar with the look of the ship, as well as with many of its crew and passengers. One passenger, Francis Brown, who had fortuitously disembarked in Queenstown, Ireland, after the first day of the voyage, had taken photographs while on board that were widely published after the disaster.

In Nacht und Eis billed itself as a "sea drama in three acts, true to life from actual reports."[9] Running forty-two minutes, it was much longer than the average dramatic film of the time. The film opened in a scene that used a real ocean liner to show the passengers boarding the ship and its departure from the harbour. Thereafter it relied on a model photographed in transit across a water-filled beer barrel for its shots of the great ship in the open sea, hitting an iceberg, and ultimately foundering (figs. 2–3). Lifeboats filled with actors bobbing in the gentle waves of the Grüpelsee near Königs Wusterhausen, southeast of Berlin, represent the survivors adrift in the North Atlantic south of Newfoundland. Despite such obvious departures from realism, *In Nacht und Eis* devised a compelling human drama out of the catastrophe. The opening scenes introduce the passengers and tell us who will survive and who will perish. We see them strolling on deck; in their cabins; playing games that provide comic relief and getting dressed for an evening's entertainment; and dining in the "elegant Café Parisienne." The captain and first mate issue commands from the bridge. Tinted film stock provides atmosphere to the radio room, where the telegraph operators tap away, and to the scenes of coal stokers vigorously shoveling fuel into the engine's furnaces. A recent commentator has called Misu's film "one of the strongest German films that survives from these years," in part because the director had already visited (or claimed to have visited) America, where he learned from D. W. Griffith and other pioneers of the narrative cinema to use close-ups and parallel and continuity editing to create dramatic tension, to show simultaneous events from different perspectives, and to move the story forward logically and understandably.[10] With such techniques a director can portray a disaster, or any historical event, as an affective and compelling drama composed of various elements unfolding over time. Romance, social commentary, sensuality, comedy, and quick character studies present individuals at the mercy of elemental and historical forces beyond their understanding or control, which proceed relentlessly, even as normal life goes on.

Beckmann, by contrast, presented the sinking of the *Titanic* as an impersonal and undramatic event. The painting's major elements are composed diagrammatically, organized into two neat, intersecting diagonals. One diagonal runs from right foreground to left background and consists of four parallel lifeboats filled with largely faceless figures. The other runs from left foreground to right background, from two capsized boats with figures struggling to hold onto their hulls to a boatload of totally faceless figures and a pyramidal chunk of iceberg. The *Titanic*'s stern is obscured by the iceberg; the bow and bridge are fully visible. The great ship seems to sit at the horizon line, immobile and strangely small in scale. Despite the churning sea and struggling figures, the lack of dramatic intensity or focus renders the painting lifeless. In the front right boat, for instance, four women surround a child. These are among the few figures whose faces are clearly visible. Their expressions seem resigned and almost detached from what is going on around them. If any prototype comes to mind, it would the familial group huddled on the benches of Daumier's *Third-Class Carriage* (1863), stolidly traveling to their destination. Daumier's picture, though, explicitly declared the working-class affiliation and ambience of its subjects. It also organized them into a group resembling the Holy Family, pointing out class divisions and deprivations while proselytizing for the nobility of the poor. In *Titanic,* by contrast, it is hard to figure out just what Beckmann intended viewers to feel about his boatloads of victims.

Like eighteenth- and nineteenth-century history paintings, or Courbet's Realist revisions of the genre to include everyday scenes, *Titanic*'s large format asserts the painting's and the subject's significance. The scale of the work contributes to what Wolfgang Kemp calls an artwork's "reception aesthetic." Whereas reception history typically concentrates on the social context coloring spectators' responses to works of art, and traces changing responses over time, reception aesthetics looks also at aspects intrinsic to the artwork—how its format, composition, and formal handling help to determine its reception. One issue Kemp identifies in a figural work such as *Titanic* is the painting's "forms of address," the diegetic relationship of its actors "toward one another and toward the beholder."[11] Beckmann's *Titanic* creates no such compelling relationships, either internally or externally. The figures within the painting form no compelling relationships, nor is the spectator "sutured," to use a term common in cinema studies, to the drama of the scene through identification with its participants. This could be construed as a strength: Beckmann's *Titanic* captures the random chaos and pointless suffering of disaster victims more realistically perhaps than does, for instance, the more highly organized and didactic *The Raft of the Medusa,* Géricault's mammoth 1819 Romantic masterpiece, which also depicted a contemporary shipwreck and with which *Titanic* has often been compared. When the British art critic Charles Darwent made this comparison in 2003, he noted that Beckmann's passengers "are merely wet and scared" in contrast to Géricault's dramatic figures.[12]

Beckmann had large ambitions for *Titanic* and for himself. Born into a bourgeois family in Leipzig on February 12, 1884, and educated at the Grand Ducal Art School in Weimar from 1900 to 1903, Beckmann first made a name for himself as an artist in Berlin between 1906 and 1914. In 1906 he began showing with the Berlin Secession, the Prussian capital's leading organization of artists with a modern outlook, in their yearly exhibitions in a large exhibition space on the fashionable Kurfürstendamm.[13] In 1907 he built a private house and studio in what the art critic Karl Scheffler called the "shabby northeastern suburb" of Berlin-Hermsdorf, and he also spent time in Florence.[14] In his *Self-Portrait in Florence* (1907, fig. 4) the light and flora of Tuscany form a loosely painted backdrop to the solidly built (and painted) pink-cheeked young man in the black suit staring resolutely at us, his cigarette a white diagonal paralleling the crisp line of his turned-back collar. All the world is Beckmann's stage, where he can present himself and assert his painterly possession.

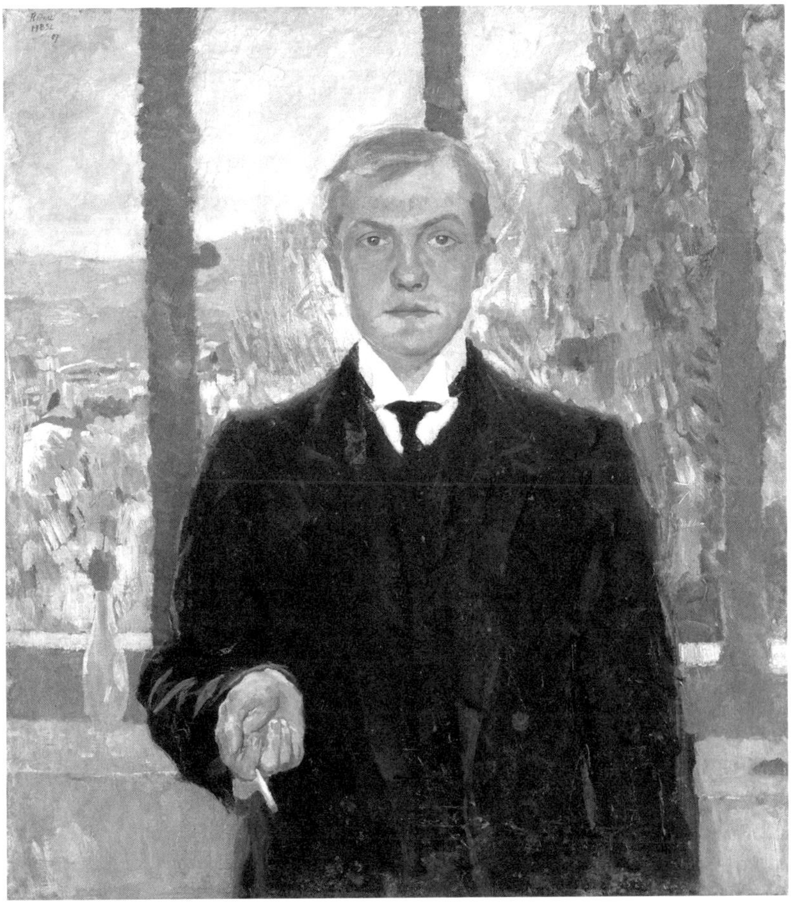

FIGURE 4. Max Beckmann, *Self-Portrait in Florence,* 1907, oil on canvas, 98 × 90 cm. Hamburger Kunsthalle. Art © 2010 Artists Rights Society (ARS), New York/VG Bild-Kunst, Bonn. Photo: Bildarchiv Preussischer Kulturbesitz/Art Resource, NY.

In 1908 Beckmann returned to Berlin and the house designed by his wife, Minna Beckmann-Tube, who gave birth to their son Peter there. In 1910, at the age of twenty-six, Beckmann was elected to the executive board of the Secession, presided over by the venerable Impressionist Max Liebermann; Beckmann was by far the youngest member of the council. In 1913 the first monographic treatment of Beckmann's art, by Hans Kaiser, was published by the important Berlin dealer Paul Cassirer, who that year also staged a retrospective of forty-seven Beckmann paintings in his gallery.

The reception of Beckmann's *The Sinking of the Titanic* on its first showing in Berlin in 1913 was dismal and dismaying to the artist.[15] Beckmann scholar Charles Haxthausen ascribes the painting's poor reception to the large presence, for the first time at the Secession, of Expressionist works: "Measured against these entries, which were finding an increasingly favorable response, Beckmann's grandiose composition must have looked especially anachronistic."[16] Not surprisingly, the leading Berlin Expressionist journal, Herwarth Walden's *Der Sturm,* published a negative, sarcastic review of the painting—written before the painting had been completed or exhibited.[17]

Probably even more damning was the criticism leveled at the finished painting by the art historian and critic Curt Glaser, who compared *Titanic* unfavorably to Géricault's *The Raft of the Medusa.*[18] It is true that *Titanic* lacks the *Raft's* compelling composition, achieved through the powerfully interconnected diagonal movement from bottom left to top right, as well as the human drama that emerges on close examination of the individuals forming the pyramidal pile. Instead, Beckmann's emphasis falls more on the water and the general situation rather than on the people and their response to it. A more appropriate precursor would be Manet's Realist *The Escape of Rochefort* (1880–81, fig. 5). Linda Nochlin, the groundbreaking feminist art historian and leading scholar of nineteenth-century Realism, has described *The Escape of Rochefort* in terms that could also be applied to Beckmann's *Titanic.* According to Nochlin, Manet "avoids the traditional rhetoric of heroism. . . . [He] refuses to endow it with the pathos of its great seagoing predecessors, Géricault's *Raft of the Medusa* or Delacroix's *Christ on the Lake of Genasareth.*"[19] Because of its theme, *Titanic* was compared to Géricault's work, and Beckmann himself was referred to as "the German Delacroix." But, like Manet, he in fact avoided Romantic rhetoric in favor of Realist specificity. Beckmann's *Titanic* lacks compositional climax or narrative focus. It reports matter-of-factly on a specific event rather than *melodramatically* asserting that there is a general lesson to be learned from it. There are no heroes for Beckmann to highlight: humanity is not being put to the test, only masses of largely undifferentiated victims.

In his review of the 1913 Berlin Secession exhibition Glaser went on to declare that Beckmann's handling was inferior even to that of "a half-parodic representation of the same events shown in the Indépendants in Paris by an imitator of Henri Rousseau," which Glaser said better summed up the theme. Providing historical evidence for Haxthausen's assertion that contemporary viewers saw Beckmann's work as outdated in relation to Expressionism, Glaser ended his gloss on Beckmann by stating that such "concentration on the essential" was most promisingly demonstrated in the small works of the Expressionist Erich Heckel—which in scale, subject, and style represent the antithesis of Beckmann's *Titanic.*[20]

In his story "The Open Boat" (1897) the Naturalist American writer Stephen Crane famously observed that "shipwrecks are apropos of nothing." They simply happen and thrust their victims into physical and psychological situations for which they could hardly be prepared, and which therefore have the potential to reveal some of what lies deep within them. How unprepared characters respond to such sudden, random crises heightens the identification for readers of stories like Crane's, or of spectators of *Titanic* films.[21] Anyone could end up in an open boat.

Film has been particularly adept at constructing stories based on disasters, and at developing meanings for them where there might be none in real life. Such was already the case in 1912–13. Brigitte Peucker, a leading scholar of the relationship between film

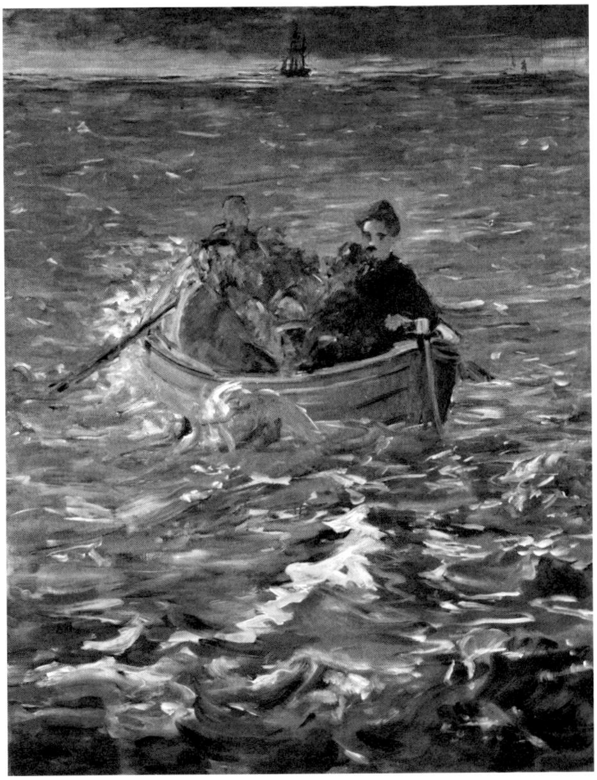

FIGURE 5. Edouard Manet, *The Escape of Rochefort,* 1880–81, oil on canvas, 143 × 114 cm. Kunsthaus Zürich. Photo © 2010 Kunsthaus Zürich. All rights reserved.

and the other arts, has theorized that silent films, and film in general, in comparison with the arts of literature and painting, more effectively create an uncanny semblance, a simulacral world of "images of moving bodies" that lodge in the viewer's imaginary to stand in for the real. The real that these moving bodies ultimately replace is haunted with anxiety, "an underlying fear of castration and death," the types of fears spectators displace onto stories of dramatic shipwrecks and other challenges to human existence and subjectivity.[22] With the procession of this simulacrum across the twentieth century and into the twenty-first, the real more and more becomes an adjunct to the imaginary realm, rather than the imaginary being a supplement to the real. Cinema's spectacle of fragmentation, horror, death, and disaster provides a means for modern and postmodern subjects to negotiate mortality as well as more specific current events, such as those Beckmann sought to depict in his early works *Large Death Scene* (1906), *Scene from the Destruction of Messina* (1909, inspired by an earthquake), and *Titanic*. Indeed, through its effectiveness at this negotiation, cinema has assumed a religious and ritual function, largely supplanting that of painting, sculpture, or other traditional, static arts, as Walter Benjamin theorized in his famous 1936 essay "The Work of Art in the Age of Mechanical Reproduction." According to the Benjamin scholar and historian of the early cinema Miriam Bratu Hansen, film in the early twentieth-century was "not just one among a number of perceptual technologies, nor even the culmination of a particular logic of the gaze; it was above all (at least until the rise of television) the single most expansive discursive horizon in which the effects of modernity were reflected, rejected or denied, transmuted or negotiated."[23]

Only recently have Beckmann's interpreters begun to assert that representational forms other than Expressionist paintings—particularly photography and film—rendered his attempt to depict contemporary history in *Titanic* truly anachronistic.[24] In a 2003 exhibition catalogue, Sean Rainbird stressed that Beckmann had to contend with the quick dissemination of "survivor's stories, and photographs and sketches made on the scene." He also referred to cinema as a cause in the demise of history painting as a genre, stating that it "proved insufficient to satisfy demands in an age where photography, journalism and early cinematic technology could capture and distribute contemporary events with far greater speed and verisimilitude."[25] Painting competed, however, with the developing aesthetic of narrative film, as well as with "cinematic technology," for primacy in the depiction of history. The ability of cinema to set the photographic image in motion and to use editing, sets, costumes, acting, and music to create a simulacrum of the world—an insubstantial world, as Peucker argues, that *appears* remarkably "real," convincing and moving—helped to sink efforts such as Beckmann's *Titanic*.

In his 1996 Beckmann monograph Peter Selz, too, compared *Titanic* to film: "Certain details of the convoluted action are infused with a vitality much like that soon to be seen in mob scenes on film. In fact, the whole picture resembles a frame from an old newsreel, although it goes beyond the melodramatic reportage."[26] Selz's apt observation suggests that the painting's lack of melodrama is a virtue, though because it lacks melodrama—or any drama—it fails as a compelling historical representation. Melodrama in film, as in Géricault's *Raft*, heightens the drama but also dramatically personalizes feelings to represent history effectively and affectively, if not accurately. Beckmann's painting depersonalizes without effectively historicizing. And, as Selz points out, Beckmann's painting reads like a single movie frame rather than like a moving image.

Cinema's Paris and Berlin debuts as collective public entertainment in 1895 built on and developed a hunger for moving pictures, which had earlier been fed by individual viewing apparatuses such as the zoetrope and kinetoscope. The scale of the projected public image links it to the collective spectator experience of the painted panorama and history painting. In his 1934 essay on the cinema, Erwin Panofsky, among the best-known and most important interpreters of Medieval and Renaissance art, keenly aware of motion pictures' growing power vis-à-vis paintings, compared their collective creation to that of the great Gothic cathedrals. Panofsky also fixed on motion and time, identifying the "dynamization of space" and "spatialization of time" as the "unique and specific possibilities" that enabled moving pictures to entertain and enthrall the twentieth-century mass audience.[27] Musical accompaniment to the moving image heightens affect and helps transform drama into melodrama.[28]

In his film *In Nacht und Eis,* Misu, cutting between scenes of the ship, the passengers, the crew, and the elements, showed that he knew that the formula for a successful historical film was to convert a disaster (or any event) into a melodrama, using romance, social commentary, and quick character studies to portray particular individuals and allow audiences to identify with them and their fates. With montage and movement, film can portray the simultaneity of individual incidents within an overall progression of events. Rising water spatializes the passage of time and foreshadows the inevitable end, while the repetitive movements of coal stokers and telegraph operator mimic the mechanical projection of film itself, sixteen frames per second, as both the obvious and embedded kinetic of film re-creates the rapid progress of this modern event. When the ship actually hits the iceberg, Misu shows the moment successively in different shipboard locations—breaking with a linear diegesis to dramatize how individuals simultaneously experienced the impact.

Misu focused on the heroic efforts of the wireless radio operator to send out SOS signals, even as the icy water surrounded him. The captain relieves him of his duties, but the radio man chooses to go down with the ship. He occupies the same position, dramatically and symbolically, as the figure at the apex of the human pyramid in Géricault's *Raft of the Medusa*. Each rises above the despair of the situation to embody the heroic human spirit seeking to make contact with unseen potential rescuers. If the hero does not succeed in the represented scene, he yet does so in relationship to the spectators viewing it. As viewers recognize his attempt, he makes contact with them: they complete the picture and "save" the hero in memory. The fact that his efforts pass unnoticed within the drama of the film only heightens spectators' empathy with him. Film celebrates such rescues of the heroic, human subject—individualized, dramatized, lifted above the mass of humanity—over and over again during the twentieth century and thus responds to and provides the model for the era's mass perception of history as a series of individual narratives. As the film scholar Anton Kaes asserts, "Historical films . . . do not show isolated pictures of accidental, contingent events but select, narrativize, and thereby give shape to the random material of history."[29] That shape makes room for the spectator to enter the picture.

The sinking of the *Titanic* was perfectly suited to the romance, class conflict, heightened emotionalism, and atmospheric musical accompaniment that characterize melodrama as a genre; as a narrative it allegorized both the early twentieth century's overestimation of technology and its new class realities. The most up-to-date and advanced engineering foundered in its encounter with a random and common creation of nature. Class affiliations, indicated by the price of the ticket rather than a person's title or, in the case of the crew, uniform and duties, determined one's life on board ship and chance for survival during a disaster. In 1913 European audiences flocked to a 113-minute, fully melodramatic Danish production of Gerhard Hauptmann's shipwreck saga *Atlantis*, which featured a three-way romantic plot involving an upper-class husband and wife and an immigrant woman in steerage.[30] Although the story was not based on the *Titanic*, the film's reception was conditioned by the *Titanic* disaster. Modern mobility, both physical and social, gave steamship disasters great appeal as a metaphor for the awkward demise of the old world order and uncertain birth of the new.

As an object of mass veneration and official political concern, film in the early twentieth century trumped painting, and Misu trumped Beckmann. The makers of *In Nacht und Eis* issued a barrage of publicity before the film's release. Pre-release advertisements in trade publications noted that theaters booking the film would receive two printed color posters and numerous smaller ones. The color poster, created by the Ernst Maier poster press of Ludwigsburg, frames a graphic black-and-white image in a bright red border (fig. 1). The disaster is represented in a woodcut, the coarse grain and simplified form and content of which recalls contemporary German Expressionism, though without Expresssionism's tendency toward angular forms and distortions. Unlike Beckmann's crowd scene, the poster image presents only five figures in the rippling waves of water, one of which gestures back toward the sinking ship. The poster refers to the film as *Der Untergang der Titanic* rather than *In Nacht und Eis*, probably so that the subject matter of this "great true-to-life sea drama in three acts" would be clear. The poster claims that the film is a hit *(Schlager)*, even a *Sensations-Schlager* (sensational hit), though this does not appear to have been the case. No advertisements or reviews seem to have appeared in the general press after the film's premiere.[31] In my own search through more than a dozen prominent and not-so-prominent Berlin newspapers from August and September 1912, I found no reviews of any popular entertainment films and only a few advertisements.[32] The fact that Berlin was saturated with the *Titanic* theme through photographs, posters, reportage, and Misu's "sensational" mass entertainment film also probably contributed to the critical unease that greeted Beckmann's importing a theme from popular mass culture into the "high" art setting of the Secession.

Misu's film, like all films screened in Berlin after a 1906 Prussian police order , had to pass the censors before it could be shown to the public anywhere in Germany.[33] In largely Catholic Bavaria the film was banned. Hansen has argued that attempts to regulate and even censor the cinema attest to its "potential as a public sphere," an arena for the free exchange of information and ideas, and to official attempts to hinder it from fully functioning as that.[34] Cinema was both controlled and uncontrollable. Film content could to some extent be controlled. Its reception was less controllable. As Hansen has shown, individual responses among early filmgoers, differentiated along class and gender lines, were difficult to predict or control. A man and woman, for instance, might respond very differently during a viewing of *In Nacht und Eis* to the sight of a woman's undergarments as she dresses herself in her stateroom for an evening at the "Café Parisienne." Spectators from different classes might respond differently to the scenes of eating and drinking, as well as to the promise and reality of well-heeled passengers going down with the ship. Cinema is consumed across class and social barriers. Its potential and real audience is construed to be not the readers of a particular newspaper, or the members or interested public of an artistic group such as the Secession, but the masses in the streets who are susceptible to color advertisements. For this reason the police, as well as intellectuals across the political spectrum, were concerned that it might present a threat to public order and decorum. Moreover, given the prevalence of literary adaptations such as *Atlantis,* many intellectuals, as Kaes has written, "deplored the debasement of 'high' art translated into the unrefined language of film."[35]

Beckmann's *Titanic* remained within the realm of "high" art but sought to convey a story more suited to the aesthetic devices of film and to elicit the kind of emotional response that had migrated to film spectatorship. Surrealist leader André Breton described the experience of "the solitary spectator," especially of the early cinema, as being "lost in the middle of these faceless strangers" and passing "through a critical point as captivating and imperceptible as that uniting waking and sleeping. . . . [T]he way others go to church . . . quite independently of what is playing, it is there that the only *absolutely modern* mystery is celebrated."[36] The movie theater can thus be the site of the kind of surreal, marvelous, and potentially transformative experience that Walter Benjamin famously summed up as the "creative overcoming of religious illumination . . . *profane illumination*."[37] Throughout his life Beckmann was drawn to the cinema, enjoying not only watching films but also "the ambiance of the movie theater, whether fussy Dutch play houses, a rundown little theater in St. Louis, or the exotic cinemas of New York."[38]

Benjamin, contrasting the painter and the filmmaker, states that "the painter maintains in his work a natural distance from reality, the cameraman penetrates deeply into its web. There is a tremendous difference between the pictures they obtain. That of the painter is a total one, that of the cameraman consists of multiple fragments which are assembled under a new law."[39] In *Titanic* Beckmann acknowledged but failed to abide by or respond to the new law: he painted a scene whose Realism was cinematic but, like a single frame of a film, as Peter Selz has remarked, lacked editing and provided only one point of view. A static scene without temporal or narrative progression, in the age of photography, moving pictures, and the cinema, his painting was deemed inappropriate and inadequate to the communication of its historical and narrative theme.

A 1913 photograph shows Beckmann in front of *Titanic* in his studio, seated next to the figure of a man struggling to gain access to a lifeboat (fig. 6).[40] The scene seems carefully staged, including the arrangement of the paintings to the right and left of *Titanic.* With the nude figure of *Resurrection* to the left and *Large Death Scene* to the right, the photograph shows the painter tending already toward the sacral associations of the triptych format, whereby the large, contemporary history painting at the center may take on the association with a Last Judgment. Alternatively, reading the images left to right, the photograph can be seen as a cycle-of-life image, related to works by Edvard Munch or Paul Gauguin.

If this photograph was as carefully staged as many scholars contend (see note 40), why were other objects, such as an easel, on which the artist's overcoat and bowler hang, included? These things could easily have been moved out of range, or the photograph could have been framed without them, or they could have been cropped during print-

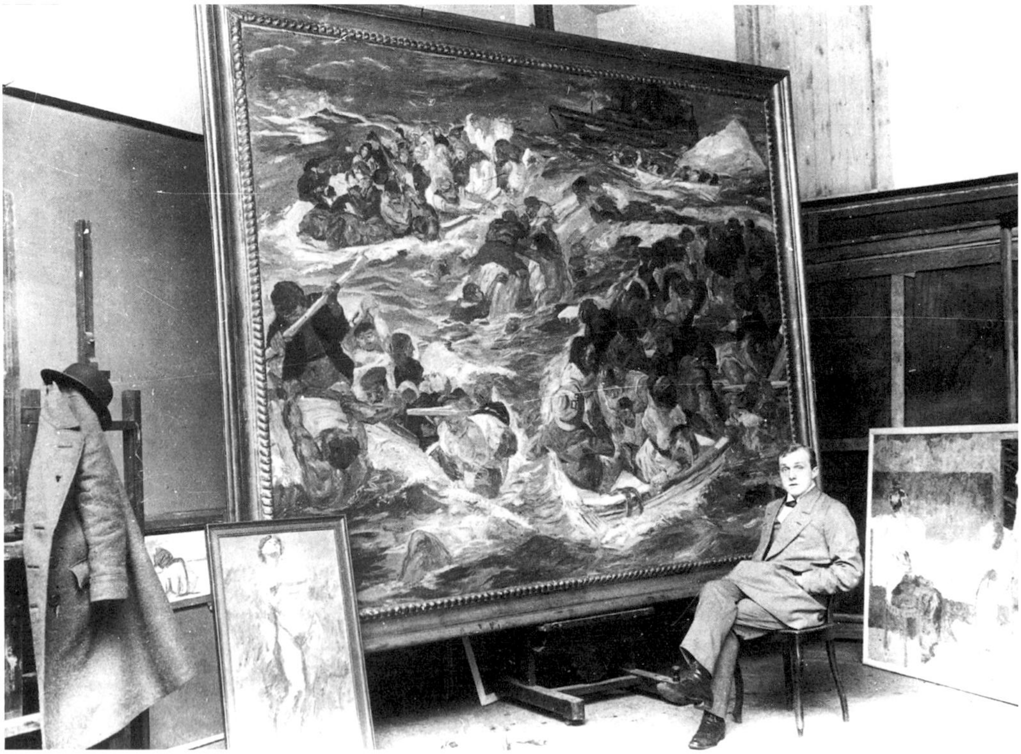

FIGURE 6. **Beckmann in his studio with *The Sinking of the Titanic,* 1913. Art © 2010 Artists Rights Society (ARS), New York/VG Bild-Kunst, Bonn. Photo: Bayerische Staatsgemäldesammlungen–Max Beckmann Archiv.**

ing. Yet they are there. The easel fixes the location as the studio of the painter, not a gallery, and thus situates us in an intimate, creative space. The photograph is a studio scene, a genre whose famous examples include works by Velázquez, Rembrandt, Vermeer, and Judith Leyster; the genre may hae originated in depictions of St. Luke portraying the Virgin, like the one by Rogier van der Weyden. The hat and coat hanging on the easel give Beckmann's studio scene a sense of "informality"—as if the photograph had not been carefully staged. The sporty bowler hat marked its wearer as a modern man, as Fred Miller Robinson has noted. It was more durable and utilitarian, and less expensive, than a top hat and without any of that hat's aristocratic associations.[41]

What if the photograph had included only these items and cropped out Beckmann and his painting? And what if Beckmann had presented such objects, and not the painting, to the Secession? These are hypothetical questions. But the possibility of presenting such objects as art was being raised at exactly the time that Beckmann first presented *Titanic* for public exhibition. In the years just before World War I, artists across Europe were raising fundamental questions about the status of the traditional artwork, the representation of objects in art, and objects in and as art. Beginning in 1912 Picasso and Braque introduced into their Cubist collages fragments of paper cut directly from and often referring directly to the real world. Printed bits of newspapers or sheet music asserted the artwork's thematic connection to the world outside its frame and its independent status as a real, material construction in the world. In the collage *Still Life with Chair Caning* (1912) Picasso employed an oval of rope as a frame. The rope transformed the frame into both a real part of the artwork and a part of the real world: that which generally separates the two, fully belonging to neither, was reconceptualized and rematerialized as that which ties together and belongs to both. Inspired by his visit to Picasso's studio in Paris, the Russian Constructivist Vladimir Tatlin began in that same year, 1914, to create his intensely material relief constructions, shown the next year in the innovative "0.10" exhibition in St. Petersburg (then Petrograd), along with Kasimir Malevich's monochromatic geometric abstract paintings, arranged from floor to ceiling and across the corner of the room in an environmental installation. Dadaists such as Grosz and Höch would soon seize on collage, construction, and exhibition installation and develop them further, utilizing them especially for political commentary disparaging the old world order. At the time of Beckmann's Realist *Titanic,* Robert Delaunay, Wassily Kandinsky, František Kupka, Piet Mondrian, and other abstract painters were eliminating representational imagery from their paintings. But they and their supporters believed that paintings that did not represent objects could contain just as much—perhaps even more—content and meaning as could representational painting. And in 1913 Marcel Duchamp first demonstrated the readymade work of art, a utilitarian object, such as a bicycle wheel, deprived of its practical function and re-presented in an artistic context with a new function: as artwork.

Had Beckmann participated in these revolutionary revisions of Western art's representational tradition, and its modern tendency to segregate artworks from other objects in the world, and had he presented his easel, hat, or coat to the Secession, they would have been rejected as surely as another progressive artists group, New York's Society of Independent Artists, rejected Duchamp's urinal *Fountain* in 1917 (see fig. 86). Beckmann would have been simultaneously mining the same vein as Duchamp, whose readymades began to call into question the traditional concept of the art object as crafted, expressive studio product. Seen within this art historical context, Beckmann's hat and coat represent the contemporaneous, modern challenge to the traditional artwork—the potential transformation of standard objects into artworks and the definite transformation of artworks into objects that in this secular age depend on institutional standards to confirm them as art, and are therefore subject to contextually specific criticism that constantly reframes them. How *Departure* met this challenge and maintained Beckmann's commitment to representational painting is my subject in the remainder of this chapter. How other objects created by German artists in a variety of formats and styles did so throughout the twentieth century will be the focus of the remaining chapters.

Departure Arrives

With *Departure,* the first and most famous of his nine triptychs, Beckmann took on the cinema, creating movement within each of the painting's panels and forcing the spectator's eye to jump from one to the other across the blank space between them. Like cinematic jump cuts, and unlike continuity editing, the scenes do not progress seamlessly forward.[42] Looking from one panel to another, we sense temporal gaps but are not sure whether we have moved backward or forward in time, nor do we know the duration of the intervals. At the time he painted *Departure* Beckmann was also experimenting with a form of painterly continuity editing, creating single canvases with multiple images within them and at least once referring directly to the cinema. As the art historian Barbara Stehlé-Akhtar points out, "*Filmatelier* (*Film Studio,* 1933) is one of the earliest examples. It is not a coincidence that it was painted in Berlin at the same time as the triptych *Departure* because the concept of scenic plurality had always interested him."[43] Beckmann painted *Filmatelier* in July 1933, inspired by a visit he and his wife had made to the Ufa film production studio outside Berlin in Potsdam-Babelsberg, with the hope of watching Marlene Dietrich perform for the cameras.[44] Dietrich did not appear, however, so the couple instead toured the studio, and Beckmann took note of the sets and equipment, which he later included in *Filmatelier.* The German art historian Olaf Peters has asserted that Beckmann originally conceived of *Departure* as three independent paintings and united them into a triptych specifically under the influence of this film studio experience, the painting of *Filmatelier,* and contemporary political events in Germany.[45]

Beckmann's choice of the triptych format, his portrayal of movement within the work, and the movement of the object itself from Germany to the United States have contributed to *Departure*'s historical significance. Beckmann did not seek to depict contemporary history directly. Instead, whereas he intended that the painting's imagery and form should serve as historical allegory, the object itself became a historical actor. In the following chapters I shall discuss other methods and materials German twentieth-century artists have employed to create artworks that convey historical meanings, and the history that these objects have subsequently enacted, seeking to account contextually for their reception histories and materially and formally for their reception aesthetics.

The triptych format, which is key to *Departure*'s effect, was unprecedented in Beckmann's work at that time. But Beckmann was not the only prominent painter in Weimar Germany to revive this format and its sacred associations. *Departure* was preceded by, among others, Otto Dix's triptychs *Big City* (1928) and *The War* (1929–30).[46] A member of the politically active late-Expressionist Dresden Secession group and a guest of the Berlin Dadaists during and just after World War I, in which he saw extensive combat, Dix, in using dramatic and dynamic formal distortions and collage constructions, especially those depicting wounded war veterans, challenged normative conceptions of artistic beauty and the art object in the service of caustic social commentary (see fig. 10, in which Dix's *War Cripples* can be seen to the left). In the 1920s Dix, like many artists, turned to the more traditional formats and the sober reportorial style of the New Objectivity *(Neue Sachlichkeit)*.[47] Beckmann had never fully embraced Expressionism, and Dadaism was totally foreign to him. He was less extreme than Dix in rejecting painting's traditions in the 1910s and in turning to a more traditional style and technique in the 1920s. Dix's triptychs are more clearly indebted to sacred prototypes than Beckmann's —his *The War* includes a predella, for instance. Dix's slick, glazed surfaces recall Northern Renaissance masters such as Holbein, whereas his often brutal and gory imagery calls to mind Matthias Grünewald. Dix, though, remained more clearly critical of contemporary culture than Beckmann, whose social criticism was always somewhat indirect, less caustic, and lacking in irony. Beckmann was more concerned than Dix with preserving representational painting as a viable and dignified art form, in an era when abstraction, collage, montage, construction, and the readymade challenged its contemporaneity, and when artists such as Dix and the Berlin Dadaists reviled what they thought to be painting's pretensions. Beckmann remained more of a painter's painter. He sought to create spatial effects that would be recognizably modern as measured against the standard of Picasso, whom he saw as his greatest rival and challenge.[48] With the triptych format, Beckmann could paint representationally and still respond both to Cubist fragmentation and abstraction, and also acknowledge the artwork's objecthood and relationship to its setting.

In *Departure* the three-part segmentation of the painting calls attention to the materiality of each panel. Even as it makes a sacred association, *Departure* affirms painting as profane, material object, presented in a particular place. Its meaning is not transcendent; it is contingent—upon the internal arrangement and relationship of the panels themselves and on the painting's location within a specific physical, historical, cultural, and discursive environment, all of which become part of the piece literally and figuratively. The object's presentness is place, codetermining interpretations of its complex allegorical imagery.

Internally and historically, *Departure* invokes movement: of the spectator's eye between the panels of the triptych, of the king and queen in the central panel across the water, of the drummer's march in the right panel from left to right, and, of course, of the thing itself, the art object, to America. The triptych format and Beckmann's personal and esoteric allegorical "world theater" has enabled readings in which *Departure* becomes not only a symbolic but also a real embodiment of the survival of art itself.[49] Against the age's desacralization and disenchantment, Beckman "the tightrope walker," as he referred to himself, sought and in *Departure* achieved, the reenchantment of the reproducible but unique work of art through direct identification with the "aura" of the individual artist as complex, creative hero. *Departure* thus rewarded Beckmann's "trust in objects" by adopting the triptych format and its sacred associations and developing an iconography and a painting style that could reinvest painting with a seemingly magical aura, now endowed with modern movement.

Throughout Beckmann's career, his work, while not exclusively dark and contrarian, repeatedly depicted human beings involved in elemental struggles—with nature, with others, with the self. Beckmann's depictions of struggle could be inspired by specific events, such as a city-shattering earthquake in *The Destruction of Messina;* the sinking of the *Titanic* in the painting by that name; or the violence of World War I, the social upheaval of Germany's November Revolution, and the ensuing reaction to it in *The Night* (1918–19), the packed composition and angular distortions of which took Beckmann as far as he ever went toward Expressionism. In later large-scale works the sources for his paintings are more obscure, as in *The Organ Grinder* (1935), triptychs such as *The Actors* (1941–42, fig. 7) and *Blindman's Buff* (1945), or the single and singular image of a man suspended in midair, head-down, his back to us, in *Falling Man* (1950). Many of Beckmann's most memorable images suggest simultaneously the horror of the world and the painter's defiant depiction of it, at once gruesome and matter-of-fact—close-up images in which paint expresses his commitment to a representational modernism, asserting its physical presence on the surface of the painting while also depicting objects. His later work constantly refuses straightforward narration, encoding defiant gestures in elaborate allegories.[50] Characters such as the recurring bellhop, depicted blindfolded and holding a fish in the right wing of *Departure,* seem contemporary. But they are most often cast in dramas detached from any specific time and mingle with figures from other periods and traditions such as the drummer dressed in Louis XI style, who was interpreted by many commentators as a reference to the bombastic rabble rousing of the Nazi party. While the figure bound upside-down with a lamp-holding woman in attendance may suggest the crucifixion of Paul observed by an angel, the art historian and painter Charles Kessler suggests that the three figures of attendant, man, and woman "echo two sublime tragic scenes": the expulsion of Adam and Eve from Eden and "the classical representation of Orpheus and Eurydice being guided from the underworld by Hermes."[51] The variety of possible identities of Beckmann's players allows them to function simultaneously as actors in the drama of twentieth-century German history and as archetypal characters involved in a universal struggle between good and evil. The bellhop could alternatively be read as a uniformed usher in a theater or in one of Beckmann's beloved movie houses, a context that Kessler also suggests informs the setting of the right wing. Thus the architectural settings of left and right panels, for Kessler, are both ritualistic and "hallucinatory"—the columns in the left panel suggesting a "pagan temple" and the architecture of the right a dingy movie theater.

When *Departure* arrived in New York in 1938 curators and art critics interpreted it as a cautionary tale in opposition to the Third Reich and as an allegory of the modern artist—representing individualism in general—as a major victim of the regime. *Departure* was begun in 1932, before the Nazis came to power, and, as Peter Selz's research has confirmed, its three paintings were completed in 1933, four years before Beckmann's actual emigration to Holland and fourteen before he crossed the Atlantic. In America, though, the triptych became early and forever associated with Nazi oppression

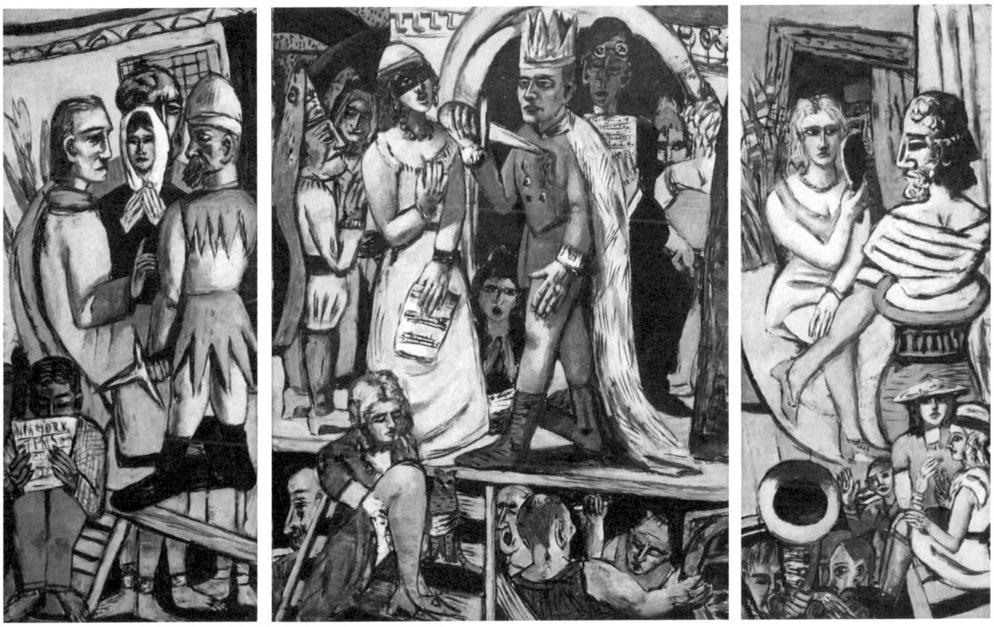

FIGURE 7. **Max Beckmann, *The Actors,* 1941–42, triptych, total size 199.4 × 83.7 cm. Harvard Art Museum, Fogg Art Museum, Gift of Lois Orswell, 1955.174.A-C. Art © 2010 Artists Rights Society (ARS), New York/VG Bild-Kunst, Bonn. Photo: Kaya Kallsen, © President and Fellows of Harvard College.**

and exile, Beckmann's flight, the flight of other artists, and the export and saving of this work and other "degenerate" artworks. The painting thus provided a dramatic, one might say melodramatic, focus for this unfolding narrative.

The first American showing of *Departure* was at Curt Valentin's Buchholz Gallery in New York in January 1938, where it was dated 1932–35, which even more specifically associated it with the artist's response to Nazi brutality.[52] Carlyle Burrows, the reviewer in the *Herald Tribune,* was equivocal about *Departure,* which he said "records the horrors of the world with a deep impassioned cynicism," but emphatic in describing Beckmann as "one of the more original and potent innovators shelved by the Nazis."[53] The critic in *Parnassus,* too, identified *Departure* with Beckmann's persona, and with the historical flight of German artists from the Nazis, seeing in the painting "an expression of painful, personal emotion, for which the solution is found only in the central panel; in other words, in departure or flight."[54] Jacob Kainen, a critic, artist, and, later, curator of prints at the Smithsonian Institution, gave the Beckmann show its most detailed review. Published in the socialist *Daily Worker,* this review is the most overtly political and also the most specifically personal, and melodramatic, in identifying Beckmann's wife, Quappi, as the mother figure in the central panel.

> The large, three-paneled "Departure" gives the show away. The two flanking panels show scenes of inhuman torture where people are bound, gagged, and cut into pieces. The

central panel is a close-up of hooded figures in a small boat making for the open sea and the blue horizon. One of the figures is Beckmann's wife. Since the artist left Germany two years ago, the date of the completion of the picture, the meaning is clear. Beckmann was yearning for the time when he would leave the country which dishonored its art and oppressed its people. Hence, the title "Departure."[55]

The painting was first shown at the Museum of Modern Art in 1939, in the exhibition "Art in Our Time," which celebrated the museum's tenth anniversary and coincided with the New York World's Fair. Reproduced in the catalogue, it was dated 1937 and captioned: "*Departure* refers symbolically to his exile, caused by official disapproval of his art."[56] MoMA acquired *Departure* in 1942, after a lengthy negotiation with Kurt Valentin, in exchange for a still life by Georges Braque.[57] In January of that year *Departure* was a central work in a Beckmann exhibition at the Chicago Arts Club, where the *Chicago Daily News* headlined its positive and cinematic review: "Beckmann Spectacular, Melodramatic."[58]

In the summer of 1942 *Departure* was the centerpiece of "Free German Art," a show of recent acquisitions at MoMA organized by the museum's director Alfred H. Barr, Jr.[59] In his press release, Barr did not specifically connect the imagery of *Departure* to Beckmann's own story, but he did interpret this painting in particular and art objects in general as both objective embodiments of exile and metaphors for America's role in assuring the survival of the "human spirit."

> German artists of spirit and integrity have refused to conform. They have gone into exile or slipped into anxious obscurity. . . . Their paintings and sculptures, too, have been hidden or exiled. . . . But in free countries they can still be seen, can still bear witness to the survival of free German culture which finds its arch[e]type in Goethe, and its living exemplars, so far as the other arts are concerned, in the musicians, Hindemith and Schoenberg, the architects Gropius and Mies van der Rohe, the writers Mann and Werfel. These men and their works are welcome here. . . . The group of acquisitions now placed on view is dominated by the Beckmann triptych *Departure*. This monumental work, perhaps unrivalled among German paintings of our century . . . whatever its obscurity of detail, can have but one meaning: the triumphant voyage of the human spirit through and beyond the agony of the modern world.[60]

Departure became the best-known twentieth-century German painting in an American collection in the second half of the twentieth century. In New York, its proximity in the Museum of Modern Art collection to *Guernica* metonymically encouraged the reading of it, too, as a political exile. The MoMA curator James Thrall Soby wrote in 1949 that *Departure,* "one of the major works of art our century has thus far produced . . . often hung in the Museum of Modern Art on the same floor with Picasso's *Guernica*. Between them, the two so different works furnish proof that modern art's symbolism can be as forceful, moving and impressive as anything produced in earlier centuries."[61]

Guernica and *Departure* also formed a pair in Kessler's 1950s interpretation of *Departure.*[62] He found both paintings "large, forceful, and topical," though he noted that *Departure's* topicality was less specific to a particular event, lending it "something of the hieratic or liturgical timelessness of medieval Christian art." Though not connected to a specific event, such as the bombing of the Basque town that inspired *Guernica, Departure* was more intimately connected to Beckmann's consistent artistic concerns and his personal experience. For Kessler, *Departure* spirals out from the artist himself to operate on three levels: the personal, the historical, and the religious or philosophical.

Departure has been reproduced and discussed in nearly every survey book of modern art.[63] It was afforded a color plate in the first and all subsequent editions of Janson's *History of Art,* representing the political side of modern art—as personal struggle—in this most canonical general textbook of art history. In the early editions Beckmann's painting was dated 1932–35. It was described (in text that remained unchanged up to the most recent edition) as "completed when, under Nazi pressure, he was on the point of leaving his homeland. . . . The stable design of the center panel . . . with its expanse of blue sea and its sunlit brightness, conveys the hopeful spirit of an escape to distant shores. After living through the Second World War in occupied Holland, under the most trying conditions, Beckmann spent the final three years of his career in America."[64] The contemporary painter Eric Fischl has testified to the continuing influence of *Departure's* intriguing web of references. Fischl cited it in 1982 as the work that made him feel that abstraction had become "bankrupt," the work that emboldened him to pursue his own richly referential, unctuously surfaced, and cinematically edited paintings, which often suggest puzzling narratives: "I could grasp the intention of the picture exactly, without understanding the allegory. . . . I could hook up certain parts of the image to political violence or historical moments or religious values—all those things that belong to the general culture."[65]

In discussing *Titanic* I posit that not only changing painting styles but also changing artistic technologies and genres, especially melodramatic narrative cinema, rendered Beckmann's large Realist painting outdated. With *Departure,* in contrast, Beckmann found a form and imagery that could compete with and supplement the cinema, which was also developing exile as a theme—especially in the work of Hollywood's large exile community—at the time *Departure* came to America.[66] In 1941, in the film *So Ends Our Night,* based on Erich Maria Remarque's novel *Flotsam,* Frederic March is pursued on his flight from Nazi Germany by an evil German character played by Erich von Stroheim. Two years later Hollywood produced an infinitely better-known and more successful film dealing in its own way with exile. *Casablanca* became the sixth most profitable film of 1943, earning $4.15 million.[67] According to one of its screenwriters, Howard Koch, the task at hand was to "develop a serious melodrama of present-day significance."[68]

With his portrayal of the individualist, isolationist, but freedom-loving and fascist-hating American expatriate Rick Blaine, Humphrey Bogart arrived as a major star and

Casablanca "became an anthem of American's commitment to the war."[69] This anthem played America's commitment as the leading man's personal, male, and romantic (in all senses of the term) choice. Contemporaneously with Bogart's arrival as a major star, and *Departure*'s arrival in New York, Lewis Mumford theorized the need for the emergence of a "new man" in defiance of the era's traumas. In *The Condition of Man* (1944) he wrote, "The period through which we are living presents itself as one of unmitigated confusion and disintegration. . . . Now, as once before in the disintegrating classic and medieval worlds, the achievement of a new personality, a new attitude toward man and nature and the cosmos, are matters of life and death. We must recapture once more our sense of what it is to be a man."[70] The central panel image in *Departure* of the king and queen, often assumed to represent Beckmann, the hero, and his wife, Quappi, traveling over the water to escape the quasi-medieval brutalities of the side panels, was interpreted by such critics as Elisabeth McCausland in the magazine *Parnassus* as the journey of an at once ancient, mythic, cosmic—and contemporary—human couple, away from the devastated European continent to the wide-open spaces of America, in which they might once again flourish freely. This was the object's story more than it was any story told within the object. As McCausland also stated, the internal content of the work's allegorical imagery remained unclear. But as Barr asserted in the press release for the 1942 "Free German Art" exhibition, and as became the dominant interpretation for its American audience, *Departure,* "whatever its obscurity of detail," seemed ultimately to be about "the triumphant voyage of the human spirit through and beyond the agony of the modern world."

Casablanca's narrative emphasis on individual characters parallels the reception of *Departure* as a work that tells both its own and its creator's exile stories. The imagery used in another film about exile, *The Seventh Cross* of 1944, more closely resembles that of *Departure.* Like *Departure, The Seventh Cross* draws on Christian imagery. *The Seventh Cross* derives from a best-selling novel by Anna Seghers, "a German exile on the run," as Jan-Christopher Horak, a scholar of film and European exiles, termed her; Seghers was a leading social realist novelist and committed Communist whose journeys in exile took her to Paris, New York, Mexico City (where she spent the war years), and finally, after the war, back to East Germany.[71] In 1942 her novel was a Book-of-the-Month-Club selection in the United States, where it sold some 600,000 copies. The novel's Christian symbolism became even more pronounced in the 1944 film adaptation, in which Spencer Tracy plays Georg Heisler, one of seven concentration camp escapees on the run across Germany. When the first six are apprehended, they are tortured and hung from crosses before being executed. Stylistically, the film's mise-en-scène, as Horak has asserted, departs from Seghers's realism to be more expressionistic—which may well have been a result of its being the collaborative project of such Central European exiles as the Austrian director Fred Zinnemann, the German camera man Karl Freund, and the scriptwriter Helen Deutsch.[72]

Beckmann's style in *Departure,* and even more so, in his later works, relates to the contemporaneous development of film noir in American cinema. The noir film of the late 1940s combined German Expressionist style and Hollywood narrative to convey viscerally the experience of exile—its uncertainty, bitterness, and cynicism, as well as the exile's sense of being suspended between cultures.[73] The stylistically and thematically "dark" cinema was pioneered in the early 1940s by émigrés such as Otto Preminger, Fritz Lang, Robert Siodmak, and Billy Wilder, whose shared worldview, film scholars argue, "was shaped by their bitter experience of living in and then escaping from a nation that had lost its mind."[74] The dark and ambiguous world of film noir is also the world of Beckmann's late works, where contemporary conflicts take on mythic proportions and are rarely resolved. In some works, among them Beckmann's *Actors* triptych of 1941–42 and Howard Hawks's 1946 noir film *The Big Sleep*, it is almost impossible to sort out the various characters and trace coherence in a twisting plot. Each work has a central character, though: the private detective Philip Marlowe in *The Big Sleep;* the crowned figure (with features resembling Beckmann's) who plunges a huge dagger into his chest in *The Actors*.[75]

The lack of linear narrative in both film and painting, though, makes them appropriate in style to their themes and their times. According to a prevalent scholarly interpretation, film noir "was European art cinema in disguise, a calculated assault on classical cinema that grafted the exiles' experience of displacement and artistic blockage directly onto the syntax of Hollywood filmmaking."[76] Noir films convey covert content through style. Similarly, Beckmann's noir tableaus employ stylistic devices for thematic ends: compositions crowded with figures and objects placed in close proximity but with no obvious connections among them, angular forms, and an atmosphere defined largely by the artist's ample use of deep black paint.[77]

Like noir films, Beckmann's late paintings confound attempts to sort out coherent narratives. At the time of *Titanic*, cinema was developing techniques to narrate stories of contemporary concern logically and compellingly. Painting could not compete. In the era of noir, influence flowed in the opposite direction: Hollywood film adopted stylistic strategies that had been developed in Expressionist visual art and theater and then incorporated into German film. Hollywood used these strategies not to narrate but instead to evoke what Mumford called the "unmitigated confusion and disintegration" of the age. *Departure* arrived in New York from a Germany in which Adolf Hitler was the popular and all-powerful leader. The painting's interpretation occurred as the world learned that mankind now possessed not only the technological, scientific, and organizational means to engineer its own destruction but also the ideological fanaticism and ruthlessness to carry out such destruction. *Departure* did not offer a narrative describing, representing, or explaining any of this. But its own story became a representative of it all, as well as of the possibility of civilization's survival.

In 1947 Beckmann was photographed sitting in front of *Departure* in the Museum of Modern Art (fig. 8). In contrast to the 1913 photograph of Beckmann with *Titanic*, the photograph of the sixty-three-year-old Beckmann with his work presents a more asser-

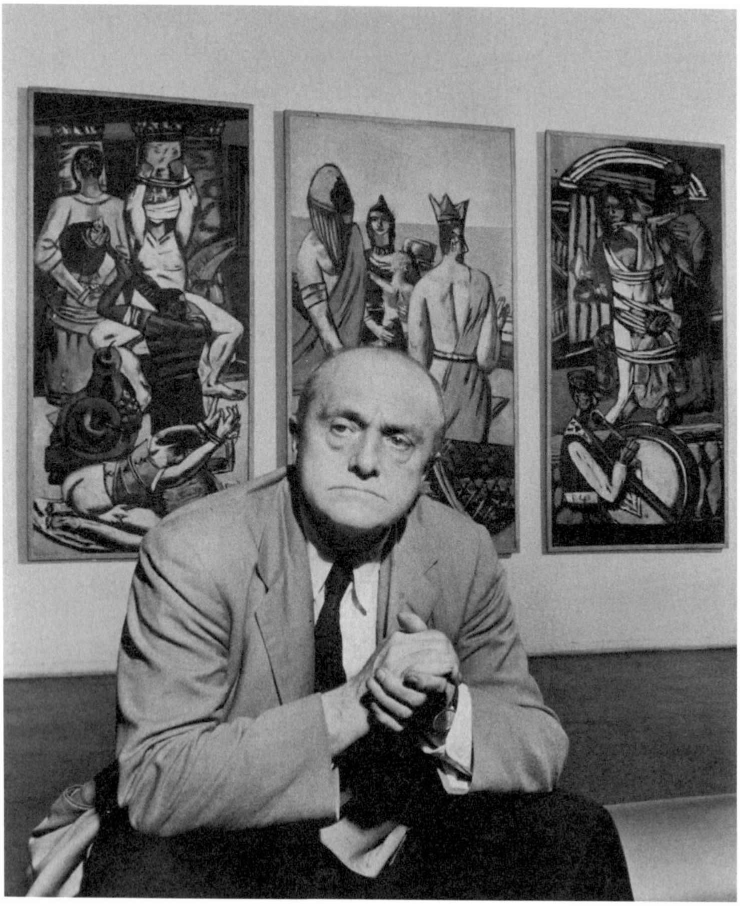

FIGURE 8. Max Beckmann in front of his triptych *Departure* (1932–33) at the Museum of Modern Art, New York, 1947 (photographed by Geoffrey Clements). Art © 2010 Artists Rights Society (ARS), New York/VG Bild-Kunst, Bonn. Digital image © The Museum of Modern Art/Licensed by Scala/Art Resource, NY.

tive museum-quality image of both the artist and the art object. His art and its specific museum setting serve as a backdrop for the public expression of his private persona, mature now and ready for public consumption. Common to both photographs, however, is the identification of a painting with the artist as the product of his individual genius, masculine and sovereign. Something of "a performative conception of artistic subjectivity" is at work in Beckmann's self-presentation in both photographs and paintings—although without the postmodern irony that the art historian Amelia Jones associates with artists from Andy Warhol in the 1960s to the present.[78]

Beckmann and *Departure* are shown not in the artist's studio amid other paintings and personal paraphernalia, but in the Museum of Modern Art. Now he and his imposing head, made familiar in his many self-portraits, dominates the painting. Painter and painting in New York are players in a larger drama—or melodrama—of exile, displacement, and ultimate individual triumph. *Departure* and Beckmann have survived the "shipwreck of modernity" and the Blakian "horror of the [modern] world" to find permanent refuge in New York.[79]

Postscript in the Present: *Departure* Returns to Berlin

Beckmann's *Departure* returned to Berlin for the first time in 2004, as part of the blockbuster exhibition "MoMA in Berlin" held at the Neue Nationalgalerie while MoMA's Manhattan building was undergoing renovation and expansion. A correspondent for the *New York Times* reported on the historical resonances of this return of the repressed: "In a show nearly devoid of German masters, this painting *[Departure]* stands out as a statement about the exhibition itself. A few years after it was made, Germany's great painters were forbidden to create art. The Gestapo would search their studios and homes, feeling the paintbrushes to see if they were wet. Many artists went into exile or died disillusioned." Museum director Peter-Klaus Schuster stated in his speech at the opening: "For the Neue Nationalgalerie this is the return of the modern, what Berlin could have been had it not been for Hitler and later the isolation of East Germany"; and Glenn Lowry, the director of the Museum of Modern Art, commented: "The works take on a new meaning that makes them contemporary in the moment. It's a dialogue between art and history."[80] A main argument of this book is that the art object is always "contemporary in the moment," defined and redefined in the ever-changing present.

2 Lost and Found Dada Objects and Subjects

George Grosz, Hannah Höch, and German Jewish Identity

Hannah Höch's most famous work, the photomontage *Cut with the Kitchen Knife Dada through Germany's Last Weimar Beer-Belly Cultural Epoch* (1919–20, plate 3), left her possession for exhibition only twice. The first time was just after its completion, in the summer of 1920, for the First International Dada Fair in Berlin (fig. 9). The next was in 1961, for her solo exhibition at the Galerie Meta Nierendorf in Berlin, from which Berlin's National Gallery purchased it for five thousand marks. George Grosz's lost 1917–18 collage-painting *Germany: A Winter's Tale* (plate 4) was also displayed at the 1920 Dada Fair (fig. 10). Exhibited often in that period, it was last seen in 1933 in the Berlin apartment of Wieland Herzfelde, who abandoned it when he fled Germany just after the Nazis came to power.

The Dada Fair was the central event of the Berlin Dada movement, not only displaying many key works but also deploying many of Berlin Dada's most characteristic and innovative strategies. Its cacophony of paintings, collages, montages, assemblages, puppets, and signage decried artistic hierarchies (fig. 11). Calling the event a fair *(Messe)* aligned it with commerce rather than culture and with commercial gatherings of limited duration (such as today's influential annual Frankfurt Book *Messe*), in this case one that took place from June 30 to August 25, in the *Kunstsalon* (art salon) of the book dealer Dr. Otto Burchard.[1]

For the Berlin Dadaists, photography, publicity, and propaganda in all their forms were more than a means of publicizing their art, they were their art. They conceived their exhibitions and performances as creative events: the Dada Fair was an assemblage of interconnected elements, including the Dadaists themselves. They staged and distributed many publicity photographs, promulgating their rebellion against artistic decorum and tradition. Beckmann's photographs with *Titanic* and *Departure* presented him and his works in his studio and a museum. Photographs of the Dada Fair, on the other hand, grant the viewer no access to the artist's intimate, creative realm, and the artwork none to museal display and preservation. Embracing collaboration, iconoclasm, impermanence, and reproducibility, the Berlin Dadaists called into question the artist as an individual producer and the unique object as the avatar of artistic meaning and

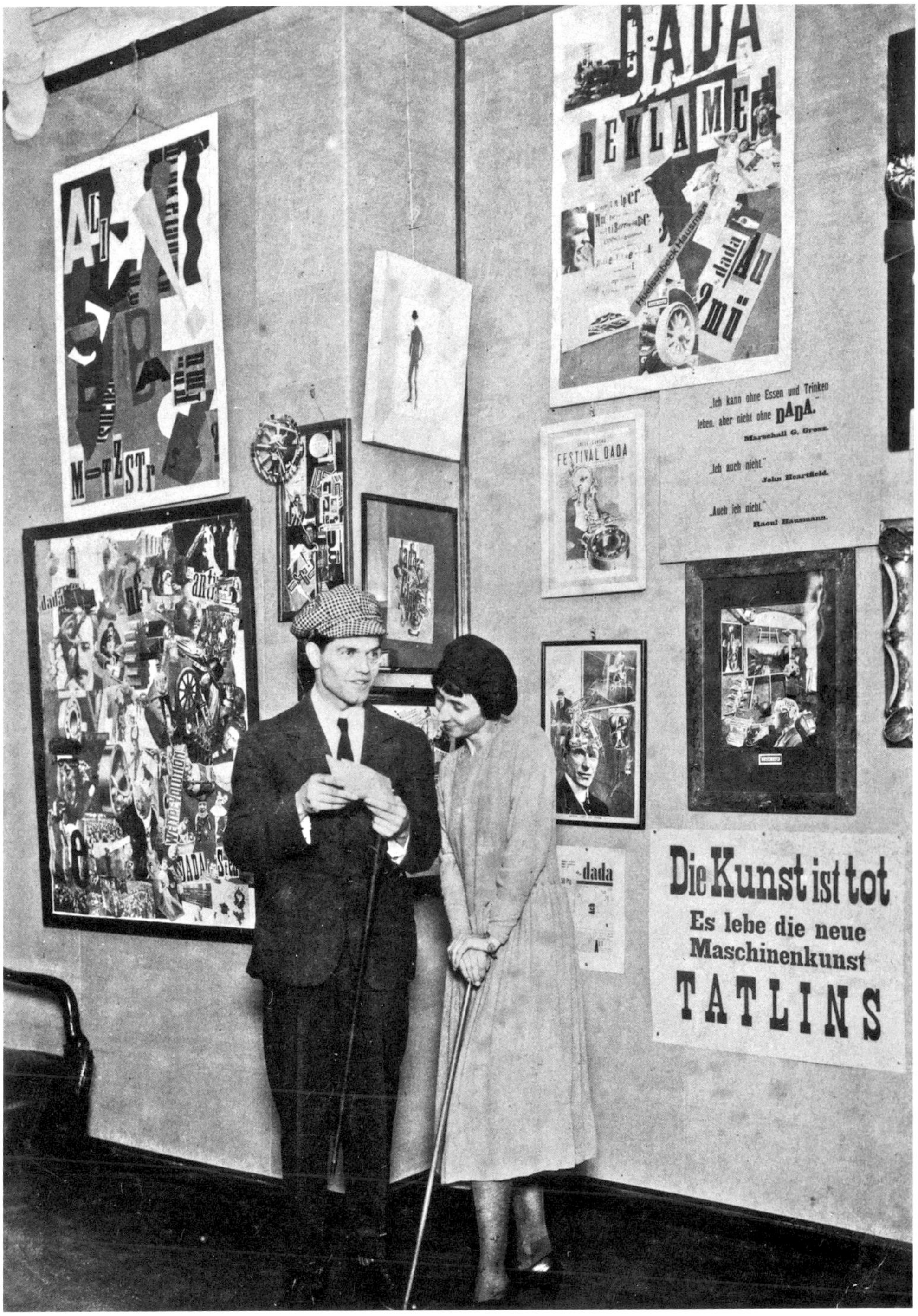

FIGURE 9. Raoul Hausmann and Hannah Höch at the First International Dada Fair, Berlin, June 30, 1920. Photo: Hannah-Höch-Archiv, Berlinische Galerie, Landesmuseum für Moderne Kunst, Fotografie und Architektur.

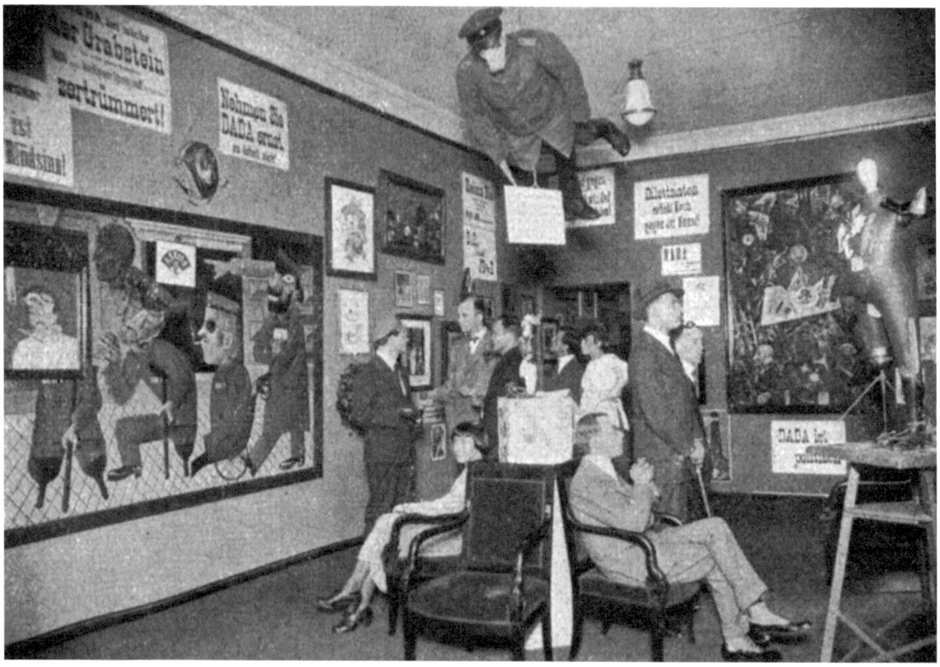

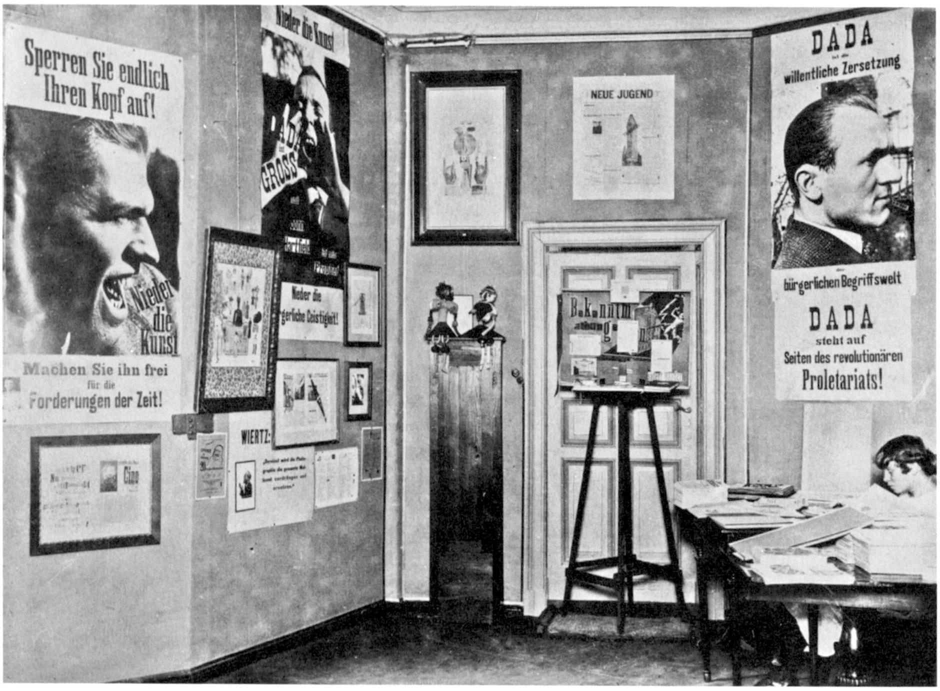

FIGURE 10. First International Dada Fair, Berlin, June 30, 1920, with Hannah Höch (seated at left), George Grosz (in hat, standing, to right), and Grosz's *Germany: A Winter's Tale* (behind on right wall). From *Dada Almanach,* edited by Richard Huelsenbeck (Berlin: Erich Reiss Verlag, 1920). Photo: International Dada Archive, University of Iowa Libraries. FIGURE 11. First International Dada Fair, Berlin, June 30, 1920, with Höch's Dada dolls (on pedestal in center) and "Dada stands beside the revolutionary Proletariat!" poster with photograph of Grosz's profile (to right). Höch art © 2010 Artists Rights Society (ARS), New York/VG Bild-Kunst, Bonn. Photo: Hannah-Höch-Archiv, Berlinische Galerie, Landesmuseum für Moderne Kunst, Fotografie und Architektur.

value. The reception history, however, of *Cut with the Kitchen Knife Dada* and *Germany: A Winter's Tale* demonstrates that objects, even Dada objects, matter.

The loss of *Germany: A Winter's Tale* has limited its interpretation, especially its debt to the great German Jewish poet Heinrich Heine. Berlin Dada's general involvement with Jews, and with questions of German Jewish identity, has been only haltingly recognized. *Cut with the Kitchen Knife Dada* provocatively displays many images of prominent modern German Jews, including Albert Einstein, Kurt Hiller, Karl Marx, Max Reinhardt, Else Lasker-Schüler, the Jewish Dadaist Walter Mehring, and the half-Jewish brothers Wieland Herzfelde and John Heartfield. Moreover, it refers to and is informed by the ideas of the messianic Jewish philosopher Salomo Friedlaender, the only person beside Höch who is named in one of the montage's text fragments.

The creator of this canonical montage, Anna Therese Johanne Höch, was born into a bourgeois Protestant home in the Thuringian city of Gotha in 1889.[2] The eldest of five siblings, she exhibited, from an early age, ample artistic skill and a precise graphic sensibility. In 1912 she left her provincial home and moved to Berlin to study painting at the Charlottenburg School of Applied Arts. She began almost immediately to attend exhibitions at Der Sturm gallery, where she was exposed to Italian Futurism, Cubism, and especially German Expressionism. In April 1915 she first met Raoul Hausmann, either at Der Sturm or in the library of the School of the Museum of Applied Arts, where she had begun her studies with Emil Orlik in January.[3] Höch and Hausmann quickly became lovers and artistic collaborators. She began to modify her name at this time, dropping Johanne and adopting the unusual spelling Hannah, instead of Hanna or Hanne, as a shortened form of Johanne.[4] Except for the years 1926–29, when she lived with her female partner Til Brugman, a Dutch writer, in The Hague, Höch lived in Berlin all her life. Like Grosz, she found an artistic home in the culture of the German metropolis. Unlike most of her male Berlin Dada compatriots, Höch did not leave Germany during the Nazi period. She survived in isolation in the Berlin suburb of Heiligensee, where she moved in 1939, and died in 1978, in the interim years tending her garden, producing art, and maintaining her extensive archive of Dada objects and documents. Since the 1960s, and especially after her death, Höch's work, particularly the Weimar photomontages, has become increasingly prominent. Recognition of its prescience vis-à-vis contemporary artistic movements and social concerns—from Assemblage, Pop, and Fluxus in the 1960s through postmodern appropriation, especially by feminist artists such as Barbara Kruger, in the 1980s, to postcolonial studies today—has helped it to reemerge.[5]

George Grosz, born Georg Ehrenfried Gross, into a working-class, Protestant family in Berlin in 1893, spent his first five years in the city and, when his father's restaurant failed, two in the Pomeranian village of Stolp. After his father's death in 1900, his mother moved the family back to Berlin, where they lived under straitened conditions, experiencing what Grosz's biographer M. Kay Flavell has called "the grey tenement life of a proletarian family in the big city."[6] He studied at the Saxon Royal Academy of Art in Dresden from 1910 to 1912 before returning to Berlin, where, like Höch, he continued his studies at the School of the Museum of Applied Arts. After service in the war, he made Berlin his home as well as his artistic *locus* until 1932, when the offer of a teaching post at the Art Students League brought him to New York; he was back in Berlin in later 1932 but returned to the United States and the Art Students League in January 1933, shortly before Hitler became chancellor. He became an American citizen but in 1954 returned to Berlin, where he collapsed on the stairs to his apartment at 5 Savignyplatz, in which he died in the early morning of July 6.

Grosz is probably the best known of the Berlin Dadaists to both art historians and the general public in his two homes, Germany and America. His fame rests on several pillars. His paintings, often reproduced, are also represented in prominent collections. The Cubo-futuristic *Funeral of the Poet Oscar Panizza* (1917), for example, is in the Stuttgart State Gallery, and *Republican Automatons* (1920) is in the New York Museum of Modern Art. (The latter features well-dressed human robots, which derive from Dada's interest in human-machine hybrids, and also relates to the mysterious mechanomorphs created by such Italian Pitura Metafisica artists as Giorgio de Chirico.) MoMA also owns and often displays Grosz's signature Neue Sachlichkeit (New Objectivity) portrait *The Poet Max Herrmann-Neisse* (1927). Berlin's National Gallery has *Pillars of Society* (1926, fig. 12), which can be related to his *Eclipse of the Sun* of the same year, which belongs to the Heckscher Museum in Huntington, Long Island, where Grosz lived during his American period. *Pillars of Society* and *Eclipse of the Sun* illustrate Grosz's stylistic transition from Dada to the New Objectivity, but they also document his continued caustic criticism of Weimar Germany.

Grosz created and distributed some of the most remarkable and memorable political graphic art of the twentieth century. In series such as *The Face of the Ruling Class*, published in 1921 by the Malik Press, which he helped found with his Communist Dada colleagues, the brothers John Heartfield and Wieland Herzfelde, he savagely criticized postwar Germany, especially the alliances struck between politicians, militarists, and capitalists. The book's fifty-seven drawings portray the violence of World War I as a prelude to class war. In one image, the upper register is drawn in a stiff and sober reportorial style (fig. 13). Men who have just marched back from war have been redeployed to report to factories at dawn, with tools rather than rifles over their shoulders. Meanwhile, below, undulating lines evoke the bestial overindulgences of capitalists and officers who gorge themselves on liquor and prostitutes and smoke. Grosz's unflinching critique of Weimar society and commitment to the broad distribution and easy legibility of his message—to using art as a political weapon—influenced younger socially and politically engaged critical Realists in Germany and elsewhere, directly and indirectly. At the Art Students League his students in the 1930s included the great African-American painter, collage artist, and cartoonist Romare Bearden and, some twenty years later, the Pop painter James Rosenquist. Bearden later compared Jacob Lawrence's depictions of

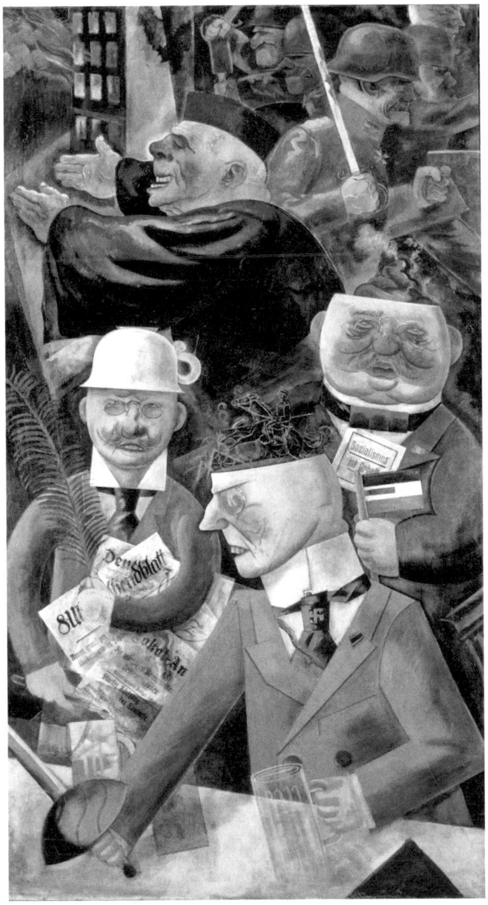

FIGURE 12. George Grosz, *Pillars of Society,* 1926, oil on canvas, 200 × 108 cm. Nationalgalerie, Staatliche Museen zu Berlin. Art © Estate of George Grosz/Licensed by VAGA, New York, NY. Photo: Bildarchiv Preussischer Kulturbesitz/Art Resource, NY.

Depression-era Harlem to Grosz's vision of Germany in the 1920s, and one can also see parallels to Grosz in the work of the Mexican muralist José Clemente Orozco and other artists who sought both to comment on and to influence contemporary history through their art.[7]

By the time Dada erupted in Berlin in 1918, Grosz and Höch had both finished their training at the School of the Berlin Museum of Applied Arts. From her arrival in Berlin in 1912 until the school closed at the outbreak of the war, Höch studied glass design—including painting, stained glass, and mosaic—at the Charlottenburg School of Applied Arts.[8] Grosz, returning to Berlin in 1912, enrolled in the Museum School, and in the spring of 1913 he went to Paris for eight months. Grosz and Höch both worked at the Museum School with Emil Orlik, a Bohemian Jew, born in Prague, best known for his Jugendstil book illustrations and posters, such as his 1901 poster for Max Reinhardt's cabaret revue *Schall und Rauch* (Sound and smoke). Orlik was also a travel illustrator, a printmaker influenced by his studies in Japan, a photographer, and, in the 1920s, a

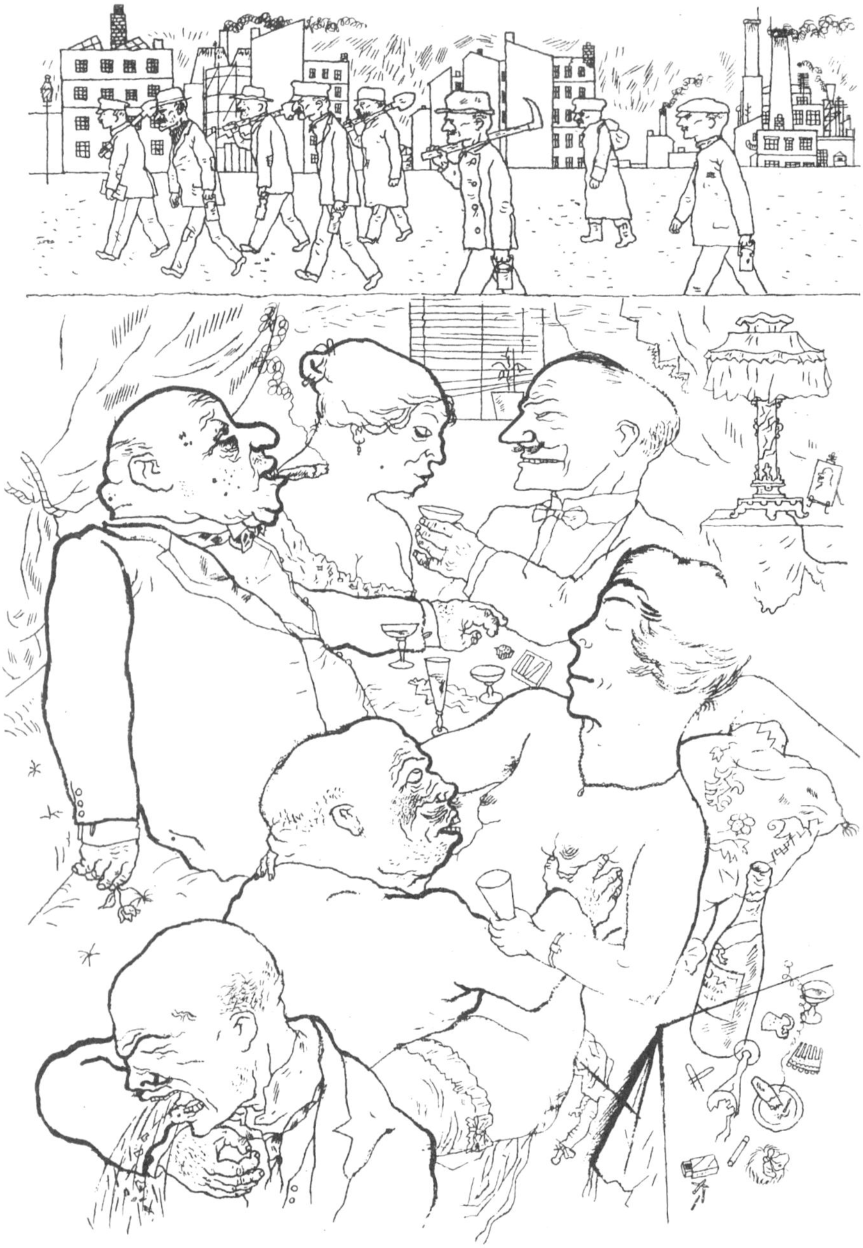

FIGURE 13. George Grosz, *Früh um 5 Uhr!* (Around 5 A.M.!), lithograph from *Das Gesicht der herrschenden Klasse* (Berlin: Malik Verlag, 1921), 54. Art © Estate of George Grosz/Licensed by VAGA, New York, NY. Photo: International Dada Archive, University of Iowa Libraries.

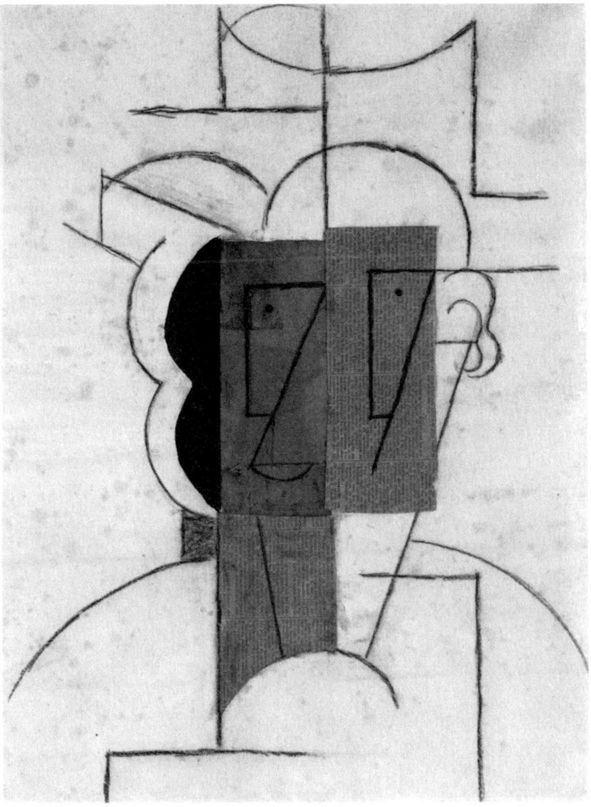

FIGURE 14. Pablo Picasso, *Man with a Hat,* 1912–13, collage, pasted paper, charcoal, and ink on paper, 62.2 × 47.3 cm. The Museum of Modern Art, New York. Art © 2010 Estate of Pablo Picasso/Artists Rights Society (ARS), New York. Digital image © Museum of Modern Art/Licensed by SCALA/Art Resource, NY.

portraitist in the New Objectivity style.[9] Under the multifariously adept Orlik, in whose class Grosz and Höch both enrolled from 1915 to 1917, the two artists practiced designing books and posters, studying what art and design schools today refer to as "communication design."[10] Höch learned a variety of graphic techniques from Orlik and his colleague Oskar Bangemann, who taught her wood engraving. In 1916 she produced what has been called her first collage, *White Clouds,* by cutting up proofs for one of her wood engravings; however, it is also claimed that by 1907 she and her mother had already collaborated on pasted-up pictures, or *Klebebilder.*[11]

In 1912 the pioneer Cubists, Pablo Picasso and Georges Braque, began pasting into their paintings and drawings trimmed pieces of construction paper or commercially printed materials such as oilcloth chair caning and, especially, newspaper fragments. Cubist collages often still relied on drawing or painting for their compositional structure: much of their excitement derives from the tensions in form and content generated by the dialogue between handmade and machine-made elements (see fig. 14). The Berlin Dadaists, in contrast, often abandoned drawing and painting altogether and instead "assembled" works using numerous photographs and photomechanically produced elements. They called the resulting creations photomontages.[12] In *Cut with the Kitchen Knife Dada,* Höch drew only with scissors, cutting around the selected photographs and text in straight or curving contours, and recombining the elements into a complex new whole.[13] Her companion and collaborator, Raoul Hausmann, explained, "We called this process 'photomontage' because it embodied our refusal to play the part of the artist. We regarded ourselves as engineers, and our work as construction: we assembled (in French: *monter*) our works, like a fitter."[14] Höch's and Hausmann's works and activities were attuned technologically to their times. They accepted the ascendancy of film, photography, and other forms of mass communication that edit and re-present the world, forming new wholes out of multiple fragments. With her extensive background in scissor work and the graphic skills evident even in juvenile drawings, Höch, in her montages, exhibited greater technical facility and compositional clarity than any other Dadaist.[15]

During the war Grosz worked with the Herzfelde brothers and their Verlag Neue Jugend, designing and distributing highly political, proto-Dadaist books, pamphlets, and *Die Neue Jugend,* a journal whose license Wieland Herzfelde acquired in 1916. These publishing activities led to the founding in 1917 of the Communist Malik Verlag, which published the single issue of *Jedermann sein eigner Fussball* (Everyman his own soccer ball), in February 1919, and the journal *Die Pleite* (Bankruptcy, 1919–24) (figs. 15–16). Grosz also collaborated with John Heartfield to make at least one animated film during the war for the German propaganda ministry, in 1917–18.[16] Höch began to work for Ullstein Verlag, publisher of mass market illustrated magazines, in 1916, continuing until 1926 to spend three days a week there, from nine in the morning until three in the afternoon, creating illustrations, especially of embroidery and lace designs, for magazines such as *Die Dame* (The lady).[17] Through her work for Ullstein she gained ready access and insight into the popular press, from which she culled photographic images to create her photomontages.

The editing of images in montage practice established a technical foundation for Berlin Dada's relationship to film. Perhaps more significant, as the film historian Thomas Elsaesser has argued, Berlin Dada and early film exploited similar conceptions of spectatorship and pleasure. "What was Dada in regard to cinema," he writes, "was not a specific film, but the performance, not a specific set of techniques or textual organization, but the spectacle."[18] Like early films such as Mime Misu's *In Nacht und Eis,* the public spectacle of the 1920 Dada Fair was subject to censorship. Several participants and the gallerist Otto Burchard landed in court for their provocative display. Soldiers confiscated Malik publications such as *Jedermann sein eigner Fussball,* and Herzfelde was imprisoned for several weeks in March 1919, though never charged with a crime or tried.[19] The harsh response of the Social Democratic government—which consolidated its power by striking an alliance with the right-wing military—to the Berlin Dadaists' activities attests to the latter's "success" in bridging the gap between fine art, mass communication, popular entertainment, and political provocation.

Dada had been announced in 1916 at the Cabaret Voltaire in Zurich. Hans Richter, who participated in Zurich Dada and closely observed Berlin Dada, later wrote of Dadaism

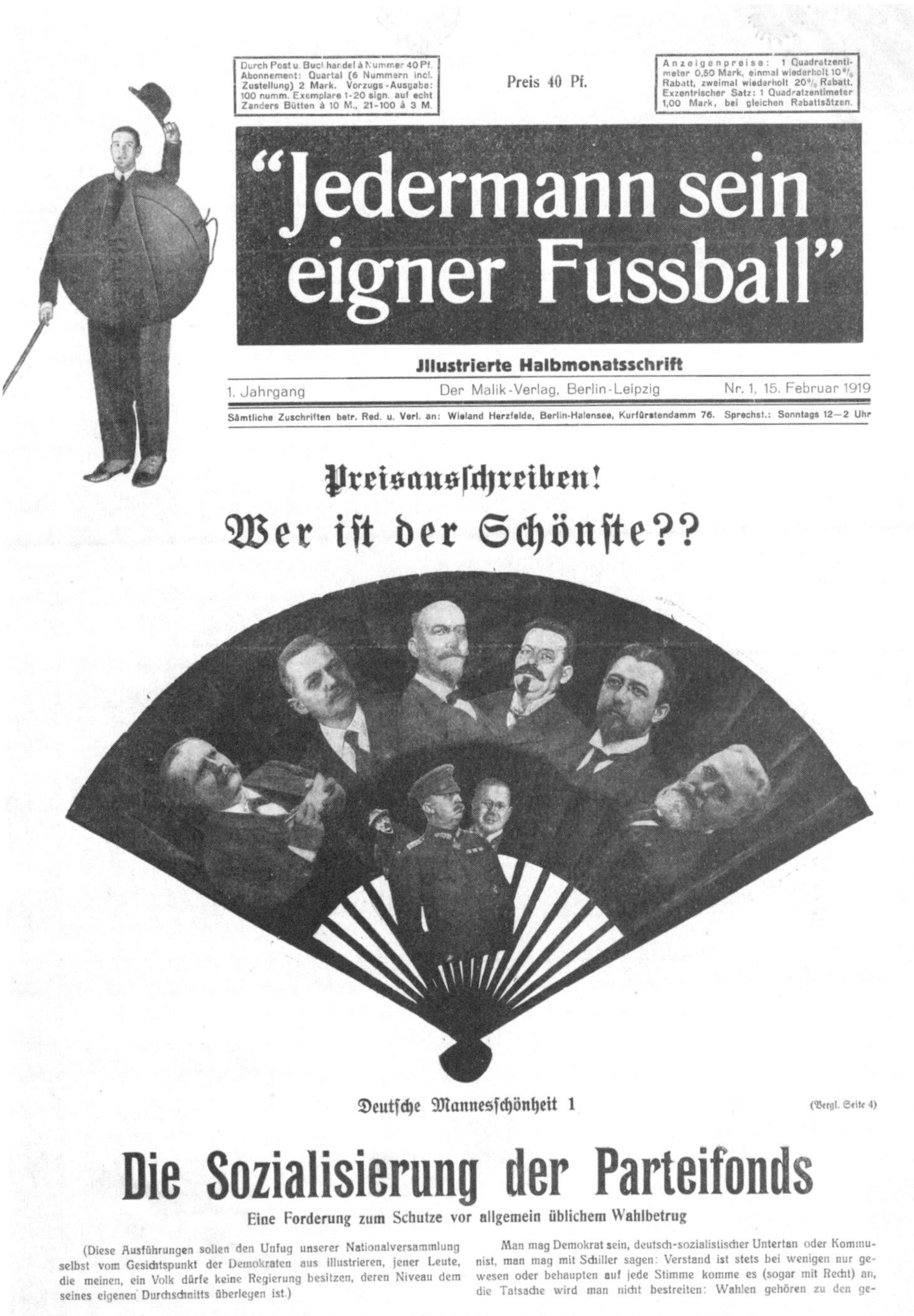

Durch Post u. Buchhandel à Nummer 40 Pf. Abonnement: Quartal (6 Nummern incl. Zustellung) 2 Mark. Vorzugs-Ausgabe: 100 numm. Exemplare 1-20 sign. auf echt Zanders Bütten à 10 M., 21-100 à 3 M.

Preis 40 Pf.

Anzeigenpreise: 1 Quadratzentimeter 0,50 Mark, einmal wiederholt 10 % Rabatt, zweimal wiederholt 20 % Rabatt. Exzentrischer Satz: 1 Quadratzentimeter 1,00 Mark, bei gleichen Rabattsätzen.

“Jedermann sein eigner Fussball”

Jllustrierte Halbmonatsschrift

1. Jahrgang — Der Malik-Verlag, Berlin-Leipzig — Nr. 1, 15. Februar 1919

Sämtliche Zuschriften betr. Red. u. Verl. an: Wieland Herzfelde, Berlin-Halensee, Kurfürstendamm 76. Sprechst.: Sonntags 12—2 Uhr

Preisausſchreiben!

Wer iſt der Schönſte??

Deutſche Mannesſchönheit 1 (Vergl. Seite 4)

Die Sozialisierung der Parteifonds

Eine Forderung zum Schutze vor allgemein üblichem Wahlbetrug

(Diese Ausführungen sollen den Unfug unserer Nationalversammlung selbst vom Gesichtspunkt der Demokraten aus illustrieren, jener Leute, die meinen, ein Volk dürfe keine Regierung besitzen, deren Niveau dem seines eigenen Durchschnitts überlegen ist.)

Man mag Demokrat sein, deutsch-sozialistischer Untertan oder Kommunist, man mag mit Schiller sagen: Verstand ist stets bei wenigen nur gewesen oder behaupten auf jede Stimme komme es (sogar mit Recht) an, die Tatsache wird man nicht bestreiten: Wahlen gehören zu den ge-

FIGURE 15. Title page, *Jedermann sein eigner Fussball* (Everyman his own soccer ball), no. 1 (unique issue; 15 February 1919), edited by Wieland Herzfelde (Berlin and Leipzig: Malik Verlag). Illustrations: (top) John Heartfield, *Wieland Herzfelde as “Progress Dada,”* and (bottom) George Grosz, *Galerie deutscher Mannesschönheit, Preisfrage “Wer ist der Schönste?”* (Gallery of German male beauty, prize question “Who is the most beautiful?”). Heartfield art © 2010 Artists Rights Society (ARS), New York/VG Bild-Kunst, Bonn. Grosz art © Estate of George Grosz/Licensed by VAGA, New York, NY. Photo: Research Library, The Getty Research Institute, Los Angeles, California.

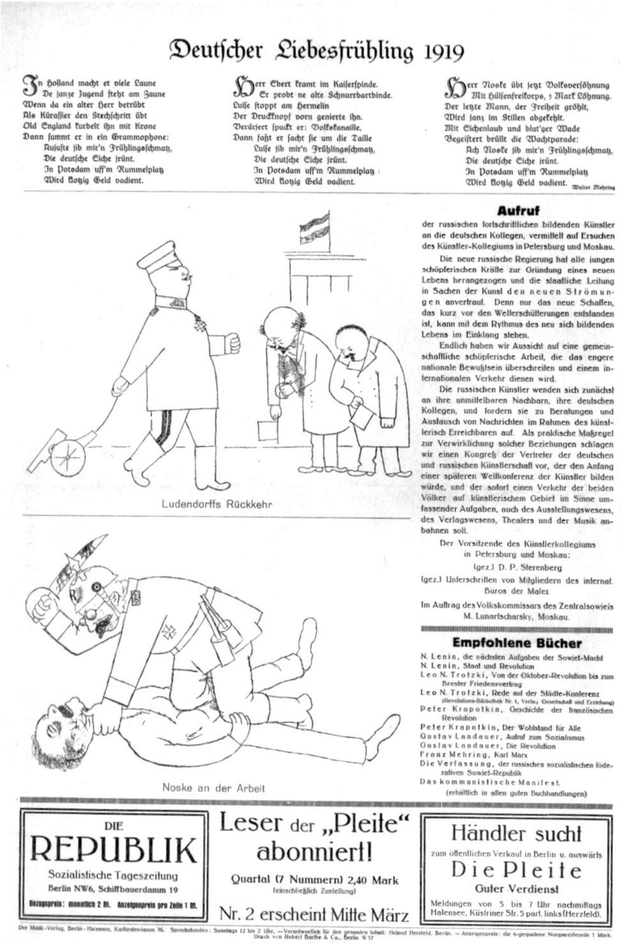

Deutscher Liebesfrühling 1919

In Holland macht et viele Laune
De janze Jugend steht am Zaune
Wenn da ein alter Herr betrübt
Als Kürassier den Stechschritt übt
Old England kurbelt ihn mit Krone
Dann summt er in ein Grammophone:
Aujuste jib mir'n Frühlingsschmatz,
Die deutsche Eiche jrünt.
In Potsdam uff'm Rummelplatz
Wird flotzig Geld vadient.

Herr Ebert kramt im Kaiserspinde.
Er probt ne alte Schnurrbartbinde.
Luise stoppt am Hermelin
Der Druckknopf vorn genierte ihn.
Verärjert spuckt er: Volkskanaille,
Dann faßt er sacht sie um die Taille
Luise jib mir'n Frühlingsschmatz,
Die deutsche Eiche jrünt.
In Potsdam uff'm Rummelplatz
Wird flotzig Geld vadient.

Herr Noske übt jetzt Volksversöhnung
Mit Hülsenfreikorps, 5 Mark Löhnung.
Der letzte Mann, der Freiheit gröhlt,
Wird janz im Stillen abgekehlt.
Mit Eichenlaub und blut'ger Wade
Begeistert brüllt die Wachtparade:
Ach Noske jib mir'n Frühlingsschmatz,
Die deutsche Eiche jrünt.
In Potsdam uff'm Rummelplatz
Wird flotzig Geld vadient.

Walter Mehring

Aufruf

der russischen fortschrittlichen bildenden Künstler an die deutschen Kollegen, vermittelt auf Ersuchen des Künstler-Kollegiums in Petersburg und Moskau.

Die neue russische Regierung hat alle jungen schöpferischen Kräfte zur Gründung eines neuen Lebens herangezogen und die staatliche Leitung in Sachen der Kunst den neuen Strömungen anvertraut. Denn nur das neue Schaffen, das kurz vor den Welterschütterungen entstanden ist, kann mit dem Rythmus des neu sich bildenden Lebens im Einklang stehen.

Endlich haben wir Aussicht auf eine gemeinschaftliche schöpferische Arbeit, die das engere nationale Bewußtsein überschreiten und einem internationalen Verkehr dienen wird.

Die russischen Künstler wenden sich zunächst an ihre unmittelbaren Nachbarn, ihre deutschen Kollegen, und fordern sie zu Beratungen und Austausch von Nachrichten im Rahmen des künstlerisch Erreichbaren auf. Als praktische Maßregel zur Verwirklichung solcher Beziehungen schlagen wir einen Kongreß der Vertreter der deutschen und russischen Künstlerschaft vor, der den Anfang einer späteren Weltkonferenz der Künstler bilden würde, und der sofort einen Verkehr der beiden Völker auf künstlerischem Gebiet im Sinne umfassender Aufgaben, auch des Ausstellungswesens, des Verlagswesens, Theaters und der Musik anbahnen soll.

Der Vorsitzende des Künstlerkollegiums
in Petersburg und Moskau:
(gez.) D. P. Sterenberg

(gez.) Unterschriften von Mitgliedern des internat. Büros der Maler

Im Auftrag des Volkskommissars des Zentralsowjets
M. Lunartscharsky, Moskau.

Empfohlene Bücher

N. Lenin, die nächsten Aufgaben der Sowjet-Macht
N. Lenin, Staat und Revolution
Leo N. Trotzki, Von der Oktober-Revolution bis zum Brester Friedensvertrag
Leo N. Trotzki, Rede auf der Städte-Konferenz (Revolutions-Bibliothek Nr. 1, Verlag Gesellschaft und Erziehung)
Peter Krapotkin, Geschichte der französischen Revolution
Peter Krapotkin, Der Wohlstand für Alle
Gustav Landauer, Aufruf zum Sozialismus
Gustav Landauer, Die Revolution
Franz Mehring, Karl Marx
Die Verfassung, der russischen sozialistischen föderativen Sowjet-Republik
Das kommunistische Manifest.
(erhältlich in allen guten Buchhandlungen)

DIE
REPUBLIK
Sozialistische Tageszeitung
Berlin NW6, Schiffbauerdamm 19
Bezugspreis: monatlich 2 M. Anzeigenpreis pro Zeile 1 M.

Leser der „Pleite" abonniert!
Quartal (7 Nummern) 2,40 Mark
(einschließlich Zustellung)
Nr. 2 erscheint Mitte März

Händler sucht
zum öffentlichen Verkauf in Berlin u. auswärts
Die Pleite
Guter Verdienst
Meldungen von 5 bis 7 Uhr nachmittags Halensee, Küstriner Str. 5 part. links (Herzfeld).

Der Malik-Verlag, Berlin-Halensee, Kurfürstendamm 76. Sprechstunden: Sonntags 12 bis 2 Uhr. — Verantwortlich für den gesamten Inhalt: Helmut Herzfeld, Berlin. — Anzeigenpreis: die 6-gespaltene Nonpareillezeile 1 Mark. Druck von Robert Barthe & Co., Berlin W 57

FIGURE 16. **George Grosz, "Ludendorffs Return" and "Noske at Work," illustrations in *Die Pleite* 1 (Berlin: Malik Verlag, 1919). Art © Estate of George Grosz/Licensed by VAGA, New York, NY. Photo: International Dada Archive, University of Iowa Libraries.**

that it "was not an artistic movement in the accepted sense; it was a storm that broke over the world of art as the war did over the nations."[20] The Zurich Dadaists rejected World War I, as well as the bourgeois conception of art, as a realm of higher spiritual values in which one could find refuge both from mundane everyday reality and from cataclysmic current events. Gathering in neutral Switzerland, they staged agitational cabaret performances in the Cabaret Voltaire, a name the Dadaists chose in homage to the French rationalist and satirist. This international group of young writers and artists included the Germans Hugo Ball, Richard Huelsenbeck, Emmy Hennings, Max Oppenheimer, Hans Richter, and Arthur Segal. Like the Zurich Dadaists Tristan Tzara and Marcel Janco, Segal was of Romanian Jewish origin.[21] Other active participants included Hans (Jean) Arp, born in the Alsace when it was under German control; the Swiss Dada painter and designer Sophie Täuber, who would marry Arp; the Dutch painter Otto van Rees; and the Bohemian writer and psychologist Dr. Walter Serner (born Walter Seligmann, in Karlsbad). Dada rejected what had passed for an avant-garde artistic culture immediately before the war. Fauvism, Cubism, and Expressionism all seemed to belong to a culture of bourgeois comfort and individualistic aspiration that had proved incapable of responding adequately to mechanized carnage. The Dadaists' poetic outpourings attempted to replace stultifying national languages with an avant-garde Esperanto. Not wanting to be another "ism" tacked on to an existing word, they gave their movement a nonsensical name with international associations. *Dada* in Russian or Romanian means "yes, yes." In French, a *dada* is a wooden horse. In German, it means "there, there." And in English and many other languages it has infantile associations. The Dada youths returned to an inchoate, primitive, transnational form of communication. They demanded attention. But while Dada demands were often phrased in infantile form, they were based in the deadly serious experience of war and revolution and were a mature demand for a better, internationally cooperative future.[22]

Epochal technological advances in the late nineteenth and early twentieth centuries—the automobile and the machine gun (1885), wireless radiotelegraph communications and projected motion pictures (1895), the Wright brothers' flight at Kitty Hawk (1904), Ford's mass production of automobiles (Model Ts began to roll off the assembly line in 1908)—when mobilized for war, left much of "the generation of 1914" in a state of shock.[23] Walter Benjamin, born in Berlin in 1892, wrote in his 1936 essay "The Storyteller": "With the end of the World War a process began to become apparent which has not halted since then. . . . A generation that had gone to school on a horse-drawn streetcar now stood under the open sky in a countryside in which nothing remained unchanged but the clouds, and beneath these clouds, in a field of force of destructive torrents and explosions, was the tiny, fragile human body." No artists registered more acutely than the Berlin Dadaists this generation's shock and outrage at the war and its aftermath—in their work, their activities, and their sense that they performed for "an audience of traumatophiles."[24] Reporting from Berlin for the *Chicago Daily News*, Ben Hecht, a friend of George Grosz who later became a prolific Hollywood screenwriter, described a Dada evening in May 1919 at the I.B. Neumann gallery as a form of group therapy, "one of the many new fantastic outlets for the neurasthenia which grips the souls and bodies of the German people."[25]

Richard Huelsenbeck returned to Berlin from Zurich in 1917 and proclaimed Dada in a speech delivered on February 23, 1918, at the gallery of Israel Ber Neumann, "I.B." for short in Berlin, and "J.B." when he moved his gallery to New York in the early 1920s. Neumann hosted the first three events, which were organized by the Herzfeldes' Neue Jugend group in 1916–17, and the Dadaists held their first Berlin exhibition at Neumann's in April–May 1919.[26] The art historian Joan Weinstein points out that many artists who had been associated with the Expressionist Der Sturm gallery switched to Neumann, "the art promoter in Berlin most closely identified with the [November 1918] revolution."[27] Unlike Der Sturm gallery director Herwarth Walden (born Georg Lewin), Neumann had not changed his name, so his Jewish ethnicity was writ large on gallery signs and letterheads associated with Dada's first and subsequent appearances in Berlin. The writer Walter Mehring later described a "Dada matinee" at Neumann's as an explicit response to the war: "In the turnip winter 1917/18 one had the feeling the war would never end.... It became clear to the Dadaists that we needed to intervene by any means necessary to try to cure this purposeless situation."[28]

Wieland Herzfelde was involved with Berlin Dada primarily as a publisher. This gave him a central role in the movement. Berlin Dada strove to be totally up-to-date and competitive in Berlin's rapidly changing media environment. The leading scholar of Berlin Dada, Hanne Bergius, has observed that the Berlin Dadaists recognized and exploited "the power of the media at a moment in which the initial effects of a structural transformation of publicity were becoming discernable."[29] Journals such as the *Berliner Illustrirte Zeitung*, for instance, tried to attract passers-by on the increasingly crowded urban streets by printing photographs prominently, rather than relying on subscription sales mailed directly to the homes of devoted longtime readers (see fig. 25). Over a hundred daily newspapers vied for the distracted, rushing Berlin urbanite's attention. The historian Modris Eckstein has argued that the "most striking features of the German press on the eve of the First World War were its abundance, its decentralization, and its growing commercialization and politicization."[30] In such a context, the Berlin Dadaists understood the power of and necessity for daring publishers such as Herzfelde, and of slogans, catchphrases, striking images, and defined political positions. As would-be media stars, they reveled in nicknames defining the breadth and content of their movement and proclaiming their particular roles in it: Dadasoph Hausmann, Weltdada Huelsenbeck, Oberdada Johannes Baader, Heartfield the Monteurdada, Progressdada Wieland Herzfelde, Pipidada Walter Mehring, Grosz the Propagandada. Hannah Höch, the only woman playing a major part in their activities, lacked both a title and a distinct role.[31]

In a carefully staged publicity photograph of the Dada Fair, Höch and Hausmann, who were from 1915 to 1922 a sometimes tender but more often tempestuous couple, stand before some of their works (fig. 9).[32] His right arm just impinges on her *Cut with the Kitchen Knife Dada*, and her left arm overlaps his collage *Tatlin at Home*. Both titles allude ironically to domestic settings. The images presented by the artists themselves, though, like those in their montages, suggest a mobile bohemian existence. The bourgeois home is something to escape and dissect. The Höch scholar Jula Dech describes the photograph as follows: "Höch and her lover Hausmann in an artificial pose in front of her *Kitchen Knife* collage"; she points out elsewhere that Höch, in her beret, is every bit the Dada Dandy, the sophisticated and somewhat satiric urban flaneur, just as Hausmann, wearing a driving cap and a monocle, is the pseudo-sportsman.[33] Bergius informs us that Höch was proud to have acquired a pair of American shoes to wear to the fair, where she cut a stylish, mobile figure.[34] Striking a contrapposto pose, in contrast to his more static position, she is better attuned to the Weimar "New Women" that most recent Höch scholars see as the active heroines, women on the move, montaged into *Cut with the Kitchen Knife Dada.*

German museums did not acquire Höch's works until after World War II. Höch and her works survived the Nazis' "degenerate art" action, which limited its pillaging to public collections, because the museums considered neither the work nor the artist important. If her work is now recognized as fundamental to any understanding of montage, Berlin Dada, and Weimar culture—and, indeed, to twentieth-century art and culture in general—it was at the time all but ignored outside her own avant-garde circle, as was she. Unlike most of her Berlin Dada compatriots, she was not compelled to flee Germany during the Nazi period. She survived in isolation in the Berlin suburb of Heiligensee, where she tended her garden, produced art, and maintained her own Dada archive, a rich source of primary information on Berlin Dada. Housed at the Berlinische Galerie since the 1980s, this archive has now been carefully catalogued, analyzed, and, in part, published.[35] Since its acquisition by the National Gallery in 1961, *Cut with the Kitchen Knife Dada* has been seen as her major work, as well as the single most important surviving visual document of Berlin Dada. Before its acquisition by the museum, *Cut with the Kitchen Knife Dada* went unremarked, mentioned by name in the catalogue of the Dada Fair but nowhere else.

Grosz's *Germany: A Winter's Tale,* in contrast, was reproduced and discussed early in its life, for example in Willi Wolfradt's Grosz monograph of 1921, Salomo Friedlaender's critical Grosz study of 1922 (published under Friedlaender's pen name, Mynona), and as the central image in a newspaper account of July 1920 satirizing the Dada Fair.[36] Some two hundred eighty-five Grosz works were seized from German museums and galleries in the "degenerate art" action, and five of his paintings, two watercolors, and thirteen graphics were shown in the 1937 Munich exhibition, one wall of which, the "Dada Wall"—and perhaps the exhibition concept of mixing artworks with derogatory texts, posters, and slogans—was inspired by the Dada Fair itself (fig. 17). But *Germany: A Winter's Tale* was not among the works seized or shown.[37] Wieland Herzfelde wrote in 1946, "The painting is lost; it disappeared early in 1933 from my apartment, which I could not enter after the Reichstag fire."[38] The Berlin Dadaists' commitment to publicity, though, enabled the image to survive, reproduce, and mutate. Herzfelde states that as soon as the collage-painting was completed, the Malik Verlag Dadaists immediately shot a seven-color transparency. The Malik publisher then used elements from it in different contexts, such as Huelsenbeck's 1920 book *Deutschland muss untergehen!* (Germany must go under!), where the three figures at the bottom of the painting, the general, the minister, and the teacher, appear separately on the cover and on pages 9 and 11,

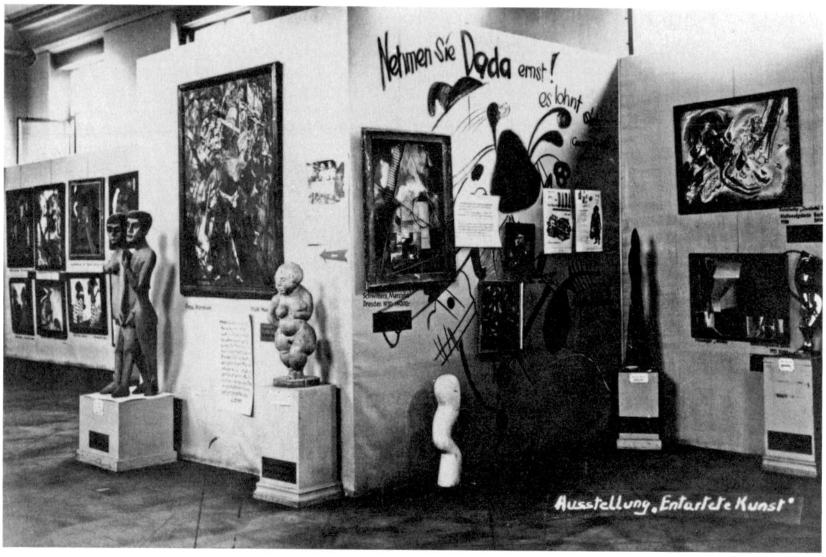

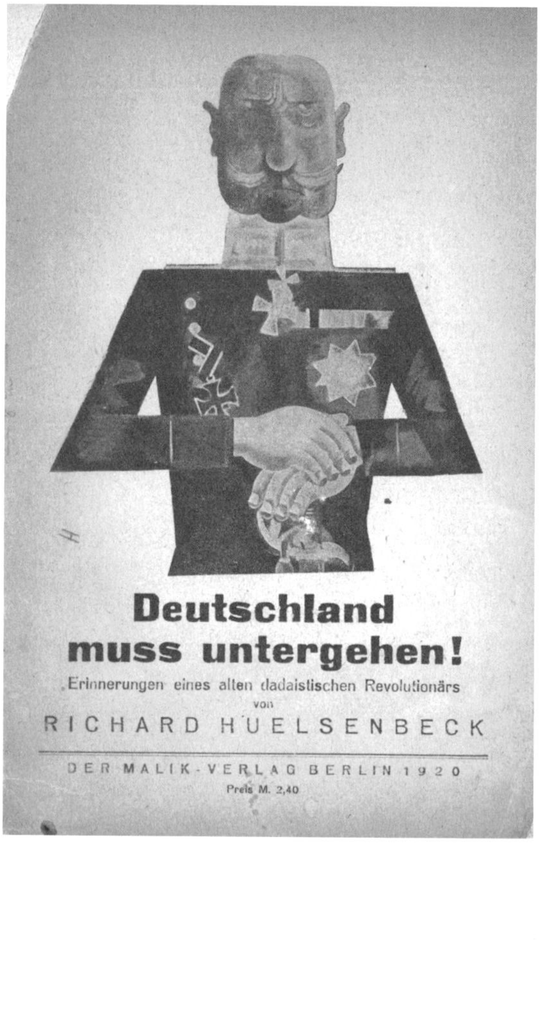

FIGURE 17. Postcard featuring the "Dada Wall" at the "Degenerate Art" exhibition, Munich, 1937. Photo: Hannah-Höch-Archiv, Berlinische Galerie, Landesmuseum für Moderne Kunst, Fotografie und Architektur. FIGURE 18. Front cover of Richard Huelsenbeck's *Deutschland muss untergehen!* (Berlin: Malik Verlag, 1920). Photo: International Dada Archive, University of Iowa Libraries.

putting a repugnant face on the German establishment that the Dadaists hoped to bring down (fig. 18). The whole painting reappeared in black and white and later as a color plate in H. W. Janson's *History of Art,* where its imagery and status as a lost work allowed it to represent both the chaos of World War I and the war's aftermath and Nazi destruction.[39]

More recent art history has not granted *Germany: A Winter's Tale* nearly as much analysis as *Cut with the Kitchen Knife Dada*. The lack of close readings derives from the unavailability of the thing itself, with its complex structure and imagery, for direct study and interpretation. Had it survived, it would almost certainly be in the possession of a major museum. The museum's curatorial staff would be responsible for interpreting it, and for providing access and resources for others to do so.[40] Known only in reproduction, *Germany: A Winter's Tale* has been interpreted only generally, as a translation into paint of the political critique of Wilhelmine and early Weimar elites and society of Grosz's graphics: painted caricatures amid a kaleidoscopically Futurist image of apocalypse.

Cut with the Kitchen Knife Dada's myriad pictorial elements, cut directly from the booming popular press of 1919, remain available for firsthand study. In recent years they have been very directly connected to that time and place, with great iconographic specificity. Biographical information about Höch and social facts of her time, the work's title, and specific pictorial elements in it support feminist analyses of the montage. Höch was a liberated, independent, professional woman who advocated universal suffrage and reproductive rights. She was a highly sophisticated artist, moreover, working among ambitious and often arrogant men, including Grosz—who opposed her inclusion in the Dada Fair—and had to struggle for any acceptance or recognition she achieved. *Cut with the Kitchen Knife Dada* includes prominent pictures of other professional women, especially writers, artists, and performers. It also includes a map, at the lower right, that highlights European countries in which women had achieved the right to vote (fig. 21). Höch's face overlaps this map and connects it with a photograph of a train on which Hausmann's profile emerges from the next window to the left. The title refers to a domestic item, typically used by women to serve men, but here transformed into an implement to dissect a conservative, patriarchal culture, summed up by the typically male beer belly.[41] Since Hanne Bergius's and Jula Dech's pioneering work of the mid- to later 1970s, interpretations have stressed these elements as connecting the work to the emergence of the Weimar New Woman: professionally active, short-haired, liberated women; publicly and professionally active to the extent the culture allowed; and, like Höch, demanding more. Höch's presentation of the New Woman, as the American art historian Maud Lavin has argued, is not unambiguous. Like all the images in the montage and the total *gestalt,* it is complex and multiple, and it oscillates between celebrating liberation, critiquing recalcitrant reality, and ironically deflating stereotypical aspects of New Woman ideology.

Feminism has also had an impact on Grosz scholarship, if not directly on analyses of

Germany: A Winter's Tale. The art historian Barbara McCloskey, who wrote a book on Grosz's relationship to the Communist Party, has observed that since the late 1980s the work of the women art historians Bergius, Kathrin Hoffmann-Curtius, Beth Irwin Lewis, and Maria Tatar has explored the theme of *Lustmord* and the pervasive depiction of sexual violence against women in Grosz's work.[42] These scholars have not condemned Grosz for his images of rape and murder, interpreting them as a reflection of a social problem and Grosz as a typically sexist man of his times who at least had the acuity to diagnose this condition and not to aestheticize it. Nevertheless, Grosz's depictions of women are commonly characterized as misogynist.[43]

The interpretive turn I shall now take, to examine the involvement of these works and Berlin Dada with Jewish thematics and individuals, is connected, like the feminist turn, to broader social forces—the interest since at least the 1980s in multiculturalism and questions of identity—and these forces' impact on recent scholarship.[44] Until the mid-1990s art history had little to say about Jewish identity in modern art, but that situation has begun to change.[45] Until very recently almost no scholarship considered Dadaism, especially Berlin Dada, in this light—a remarkable gap, given the monumental amount of research, its diversity of approach, and its sophistication.[46] Aside from Lavin, who has interesting things to say about Jewish liberals in Weimar and Höch's association with them as an employee of the Ullstein Verlag, as well as about the "Jewish anti-Semite" Otto Weininger and his gender theorizing, neither she nor any other scholar of art history has attempted to read images of Jews in Höch's work, or commented on the broader implications of the association of Berlin Dada with Jews.[47]

In emphasizing these works as objects—along with the loss of one and survival of the other, and the issue of Jewish identity—I study not only the context of their creation but also the subsequent history of Germany, especially the Nazi's accession to power in 1933. That regime's brutal policies toward liberated women, modernist art and artists, and Jews renders the history of these works all the more significant. The contexts surrounding the disappearance of *Germany: A Winter's Tale* and the reappearance of *Cut with the Kitchen Knife Dada* have conditioned their interpretation. Grosz's work has functioned as a lost and silenced victim of the regime and Höch's as an eloquent survivor.

Jews in Dada's Texts

The first issue of the Berlin journal *Dada,* produced in June 1919 by Huelsenbeck, Baader, and Hausmann, and listing Tristan Tzara as an international guest, includes at top right on the first page the Hebrew word כשר—kosher—near the picture of a cow (fig. 19).[48] Other examples of Hebrew, and specifically כשר, had already appeared in the catalogue of the Cologne Dada exhibition "Dada Vorfrühling" (Dada pre-spring) in

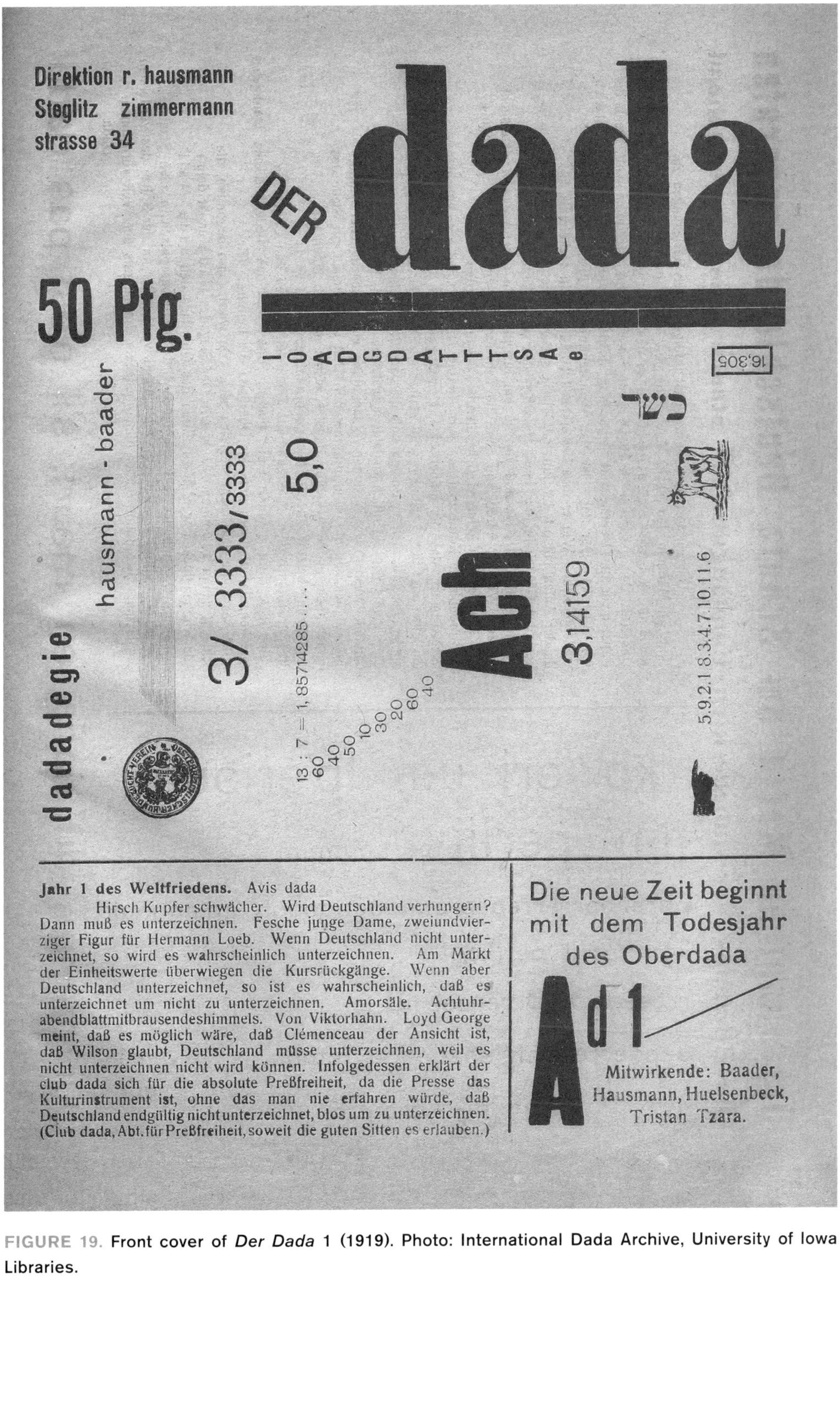
Direktion r. hausmann
Steglitz zimmermann
strasse 34
DER dada
50 Pfg.
dadadegie
hausmann - baader
3/ 3333/3333
5,0
Ach
3,14159
13 : 7 = 1,85714285....
5.9.2.1 8.3.4.7.10.11.6
16,305

Jahr 1 des Weltfriedens. Avis dada

Hirsch Kupfer schwächer. Wird Deutschland verhungern? Dann muß es unterzeichnen. Fesche junge Dame, zweiundvierziger Figur für Hermann Loeb. Wenn Deutschland nicht unterzeichnet, so wird es wahrscheinlich unterzeichnen. Am Markt der Einheitswerte überwiegen die Kursrückgänge. Wenn aber Deutschland unterzeichnet, so ist es wahrscheinlich, daß es unterzeichnet um nicht zu unterzeichnen. Amorsäle. Achtuhrabendblattmitbrausendeshimmels. Von Viktorhahn. Loyd George meint, daß es möglich wäre, daß Clémenceau der Ansicht ist, daß Wilson glaubt, Deutschland müsse unterzeichnen, weil es nicht unterzeichnen nicht wird können. Infolgedessen erklärt der club dada sich für die absolute Preßfreiheit, da die Presse das Kulturinstrument ist, ohne das man nie erfahren würde, daß Deutschland endgültig nicht unterzeichnet, blos um zu unterzeichnen. (Club dada, Abt. für Preßfreiheit, soweit die guten Sitten es erlauben.)

Die neue Zeit beginnt mit dem Todesjahr des Oberdada

Ad 1

Mitwirkende: Baader, Hausmann, Huelsenbeck, Tristan Tzara.

FIGURE 19. Front cover of *Der Dada* 1 (1919). Photo: International Dada Archive, University of Iowa Libraries.

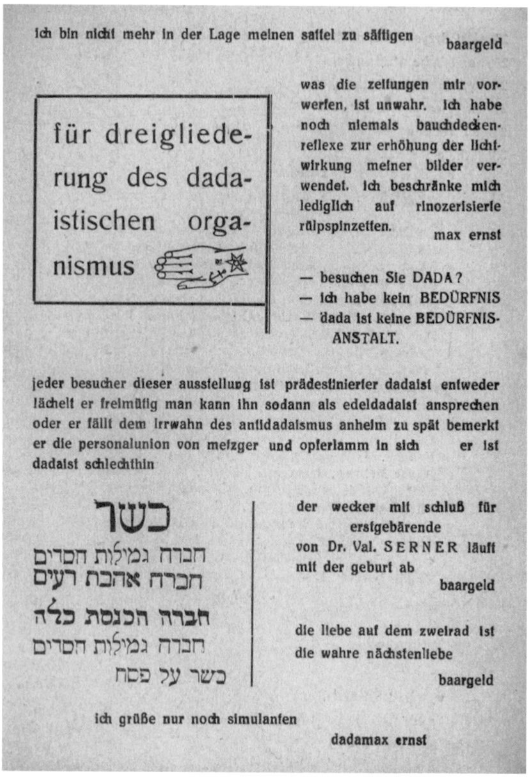

ich bin nicht mehr in der Lage meinen sattel zu sättigen
baargeld

für dreigliederung des dadaistischen organismus

was die zeitungen mir vorwerfen, ist unwahr. ich habe noch niemals bauchdeckenreflexe zur erhöhung der lichtwirkung meiner bilder verwendet. ich beschränke mich lediglich auf rinozerisierte rülpspinzetten.
max ernst

— besuchen Sie DADA?
— ich habe kein BEDÜRFNIS
— dada ist keine BEDÜRFNIS-ANSTALT.

jeder besucher dieser ausstellung ist prädestinierter dadaist entweder lächelt er freimütig man kann ihn sodann als edeldadaist ansprechen oder er fällt dem irrwahn des antidadaismus anheim zu spät bemerkt er die personalunion von metzger und opferlamm in sich er ist dadaist schlechthin

כשר
חברה גמילות חסדים
חברה אהבת רעים
חברה הכנסת כלה
חברה גמילות חסדים
כשר על פסח

der wecker mit schluß für erstgebärende von Dr. Val. SERNER läuft mit der geburt ab
baargeld

die liebe auf dem zweirad ist die wahre nächstenliebe
baargeld

ich grüße nur noch simulanten
dadamax ernst

FIGURE 20. Back cover of *Dada Ausstellung: Dada-Vorfrühling,* exhibition catalogue for "Dada Pre-Spring" at Brauhaus Winter, Cologne, April 1920. Photo: International Dada Archive, University of Iowa Libraries.

April 1920, an event the German Dada scholar Bettina Schaschke interprets as a precursor to the Berlin Dada Fair. In the Cologne catalogue five more lines of handwritten doggerel in Hebrew appear under כשר (fig. 20). The passage reads "KOSHER / Society for granting charity / Society for love between friends / Society for bringing in of brides / Society for granting charity / Kosher for Passover."[49] The author of these lines was probably the German-Jewish journalist and art historian Lou Straus-Ernst, born in Cologne in 1893 and murdered at Auschwitz in 1944, who married Max Ernst in 1918. Straus-Ernst helped to organize Cologne Dada events. According to her son, the painter Jimmy Ernst, born in 1920, she also showed her collages in the Dada prespring exhibition.[50]

European Jewry provided these German Dadaists with a precedent for a language that, like Hebrew and a kosher diet, was specific to the Jewish and the Dada diaspora. The Romanian Jew Tzara had attempted before the war to construct a global language for initiates, a system of pure sounds that would convey meaning to insiders but seem garbled and nonsensical to outsiders.[51] Sometimes, though, there is sense in nonsense:

a critic writing about the raucous matinee performance at the Tribüne Theater in Berlin on December 7, 1919, declared the Dadaists to be "Meschuggas" (Yiddish for "crazies") and asked, "But who doesn't recognize that while the 'Meschuggas' display is in part raging youthful desire, it's also in part a masquerade, under cover of which the Dadaists boldly pursue their satiric craziness, their crazy satire."[52] The seriousness of Berlin Dada's seemingly nonsensical demands and gallows humor can be measured only in the context of the war and postwar years. In a handwritten chronology prepared in 1949 Hannah Höch reflected: "Dada was a revolt by visual and other artists against the system that brought on the First World War. We wanted freedom."[53]

During the war, Wieland Herzfelde and John Heartfield founded the Malik Press to print and distribute Berlin Dada graphics and books. The Herzfeld brothers, to revert to their birth name, were sons of the socialist and ethnically Jewish writer Franz Herzfeld, whose pen name was Franz Held. Exiled from Germany for writing a supposedly blasphemous poem in 1895, Herzfeld and his wife, the anarchist Alice Stolzenberg, abandoned their children, and both died while incarcerated in an Austrian sanatorium.[54] According to John Heartfield's first wife, Barbara (writing in 1942), after their parents' deaths the Herzfeld children each had an inheritance of about sixty thousand marks, administered by their uncle, Joseph Herzfeld—a prominent Jewish lawyer and left-wing politician in Berlin—which provided them each with a monthly allowance of fifty marks until the money lost all value in the postwar inflation.[55] Walter Mehring reported that the Herzfelds' inheritance helped finance their activities, specifically the printing and distribution of *Jedermann sein eigner Fussball.* Probably not by coincidence, Mehring was also the son of a German-Jewish author who had been charged with blasphemy: Sigmar Mehring, who preceded Kurt Tucholsky as editor of the humor magazine *Ulk.*[56] According to Mehring, the Malik Press promoted *Jedermann* by hiring a band, as well as raucously hawking the publication from a carriage driving through Berlin, and they sold all seventy-six hundred copies.[57]

Walter Mehring's head appears in the bottom-right corner of *Cut with the Kitchen Knife Dada,* just below the heads of Hannah Höch and Raoul Hausmann, glancing back toward the bodiless head of Albert Einstein in the top-left corner (fig. 21). Höch placed Mehring's head on the body of a muscleman, a pairing Bergius interprets as a caricature of the *Pipidada*'s (wee-dada's) "dainty appearance."[58] The depiction also makes Mehring the literal, dadaistic, and absurd embodiment of the call for buff twentieth-century "Muscle Jews" *(Muskeljuden)* issued by Max Nordau, the Zionist author of *Entartung* (Degeneration, 1892). Muscle Jews would replace the nineteenth century's "thin-chested 'coffeehouse Jews' "—exactly what Mehring was in the flesh.[59]

Another prominent "coffeehouse Jew" and an inspiration for Dada, the poet Else Lasker-Schüler, appears in *Cut with the Kitchen Knife Dada* as if wearing a huge hat, ornamenting the chest of the shadowy image of Kaiser Wilhelm II in the upper right (fig. 22). The Malik Press took its name from the eponymous hero of Lasker-Schüler's antiwar novella *Der Malik,* an "Oriental," that is, Middle Eastern, prince. Wieland Herz-

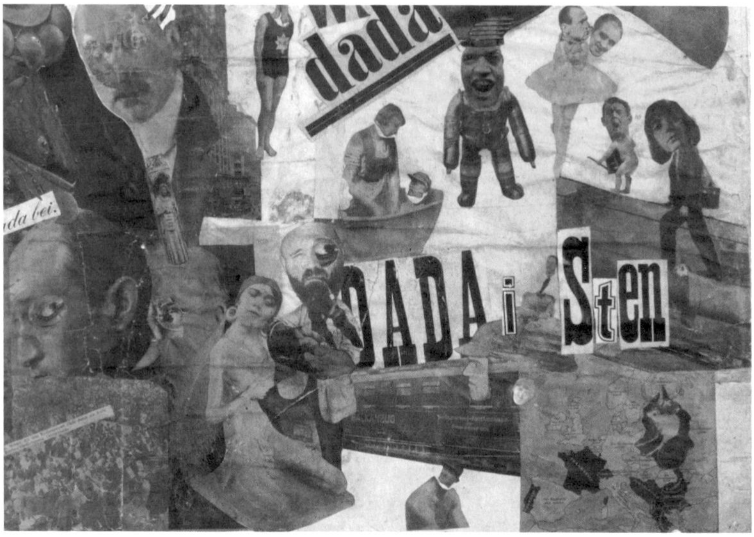

FIGURE 21. Hannah Höch, *Cut with the Kitchen Knife Dada* (detail of plate 3, bottom right). Art © 2010 Artists Rights Society (ARS), New York/VG Bild-Kunst, Bonn. Photo: Bildarchiv Preussischer Kulturbesitz/Art Resource, NY.

felde first met Lasker-Schüler in 1913, the year she published her volume of *Hebräische Balladen* (Hebraic ballads). At seventeen he attended a recital of her poems and rapturously described her performance as "not language, but song, like the magical prayer of an oriental prophetess."[60] When the Herzfeld brothers moved to Berlin, Lasker-Schüler introduced them to the Expressionist avant-garde at her favorite coffeehouse, the Café des Westens, where she was at the center of a bohemian group that also included, according to Herzfelde, Johannes R. Becher, Alfred Wolfenstein, Ferdinand Hardeköpf, Jakob von Hoddis, Theodor Däubler, and Salomo Friedlaender. Lasker-Schüler wrote a poem, "Es war eine Ebbe in meinem Blut" (My blood was at low tide), dedicated to "the two dear brothers, Helmut and Wieland Herzfelde," around 1915.[61] According to Herzfelde, it was Lasker-Schüler who engineered the ruse to convince Heartfield that he was mentally unfit for military service.[62] Under Lasker-Schüler's influence Wieland Herzfelde published his first book, *Sulamith* (1917), a luxury edition of love poems written in 1915–16, printed on rich Japan paper, available in a signed and numbered edition of one hundred, dedicated to his brother, and with an embossed cover bearing George Grosz's first book design.[63] The Old Testament character Shulamite, the sensuous Jewish heroine of the Song of Songs, provides a thinly veiled surrogate for the "oriental prophetess" Lasker-Schüler.

Der Malik: Eine Kaisergeschichte mit Bildern und Zeichnungen (The Malik: The story of an emperor, with pictures and drawings) appeared in three installments, in Franz Pfemfert's Berlin Expressionist journal *Die Aktion,* in 1913–14, in the Innsbruck Ex-

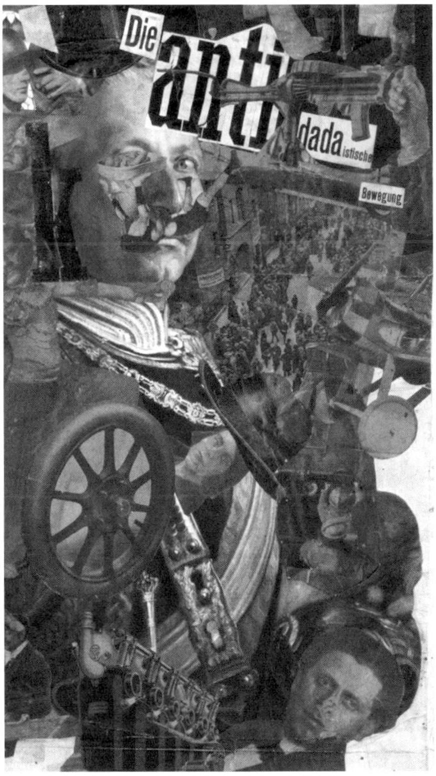

FIGURE 22. Hannah Höch, *Cut with the Kitchen Knife Dada* (detail of plate 3, right center). Art © 2010 Artists Rights Society (ARS), New York/VG Bild-Kunst, Bonn. Photo: Bildarchiv Preussischer Kulturbesitz/Art Resource, NY.

pressionist journal *Der Brenner* in 1914, and, finally, in Grosz, Heartfield, and Herzfelde's *Neue Jugend*, in 1916–17. The first part of *Der Malik* consists of a series of imaginary letters to the Blue Rider painter Franz Marc. In the seventh letter Lasker-Schüler provided the Herzfeld brothers a brief for their press and the journals and books it would produce: "I will found a journal: The Wild Jews; an art-political journal."[64] Malik Press went on to publish radical art-political journals that were banned during and after the war, such as *Die Pleite*, which savagely attacked the conservative backlash against Germany's November 1918 Revolution.

The art historian Carl Einstein, already well-known for his pioneering 1915 study *Negerplastik* (Negro sculpture), was involved with the Dada group in the formative years 1917–19 but afterward distanced himself. According to Walter Mehring, Einstein suggested the name *Die Pleite* for the Malik journal.[65] The learned Einstein, son of a cantor and lay rabbi from the Rhineland, was no doubt aware of the derivation of the German word *Pleite* (bankruptcy) from the Yiddish *pleto*, and ultimately from the Hebrew *plejta* (flight, in this usage: flight from debt).[66]

The war years were formative for Dada and Höch artistically, intellectually, and personally. During the war Höch met Salomo Friedlaender, a Polish-born Jewish philosopher, critic, and author of "grotesque" stories published under the name of Mynona ("anonym," reversed). Höch and Friedlaender first met at one of the regular gatherings at Ludwig Meidner's apartment in Berlin-Wilmersdorf, which was also where Wieland Herzfelde first met George Grosz and Raoul Hausmann. As the war ground on, Meidner became increasingly religious. In the aftermath of the earth- and sanity-shattering cataclysm of war, which he often portrayed in his "apocalyptic landscapes," Meidner became a practicing orthodox Jew. Höch frequented these evenings, as did Friedlaender, and it is likely that the discussion sometimes turned to Zionism and questions of Jewish identity.[67] It was at this time that Höch adopted the more Jewish spelling of her first name.

In his "Dadaistic Manifesto," a speech delivered at the Neumann Gallery in April 1918, Richard Huelsenbeck declared that the Dadaist is an artist only by accident and incidentally: often he needs rather to be a *Kaufmann,* a merchant, trader, or dealer, more at home at a trade fair than at an art exhibition.[68] This statement certainly reflects the Dadaists' rejection of the art museum's elitist associations and embrace of the commercial world. The term *Kaufmann* (often rendered in translations imprecisely as "businessman") also affiliates the Dadaists with Jews: though not exclusively so, it is commonly a Jewish name, and the profession of Kaufmann is strongly associated, if often stereotypically, with Jewish occupations and identity. Witness the character of Shylock in Shakespeare's "Merchant of Venice"—*Der Kaufmann von Venedig.*

Finding a Jewish presence in the Dadaists' use of words such as *Kaufmann* may appear to overreach and even come uncomfortably close to repeating the Nazis' official conflation of art they considered "degenerate" and "insane" (like Dadaism) with "the Jewish spirit" and, especially, the "Jewish art trade"—represented by such prominent Jewish gallerists as Neumann, Walden, and Alfred Flechtheim. But NS-German ideology and policy had a long prehistory. As Bergius points out, a report on the post-Dada Fair trial, published in the ultranationalist *Deutsche Zeitung,* claimed to discern a secret conspiracy linking Jews, especially Jewish art dealers and merchants, and subversive anti-German art; these charges were given intellectual validity by the prominent historian Werner Sombart's book *The Jews and Modern Capitalism* of 1911, crudely repeated in Hitler's *Mein Kampf* in 1925, and brought home in the bullying Nazi campaign against "degenerate art":

> After the Dada exhibition, [Grosz's portfolio *The Face of the Ruling Class*] is perhaps the most shameless thing to have emerged from this circle. . . . *The Face of the Ruling Class* never bears Jewish traits. Not one single caricature is directed against Semitic capitalism and Semitic racketeering. Well, Groß(!), after all, has to obey his instructions. Connections could not become any clearer.[69]

When Fritz Kaiser, who wrote the guide to the Nazi "Degenerate Art" exhibition of 1937, condemned the interest of modernist artists in Hans Prinzhorn's *Artistry of the Mentally Ill,* a 1923 anthology of artworks created by patients in Prinzhorn's Heidelberg

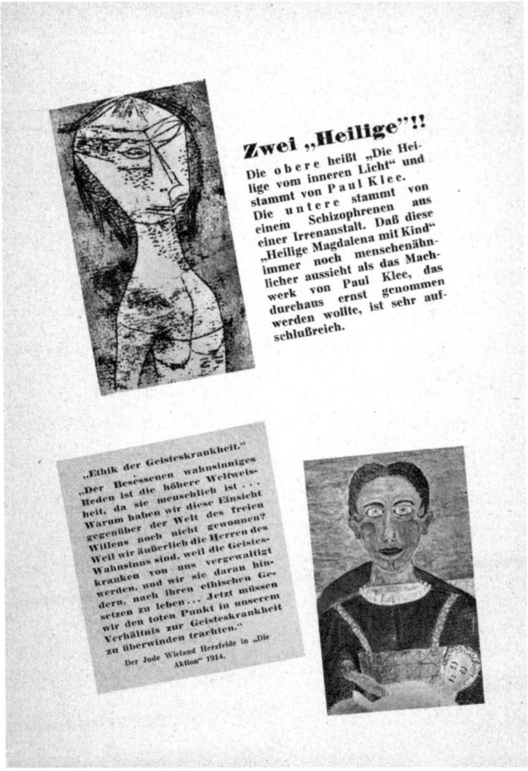

Zwei „Heilige"!!

Die obere heißt „Die Heilige vom inneren Licht" und stammt von Paul Klee. Die untere stammt von einem Schizophrenen aus einer Irrenanstalt. Daß diese „Heilige Magdalena mit Kind" immer noch menschenähnlicher aussieht als das Machwerk von Paul Klee, das durchaus ernst genommen werden wollte, ist sehr aufschlußreich.

„Ethik der Geisteskrankheit."

„Der Besessenen wahnsinniges Reden ist die höhere Weltweisheit, da sie menschlich ist . . . Warum haben wir diese Einsicht gegenüber der Welt des freien Willens noch nicht gewonnen? Weil wir äußerlich die Herren des Wahnsinns sind, weil die Geisteskranken von uns vergewaltigt werden, und wir sie daran hindern, nach ihren ethischen Gesetzen zu leben . . . Jetzt müssen wir den toten Punkt in unserem Verhältnis zur Geisteskrankheit zu überwinden trachten."

Der Jude Wieland Herzfelde in „Die Aktion" 1914.

FIGURE 23. Page 25 from Fritz Kaiser's *Führer durch die Ausstellung Entartete Kunst* (Berlin: Verlag für Kultur-und Wirtschaftswerbung, 1937), with (clockwise from top left) Paul Klee's lithograph *The Saint of the Inner Light* (1921), "Two 'Saints,'" a picture by a mentally ill patient and an excerpt from Wieland Herzfelde's "Ethic of the Mentally Ill" (1914). Klee art © 2010 Artists Rights Society (ARS), New York/VG Bild-Kunst, Bonn. Photo: Research Library, Getty Research Institute, Los Angeles, California.

clinic, he reproduced a work by Paul Klee next to one by a schizophrenic, and linked them to Berlin Dada and Jews by captioning them with a quotation from the man he referred to as "The Jew Wieland Herzfelde" (fig. 23).[70]

One might not think of the many Jews one sees in *Cut with the Kitchen Knife Dada* first and foremost as Jews. One might have a similar response to Heinrich Heine, much of whose writing does not deal with Jewish themes. But though neither Heine nor the Jews depicted in *Cut with the Kitchen Knife Dada* were associated solely with engagement with "Jewish" issues, in the Germany in which they gained notoriety their Jewish origins were always part of their public personae. As the eminent cultural historian Peter Gay, born Peter Fröhlich in Berlin in 1923, points out: "Everyone understood—everyone, philo-Semite and anti-Semite alike—that even those former Jews who had repudiated Judaism by religious conversion to Christianity or legal disaffiliation from the Jewish community, were still somehow Jews. . . . Berlin was full of Jewish agnostics, Jewish atheists, Jewish Catholics, and Jewish Lutherans."[71] There was no monolithic Jewish subject in Wilhelmine or Weimar Germany, and a large gap existed between German and Eastern European Jews. But as Gay asserts, despite the assimilation that had taken place since the opening of the ghettos and emancipation of German Jews, being Jewish always mattered in Germany, as did the deep association with Jews that characterized German Expressionism and Dadaism—in relationships that went beyond necessity and were mutually respectful if not always uncritical (in other words, normal).

The neglect of Jewish content in *Cut with the Kitchen Knife Dada* owes much to its reemergence in Germany at a time of reticence and reluctance to acknowledge either the destruction of Germany's Jews or Jews' contributions to German culture. Interpretation of Höch's montage began just as the situation was about to change, in 1968. But other political and art-political issues seemed more pressing and pertinent to *Kitchen Knife*'s interpretation in that tumultuous political year, and that has remained the case until now. Initial analysis was limited to the mechanics of montage as an artistic practice, and to Berlin Dada's revolt against Wilhelmine authority and Weimar reaction. Since the late 1970s, the montage's mobile, feminist discourse on gender and its mechanical imagery have dominated the discussion. These are important to the work but do not exhaust the forms of difference it thematizes. Issues of Jewish identity formed another long-neglected component of Berlin Dada's revolt against dominant social structures and conceptions of Germanness.

It is correct but incomplete to translate the name of the highpoint of the Berlin Dadaists' activities, *Die Erste Internationale Dada-Messe,* as The First International Dada Fair. *Messe* also has another meaning, beside that of trade fair, that is lost in translation but seems to have impressed itself on many German interpreters of the Dada Fair and of *Germany: A Winter's Tale. Die Messe,* a feminine noun in both meanings, is also the Catholic Mass. In German sources, from early on, the *Dada-Messe* has often been seen as an anti-Mass, an attack not only on the institutions of state and of art but also on the institutional symbols and ceremonies of Christianity at its most ritualistic.

Heartfield's and Rudolf Schlichter's *Prussian Archangel,* with its papier-mâché pig's head and Prussian officer's uniform, hangs over this grotesque satire (fig. 10). Like Grosz's portfolio *Gott mit Uns* (God is with us), it was used as evidence against Grosz, the exhibition's host, Otto Burchard, and Baader, Herzfelde, and Schlichter when all of these men were charged with having insulted the military.[72] The charge and subsequent trial could only have affirmed that the fair/Mass had fulfilled some of its intentions. During and after World War I, Germany and other nations mobilized Christian imagery to promote the myth of the "nobility of death" and the righteousness of the war, as expressed in the *Kriegsmesse* (Mass in Time of War, such as Haydn's 1796 *Missa in tempore belli*).[73] In the postwar period this myth combined with an increase in anti-Semitism, and, as the historian George Mosse has argued, the "exclusion of Jews from many significant social organizations and the *Männerbunde* [men's associations]."[74] The Dadaists responded by staging an inclusive antiwar anti-Mass. Rather than mourn the victims of the war, the *Dada-Messe* attacked those they held responsible for the war, the figures of authority in Wilhelmine Germany: the imperial government, the military, and the Christian clergy.

By attacking Christianity and its clergy and rituals, the Berlin Dadaists lashed out at the beliefs to which most of them had been born, and which they now, to a man and woman, rejected. Baader, the "Oberdada" and self-proclaimed "President of the Globe," sent calling cards with his image framed in a six-pointed star, the Star of David, and famously disrupted a service in the Berlin Cathedral in November 1918 by screaming, "Jesus Christ means nothing to you!"[75] Identification with Jewry provided a precedent for the historical rejection of false messiahs and contemporary pillorying of *Scheinheiligen* (false holy ones, or hypocrites). Grosz's *Germany: A Winter's Tale* clearly identifies as hypocrites those who, in the name of the powers of church, state, and school—the "unholy trinity" of minister, general, and teacher in the lowest register of the collage-painting—had sent a generation to dismemberment and death.

At the time Grosz created and showed *Germany: A Winter's Tale,* Heinrich Heine was being analyzed and defended by philo-Semitic German literary historians (for example, Max Fischer, in his book of 1916, *The German Jew Heinrich Heine*), and attacked by anti-Semites (particularly the influential encyclopedist Adolf Barthels). Grosz's satiric attitude toward Germany, Germanness, and governmental and religious institutions and power, and several pertinent pictorial elements of Grosz's *Germany: A Winter's Tale* correspond to Heine's attitude and his poem's iconography. In the upper right of the painting, Grosz, as Heine had done in his time, identifies and critiques the convergence of sources of power in Imperial Prussia, displaying the word *Kaiser* as printed on a coal briquette— literally a power source—beneath the recently completed Berlin Cathedral, the Kaiser's *Dom,* whose spiked-helmet dome connects the church, the military, and Imperial German pretensions—as does, of course, the "unholy trinity." Grosz, who reveled in role-play—as a *Kaufmann* from Holland, a boxer, a violent rapist, an American, Salvador Dalí—also takes on the role of German Jew in his self-portrait in profile at the lower left. Like Heine, writing his poem as an exile in Paris, Grosz is the outsider as insider and insider as outsider—a knowing, internal, but marginalized critic of the dominant Christian Prussian culture and its discontents.[76] Grosz was convincing in this role: Salomon Wininger's Jewish biographical encyclopedia in 1927 misidentified him as a prominent Jewish artist, an error that may go back to the main witness for the prosecution in the Dada Fair trial, who intimated that the entire event was a Jewish conspiracy.[77]

Berlin Dada, part of a broader Dada diaspora, was specific to its time and place. By 1914 the population of Berlin had grown to about two million. With the incorporation of several suburbs in 1920, the population reached about four million.[78] About two hundred thousand of Berlin's residents were Jews, approximately 5 percent of the city's population and ten times the percentage in the total German populace. The two most prominent Jews in Berlin were probably the foreign minister, Walter Rathenau, and the scientist Albert Einstein, who spent as little time in the city as possible after Rathenau's murder by an anti-Semite in 1922. Many Berlin Jews were prominent in the arts, education, and publishing—having established such presses as Mosse and Ullstein. But,

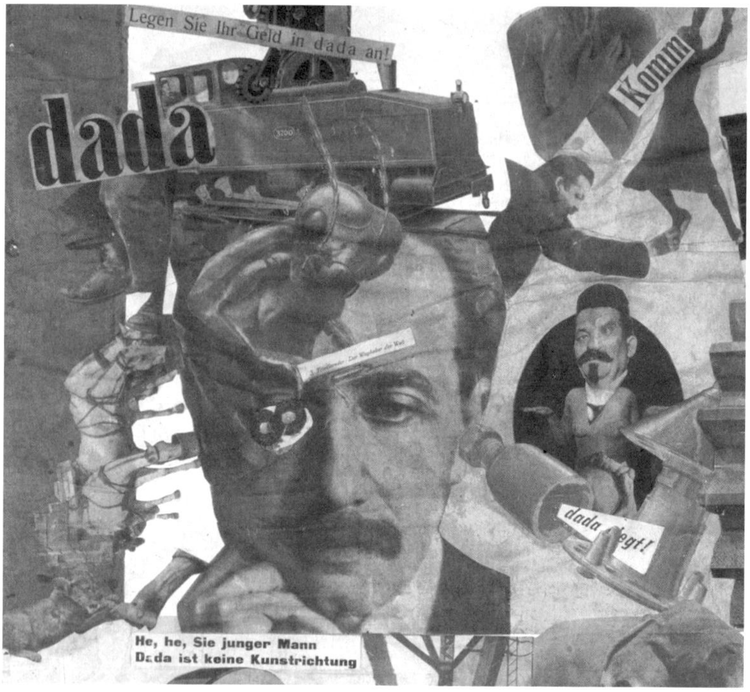

FIGURE 24. Hannah Höch, *Cut with the Kitchen Knife Dada* (detail of plate 3, top left). Art © 2010 Artists Rights Society (ARS), New York/VG Bild-Kunst, Bonn. Photo: Bildarchiv Preussischer Kulturbesitz/Art Resource, NY.

most were as obscure as the fifteen thousand Eastern European Jewish refugees who streamed into the city during and after the war, to whom Einstein, at that time, lent his support as a world figure, a Jew, a professor, and a Berliner. In an article in a Mosse Press newspaper in December 1919, he declared: "With regard to the agitation against Eastern European Jews . . . such a summary verdict is tainted by its appeal to strongly anti-Semitic instincts, deflecting attention from the real causes of today's dire conditions. . . . Germany's recovery can by no means be accomplished by using force against a small, defenseless fraction of the population."[79]

The most prominent image in Höch's montage is the portrait photograph of Einstein in the top left, taken by the Polish-born Jewish photographer Suse Byk, one of a number of successful Jewish women photographers practicing in interwar Berlin: others included portraitist Lotte Jacobi, who also photographed Einstein, and Ellen Auerbach and Grete Stern, who used their nicknames for their advertising firm, Ringl + Pit (fig. 24). By 1913 Byk owned and operated a portrait studio on the Kurfürstendamm.[80] Her Einstein portrait, clearly credited to her, appeared on the cover of the December 14, 1919, edition of the Ullstein Press journal *Berliner Illustrirte Zeitung* (figs. 25–26). It bore the caption "A New Giant in World History." The publication of this portrait and the accompanying article were part of the worldwide media frenzy

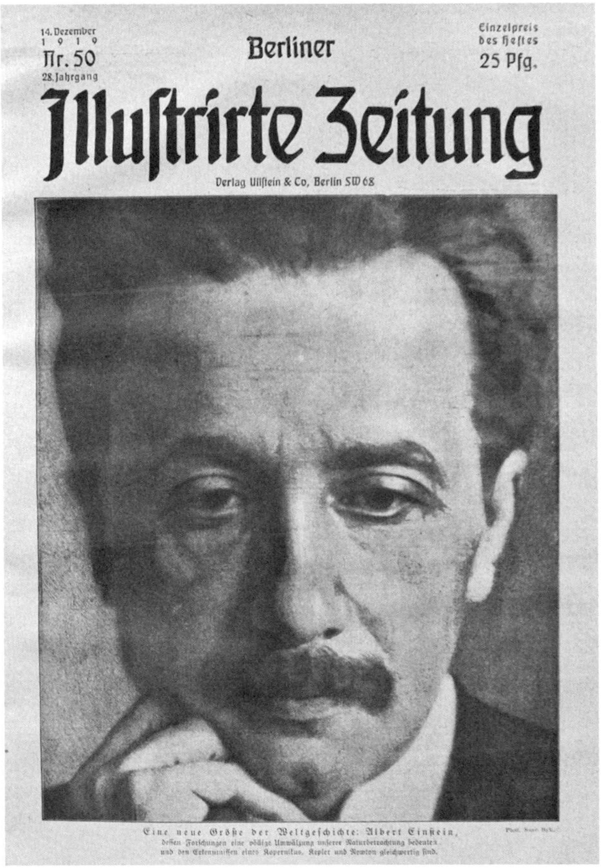

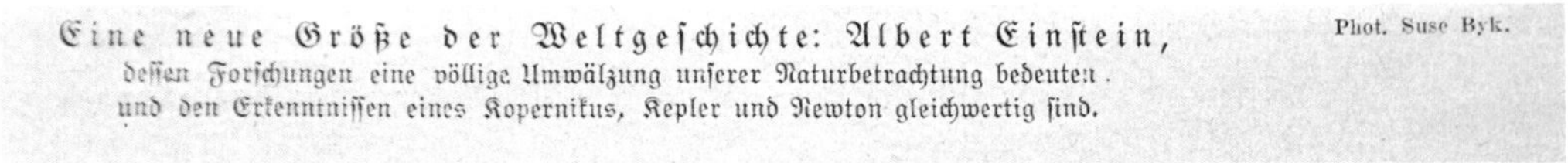

FIGURE 25. Cover of *Berliner Illustrirte Zeitung* (14 December 1919), with Suse Byk's photograph of Albert Einstein. Photo: Greg Wendt, Morris Library, Southern Illinois University Carbondale. FIGURE 26. Detail of fig. 25. Photo: Greg Wendt, Morris Library, Southern Illinois University Carbondale.

that turned Einstein the scientist into Einstein the genius-celebrity, set off by the British Royal Astronomical Society's confirmation of his general theory of relativity in November 1919.[81]

Many German scientists found Einstein's revolutionary ideas deeply unsettling on both scientific and ethnic grounds—which they suspected must be connected. The front-page publication of Byk's respectful, thoughtful portrait asserted the Ullstein Press's position against such attacks.[82] Höch, as an Ullstein employee, also clearly took a side in this struggle (fig. 27): in *Kitchen Knife,* Einstein's brain supports a steaming "dada" engine, paralleling the Orient Express that her own head couples with the women's suffrage map at lower right, and juxtaposed to the "the anti-dadaist movement" emanating from Emperor Wilhelm II's brow in the top right. These compositional arrangements are key to the interpretation I shall advance in the next chapter.

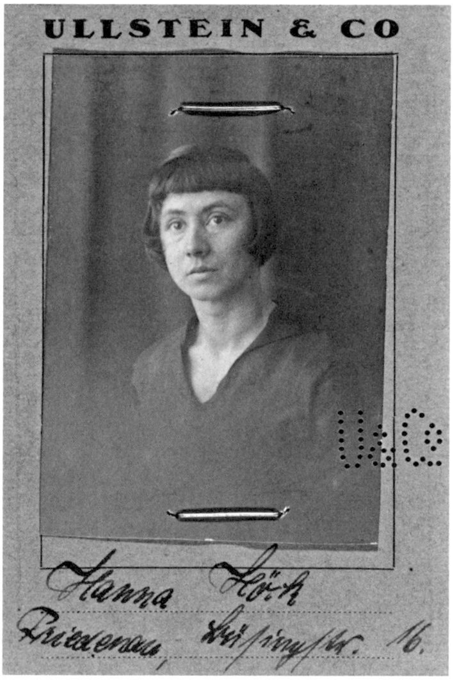

FIGURE 27. Hannah Höch's employee ID, 1916. Photo: Hannah-Höch-Archiv, Berlinische Galerie, Landesmuseum für Moderne Kunst, Fotografie und Architektur.

On the penultimate day of the First International Dada Fair, August 24, 1920, the Working Group of German Natural Scientists for the Preservation of Pure Science staged its own public event in the Berlin Philharmonic concert hall. Anti-Semitic pamphlets were distributed outside, while inside the nationalist and anti-Semitic writer and researcher Paul Weyland castigated Einstein's work in terms that testify to the Berlin Dadaists' success in publicizing their activities and affinities, and to their negative identification with the "Jewish element" of German culture.[83] Weyland condemned Einsteinian relativity as "scientific Dadaism."[84]

3 Objects of Interpretation

Grosz's *Germany: A Winter's Tale*

My feelings were realized in a large, political painting which I called *Germany: A Winter's Tale* after an epic by Heinrich Heine. At the center sat the eternal German bourgeois, fat and frightened, at a slightly unsteady table with the morning paper and a cigar. Below, the three pillars of society: Army, Church, and School (the schoolmaster carrying a cane painted in the national colors). The bourgeois holds tightly to his knife and fork, as the world sways about him. A sailor, symbolizing the revolution, and a prostitute completed my personal image of the times. —**GEORGE GROSZ, *AUTOBIOGRAPHY* (1983), 114**

Grosz could not have finished *Germany: A Winter's Tale* prior to late December 1918. At that time, along with Heartfield and Herzfelde, he joined the Spartacist League led by Rosa Luxemburg and Karl Liebknecht, hoping to participate actively in turning the November Revolution that had toppled the monarchy and ended World War I into a Soviet-style Communist revolution. But when Luxemburg and Liebknecht were murdered by Berlin police in January 1919, those radical hopes were shattered. The governing liberal Social Democrats and conservatives in the military and business had struck an alliance. The most militantly reactionary elements in the military, the Free Corps militias, from which Nazi storm troops would be recruited, were employed to put down any further Communist agitations.

This tumultuous period forms the backdrop to *Germany: A Winter's Tale*. The first explicit reference to the painting appeared in spring 1919, when Grosz included it in the first Berlin Dada exhibition at Neumann's.[1] Kurt Glaser reviewed the show admiringly, especially "this George Groß's large picture in which he gruesomely mocks himself and his prophets and Chagall and Futurism. . . . In a Futurist way houses and people and things are all thrown together chaotically, newspaper pages and ration cards are pasted to the canvas and this huge, amazingly witty picture puzzle reveals a full-blooded derision for the German philistine, compared to which Heinrich Mann's *Untertan* is harmless satire."[2] Glaser continued, saying that the philistine seated at the central table is not the target here—he is only trying to satisfy his needs—but rather the "false prophets and saints," representing the established powers of German society depicted at the bottom of Grosz's painting. According to Glaser, the Dada exhibition also attacked Expressionists such as the "activist" writer Kurt Hiller, whom the Dadaists saw as overly committed to bourgeois artistic conceptions.

In spring 1920 Grosz again showed *Germany: A Winter's Tale,* this time in an exhibition at the Hans Goltz gallery, in Munich, coinciding with a special issue of the journal *Der Ararat,* with essays by Leo Zahn and Willi Wolfradt. Wolfradt's *Ararat* text concentrated on Grosz's syphilitic *Adventurer* of 1916 and advanced a theory of Grosz's "infantilism."[3] Zahn traced the genesis of Grosz's graphic work to the graffiti markings of "bitter urban youths on city walls." Grosz's paintings, in contrast, were dynamic and apocalyptic examples of "Futurism, the modern big city art par excellence." Zahn argued that *Germany: A Winter's Tale* synthesized infantile graffiti and apocalyptic Futurism. While neither Zahn nor Wolfradt named *Germany: A Winter's Tale,* Zahn must have been referring to this work because he, like Glaser, mentioned collaged elements—the newspaper and bread ration labels on the table in the picture's center—which he claimed introduced "naturalism, the appearance of a tangible materialism," into a picture that otherwise produced a dreamworld "vision."

Another article reproducing and discussing *Germany: A Winter's Tale* appeared in 1920 in Paul Westheim's journal *Das Kunstblatt* (The art sheet).[4] Alfred Salmony referred to the "decorated military man, blessings-dispensing war minister, and Goethe professor with cane at the feet of the philistine *[Spießer]*" as "a hideous trinity."[5] Salmony also called attention to the collaged elements and Futurism but referred the reader to the Expressionist writer Theodor Däubler's essay of 1917 in *Kunstblatt,* which includes a discussion of *The Adventurer,* for an "incomparable description" of Grosz's work. In that essay Däubler also described a Grosz nocturnal work as both Futurist and dreamlike; in it, he writes, "one can encounter a revenant," the dead come back to life. The half moon pasted in the sky, like the one in the top left of *Germany: A Winter's Tale,* "was paraphrased in a poem by Grosz: silvery, kitschy moonlight." The reference to "kitschy" images of the moon is certainly appropriate, for Grosz collected kitsch postcards, some of which provided him with motifs.[6] Wolfradt also detected "hybrid beings" *(Mischwesen)* in Grosz's *Adventurer,* which describes and derides a woman for her mixture of Polish and Jewish blood *(Mischblut polnisch-jüdisch):* "The fat female image, mixed-blooded Polish-Jewish, appropriately enjoys herself in her silk stockings and carnival boots."[7]

Willi Wolfradt published a monograph on Grosz in 1921, in which he discussed *Germany: A Winter's Tale* in depth, calling attention to the colorful, unctuous oil painting and the collaged elements: Wolfradt interpreted the painting as transitional between *The Adventurer* and assembled constructions by Grosz, Heartfield, and Schlichter at the Dada Fair.[8] Grosz himself later declared *Germany: A Winter's Tale* to be the "high point" of the Dada Fair, his "most important" oil painting; he claimed that it "exerted decisive influence on the veristic painting that has since become popular."[9] When a Berlin illustrated paper published a satirical article mocking the Dada Fair, *Germany: A Winter's*

Tale was the central illustration, attesting to and probably influencing Grosz's high estimation of its impact.[10] By "veristic painting" Grosz meant what has come to be known as the New Objectivity of the 1920s, the Realist style to which Beckmann, Dix, Grosz, and many other artists migrated. It was given its name by the exhibition "Die Neue Sachlichkeit" (The New Objectivity), organized in 1923 by Gustav Friedrich Hartlaub for the Mannheim Kunsthalle, where it opened in 1925. The exhibition was seen subsequently in Dresden and Chemnitz and included *Germany: A Winter's Tale.*

Kurt Glaser, who was the first critic to write about the work in 1919, was also the last to write about it from direct observation, in 1929. Seeing it again in the retrospective exhibition "10 Jahre Novembergruppe" (Ten years of the November Group), toward the end of the Weimar Republic's relatively stable Stresemann era, Glaser felt distanced enough from the revolutionary days that had given the November Group its name to comment that "after ten years Dix's *Barricades* and Grosz's *Winter's Tale* have become curiosities that belong by now in a panopticon of the revolutionary period."[11] Grosz's reference to Heine played no explicit role in these contemporary interpretations. More recent discussions give only passing notice to it.[12] Little has been made of the open reference to Heine, and specific elements of the work that relate to Heine's poem have been left unexamined.

Heine, born into a Jewish family in Düsseldorf in 1797, grew up as Harry Heine in the Rhineland, where he studied Greek, French, and Hebrew (fig. 28).[13] In Berlin in the early 1820s he participated in the intellectual salon presided over by Rahel Varnhagen von Ense, a converted Jew; this circle included Alexander von Humboldt, Hegel, the historian Leopold von Ranke, and the poet Peter von Chamisso. Frederic Ewen has called Rahel Varnhargen Heine's "guardian angel," claiming that she was "attracted by this Byronic, wayward, slight and pale poet, dressed like a dandy, blond-haired, retiring, melancholy and ironical. He was a Jew—already racked by *'Judenschmerz'*—seeking to understand his relation to his own people."[14] Heine famously placed his conversion to Christianity in 1825 in a pragmatic context, unrelated to belief: "A baptismal certificate is a ticket of admission to European culture."[15] For Jews like Heine, desire to become the Enlightenment ideal of a "world citizen" who could wear many costumes often meant renouncing a specifically Jewish identity. During a mutually derisive literary exchange that lasted from 1827 to 1830, though, the poet Count August von Platen mocked Heine's Jewish origins, while Heine ridiculed Platen's homosexuality. Responding to the failed liberal revolutions of 1830 and rising nationalism and anti-Semitism in Germany, Heine left Hamburg for a long exile in Paris, where he died in 1856. Heine wrote *Germany: A Winter's Tale* (1844) after traveling back to Germany for the first time in a dozen years.[16]

In 1916 Max Fischer published his short, accessible book *The German Jew Heinrich Heine.* Fischer dismissed the idea that a fundamental mean-spiritedness caused the poet to take an ironic and sometimes scornful stance toward Germany, especially in picaresques such as *Germany: A Winter's Tale.* "Irony is the sister of pain . . . especially

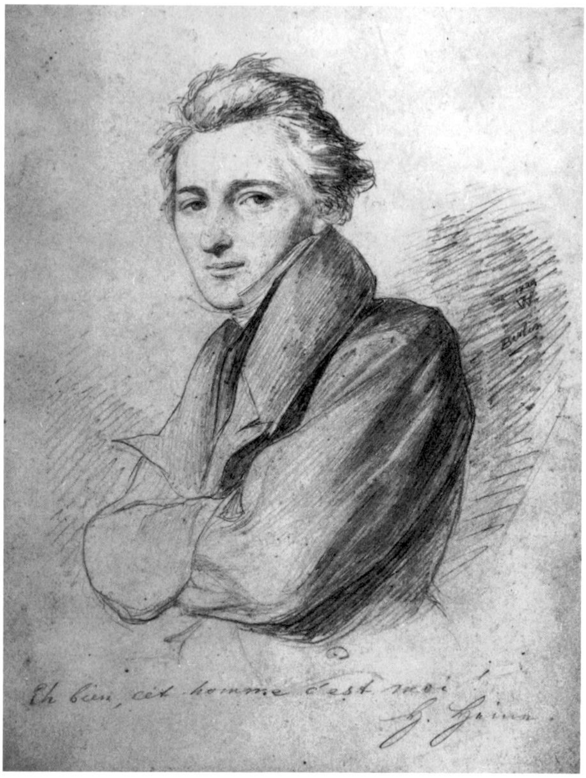

FIGURE 28. Wilhelm Hensel, *Heinrich Heine*, 1829, pencil on cardboard. Kupferstichkabinett, Staatliche Museen zu Berlin. Photo: Bildarchiv Preussischer Kulturbesitz/ Art Resource, NY.

pronounced in the soul of the Jew," Fischer wrote—even, and perhaps especially, in the convert.[17] Fischer's book caught the attention of both Jews and non-Jews. The Kabbalah scholar Gershom Scholem, in *From Berlin to Jerusalem,* the memoir of his early years, noted that he read Fischer and was surprised that a non-Jewish German scholar would devote serious and sympathetic attention to the question of Heine's Jewish identity.[18] But Heine's affinity for France, his political liberalism, and above all, his Jewishness rendered him anathema to German nationalistic and anti-Semitic intellectuals. Foremost among them was the literary historian Adolf Bartels, who was read widely in the 1920s and provided intellectual support to Nazi ideology.[19] In January 1920 Bartels sketched the positions and categorized the combatants in the historical and current "struggle between internationalism and nationalism." He aligned the recent revolution with internationalism and the triumph of "Judaism over the Germans." In an implicit swipe at Fischer, he declared that true German intellectuals "are just as little taken in by the hazy idealism with which democracy has done its hawking for a hundred years as by the business culture of the international Jew. . . . There do exist German fools who still declare Heinrich Heine a great writer. . . . But we no longer let them annoy us; long have we learned to laugh at them. . . . The Jewish virtuoso will amount to nothing more than a curiosity for literary researchers."[20]

There is no indication that Grosz worked literally from the Heine poem or that he was a particular devotee of Heine or his work. It cannot be unimportant or coincidental, however, that he named what he and his supporters then considered his best work after one of Heine's most famous satiric poems, just when Heine's ethnic identity was being attacked and defended. Grosz was not the only artist to do so in the context of the November Revolution. "Das neue Wintermärchen" (The new winter's tale), a poem by the twenty-year-old screenwriter and actor Hans Heinrich von Twardowski, appeared in the humor magazine *Ulk,* after editorship had passed from Walther Mehring's father Sigmar to Kurt Tucholsky, and just as Grosz was completing his painting.[21] Like Grosz in his painting, as Sherwin Simmons notes, Twardowski caricatured and commented on contemporary events, using the reference to Heine to call attention to the seriousness of the satire.

Connecting Grosz's painting and Heine's poem is not a matter of identifying exact motifs translated into visual form in the painting. As Grosz indicated in a letter of 1945 to the exiled Frankfurt School theorist Max Horkheimer, that was not the way he worked.[22] Rather, Grosz's satirically mocking tone toward Prussian imperial pretensions and symbols echoes Heine's, as does his jaundiced attitude toward the church and certain sacred cows of Germany's literary culture, and his keen eye for *echt deutsch* food, clothing, and companions. But whereas previous commentators have seen Grosz's *Winter's Tale* as pure, negative satire, I note a Heinian sympathy for some of what he mocks: not for the "unholy trinity" of army, church, and school that became the poster image of the Germany that the Dadaists wanted to destroy and basis for the unstable *Pillars of Society* in Grosz's painting of 1926 (fig. 12), but for the "fat and frightened" German bourgeois at his "slightly unsteady" table, whom Wolfradt identified as a reserve officer trying to enjoy a simple meal amid threat and chaos.

The satirist can skewer most effectively something he or she truly knows. The outsider in a culture—the Jew in Central Europe, the African American in the United States, a woman under patriarchy, the avant-garde artist everywhere—is always a keener observer than the majority insider of the dominant culture's vices and virtues. Grosz, in both his satiric love-hate relationship with Germany and Germans and his self-defensive adaptive strategies, played, among his other roles, that of the Jew, as Heine played that of the gentile.[23] Grosz's profile glowers at the minister's Bible, appearing like a spirit image in dark silhouette illuminated from behind, with an orange circle on the temple, which Wolfradt in 1921 interpreted tentatively as a self-inflicted wound, a sign of imminent suicide.[24] Where the other figures are light, Grosz is as dark and hook-nosed as Judas shown in profile as a Jewish caricature in Castagno's Renaissance *Last Supper.*[25]

Heine's poem *Germany: A Winter's Tale* tells the story—partly in dream imagery that probably appealed to Grosz at a time when many of his works were nocturnes—of Heine's 1843 trip to Germany, his first since moving to Paris in 1831 and being censured (and censored) by the Prussian government in 1835. The poem begins:

It was in November, that dreary month;
the days were growing shorter;
The winds ripped all the leaves from the trees;
And I came to the German border.[26]

The reference to "that dreary month" of November also relates to the genesis of Grosz's painting. In November 1918, when Grosz was still working on the painting, Germany's November Revolution succeeded in bringing down the German monarchy (with outside pressure from the Allies and Wilson's Fourteen Points) but did not succeed in unseating Germany's ruling elites. The newspaper that Grosz collaged onto the table in the center of *Germany: A Winter's Tale* is dated December 21, 1918, showing that Grosz was still involved with the work throughout this tumultuous period (fig. 29). The headline, "A Republic for Upper Silesia," reports anxiously on the possibility that Germany might lose territory in the east as a result of losing the war, an outcome conservatives attributed to a domestic "stab in the back" by internal German opponents.[27] On January 16 the same newspaper, the conservative, nationalistic *Berliner Lokal-Anzeiger,* reported on the police murder of Luxemburg and Liebknecht and claimed that they had been killed by an angry crowd of citizens.[28]

The third chapter of the poem presents motifs and images that reappear in Grosz's painting—though not as direct translations. Heine heads to Aachen and visits Emperor Charlemagne's tomb. Domes appear as symbols of the Holy Roman Empire. But quickly the references point to contemporary details—for example, the spiked helmets that the Prussian cavalry had begun to wear during Heine's exile and which were ubiquitous in Grosz's time in the Prussian officer class. A spiked dome also appears in the top right of Grosz's painting. As Bergius points out, this dome refers not only to Prussian helmets but also to the Berlin Cathedral (the *Dom*), which had been completed in 1905 under imperial patronage. The Dom, site of Baader's November 1918 anticlerical outburst, thus refers to the alliance of church, military, and imperial state. Grosz's painting spells out this connection and brings it surreptitiously down to earth: the spiked helmet/dome in the collage-painting rises just above the word *Kaiser* (emperor), which here derives from an advertisement for a brand of coal.

In Heine's third chapter we also read: "Milling around on Aachen's streets / The dogs were humbly imploring: / 'Oh stranger, give us a little kick! / Life has become so boring.' " The dog in Grosz's work needs a kick to awaken to the nightmare of history that surrounds him. From Cologne, Heine proceeds on to Hagen—where he eats "good old German" food: "Hail to thee, dear sauerkraut!" thus affectionately satirizing Germany's, and his own, appetite for sausages and pickled cabbage. But the empire gets no sympathy either from Heine or from Grosz. In a dream, Heine encounters "Old Redbeard," Emperor Frederick Barbarossa, and the two men enter into dialogue. They discuss the Enlightenment Jewish philosopher Moses Mendelssohn and other individuals and events since Barbarossa's medieval reign, and after the conversation the poet con-

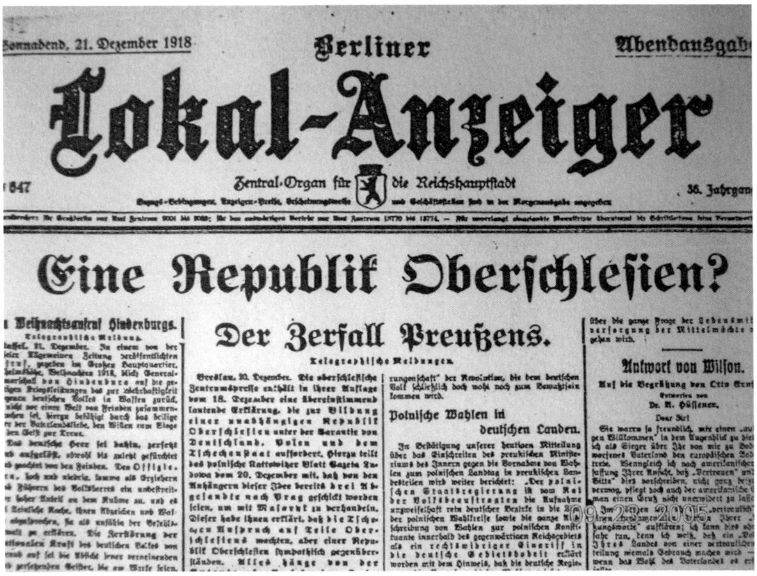
Sonnabend, 21. Dezember 1918

Berliner

Abendausgab

Lokal-Anzeiger

Zentral-Organ für die Reichshauptstadt

36. Jahrgan

Eine Republik Oberschlesien?

Weihnachtsaufruf Hindenburgs.

Der Zerfall Preußens.

Polnische Wahlen in deutschen Landen.

Antwort von Wilson.

FIGURE 29. Front page of *Berliner Lokal-Anzeiger* (21 December 1918). Photo: Author.

cludes: "Considering how matters stand, / We need no king at all." Clearly, this is also the sentiment of Grosz's painting and of all his activities as a member of the Communist wing of Berlin Dada.

Much of Heine's poem is set in his native Rhineland—that border area occupied by the French at the end of the war that became a nationalist symbol of Germany's humiliation. Heine then crosses the German countryside to his last German home, Hamburg. The countryside also appears in Grosz's painting, as the apocalyptic urban landscape of crashing skyscrapers, smoking factories, and leaning cathedrals gives way in the left background to snow-covered pointed peaks and a castle—elements foreign to Grosz's Berlin but at home in Heine's satiric German travelogue.

German food and drink play a central role in both Heine and Grosz. Both exhibit sympathy for German tastes. Certainly Grosz's philistine is a caricature, drinking beer, from a bottle labeled with an Iron Cross, which the Dadaists disdained as stereotypically and grossly German (they preferred red wine), convinced too that it promoted ignorant obedience to authority. "With a stomach filled up with beer and stuffed like you're pregnant with sauerkraut you'll believe anything," Grosz wrote in a letter to his friend Robert Bell in 1917.[29] But there is no hint here, as in so many of Grosz's other gustatory images, of oncoming indigestion or vomit (fig. 13). Grosz painted this work during a time of widespread hunger. The numbers on the bread labels collaged onto the table refer to the weekly rations of bread and butter. The bone at the center of the plate is better food for the sleeping dog than for a human. Two indistinct blobs fill out the plate. The eater, lucky to have some sustenance, is no libertine gorging himself.

Heine, traveling from France to Germany, focuses repeatedly if ambivalently on German food. After leaving Aachen and traveling to Cologne he gets hungry: "My appetite. The dish of ham / And omelets tasted fine. / And since it was salted very well / I washed it down with wine." Like the Dadaists, Heine preferred wine to beer—but he drinks too much and is driven out into the streets, where he encounters the pointed tower of the city's still unfinished Gothic cathedral, its structure similar to the red cathedral above the eater's head in Grosz's painting. After falling asleep Heine dreams of the Three Holy Kings—Cologne's cathedral contains the famous reliquary of the Magi—come to life as skeletons and, holding scepters, demanding Heine's "awe and admiration." Hanne Bergius suggests that the composition of *Germany: A Winter's Tale* derives from a medieval Romanesque church tympanum, the area over a door often including a depiction of the Last Judgment. For her, the soldier with his knife takes the place of the Judge of the World, the general becomes an archangel, the teacher is the devil, and the minister is an angel of salvation.[30] Employing a medieval format to mock traditional Christian imagery and ritual is consistent with Berlin Dada practices, but such a specific antiquarian, iconographic program seems contrary to Grosz's approach. Like Heine's poem, the painting portrays past and present simultaneously. Grosz takes certain images and attitudes from Heine and interpolates them into subjects and objects from his own milieu. The three figures, then, are the conservative preacher, military man, and schoolmaster of Grosz's time and place, as every commentator on the painting noted, but they also function like the "Drei Totengerippe," the three skeletons, from Heine's seventh chapter, line seventy-seven, as harbingers of death.

The preacher bears three crosses—the one on the bible Grosz scowls at, a bloodstained one around his neck, and, on his chest, an Iron Cross like the one worn by the military man to his right, which identifies the preacher as a military minister. Four more crosses rise up through the window frames of the building behind him. Under the cathedral's lamp, to the left of the table, two horses draw a hearse toward a grandfather clock that reads seven o'clock and also has a cross at three o'clock and one beneath its frame. To the right of the central figure a grave robber carts away a casket and cross in a wheelbarrow. Other figures integrated into the scene next to and behind the sailor, who is moving toward a prostitute, rob and fight one another in a Hobbesian war of all against all. The cross's time as a symbol of redemption has run out—its power is political and its value material—and the "war minister" gives his hollow blessing to the dead and dying.

The teacher's stick, both a walking cane and a crop for disciplining students, is festooned with ribbons in nationalist, monarchical colors: the black, white, and red of the right-wing prowar parties, as opposed to the more liberal republican black, red, and gold. At the point of that stick appears the word "*Papestr.*" This abbreviation combined with other references in the texts of the collage-painting, underlines the central theme of the work: power, the creation and abuse of power by intertwined hierarchies melded together in wartime and postwar Germany. *Papestr.* is an abbreviation for General-

Pape-Street, which in Berlin was the location of the military barracks to which Grosz and many other young men reported for physical examinations for military service.[31] In the world of *Germany: A Winter's Tale,* hovering over the teacher's stick, its sound similar to "Papa," as well as to *Papst* (pope), *Papestr.* indicts the intertwined patriarchal power structures of the church, the military, and the education systems.[32] The unholy trinity at the bottom of the painting represents this word-made-flesh. The word *Papestr[aße]* and reference to that specific street also locates *Germany: A Winter's Tale*—in Dadaist practice, as demonstrated at the Dada Fair—as a precursor to the *Prussian Archangel* (fig. 10). The Dada scholar Brigid Doherty points out that the hanging construction explicitly refers to the Tempelhof military drill grounds.[33] In military procedures the physical examination comes before the drill, and in Dada procedures, as Wolfradt argued, the collage-painting *Germany: A Winter's Tale* comes before the assembled archangel as object.

Another instance of intermixing power is suggested at the top right, where the dome referring at once to church, military, and empire rests on a lump of Kaiser coal, an advertising image Grosz derived from a commercial decal he pasted in a sketchbook of March–August 1918, which also includes other references to the painting.[34] Burning coal produces power, in cities as well as on ships such as the *Titanic* and the military vessels manned by seamen like the sailor in an enlisted man's uniform to the right of the table, heading toward a prostitute. It provides the fuel emitted from the smoke stacks of the factory, or power plant, and from the steaming locomotive behind the church and to the left of the Prussian church/helmet. Power produces heat and also light, which is referred to just below the piece of Kaiser coal. The text below the brand name Kaiser derives from an Osram light bulb advertisement. A bar underscoring the word and the "m" of Osram both intersect the light bulb to the right.[35] Here, too, *Germany: A Winter's Tale* acted as the precursor to and linked up with an assemblage at the Dada Fair: the head of the assemblage figure "The Middle-Class Philistine Heartfield Gone Wild" (visible at right, fig. 10) was a real, trademarked Osram bulb.[36]

In *Germany: A Winter's Tale* electric light provides illumination for a train emerging from a tunnel beneath the Osram ad, as well as for the lamp next to the cathedral to the left; these are the only sources of man-made illumination in this nocturnal scene.[37] On the building to the right of the sailor appear the letters E and R, a fragment of a frieze inscription typically used to identify the function of Berlin business or industrial buildings. The R is obscured by a form in front of it that looks like flames and smoke rising from a smoldering pile of coal. Another letter, which touches the R's extender, is even less legible. I venture, though, that Grosz is here providing the first letters and a symbol identifying this building as an *Erzhütte,* a smelting works, or *Erzgiesserei,* a foundry, where the intense heat produced by burning coal or coke melts down, reshapes, and combines *(zusammenschmelzen)* metals to produce new forms and alloys. In 1921 Willi Wolfradt interpreted *Germany: A Winter's Tale* as "melting together" all of Grosz's key motifs to that time ("die ganze Motivwelt des

George Grosz zusammenschmelzt"). The city, the country, and, especially, the empire, military, educational system, and capitalist industry—the sources of social, political, and economic power—melt, blend, and combine.

At the center of the scene sits the destabilized reservist, among neither the despised "pillars of society" below nor the groups that during the "turnip winter" stole from one another or sold their bodies for sex or military service. Contemporary critics, such as Salmony and Wolfradt, referred to this reserve officer at the table as a *Spießer,* which Doherty has translated as "Middle-Class Philistine." She also notes, in analyzing the light-bulb-headed assemblage, that "The middle-class Philistine Heartfield gone wild" *(Der wildgewordene Spießer Heartfield),* could refer to and derive from a seventeenth-century term for a member of the civilian militia armed with a pike.[38] The *Spießer* in *Germany: A Winter's Tale* is both the middle-class philistine and the uniformed militiaman, wielding his knife and fork like daggers and using his table as a shield. Glancing furtively to his left, he protects his body from what Benjamin described as the World War I era's "destructive torrents and explosions" and defends his meager German winter's repast.

Höch's *Cut with the Kitchen Knife Dada through Germany's Last Weimar Beer-Belly Cultural Epoch*

This morning I made a quick decision to go to the National Gallery (Schloss Charlottenburg). I had not yet seen my big collage, "Cut with the Kitchen Knife," there. It's hung nicely and actually looks quite respectable. My anxiety that it wouldn't hold up had grown and grown. But this is a real relief. During the quarter-of-an-hour I was around it I noticed that everyone who came by showed quite an interest in the work. And to my satisfaction it didn't seem sensational, but peaceful and balanced. It's been there about a year and I had not yet had the courage to go see it. —**HANNAH HÖCH, DIARY ENTRY OF 16 FEBRUARY 1963 (HHA)**

Höch's first important interpreter, the art journalist Heinz Ohff, wrote in 1982 about *Cut with the Kitchen Knife Dada:* "This montage stands as one of the great cultural-political statements of the post World War generation, a confession of fundamental societal importance and one of the most important works of these years."[39] This evaluation, neither eccentric nor hyperbolic, reflects the prominence of Höch's work since the 1960s, when interpretations first started appearing.[40] Since then, gender has been the lens through which critics have viewed her art—her status as a female artist was first viewed patriarchally and then, beginning in the 1970s, from several feminist positions. In 1989 feminist art historians convened in Berlin for a Höch centennial symposium—the first ever, its organizers claim, devoted to a woman artist.[41]

Until the late 1960s *Cut with the Kitchen Knife Dada* occupied a less privileged position in assessments of the artist's work, of Berlin Dada, and of twentieth-century art. Höch's own attitude toward the work was paradoxical. After the 1920 Dada Fair she did not show it again publicly until the gallery show of 1961 from which the Berlin National Gallery purchased it, though she had many opportunities to do so.[42] She did not show it as one of her five works in the 1920 November Group exhibition, staged as a section of the "Great Berlin Art" exhibition (Kunstausstellung Berlin 1920), because it ran concurrently with the Dada Fair.[43] The next year, though, it would have been available and would certainly have been appropriate for the November Group exhibition, which included a catalogue text by Raoul Hausmann.[44] She seems generally to have preferred showing recent work in her exhibitions. Eberhard Roters quotes her in the 1970s sighing to him, "I don't even want to hear the word Dada anymore, but people don't want anything else, so I have to go into it."[45] In 1954 Edouard Roditi published an interview with Höch in the journal *Der Monat*. The translation of this interview—in *Arts* magazine in December 1959 and again in Lucy Lippard's anthology *Dadas on Art*—hastened Höch's international rediscovery. Typically, though, the interview devotes more attention to her memories of the Dada milieu and her Dada compatriots (especially Grosz, who had just died) than to her own work.[46] *Cut with the Kitchen Knife Dada,* on the verge of being "refound" and elevated to being considered her major work and a major document of the movement, receives no mention in the interview, not even an implicit mention when she asserts that the Berlin Dadaists' most original and lasting artistic contribution was that of their having been "the first artists to discover and develop the artistic potential of photomontage."[47]

Höch declined to show *Cut with the Kitchen Knife Dada* in a number of exhibitions where it would have fit perfectly—among them the German Werkbund exhibition "Film und Foto" of 1929. She sent some seventeen works to this Stuttgart show, but *Cut with the Kitchen Knife Dada* was not among them, even though it demonstrates connections between cinematographic editing, photographic reproducibility, avant-garde photomontage, and mass culture. The movie star Asta Nielsen, included along with other prominent cultural figures in *Cut with the Kitchen Knife Dada,* as well as in the 1925 painting *Roma,* which she exhibited often, demonstrates Höch's sensitivity to the developing film "star system" and its relation to other forms of fame.[48] She did not send it to photography and film exhibitions in Brussels in 1932 or 1934, or to her large solo exhibition in 1934 in Brno, Moravia (now in the Czech Republic), where she showed forty-two photomontages.[49] The work's large size and fragility may have motivated her decision to keep it safely at home.

Peter Boswell, the cocurator of the Walker Art Center's 1996 Höch retrospective exhibition, has attributed her reluctance to show Dada-era works after the Dada Fair to both her awareness that painting was a more established art form than montage—and her desire for recognition as a painter—and the specific connection of Dada works to the Berlin of 1919–20.[50] The response of one reviewer, Joseph de Gruyter, to her large exhibition of watercolors and photomontages at Galerie d'Audretsch in The Hague in 1935 confirms the lesser status of montage: he admired her photomontages as "now and then brilliant in their own way" and suggested that works such as *Seven-Mile Boots* contain Freudian and surrealist associations. But he questioned whether these works, with their heterogeneous sources and compositions, "wholly count . . . within the domain of art."[51] Nonetheless, Höch continued to create photomontages until her death. After 1929 she showed these works in many exhibitions and seems to have believed in their status as art throughout her career. She wrote and spoke on several occasions about photomontage as a significant twentieth-century art form, extolling its potential as individual creative expression as well as acknowledging its role in advertising and propaganda.[52] She often showed her later photomontages in November Group exhibitions in Berlin and in exhibitions in Stuttgart, Brussels, and Brno; and she showed her 1930 montage *Love in the Bush* in a 1931 Berlin photomontage exhibition organized by Cesar Domela-Nieuwenhuis, which also included whole sections devoted to the Bund Revolutionärer Künstler Deutschland (Union of German revolutionary artists) and to artists from the Soviet Union.[53]

After World War II Höch began to show in Berlin at the Gerd Rosen gallery, the first gallery to reopen amid the destruction and begin showing modern art. In February 1946 she took part in the "Fantasten" (Fantasms) exhibition, where, in accordance with the theme, she showed her more recent surrealistic paintings. In December 1946 Rosen staged "Photomontage from Dada to Today," for which he issued a small brochure featuring a text by Höch. In this text she discussed the studio ambience leading up to the Dada Fair ("For weeks the artists' studios were like waste baskets") and referred to the importance of the "Film und Foto" exhibition and the relation of montage to the films of René Clair, Man Ray, and Eisenstein, remarking that after 1933 photomontage was used "only for propaganda purposes" (in a handwritten note she corrected that to "almost only"). This text offers no hint that she considered photomontage a less respectable art form than painting. Her handwritten list of works suggests that she again kept *Cut with the Kitchen Knife Dada* out of the show.[54] In 1948 Dorothy Miller, of the New York Museum of Modern Art, invited Höch to participate in a collage exhibition. In letters to Höch, Miller specifically requested Berlin Dada works by her and her colleagues. Höch provided the museum with a photomontage from 1919 by Baader, one by Hausmann of 1924, and three of her own works, including one from the Dada period, but again not *Cut with the Kitchen Knife Dada*. A few years later she exhibited a work with explicit connections to Berlin Dada at the Sidney Janis gallery's 1953 show "Dada, 1916–1923." She provided the gallery with twelve key works from her collection, including three works by Hausmann—the wooden head *Spirit of the Age*, the photomontage *Tatlin at Home*, and a drawing, *The Iron Hindenburg*—as well as her own photomontage *Dada Rundschau*, which, she noted, was "shown in 1920 at Dada exhibition at O. Burchard, Berlin."[55] In postwar New York, where one might see Albert Einstein working in the reading room of the New York Public Library, might spectators have noticed the prominence of Jews in *Cut with the Kitchen Knife Dada*?

In 1958 she sent twenty-one works dated 1918 to 1923, but again not *Cut with the Kitchen Knife Dada*, to the Düsseldorf Art Union show "Dada: Documents of a Movement." This important exhibition helped revive interest in Dada in Germany and throughout western Europe, especially in connection with developments in contemporary art such as Neo-Dadaism, beginning in the mid-1950s with the collage works of Robert Rauschenberg and Jasper Johns and continuing with Wolf Vostell and other Fluxus artists.[56]

Cut with the Kitchen Knife Dada's close association with Berlin Dada may have made Höch see it as dated. As her diary entry after viewing it at the Berlin National Gallery indicates, she feared people would not spend enough time looking at it or know enough about Berlin in 1919–20 and Berlin Dada's mission to appreciate its complex references and technique. It may also have reminded her of her painful relationship with Hausmann and his role in the work's genesis and single exhibition. Hanne Bergius, for instance, reports that Höch told her that she omitted from the work any image of Berlin Dada's founder, Richard Huelsenbeck, at Hausmann's request.[57]

Höch certainly valued *Cut with the Kitchen Knife Dada*. When she finally showed it in 1961, the price she and her dealer gave it was more than three times that of any of the other montages in the show, though still less than several of the oil paintings. A reviewer of that show declared that "*Cut with the Kitchen Knife,* the name of one of her earliest collages, is a fierce call for accountability. At that time she had just as much 'engagement' as George Grosz!"[58] The Berlin National Gallery purchased it, along with *Collage with Arrow* of 1919.[59] Höch's diary entry recounting her first viewing of it at the museum demonstrates her trepidation about viewers' responses but also her pride at its having gained a place there—geographically close but historically, institutionally, and culturally very distant from the Kunstsalon Burchard in 1920.

In 1968 Eberhard Roters, the director who acquired the work for the New National Gallery, which had moved from Charlottenburg Palace to its Mies van der Rohe building near Potsdamer Platz, produced the first iconographic study of *Cut with the Kitchen Knife Dada,* a brief text, prepared with Höch's assistance, identifying some of its main figures and features.[60] The German art historian and artist Gertrude Jula Dech went further in her 1981 doctoral dissertation to unravel its iconography and connect it to both the technique of montage and the social and political context of Berlin Dada.[61] She pared down the detail of her findings and made them more broadly contextual in a book devoted to the montage published in 1989.[62] Dech's careful research remains essential to such interpretations as those offered by Maud Lavin and Maria Makela, which are centered on gender.

Hanne Bergius, who knew Höch in the 1970s, began the steady critique of her marginalization in the first feminist reading of her work, published in the catalogue of the Höch retrospective exhibition of 1976 seen in Berlin and Paris.[63] Prior to that essay, there had been numerous references, generally by men, to Höch as a woman artist. These were often paternalistic and almost never recognized the political dimensions of gender. Even Heinz Ohff, who did great service to Höch studies by producing the first monograph on the artist, in 1968, and writing numerous supportive newspaper reviews of her work, nevertheless referred to her as "Dada's *Dornröschen*" (Dada's Sleeping Beauty), and to the 1961 exhibition as the overdue prince's kiss that had brought her out of her self-imposed obscurity.[64] When the national art magazine *Das Kunstwerk* (The artwork) produced a special 1964 issue devoted to art in Berlin, it reprinted the Ohff text, which stated that Höch "has always cultivated a very female, almost tender Dadaism."[65]

In 1964 the influential art historian and critic Will Grohmann—generally more identified as a supporter of postwar abstract artists such as Willi Baumeister and Ernst Wilhelm Nay, gave his support, too, to Höch, writing the catalogue essay, presenting the opening address for her seventy-fifth birthday exhibition at Nierendorf, and reviewing the exhibition for the influential *Frankfurter Allgemeine Zeitung*.[66] "In her art," he wrote, "she is always a woman and never doctrinaire. She maintains a connection with nature" and is, he continues, as at home with abstraction as with satire. For Grohmann, Höch's abstractions during and after World War II separated her from her more stridently political and representational colleagues, such as Heartfield, who was active at that time in theater design in East Berlin, and Grosz, and connected her work to broader, international trends in surrealistic abstraction, such as Baumeister, Nay, and American Abstract Expressionists.

In her book of 2000 Hanne Bergius has presented the most exhaustive identification of *Cut with the Kitchen Knife Dada*'s individual elements within an overall analysis and interpretation of the montage and of Berlin Dada in general.[67] Like anyone discussing Höch and *Cut with the Kitchen Knife Dada*, I am indebted to Dech and Bergius for their research and painstaking identification of individuals and elements in the montage. Both scholars provide compelling interpretations of the work and of Berlin Dada, influenced by concerns at the time of their writing. These concerns are primarily feminist for Dech (as for Lavin and Makela), whereas Bergius's Nietzschean interpretation also encompasses interest in cyborgs and the "post-human condition." Without questioning the validity of those readings—Lavin emphasizes that Höch's montage practice enables a variety of readings—I want to shift the emphasis from gender and technology as threats to traditional phallocentric and/or biologically driven notions of bodily integrity and psycho-political identity, to the issue of Jewish identity, which is also grounded in Höch's work and certainly challenged the culture Höch so skillfully cut up and reassembled.

Dech points out four compositional zones or groupings in the work, all oriented toward the edges of the 114- by 90-centimeter rectangle, and all seeming to spin centrifugally around a more open center. She terms this an "X"-like composition, in which the lower left and upper right are more densely filled than upper left and lower right. Like Grosz's *Germany: A Winter's Tale*, Höch's montage reflects the contemporary fascination with the city and skyscrapers. Höch connects this fascination specifically to New York.[68] At the top right appear the four towers of the Hotel Pennsylvania, which opened in 1919. In contrast to Grosz's work, the buildings in Höch's city do not blend as in a kaleidoscope but are edited into distinct and sequential frames, as in a film. Wall Street buildings stand in the bottom left. These structures, housing the center of finance capitalism, are intercut with scenes from Berlin, so that Wall Street appears to be filled with masses of people—a demonstration of children (with Höch's initials HH superimposed on them)—and to be contiguous with streets in front of Berlin's palace and the meeting of the Weimar parliament.[69]

Most commentators have pointed to those denser areas toward the edges as those of the "anti-Dadas," the masses of people in the lower left and in the upper right near the face of Kaiser Wilhelm II with the words *"Die anti-dadaistische Bewegung"* (the anti-Dadaistic movement) punctuated by a machine gun aimed at his brow (fig. 22). In the lower right of the "X" are the Dadaists themselves: Hausmann, whose yelling face is attached to the body of a swim-suited female diver; and John Heartfield, whose head is superimposed on the body of a baby being bathed by a woman (fig. 21). Albert Einstein's head dominates the upper left (fig. 24). Dech points out that Einstein's pose is the "classic thinker position," head propped on hand: Bergius adds that this pose alludes to the allegorical figure of melancholy.[70] Einstein has the sign of infinity in his right eye—he sees the unending—above which an earwig climbs over his brow, seeming to hold the legend *"S. Friedlaender: der Waghalter der Welt"* (S. Friedlaender: The driver/balancer/judge of the world).[71] Bergius argues that Höch, with this reference to the Salomo Friedlaender essay, first published in 1915 in the Expressionist pacifist journal *Die Weissen Blätter,* "concealed the concept of the *Kitchen Knife* montage." Bergius reads the montage as a "grotesque political allegory," citing Friedlaender's short "grotesques"—often uncanny, gruesome moral fables.[72] Such stories have roots in the Romantic era in stories like E. T. A. Hoffmann's "Sandmann." For Bergius, the *Mischwesen* (hybrids) in these stories, and in Höch's montages, stage a precarious balancing act of opposites—human/animal, machine/human, male/female, Dadaist/anti-Dadaist. In *Cut with the Kitchen Knife Dada* these oppositions are to be reconciled by the will of a "*Weltperson*"—a worldly person. Einstein, for Bergius, is that "contemplative *Weltperson*": a Nietzschean, Apollonian, superman, whose gaze into the infinite allows him to occupy the calm, conceptual center of a spiritual and pictorial storm, the intellectual equivalent of the bodily balancing act demonstrated at the physical center of the montage by the gracefully pirouetting figure of the dancer Neddy Impekoven, costumed as one of the craft artist Lotte Pritzel's dolls.[73]

Women, as many commentators have pointed out, are Höch's moving, active subjects; her male figures are generally more static. Maria Makela asserts: "Let there be no mistake: it is the women of *Cut with the Kitchen Knife* who animate the work both formally and conceptually."[74] Above Impekoven's body hovers the head of the graphic artist Käthe Kollwitz, which is at once a ball tossed by the dancer, the dancer's severed head, and a trophy skewered and held aloft on a lance by an animal trainer. The treatment of Kollwitz's head both honors and scorns her: Germany's most prominent woman artist of the day occupies a central position in the montage, but as a traditionalist in compari-

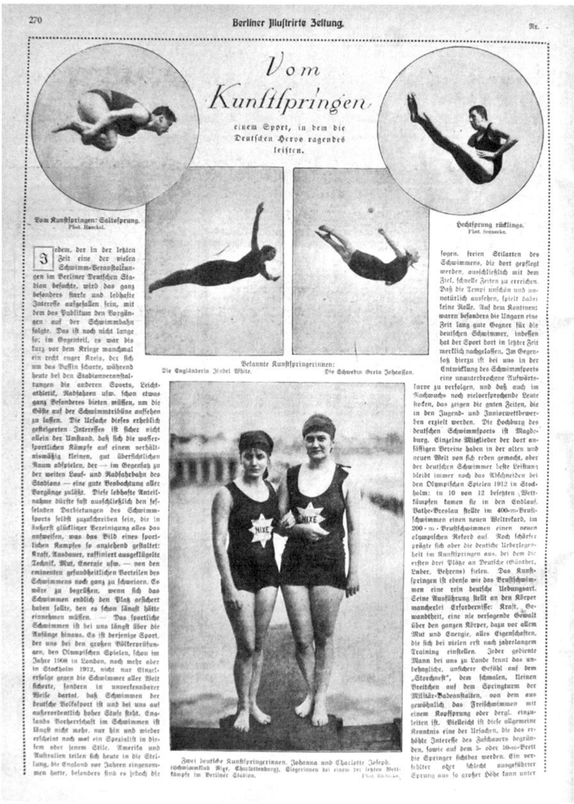
270 Berliner Illustrirte Zeitung

Vom Kunstspringen

FIGURE 30. "Vom Kunstspringen," *Berliner Illustrirte Zeitung* (20 July 1919). Photo: Greg Wendt, Morris Library, Southern Illinois University Carbondale.

son to the Dadaists, her placement there is ambivalent. Many wheels—gears, ball bearings, automobile tires—reiterate the centrifugal movement of images around the dancer. These machine parts relate to the Dadaists' fascination with technology, evident also in the work of Marcel Duchamp, Francis Picabia, and others.

The head of the Dadaist Johannes Baader, set between those of the Communist revolutionaries Karl Radek and Lenin, is attached to the body of a female diver (a *Kunstspringerin,* literally an art-jumper who competes in *Kunstspringen,* high diving, fig. 30). Baader's head rests on the body of Charlotte Joseph, which in turn stands on the chest of Johanna (or Hanna) Joseph, the German national champion in the three-meter dive in 1919 and 1920.[75] As Höch plays on the names for diving and art, she plays too on Baader's name: *baden* means to bathe; a *Schwimmbad* is a swimming pool, but *Bader* is also an archaic word for a barber or surgeon—one who cuts heads with scissors, or bodies with knives. From such play Höch creates one of her Dadaist *Mischwesen.* Baader's head, which on his calling card was framed by a six-pointed star, is placed above the diving suit of the Charlottenburg Nixe (Mermaid) woman's swimming and diving club, which is adorned by an eight-pointed star on the chest. Charlotte Joseph's head, turned sideways, reappears as the left eye of Count von Mirbach, the mustached man whose bald head supports the pirouetting figure of Impekoven and an African

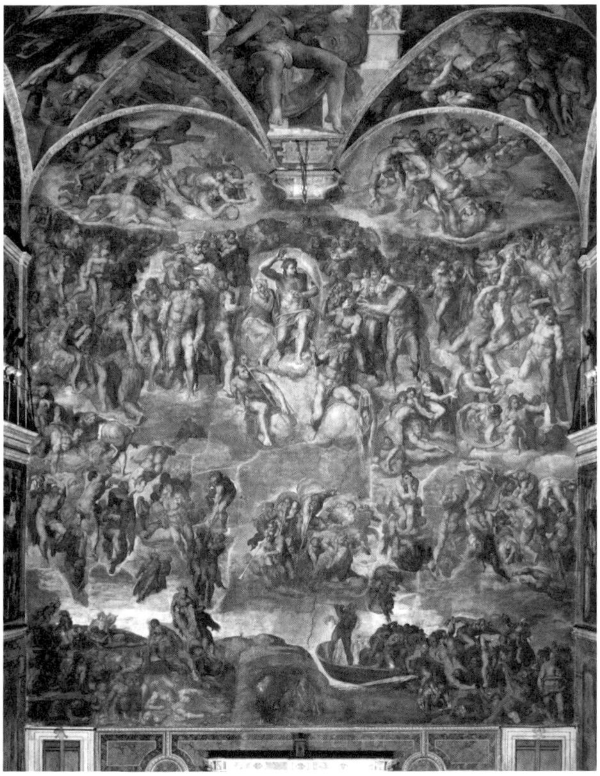

FIGURE 31. **Michelangelo, *The Last Judgment* (prior to cleaning), 1536–41, fresco. Sistine Chapel, Vatican Palace, Vatican State. Photo: Scala/Art Resource, NY.**

okapi. The composition suggests changing, unstable positions with figures rising, falling, and spinning, like divers practicing *Kunstspringen*.

At bottom left Höch alludes to a passage from Nietzsche's *Beyond Good and Evil* that informed Berlin Dada: "When nothing else today has a future, perhaps it's our laughter that still has one."[76] Höch quoted this line in the guestbook at Alfred Richard Meyer's house in Munich, on her way to Rome after the Dada Fair: "Dada is no bluff. If nothing else has a future today, perhaps it's our laughter that still has a future."[77] Her initials, HH, painted in bold, orange letters on a piece of paper superimposed onto the crowd, provide the hottest intervention of color into the primarily black-and-white montage. A bit of cool blue construction paper in the top left offers the only other color. In German, Höch's bold initials yell "HaHa!" the equivalent of an "Aha!" exclamation in English, and the onomatopoeic reading in English continues to resound today as a DaDa laugh.[78]

Like *Germany: A Winter's Tale, Cut with the Kitchen Knife Dada* presents a contemporary Last Judgment as part of the Dada anti-Mass. Höch's balletic central figure, like the muscular figure at the center of Michelangelo's centrifugally composed Sistine *Last Judgment* (1536–41, fig. 31), conducts the proceedings.[79] Here, too, we have a crowded, almost all-over composition, with circular movement around a central figure in a void, with figures rising and falling around it. The figure composed of the head of the Austrian writer Mechthild Lichnowsky, set atop the body of a skater, flies upward from left to right, above the Weimar assembly and into the side of a ball-bearing casing. On the right the chain-like figure consisting of the Josephs' bodies and Baader's head seems to descend, mirroring the famous figures being pulled down to hell in Michelangelo. At the very bottom center an orchestra plays music to accompany this apocalypse.

One of the most problematic words in the brilliantly provocative title of the work has always been *letzte*—last. How could this be the "last" Weimar beer-belly cultural epoch, when, in fact, the Weimar Republic had just begun at the time the work was created and titled? Did Höch really mean "most recent"? As Dech points out, this confusion has sometimes led to the substitution in the title of *erste* (first) for *letzte,* despite the use of *letzte* in the Dada Fair catalogue.[80] If we interpret the image as a Last Judgment the term *letzte* remains appropriately and Dadaistically problematic. In using *letzte* Höch did not allude directly to the Last Judgment—which in German is called *das jüngste Gericht.* If *jüngste* had been used instead of *letzte* in the montage's title, though, it would imply "recent" and not last, as in the phrase *in der jüngsten Vergangenheit* (in recent years). It would also make the connection to the Christian theme too explicit to appeal to Höch's subtle intellect. Using *letzte* in a properly Dadaistic method of substitution, Höch has her cake and eats it too, cut with both a kitchen *(Küchen)* and a cake *(Kuchen)* knife—two variations on the title that arose in later years and that Höch tolerated.[81] This, then, is both a Last Judgment *and* a cutting up of "the most recent" Weimar beer-belly epoch. Like Grosz's *Germany: A Winter's Tale,* Höch's montage is topical and allusive, referring at once to the present and recent past as well as to a well-known literary source and its associations.

For Maud Lavin, as for Bergius, *Cut with the Kitchen Knife Dada,* and Höch's work in general, functions according to "a dialectic . . . between anger and pleasure, and, for the viewer, an oscillation between ironic distance and intimate identification."[82] For both of these authors the work is allegorical, presenting a utopian vision that might reconcile the supposedly contradictory elements of human identity problematizing the human subject in the new social order emerging after World War I—male and female, gay and straight, machine and human. For Lavin this vision expresses a longing for a future not fully imagined that relates to the theories of the messianic Marxist Jewish philosopher Ernst Bloch, and to his idea that avant-garde artworks can harbor intimations of "not yet conscious knowledge." In Bergius's case the utopian project is to create a Nietzschean "superbeing," at once Apollonian and Dionysian, mental and physical, "wee" and muscular: *Mischwesen.*

According to Bergius, Höch's Einstein alludes to the Golem, the mythical giant who physically protected the Jews of the Prague Ghetto. The words superimposed onto Einstein's brow *("S. Friedlaender: der Waghalter der Welt")* "no doubt at the time could also be read as a reference to the Golem," as presented in Gustav Meyrink's novel of 1915 and Paul Wegener's films of 1915, 1917, and 1920. "In the magic of words the polar forces of creation and destruction unite. For Hannah Höch, Einstein, possessor of natural scientific knowledge, was *Waghalter der Welt.*"[83] Despite this insight, neither the word

"Jew" nor the concept of Jewish identity are ever written into Bergius's text. Friedlaender's or the Golem's relationship to Jewish messianic thought, and what Einstein as a Golem might mean in this social context, as well as Höch's witty parodies and ripostes to stereotypes circulated by anti-Semites (some of whom, like Max Nordau, were themselves Jewish) hover somewhere around the discussion, as if unspeakable.[84]

The faces of three German Jews—Einstein, Kurt Hiller, and Max Reinhardt, all identified by Roters and so by Höch—form a compositional triangle inscribed into the apocalyptic, centrifugal world of the montage (fig. 32). The three points of the triangle—Höch employed a common compositional schema even if she did not consciously plan it—fall on the bridge of each man's nose, between the eyes.[85] One long side links the bridge of Einstein's nose to Reinhardt and runs through the mechanical device that projects like a hearing aid from Einstein's left ear, from which emerge the words *dada siegt!* (dada victorious!). The other long side follows the V of a power stanchion that for Bergius seems to support the Einstein portrait. She identifies its source as an illustration of a wireless communication system.[86] The triangle gains formal structure from the placement of the ball-bearing casing above Hiller and a wheel to Reinhardt's left, on opposing sides of the triangle emanating from Einstein. Animals, technology, people, and the dancer of the apocalypse lie within the triangle. Its base runs between Hiller and Reinhardt, and below it is the zone of the Dadaists.[87]

Studies of Höch have stressed that in her montage work she was the most calculated and precise of the Dadaists—creating well-planned and composed compositions and carefully selecting her source photographs. *Cut with the Kitchen Knife Dada*'s status as an exception to this general rule has been overstated.[88] Although it is formally more various and complex than most of her other montages, complexity does not preclude careful selection and composition, even if both proceeded intuitively. It would be remarkable if Höch had forsaken her artistic training and outlook in this one major work. Instead, the work's multiple, interconnected images and structures reward multiple readings. Its constituent parts and their recombination constitute a fractured mirror image or critical cross section of early Weimar, when opportunities for Jews, as for women, were both expanding and facing challenges. In addition to advocating women's empowerment, Höch's work presents a vision of possible roles and potential dangers for Weimar German Jews.

Höch chose the posed studio portrait by Suse Byk to represent Einstein as thinker, embodiment of the *vita contemplativa,* at the apex of the triangle. Einstein was more often portrayed in pursuits that humanized him, such as playing his beloved violin, sailing on the Wannsee, relaxing at his summer home in Caputh near Potsdam, or speaking in public (fig. 33).[89] But Byk and Höch emphasized the invisible thinking whose otherworldly power made Einstein famous. By using a portrait that shows Einstein thinking, his eyes averted from the viewer and suggesting interiority, Höch connected his vision—his thoughts—to the apocalyptic world of the montage itself.[90] The clarity of the photographic image of Einstein, which contrasts to the shadowy emperor in the top right,

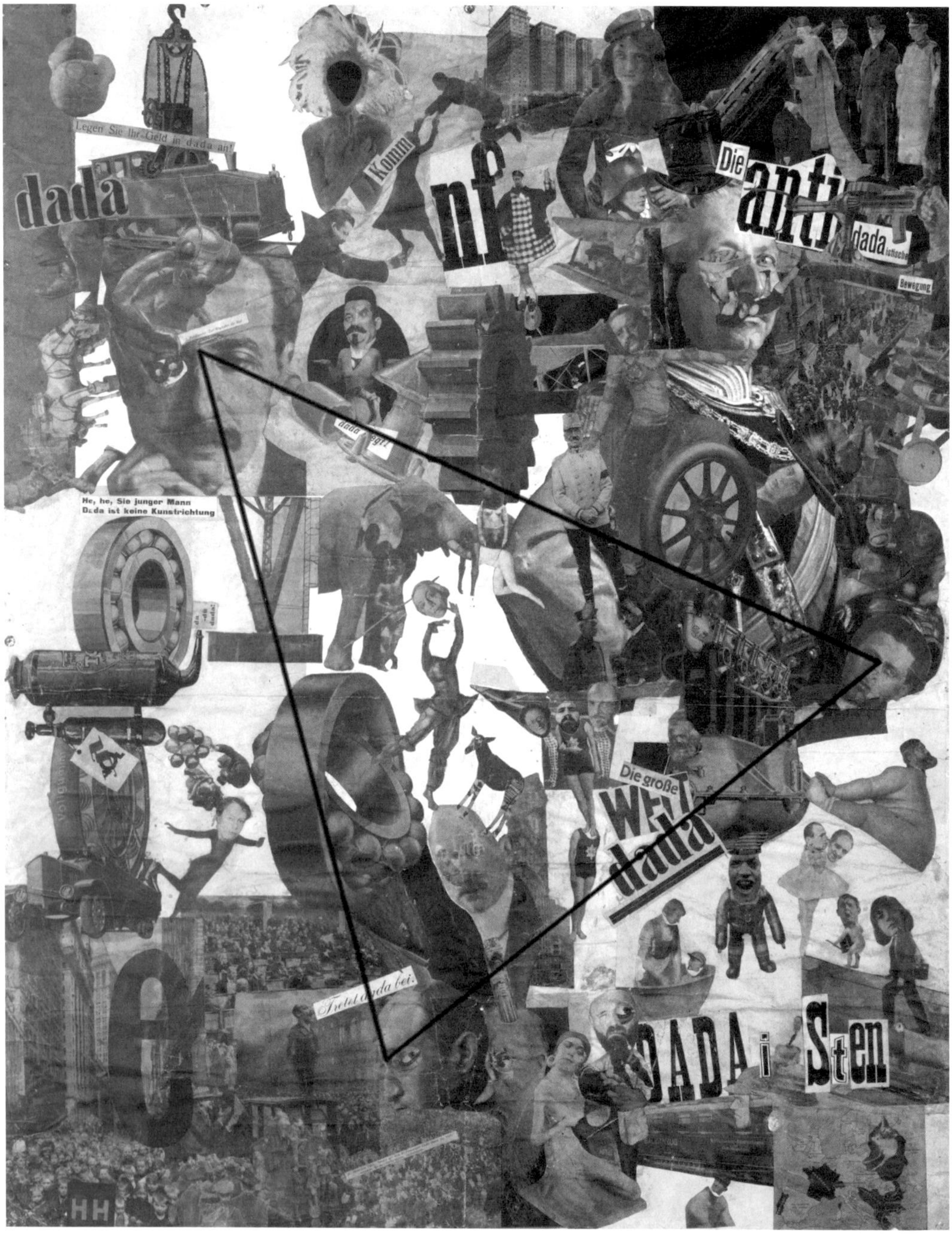

FIGURE 32. Triangle between three German faces in Hannah Höch's *Cut with the Kitchen Knife Dada* (see also plate 3). Art © 2010 Artists Rights Society (ARS), New York/VG Bild-Kunst, Bonn. Photo: Bildarchiv Preussischer Kulturbesitz/Art Resource, NY; with triangle added by Eric Peterson, Visual Resources Collection, SoAD, Southern Illinois University Carbondale.

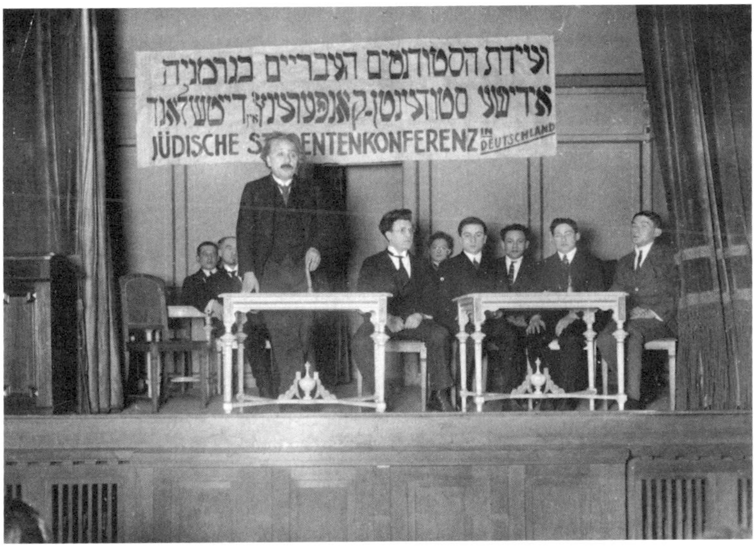

FIGURE 33. Albert Einstein at a Jewish students' conference, Berlin, 1924. Photo © Stiftung Neue Synagoge Berlin–Centrum Judaicum.

emphasizes the clarity of his vision. Höch pasted a photograph of two rubber tires over his right eye, forming an infinity sign. As Dech and Bergius have pointed out, Einstein the genius has insight that extends beyond normal human sight.

Max Reinhardt—the performer, stage artist, and director—resides near the right edge of the work, midway between top and bottom (fig. 22). The axis of the triangle that would have come to rest on his nose instead rests on the extended index finger of a female hand, with a ring on its finger and bracelet around its wrist, that Höch pasted over his most "Jewish" feature, his nose—the feature that the cultural historian Sander Gilman linked in caricatures and popular discourse with the Jew's "questionable" sexuality.[91] The Viennese Jew Max Goldman, transformed into the Berlin impresario Max Reinhardt, represents an attempt to reinvent the self by skillfully combining the life of mind and body. He is, however, as the extended index finger on his nose points out, still *indexically* connected to his origins—by virtue of being a Jew rather than symbolizing or playing one. His image is thus the one that corresponds most closely to that of the female Dadaist Höch—who includes her self-portrait in the Dadaist zone below Reinhardt, also in a frontal photograph of her face. Reinhardt's success in the legitimate theater of Berlin made him suspect to many Dadaists. But he had earned fame initially in the very sphere—performance—where they were active and through which they hoped to generate publicity, at the Schall und Rauch (Sound and smoke) cabaret. Höch's teacher Emil Orlik had designed the poster for the cabaret's opening in 1901; the Berlin Dadaists Grosz, Heartfield, Herzfelde, Mehring, and Höch began to contribute to it in 1919.[92] By that year Reinhardt's theater had moved into a large building, where he staged full-scale productions upstairs, and the Schall und Rauch cabaret, directed by Rudolf Kurtz, performed in the basement. In December 1919 Schall und Rauch premiered a satiric puppet show, *Simply Classical*, written by Mehring, with puppets by Heartfield and Grosz. Mehring's most famous song for that cabaret, "Heimat Berlin" (Our home, Berlin) features a protagonist rushing about at *Berliner Tempo* (Berlin speed) complaining that there was "No time. No time to lose."[93] This image was quickly translated into the colloquial description of Berliners' *jüdische Hast* (Jewish haste), conflating all Berliners with Jews. At the same time Mehring's Berlin odes turned sharply critical: "An Ufa film / Hails Kaiser Wil'm / Cathedrals wag reaction's flag, /With swastikas and poison gas, / Monocles won't let hooked noses pass. / On to the pogrom / In the hippodrome!"[94] Like Grosz's *Germany: A Winter's Tale*, mass culture (the hippodrome), Christian symbols, and government forces merge, which Mehring links to anti-Semitism. Hausmann and Wieland Herzfelde also participated in Schall und Rauch, and the April 1920 edition of the journal associated with the cabaret featured on its cover two of Hannah Höch's puppets, which were later shown at the Dada Fair (fig. 11).[95]

No longer an "underground" performer, though still marginal, Reinhardt floats precariously near the anti-Dadaists above him, presided over by the image of Kaiser Wilhelm II. The emperor's face is the only image as large as Einstein's—the two men represent opposing ideals (Einstein labeled "dada" above his head, the emperor "anti-dada"). The kaiser is further distanced from the other individuals in the montage, one might say "relativized," in that his head and torso are presented not in a photographic portrait but in a photographic reproduction of a painting. Unlike the crisper photographs from life, such as the Byk Einstein photograph, Kaiser Wilhelm's image appears hazy and includes visible brushstrokes. The kaiser's sepia-toned, ghost-like appearance represents an outmoded and now deposed form of power, as painting represents to the Dadaists an outmoded form of representation. Twentieth-century power, like class designations on board the *Titanic*, derives now not from inherited title but from wealth—indicated by the businessman's top hat that replaces the kaiser's crown.[96] The kaiser's mustache is composed of two inverted wrestlers, and his chest is decorated not only with medals but also with the photograph of Else Lasker-Schüler in an enormous man's hat. The Jews Reinhardt and Lasker-Schüler—performer and poet—present retorts to Germanic imperial pretensions and the physical power of wrestlers. Reinhardt and Lasker-Schüler are therefore proto-Dadaists. But they also risk losing their outsider status by courting favor with those in power, becoming too respectable, and being relegated to ornaments of the faded Wilhelmine culture.

At the other angle of the triangle, near the bottom center of the montage, resides the profile of the Expressionist Kurt Hiller, son of a *Kaufmann* father and descended on that side from "famous rabbis, on his mother's from socialists."[97] He was not a figure the Dadaists admired—but one they had to reckon with and one with whom, perhaps, Höch identified. In declaring Dada a "club" that anyone can join and "not a pretense for the ambition of a few literary types," Huelsenbeck and company rejected Hiller's elitist

Activist movement that held revolutionary change required leadership from artists and intellectuals of quality and sophistication.[98] The Dadaists rejected this idea in favor of unbridled freedom of expression. Prefiguring the neo-avant-garde professor Joseph Beuys's declaration that "everyone is an artist" and his admission of any applicant to his class at the Düsseldorf Art Academy in 1970, they invited the fifteen-year-old Hans Citroen to show with them at the Dada Fair. Though she may not have sympathized with his elitism, Hiller's advocacy of sexual freedom and abortion right probably appealed to the sexually progressive Höch, who by this time had had two abortions. In an article of 1913 Hiller argued against Statute 175 of the Wilhelmine penal code, which prohibited homosexuality, and in 1922 published a book labeling that law "the disgrace of the century."[99] Höch pasted over Hiller's eye a monocle (fig. 21). Hausmann and other Dadaists wore one as a satirical provocation against Prussian norms. In the 1920s the monocle became a sign of a woman's lesbian orientation, as in Otto Dix's *Portrait of Sylvia van Harden* of 1926.[100] In Höch's montage, though, Hiller represents the failure of the activist's intellectual position, his head squeezed between parallel text clippings, each on a diagonal: below, the montage's title, clipped from the Dada Fair catalogue, and above, the slogan *Tretet dada bei!* (Join dada!), shouted to a crowd by a man standing on the roof of a carriage.[101] This diagonal proceeds just below Count Mirbach's high collar and is extended by the word *dada,* beneath Marx, and the words *Die große* (the great) along the axis leading to Reinhardt. The first version of the montage, shown at the Dada Fair, did not include the slogan *Die große Welt dada,* now found next to the figures of the divers, but the word *Weltrevolution* (world revolution) in red letters set parallel to the body of the lower diver; they are visible to the left of Raoul Hausmann's arm in the photograph of Hausmann and Höch at the Dada Fair (fig. 9).[102] The movement from Hiller toward Reinhardt, however, was already implied by the eye in Hiller's monocle, which looks back in that direction. Hiller, though, remains oblivious to entreaties to join inclusive movements such as Dada, the "World Revolution," or the "Great World dada." Bodiless, with his bald head in profile, he is too cerebral to be truly "active" in a Dadaistic sense, isolated from the masses of spectators indicated by the crowds around him and the object's spectators, who are implicit subjects of address of all those other, frontal faces, such as Höch's, peering out of the montage.

By attacking Hiller's left-wing Nietzschean position, the Communist wing of Berlin Dada (Grosz, Heartfield, Herzfelde) created a rift with another left-wing Nietzschean, Salomo Friedlaender (fig. 34). Friedlaender responded by attacking Grosz in his 1922 monograph. For Friedlaender, as for Höch, Grosz had drifted too far into caricature in the service of party politics.[103] Friedlaender instead advocated for the properly Nietzschean oppositional intellectual a position of "creative indifference," a phrase he used as the title of his best-known philosophical work. Friedlaender advocated criticism of the commonplace, independent of any specific party or political affiliation.[104] In every sense, the Friedlaenderian position—that of the ironist, the word player, the creator of hybrid, "grotesque" creatures—is much more Höch's than Grosz's.

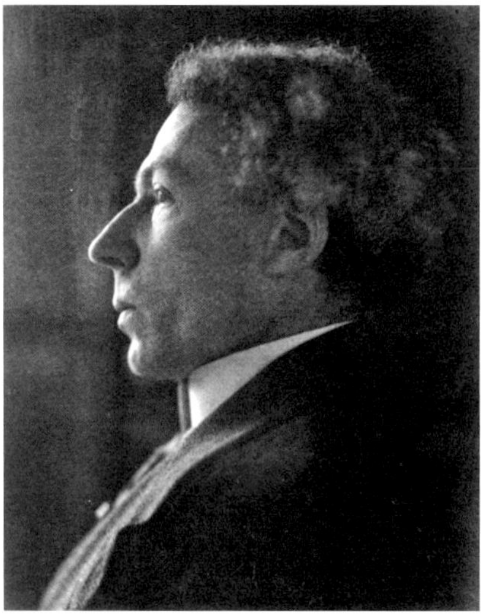

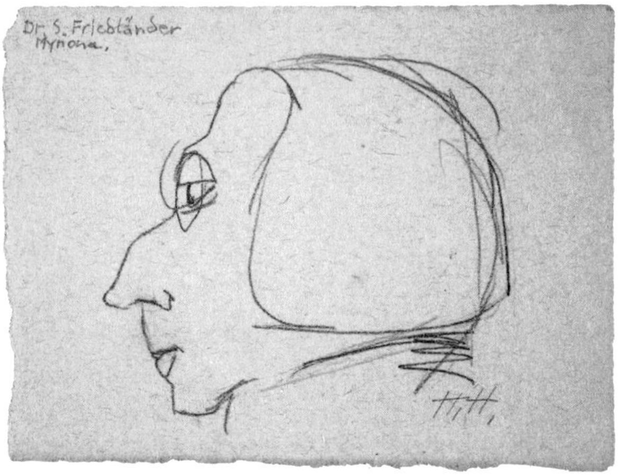

FIGURE 34. Grete Leistikow, *Untitled* (Salomo Friedlaender, aka Mynona, 1871–1946), 1921, silver gelatin print. Photo: Hannah-Höch-Archiv, Berlinische Galerie, Landesmuseum für Moderne Kunst, Fotografie und Architektur. FIGURE 35. Hannah Höch, *Dr. S. Friedlaender Mynona,* ca. 1922, pencil. Art © 2010 Artists Rights Society (ARS), New York/VG Bild-Kunst, Bonn. Photo: Hannah-Höch-Archiv, Berlinische Galerie, Landesmuseum für Moderne Kunst, Fotografie und Architektur.

The intellectual historian Anson Rabinbach groups Friedlaender among the "Jewish Nietzscheans" in analyzing the tradition of Jewish intellectual messianism—a theologically inflected but often secular strand of utopian thinking from the years before and after World War I. Rabinbach calls Friedlaender "an extraordinary figure on the fringes of the Oskar Goldberg circle of modern Jewish 'Kabbalists,' " whose major book *(Schöpferische Indifferenz,* translated as *Creative Indifference)* "is a form of Jewish apocalypticism" distinct from the theological messianism of Walter Benjamin or Ernst Bloch.[105] Friedlaender critiqued Bloch in an essay published in Kurt Hiller's journal *Ziel* (Goal) in 1919.[106]

Höch probably met Friedlaender at Meidner's and through Raoul Hausmann, "the Dadasoph," who was much taken with this Jewish mystic's brand of Nietzscheanism. Friedlaender, Baader, and Hausmann planned to publish a journal, *Die Erde* (The earth), together in 1915. Höch studied Friedlaender's texts, which probably formed her first introduction to philosophical writing.[107] She and Friedlaender became very close—she executed four graphic portraits and one painting of him, and he wrote her love letters and poems.[108]

Höch's graphic portraits of Friedlaender border on caricature (fig. 35). By portraying him in physiognomic profile in line drawings and silhouette cutouts, she emphasized the most "Jewish" of his attributes, his long, hooked nose. These images, certainly not derogatory, are celebratory—Höch portrays Friedlaender with the broad forehead and shock of hair emphasized in the Austrian graphic artist Alfred Kubin's written descrip-

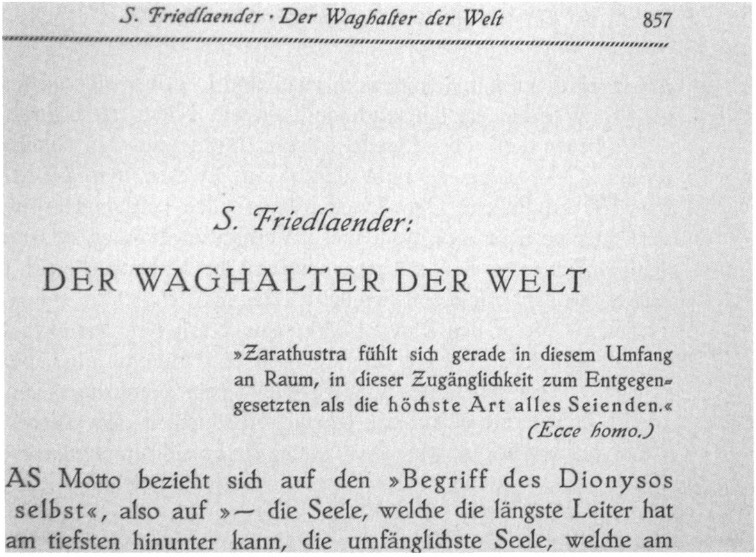
S. Friedlaender · Der Waghalter der Welt 857

S. Friedlaender:

DER WAGHALTER DER WELT

»Zarathustra fühlt sich gerade in diesem Umfang an Raum, in dieser Zugänglichkeit zum Entgegengesetzten als die höchste Art alles Seienden.«
(Ecce homo.)

AS Motto bezieht sich auf den »Begriff des Dionysos selbst«, also auf »— die Seele, welche die längste Leiter hat am tiefsten hinunter kann, die umfänglichste Seele, welche am

FIGURE 36. S. Friedlaender, "Der Waghalter der Welt," *Die Weissen Blätter* (July 1915). Photo: Author.

tion of him, and confirmed in a profile photograph by Grete Leistikow, but Höch also shows him with a slightly smiling and sensuous mouth, featuring a long upper and full lower lip.[109] This is not the rapacious and libertine hook-nosed Jewish businessman of anti-Semitic caricature but an eroticized Jewish intellectual, emphasizing the positive in what Sander Gilman has analyzed as a shifting positive/negative association in gentile culture "between the Jew's sexuality and the Jew's nose."[110] In Höch's drawing, the nose is portrayed not as sign of the Jew's emasculation, the stereotype connecting a large, "deformed" nose to a small, mutilated (i.e., circumcised) penis, but a sign of physical distinction appropriate to his intellect.[111]

While *Cut with the Kitchen Knife Dada* presents the Friedlaenderian position, not least in its subtle allusions and wordplay, Mynona himself is absent as image but, like the unpicturable Jewish messiah, present as the only other person, beside Höch herself, named among the text fragments. A form of Höch's name is included in the snippet of text from the Dada Fair catalogue pasted beneath Hiller's profile.[112] "S. Friedlaender" and the name of his essay, "Der Waghalter der Welt," run across Einstein's brow (fig. 24). That essay appeared first in July 1915, in René Schickele's pacifist journal *Die Weissen Blätter* (White sheets, or papers), which is the source for Höch's clipping (fig. 36). In the montage this text fragment is held aloft by an earwig, just above the point of the Einstein-Reinhardt-Hiller compositional triangle, and on a diagonal that parallels the text fragment with Höch's name and the work's title at the bottom of the montage. The superimposition of the life-size earwig on Einstein's smaller-than-life forehead inverts the scale, transforming the insect into a monstrous aberration. Legend has it that the earwig crawls into the ear cavity, surreptitiously inhabiting its host's body. The connection to Einstein and Friedlaender here might also suggest the anti-Semitic association of Jews with body-defiling vermin. Although this association stems from anti-Semitic sources, it can also inhabit the Jew's self-conception and erupt monstrously and unexpectedly, as in Gregor Samsa's transformation into an *ungeheueres Ungeziefer* (a monstrous vermin) in Kafka's famous novella *Die Verwandlung (The Metamorphosis)*. Kafka's story, written in 1912, first appeared in *Die Weissen Blätter* in the October–December 1915 issue, a few months after Friedlaender's "Der Waghalter der Welt." Höch had probably already read it there: she also owned a copy of the first edition (1915) of Kafka's story in book form.[113]

While many plausible interpretations have been offered for Gregor's transformation, Samsa in his barricaded bedroom is also the entomological embodiment of Kafka himself, and his name is the orthographical equivalent of Kafka's (in a play on words that Höch would have recognized).[114] Kafka, as artist, German speaker, and Jew, belonged to minorities relegated to marginality in Prague's business world (he worked by day in insurance) and in Christian Czech culture. As a Prague Jew he also spent his youth in the same ghetto as Höch's and Grosz's teacher Emil Orlik. The earwig emerging from Einstein's head and holding aloft Friedlaender's name and credo is thus a sign not only of these intellectuals' powerful thoughts but also of the reemergence in postwar Germany of anti-Semitic conceptions of Jews—"scientific Dadaism"—with their power to become internalized self-images, and of the need to find the means to combat or escape them.[115] The views of Einstein, Reinhardt, and Hiller form a trinity of Jewish identity and alterity, presented, like the rest of the montage, both positively and negatively, a balancing of different possibilities in this image that, in an appropriately Friedlaenderian way, is at once playful, apocalyptic, and utopian.

During the final weeks of the First International Dada Fair, internationalism and philo-Semitism came under direct attack. The German Workers' Party (Deutsche Arbeiter Partei, DAP), founded in 1919 in Munich, changed its name in August 1920 to the National Socialist German Workers' Party (Nationalsozialistische Deutsche Arbeiterspartei, NSDAP, Nazi for short). Point 2 of its program, announced in February 1920, called for abolishing the Treaty of Versailles; point 4 called for the exclusion of Jews from the German body politic.[116] George Grosz later commented on the struggles of 1919: "Out on the street one group of white-shirted men was marching to the slogan of '*Deutschland, erwache! Juda, verrecke!*' (Wake up, Germany! Jew, drop dead!)."[117] On March 13, 1919, Hannah Höch noted in her daybook: "Revolution." That morning, troops of the radical right-wing Free Corps Erhard Brigade had "marched through the Brandenburg Gate toward Berlin in armored vehicles and with swastikas on their helmets."[118]

Women call up, energize, and nimbly dance and fly through Höch's brilliant last judgment of Germany's last Weimar beer-belly cultural epoch, a world still too dominated by fat beer-swilling men. At bottom right, the realm of the Dadaists, Höch's lover Hausmann screams in defiance, his body a deep-sea diving suit. To his right, Grosz's head is grafted onto the body of a ballerina, while to his left John Heartfield receives a baby bath from a woman dressed in traditional German costume, her head that of the dancer Impekoven.[119] The male Dadaists, true to their name, express themselves viscerally, revert to childish forms of protest, play out infantile fantasies that oscillate between helplessness and omnipotence, dream themselves dancers. The Jewish intellectuals Einstein, Reinhardt, and Hiller, in contrast, reflect on their next moves with all due seriousness. The triangle formed by their faces is a hierarchical diagram, with Einstein at the top, Reinhardt in the middle, and Hiller at the bottom. This compositional schema, though, connects them, suggesting a collective weighing of different strategies to survive this apocalypse. Still static, though, the montage's carefully selected images and their arrangement into a coherent if complex overall composition suggests that they would do well to follow the more mobile women's lead and join the engine representing Einstein's train of thought in the top left (labeled "dada" and with the slogan "invest your money in dada!" coming out of its smokestack) to the passenger car of Höch's train of action in the bottom right (in the area of the Dadaists and labeled "Dadaists"), and together ride into a Dadaist future that is friendly to feminists and enlightened Jews.

Like Hannah Höch, however, we should not limit our attention to those well-known intellectuals and artists. What of those nimble, lively *Kunstspringerinnen?* Of a Berlin resident named Charlotte Joseph, perhaps the woman diver on whose body Baader's head resides, we read chilling words on which further commentary chokes (whether this is indeed the same Charlotte Joseph or not): "Joseph, Charlotte, born 12 February 1897 in Leipzig, Wilmersdorf, Uhland Street 54–55; 24th transport of 9 December 1942, Auschwitz; Place of death: Auschwitz, lost."[120]

Germany: A Winter's Tale and *Cut with the Kitchen Knife Dada* were extraordinarily attuned to their times and those to come, and not only in the former's pillorying of church, state, and educational establishments or Höch's exploration of the New Woman. The Jewish presence inscribed into these works is not unambiguously positive. But by presenting a variety of images of Jews and referring to complexly multifaceted German-Jewish sources, they refute the characterization of German Jews by the influential historian Heinrich von Treitschke as unambiguously "our misfortune." Predicting and influencing Werner Sombart and, like him, providing intellectual legitimation for anti-Semitism, von Treitschke argued that German Jews should lose all outward signs of their ethnicity and religion and assimilate to German gentile culture so that the newly formed nation would not degenerate into an "age of German-Jewish bastardized culture—*Mischkultur.*"[121] Hanne Bergius has documented how Dada promulgated just such a *Mischkultur* as an antidote to the concept of *Deutschtum* (or any singular national or personal identity), which the Great War and its aftermath revealed as morally bankrupt and inherently dangerous. Grosz's and Höch's object lessons continue to teach today.

Postscript in the Present: Signs of Jews in the Bavarian Quarter

Albert Einstein returned to Berlin art in September and October 2005. In the spirit of Berlin Dada, the Swiss artist Christoph Büchel sought to blur the borders between art and mass communication and to provoke public response and even outrage with his contribution to the exhibition "Einstein Spaces," part of the centennial celebration of Einstein's 1905 *anno mirabilis* (fig. 37). From 1918 to 1932 Einstein lived in an apartment in Berlin at Haberland Street 8, in the so-called Bavarian Quarter in Berlin Schöneberg, where many streets and squares are named after Bavarian locales.[122] "Einstein Spaces" invited nine international artists to create pieces in areas significant to Einstein's Berlin years. Among them, Christian Boltanski's installation intoned the relativity of time at the Oranienburger Street Synagogue, and Franz West's two signs—EIN and STEIN—sailing about on the Templiner See near Einstein's summer house at Caputh, invoked curvatures in space. Büchel erected a huge billboard at the corner of Haberland and Bamberger streets announcing a (fictitious) cooperative project between the German and Israeli governments, whereby a piece of the Berlin Wall would be used as part of the barrier wall between Israel- and Palestinian-controlled territories, and an element of the Israeli wall would be installed in Berlin as public sculpture.

Other signs in the Bavarian Quarter have long referred to Jews. In 1993 Renata Stih and Frieder Schnock installed their well-known and much praised project, *Places of Remembrance in the Bavarian Quarter/Memorial in Berlin-Schöneberg.* This piece consists of eighty small signs, each attached to a light or street post. Each sign bears a simple graphic depiction of an object or image on one side, with text on the other. The texts are mainly decrees issued between 1933 and 1945 that gradually limited Jewish residents' rights and ultimately deported them to their deaths. A few of Stih's and Schnock's texts are personal testimonies to the results of those decrees. The objects pictured on the signs generally relate to their text. For example, the reverse of the sign picturing a simple iconic plug has a decree of 1943 declaring that Jews may no longer own electric appliances (fig. 38). As the cultural historian Bill Niven points out, in structuralist terms, the image and the text point out a gap between "signifier" and "signified"—the plug, which should represent electric power, actually denotes the absence of power for Jews.[123] *Places of Remembrance* assiduously documents the escalation of persecution from petty annoyance to real hardship and mass murder, implicitly calling for vigilance in the present about human rights abuses, small and large. Strollers encounter the signs dispersed throughout the neighborhood, spatializing the dispersal of persecution. Some signs are placed strategically in relation to a nearby business, office building, or landmark.[124]

Stih and Schnock's work relates to the contemporaneous project of the American art collective REPOhistory, especially their Lower Manhattan Sign Project, which used a similar format of graphics and text to recount aspects of the "negative past" of colonialism and slavery to counter the generally celebratory mood of the five-hundred-year anniversary of Columbus's "discovery" of America.[125] It is also almost a textbook updating of

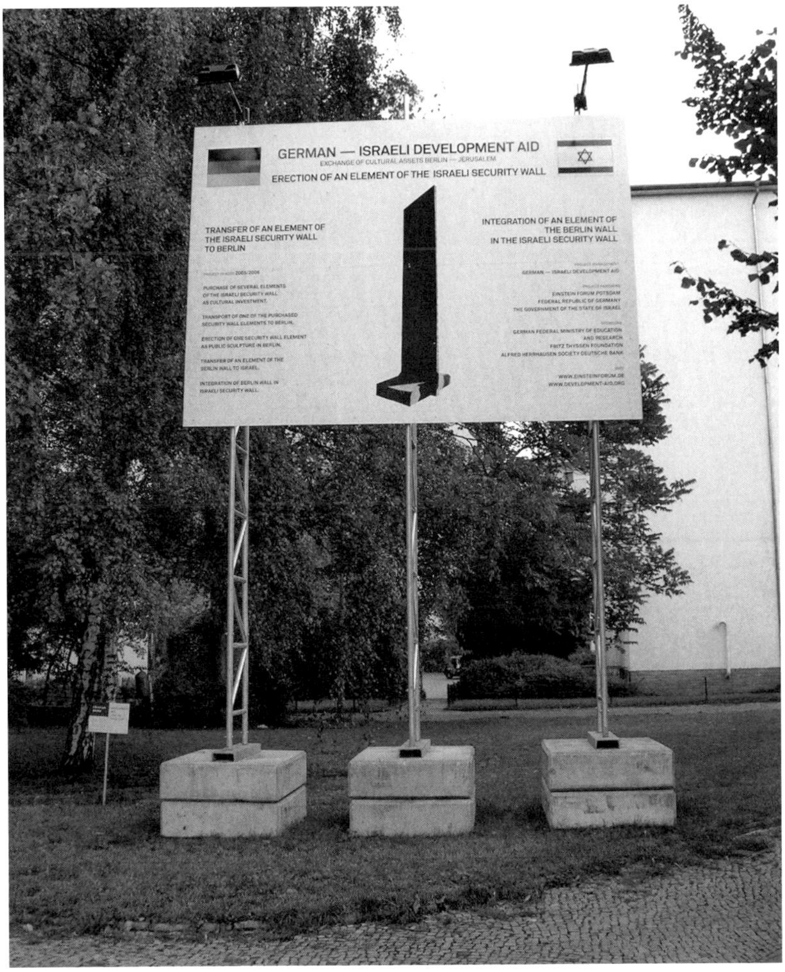

FIGURE 37. **Christoph Büchel, *German-Israeli Development Aid*, 2005/6, installation at "Einstein Spaces" exhibition, Bavarian Quarter, Berlin. Photo: Author.**

the project of Pierre Nora, who developed ideas from the classicist Francis Yates to document France's *Lieux de mémoire* (places, or sites, of memory). As the historian Patrick H. Hutton explains, Greek and Roman rhetoricians in antiquity developed the art of mnemonics, the use of signs and symbols to evoke memories. To do so, they "utilized a dual repertoire of places and images. They conjured up striking images, to which they attached the ideas they wished to remember, and then located them within imaginary frameworks that served as paths for their narrative walks through the past."[126] Nora attempted to transpose these techniques to the study of monuments and "sites of memory" in modern France, especially monuments, buildings, and landscapes that evoke an individual historical memory and together produce a composite image of the nation's history. Stih and Schnock return to the rhetoricians, to simple graphic signs (in both senses of

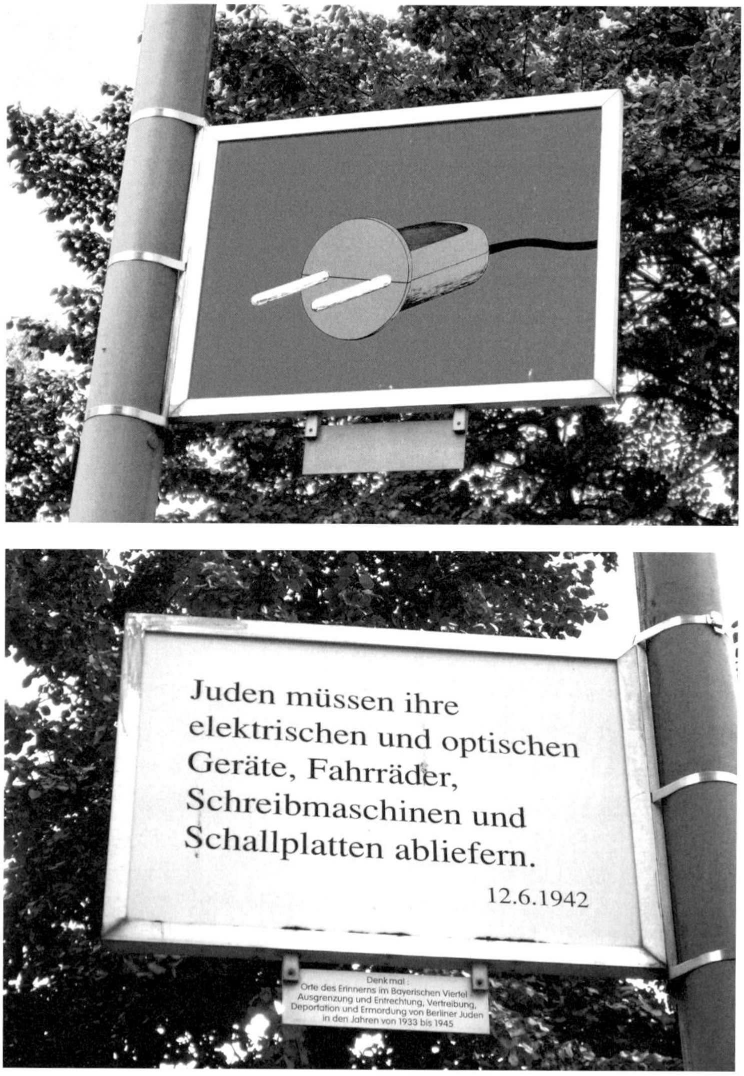

FIGURE 38. Renata Stih and Frieder Schnock, *Places of Remembrance in the Bavarian Quarter/Memorial in Berlin-Schöneberg,* 1992: "Jews must turn in their electrical and optical devices, bicycles, typewriters and records. 12 June 1942." Art © 2010 Artists Rights Society (ARS), New York/VG Bild-Kunst, Bonn. Photo: Author.

the word) attached to text, to place, and to the perambulation of an individual through an urban landscape. The past is thus inscribed into contemporary everyday experience, such as shopping or waiting for the bus. Juliet Koss, writing of her experience living now in the presence of the Bavarian Quarter's signs of Jewish persecution during the Nazi past, has expressed annoyance at the piece. She reports never encountering, in two years of living in the neighborhood, people who actually noticed or interacted with the signs. As an art historian and a Jew, she did. Her irritation derived from her conclusion that the signs ultimately targeted and excluded her as a Jew, relegating Jews to a special and distinct category as victims while also reifying an old and rigid distinction between Germans and Jews—assuming Jews to be invisible today and have no life in Berlin and present-day Germany, which is, in fact, a polyglot, multiethnic, cosmopolitan *Mischkultur.*

Koss offered as her new favorite memorial project what seems to have become an "underground" hero among German Holocaust memorials, Gunter Demnig's *Stolpersteine* (Stumble stones, or Stumbling blocks—see frontispiece), little bronze plaques installed throughout Germany amid the cobblestones in front of houses from which Jews and other victims were deported and murdered by the Nazis, naming the victims but keeping silent as to the mechanisms, causes, effects, and even person responsible for the remembrance. These plaques were also the anonymous heroes of Arthur Danto's review in *The Nation,* on October 17, 2005, of Peter Eisenman's recently completed work in Berlin, the *Memorial to the Murdered Jews of Europe,* Germany's national Holocaust memorial. The strength of Demnig's project resides in part in the anonymity of the artist and the identification of the victims. Misha Berson, an American commentator writing in the *Seattle Times,* also stumbled on Demnig's plaques. He researched them and, like Danto, contrasted them with Eisenman's monumental field of mute pillars: "More than anything else on my trip, the stumble stones made real to me the lost Jews of Berlin and the righteous impulse to honor them." Berson's complaint about the Eisenman memorial is similar to Koss's criticism of the Stih and Schnock piece: both object to the singling out of Jewish victims as contemporary "ghettoizing." There is, however, a "damned if they do, damned if they don't" problem here, because a central weakness of many memorials to Nazi victims in Germany has been their vagueness about the fact that terror against all Jews was fundamental to the ideology, legal structure, and program of action of the Nazi state. This is a specific strength of Stih's and Schnock's piece.

Christoph Büchel's provocative work for "Einstein Spaces" may indicate a gradual "normalizing" of the discourse on the German-Jewish relationship. More than any other work in "Einstein Spaces," his billboard blurred the boundaries between art and non-art. Its blurring of distinctions between public art and public signage reflects developments in contemporary art, such as Jenny Holzer's LED displays, Barbara Kruger's billboards, and the work of Edgar Heap of Birds exposing hidden histories and embedded stereotypes in North American culture, as well as projects by Stih and Schnock and REPOhistory. Büchel's work had little or no connection with Einstein, beyond his being a Jew and Israel a Jewish nation whose creation he supported. Using the Einstein Year as an opportunity to criticize contemporary Israeli politics has its distasteful aspects. However, linking the exploration of German-Jewish relations with criticism of Israel certainly heightened the piece's abrasive, even offensive, qualities, and thus the billboard, in representing an homage to Berlin Dada tactics, certainly captured the Berlin Dada spirit.

4 *Absender: ich*

Willi Baumeister's Anti-Nazi Works as Objects of (S)exchange

Postcard Studies

During the Third Reich, the "degenerate" artist Willi Baumeister created a remarkable series of postal artworks in which he used reproductions of works by the leading Nazi painter, Adolf Ziegler (plate 5 and figs. 39–40). These mobile art objects engaged history and politics directly and personally, as is appropriate to their format. Postcards involve both the sender and the recipient in an intimate communicative relationship. The historian analyzing them, as Jordana Mendelson has observed, can also become personally involved, invested, and identified with these objects of exchange and collection that we apprehend in language, as image, and as objects that we touch:

> Postcard studies implicate the author in ways that perhaps other media may not. The postcard disallows disinterested analysis because as historians dealing with these objects we cross the line that has been drawn between realms of culture considered worthy of public interest and those that are more often associated with private passions.[1]

Postcards played an important role in Dadaist practice, as they already had in that of the German Expressionists, many of whom, like Franz Marc, drew individual artworks on blank cards to send to friends. According to Höch and Hausmann, their photomontages were inspired by World War I field postcards depicting generic battle scenes, into which a soldier could paste his own image.[2] Hausmann's postcard correspondence includes his defacing of a *Sturm* postcard featuring the face of its leader, Herwarth Walden, with *"section du merde"*—shit section—written across his forehead, among other insults.[3]

Postcard correspondence was also central to Grosz's and Heartfield's competing claim to have "invented" photomontage. In his infamous, farcical identification of a single, originating moment for photomontage, Grosz wrote: "In 1916, when Johnny Heartfield and I invented photomontage in my studio at the south end of the town at five o'clock one May morning . . . we pasted a mischmasch of advertisements for hernia belts, student song-books and dog food, labels from schnaps- and wine-bottles, and

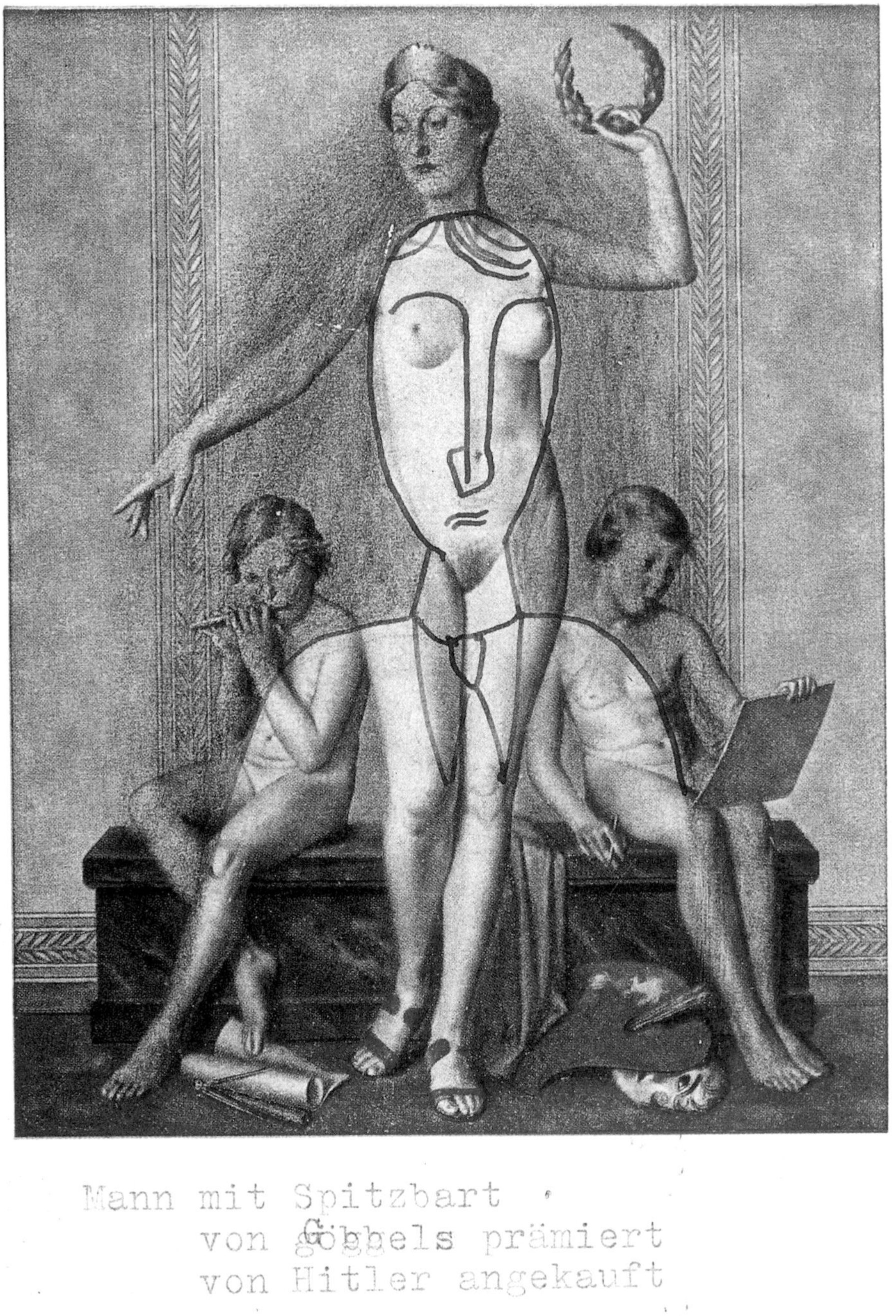

FIGURE 39. Willi Baumeister, *Mann mit Spitzbart, von Göbbels prämiert von Hitler angekauft* (Man with goatee, premiered by Göbbels/göggels, bought by Hitler), ca. 1941, altered postcard of Adolf Ziegler's *Goddess of Art* (1938). Art © 2010 Artists Rights Society (ARS), New York/VG Bild-Kunst, Bonn. Photo: Archiv Baumeister im Kunstmuseum Stuttgart.

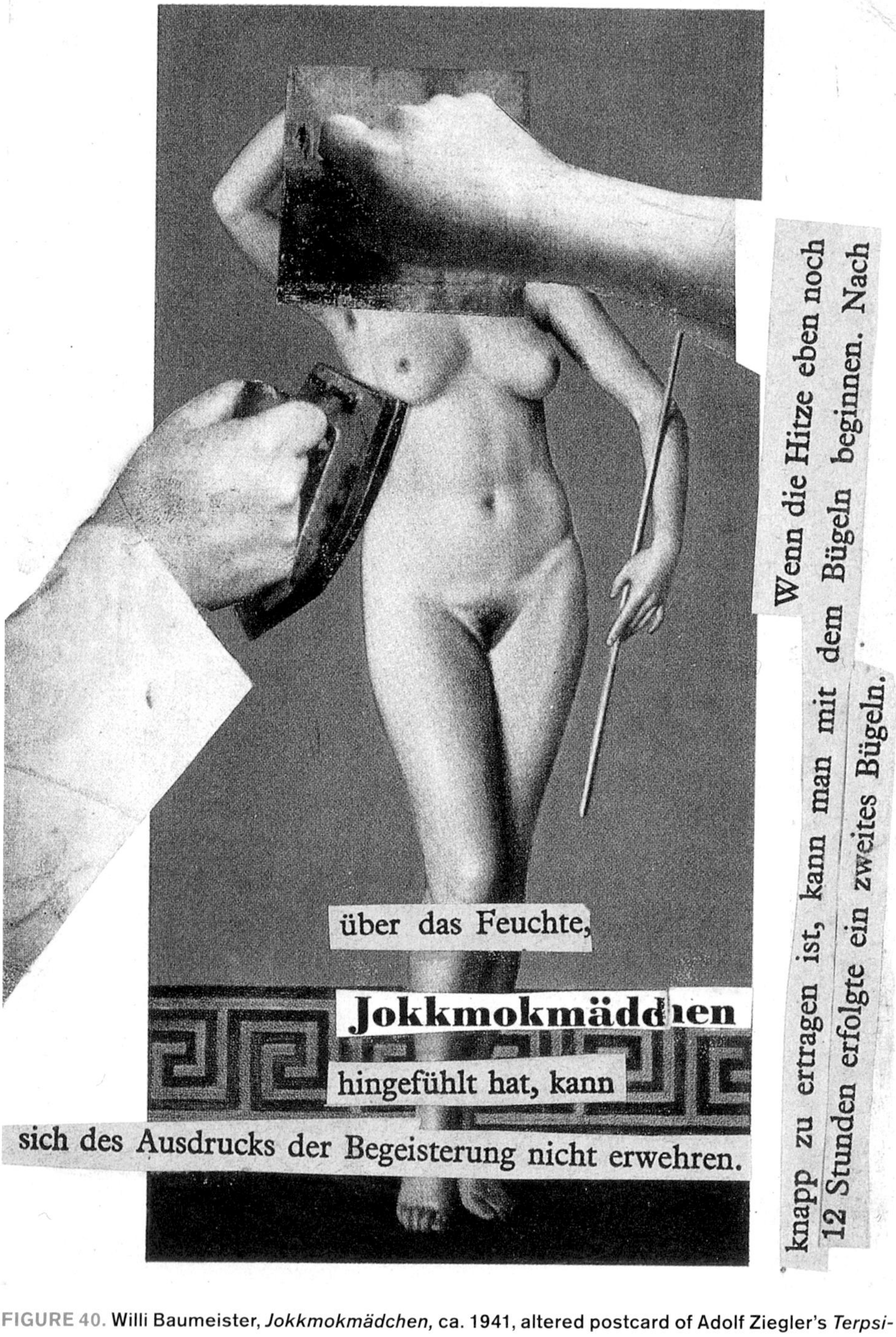

FIGURE 40. Willi Baumeister, *Jokkmokmädchen,* ca. 1941, altered postcard of Adolf Ziegler's *Terpsichore* (1937). Art © 2010 Artists Rights Society (ARS), New York/VG Bild-Kunst, Bonn. Photo: Archiv Baumeister im Kunstmuseum Stuttgart.

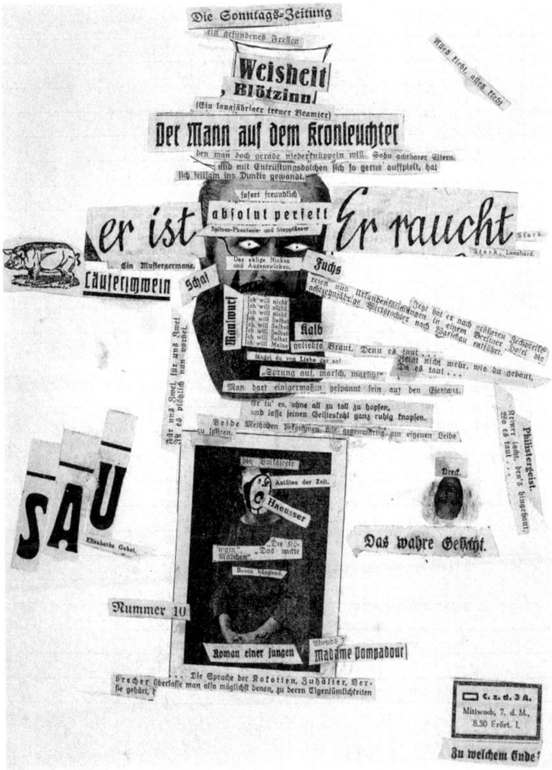

FIGURE 41. Willi Baumeister, *The Man on the Candelabra*, ca. 1916, collage and ink on paper. Art © 2010 Artists Rights Society (ARS), New York/VG Bild-Kunst, Bonn. Photo: Archiv Baumeister im Kunstmuseum Stuttgart.

photographs from picture papers, cut up at will in such a way as to say, in pictures, what would have been banned by the censors if we had said it in words. In this way we made postcards supposed to have been sent home from the Front, or from home to the Front."[4] In a time of war and censorship, Grosz and Heartfield employed montage postcards for clandestine communication.

As a soldier on the Eastern Front in World War I, Willi Baumeister sent home preprinted field postcards *(Feldpostkarten)*. On leave in Vienna in 1915 and 1916, though, he came into contact with the circle around Karl Kraus, the editor of the journal *Die Fackel* (The torch), which included the writer Peter Altenberg and the architect Adolf Loos. Baumeister picked up on Kraus's verbal collages skewering common wisdom and received ideas, and began precociously in 1916 to create satirical collages of cut-up newspaper fragments that one scholar has recently claimed "ushered in Dada montaging, such as in the work of Hannah Höch" (fig. 41).[5]

Baumeister refrained from collaging his *Feldpostkarten*. He did, however, exchange collaged letters with Oskar Schlemmer, his best friend, a fellow Stuttgart art student and artist, and a future Bauhaus master, who was also in the army, stationed in the west. At the time of the November Revolution, Baumeister wrote on a field postcard in his typically understated manner to his family: "In Germany there appears to be relative disorder. . . . If you all have enough to eat, then everything else is irrelevant! Things continue to go very well for me, and I'm extraordinarily happy that the end of the war is in sight."[6] A few weeks later, after the revolution had toppled the monarchy and in apparent disregard of ultramontane censors, he wrote: "How wonderful it is to be certain that I will finally be free from the agonizing soldier's existence and that the dark conditions of war are now gone, as is the supreme sorcerer, Wilhelm II."[7]

About twenty years later, in Nazi Germany, Baumeister created Dadaistic postcard collages and montages that commented on art and politics and the politics of art in a most subtle and subversive way. Postcards proliferated in Nazi Germany. The government not only encouraged their production and use in correspondence, it also policed their imagery, attempting to repress the circulation of unorthodox or transgressive images.[8] Views and art approved by the state circulated as private and public affirmations of that state's values, bearing official stamps, many featuring a profile portrait of Hitler. The Nazi's security apparatus took an interest not only in the images that circulated but also in their quality. A "Report from the Reich" of 1940—one of the many policy advisories by the Nazi security service based on its operatives' observations of civilian behavior—concerned the images on field postcards: "Extremely kitschy field postcards are turning up in shops in ever greater quantities. . . . [F]ield postcards should be created featuring, for example, good, racially unobjectionable girls and women from the area of operation, figures from German history, the leadership of the movement and military or contemporary artworks."[9] The contemporary artworks recommended were by such painters as Ivo Saliger and Adolf Ziegler and such sculptors as Arno Breker and Josef Thorak, whose works were shown beginning in 1937 in the annual "Great German Art" exhibition in the House of German Art in Munich. In mass distribution, reproductions of these academic works were to offer evidence that contemporary art had been "cleansed" of modern "degeneracy."

Unaltered, the postcard on the cover of the literary scholar Jay Prosser's *Second Skins: The Body Narratives of Transsexuality* (1998) displayed one of these approved works of Third Reich art, the Greek muse Terpsichore, portrayed by Adolf Ziegler, the leading Nazi painter and organizer of the 1937 "Degenerate Art" exhibition (fig. 42).[10] Willi Baumeister visited both the Munich showing of the "Degenerate Art" exhibition, where four of his paintings were on display, and the concurrent "Great German Art" exhibition of Nazi-approved art, which included Ziegler's *Terpsichore;* among the postcards he acquired was one of this work. It may seem surprising that a "degenerate artist" visited this exhibition pillorying his work, but Baumeister's visit appears not to have been unusual. Although Hannah Höch had no works in the show, she identified with those artists who did, including her Berlin Dadaist and Expressionist friends, such as the Jews Ludwig Meidner and Otto Freundlich, one of whose sculptures was reproduced on the cover of the guide to the exhibition. Höch visited four times, twice in Munich in 1937 and again in Berlin and Hamburg in 1938.[11]

Baumeister visited the Munich "Degenerate Art" exhibition twice. Back home in Stuttgart, he altered some of the postcards he had acquired at the "Great German Art"

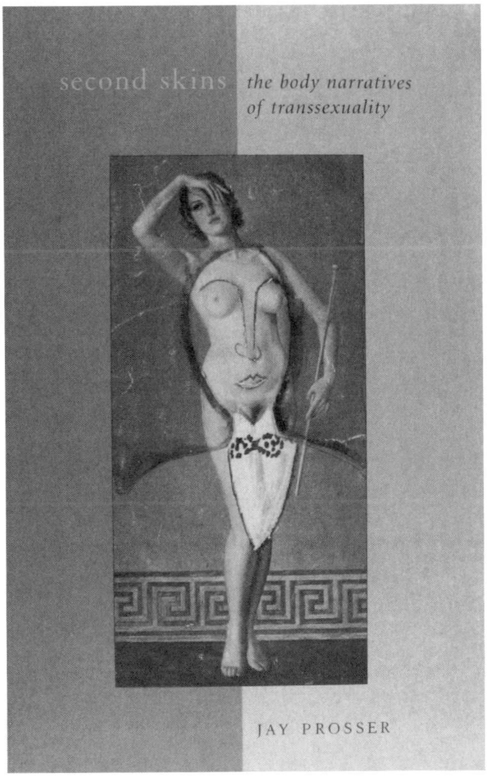

FIGURE 42. Cover of Jay Prosser's *Second Skins: The Body Narratives of Transsexuality* (New York: Columbia University Press, 1998), with Willi Baumeister's *Man with Goatee II* (ca. 1941, altered postcard of Adolf Ziegler's *Terpsichore*). Book © 1998 Columbia University Press, reproduced with permission of the publisher. Baumeister art © 2010 Artists Rights Society (ARS), New York/VG Bild-Kunst, Bonn. Photo: Visual Resources Collection, SoAD, Southern Illinois University Carbondale.

exhibition. He drew on the one of Ziegler's *Terpsichore* to transform the blond, willowy Greco-Nordic nude into a bearded "Man with a Goatee," with breasts as bulging eyes and pubis as pointed beard. Prosser, who studies transgender themes in literature, has told me that he was unaware of the specifics of this history, but, having seen exactly this postcard in London in the 1995 exhibition "Art and Power: Europe under the Dictators," he suggested it as a cover illustration for *Second Skins*. It seemed to him related to the theme of his book: the potential of narratives of transgendered bodies to escape binary oppositions of male and female, hegemonic and resistant.

Prosser chose the postcard's altered image for "the transsexual connotation—the suggestion of change"—and for the "the notion of rewriting" suggested by Baumeister's drawing on it.[12] Baumeister had rewritten the Ziegler card, and Prosser rewrote the "Baumeister." Prosser's use of this image can be viewed as what the literary theorist Harold Bloom calls a "strong misreading"—*"an act of creative correction that is actually and necessarily a misinterpretation"*—that rewrites the work and inscribes it into a new context that may seem to have little to do with the work's "origin" but actually increases rather than diminishes the rewritten work's resonance and meaning.[13]

In previous writings I have examined these works in relationship to their specific political and artistic context and suggested revising the interpretation of Baumeister as an abstract artist who was withdrawn from the world, especially during his "inner emigration" in Nazi Germany—and recognizing his consistent engagement with the social and political world.[14] While his engagement was rarely as direct as in these works, they are not unique in his oeuvre.

Prosser's misreading inspires my own rereading and rewriting of this and other works (usually, but not always, postcards) in which Baumeister altered reproductions of Nazi-approved art into scurrilous anti-Nazi images and objects. Baumeister himself was already engaged in a productive "misreading" of Nazi art when he employed Duchamp's tactic of "correcting" or "rectifying" a readymade—for example, his famous correction of a reproduction of the Mona Lisa into *L.H.O.O.Q.* in 1919, a strategy also employed in George Grosz's and John Heartfield's "corrected" masterpieces.[15] In this chapter I focus on these works as objects and images circulating both in the political sphere (defined by the narrow and unnuanced opposition between "Nazi and anti-Nazi art") and in personal, professional, and eroticized economies of (s)exchange.[16] With these backgrounds, the cover of Prosser's book suggests reading these composite images as both "shemales" and another form of *Mischwesen,* the *Mischling* mixture of Jewish and German "racial" identity.

Baumeister's corrections directly confronted the public ideology of Nazi art. And they did so more personally and pointedly than any commentator has previously noted. By reinscribing and sending them, Baumeister himself engaged in a gendered and "racial" rewriting of the self. The literary theorist Naomi Schor, in a pioneering scholarly study of postcards, pointed out that the "association of femininity with postcard writing" also engendered "a transfer of the traditional association of femininity with letter writing to a new mode of written communication, further reinforced by the association of the feminine with the trivial, the picturesque, the ephemeral."[17] Before I first published on them in 1989, Baumeister's postal and other Dadaistic works had never been included in discussions of his work. As Mendelson asserts, they "cross a line" and transgress the conventional limits of this artist's art or career.[18] They were considered too "trivial"—and thus, as Schor suggested, already gendered female—to count as components of Baumeister's (male) artistic production.[19]

Baumeister's postcard works disrupted—even as they participated in—the Nazi's system of image circulation. In Nazi Germany Baumeister's images circulated but once, and not as "Baumeisters" but as private, subversive messages for friends, not intended for display. Their singular historical and political interest rests on their having been made and circulated as critical commentaries on reproductions of Nazi-approved art. Writing in 1989, I called them "oppositional" works, a classification of anti-Nazi activity one critical degree less militant than "resistance."[20] Although clearly anti-Nazi, they were not created and disseminated as part of an active resistance movement, in contrast to John Heartfield's photomontages (fig. 97), for instance, which also circulated as postcards.[21]

Baumeister created at least four postcards transforming Ziegler's *Goddess of Art* or *Terpsichore* into *Mann mit Spitzbart* (Man with goatee, or pointed beard).[22] Those that he mailed are dated from August to November 1941. Each one has a subtitle typed either

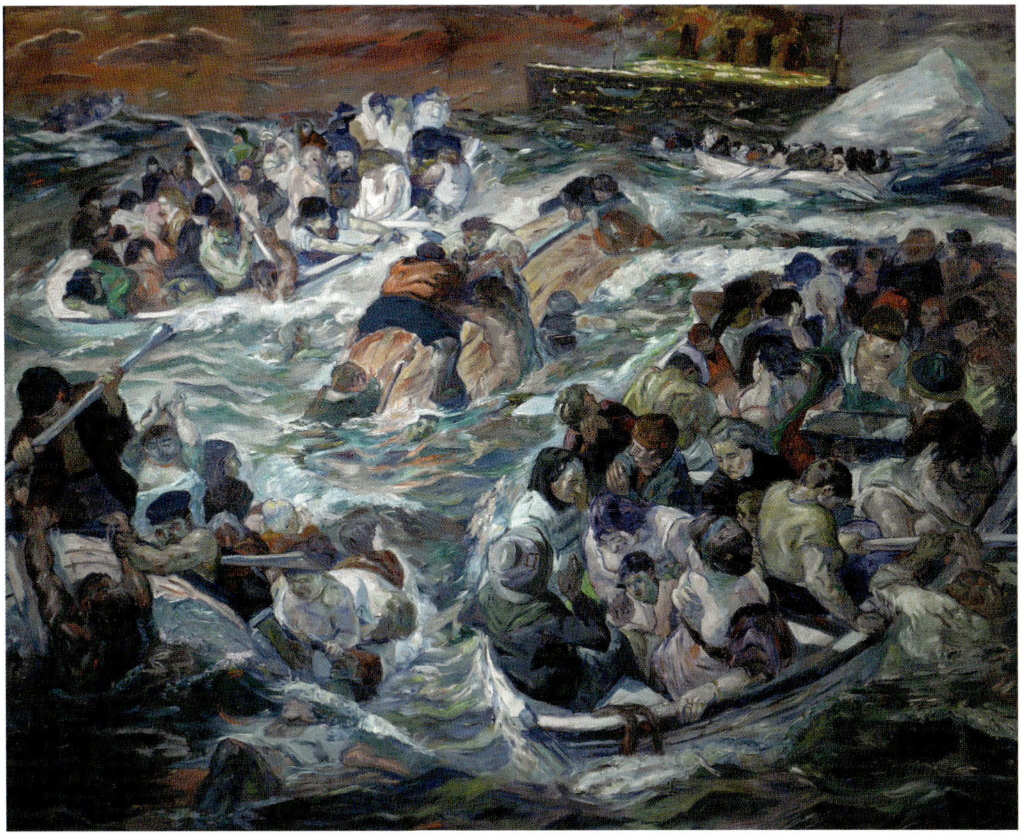

PLATE 1. Max Beckmann, *The Sinking of the Titanic,* 1912–13, oil on canvas, 265 × 330 cm. Saint Louis Art Museum, Bequest of Morton D. May. Art © 2010 Artists Rights Society (ARS), New York/VG Bild-Kunst, Bonn. Photo: Saint Louis Art Museum.

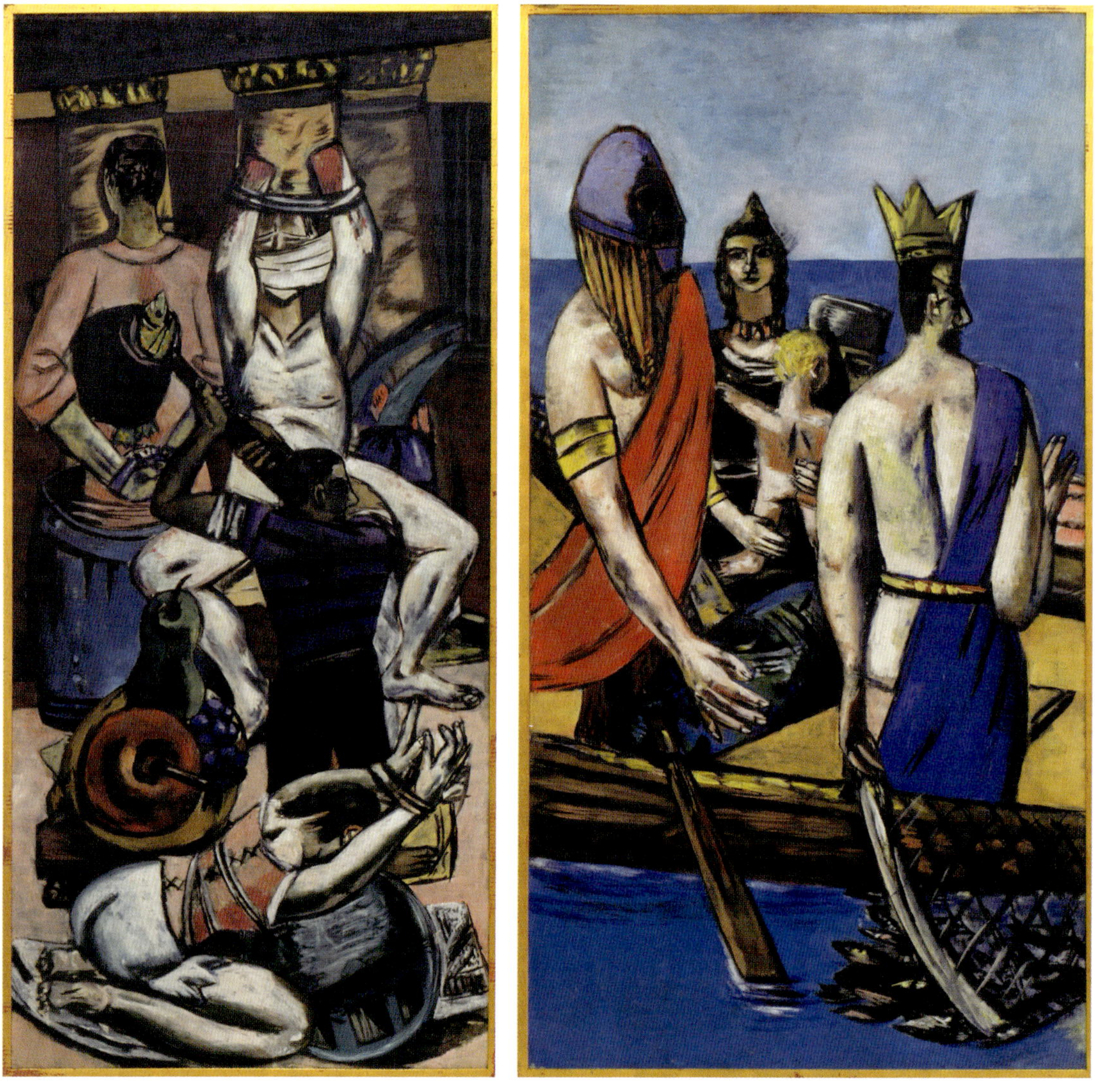

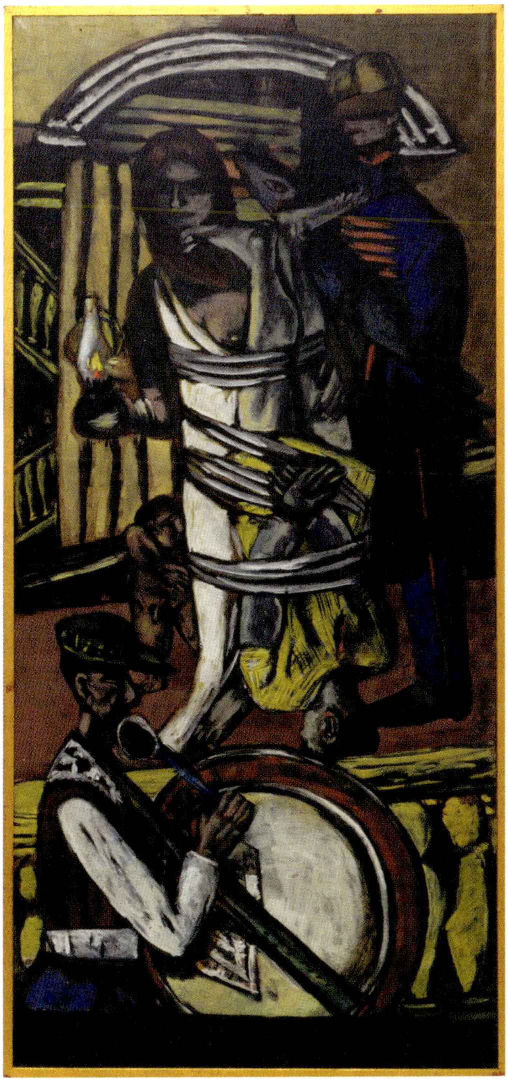

PLATE 2. Max Beckmann, *Departure,* 1932–33, oil on canvas, triptych, center panel 215.5 × 115 cm, side panels each 215.5 × 99.5 cm. The Museum of Modern Art, New York. Art © 2010 Artists Rights Society (ARS), New York/VG Bild-Kunst, Bonn. Digital image © The Museum of Modern Art/Licensed by Scala/Art Resource, NY.

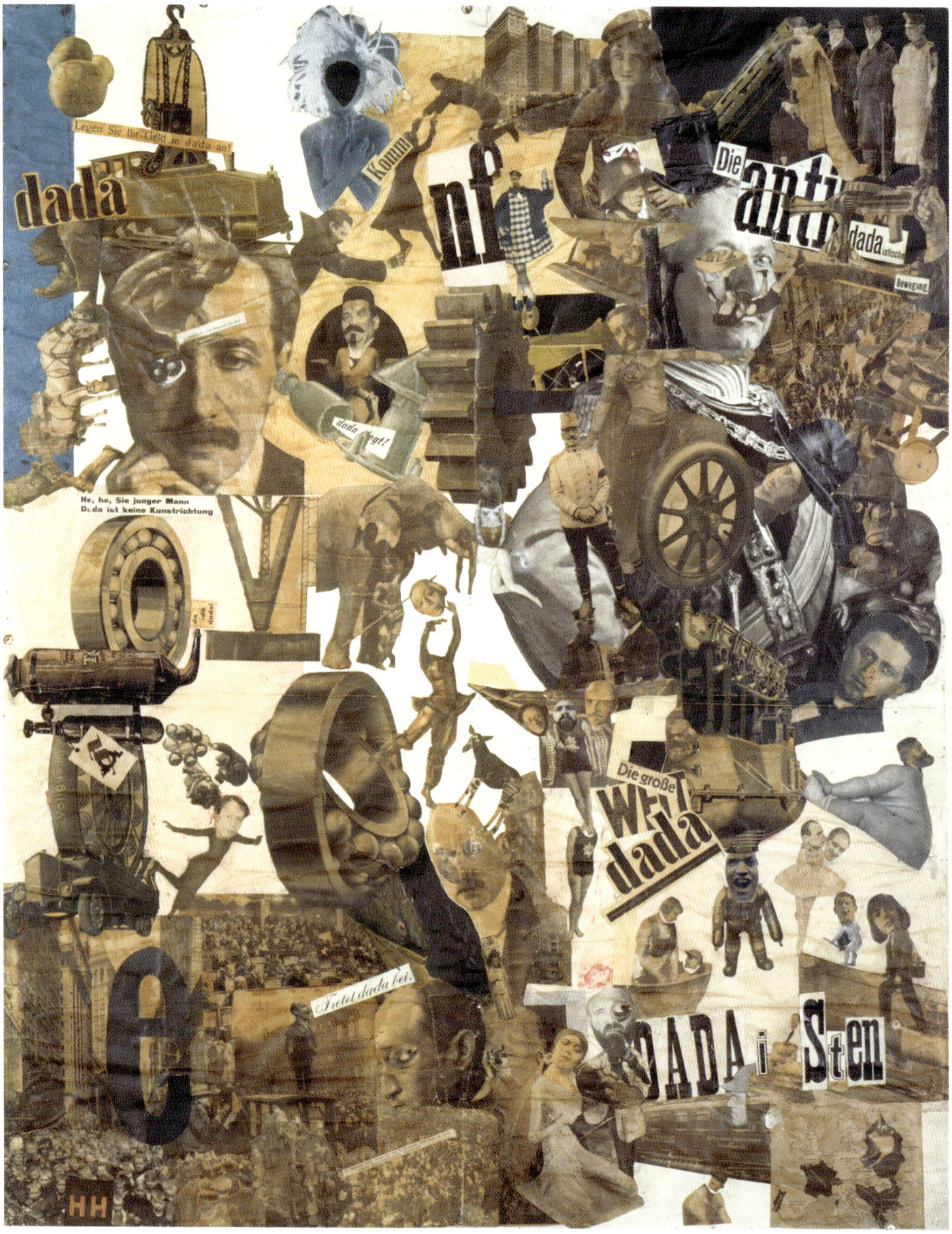

PLATE 3. Hannah Höch, *Cut with the Kitchen Knife Dada through Germany's Last Weimar Beer-Belly Cultural Epoch,* 1919–20, collage, 114 × 90 cm. Nationalgalerie, Staatliche Museen zu Berlin. Art © 2010 Artists Rights Society (ARS), New York/VG Bild-Kunst, Bonn. Photo: Bildarchiv Preussischer Kulturbesitz/Art Resource, NY.

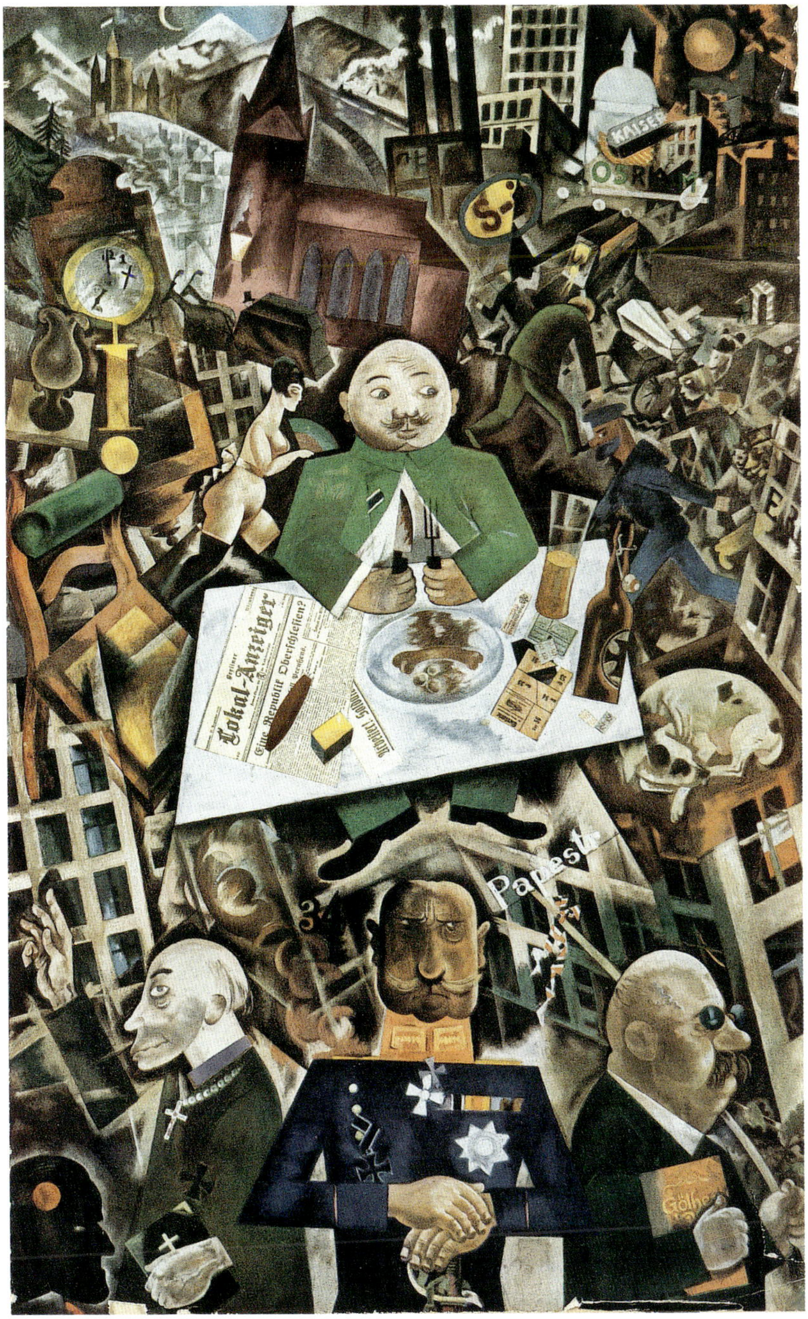

PLATE 4. George Grosz, *Germany: A Winter's Tale,* 1917–18, oil and collage on canvas, lost. Art © Estate of George Grosz/Licensed by VAGA, New York, NY. Courtesy Kunstsammlung, Archiv der Akademie der Künste, Berlin. Photo: AdK, Berlin, George-Grosz-Archiv.

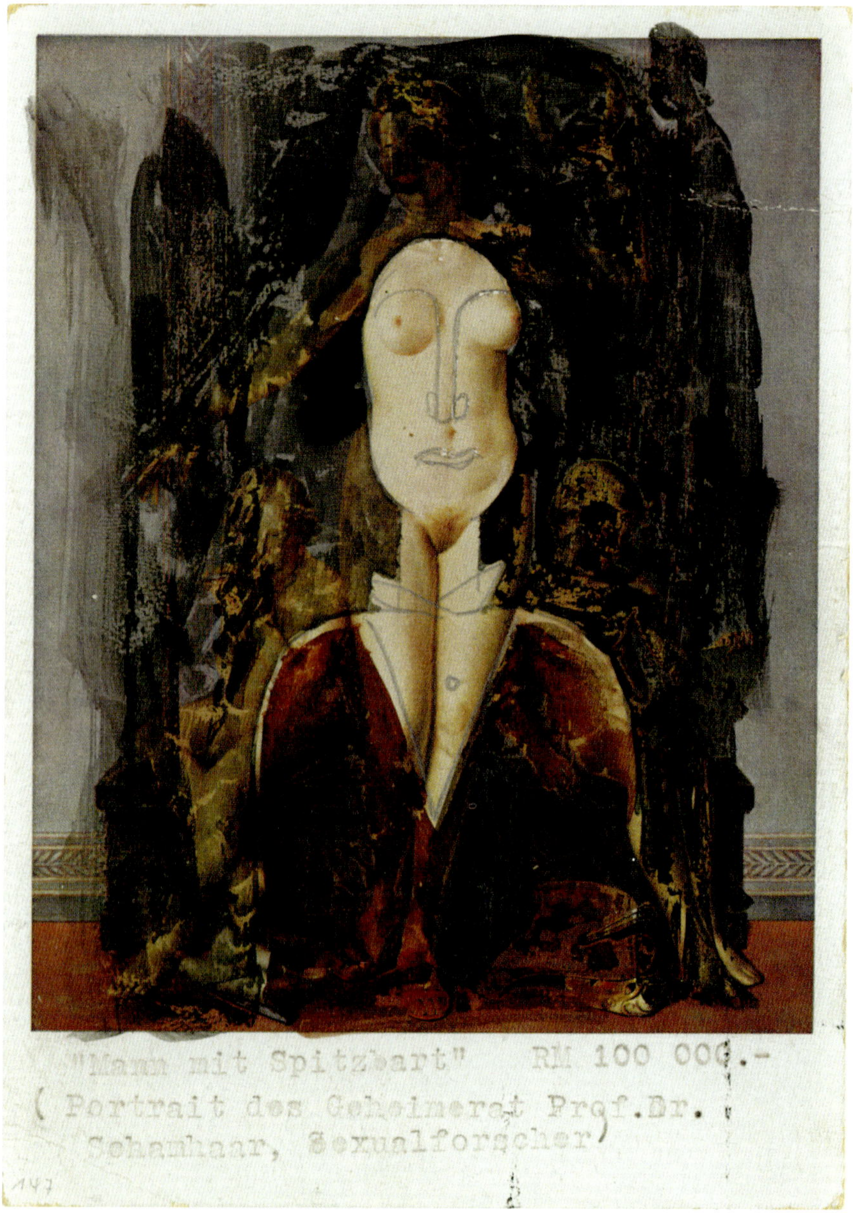

PLATE 5. Willi Baumeister, *"Mann mit Spitzbart" RM 100 000.- (Porträt des Geheimrat Prof. Dr. Schamhaar, Sexualforscher)* ("Man with goatee" 100,000 Reichmarks [Portrait of Privy Council Prof. Dr. Pubic Hair, sexual researcher]), 1941, altered postcard of Adolf Ziegler, *Göttin der Kunst.* Altonaer Museum für Kunst und Kulturgeschichte, Hamburg. Photo: Stiftung Historische Museen Hamburg-Altonaer Museum.

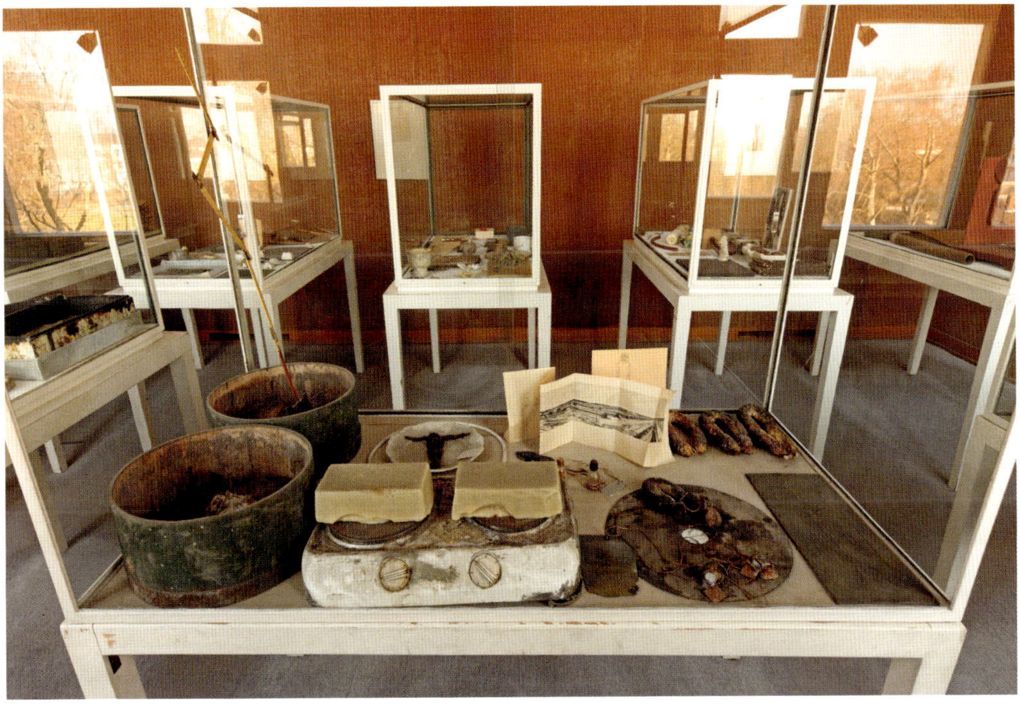

PLATE 6. Joseph Beuys, *Auschwitz Demonstration,* 1956–64, mixed-media installation. Art © 2010 Artists Rights Society (ARS), New York/VG Bild-Kunst, Bonn. Photo: Hessisches Landesmuseum Darmstadt.

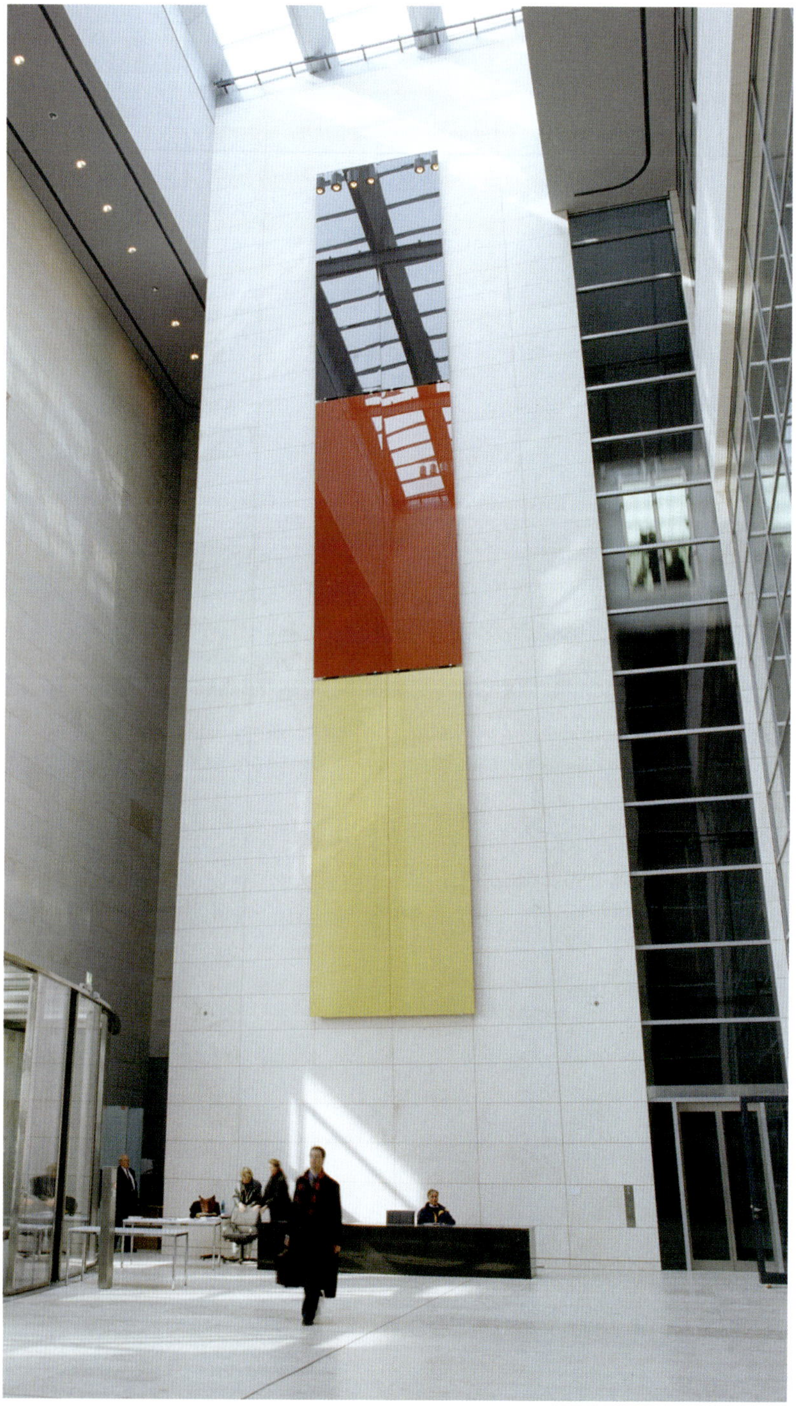

PLATE 7. Gerhard Richter, *Schwarz, Rot, Gold/Black, Red, Gold,* 1999, glass covered with gray enamel, 2043 × 296 cm. Collection Deutscher Bundestag. Art © Gerhard Richter; courtesy Marian Goodman Gallery, New York/Studio Gerhard Richter. Photo: Stephan Erfurt.

on the bottom border or on the back, such as *Katal. Nr. 001 "Herr mit rötl. Spitzbart" Gold. Staatsmedaill. Preis netto RM 100 000.-* (Catalogue no. 001, "Man with reddish goatee," state gold medal, net price 100,000 Reichsmarks), which appears on a card he sent to his friend Heinz Rasch on August 27, 1941. Perhaps the most explicit political content is in the unsent card (fig. 39) he titled *Mann mit Spitzbart, von Göbbels prämiert von Hitler angekauft* (Man with goatee, premiered by Göbbels/göggels, bought by Hitler), in which Baumeister double-struck the letters gg and bb on his typewriter so that Propaganda Minister Göbbels's name also became, simultaneously, "göggels," a play on the Swabian and also archaic pronunciation of *Gockel* (cock or rooster), as *Göggel.*[23] On August 26, 1941, he posted *"Mann mit Spitzbart" RM 100 000.- (Portrait des Geheimrat Prof. Dr. Schamhaar, Sexualforscher)* ("Man with goatee" 100,000 Reichmarks [portrait of Privy Council Prof. Dr. Pubic Hair, sexual researcher]) to Dieter Keller (plate 5).[24] In a letter to Baumeister dated September 9, 1942, the journalist Wilhelm Arntz responded to "Prof. Dr. Pubic Hair" and other cards he had received from Baumeister: "All this prattle about primitive art is nonsense. Certainly there is primitive art: the pretty color postcards that you have painted over so suggestively point that out to us."[25]

Arntz's comment confirms that Baumeister's cards were received in their time as political and artistic critiques. But they were also souvenirs of his and his male friends' encounter with the eroticized political art and politicized erotic art of the Third Reich. A newspaper review of an exhibition in which Baumeister's postcards were shown reproduced the postcard of Ziegler's *Terpsichore* of 1937 that Baumeister had altered into *Jokkmokmädchen* (fig. 40) and captioned: "A Genuine Porno," or prostitute.[26] Baumeister's postcard works satirize, even as they themselves exploit, the sterile eroticism of the Ziegler maidens. Baumeister's exchanges also evoke the displacement of homoerotic urges common in boys' school pranks. In addition, they involve control, not only of Nazi-sponsored art but also of the female image and unruly, polymorphously perverse desires. Desire for the recipient, for the image itself, for control, all are symbolically enacted by defacing an image and object, both gendered female, and posting it to a male friend.

Jacques Derrida, in *The Postcard,* considers some erotic dimensions of the exchanges among the sender, the image, and the recipient of a postcard. Derrida obsesses over a postcard reproducing a medieval manuscript image of Socrates writing as Plato watches. Derrida's readings multiply like the reproduced image on the postcard: the one image becomes many readings (or, really, writings) of it, parceled out in small amounts and distributed privately. To be sent they must be stamped—and stamps themselves become an object of love. Derrida writes, "It's new, the love of stamps, in me, it's not a collector's love but only a sender's love."[27] For Derrida, the sender's love of the stamp is distinct from that of the stamp collector's. The collector never licks his stamp, never sends a bit of his own spittle, concealed, to a recipient. For him both body fluid and stamp are too precious to part with. The recipient of this gift may be distracted by the image on the other side, the stamp and postmark, and the author's own inscription—but the essence of the stamped card, before self-adhesives, and excepting prefranked cards, is that it was purchased and then licked: the sender invests in the correspondence economically and bodily.

The sender engages in a generous, but also sadistic, exchange. The stamped and sent postcard is a gift to the recipient, but it declares that the sender has had some real experience, while the correspondent receives only its picturesque trace. The stamp or postcard collector, by contrast, is characteristically anal and retentive, obsessively holding onto and ordering his horde of printed images. A Google search for "Jokkmokmädchen" yields one hit: "Patrick's Website: Postcards & The Female Nude." This collector, curator, and Web site creator announces that he "welcomes you to his website, Postcards & the Female Nude. The Main Criterium: The card must show at least a female nude (partial or complete)."[28] Patrick, though, does not own the "original" *Jokkmokmädchen* made by Baumeister on a Heinrich Hoffmann Press postcard depicting Ziegler's *Terpsichore*. What he owns is card 9 of series 194, "Artists' Postcards I," reproducing a work from the collection of the Altonaer Museum in Hamburg, produced by Gebr. König Postcard Press in Cologne, and now out of print. I own several examples of this card, too. I named the original "Jokkmokmädchen" in 1989, interpreted it, and declared it the "masterpiece" among Baumeister's postal works. The pasting of the caption "Jokkmokmädchen" (Maiden from Jokkmok) infiltrates the "classical" muse with the conception of "Nordic" beauty lurking behind it and pushes it ad absurdum by referencing a Lapland village lying beyond the Arctic Circle and blessed with the Dadaistic name Jokkmokk.[29] As I argued then, when Baumeister pasted over of the torso and head of the figure, with his own hands holding plaster-smoothing implements, he also referred to the racist and sexist highlighting of body parts, particularly breasts and nipples, in Nazi aesthetic tracts—for example the architect Paul Schultze-Naumburg's *Nordische Schönheit: Ihr Wunschbild im Leben und in der Kunst* (Nordic beauty: Its ideal image in art and life).[30] But despite my part in gaining recognition for Baumeister's work, my "Jokkmokmädchen" is no rarer or more precious—or more permanently fixed in any system of ordering—than Patrick's. Although I put it into circulation in museums and scholarly publications as an anti-Nazi work, when it circulates now in cyberspace, it is ordered only by category, that of the female nude, along with other images of unclothed women that have throughout the ages been created by artists, disseminated in reproduction, and, now, made freely available by Patrick on the Web.

On Patrick's Web site nothing is for sale. Patrick wants only to share these images while he preserves and retains his objects, his postcards. This is pure circulation: no ink, no stamps, and no spit, just hits, links, and images. He expresses his passion for cards in what seems a cleaner, less personal form than Derrida's or Baumeister's pre-Internet correspondence. Derrida and Baumeister were always personally present in and on the card. Patrick, in contrast, the collector and also the curator, exposes to us not himself but only his cards, which he loves, orders, and retains, and from which he and we can freely take our pleasure.

Perhaps in intervening in a totally different time and place, I sought to invest what

Arntz called "pretty color postcards" with an "aura" inappropriate to the category of "authentic" artworks as "Baumeisters." As Duchamp's readymades demonstrated, in the modern world exhibition makes art. Public display invests what Benjamin called "post-auratic" objects, which are subject to mechanical reproduction, with the aura of ritual art objects. Their placement in art museums threatens to obscure rather than clarify their political, and postal, trajectories. "To an ever greater degree the work of art reproduced becomes the work of art designed for reproducibility," Benjamin observed. "But the instant the criterion of authenticity ceases to be applicable to artistic production, the total function of art is reversed. Instead of being based on ritual, it begins to be based on another practice—politics."[31] Perhaps I participated in moving these postcards back from the practice of politics to the performance of ritual. In this I would not be alone. Although they appear to attack and seek the destruction of the fetishized art object, Dada strategies employed ordnance that survives not only as souvenirs or mementos but also as artworks, and, as such, as evidence of a battle lost. Readymades reappear in limited editions; montages such as Höch's *Cut with the Kitchen Knife Dada* become prized works in state collections and objects of involved and often fruitful iconographic as well as ideological analysis, as well as commodities to be massively reproduced, sold, and sent in postcard form. It was as such an object on display in a museum that Prosser came upon the object bearing the image that landed on the cover of his book. Once relocated there, though, its Dadaistic, destructive thrust against tradition "hit the spectator like a bullet," in Benjamin's memorably ballistic image.[32] With Prosser's intervention, Ziegler's painting (an artwork to be exhibited), Hitler's trusty photographer and propagandist Heinrich Hoffmann's postcard of it (an image to circulate), and Baumeister's reworking of that image and object (a projectile weapon), as well as my own rewriting of it (again as artwork), have been shot again into another realm.

A Modernist Artist in Modern Germany

Baumeister's anti-Nazi collages remained obscure until the 1990s. Considering them a part of his oeuvre disrupts two interconnected art historical narratives that until then structured assessments of his career. In the first, Baumeister transmits prewar modernism into the postwar era by means of a personal journey from work to work, from the 1920s to the 1950s, that culminated in his late mythic abstractions. In the second, he represents artistic "inner emigration" in Nazi Germany, turning away from all that was happening around him to find refuge in his private, autonomous, artistic development. His work paralleled developments in Parisian modernism, from the Constructivism of his friends Léger and Le Corbusier in the 1920s, through Arp's and Miró's biomorphic Surrealism in the 1930s and 1940s, to *Informel* abstraction in the early 1950s (figs. 43–44).[33] In Germany he is referred to as one of the masters of "classic modern" painting.[34]

After the Nazi suppression of modern art from 1933 to 1945, Baumeister's work, for many people in postwar Germany, functioned as the local, living, visible embodiment

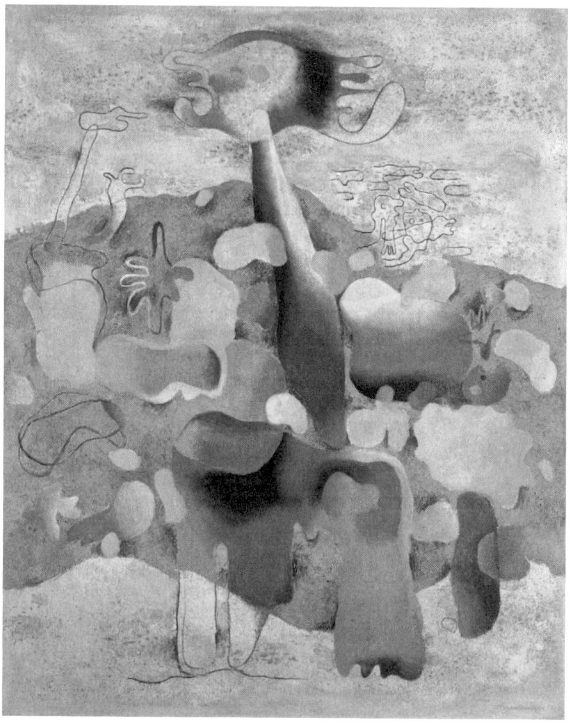

FIGURE 43. Willi Baumeister, *Rock Garden,* 1939, oil on canvas, 101 × 81.5 cm. Private collection. Art © 2010 Artists Rights Society (ARS), New York/VG Bild-Kunst, Bonn. Photo: Archiv Baumeister im Kunstmuseum Stuttgart.

of modern art's tenuous survival and unlikely further development. In 1947 Baumeister was pictured on the cover of the mass-circulation magazine *Der Spiegel* (fig. 45). In 1956, shortly after Baumeister's death, the British art critic and cultural attaché to Germany, John Anthony Thwaites, wrote: "He had been in a special sense the father of all postwar German art. Not only his pupils, but practically the whole new generation he taught what a modern picture is. If the new painters are free of epigonal expressionism, can use the new picture space, the new dynamic form, have something of the four-dimensional vision of our time, they owe it in the main to him. He transmitted the heritage of Kandinsky and Klee."[35] This assessment coincides with that of the only comprehensive monograph on the artist, the last and most extensive of three written by Will Grohmann, published in German in 1963 and English in 1965.

Baumeister developed his motifs and his style in expansive and often repetitive series. Grohmann wrote in 1952 about Baumeister's heterogeneous oeuvre: "He follows a line until it becomes sterile, he thrusts forward in another direction, tries the opposite, and is not afraid to grasp a discovery and carry it further. This results in a zig-zag course which only becomes understandable when one surveys longer periods of his work."[36] Over these longer periods, according to Grohmann's authoritative last monograph, one notices that "year by year he moved further away from superficial topicality and closer to the unknown: to abstraction."[37] The influential postwar critic Werner Haftmann, too, saw in Baumeister's career steady development toward abstraction along "an inward route, that led straight

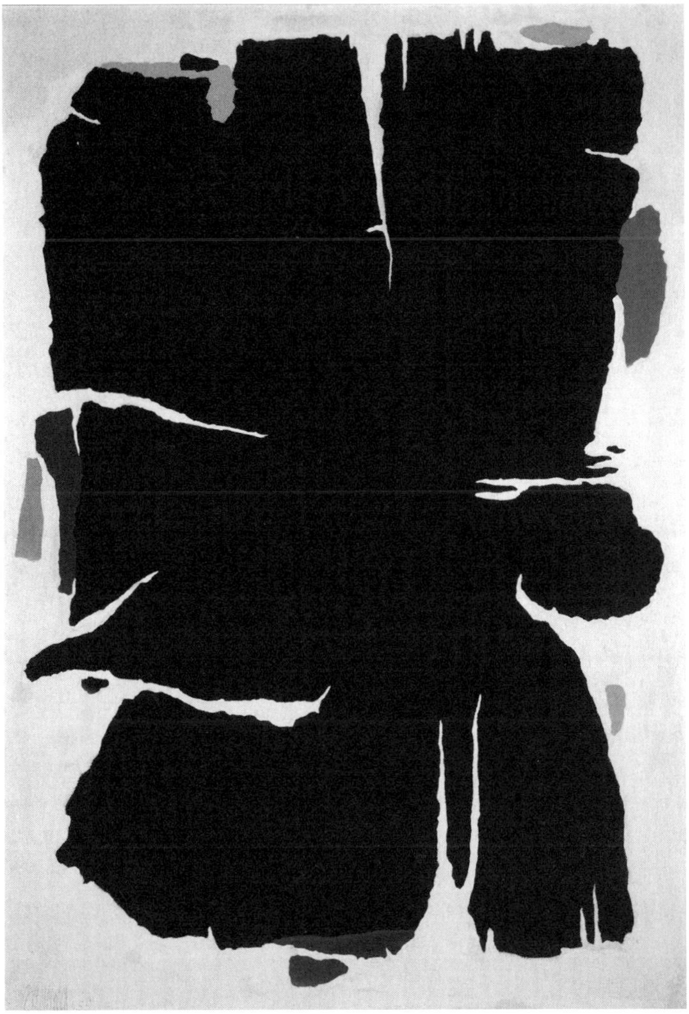

FIGURE 44. Willi Baumeister, *Aru 5,* 1955, oil and synthetic resin on board, 185 × 130 cm. Nationalgalerie, Staatliche Museen zu Berlin. Art © 2010 Artists Rights Society (ARS), New York/VG Bild-Kunst, Bonn. Photo: Bildarchiv Preussischer Kulturbesitz/Art Resource, NY.

into mythic realms, leaving any representational starting point behind."[38] In post–World War II Germany, critics invoked Picasso to validate Baumeister's diverse career.[39] After the Nazi's suppression of artistic freedom and during the Cold War his "zig-zag course" was also often interpreted as the symbolic exercise of individual freedom, with each stylistic nuance, choice, transition, or about-face as evidence of an unquenchable thirst for artistic and personal freedom, affirming the Western promise of personal autonomy.

The concept of "internal exile" appeared almost immediately after the German capitulation in 1945. Walter von Molo and Frank Thiess proposed that some non-Nazi German writers who had stayed in Germany had preserved their artistic and spiritual

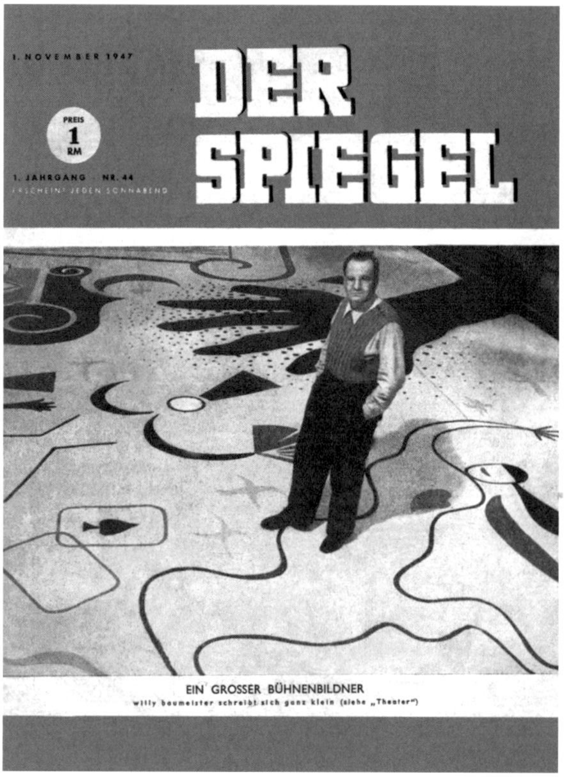

FIGURE 45. **"A Great Scenic Artist: Willy Baumeister Signs Himself Small." © *Der Spiegel*, 1 November 1947.**

integrity, and so that of Germany itself, in an artistic "*inner space,* that Hitler could not conquer despite all his efforts."[40] In the visual arts, "inner emigrant" status has generally been conferred upon any artist whose work was considered "degenerate" and who did not leave Germany. Emil Nolde's work has provided the model of the art of inner emigration. Despite his anti-Semitism and his joining the Nazi Party in 1920, Nolde was among the artists attacked after the Nazi Party congress of September 1934. At that congress Hitler denounced both Goebbels's favored Expressionism, which would have supported Nolde, and the folksy, rustic old-German style promoted by the leader of the Combat League for German Culture, Alfred Rosenberg. Nolde became one of the few artists actually forbidden after 1941 not only to exhibit but also to work as an artist. His subsequent small, atmospherically abstract studies, the so-called unpainted pictures, seem to embody the forced isolation of the inner emigrant "painting for no one," yet generalize this historically specific situation into a sublime, private, universal artistic state of contemplative and melancholic aesthetic experience.

There was no danger that Baumeister or his work could be construed as particularly "Germanic," in either an Expressionist or folkish sense. Modern painting, for Baumeister, derived from Cézanne, especially his painstaking modulation of the painted surface. Emotive expressionism was anathema to him.[41] There is no evidence that he was either anti-Semitic or overly nationalistic. Peter-Klaus Schuster, general director of the

Berlin State Art Museums, has portrayed Baumeister and his work as paradigmatic of inner emigration. He writes that Baumeister, because of his isolation during the Nazi years, enjoyed an "intensification of his artistic life" which made it possible for him to concentrate "on what is essential . . . [devoting] himself completely to the unknown world of abstract art." Baumeister's abstraction, for Schuster, expressed "the opposition adopted by the 'Inner Emigration' to the official art-for-all of the authorities. It is the ideal of an art for no one which derives its mandate and its consummation from within itself and which, for this very reason, is an expression of absolute freedom. . . . Baumeister's abstract art showed no signs of adaptation but it demonstrated resistance only in so far as it was totally unpolitical and paid no regard to anyone."[42]

Baumeister developed his ideas on modern art in a book he worked on from 1943 to 1945, and published in 1947, titled *Das Unbekannte in der Kunst* (The unknown in art). It formed the basis for his famous confrontation with the antimodernist art historian Hans Sedlmayr at the 1950 Darmstädter Gespräch (Darmstadt discussion) symposium.[43] In *Das Unbekannte in der Kunst* Baumeister presented a universal history of art, from prehistory to the present, unified by the idea that art can progress only if it transforms common vision into deeper insight. Experimental artists lead viewers into hitherto unknown realms of pure optical experience, opening their minds and consciousness to accept the inability of humans to comprehend fully the sources and limits of knowledge. His theory combined a Hegelian conception of art's dialectical progress toward ever greater purity with a Kantian idea that the noumenon—the essence of a phenomenon—would remain forever unknown. *Das Unbekannte* also drew on the mystical theories and organic metaphors of Wassily Kandinsky, Paul Klee, Goethe, Meister Eckhart, and Lao Tze.

The history of art, according to *Das Unbekannte,* presents "the history of mankind in purified form."[44] Only autonomous art can achieve this state of purity, a state separate from and superior to everyday life. These ideas became axiomatic in the postwar period, when *Das Unbekannte in der Kunst* was among the first books to explain and justify modernist art theoretically and historically for a still skeptical German public. Baumeister wrote at the very time the New York School painters Adolph Gottlieb, Mark Rothko, and Barnett Newman were reacting to a hostile critic by declaring "art is an adventure into an unknown world, which can be explored only by those willing to take the risks."[45] *Das Unbekannte in der Kunst* offered a similar defense of high modernism's march to abstraction but responded to a much stronger threat. Baumeister wrote: "The artistic human being is the ultimate human being, the essential human being. He is receptive to all stimuli, collaborates with them, enriches them. In order that the unknown be manifest in its purist form, the artist places no value on presenting his mysteries in a familiar form."[46] Baumeister's commitment to artistic autonomy and abstraction has its roots in his inner emigration under the Nazis, whose war on "degenerate art" met little resistance from the German population. Because his art represents a response to real world forces and actual attacks on both him and his work, we should question whether it really represented a withdrawal into inner emigration.

Baumeister's artistic route was in fact less inward and private than Grohmann and Haftmann or, more critically, Schuster, have claimed. As I have argued elsewhere, in what one commentator has called a third way of assessing Baumeister's significance (if Grohmann's biographical approach is the first and the hermeneutic and formalist interpretations of the Swiss art historian and aesthetician Gottfried Boehm are the second), in Baumeister's work and career we can observe and test the efficacy and significance of modernist artistic practice in Germany from before World War I to after World War II.[47] From this perspective, Baumeister's anti-Nazi collages (along with *Das Unbekannte in der Kunst*) look like practical adaptations to the exigencies of life and work by a twentieth-century modern artist in Germany, a rather remarkable move that until 1989 resisted interpretation by both his admirers and detractors.

Baumeister's career between the wars connected directly to cultural and political developments in Weimar Germany and also reflected artistic tendencies throughout Europe. In 1919 Baumeister and Schlemmer, thirty-year-old war veterans, became nominal students again at the Stuttgart Academy. They began agitating for the reform of the school, especially during their unsuccessful campaign for the appointment of Paul Klee as successor to their retiring professor, Adolf Hölzel. The Üecht (New dawn) group was the organizational center of the Hölzel circle's agitations.[48] On the morning of October 25, 1919, when the Üecht group's first exhibition was to open in downtown Stuttgart, Schlemmer, his fiancée, Helena Tutein, and Baumeister's girlfriend, Paula Falschebner, were arrested on suspicion of activities in support of the Spartacist League. Some of the paintings Baumeister showed in the Üecht exhibition were explicitly political, with their titles the dates of current events such as the murders in Berlin of the Spartacist leaders Rosa Luxemburg and Karl Liebknecht.[49] In response to the Üecht group exhibition, a hostile article appeared, unsigned, in the November 12 *Süddeutsche Zeitung*, entitled "Kunst und Bolschewismus" (Art and bolshevism), whose author railed against the exhibition as the work of "people with pea-brains infected by the bolshevik-bacillus." Predicting the strategy the Nazis employed in 1937, and paralleling contemporaneous anti-Semitic attacks on the Berlin Dadaists, the author called for "an iron-clad protest by our artists, critics, and professors against this brand of art and the concerns (better, Cohncerns) that stand behind this movement."[50]

Baumeister and Schlemmer, in their first theater designs, addressed this volatile environment, seeking constructive, performative applications for their visual and social ideas. Baumeister designed the production for the Stuttgart premiere on January 27, 1920, of *Die Wandlung* (The change), by the radical Expressionist playwright and political prisoner Ernst Toller, one of the bohemian Jewish leaders of the short-lived Bavarian Soviet Republic of 1918–19 (fig. 46). At the same time, Baumeister began to work in geometric, constructivist but figural abstraction. His relief *Mauerbilder (Wall Pictures)* implicated the spectator's body by means of confrontation and simplification, guiding visitors through the constructivist interiors of German Werkbund exhibitions (fig. 47).[51]

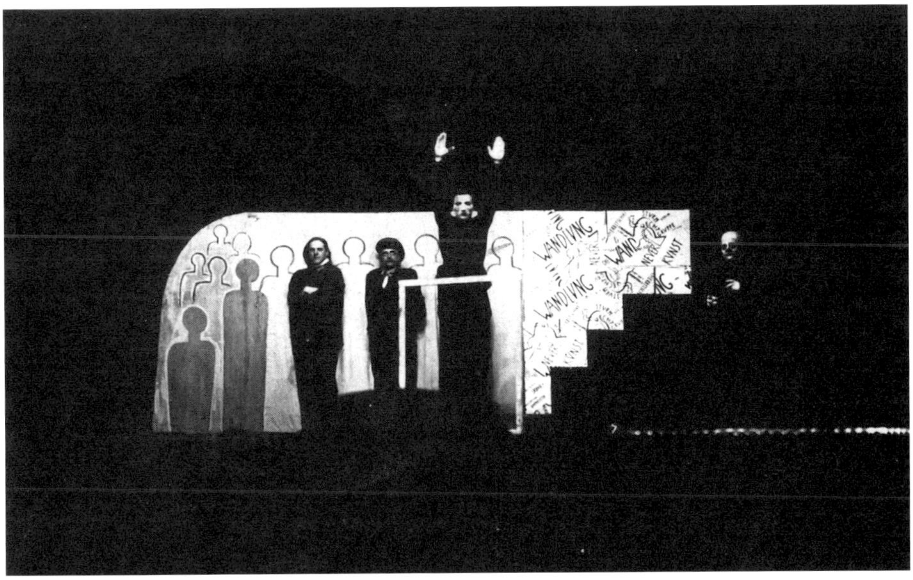

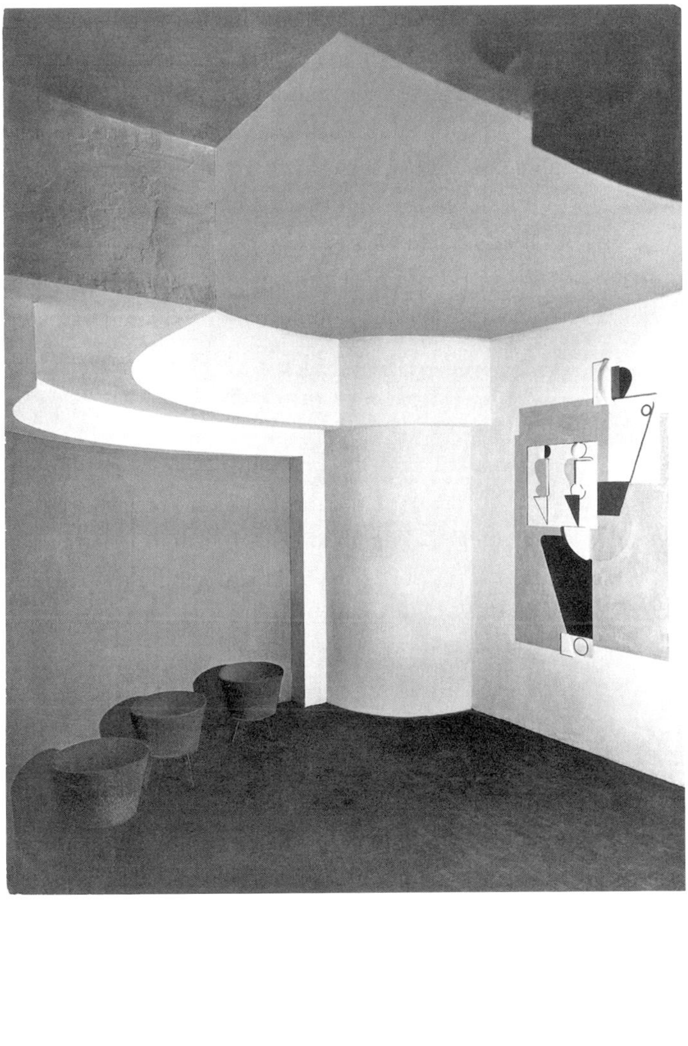

FIGURE 46. Willi Baumeister, sets and costumes for Ernst Toller's *Die Wandlung,* 1919, Stuttgart. Art © 2010 Artists Rights Society (ARS), New York/VG Bild-Kunst, Bonn. Photo: Willi Baumeister Archiv, Kunstmuseum Stuttgart. FIGURE 47. Willi Baumeister, *Wall Pictures,* relief in a space designed by Richard Döcker, "Werkbund" exhibition, Stuttgart, 1922. Art © 2010 Artists Rights Society (ARS), New York/VG Bild-Kunst, Bonn. Photo: Archiv Baumeister im Kunstmuseum Stuttgart.

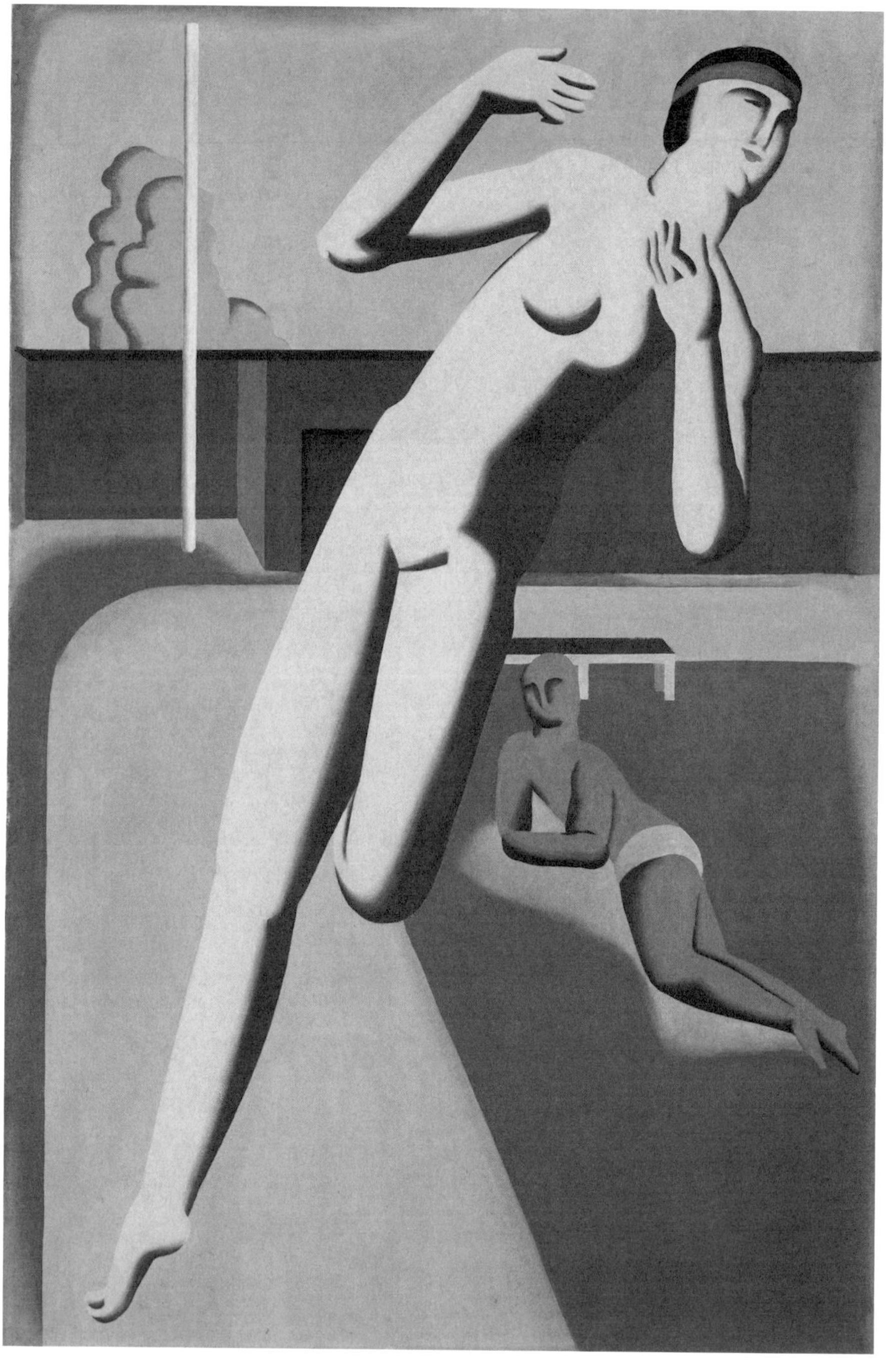

FIGURE 48. Willi Baumeister, *Female Runner II,* 1925, oil on canvas, 120 × 80 cm. Staatsgalerie Stuttgart. Art © 2010 Artists Rights Society (ARS), New York/VG Bild-Kunst, Bonn. Photo: Staatsgalerie Stuttgart.

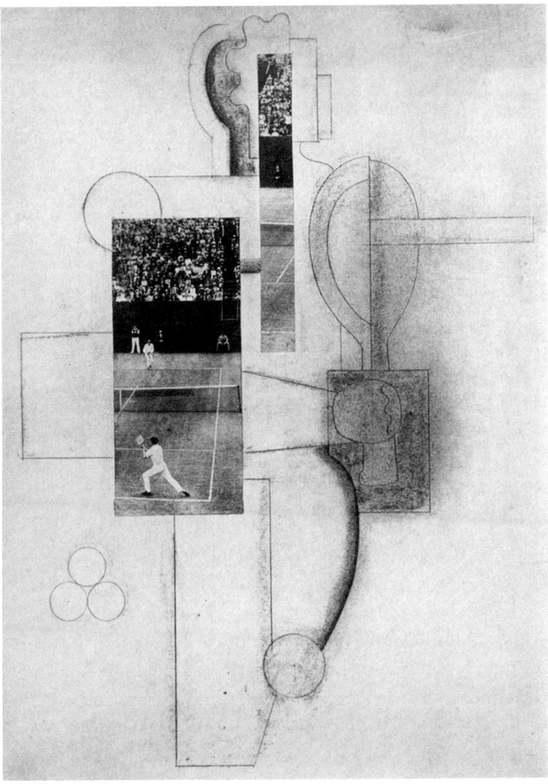

FIGURE 49. Willi Baumeister, *Tennis,* 1927, collage with pencil and charcoal, 42 × 30.5 cm. Art © 2010 Artists Rights Society (ARS), New York/VG Bild-Kunst, Bonn. Photo: Archiv Baumeister im Kunstmuseum Stuttgart.

The series of sport-named works that he began to produce in 1924 presented athletes as concentrating fully on the perfection of their skill and technique, thus exemplifying a modernist ideal. Baumeister's sport pictures, though, contradict the autonomous development of the artist's work. He moved from geometric abstraction to more "objective" representation under the influence of the increased social prominence of competitive spectator sports in the 1920s—a theme that attracted many artists—and not because of the internal development of his craft.[52] Baumeister's inclusion of spectators in his sport paintings and photocollages relate them to the Brechtian celebration of sport for its appeal to a mass audience (figs. 48–49).[53] These works also reflect the widespread turn to greater *Sachlichkeit* (objectivity) in German art during the period of relative stability in the Weimar Republic from 1923 to 1929 and represent part of a general European and American return to more representational art between the wars. Four of Baumeister's paintings in this style were included in the "Degenerate Art" exhibition.

Baumeister's *Sachlichkeit* also extended into his commercial art practice, in which he advocated the "new typography" of lowercase sans serif typefaces and bold geometric designs—such as in his design for a commemorative stamp for the Werkbund's famous modernist housing exhibition "Die Wohnung" (The residence), often referred to as the Stuttgart Weissenhofsiedlung exhibition, of 1927 (fig. 50). Along with Kurt Schwitters and Jan Tschichold, he was a founding member of the Circle of New Commercial De-

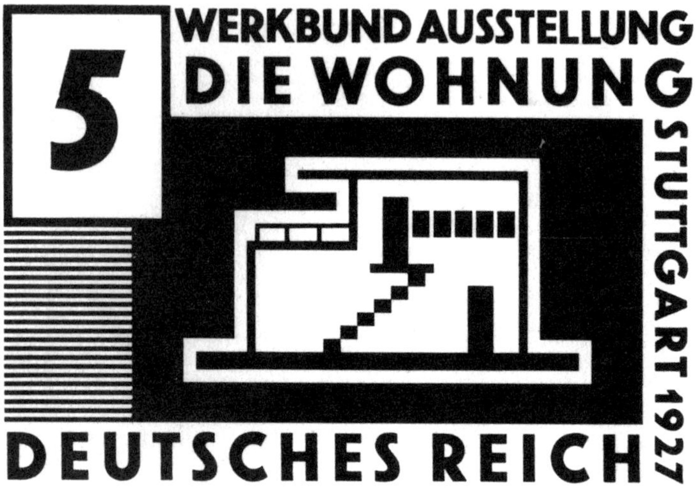

FIGURE 50. Willi Baumeister, commemorative stamp design for Weissenhofsiedlung exhibition "Die Wohnung," 1927. Art © 2010 Artists Rights Society (ARS), New York/VG Bild-Kunst, Bonn. Photo: Archiv Baumeister im Kunstmuseum Stuttgart.

signers and in 1928 was appointed professor of typographical and applied design at the Frankfurt Städel Art School, where Max Beckmann held the professorship in painting. Baumeister designed the progressive architecture and planning magazine *Das Neue Frankfurt,* published by the Frankfurt city planner Ernst May, from October 1930 to its final issue in March 1933.[54] He became a member of the Oktobergruppe (October Group), an organization of architects, artists, graphic designers, and city planners founded in Frankfurt in 1928 with a goal of researching and publicizing modernist designs from the Soviet Union. In that year another group with the same name was established in Moscow, which included El Lissitzky, Sergei Eisenstein, and Diego Rivera. Frankfurt's October Group included the architects and designers Max Cetto, Josef Hartwig, and Eugen Kaufmann, the artist Robert Michel, and the art historian Joseph Gantner.[55] Baumeister also became involved with the group Das Neue Frankfurt, a national organization devoted to the magazine's principles.[56]

Baumeister's writings of this period reinforced his design practice, linking applied and fine art. His essays of the 1920s appeared mainly in architecture and design journals. He developed his thinking about art in his diary and in his correspondence, especially in the letters he wrote to the architect Heinz Rasch. In all of his writings he stressed modernism's move away from the imitation of the natural world toward personal, idiosyncratic, and purely formal art. But his writings and art of the 1920s often posited abstract modernist art as a constituent element, first constructive and then reflective, of a specifically modern social and built environment.[57]

In 1929–30 Baumeister's paintings and graphics began to change from mechanical and objective form to biomorphism and greater abstraction, inspired both by his personal study of prehistoric art and his contact with Parisian Surrealism. The art historian René Hirner has suggested that the controversy in the Frankfurt press over the 1929 purchase, partially financed with funds donated by the public, of Baumeister's 1929 painting *Atelier III* by the Frankfurt Municipal Gallery, was the catalyst for turning Baumeister's intellectual interest in the art of the distant past into artistic practice.[58] *Atelier III* was geometrically styled and resembled Picasso's *The Studio* (1927–28). But the picture within the picture, sitting on the painter's easel, hints at Baumeister's own developing curvilinear abstraction. The outcry against the purchase of Baumeister's painting rehearses other similar attacks on modern painting grounded in style. But economic hardship and political turmoil in the years of the Weimar Republic's collapse provided a new focus for this reactionary opposition.

The press campaign against *Atelier III* was part of a broader attack on modernist art in Germany that was symptomatic of the accelerating downward slide after 1929 of Weimar Germany's already fragile liberal institutions, propelled by the erosion of the economy and the destabilizing of political leadership. In 1929 and 1930 the relatively stable Stresemann era ended, the extreme left ascended briefly, and the extreme right more fatefully arose. On October 3, 1929, Foreign Minister Gustav Stresemann died. It was he who had negotiated skillfully with the Allied powers the terms by which Germany might recover from World War I. On October 24, 1929, the New York stock market crashed, whereupon American banks began recalling loans. In Germany, as elsewhere, economic uncertainty and unemployment rose. In the German national elections of September 14, 1930, the result was ominous: the Communist Party became the third most powerful force in the Reichstag, with seventy-seven seats, and "Wilhelm Frick led 107 rowdy, brown-shirted Nazis into the company of the stunned assembly."[59] The National Socialists became the second most powerful faction in the parliament. Previously occupying only twelve seats, they now had more than any party except the Social Democrats, who held 143 seats.

As the period of crisis began, in February 1929, the Nazi ideologue Alfred Rosenberg founded the antimodernist, racist *Kampfbund für Deutsche Kultur* (Combat league for German culture), which issued an appeal for members to battle "today's cultural decline" by informing "the German people about the interconnection of race, art, learning and moral . . . values."[60] When Wilhelm Frick became minister of education in Thuringia in January 1930, prior to his ascension to the national Reichstag, he appointed the architect Paul Schultze-Naumburg director of the Weimar School of Applied Art, the successor of the Bauhaus, which had already fled from Thuringia to less reactionary Dessau in 1925. Schultze-Naumburg's racist tract *Kunst und Rasse* (Art and race) had appeared in 1928, and one "achievement" of his brief tenure as director of the Weimar School of Applied Art was an act of vandalism against modernist art, the destruction of Oskar Schlemmer's murals in the original Weimar Bauhaus buildings.[61]

In November and December 1929 Baumeister exhibited at the Frankfurt gallery of

Gustav Kahnweiler, the brother of the pioneering dealer and theorist of Cubist painting Daniel Henry Kahnweiler. Georg Swarzenski, director of the museum and the school at the Städel, purchased *Atelier III* from Kahnweiler for the municipal art collection. Reacting to the reproduction published in the December issue of *Das Neue Frankfurt,* Frankfurt's conservative press protested the purchase. On January 9 the *Frankfurter Nachrichten* reprinted the reproduction of the painting from *Das Neue Frankfurt* and protested that under the present bleak economic conditions the public had a right to know about the "exercise of a kind of artistic and cultural dictatorship that allows for the purchase by the 'Städel' of the 'artwork' reproduced here. . . . Even in these hard times there remains money for this type of 'art.' "[62]

Baumeister protested against the reproduction of the painting without his permission and requested a payment of sixty marks. The editors of *Frankfurter Nachrichten* paid him, but they exploited Baumeister's naive demand by arguing that modernist artists were opportunistic and venal.[63] By early 1931 the influential *Frankfurter Zeitung* had joined in condemning Baumeister and his work. On the occasion of an exhibition at the Frankfurt Kunstverein (art union), the critic Ernst Benkard accused the "Swabian Avant-gardist" of exhibiting works resembling those of a schizophrenic.[64] Baumeister, reacting to the use of the term "schizophrenic," sent the editor of the *Frankfurter Zeitung* a passage from a letter Le Corbusier had written him, in which the architect stated that "since 1920, your point of departure has been healthy *(sain)* and interesting."[65] Baumeister also wrote to Paul Westheim, one of Weimar Germany's most influential supporters of modern art and the editor of *Das Kunstblatt* (The art sheet). Westheim published an astute answer to Baumeister:

> *Willi Baumeister:* You send us an excerpt from a letter from Le Corbusier, who writes you: "I am pleased to see the fine bearing of your work. Everything is eminently pictorial. The drawings are very beautiful. Since 1920 your point of departure has been healthy and interesting. You can move into the future with confidence." At the same time you send us an excerpt from the *Frankfurter Zeitung,* in which Benkard writes: "Here (with Baumeister) one could say that a schizophrenic is illustrating technical plans, mathematical proofs, or scholarly diagrams." Last year they already referred to you there as a "clinical case," which you apparently didn't take as flattery. We don't want to get mixed up in all these medical diagnoses, in any case not without consulting a specialist as to whether Corbusier's "healthy" or Benkard's "schizophrenic" is correct. But why don't you want to be a bit crazy?! Would you rather be thought of as one of the usual bourgeois philistines? And schizophrenia? These days craziness is practically synonymous with artistic originality. Just take a look at the book *Art and Race* by Schultze-Naumburg. Kokoschka, Schmidt-Rottluff, Picasso—all schizophrenic. One could be in no better company.[66]

Paul Schultze-Naumburg's "racial-biological" aesthetic, according to Westheim's 1938 essay explicating and critiquing it, was grounded in the belief that all artworks are expressions of the artist's own body, and that this body is racially constituted. "Healthy," upright, Germanic artists will express themselves clearly and without distortion, whereas racially impure artists will produce distorted works betraying their creators' lack of bodily integrity. Westheim pointed out about Schultze-Naumburg's analysis: "The deformation of natural appearances by Picasso or Klee, which is a form of expression, no longer needs to be investigated or even recognized as a stylistic principle: it is biologically grounded. Thus the explanation is that the artist who paints such deformed bodies, must himself have a deformed physique, that is, must have a heredity that is 'degenerate,' 'diseased' and so forth."[67] Schultze-Naumburg's arguments laid the groundwork for Nazi Germany's "degenerate art" campaign, which went hand in hand with internments, sterilizations, and murder.

Sander Gilman has examined the modern stereotypes of "the madness of the Jews," and of the "the mad as artists," exposing links between madness, otherness, and modern art that the Nazis adopted and exploited. The Nazis' one original "contribution" to this discourse was that they "took the equation artist = mad = Jew as a program of action."[68] As a longtime champion of avant-garde art, and as a Jew, Westheim stood very much in the line of fire of those who claimed that modern art was a symptom of the madness endemic to modernity. Aware of how the wind was blowing in 1931, Westheim used irony to express the danger inherent in simply substituting Le Corbusier's diagnosis of mental fitness for Benkard's of schizophrenia: it legitimized Benkard's methodology and thus risked legitimating that of Nazi "aesthetics" as propounded by Schultze-Naumburg. Anticipating the implementation of a political policy based on such notions, Westheim, shortly after the Nazi assumption of power, fled first to Paris and later to Mexico.[69]

During the two months that separated Adolf Hitler's assumption of office as chancellor of Germany, at the end of January 1933, and Baumeister's dismissal from his teaching post in Frankfurt, at the end of March, the Nazi Party's national newspaper, the *Völkischer Beobachter*, singled out Baumeister for ridicule in an anti-Semitic tirade against modernist art. The article turned Westheim's prescient warning to Baumeister on its head by reprinting one line of it, divorced now from its context and stripped of irony, as proof that modern artists and Jews were linked advocates of insanity: "But why don't you (Willy Baumeister) want to be a bit crazy?!"[70]

From the years between the economic collapse of 1929 to Hitler's assumption of the chancellorship, even avowed apolitical artists such as Baumeister saw their friends, colleagues, and adversaries politicized and became aware that their own livelihoods and even their lives were political issues. On May 30, 1932, Baumeister noted in his diary: "Collapse of the Brüning cabinet. This the apparent end of the democratic epoch."[71] When he visited the painter Otto Meyer-Amden in Switzerland at the end of summer 1932, Baumeister wrote in his diary that this friend from his Stuttgart student days now supported Hitler's National Socialist Party.[72] When Meyer-Amden died in January 1933 Baumeister noted about him, before going on to praise the originality of his art: "He was also politicized. He became extremely Germanic and read all the National Socialist newspapers and brochures."[73]

Baumeister's dismissal from his teaching position, a minor detail amid the monstrous crimes of the Third Reich, exemplifies *Gleichschaltung* (coordination), the process of amalgamating institutions into the Nazi system. The timing and the methodology of the attack on and subsequent dismissal of Baumeister coincided with the Nazi's consolidation of absolute power. The attack on Westheim and Baumeister in the national newspaper of February 25 had been preceded a few days earlier by an attack in the local Frankfurt party organ, the *Frankfurter Volksblatt*. In his diary entry for February 22 Baumeister noted, "November Criminal in the applied arts. Headline in bold over an article attacking me in the *Frankfurter Volksblatt*. False things are asserted there."[74] Baumeister sent a letter to the editor protesting these "false things." The newspaper responded that it had not been its intention to slander him individually, for a typographical error had led to his being singled out as a "November Criminal" *(November Verbrecher)*, while their manuscript referred instead to the "November Crime" *(November Verbrechen)*, by which "an entire cultural tendency" was meant—the November Revolution and Weimar Republic.[75]

On February 27 Baumeister noted in his diary the perpetration of a minor act of terrorism against him: "Working on paintings despite all threats. A slanderous symbol is drawn on my studio door in an unknown hand."[76] On the same day the Reichstag was burned to the ground in a major act of terrorism probably engineered by Hitler to increase the public perception that only a single strong leader could enforce order. The way was thus clear for the so-called Enabling Act, issued on March 24, 1933, which granted Hitler dictatorial powers and allowed him to terminate summarily the contracts of undesirable civil servants, including Baumeister, Beckmann, and other teachers at the Frankfurt Art School. On March 29, a letter announced to the new administrators of the school that "in order to be able to restructure the Art School as fundamentally German and rooted in craft, Professor Baumeister, Professor Scheibe, Professor Schuster, and Misters Hartwig and Beckmann as well as Miss Schöff should be terminated at the nearest possible date."[77] On the same day a letter from the editors of the *Frankfurter Volksblatt* to Baumeister answered his protest against their most recent defamation of him: "Our judgment of your artistic work has long been final. . . . However the matter may now stand, we reject you as a German artist, and regret that you cannot express your German thoughts in any other form."[78]

A letter of March 31 officially severed Baumeister from further employment at the Frankfurt art school. In his diary he noted with resignation: "I was never active politically. (Should I take action against the dismissal? No.—) The issue is my 'bolshevistic' art."[79] Seven grounds for the dismissal were enumerated in a position paper of the provisional director of the school, dated April 22, 1933, including his association with Jewish art dealers, publishers, and critics such as the gallerist Alfred Flechtheim and the Frankfurt art critic Sascha Schwabacher; membership in the October Group; and admiration for Picasso.[80] Baumeister was given eight days to clear his Frankfurt studio. On April 7 he wrote in his diary: "I pack up the apartment. Departure for Stuttgart. Mother, Margrit, and Krista arrive safely. What now?"[81]

Baumeister's Postcards Unmaled: Portraits of the Artist as Cigar Smoking, Circumcised, Shemale

One can feel simultaneously enlightened and misled by the large exhibitions currently [1995–96] in London and Berlin, both of which present art produced under the great dictatorships. Public and private are set side by side. Here (in London) are the intolerable public nudes of the Nazi Arno Breker. And here too are the private doodles of the anti-Nazi Willi Baumeister, transforming the genitals, on a photograph of Breker's serpent-slaying *Avenger,* into the face of a serious young man with a large spotted bow tie. [fig. 51] **—JAMES FENTON, "SUBVERSIVES,"** ***NEW YORK REVIEW OF BOOKS***

James Fenton's *New York Review of Books* report on the exhibition in which Jay Prosser saw the Baumeister works to which we now return correctly cites a split between the public figure and the private gesture.[82] This public/private dialectic controlled conditions of meaning for each work, as well as of the life of each artist, in Nazi Germany. Arno Breker's colossal reliefs were designed for the heart of Nazi Germany, Albert Speer's planned North-South Axis in Berlin.[83] Breker's work of the 1920s featured fragmentary forms and active surfaces emphasizing the physicality of sculpture itself and the physical engagement of the sculptor in the studio with the piece. Nazi-period pieces such as *The Avenger,* on the other hand, were cast by teams of art workers at the vast Arno Breker Works, a foundry located near the eighteenth-century castle of Jäckelsbruch that Breker acquired as a gift from Hitler in 1940.[84] Such works deployed smoothly packaged heavily muscled bodies striking contrived poses to "unsettling and latently threatening effect."[85] It is this threatening effect that Baumeister, working at home as a "degenerate artist," undermined in his "private doodle," using ridicule and irreverent, adolescent, Dadaistic humor as weapons of self-defense.

Breker's *Avenger* was to be "timeless" in its pseudo-Classicism, and to provide an idealized self-image of Nazi Germany's ruling elite.[86] The philosopher Wolfgang Fritz Haug has described such objects as "the body of a state-regulated self-control, of an imperialistic mechanism, subordinated and superior at the same time."[87] The body on display is a self-consciously and grotesquely "perfect" male specimen, fending off the erotic access it encourages male spectators to seek by means of its pose of aggressive, vengeful authority. The naked figure, poised to decapitate a huge serpent that rises from between his legs, embodies what Klaus Theweleit has identified as one of the storm trooper's problems and its "solution": "You should love men, but you are not allowed to be homosexual . . . the best thing is to obey and repress the contradictions."[88] Breker's figures suggest that erotic energies generated among men can and should

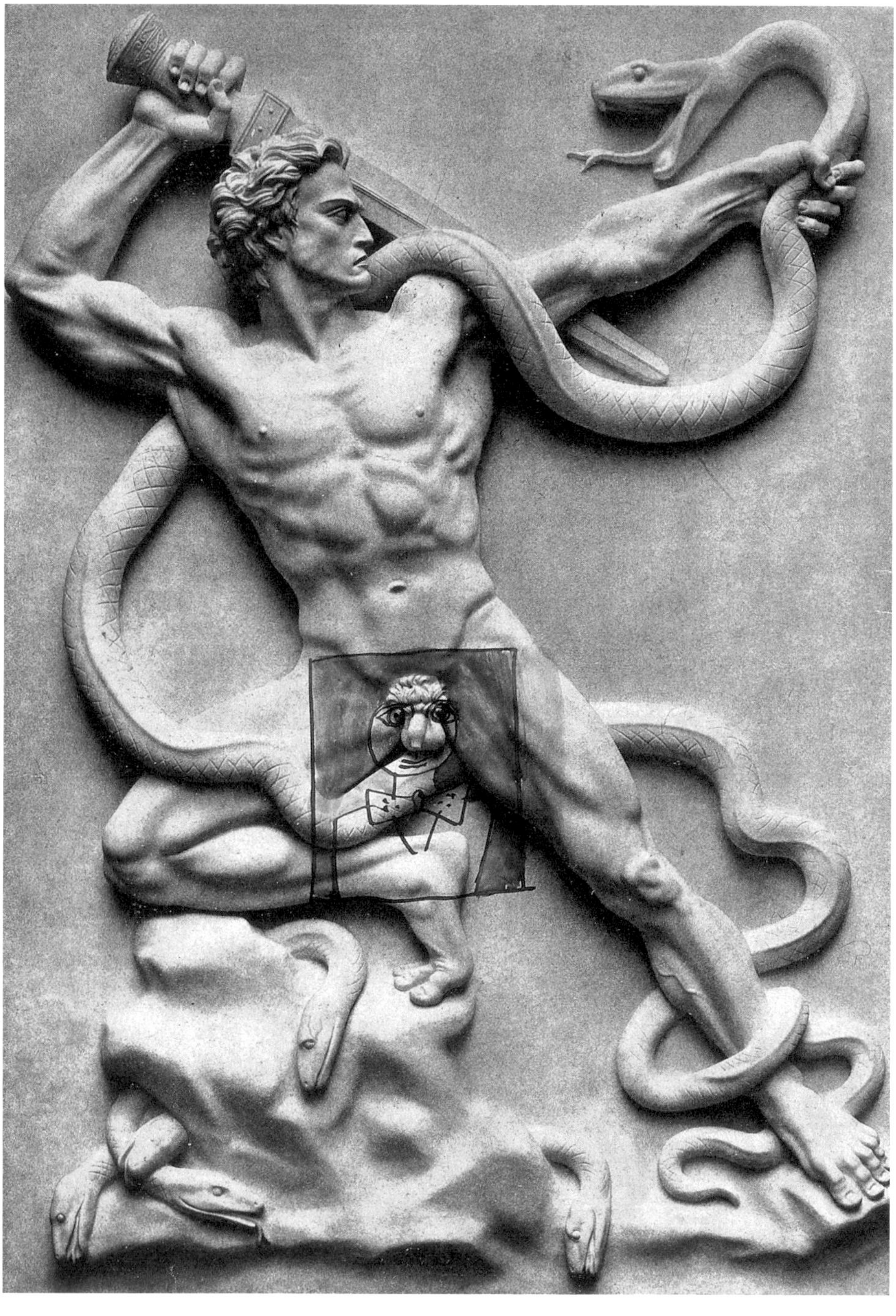

FIGURE 51. Willi Baumeister, *Altered Avenger,* pen-and-ink drawing on Arno Breker's *The Avenger,* reproduced in "Die Grosse Deutsche Kunstausstellung 1941, II," *Kunst dem Volk* (September 1941), 12. Art © 2010 Artists Rights Society (ARS), New York/VG Bild-Kunst, Bonn. Photo: Archiv Baumeister im Kunstmuseum Stuttgart.

be sadistically sublimated into violence against "acceptable" targets: liberated women, Jews, homosexuals, gypsies, Communists.

The object of the Avenger's hostility, the snake that coils suggestively through the legs, offering its hissing head to his sword, stands for those *Gemeinschaftsfremde* (foreigners to the community, in other words, "others") to be eliminated. Snakeheads particularly proliferate in the representation, oozing out of the rock beneath the Avenger's feet.[89] They are a symbolic concatenation of largely undifferentiated "antisocial" elements that the Nazis feared would contaminate, and ultimately castrate, the martially eroticized Aryan (male) body of the *Volk*. Heinrich Himmler, for one, saw that threat of contamination in homosexuality. "Wilhelm Frick, future Nazi Minister of the Interior, then a Nazi Reichstag deputy, introduced a bill in 1930 calling for the castration of homosexuals, 'that Jewish pestilence.' "[90]

The sword, a phallic symbol of state-regulated power, must castrate the "other," who is feared precisely as a potential castrator, a crippler of the male life force. As Freud observed:

> To decapitate = to castrate. . . . The hair upon Medusa's head is frequently represented in works of art in the form of snakes, and these once again are derived from the castration complex. It is a remarkable fact that, however frightening they may be in themselves, they nevertheless serve actually as a mitigation of the horror, for they replace the penis, the absence of which is the cause of the horror. This is a confirmation of the technical rule according to which a multiplication of penis symbols signifies castration.[91]

If Breker's *Avenger* embodies the revenge of the state-sponsored phallus on some repressed desire for the "other," Baumeister's "correction" could be called "Revenge of the Penis." He cuts this symbolic representation of supposedly limitless phallic power down to actual penis size. In so doing Baumeister reveals repressed meanings and vulnerability lurking in the posturing of Breker's figure.[92] Baumeister frames the Avenger's penis and uses the frame to focus our gaze on its anthropomorphized form. His doodle contrasts the "classical" timeless profile of the Avenger with the goofy frontal view of the penis-nosed man. This humorous juxtaposition transforms the "natural" back into art and artifice, unveiling the production and reproduction of monumental, naturalistic, "timeless" sculpture as a staged exercise in illusionism, the smoke and mirrors behind which lurked a murderous, but in no sense coherent, ideology. Toby Clark, reproducing this as the first image in his *Art and Propaganda in the Twentieth Century* (1997), characterized Baumeister's doodle as "not just an impudent joke . . . [but as] a brave act which brilliantly exposed the face of bureaucratic evil hidden behind a pompous mask of heroism," and he compared it to the defiant public art of the Chinese prodemocracy students in Tiananmen Square in 1989.[93]

Baumeister was working as a "producer" in Benjamin's sense: creating an oppositional space for his work that disrupted the otherwise seamless surface of the dominant cultural apparatus. In so doing he produced work that was utterly incompatible with that apparatus and uncontainable by it. He used what Benjamin identified as the "revolutionary strength of Dadaism," which "consisted in testing art for its authenticity."[94] That real ink lying on the surface of the slick Breker reproduction that appeared in *Kunst dem Volk* (Art for the people), a journal published in Vienna by Hitler's personal friend and official photographer, Heinrich Hoffmann, "exposed" Breker's work as ridiculous and effectively defused what must have been, for a "degenerate artist," its rather terrifying threat.[95]

And it may have been even more personal, and no less political, than that. In *Transgressions: The Offences of Art* (2002) Anthony Julius posits transgression as a significant genre of modern art. Baumeister's "Altered Avenger" serves as one of his typological examples.[96] Julius contributes an important new reading of this image. For Julius, a lawyer and cultural historian best known academically for his controversial *T. S. Eliot, Anti-Semitism, and Literary Form* (1995), Baumeister's "mischievous graffito" exemplifies transgressive art that is politically resistant to a political structure so oppressive to the artist that it renders the artist's compliance with it, the artist's very life under it, impossible. Furthermore, Julius perceptively points out, Baumeister achieves in his doodle a refunctioning of the anti-Semitic "racial" stereotype of the Jew. "With wonderful subversive mockery, Baumeister makes comedy out of the heroic nude by Breker, Hitler's favorite artist. He too is an avenger, not throttling the snake but framing the phallus. He avenges those artists whose work has been suppressed—throttled—by the Nazis. The penis becomes a long nose, the face a Jewish caricature that mocks the Nazis' deepest, most fantastical fears about the emasculating effect of Jewish power."[97] This is an extremely suggestive observation, particularly in light of a number of interrelated issues having to do with Jewish stereotyping, Baumeister's biography, and Baumeister's own conception of these anti-Nazi works.

Baumeister considered some of his anti-Nazi doodles and collages self-portraits.[98] Next to Baumeister himself, the architect Heinz Rasch, to whom Baumeister sent some of the postcards, is the person most closely associated with them. Baumeister and Rasch became friends in 1924, when they helped set up a Werkbund exhibition in Stuttgart, as they did again in 1927, when they worked together on the Weissenhofsiedlung exhibition. They were very close during the Nazi period. At the request of the Wuppertal paint manufacturer Kurt Herberts, Rasch organized a research institute for the study of historical painting techniques that operated in Herberts's factory from 1937 to 1944.[99] In Wuppertal, Baumeister, Schlemmer, the painter Georg Muche, the architect Franz Krause, the art historian Hans Hildebrandt, and Hildebrandt's wife, Lily, who was a painter and Jewish, and others carried on researches into the properties and application of various artistic media.[100] Herberts published the results of their work under his own name and in exchange protected them from war-related duties. In some of Herberts's publications, Baumeister paintings inspired by prehistoric cave paintings were reproduced not as works by the artist but as technical replications of Paleolithic paintings. All the text of *Jokkmokmädchen* (fig. 40), like the photographs of

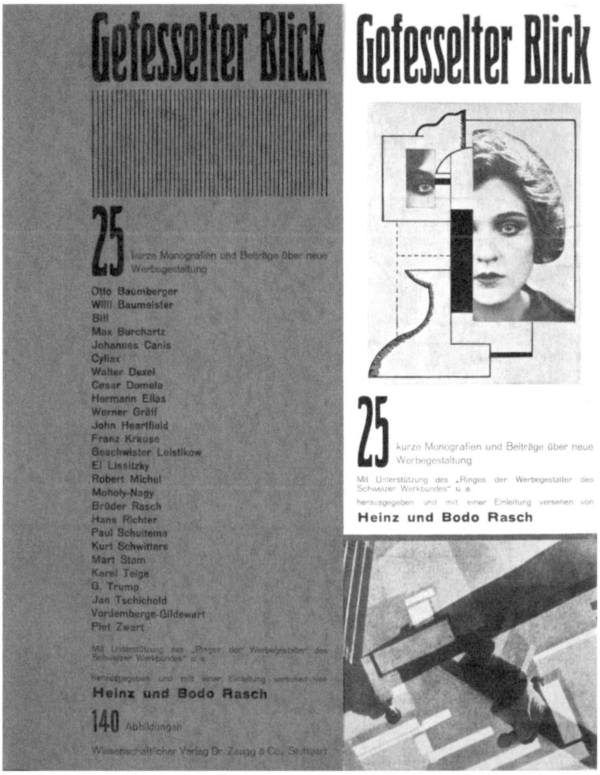

FIGURE 52. **Cover of Heinz and Bodo Rasch's anthology *Gefesselter Blick* (1930), with Willi Baumeister's *Head* (ca. 1923, pen and ink over pencil, collage of black paper and photograph on light brown cardboard, 35 × 24.8 cm). Art © 2010 Artists Rights Society (ARS), New York/VG Bild-Kunst, Bonn. Photo: Archiv Baumeister im Kunstmuseum Stuttgart.**

Baumeister's plastering hands, derives from one of these publications—with the exception of the eponymous *Jokkmokmädchen,* which must have been cut from the caption of an ethnographic photograph.

According to Rasch, Baumeister planned to publish the postcards and illustrated letters he had sent to friends from the 1920s until his death in 1955 under a title inspired by commercial postcards bearing the word *Absender* (sender) and then a space for the individual sending the card to fill in his or her name. The book was to be called "Absender: *ich*" (Sender: *i* [first-person singular]). As a practitioner of the "new typography" in Weimar Germany, Baumeister was committed to the equalizing effect of lowercase lettering, as was Heinz Rasch.[101] In 1930 Rasch and his brother, Bodo Rasch, who was also an architect, published the anthology *Gefesselter Blick* (Captured glance), which summarized the work of twenty-five graphic designers associated with the Circle of New Graphic Designers, including Baumeister, Max Burchartz, John Heartfield, El Lissitzky, Moholy-Nagy, the Rasch Brothers, Kurt Schwitters, Jan Tschichold, and others.[102] Baumeister provided what is probably his best-known Weimar collage, *Head* (ca. 1923), as the cover illustration for this anthology (fig. 52).

Baumeister's hostile response to Adolf Ziegler's paintings, which thrust women back into the traditional artistic role of nude muses and goddesses, in part derives from his own taste for more active, short-haired, modern women, such as the one included in

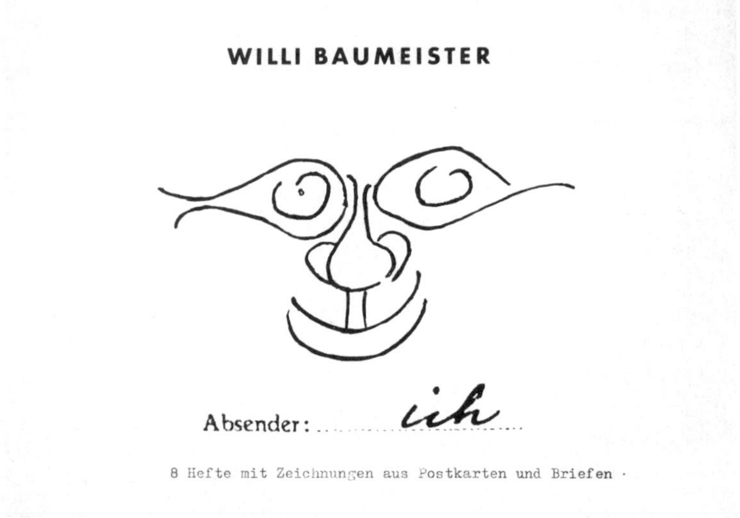

FIGURE 53. Willi Baumeister/Heinz Rasch, cover of *Absender: ich*, ca. 1969. Art © 2010 Artists Rights Society (ARS), New York/VG Bild-Kunst, Bonn. Photo: Archiv Baumeister im Kunstmuseum Stuttgart.

Head. While one should not make exaggerated claims for Baumeister's feminism, he was modernist in all senses: some of his New Objectivity paintings in the 1920s portray female agency and mobility, such as two versions of the sporty *Female Runner II* of 1925 (fig. 48), which also relate to such "New Women" of Weimar Germany as the mobile women in *Cut with the Kitchen Knife Dada* and to the androgynous image of the "garçonne."[103] In a letter to Heinz Rasch of 1925, Baumeister declared his attachment, at least aesthetically, to the short-haired active and unemotional type of the Weimar "New Woman": "Pageboy hairstyle *(Bubikopf)* going out of style? Not with me! In the opposite sex I prefer a flapper to a 'lady,' and a sporty type to a flapper, and a neutral, matter-of-fact type to a sporty type: the farther removed from the old 'rococo' ladies the better!"[104] As the art historian Joann Skrypzak points out, Baumeister's female athletes of the 1920s not only "evoke the wide-ranging plurality" of social roles that flourished then for women but "also distinguish themselves from the physically perfected athletic bodies that increasingly became a vehicle for National Socialist racial ideology."[105]

On his sixty-fifth birthday, in 1954, Baumeister presented his postcards to some friends at a local restaurant. Ten years later, long after the artist's death in 1955, Rasch presented them at the von der Heydt Museum in Wuppertal, with some of Baumeister's family present. According to Rasch, Baumeister's wife was not pleased with the presentation, and plans to publish the works were never realized, save for the self-published collection of pamphlets Rasch produced circa 1969 in Baumeister's name under the title *Absender: ich; 8 Hefte mit Zeichnungen aus Postkarten und Briefen* (Sender: i; 8 folios with drawings from postcards and letters) (fig. 53).[106]

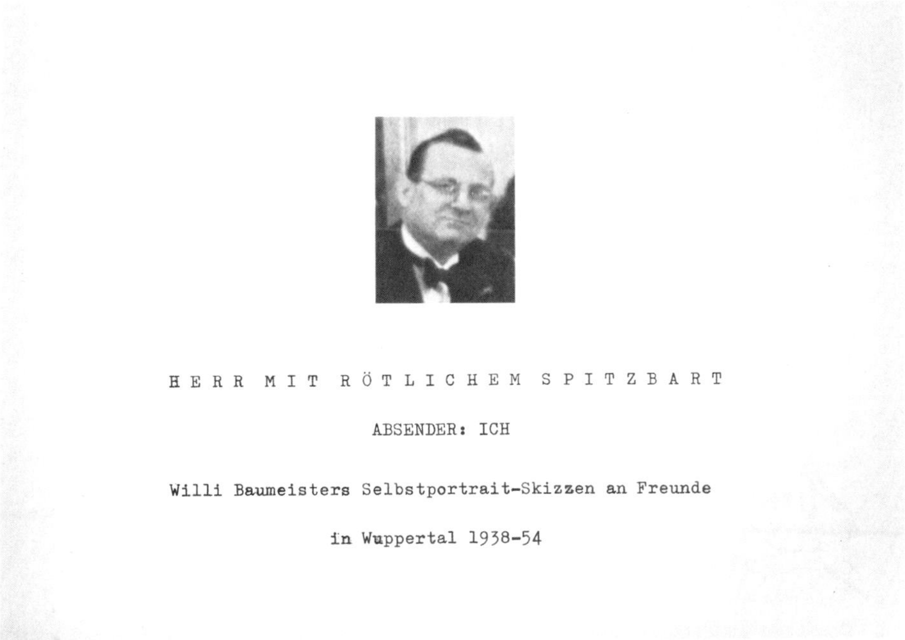

H E R R M I T R Ö T L I C H E M S P I T Z B A R T

ABSENDER: ICH

Willi Baumeisters Selbstportrait-Skizzen an Freunde

in Wuppertal 1938-54

FIGURE 54. Willi Baumeister/Heinz Rasch, "Man with Reddish Goatee," *Absender: ich,* ca. 1964. Art © 2010 Artists Rights Society (ARS), New York/VG Bild-Kunst, Bonn. Photo: Archiv Baumeister im Kunstmuseum Stuttgart.

One of the eight folios Heinz Rasch put together is called "Herr mit rötlichem Spitzbart . . . Willi Baumeisters Selbstportrait-Skizzen an Freunde in Wuppertal, 1938–54" (Man with reddish goatee . . . Willi Baumeister's self-portrait sketches to friends in Wuppertal, 1938–54). The opening image is a small head shot of Baumeister in a tuxedo, sporting a bow tie, like the one he had drawn on *The Avenger*'s penis (fig. 54). According to Rasch, works such as the one on Prosser's book cover and the portrait of "Privy Council Prof. Dr. Pubic Hair" are in fact Willi Baumeister self-portraits. Baumeister projects himself onto the woman's body, transforming himself into a shemale, making his calling card "s/he mail." Declared "degenerate" by the Nazis in 1937, Baumeister makes himself over into the epitome of *Entartung,* or "degeneration," emphasizing precisely the biological connotations of the word.[107]

Baumeister's self-portrayal relates to the Austrian Expressionist Oskar Kokoschka's 1937 riposte *Self-Portrait as Degenerate Artist,* in which he emphasized those formal qualities of modern painting that the Nazis, especially Hitler, reviled.[108] Formally, Baumeister employs Dada strategies, but he goes beyond the formal to endow the image with transgressive psychosexual and ethnic identity. This is a strategy analogous to what the historian of contemporary art Therese Lichtenstein has claimed for the Surrealist Hans Bellmer, whose notoriously perverse dolls, she claims, "constitute a fantasy: a subversion of Nazi representations and codes of normality."[109] Unlike Bellmer,

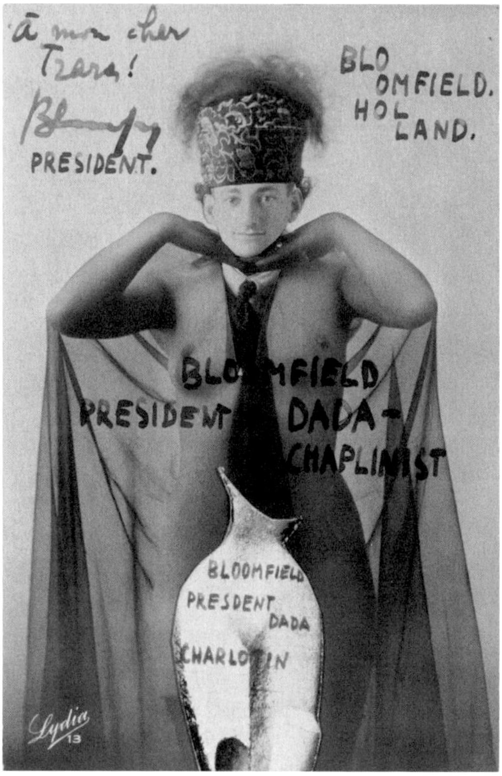

FIGURE 55. Erwin Blumenfeld, *Bloomfield: President—Dada—Chaplinist,* 1922, collage on postcard sent to Tristan Tzara, 13.4 × 8.8 cm. Art © 2010 Artists Rights Society (ARS), New York/ADAGP, Paris. Photo: Kunsthaus Zürich—© Pro Litteris, Zürich 2007.

though, Baumeister presented himself not only as a degenerate artist, like Kokoschka, but also as the Nazi's worst transgendered nightmare: the return, by approved mail, of the repressed and oppressed, of their own ideal of art and beauty transformed simultaneously into a degenerate artist, shemale, and Jew. In this regard the clearest precedent is the transgendered self-portrait by the Jewish Dadaist Erwin Blumenfeld, *Bloomfield: President—Dada—Chaplinist,* a card sent to Tristan Tzara in 1922 (fig. 55).[110]

The irreducible sign of (male) Jewish difference is the circumcised penis. Sander Gilman has studied the anti-Semitic use of circumcision in the construction of the German (and wider European) conceptions of Jewish males as inferior. "Circumcision marked the Jewish body as unequal to that of the Aryan and the male Jew as the exemplary Jew."[111] While circumcision marked the Jewish man ethnically, it confused his gender identity. Removal of the foreskin was also taken to be the "leading sign and originating occasion" for the idea of Jewish male effeminacy—of Jews not only as a "race"—as in the notions of nineteenth- and early twentieth-century "biological" and political anti-Semites—but also as of questionable sexual identity.[112] If the Jewish man was feminized, he was therefore eroticized for non-Jewish men. Yet no Jew could be totally feminized according to normative standards. "The Jewish woman" was perceived as at once hypererotic and exotic as well as intellectual and demanding—all qualities that called into question her "femininity" but also made her desirable to men who considered themselves up to her challenge. The figure around whom many of these conceptions coalesced at the turn of the century and into the twentieth was the Jewish actress Sarah Bernhardt, especially in her most famous role, as Oscar Wilde's *Salome*.[113]

The penis at the center of Baumeister's alteration of the Breker is, of course, uncircumcised. Here the uncircumcised penis becomes, as Julius pointed out, the ubiquitous, public, physiognomic anti-Semitic sign of the Jew, the hooked nose.[114] But, transformed into what James Fenton referred to as a "serious young man with a large spotted bow tie," this is, like the postcards, a form of self-portrait, and in this case the image conflates Baumeister with both Jewish caricature and actual Aryan. If this seems farfetched, it might be appropriate to note that when Baumeister created this work, he was personally concerned with circumcision both as ritual and as medical and cosmetic procedure. In 1941 he developed the condition known as phimosis, failure of the foreskin to retract, causing a penile infection necessitating circumcision. Baumeister was "made into a Jew."[115] Heinz Rasch recounts him garrulously regaling (and appalling) Schlemmer and an unnamed "lady" in a café with a detailed historical description of this procedure ("not only the Jews practice this, it's done for hygienic reasons!"), culminating in a graphic description of his own recent operation.[116]

During these years another obsession Baumeister had and indulged was cigars, which he smoked avidly and had trouble procuring during the war. He even composed a paean to them, a poem titled "Cigars," in 1943, published along with a picture of him smoking in the journal *Meta* in 1949 (fig. 56).

In Nazi Germany, cigars were also identified with Jews.[117] Though they hardly dominated the industry, by the nineteenth century Jews were strongly identified with tobacco as producers, distributors, and consumers. Anti-Semitic images, such as one found in the infamous children's primer published by Julius Streicher's Stürmer Press, *Trau keinem Fuchs auf grüner Heid und keinem Jud auf seinem Eid (Trust no fox in the hedge and no Jew in his pledge)*, pictured Jews as cigar-smoking capitalists with corrupted physiques and morals (fig. 57).

According to Gilman, "Anti-Semites, who saw tobacco as weakening the social fabric, laid its very origin at the feet of the Jews. (There is a strong association between health reform and anti-Semitism in Central Europe from the nineteenth century through to the twentieth century)."[118] The historian Robert Proctor has established that medical researchers in Nazi Germany engaged in the most advanced epidemiological studies of cancer to that time and were the first to link cancer and smoking conclusively. Armed with these findings, the Nazi Party and affiliated antismoking activists launched a battle against tobacco, smoking, and cancer—and linked these to their genocidal war on Jews, and to other actions, including the "degenerate art" action, to purge the *Volkskörper*.[119] At the opening of the 1938 "Great German Art Exhibition," Hitler railed against "contamination" of what he referred to as the "*Volkskörper*" (the folk conceived as a homogenous biological entity) supposedly spread by Jews, Communists, homosexuals, Sinti, Roma,

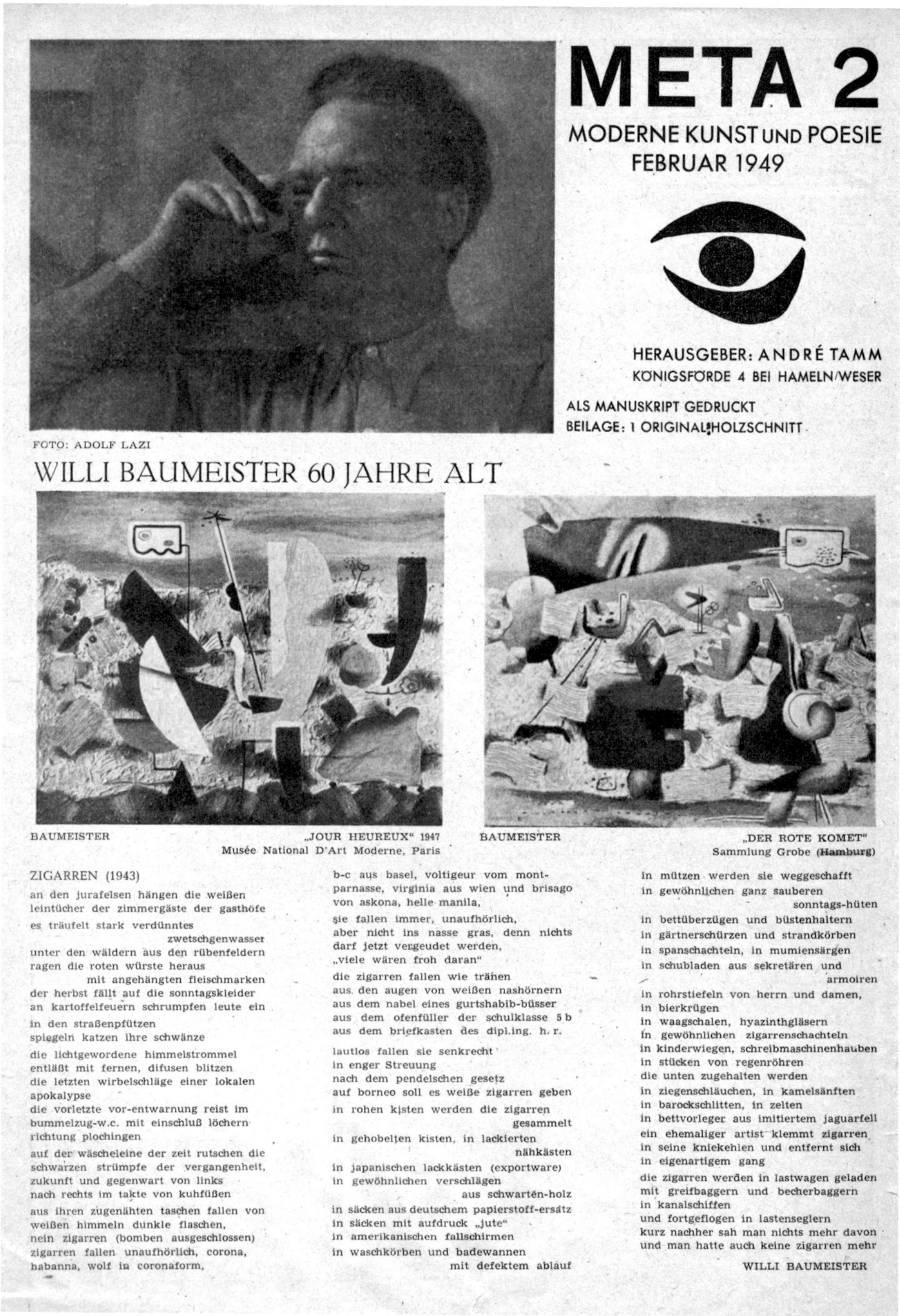

META 2

MODERNE KUNST UND POESIE
FEBRUAR 1949

HERAUSGEBER: ANDRÉ TAMM
KÖNIGSFÖRDE 4 BEI HAMELN/WESER

ALS MANUSKRIPT GEDRUCKT
BEILAGE: 1 ORIGINAL-HOLZSCHNITT

FOTO: ADOLF LAZI

WILLI BAUMEISTER 60 JAHRE ALT

BAUMEISTER „JOUR HEUREUX" 1947
Musée National D'Art Moderne, Paris

BAUMEISTER „DER ROTE KOMET"
Sammlung Grobe (Hamburg)

ZIGARREN (1943)

an den jurafelsen hängen die weißen
leintücher der zimmergäste der gasthöfe

es träufelt stark verdünntes
zwetschgenwasser
unter den wäldern aus den rübenfeldern
ragen die roten würste heraus
mit angehängten fleischmarken
der herbst fällt auf die sonntagskleider
an kartoffelfeuern schrumpfen leute ein

in den straßenpfützen
spiegeln katzen ihre schwänze

die lichtgewordene himmelstrommel
entläßt mit fernen, difusen blitzen
die letzten wirbelschläge einer lokalen
apokalypse
die vorletzte vor-entwarnung reist im
bummelzug-w.c. mit einschluß löchern
richtung plochingen

auf der wäscheleine der zeit rutschen die
schwarzen strümpfe der vergangenheit,
zukunft und gegenwart von links
nach rechts im takte von kuhfüßen

aus ihren zugenähten taschen fallen von
weißen himmeln dunkle flaschen,
nein zigarren (bomben ausgeschlossen)
zigarren fallen unaufhörlich, corona,
habanna, wolf in coronaform,
b-c aus basel, voltigeur vom mont-
parnasse, virginia aus wien und brisago
von askona, helle manila,

sie fallen immer, unaufhörlich,
aber nicht ins nasse gras, denn nichts
darf jetzt vergeudet werden,
„viele wären froh daran"

die zigarren fallen wie tränen
aus den augen von weißen nashörnern
aus dem nabel eines gurtshabib-büsser
aus dem ofenfüller der schulklasse 5 b
aus dem briefkasten des dipl.ing. h. r.

lautlos fallen sie senkrecht
in enger Streuung
nach dem pendelschen gesetz
auf borneo soll es weiße zigarren geben

in rohen kisten werden die zigarren
gesammelt
in gehobelten kisten, in lackierten
nähkästen
in japanischen lackkästen (exportware)
in gewöhnlichen verschlägen
aus schwarten-holz
in säcken aus deutschem papierstoff-ersatz
in säcken mit aufdruck „jute"
in amerikanischen fallschirmen
in waschkörben und badewannen
mit defektem ablauf
in mützen werden sie weggeschafft
in gewöhnlichen ganz sauberen
sonntags-hüten
in bettüberzügen und büstenhaltern
in gärtnerschürzen und strandkörben
in spanschachteln, in mumiensärgen
in schubladen aus sekretären und
armoiren
in rohrstiefeln von herrn und damen,
in bierkrügen
in waagschalen, hyazinthgläsern
in gewöhnlichen zigarrenschachteln
in kinderwiegen, schreibmaschinenhauben
in stücken von regenröhren
die unten zugehalten werden
in ziegenschläuchen, in kamelsänften
in barockschlitten, in zelten
in bettvorleger aus imitiertem jaguarfell
ein ehemaliger artist klemmt zigarren
in seine kniekehlen und entfernt sich
in eigenartigem gang

die zigarren werden in lastwagen geladen
mit greifbaggern und becherbaggern
in kanalschiffen
und fortgeflogen in lastenseglern
kurz nachher sah man nichts mehr davon
und man hatte auch keine zigarren mehr

WILLI BAUMEISTER

FIGURE 56. Willi Baumeister, "Cigars" (1943), in *Meta 2* (February 1949). Art © 2010 Artists Rights Society (ARS), New York/VG Bild-Kunst, Bonn. Photo: Archiv Baumeister im Kunstmuseum Stuttgart.

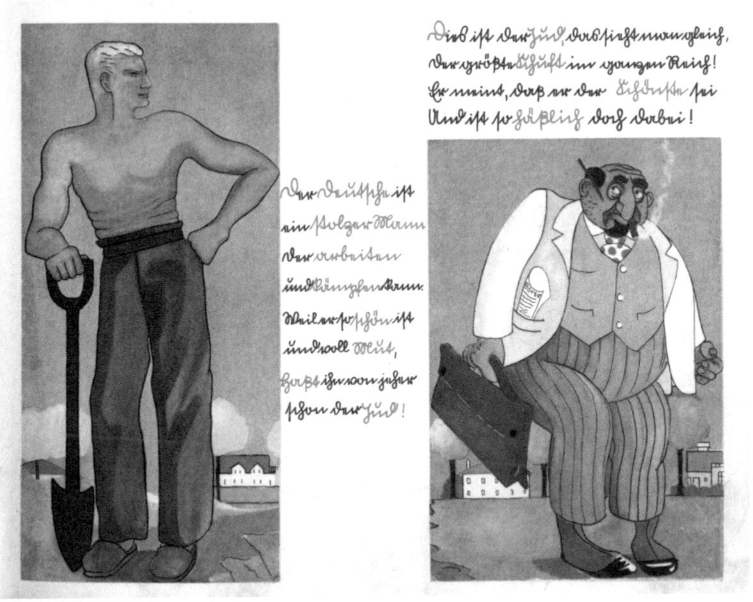

FIGURE 57. **Comparison of "the German" and "the Jew," from Elvira Bauer, *Trau keinem Fuchs auf grüner Heid und keinem Jüd auf seinem Eid* (Nuremberg: Stürmer Verlag, 1936). Photo courtesy Randall Bytwerk, German Propaganda Archive.**

and empowered women. Hitler held these groups to be responsible for "the collapse and general deterioration of Germany . . . a gradual disintegration of a unified sense of *Volk* . . . crippling of the inner and outer life force of our *Volk* . . . [and] weakening of the German *Volkskörper*."[120] Impure art and impure people were equated with cancer, rationalizing their elimination.

In his postcards and the Dadaistic doodle on the Breker reproduction, Baumeister went much farther in his defiance of Nazi concepts than any commentator, including the author of this book, has previously allowed. He iconoclastically portrayed himself to friends as a woman and a Jew, and publicly proclaiming himself a circumcised, cigar-smoking one, at that. Better yet, he became, symbolically at least, not a woman or a Jew but a transgendered, multiethnic subject continually in process, neither one nor the other but both at the same time: a *Mischwesen*. The circulating image, the postcard, the reproduction, lends itself to these transitional and transgressive states of being. Dario Gamboni, a specialist in iconoclastic art, has asserted that "Baumeister's overpainting of Ziegler's Nazi allegory . . . makes a freezed and freezing image move again, and it reveals its implicit ingredients, the male spectator and sexuality."[121] The overpainted card does indeed continue to move: it circulates as card and image, and its depiction oscillates between male and female, hovering in the vicinity of arrival at a "third sex" that encompasses both simultaneously. This blurring of the distinction between male and female flew directly in the face of Nazi ideology. Hitler declared: "The wonderful

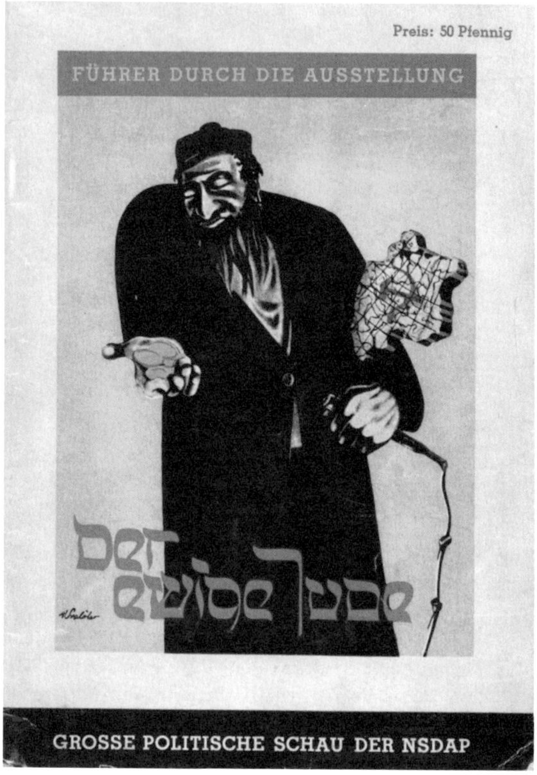

FIGURE 58. **Cover of the exhibition guidebook *Der ewige Jude* (Munich: Zentralverlag der NSDAP, 1937). Private collection. Photo courtesy Randall Bytwerk, German Propaganda Archive.**

thing about nature and providence is that no conflict between the sexes can occur as long as each party performs the function prescribed for it by nature."[122] Baumeister's transgendered self-portraits also refer to Freudian theory and its insistence "that portions of the male sexual apparatus also appear in women's bodies, though in an atrophied state, and vice versa in the alternative case. It [science] regards their occurrence as indications of *bisexuality*, as though an individual is not a man or a woman but always both—merely a certain amount more the one than the other."[123] Baumeister's self-portrait calling cards transgressed differences that were ever more sharply delimited in Nazi Germany. In a quintessential Dada gesture, he answered the charge that he was a degenerate artist with exaggeration, humor, aggression, and transgression.

These works, though, also re-create anti-Semitic stereotypes, though Baumeister was no anti-Semite. The Breker penis transformation relies on acceptance of, or at least familiarity with, the stereotype of the wiry-haired, hook-nosed Jew. In some of his transformations (see fig. 42), Baumeister also drew a long, flowing beard, like that of an orthodox Jew, a stereotype circulated in postcard form and on the cover of the guidebook to the anti-Semitic exhibition "Der ewige Jude" (The eternal Jew) of 1937 (fig. 58). The Jew as a wandering, rootless, unscrupulous scourge of rooted German culture was also the theme of the most notorious of Nazi propaganda films, *Der ewige Jude* of 1940. The montage on the film's program was dominated by the faces of two bearded

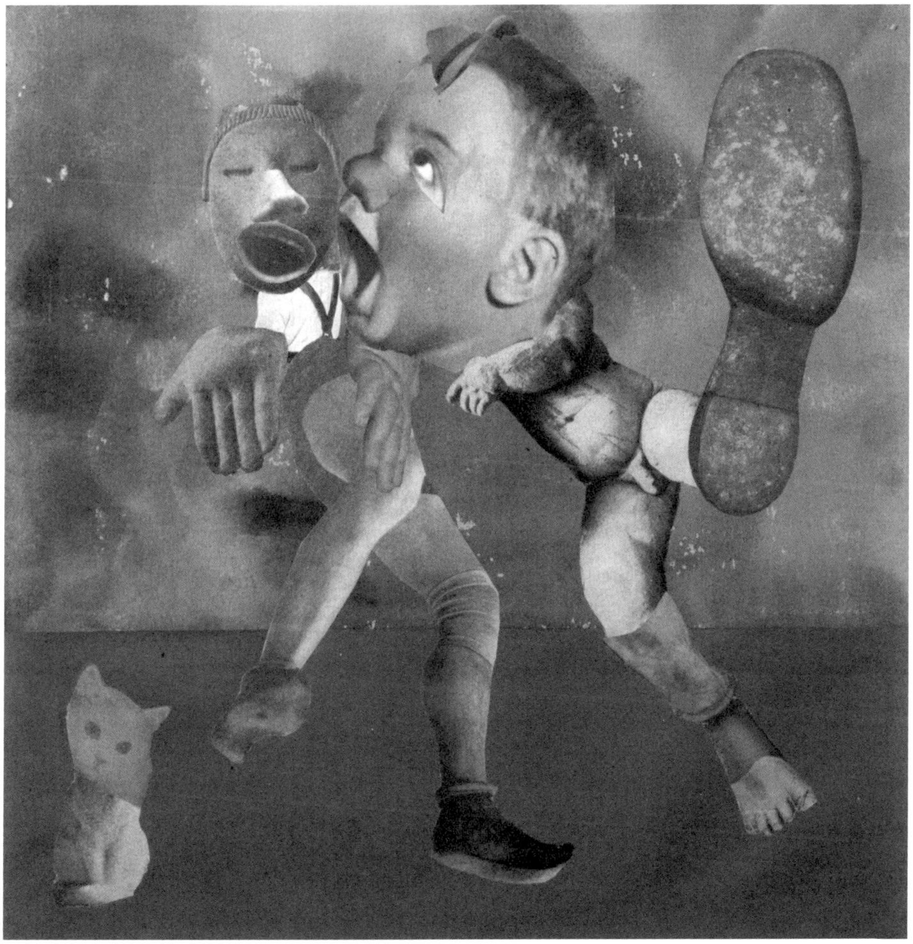

FIGURE 59. Hannah Höch, *Die ewigen Schuhplattler,* 1933, collage with watercolor, 25.2 × 26 cm. Collection Thomas Walther. Art © 2010 Artists Rights Society (ARS), New York/VG Bild-Kunst, Bonn. Photo: Hannah-Höch-Archiv, Berlinische Galerie, Landesmuseum für Moderne Kunst, Fotografie und Architektur.

young men in hats, wearing round wire-framed glasses, in front of whom Peter Lorre cowers in a pose drawn from his unforgettable performance as the child murderer in Fritz Lang's *M*. In the film, shots of ghetto residents are intercut with images of rats and cockroaches (*Ungeziefer,* or vermin, which is also Kafka's term for Gregor Samsa), and a photograph of Albert Einstein is presented as "The Jew Einstein." Hannah Höch offered a critique of the idea of the degenerate "eternal Jew" in her wittily subversive montage *Die ewigen Schuhplattler* of 1933 (fig. 59). Instead of a wandering, homeless Jew she presents these "eternal *Schuhplattler,*" Bavarian folk dancers: clumsy, off-balance, infantile—and tribally "primitive"—figures stomping out their folkish rhythms parody the idea of a reawakening and empowerment of Germany through the return to supposedly "healthy" and "rooted" indigenous Germanic cultural traditions that the

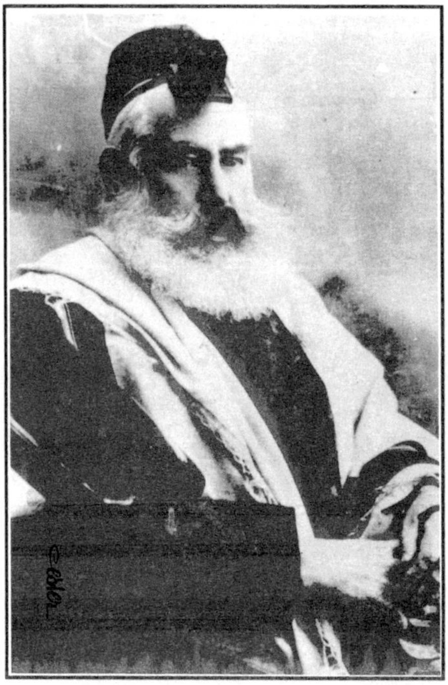

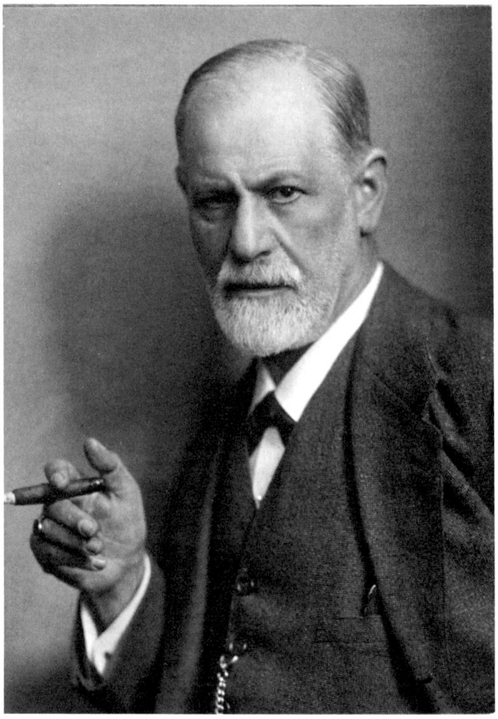

FIGURE 60. Polish postcard, Orthodox Jew, early twentieth century. Collection of the author.
FIGURE 61. Sigmund Freud, photographed by Max Halberstadt, ca. 1921. Library of Congress, Prints and Photographs Division, Sigmund Freud Collection.

Nazi Party preached in the 1920s and at precisely this time was ascending to political power to propagate.[124]

How, then, should we interpret Baumeister's privy councilor montage, *"Mann mit Spitzbart" RM 100 000.- (Portrait des Geheimrat Prof. Dr. Schamhaar, Sexualforscher)* (plate 5)? The name Prof. Dr. Schamhaar plays off the sarcastic titles applied to Adolf Ziegler by his opponents, *Reichsschamhaar-Maler* (Imperial pubic-hair painter) or *Meister des deutschen Schamhaars* (Master of German pubic hair). But there are other associations to the sexual researcher *(Sexualforscher)* Dr. Schamhaar (literally, "shame hair").

Germany's most famous early twentieth-century sex researchers were Jewish, including the "self-hating" Otto Weininger, whose best-selling 1903 study *Geschlecht und Charakter* (translated as *Sex and Character*) "went through twenty-five printings in almost as many years" and "doubled as an attack on two late nineteenth-century emancipation movements, those of Jews and women."[125] Magnus Hirschfeld founded the Institute for Sexual Research in Berlin and invented the term "transvestite." Hirschfeld, however, wore a mustache and no pointed beard, unlike Sigmund Freud. Freud's neatly trimmed, pointed beard certainly marks him generally as an intellectual but also as a secularized Jewish one—retaining the Jewish beard but also taming and grooming it

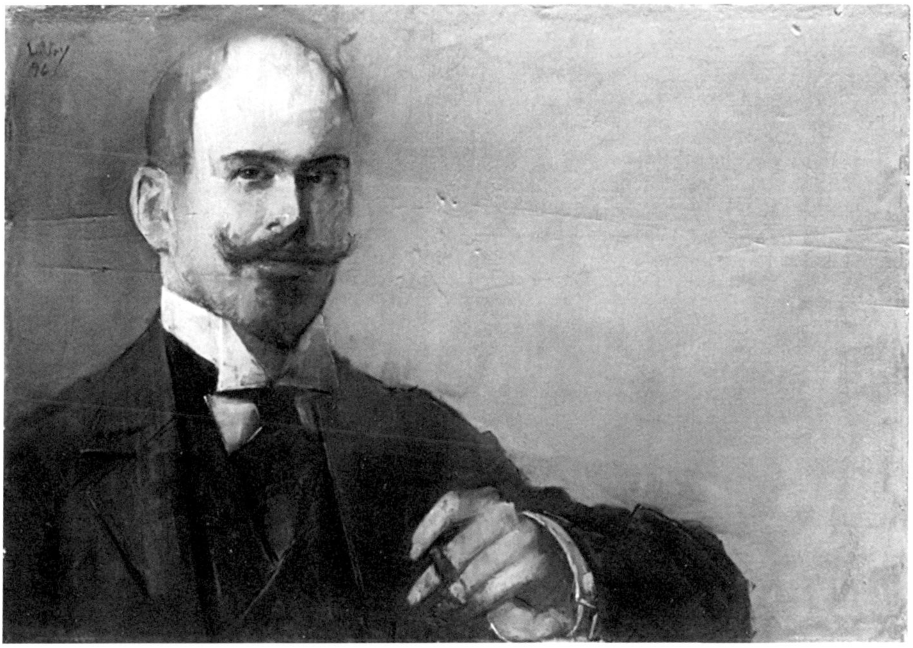

FIGURE 62. Lesser Ury, *Portrait of Walter Rathenau,* 1896, pastel on paper, 48 × 69.5 cm. Leo Baeck Institute, Jerusalem. Photo courtesy Leo Baeck Institute.

into a less specifically Jewish form (figs. 60–61). Many well-known photographs and painted portraits presented Walter Rathenau, the murdered Weimar finance minister (not a sexual researcher, but a privy council), as a similarly cultured and acculturated cigar-smoking German Jew (fig. 62).

Although there may well be unconscious connections to anti-Semitic imagery in Baumeister's anti-Nazi collages, other important anti-Nazi works that have long been admitted to his oeuvre confirm his conscious philo-Semitism. After his house in Stuttgart was bombed, as was the Wuppertal research institute, Baumeister moved with his family to the village of Urach in the Swabian Alps. After the war, in 1950, Baumeister was visited by Helmut Lehmann-Haupt, who was researching *Art under a Dictatorship,* his comparative study of German Nazi and Soviet Communist art policies. According to Lehmann-Haupt, Baumeister, "Germany's most widely recognized abstract painter," recounted to him: "In 1943 I had to stop painting altogether, because my next-door neighbor was an SS general. . . . It was then that I began to make illustrations, *Gilgamesh* and *Salome,* as a little personal revenge against this anti-Semitic business; finally Shakespeare's *Tempest.* They all were made in 1943, but published much later, after the war."[126] The *Salome* that he worked from was Oscar Wilde's version, the title role of which was closely identified with Sarah Bernhardt, "the original Salome."[127] Baumeister was certainly aware of the many "degenerate" connotations of these graphic works.

Illustration 31 of Baumeister's *Esther,* a drawing with a *frottage* ground created by

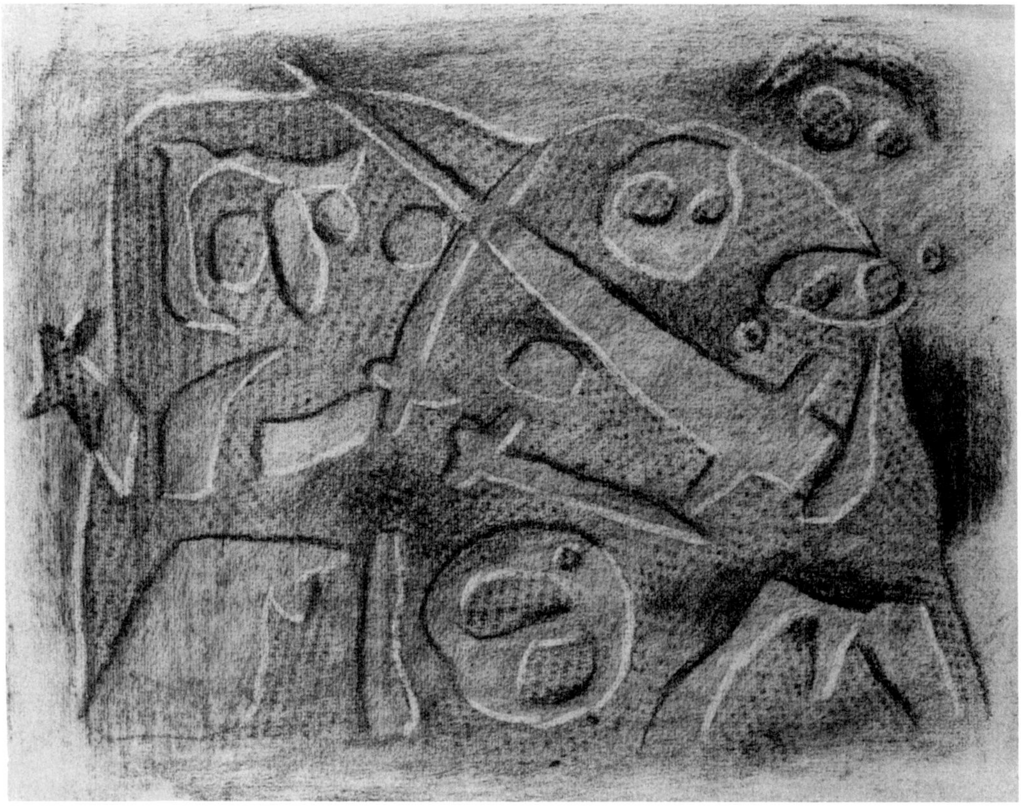

FIGURE 63. Willi Baumeister, *Esther 31*, 1943, charcoal on paper, 24 × 31.4 cm. Art © 2010 Artists Rights Society (ARS), New York/VG Bild-Kunst, Bonn. Photo: Willi Baumeister Archiv, Kunstmuseum Stuttgart.

rubbing the charcoal over paper laid on the rough floor boards of his Urach cabin, includes in the upper left a form unmistakably resembling Hebrew, a reversed letter *taw* (fig. 63). A form that could also be phallic or cigar-like (and, is a cigar ever just a cigar?) extends from the lower right to this character. It represents here a raised sword and wrenches us back to the deadly serious terms of the day, to "degeneracy" in the real, as opposed to symbolic or delusional, realms. This series was executed in June 1943, one month after the gassing of the last Jewish defenders of the Warsaw Ghetto on May 8. Baumeister appropriately devoted himself at this time to private study of and response to the Old Testament version of the story of Esther, the Jewish queen of the Persian King Ahasuerus, who with her uncle Mordecai saved the Persian Jews from the annihilation planned for them by Ahasuerus's vizier Haman, inspiring the Feast of Purim. The textual passage that inspired the drawing is attached to the back of the sheet: "Thus the Jews smote all their enemies with the stroke of the sword, and slaughter, and destruction, and did what they would unto those that hated them" (Esther 9:5, King James version). Here, too, Baumeister confronts Breker's *Avenger,* now arming Esther for this sword fight. She becomes a phallic Jewish mother, rising symbolically to the occasion.

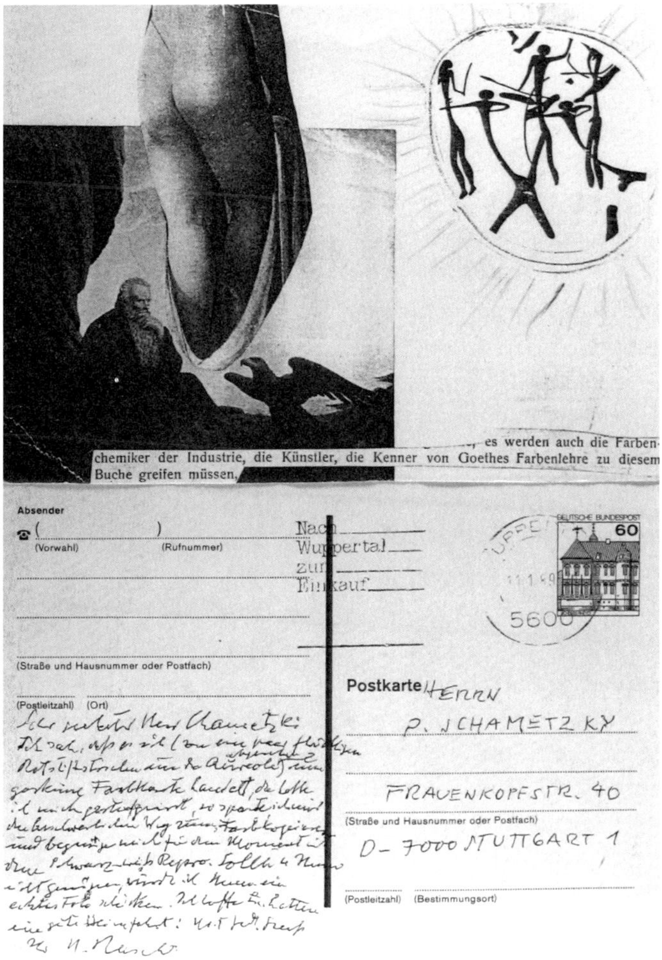

FIGURE 64. **Heinz Rasch, re-creation of Willi Baumeister's *Zarathustra* (1938), photocopy, 1989. Collection of the author. Photo: Visual Resources Collection, School of Art and Design, Southern Illinois University Carbondale.**

Postscript in the Present (Personal Correspondence): My *Zarathustra*

In the course of working on this chapter I came across a homemade postcard that I had not looked at in more than a decade (fig. 64). This postcard is a unique photocopied reproduction of the card that had gotten me started on my studies of Baumeister's anti-Nazi works, after I had come across some torn pages in his copy of the 1938 "Great German Art" exhibition catalogue and tracked down the missing images, Carl Schwalbach's *Zwei Mädchen* and Johann Benjamin Godron's *Zarathustra,* to a collaged card he had sent to Heinz Rasch during the Nazi period. In 1989 Rasch photocopied the original Baumeister collage *Zarathustra,* cut and pasted the copy to a commercial postcard, drew in orange pencil the lines emanating from the sun in the upper right, and sent it to me in Stuttgart. Rasch was in his late eighties when he made this altered replica of the card he had received almost fifty years earlier. I was around thirty when I received the replica and became another link in this chain of circulating objects and images and altering ideas.

I proceeded to send these images on, arguing that as political artworks they deserved space in the museum. However, as the cultural critic Andreas Huyssen has argued, the contemporary museum is no longer a static temple of culture endowing objects with fixed meanings that enshrine and ultimately entomb them. It is also a mass medium that attracts large and diverse audiences hungry for contact with objects and eager to formulate their own responses to them.[128] Beth Irwin Lewis, a scholar of German modernism, has studied the emergence of a mass audience for art in Germany. In a passage worth quoting at length, as it nicely sums up in figures and images the emerging phenomenon of mass artistic spectatorship that has continued to grow in the present, she writes that the audiences for modern art are "vilified by critics for having petit bourgeois philistine tastes":

> Accused by artists for laughing, even spitting on their work; bemoaned by reformers who wanted to refine and educate them, the public marched through the exhibitions. . . . 1.2 million at the Berlin Jubilee Exhibition of 1886; 3,000 viewed Fritz von Uhde's *Last Supper* in Munich during five days in 1887; 11,212 were members of the Hanover Art Society, whose seventy-third exhibition in 1905 drew more than 100,000 visitors; large audiences gathered in Dresden to hear Woldemar von Seidlitz lecture on modern art in 1897. . . . [T]he crowds in reality were old and young, silent and outspoken, elegant, respectable, absorbed, but equally noisy, unruly, disrespectful, bored, boisterous, overwhelmed, delighted, supercilious, laughing, proclaiming and eager to stop for coffee or beer.[129]

Like that of film, though to a lesser extent, modern and postmodern art spectatorship has been vast and varied. The audiences for art and film also overlap. "Film und Foto," the German Werkbund exhibition held in Baumeister's hometown of Stuttgart from May through July 1929, which including works by him and Hannah Höch, had by mid-June attracted some ten thousand visitors to look at new styles of photography and the relatively new art of photomontage, and to consider their often unconventional points of view and editing techniques in relationship to cinema by such filmmakers as Sergei Eisenstein, Dziga Vertov, Hans Richter, and Viking Eggling.[130] Attendance extended beyond Stuttgart's small avant-garde: the show attracted curious nonspecialist locals as well as out-of-town visitors.

The "Degenerate Art" exhibition drew an estimated two million visitors. This number included haters of modern art, who came to exercise the government's prescribed point of view, which was also being propagated in films, and schoolchildren and community groups bussed to the exhibition with no particular preformed opinions. But it also included "degenerate artists" such as Baumeister, colleagues such as Höch, and other supporters of modern art who came to pay their respects to the vilified works. One seventeen-year-old visitor with an interest in modern art, Peter Guenther, later became a scholar of German Expressionism in the United States.[131]

Museums today increasingly incorporate electronic media and interactive displays. Art objects are apprehended in relation to these new media, as they long have been in relation to film and other mass cultural forms. This seems to have heightened, rather than diminished, the allure of material objects. Even larger crowds than those described by Lewis throng museums today. The 2004 exhibition of works from the Museum of Modern Art at Berlin's New National Gallery that included Beckmann's *Departure* drew some 700,000 visitors, many of whom waited in line for up to four hours.[132] Why would this be the case, when images are readily and conveniently available on the Internet, for free and without a wait? It appears, as Huyssen argues, that "the new-found strength of the museum and the monument in the public sphere may have something to do with the fact that both offer something that the television screen denies: the material quality of the object."[133] We go to museums and look to objects for some material connection between our past and present. Objects themselves can also create such connections, becoming sites of memory. My *Zarathustra* card, not a museum object, still materializes histories that I have and by which I am touched.

5 Sculpture and Crime

Arno Breker

Arno Breker's name is often used to stand for Art in the Third Reich. Tradition supports this usage. For the National Socialists themselves Breker provided the perfect example of an artist employing his virtuoso talent solely to serve the regime and propagate its ideology. His career as a sculptor was singular: none of his colleagues attained such cultural political power, none received such gigantic commissions. —MAGDALENA BUSHART, "ARNO BREKER (GEB. 1900)—KUNSTPRODUZENT IM DIENST DER MACHT," *in SKULPTUR UND MACHT,* 1983, 155

At decisive moments in their careers, Arno Breker and Joseph Beuys rejected modernist sculptural autonomy and began creating objects and environments aspiring to integration into and transformation of the modern social and political world. Beginning in 1935–36, Breker's work in Nazi Germany sought to turn back the sculptural clock and reinvest this art form with monumental, permanent meaning derived from the object's awesome auratic presence in politically orchestrated public space (fig. 65). As I discuss in the following chapter, when Beuys submitted plans to the Auschwitz memorial competition in 1958 and a year later completed his only publicly commissioned war memorial, the Büderich *Memorial to the Victims of the World Wars* (see figs. 90–91), he rejected both the modernist belief in autonomy, which had been reestablished in postwar West German art by Baumeister and others, and Breker's antimodernist monumentality, which continued to inform memorial sculpture in postwar Germany (see fig. 93). Beuys's work revised Breker's legacy by offering materials and processes that maintained their humble and even crude and decidedly antimonumental identities, and environmental experiences bringing spectators into contact with these materials and their historical, discursive, and visceral associations. His later works organized materials into museum installations that interacted with and criticized their institutional settings but also used the museum's cultural authority to gain legitimacy as public statements.

Breker's work in Nazi Germany has been placed in the context of other figural sculptors of his generation, such as Wilhelm Lehmbruck and Georg Kolbe, who developed Adolf von Hildebrand's late nineteenth-century sculptural principles.[1] However, there has been little to no analysis of Breker's possible influence on the subsequent genera-

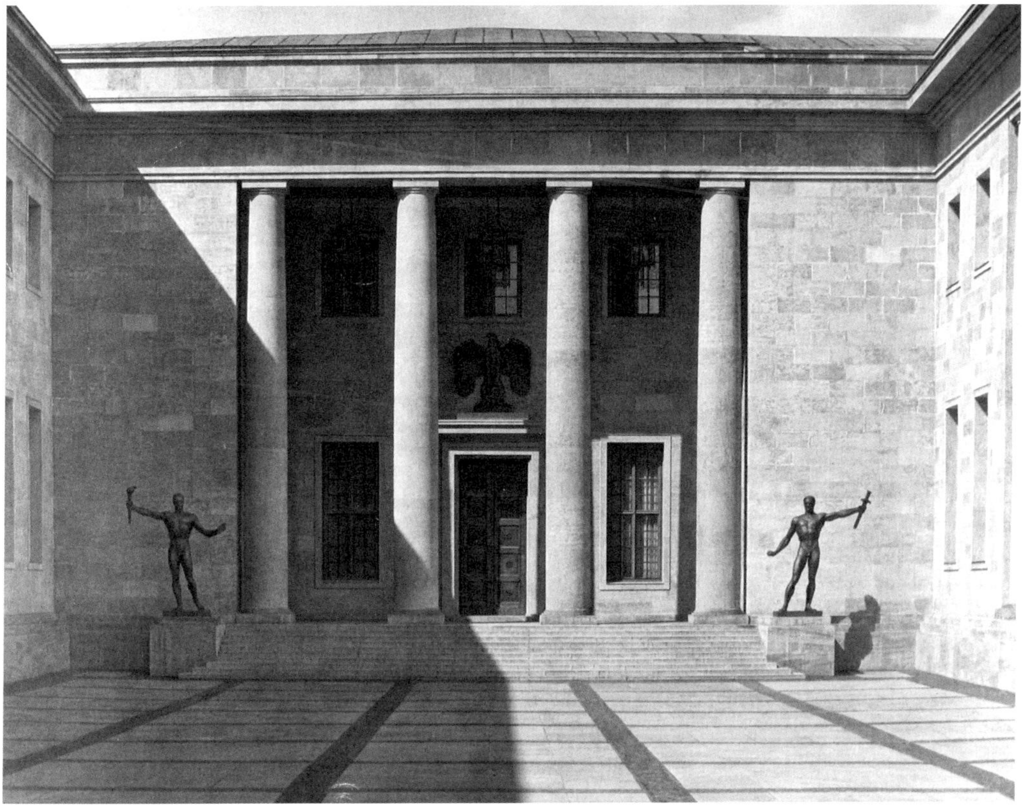

FIGURE 65. Entrance to Albert Speer's Reichs Chancellery with Arno Breker's *The Party* and *The Army,* 1939. From *Die Neue Reichskanzlei, Architekt Albert Speer,* edited by Franz Eber (Munich: Zentralverwaltung der NSDAP, 1940). Art © 2010 Artists Rights Society (ARS), New York, VG-Bildkunst, Bonn. Photo: Visual Resources Collection, School of Art and Design, Southern Illinois University Carbondale.

tion of German artists, including Beuys. Breker provided Beuys with an object lesson in sculptural presentation and an abject lesson in personal presentation, both of which were of fundamental historiographic significance in the first decades of post-Nazi German history and art history. Arno Breker's art provided Beuys a negative example to react against in his sculptural practice, and his career provided a cautionary tale motivating him to exert control over his public image and the presentation of his work. Beuys's intense confrontation with sculptural materials and formats helped shift the terrain of sculpture in Germany and beyond.[2]

Breker's Body Politics

Western sculpture, from the ancient Greeks to the moderns, has focused on the human body. Breker's Rodinesque *Torso of a Seated Man* of 1928 and Beuys's surreal *Chair with Fat* of 1964 (fig. 66) continue this tradition.[3] Breker's work, executed in plaster, consists

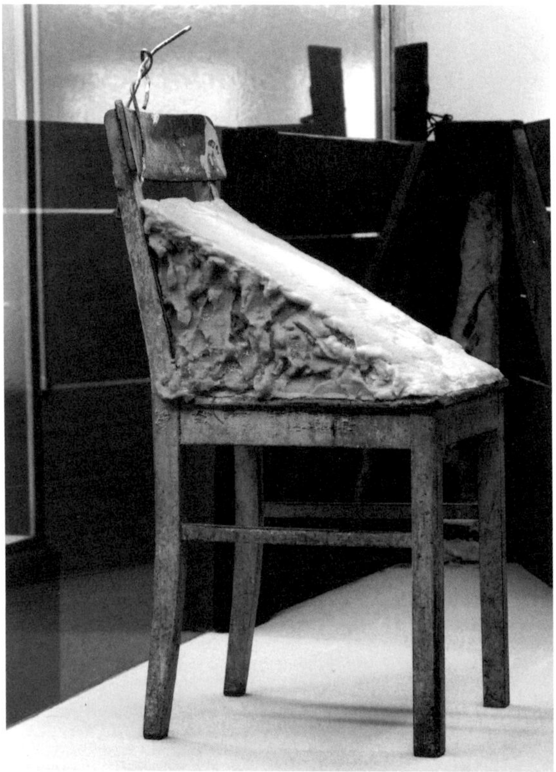

FIGURE 66. Joseph Beuys, *Chair with Fat,* 1964, wooden chair with fat, 94.5 × 41.6 × 47.5 cm. Hessisches Landesmuseum Darmstadt. Art © 2010 Artists Rights Society (ARS), New York/VG Bild-Kunst, Bonn. Photo: Hessisches Landesmuseum Darmstadt.

of a straight-backed, headless, and armless figure seated on a block of plaster with legs extended but truncated—one just below the bent knee, the other above. For the artist later known for his highly finished, smoothly packaged, muscular male figures, the mottled surface of this partial body seems incongruous, but it provides a glimpse into Breker's pre-Nazi, moderately modernist production.

Breker depicts and Beuys implies the body. Both employ modernist synecdoche, allowing the part to speak for the whole. The artist's modeling of soft material also remains visible: the process of making is inscribed into the finished object, a characteristic feature of modernist sculpture. By retaining evidence of the sculptor's touch they imply the continued presence of the body of the artist, and invite the spectator also to imagine engaging with the object physically and temporally.

In the late nineteenth and early twentieth centuries, Rodin broke with Classical finish and created a sculptural language that rephrased the traditional three-dimensional processes of carving, modeling, and casting.[4] He exploited studio accidents and mistakes to create powerful metaphors and heighten awareness of the intrinsic qualities of specific materials. Moved by the modern fragments of ancient sculpture and the unfinished works of Michelangelo, Rodin "strongly misread" these shattered remains of Classicism. Time had taken a toll on those objects; Rodin renewed sculpture by incorporating time into his. The art historian and theorist Rosalind Krauss asserts that "Rodin forces the viewer to acknowledge the work as a result of a process, an act that has shaped the figure over time. . . . [M]eaning does not precede experience but occurs in the process of experience itself."[5] The modern, post-Rodin sculptural object reaches back to incorporate the duration of its creation into its physical appearance. Its meaning is also contingent on the time spent and position taken by the viewer. Three-dimensional matter comes to embody a state of being as perpetual process, a metaphor for life itself.

Sympathetic interpreters identify Breker's viewing of Rodin's *Age of Brass* at the Düsseldorf Museum around 1915 as a formative experience, leading to his subsequent reading of the poet Rainer Maria Rilke's Rodin study of 1919.[6] From 1927 to 1934 Breker lived mainly in Paris and became well acquainted with Rodin's work. Breker's belated, neo-modern sculptures of the late 1920s, such as *Torso of a Seated Man,* mimic Rodin and so present a set of conceptual contradictions: studied spontaneity, derivative personal expression, calculated chance.

Arno Breker was born in the Rhineland town of Elberfeld, near Düsseldorf, son of a stoneworker whose business he ran during his father's service in World War I. From his return to Germany from France in December 1933 to the fall of the Third Reich in 1945, he ascended to become the Nazi leadership's most celebrated and patronized sculptor. Beginning in 1936, Breker's work represented Nazi ideology, providing highly crafted objects cultishly venerating its leaders and aggressively promoting its "racially" determined conceptions of bodily perfection. He worked closely with the architect Albert Speer in his plans to reconstruct Berlin as "Germania," the grandiose planned capital of the Third Reich, and enjoyed direct access to and influence on Hitler himself: in 1940 he accompanied Hitler on his tour of conquered Paris; in 1944 his bust of the Führer that was included in the postcard series "German Artists and the SS" also served as the catalogue frontispiece to his exhibition at the Garnisonmuseum in Potsdam (fig. 67). This odious legacy has forever tainted all his works—including works with no direct connection to the Nazi period, such as *Torso of a Seated Man.*

Breker created *Torso of a Seated Man* in the year of the first substantial critical text on his work, written by the Jewish ex-Dadaist Louise Straus-Ernst and published in the Munich-based art magazine *Die Kunst für Alle.*[7] For Straus-Ernst, Breker presented the very model of the virtuous artist, conscious of the limits and aware of the potential of his medium, and attentive to both tradition and contemporary innovations. Breker's portrait busts, in Straus-Ernst's opinion, revitalized a format neglected by modern sculptors, striking a balance between attention to facial details evoking the individual's personality and the preservation of a satisfyingly volumetric, sculptural whole (fig. 68). She described Breker's figuration as part of the general turn from "Expressionist exaggeration" but differentiated it from "bland Naturalism." Borrowing from the sculptural theories of Adolf von Hildebrandt, she observed that sculptural objects offer the viewer multiple points of view and so create a reality distinct from the rest of the world. Moving

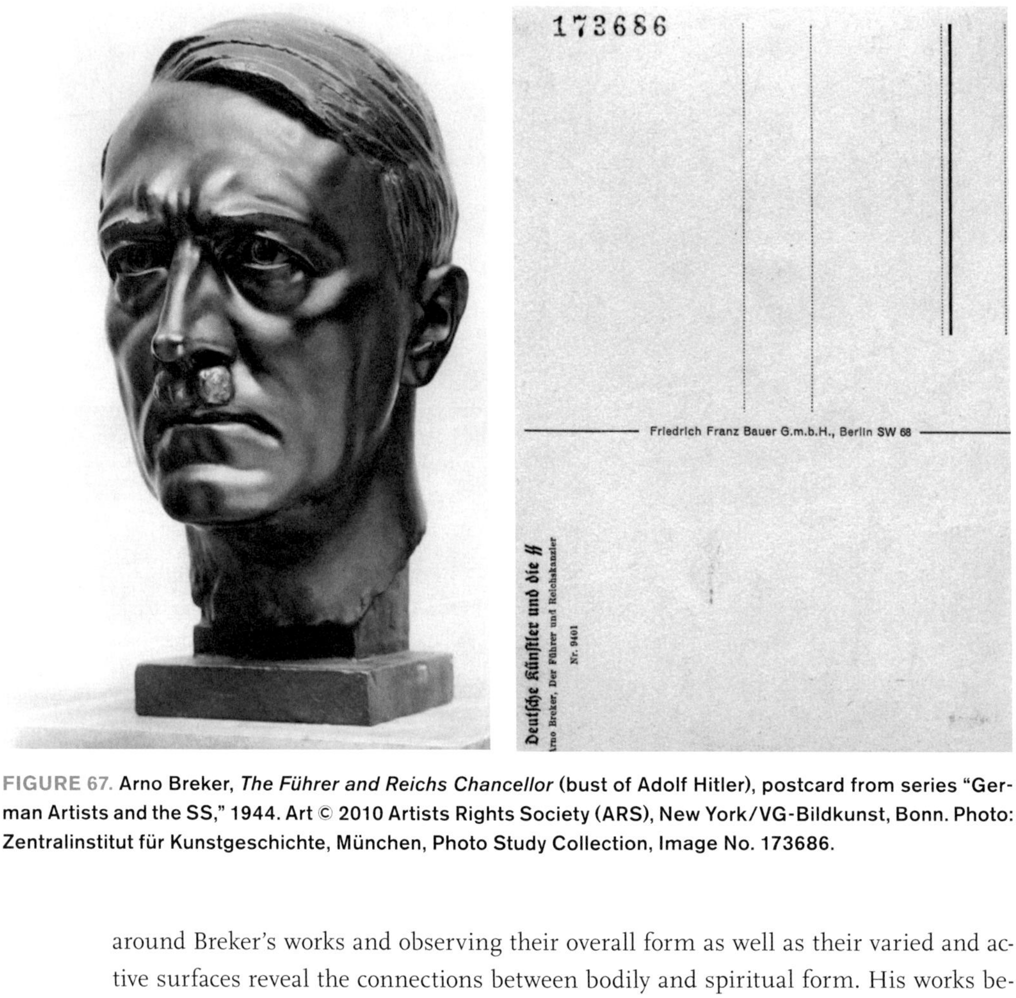

FIGURE 67. Arno Breker, *The Führer and Reichs Chancellor* (bust of Adolf Hitler), postcard from series "German Artists and the SS," 1944. Art © 2010 Artists Rights Society (ARS), New York/VG-Bildkunst, Bonn. Photo: Zentralinstitut für Kunstgeschichte, München, Photo Study Collection, Image No. 173686.

around Breker's works and observing their overall form as well as their varied and active surfaces reveal the connections between bodily and spiritual form. His works betray a "passionate almost dogged struggle with form—through strong and always tangible tension they offer incredible variety."[8] While Breker had enjoyed earlier success, as in his 1926 public commissions for a war memorial in the village of Budberg and for a reclining female figure in Düsseldorf's Rhine Park, "he is not a man for whom such early successes can prove damaging . . . for solving one problem presents for him only the opportunity to move on to new and more challenging things."

Straus-Ernst described and praised Breker's works of his Parisian period in both general terms and on specific points that foreshadow the appreciations of him and his work that would be repeated by Nazi "art commentators" discussing his National Socialist commissions. However positive Straus-Ernst's review, she obviously saw no reason to heap the kind of fulsome praise on him that began in the Nazi period, when he began to be compared with Michelangelo—nonsense of the kind that continues today among his apologists. In 1938, after Breker had made his fateful transition to more finished, monumental, and Classical works, a writer whose overall assessment of Breker laid down

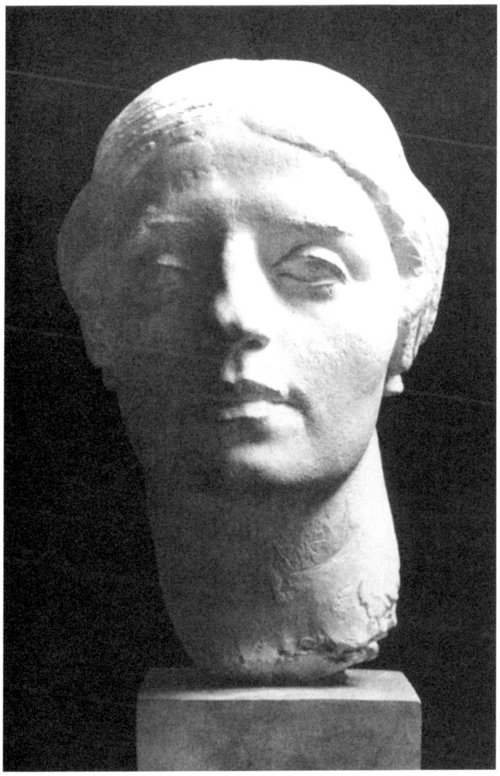

FIGURE 68. Arno Breker, *Portrait Bust of a Greek Woman*, ca. 1926. From Louise Straus-Ernst, "Der Bildhauer Arno Breker," *Die Kunst für Alle* 44 (1928–29): 374. F. Bruckmann A.G., Munich. Art © 2010 Artists Rights Society (ARS), New York/VG-Bildkunst, Bonn. Photo: Visual Resources Collection, SoAD, Southern Illinois University Carbondale.

the main guidelines that his contemporary supporters continue to follow claimed that Breker "saw, used, and overcame" Rodin.[9] Louise Straus-Ernst was by this time in exile in France—from which she would be deported to her murder at Auschwitz in 1944.[10]

Breker's first government sculptural commissions in the Third Reich were for the Berlin Finance Ministry in 1935, followed by figures of athletes for the 1936 Olympic complex (fig. 69), where his works triumphed over other figurative sculpture by Karl Albiker, Fritz Klimsch, Georg Kolbe, Josef Thorak, Joseph Wackerle, and Adolf Wamper, to become the signature works of Third Reich sculpture and Hitler's favorites.[11] Rather than accommodating his aesthetic to Nazi ideology, as some commentators contend, Breker in fact formulated a visual and material ideology of the object and of the body that informed Hitler at precisely the moment he intervened in Nazi artistic policy, from his speech on art at the party's meeting on cultural policy in late 1934 to the concurrent openings of the first "Great German Art" and "Degenerate Art" exhibitions in Munich in 1937.[12] After initial reluctance, Breker joined the party in a leadership position in 1937, after which, according to the leading American historian of the Nazi art system and the individuals involved in it, Jonathan Petropoulos, "he enjoyed a grand lifestyle."[13]

Breker courted power and reaped immense financial profit during the Nazi period.[14] Petropoulos outlines Breker's career and what he describes as a "gradual transition"

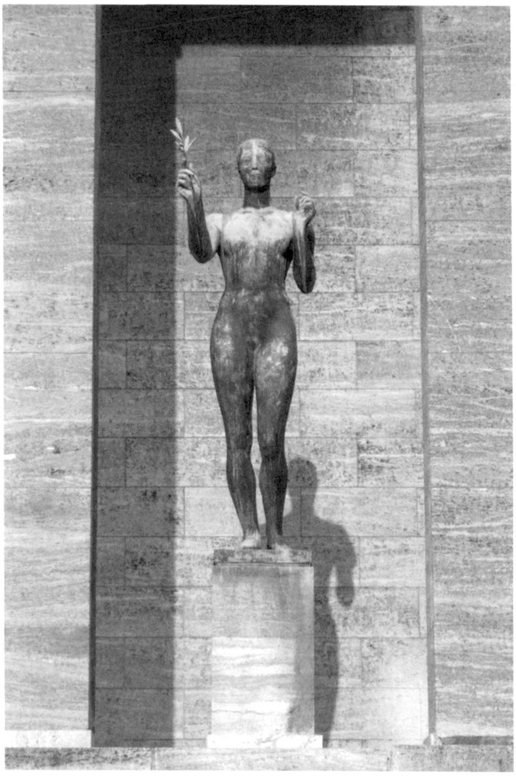

FIGURE 69. Arno Breker, *Die Siegerin* (The female victor), 1936, bronze. Reichssportfeld, Berlin. Art © 2010 Artists Rights Society (ARS), New York/VG-Bildkunst, Bonn. Photo: Marc Wellmann.

from a middle-of-the-road modernist to the most favored and powerful Nazi sculptor.[15] While he probably exploited forced laborers in the vast sculptural workshops placed at his disposal in Wriezen, northeast of Berlin, there is also evidence that Breker intervened on behalf of some persecuted artists and intellectuals. His personal intervention is credited with saving publisher Peter Suhrkamp's life following the attempt to kill Hitler in July 1944.[16] Petropoulos, though, debunks Breker's later statements and those of his supporters that he was active only as a rather innocent, naive artist in service to the state. In denazification terms his career advancement would seem to have made him a *Nutzniesser* (beneficiary) of the Nazi system, though he emerged from his 1948 investigation and trial with the more moderate categorization of *Mitläufer* (fellow traveler). He was fined one hundred marks and court costs for his activities and allowed to resume his career.[17]

Wolfgang Fritz Haug has described Breker's muscular male figures as "the body of a state-regulated self-control, of an imperialistic mechanism," the sculptural equivalent of the "armored bodies" that the reactionary modernist writer Ernst Jünger had called for in response to World War I's "storm of steel."[18] The male figures Breker produced were uniformly naked: their physiques act as their uniforms. While the men have exceptionally narrow hips, which taper in pronounced triangular form to their broad shoulders, female figures such as *Die Siegerin* (The female victor, 1936, fig. 69) deviate less from their Classical prototypes, so that even a work portraying an athletic woman and modeled after an actual athlete is presented with the broad hips, fleshy thighs, and conical breasts of a Greco-Roman Venus figure.[19] As with the male figures, the faces depart from portraiture and instead bear vaguely Classical, blank expressions topped by stylized, pseudo-Classical hair. Both male and female figures have unusually long necks and small heads, emphasizing them as portraits of the body. Breker later declared that his dedication to portray what he considered beautiful human bodies was beyond all ideology:

> I have never intended to glorify any system of government through my artistic work. I also have no intention of doing so in the future. If I glorify anything, it is beauty. The beauty of the human being, the beauty of the human body. . . . The central motif of my work has always been the human being. . . . I have striven for the ideal, humane image of mankind. Even political developments have not discouraged me from pursuing that goal. That is also true of the period of the *Third Reich*, during which I received numerous commissions dealing with the redesigning of Berlin. . . . No one who looks at my artistic work and judges it objectively can in good conscience suspect that it served to promote fascist ideology. The depiction of the human image in my way of thinking is a clear denial of everything inhuman.[20]

Contrary to his claims, Breker's aesthetic, as it developed from 1936 on, provided the visual and material embodiment of certain aspects of Nazi ideology extremely well, indeed better than that of his artistic rivals. Prior to the 1936 Olympics, for instance, Hitler favored Thorak's massive, blocky, low-definition muscle men.[21] Breker's males are generally smoother, sleeker, with body parts more clearly articulated. Significantly, Breker always stressed that his figures' bodies were modeled from life. Thorak modeled his *Boxer*, placed outside the swimming stadium at the Olympic complex, on the one-time champion Max Schmeling.[22] However, the piece's gargantuan scale and generalized physique distances it from Schmeling's actual body, while the sloping forehead, protruding eyebrows, and flattened boxer's nose resemble Schmeling's actual facial features too much to present an Aryan ideal (fig. 57). Observing the athletes training for the Olympic Games, Breker was particularly taken by decathlete Gustav Stührk's physique and that of a woman javelin thrower. Stührk continued to model for Breker, who had a studio photograph made of this relationship in preparation for the 1939 sculpture *The Herald* (fig. 70). The poses struck by the allegorical figures "The Party" and "The Army" flanking the entrance to Hitler's new chancellery building, designed by Speer in 1938, seem also to derive from these modeling sessions (fig. 71).[23] Breker's works thus formed the sculptural, material proof of Hitler's verbal assurances to the German people that they themselves were attaining a physical perfection that mirrored their cleansed inner body politics in a way not seen since Classical antiquity. Hitler intoned in 1938: "*The new era of today develops a new type of person*. Never has humanity looked or felt more like antiquity than today. Sport, competitions, contests steel millions of

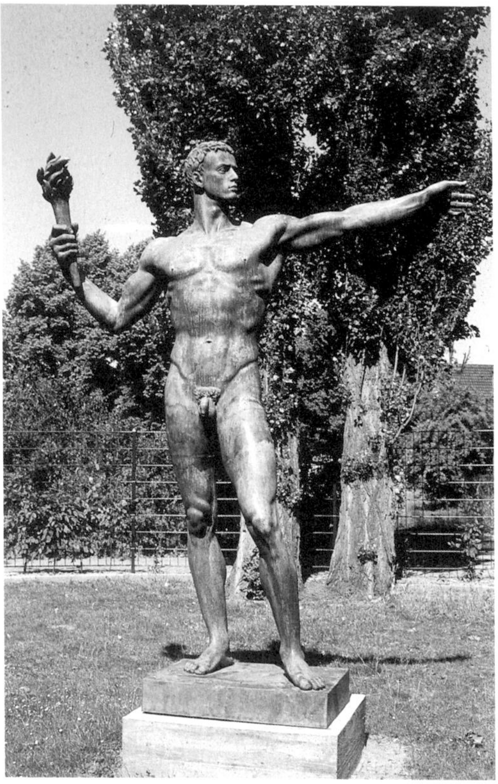

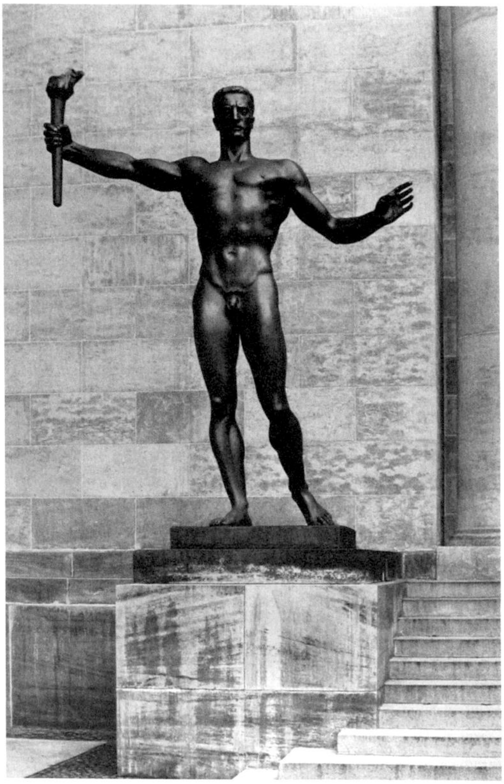

FIGURE 70. Arno Breker, *The Herald,* 1939, bronze. Museum Europäische Kunst, Schloss Nörvenich, Germany, 1993. Art © 2010 Artists Rights Society (ARS), New York/VG-Bildkunst, Bonn. Photo: Author. FIGURE 71. Arno Breker, *The Party,* 1939, bronze. Reichs Chancellery, Berlin. From *Die Neue Reichskanzlei, Architekt Albert Speer,* edited by Franz Eber (Munich: Zentralverwaltung de NSDAP, 1940). Art © 2010 Artists Rights Society (ARS), New York/VG-Bildkunst, Bonn. Photo: Visual Resources Collection, School of Art and Design, Southern Illinois University Carbondale.

young bodies and display to us more and more a form and posture that has not been seen in thousands of years, that have hardly been imagined. . . . This human form we first saw last year in the Olympic Games."[24] Breker's work, along with Leni Riefenstahl's documentary and propaganda film *Olympia,* rather than accommodating themselves to conceptions already being propounded by the Nazi leadership, actually provided Hitler with clear visual examples of the usefulness and potential appeal of Classicism at the critical moment when he was formulating, articulating, and preparing to enact a cultural policy in the visual arts. That Breker's bodies and Olympic athletes actually reflected a current trend among the "aryanizing" German population provided a justification for a cultural policy in the visual arts that rejected more obviously Germanic styles.

In his memoirs Breker recounts strolling over the grounds of the Olympic stadium with Hitler and stopping before one of his works. " 'You work from antiquity,' Hitler

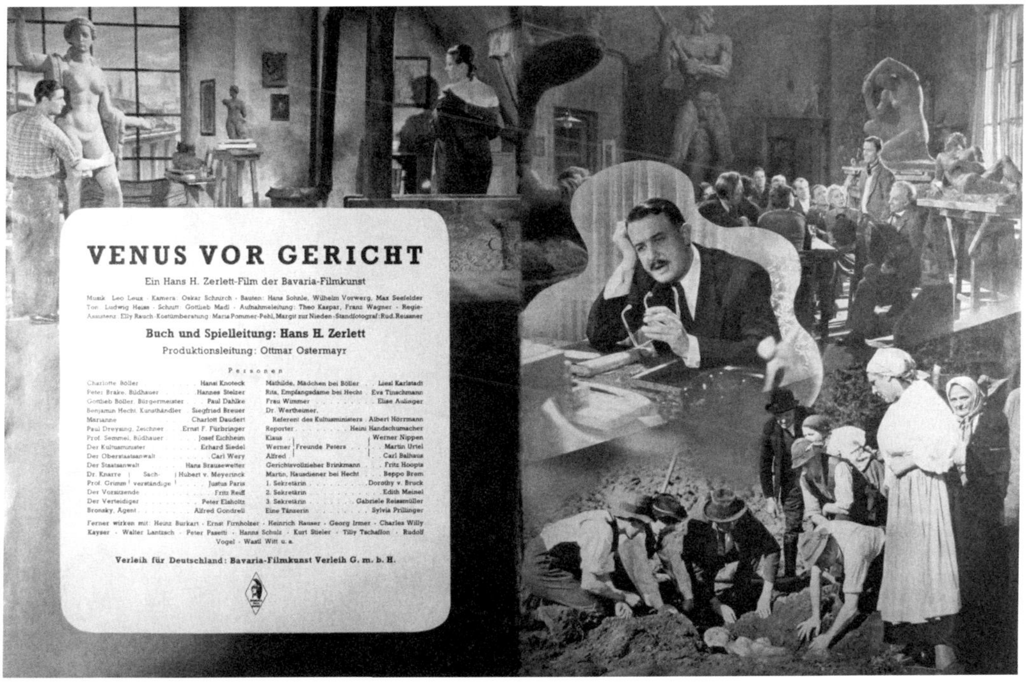

FIGURE 72. **Production information for and montage of images from *Venus vor Gericht,* from *Illustrierter Film-Kurier,* no. 3214 (Berlin-Wilmersdorf: Verlag Vereinigte Verlagsgesellschaften Franke and Co., KG, 1941), showing Peter Brake working from the model (top left), Benjamin Hecht in his gallery office (center), and the discovery of "Venus of the Fields" (bottom right). Courtesy Verlag für Filmschriften, Christian Unucka, 85241 Hebertshausen, www.unucka.de. Photo: Visual Resources Collection, School of Art and Design, Southern Illinois University Carbondale.**

asserted; I contradicted him: 'No, *mein Führer,* both my bronzes in the Imperial Sports Field are portraits of our outstanding athletes.' "[25] While he claims to have thus offended the Führer and to have received no further commissions until 1938, it appears more likely, given the statements in Hitler's speeches of 1938, that Breker was instrumental in providing him with a key idea: the promotion of Breker's Germano-neo-Neo-Classical sculpture would help legitimate Hitler's imperial pretensions by virtue of its historical pedigree in the Greco-Roman empires, while his insistence that Breker worked from life could appeal to the contemporary populaces' narcissistic desire to imagine themselves literal embodiments of an age of renewal and progress.

A later and less well-known film than Riefenstahl's *Olympia* provides even greater insight into the Nazi application of Breker's formulation that German virtue could be embodied by classicizing sculptures modeled directly from contemporary Germans. In 1941 the Bavaria-Filmkunst studio released the moralizing, romantic, and propagandistic comedy *Venus vor Gericht* (Venus on trial, fig. 72), directed by Hans Zerlett, a friend of the Nazi official Hans Hinkel.[26]

The film is set in 1930. The hero is a young sculptor in the Classical tradition, Peter

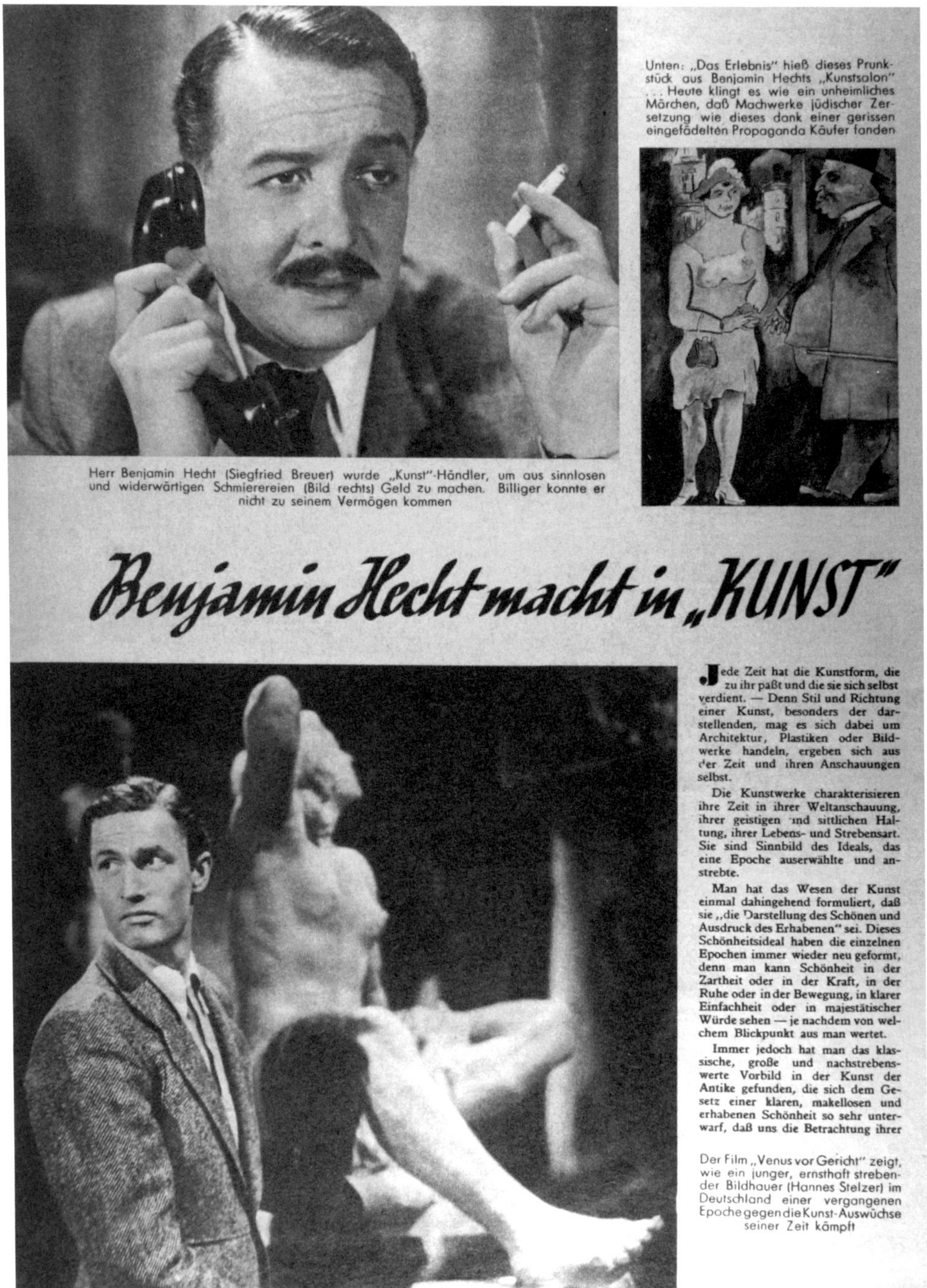

Unten: „Das Erlebnis" hieß dieses Prunkstück aus Benjamin Hechts „Kunstsalon" . . . Heute klingt es wie ein unheimliches Märchen, daß Machwerke jüdischer Zersetzung wie dieses dank einer gerissen eingefädelten Propaganda Käufer fanden

Herr Benjamin Hecht (Siegfried Breuer) wurde „Kunst"-Händler, um aus sinnlosen und widerwärtigen Schmierereien (Bild rechts) Geld zu machen. Billiger konnte er nicht zu seinem Vermögen kommen

Benjamin Hecht macht in „KUNST"

Jede Zeit hat die Kunstform, die zu ihr paßt und die sie sich selbst verdient. — Denn Stil und Richtung einer Kunst, besonders der darstellenden, mag es sich dabei um Architektur, Plastiken oder Bildwerke handeln, ergeben sich aus der Zeit und ihren Anschauungen selbst.

Die Kunstwerke charakterisieren ihre Zeit in ihrer Weltanschauung, ihrer geistigen und sittlichen Haltung, ihrer Lebens- und Strebensart. Sie sind Sinnbild des Ideals, das eine Epoche auserwählte und anstrebte.

Man hat das Wesen der Kunst einmal dahingehend formuliert, daß sie „die Darstellung des Schönen und Ausdruck des Erhabenen" sei. Dieses Schönheitsideal haben die einzelnen Epochen immer wieder neu geformt, denn man kann Schönheit in der Zartheit oder in der Kraft, in der Ruhe oder in der Bewegung, in klarer Einfachheit oder in majestätischer Würde sehen — je nachdem von welchem Blickpunkt aus man wertet.

Immer jedoch hat man das klassische, große und nachstrebenswerte Vorbild in der Kunst der Antike gefunden, die sich dem Gesetz einer klaren, makellosen und erhabenen Schönheit so sehr unterwarf, daß uns die Betrachtung ihrer

Der Film „Venus vor Gericht" zeigt, wie ein junger, ernsthaft strebender Bildhauer (Hannes Stelzer) im Deutschland einer vergangenen Epoche gegen die Kunst-Auswüchse seiner Zeit kämpft

FIGURE 73. Images from *Venus vor Gericht:* (top left) Siegfried Breuer as art dealer Benjamin Hecht; (top right) a work of "degenerate art" in Hecht's gallery, done in the style of George Grosz and captioned "a concoction of Jewish corruption"; (bottom) Hannes Stelzer as Peter Brake with one of his sculptures. From Ellie Tschauner, "Benjamin Hecht macht in 'Kunst,'" *Filmwelt: Das Film- und Foto-Magazin* (Berlin) 16 (18 April 1941): 410. Photo: Visual Resources Collection, School of Art and Design, Southern Illinois University Carbondale.

Brake, played by Hannes Stelzer (fig. 73). Brake (pronounced in German, like Breker, in two syllables: Bra-ke) seems to be based on Breker, except in one detail: in 1930 he is already a committed Nazi. Brake's commitment to the National Socialist cause is largely aesthetic and moral. Though he and the film are surely anti-Semitic, they are so because Jews control the art world and promote bad, "degenerate" art. Though Brake and his Nazi friends are willing to fight in the defense of women's, the party's, and the nation's honor, they are not overly aggressive or militarist. The film presents Brake's ideological position to be belief in beauty and truth—the same position Breker claimed for himself to his death.

The film begins with Bavarian farmers digging in their fields and unearthing a Classical torso (fig. 72). The torso comes to Berlin and is acquired by the unctuous Jewish art dealer Benjamin Hecht—whose name links him to Dadaism through the American screenwriter of the same name, a famous figure in the world of film by this time—who otherwise deals in modern, "degenerate" art. And, indeed, he does: a remarkable historical aspect of the film is that Hecht's gallery displays actual modern artworks seized by the Nazis, almost all of which are now lost.[27] After an opening shot of the Venus torso, the next work of art shown is Ernst Ludwig Kirchner's lost sculpture *The Couple,* in the window of Hecht's gallery (fig. 74). Inside the gallery are works by Paul Kleinschmidt (figs. 75–76), Richard Haizmann's *Elephant,* a painting with some resemblance to a George Grosz (see fig. 73), a sculpture by Erich Heckel, and two works that were shown on the "Dada Wall" in the "Degenerate Art" exhibition in Munich in 1937 (fig. 17): Wassily Kandinsky's *Two Kinds of Red* of 1916 (fig. 77), which had been seized from the National Gallery in Berlin, and Margarete Moll's *Female Figure,* from the municipal museum in Breslau.[28] While the "Degenerate Art" exhibition was a blockbuster show, a film such as *Venus vor Gericht* could dramatize and romanticize its message and project it to a mass audience on screens in cities and towns across Germany. It thus formed one more cog in the Nazi's "degenerate art" propaganda machine, which in addition to numerous exhibitions, books, articles, speeches, and newsreels also included this piece of popular entertainment; the film was banned by American officials from display in postwar Germany.

Hecht, more *Kaufmann,* or merchant, than true art lover, will deal anything. He sells the *Venus* to the Berlin National Gallery. Effeminate experts declare it to be a work of Praxiteles brought to German soil by the Roman legions. The *Venus of the Fields* becomes a sensation, the subject of cabaret reviews and innumerable mechanical reproductions. By this time Brake, now living as a struggling artist in Berlin, has recognized it as a work he created years before and then buried to protect the reputation of his nude model. When he comes forward to reveal the truth, Hecht and the district attorney concoct a plan to place him on trial for slander. Brake finally tracks down the model, Charlotte Böller, finding her now the wife of an older, fat, petty, immoral, anti-Nazi mayor of a small town in Upper Franconia. The handsome young couple's mutual attraction is quickly apparent, but Brake demurs from telling her the reason for his visit, realizing

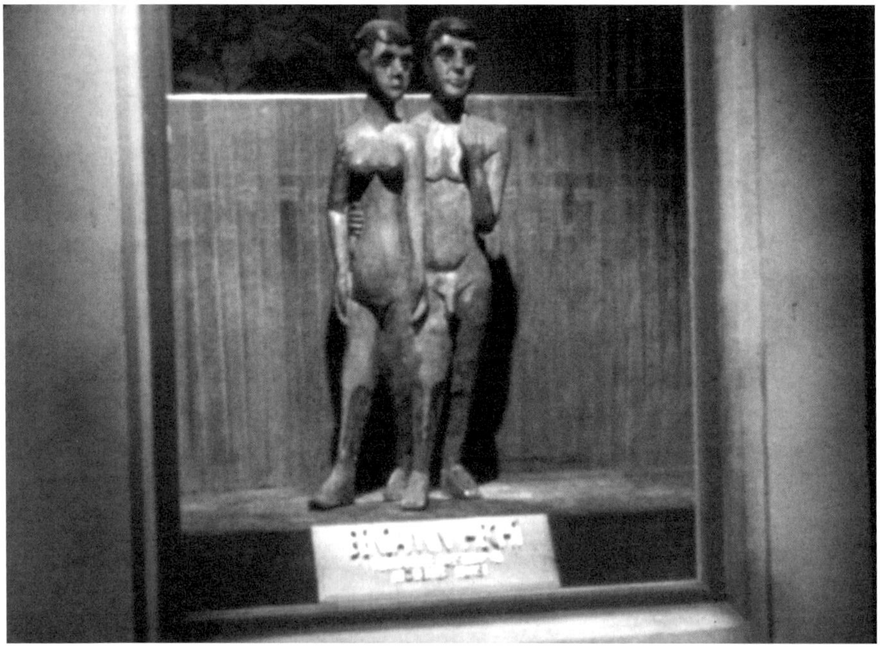

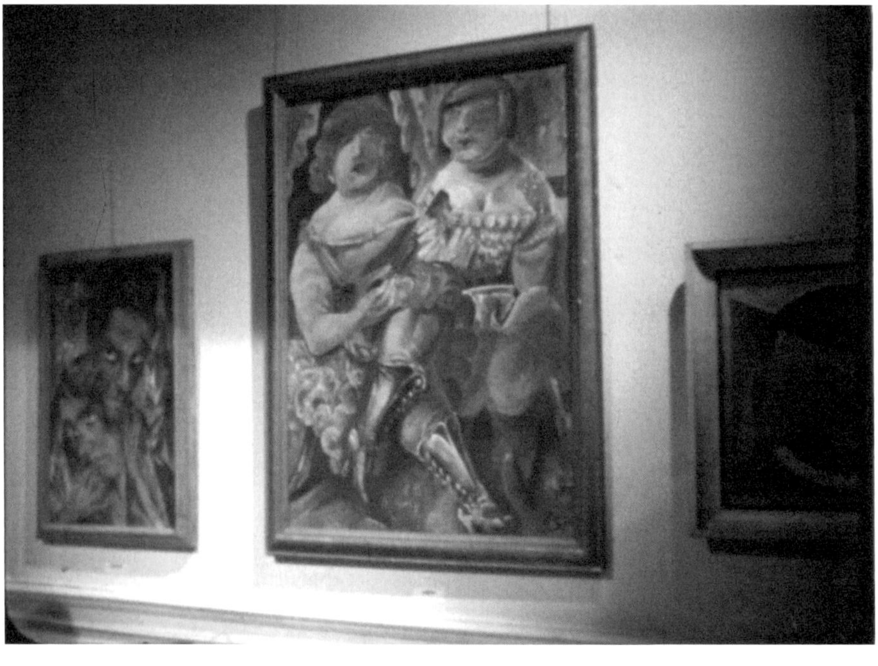

FIGURE 74. Captured frame from *Venus vor Gericht* with Ernst Ludwig Kirchner's *The Couple,* now lost. Photo © Friedrich Murnau Stiftung. FIGURE 75. Captured frame from *Venus vor Gericht* with Paul Kleinschmidt's *Duet in the North Café,* formerly in Stuttgart State Gallery, now lost. Photo © Friedrich Murnau Stiftung.

Bildwerke heute noch beinah andächtig zu stimmen vermag. Hier erreicht der künstlerische Ausdruck einen Gipfelpunkt der Vollendung. — Immer haben die Künstler aus diesen Schöpfungen gelernt und Anregungen empfangen.

Und es erscheint uns heute nahezu unfaßbar, daß es überhaupt möglich war, daß gewisse Schichten einer Zeit den Sinn ihrer „Kunst" genau in das krasseste Gegenteil verbiegen und vergewaltigen konnten: sie zur Verkörperung des Abstoßend-Häßlichen, Grauenvollen zu machen.

Menschen mit grasgrünen Gesichtern, zinnoberroten Augenhöhlen, dunkelblauem Mund und violetten Haaren, zu entstellender Formlosigkeit verurteilt — Frauenfiguren aus unförmigen Klumpen gemacht, menschenunwürdig gedrungen oder statt der Verkürzung wie ein Totenskelett mager und überdehnt. Als Gegensatz zu Schönheit und Sinn eine ins Maßlose gesteigerte Häßlichkeit und eine an Ausgeburten des Wahnsinns grenzende Sinnlosigkeit.

Das heißt: auch in dieser scheinbaren Sinnlosigkeit der „entarteten Kunst" war messerscharf ein Sinn und ein Zweck eingefangen: die Aufgabe der Zersetzung, der Zerstörung jedes ethischen Willens, der Vernichtung. In dieser Auflösung suchte der jüdisch-liberalistische Zeitgeist seinen Vorteil und seine Stärkung, er benutzte sie als eine Waffe, und der Kampf gegen den Künstler eines gesunden und idealen Empfindens war zugleich ein politischer Kampf.

Der neue Hans H. Zerlett-Film der Bavaria zeigt das Ringen eines ehrlich und anständig gesinnten jungen Bildhauers gegen diesen „Zeitgeist", wie er sich in der Handlung des Buches am schärfsten in dem jüdischen Kunsthändler Benjamin Hecht (Siegfried Breuer) verkörpert und in dem Kreis der Personen, der sich um ihn gruppiert.

Benjamin Hecht unterhält eine „Permanente Ausstellung moderner Kunst", zeitgemäße Werke von Malerei und Plastik, wo man — wie der junge Bildhauer in spöttischer Erbitterung sagt — statt der Maler selbst nur ihre Bilder aufgehangen hat.

In diesem „Salon" spielt sich eine kleine, aber sehr bezeichnende Szene ab: zwei Besucher, ein Herr und eine Dame, sind dabei, eine Mappe mit großen Blättern zu betrachten, die Fräulein Rita, eine Person mit Monokel und Herrenschnitt, die einer dieser Zeichnungen entsprungen zu sein scheint, und die Sekretärin und Vertraute des Chefs ist (Eva Tinschmann), ihnen vorlegte.

„Er" hebt prüfend eines der Blätter hoch.

Fräulein Rita unterbricht: „Pardon, mein Herr, das Bild gehört s o herum . . ." (stellt es auf den Kopf).

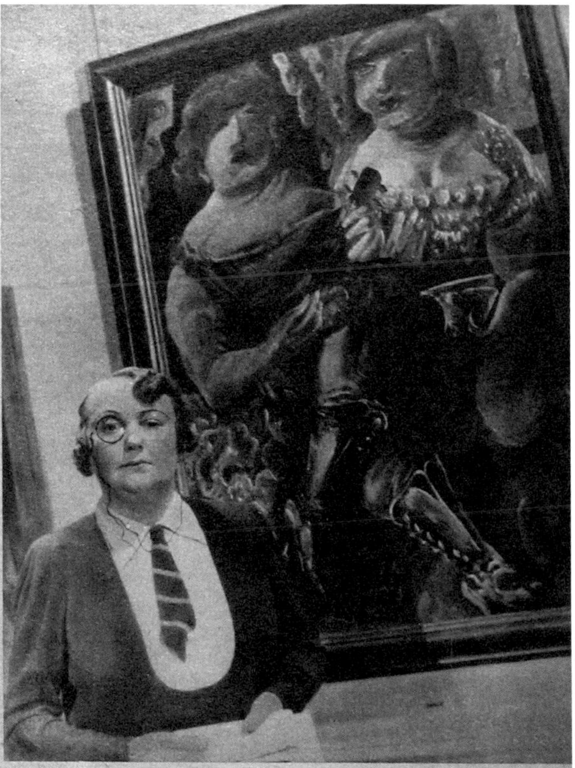

Die Empfangsdame des Salons Benjamin Hecht führt im Film „Kunstwerke" vor, die wir heute als entartet ausgemerzt haben (Eva Tinschmann)

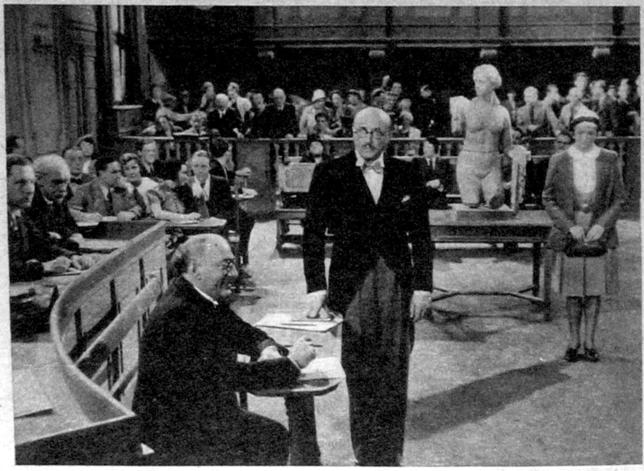

Der Herr Sachverständige (Hubert v. Meyerinck) äußert sich über die in einem Acker gefundene Venusstatue, um die ein großer Kunst-Skandal entbrannt ist (Vorn links Justus Paris, rechts Hansi Knoteck)

Aufnahmen Bavaria-Reißner

„Sie" vollerVer- und Bewunderung: „Woher die das nur weiß?"

„Er", ein angekränkelter Kunstsnob: „Man muß wohl besonders geschulte Augen haben, um diese moderne Kunst zu verstehen . . ."

„Sie": „Ach, weißt du, verstehen wäre ja noch nicht so wichtig. Aber ich möchte doch wenigstens erkennen, was auf einem Bilde ist . . ."

Konnte, fragen wir uns heute voller Entsetzen, konnte sich ein Mensch — außerhalb der Irrenhäuser — überhaupt Mühe geben, diese Machwerke „verstehen" zu wollen? — Wir schütteln heute nur die Köpfe. Dieser spukhafte Irrsinn scheint uns nur in einem einzigen Punkt in etwa begreiflich: als notwendiges Symptom einer in allen ihren Grundfesten erschütterten Zeit.

So zeigt der Film den Weg auf, den wir einmal vor vielen Jahren gegangen sind.

Er tut es, um uns zugleich nochmals und in gegenständlicher Form die Gefahr vor Augen zu führen, der wir entronnen. Denn er war nur ein Mosaikstein aus einem wohldurchdachten Bau eines verheerenden Ganzen: der Jude Benjamin Hecht mit seiner „PermanentenAusstellung" zeitgenössischer Kunst . . . *Ellie Tschauner*

411

FIGURE 76. Images from *Venus vor Gericht:* (top) Standing in front of Kleinschmidt's *Duet in the North Café,* "the receptionist *(Empfangsdame)* in Benjamin Hecht's salon presents 'artworks' that these days we have eliminated as 'degenerate'"; (bottom) trial scene with art snob giving "expert testimony" while Charlotte stands next to Brake's Venus statue. From Ellie Tschauner, "Benjamin Hecht macht in 'Kunst,'" *Filmwelt: Das Film- und Foto-Magazin* (Berlin) 16 (18 April 1941): 411. Photo: Visual Resources Collection, School of Art and Design, Southern Illinois University Carbondale.

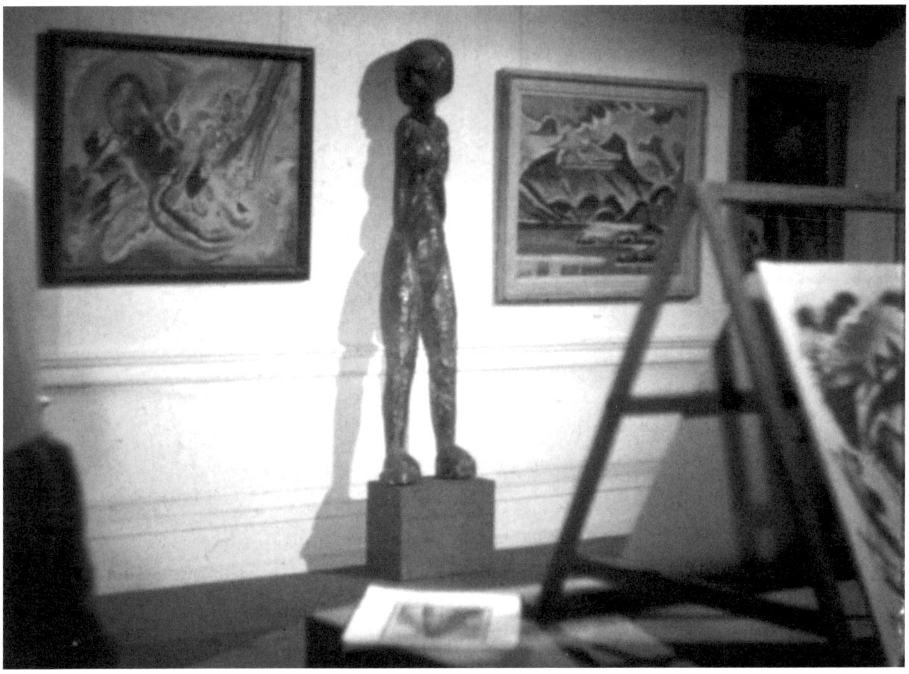

FIGURE 77. Captured frame from *Venus vor Gericht* with, at left, Wassily Kandinsky's *Two Kinds of Red* (1916), formerly National Gallery, Berlin, now lost. Kandinsky art © 2010 Artists Rights Society (ARS)/ADAGP, Paris. Photo © Friedrich Murnau Stiftung.

that in her current position it would compromise her honor. But when she hears on the radio about the Berlin trial, she appears on her own to testify on Brake's behalf, causing another sensation, and adding titillation to the film spectators' experience with the intimation that she might have to take off her clothes in court and on camera to prove her point. She remains clothed, and the word of a humble German woman carries the day (fig. 76). Charlotte provides simple, visible, homespun proof that the idiotic art expert, Dr. Knarre, is wrong. Brake is found innocent, and Charlotte leaves her husband, who had demanded a divorce, but then retracted that when he learned that they could make 1,000 marks per night if she were to perform as Venus in a Berlin cabaret. The film does not end with a flash-forward to a present in which Brake appears as a highly paid and celebrated state sculptor such as Breker, but shows the young couple on the train to Berlin, their journey together just beginning. The good Nazi gets the girl, but the struggle for truth and beauty continues.

Venus vor Gericht presents a National Socialist response to Rouben Mamoulian's melodrama *The Song of Songs* of 1933, staring Marlene Dietrich as a country girl around the turn of the century who comes to Berlin and promptly poses nude for a Berlin sculptor; gets sold by her tyrannical, tippler aunt for 1,000 marks to a lascivious count; becomes a cabaret tart; and ends up again with the sculptor. This film was banned by German censors in 1934, not for Dietrich's near (and the sculpture's explicit) nudity, or, at least not explicitly, for Dietrich's anti-Nazi sentiments, but for the negative, amoral image of German society presented in the film, as based on a 1908 German novel by Hermann Sudermann. The accurate sculpture of Dietrich (sculpted from life by Salvatore Scarpitta) makes her nude body very much the central attraction of *Song of Songs,* the object of unruly desires around which the narrative rotates and which rivets the spectator's attention. The Berlin critic Alfred Kerr traveled to Paris to see *Song of Songs* and reported in *Das neue Tagebuch* that the effect was to be "shaken by beauty."[29] *Venus vor Gericht* was designed to be less disconcerting to its audience, suggesting instead that Classical art was rooted in the native German soil and that its erotic potential could be contained by a return to traditional gender roles and bourgeois morality.

The film scholar Linda Schulte-Sasse has argued that the popular cinema of the Third Reich was structurally similar to earlier and later film.[30] This holds true for *Venus vor Gericht*. The film employs familiar narrative and entertainment devices: boy meets girl, boy loses girl, boy gets girl back; the hero is wrongly accused; things look bad for him, as only he and the audience know he is telling the truth; final vindication and happy ending. Rather than Nazi propaganda with conventional entertainment inserted, it is essentially a conventional entertainment film that includes some not very compelling Nazi propaganda. Perhaps realizing the film's weakness as a potential propaganda vehicle (the scenes of decadent Berlin nightlife look much more entertaining than Brake and his friend's *gemütliche* gatherings, and Siegfried Breuer plays a Hecht who is a more interesting and certainly less annoying character than Hannes Stelzer's Brake is), an extremely polemical article appeared in the journal *Filmwelt* in April 1941, which clearly explicated the film's ideological lessons (figs. 73 and 76). The article concentrated almost exclusively on art, juxtaposing the Classical, beautiful work of Brake to the "degenerate" work shown by the Jewish Hecht: "Artworks characterize their times and their world views, their spiritual and moral stature. . . . [T]he apparent absurdity of 'degenerate art' had a razor sharp purpose and meaning: The corruption of all ethical values . . . this spirit is embodied by the Jewish art dealer Benjamin Hecht (Siegfried Breuer) and the cabal surrounding him."[31]

In *Venus vor Gericht,* National Socialism is represented primarily as an aesthetic and ethical position. Brake testifies under oath that he worked directly from the simple German girl Charlotte because he was looking for a model who is "beautiful, noble, and natural." That is why his work could not be recognized as contemporary in 1930, since, as he says, "Today, art depicts women as gorillas." Art dealers, so-called experts, and Weimar officials lie for financial gain and to protect their reputations. Brake does not want money, or fame, but simply truth and beauty. And, most significantly, it is the simple German contemporary woman who possesses classical beauty—for Brake and Breker and in the ideological position articulated by Hitler in 1937 and restated again in 1938 as justification for the elimination of "degenerate art" such as the primitivist Kirchner in Hecht's window. In his speech opening the second "Great German Art" exhibition of 1938, Hitler asserted: "A period in which all areas of human progress are attaining the highest achievement, cultivating not only the greatest insight into intellectual matters, but also ideal physical beauty, can no longer be symbolized by the barbaric demonstrations of those backwards, stone-age, idiotizing artists. . . . The German Volk of this twentieth century is the Volk of newly awakened affirmation of life, gripped by admiration for the strong and beautiful, which has a healthy capacity to live."[32]

Venus vor Gericht and its accompanying press clarify the ideological work that Breker's figures performed in Nazi Germany.[33] As many commentators have pointed out, Breker's works of these years need to be seen within their context of creation, display, and reception. Their meanings emerged in dialectical relationship with those works and images to which they were juxtaposed—the works on view in the "Degenerate Art" exhibitions, and, for those unable to attend those shows, at Hecht's fictitious gallery in *Venus vor Gericht*. Further, as the art historian Walter Grasskamp points out, the idealized bodies and generalized features of Breker's sculptures have to be seen in relationship to the defamatory images circulated in propaganda posters and films, which specifically and primarily targeted Jews in their "racist polarization between superior, useful peoples and worthless, useless races which could be used as slaves or eliminated. . . . *Stürmer*-caricature and Breker sculpture cannot be separated from each other" (fig. 57).[34] In a society in which such comparisons were drilled into the populace from an early age, the battle that Breker's bodies fought was not limited to the sculptural or aesthetic field.

As Breker's prominence and resources grew, so too did his sculptures grow in size and dynamism. What further distinguished him from Thorak, his only rival for prominence, and even more from Albiker, Kolbe, and Wamper, is that his sculptures depict the muscles in action, in the midst of driving the figures' wills to power. Vigor and aggression characterize such pieces as the 1936 *Prometheus* (fig. 78), commissioned by the Third Reich's Propaganda Ministry and erected in front of the House of German Art in Munich in 1937; the 1939 *Readiness (Bereitschaft)*—a heavily muscled male nude with a grimacing face, who is striking an active contrapposto pose as he pulls a sword from its sheath—which was to have culminated in an over-thirty-foot-tall figure on an over-one-hundred-foot-tall Mussolini monument on Speer's new east-west axis for Berlin (at the current site of Theodor Heuss Platz); and the huge 1940–41 reliefs *The Avenger* (fig. 79) and *The Comrades* (fig. 80), which were intended for the north-south axis.[35] The German Renaissance art scholar Max Imdahl has analyzed the poses and physiques of Breker's male figures, comparing *Readiness* to Michelangelo's *David* to refute the claim that Breker was a "modern Michelangelo."[36] As Imdahl shows, not all over-life-size muscular male nudes are the same: Michelangelo's "gesture," whereas Breker's "pose." The *David* of Michelangelo moves naturally, and through carefully observed and rendered body language articulates something of the inner life of this individual, constantly processing information from the outside and responding to it physically and psychologically. Breker's figures strike depersonalizing, frozen, exaggerated postures that give symbolic form to the Nazi program to dominate the individual.[37]

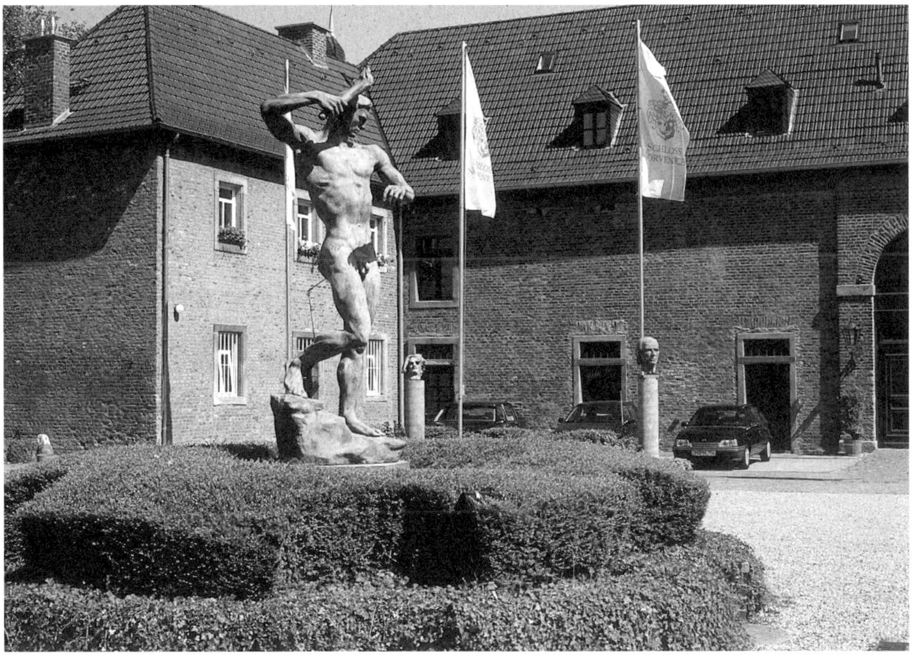

FIGURE 78. Arno Breker, *Prometheus,* 1936, bronze. Museum Europäische Kunst, Schloss Nörvenich, Germany. Art © 2010 Artists Rights Society (ARS), New York/VG-Bildkunst, Bonn. Photo: Author.

Breker's contemporary supporters have sought to normalize him as an artist by treating the Nazi period simply as a stylistic moment within his artistic career, devoid of ideological content. His dealers, Joe and Marco Bodenstine, employ self-defeating tactics when they aggrandize him as a genius on the order of Michelangelo, or in vaguely humanist and new age terms as "guardian of the image of man."[38] They want one to think "Breker," rather than "Hitler" when looking at his work. But, for nonpartisan art historians such as Magdalena Bushart (quoted at the beginning of this chapter), as well as for neo-Nazis and the general public, Breker's legacy cannot be separated from that of Hitler.[39]

Breker's modification of his sculptural style after 1935 has had irrevocable and ill effect on his artistic legacy. *The Herald* was retitled *Ewiges Leben* (Eternal life) in 1970–71 and integrated into a familial group placed in front of a hospital. Recognized as a Breker, though, the work took on associations with eugenics and the stigmatization of sick patients.[40] Breker's name also taints less ideologically charged works from the Nazi period. After the war, five relief sculptures executed in 1936 depicting saints George, Christopher, and Martin, and a male and a female torchbearer, were removed from the North Star Life Insurance Building on Fehrbelliner Platz in Berlin. The niches stand empty today, in contrast to others on the building that still contain sculptural groups, depicting workers, executed by Waldemar Raemisch, also in 1936. Raemisch is not

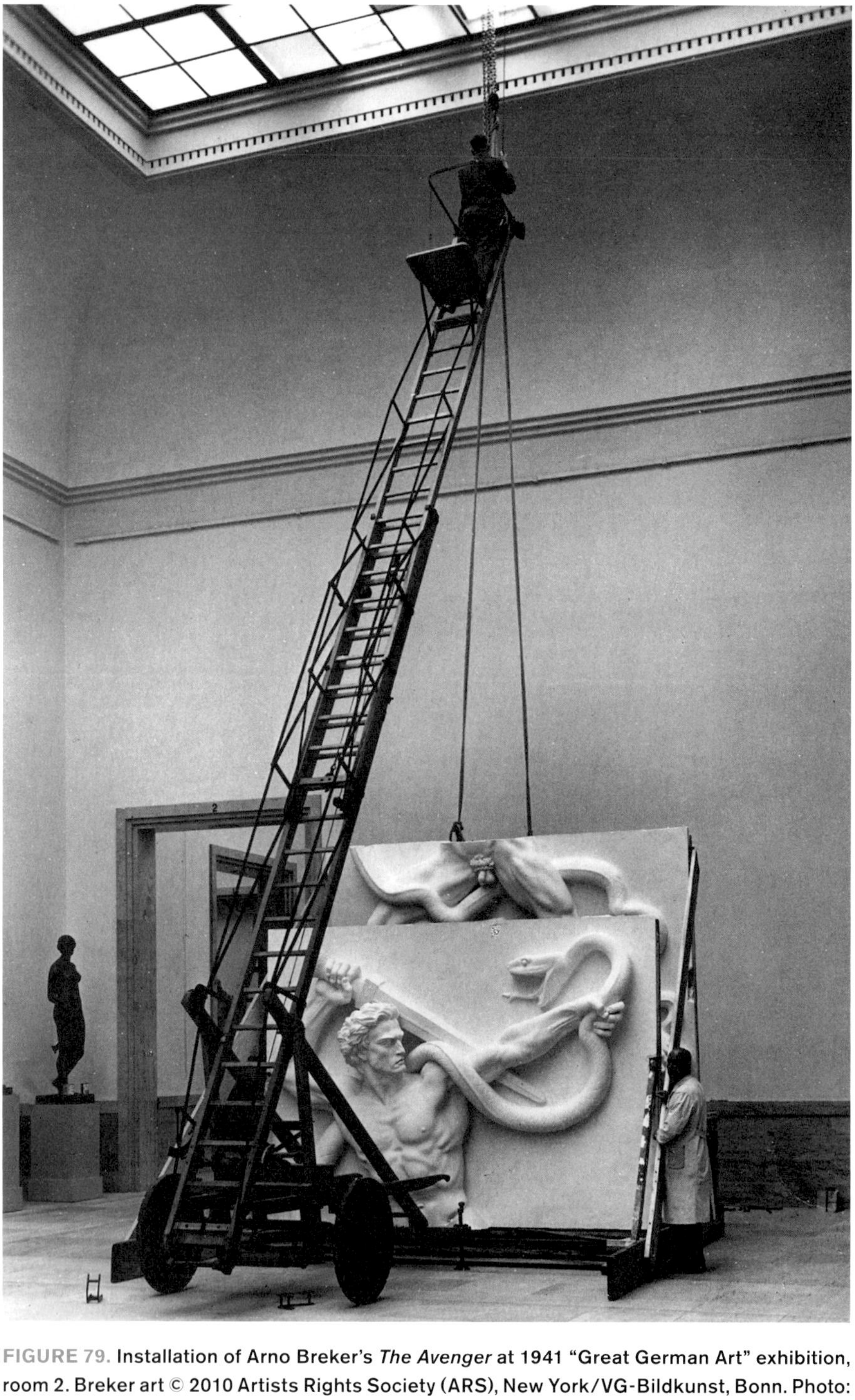

FIGURE 79. Installation of Arno Breker's *The Avenger* at 1941 "Great German Art" exhibition, room 2. Breker art © 2010 Artists Rights Society (ARS), New York/VG-Bildkunst, Bonn. Photo: Jaeger and Goergen, 1941, © Zentralinstitut für Kunstgeschichte, München.

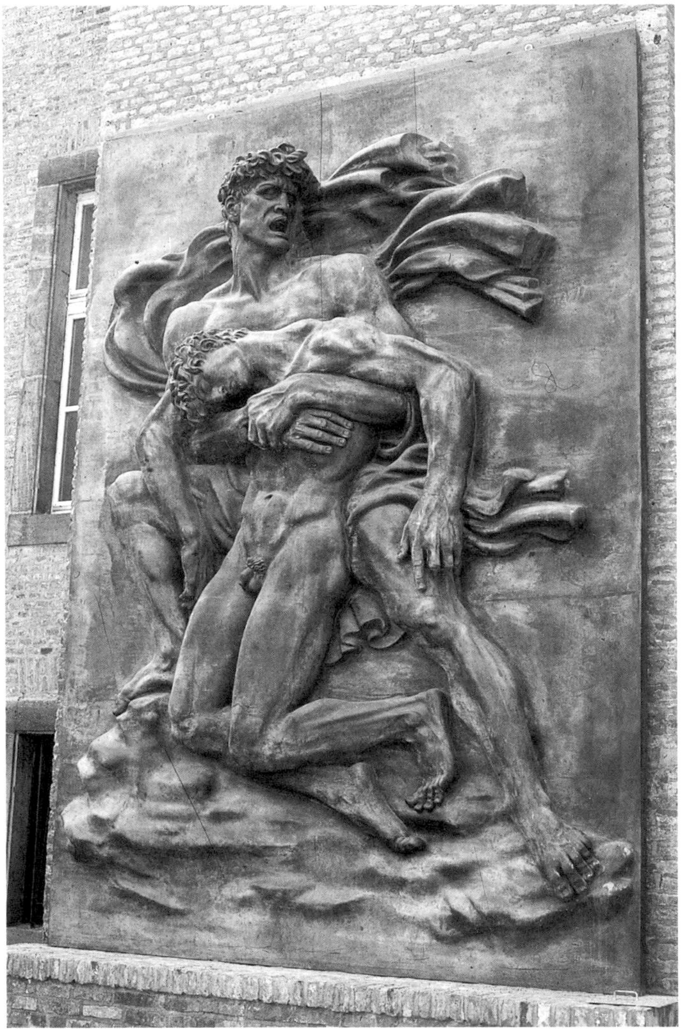

FIGURE 80. Arno Breker, *The Comrades,* 1941, bronze relief. Museum Europäische Kunst, Schloss Nörvenich, Germany. Art © 2010 Artists Rights Society (ARS), New York/VG-Bildkunst, Bonn. Photo: Author.

associated with the Nazi Party or its crimes, so his works remain in place, though iconographically and stylistically they conform to the building's function during the Nazi period just as much as Breker's did.[41]

In 1981 a Berlin gallery's attempting to show Breker's work led to street protests.[42] In 1986–87, at the same time as the *Historikerstreit* (Historians' Debate) over the "normalization" of the history of the Nazi period in general, the chocolate magnate Peter Ludwig—a patron of the Museum Ludwig in Cologne and, with his wife, an important collector of contemporary art, especially Pop—asserted that Breker's work belonged in art museums.[43] The Ludwigs commissioned bust portraits of themselves from Breker, and Peter Ludwig argued that besides being an "excellent artist" Breker merited inclusion in the art museum to give a fuller picture of German art of the 1930s and 1940s. Ludwig claimed that banishing Breker from museums actually repeated the Nazi degenerate art policy, judging historically representative works according to contemporary taste.[44] He asserted Breker's significance and innocence in terms that are typical of those used by Breker and his supporters: "Breker's art derives from mankind. He is devoted to tradition and especially to the legacy of antiquity. His monumental sculptures of the thirties demonstrate a pathos that was an international style then. His humanity is for me beyond question. That Hitler revered him doesn't make him a Nazi."[45] The same anthology that includes Ludwig's pleas for Breker, though, contains the petition "No Nazi-Art in Our Museums," signed by almost four hundred prominent German and Austrian museum directors, curators, and artists, charging Ludwig with "irresponsibility with regards to art and our democratic society."[46]

Displaying works from before and after the Nazi period has also led to controversy and protest. In 2002 Breker's 1926 *Aurora,* situated on top of a building designed by one of his teachers, the architect Wilhelm Kreis, was wrapped in burlap and planted with vines in an iconoclastic art action. In 2003 a figure of Pallas Athene, executed in a neo-Greek Archaic style and commissioned to stand in front of a school in Wuppertal in 1957, was pulled down and anti-Breker slogans written on the empty plinth. After much debate, the piece was finally reinstalled in 2005 with an explanatory plaque, now an intrinsic part of the piece, explaining that the school's students disapprove of Breker's role in the Nazi state, but also that they condemn the destruction of artworks (fig. 81).[47]

In the 1980s Breker's dealers founded a private museum in the tiny Rhineland village of Nörvenich to showcase Breker, Salvador Dalí, and the Viennese Fantastic Realist painter and antimodern art agitator Ernst Fuchs. In the 1990s the museum was renamed Museum of European Art. In the entrance courtyard, visitors to this restored German Renaissance castle are greeted by the torchbearing figure of Breker's *Prometheus* (fig. 78). Numerous Breker works decorate the grounds, while around the back of the building, attached to its exterior wall, is the sculpture garden's pièce de resistance, Breker's final, over-thirty-foot-high bronze relief of *The Comrades* (fig. 80), the plaster version of which was seen in the 1940 "Great German Art" exhibition in the House of German Art in Munich.

The debate as to whether such works should take their place in Germany's state-supported art museums (as opposed to history museums; fig. 82) has for now been settled in the negative, for reasons both ethical and pragmatic. Museums have limited space, budgets, and personnel, and, just as important, there is a limit to the amount of controversy they can withstand. Given Breker's undeniable connection to the Nazi Party and its leadership, and through them to heinous crimes, Breker's works, according to Walter Grasskamp, "besides their lack of artistic qualities, will also always function as memorials" to the victims of Nazism.[48] To display them as artworks could be considered

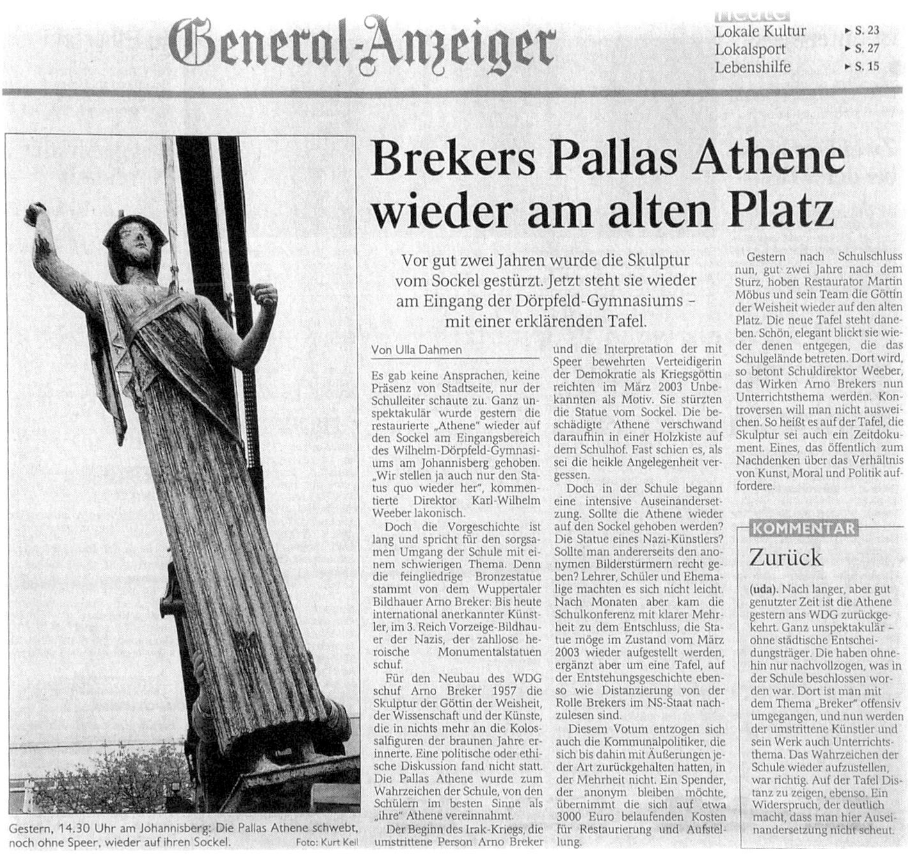

General-Anzeiger

Lokale Kultur ▸ S. 23
Lokalsport ▸ S. 27
Lebenshilfe ▸ S. 15

Brekers Pallas Athene wieder am alten Platz

Vor gut zwei Jahren wurde die Skulptur vom Sockel gestürzt. Jetzt steht sie wieder am Eingang der Dörpfeld-Gymnasiums – mit einer erklärenden Tafel.

Von Ulla Dahmen

Es gab keine Ansprachen, keine Präsenz von Stadtseite, nur der Schulleiter schaute zu. Ganz unspektakulär wurde gestern die restaurierte „Athene" wieder auf den Sockel am Eingangsbereich des Wilhelm-Dörpfeld-Gymnasiums am Johannisberg gehoben. „Wir stellen ja auch nur den Status quo wieder her", kommentierte Direktor Karl-Wilhelm Weeber lakonisch.

Doch die Vorgeschichte ist lang und spricht für den sorgsamen Umgang der Schule mit einem schwierigen Thema. Denn die feingliedrige Bronzestatue stammt von dem Wuppertaler Bildhauer Arno Breker: Bis heute international anerkannter Künstler, im 3. Reich Vorzeige-Bildhauer der Nazis, der zahllose heroische Monumentalstatuen schuf.

Für den Neubau des WDG schuf Arno Breker 1957 die Skulptur der Göttin der Weisheit, der Wissenschaft und der Künste, die in nichts mehr an die Kolossalfiguren der braunen Jahre erinnerte. Eine politische oder ethische Diskussion fand nicht statt. Die Pallas Athene wurde zum Wahrzeichen der Schule, von den Schülern im besten Sinne als „ihre" Athene vereinnahmt.

Der Beginn des Irak-Kriegs, die umstrittene Person Arno Breker und die Interpretation der mit Speer bewehrten Verteidigerin der Demokratie als Kriegsgöttin reichten im März 2003 Unbekannten als Motiv. Sie stürzten die Statue vom Sockel. Die beschädigte Athene verschwand daraufhin in einer Holzkiste auf dem Schulhof. Fast schien es, als sei die heikle Angelegenheit vergessen.

Doch in der Schule begann eine intensive Auseinandersetzung. Sollte die Athene wieder auf den Sockel gehoben werden? Die Statue eines Nazi-Künstlers? Sollte man andererseits den anonymen Bilderstürmern recht geben? Lehrer, Schüler und Ehemalige machten es sich nicht leicht. Nach Monaten aber kam die Schulkonferenz mit klarer Mehrheit zu dem Entschluss, die Statue möge im Zustand vom März 2003 wieder aufgestellt werden, ergänzt aber um eine Tafel, auf der Entstehungsgeschichte ebenso wie Distanzierung von der Rolle Brekers im NS-Staat nachzulesen sind.

Diesem Votum entzogen sich auch die Kommunalpolitiker, die sich bis dahin mit Äußerungen jeder Art zurückgehalten hatten, in der Mehrheit nicht. Ein Spender, der anonym bleiben möchte, übernimmt die sich auf etwa 3000 Euro belaufenden Kosten für Restaurierung und Aufstellung.

Gestern nach Schulschluss nun, gut zwei Jahre nach dem Sturz, hoben Restaurator Martin Möbus und sein Team die Göttin der Weisheit wieder auf den alten Platz. Die neue Tafel steht daneben. Schön, elegant blickt sie wieder denen entgegen, die das Schulgelände betreten. Dort wird, so betont Schuldirektor Weeber, das Wirken Arno Brekers nun Unterrichtsthema werden. Kontroversen will man nicht ausweichen. So heißt es auf der Tafel, die Skulptur sei auch ein Zeitdokument. Eines, das öffentlich zum Nachdenken über das Verhältnis von Kunst, Moral und Politik auffordere.

Gestern, 14.30 Uhr am Johannisberg: Die Pallas Athene schwebt, noch ohne Speer, wieder auf ihren Sockel. Foto: Kurt Keil

KOMMENTAR

Zurück

(uda). Nach langer, aber gut genutzter Zeit ist die Athene gestern ans WDG zurückgekehrt. Ganz unspektakulär – ohne städtische Entscheidungsträger. Die haben ohnehin nur nachvollzogen, was in der Schule beschlossen worden war. Dort ist man mit dem Thema „Breker" offensiv umgegangen, und nun werden der umstrittene Künstler und sein Werk auch Unterrichtsthema. Das Wahrzeichen der Schule wieder aufzustellen, war richtig. Auf der Tafel Distanz zu zeigen, ebenso. Ein Widerspruch, der deutlich macht, dass man hier Auseinandersetzung nicht scheut.

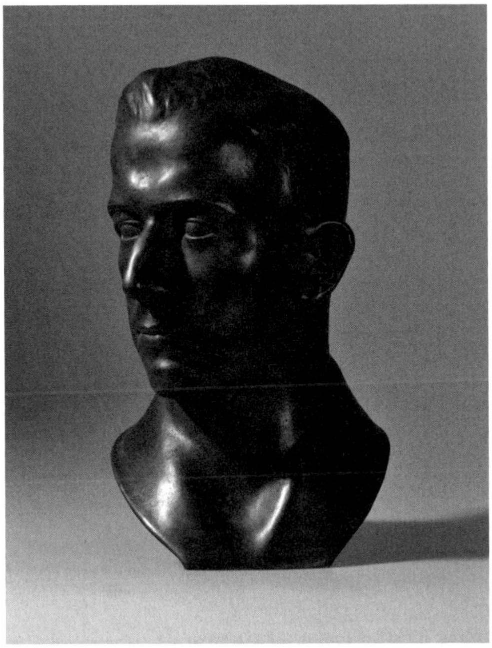

FIGURE 81. "Breker's Pallas Athene Back in Its Old Position." Article by Ulla Dahmen in *Westdeutsche-Zeitung* (8 April 2005), with photograph by Kurt Keil. Art © 2010 Artists Rights Society (ARS), New York/ VG-Bildkunst, Bonn. Photo Andreas Fischer, courtesy *Westdeutsche-Zeitung.* FIGURE 82. Fritz Koelle, *Horst Wessel,* 1936, bronze, 45 × 25.5 × 24.5 cm. Photo courtesy A. Psille/Deutsches Historisches Museum, Berlin.

an insult to the memory of those victims and risk controversies threatening the very existence of the institution, as well as the jobs of the institution's employees.

Over six hundred works that were shown in the "Great German Art" exhibitions from 1937 to 1944 and remain in the possession of the German government were stored until the mid-1990s in the old Bavarian customhouse, a massive, late nineteenth-century building looming over the rail lines leading into Munich. Scholars could view the works, largely landscape and genre paintings and nudes, by appointment. These works, including Fritz Koelle's bust of the Hitler Youth hero Horst Wessel (fig. 82), have since been moved to the German Historical Museum collection on Unter den Linden in Berlin, where some are integrated into the permanent display documenting German history that opened in June 2006, in a section devoted to the arts in National Socialist Germany and presenting them in the context of the degenerate art action. A small version of Breker's *Comrades* relief can be seen in the section of the exhibit devoted to National Socialist architecture, next to a model of Speer's planned rotunda.

The Nazis' thoroughly modern propaganda techniques—including magazine montages; propaganda newsreels such as the 1938–39 *Herrschaft in Stein* (Mastery in stone) celebrating the new architecture of designers such as Kreis and Speer, and sculpture such as Breker's; the 1944 Hans Cürlis and Arnold Franck "culture film" *Arno Breker;* and popular entertainments such as *Venus vor Gericht*—positioned the battle against modern art as a symbol of cultural regeneration through a return to traditional values. They enforced the coordination of the institutions of art into their overall system. The role Breker and his works played in this system relinquished autonomy for every object he created. His works' status as objects of history overwhelms any claims they might make to be aesthetic objects of disinterested contemplation and appreciation.

6 From Muscle Men to Fatty Remains

Joseph Beuys's Sculptural Objects Beyond Objecthood

In the case of Joseph Beuys the materials of fat and felt–with their links to his own biography and primordial mystical overtones of survival and shelter–comprise the signature appearance and functional content of his work more definitively than any stylistic hallmarks. –REINHOLD HELLER, *CONFRONTING IDENTITIES IN GERMAN ART*

Beuys's *Chair with Fat* (fig. 66) employs modeling, in the working of the soft fat, but is also assembled out of various materials and objects, including the chair. It thus continues the twentieth-century tradition of assemblage employed in various ways in Cubism, Dada, Constructivism, and Surrealism, recombining and repurposing objects and materials appropriated whole or as fragments from the world at large. Anthony Caro—the artist who Michael Fried thought might save the autonomous modernist sculptural object from minimalist theatricality—employed assemblage to much different effect, integrating materials into unified sculptural compositions that suppress the histories of the individual elements. Beuys's battered chair, fat, wax, and wire, while rescued from their prior contexts, still bear marks, scars, and a peeling skin of paint attesting to their earlier, non-art existence. The chair remains a chair, invites us to consider sitting in it, but also contains a bodily residue suggesting previous sitters: the triangle of fat on the seat, which seems to ooze out of the sides beneath the smoothly layered visible upper strata of its hypotenuse. Beuys's sculpted objects bespeak materials' multiple existences in continuous process and suggest that each thing in the world bears traces of its history, visible as a variable surface appearance that reflects a constantly changing essence. As he stated, "The nature of my sculpture is not fixed and finished. Processes continue in most of them: chemical reactions, fermentations, colour changes, decay, drying up. Everything is in a **state of change**."[1]

Breker's *Torso of a Seated Man* and Beuys's *Chair with Fat* are both fragments suggesting larger wholes. They both present partial bodies, with Beuys's piece even more truncated than Breker's: a person rendered into fat. Beuys stated: "The chair represents a kind of human anatomy, the area of digestive and excretive warmth processes, sexual organs and interesting chemical change, relating psychologically to will power. In German the joke is compounded as a pun since *Stuhl* (chair) is also the polite way of saying shit (stool)."[2] And Beuys's *Stuhl* stinks. Prior to being encased in climate-controlled vitrines, his works typically extended into their environments more powerfully olfactorily than spatially.

Each of these works is also a fragmentary relic of its creator's career. As with all of Breker's works, it is impossible not to view *Torso,* like *Pallas Athene,* as a work by "Hitler's favorite sculptor." Like most of Beuys's objects from this date on, *Chair with Fat* is, instead, firmly associated with the artist, not with any patron. *Chair* derives from one of Beuys's *Actions*—performances in which he played himself and enacted his art—and through this to his "expanded conception of art" *(erweiterter Kunstbegriff),* which linked his artistic practice to his life and conceptions for transforming the social world through, and into, art. The wire on the chair's back was used to fasten *Chair with Fat* to a wall, in an action in which the piece "was hung at various heights in a bare room where Beuys's students worked."[3] The object changed heights and punned on the artist's and the professor's varying incarnations in his student's own production, and in their perceptions of him; the German word for "professorship" is *Lehrstuhl* (a teaching or instructional chair), so Beuys's institutionally sanctioned "chair" and more personal and unruly "instructional shit" hovered over his students and permeated their working environment.

Although he did become a professor and enjoyed civil servant status (before being dismissed), Beuys, outside of his salary, studio, and benefits, received very little direct state support for his work and produced almost no "public art." Having come of age in Nazi Germany and served in the German Luftwaffe, or air force, Beuys consciously avoided government patronage. Art institutions, collectors, and the institutionalized neo-avant-garde of the postwar Western art world mediated his contact with a wider public.[4] The *Actions* from which his objects derived also helped to determine their ultimate placement and interpretation within those institutions and for the public. He worked within the institutions of art with the goal of first transforming them, and through them, transforming the larger social world.

Beuys's activities paralleled those of Americans such as Allan Kaprow and Robert Morris, both of whom he sought to collaborate with, as well as the French artists Arman and Yves Klein. Like these artists of Happenings and performances, the body of the artist was also part of his body of work. And, like Kaprow and Morris, Beuys had academic support. His teaching at and termination from the Düsseldorf Art Academy, for refusing to distinguish between artists and non-artists and allowing anyone to study with him, expressed his artistic program. But Beuys's public prominence in Germany far eclipsed that of Kaprow and Morris in the United States, or Arman and Klein in France. By the early 1980s Beuys had been the subject of over six hundred German newspaper articles, his face had appeared on the cover of *Der Spiegel* magazine, and his work was valued at about twenty million dollars (fig. 83).[5] With his fame, he was able to proclaim his artistic conceptions to a wide audience, and even to invite that audience to

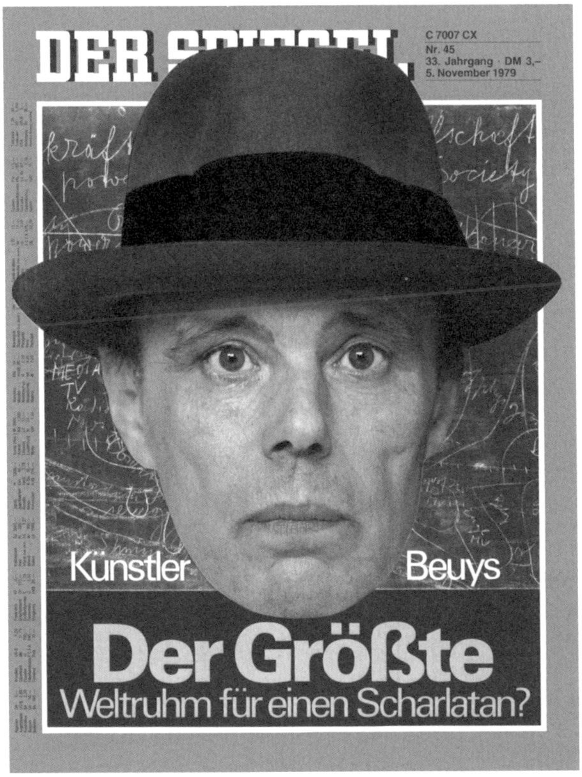

FIGURE 83. "Artist Beuys: The Greatest World Renown for a Charlatan?" © *Der Spiegel,* 5 November 1979.

adopt and become his ultimate artistic conception—"Everyone is an artist"—able to participate in art as a therapeutic, homeopathic, social activity.

Two years after Beuys's death the Viennese artist Gottfried Helnwein created a striking and odd image bringing Breker and Beuys together (fig. 84). Helnwein posed the eighty-eight-year-old Breker uncomfortably holding Helnwein's portrait of Beuys in front of his chest. The older man with furrowed brow directs the glossy, skeletal image of Beuys—like an icon painting—away from his own gaze and toward that of the viewer. The image asserts the generational relationship between Breker and Beuys as sculptors and cultural figures and also positions Breker as a pathetic father figure making public his own confused feelings after the death of an estranged son.[6] Breker is dressed in his white sculptor's smock, presenting the surgeon-like image he favored and that was the preferred self-presentation of sculptors, especially Breker, as respectable, trained professionals in the Third Reich, in contrast to prewar bohemians.[7] This was an artistic self-conception and presentation that Beuys abhorred. Looking back on his "key experiences," he recounted being revolted by a sculpture professor in the early 1950s: "He approached me almost like a surgeon, wearing a white smock, with modeling tools instead of a stethoscope. . . . He would say, 'Look, you haven't got the muscle right at all,' then he would tap on the studio model, on the muscle. As if art could be built up from the muscle."[8] In contrast to the artist as a doctor dressed for the operating theater, who

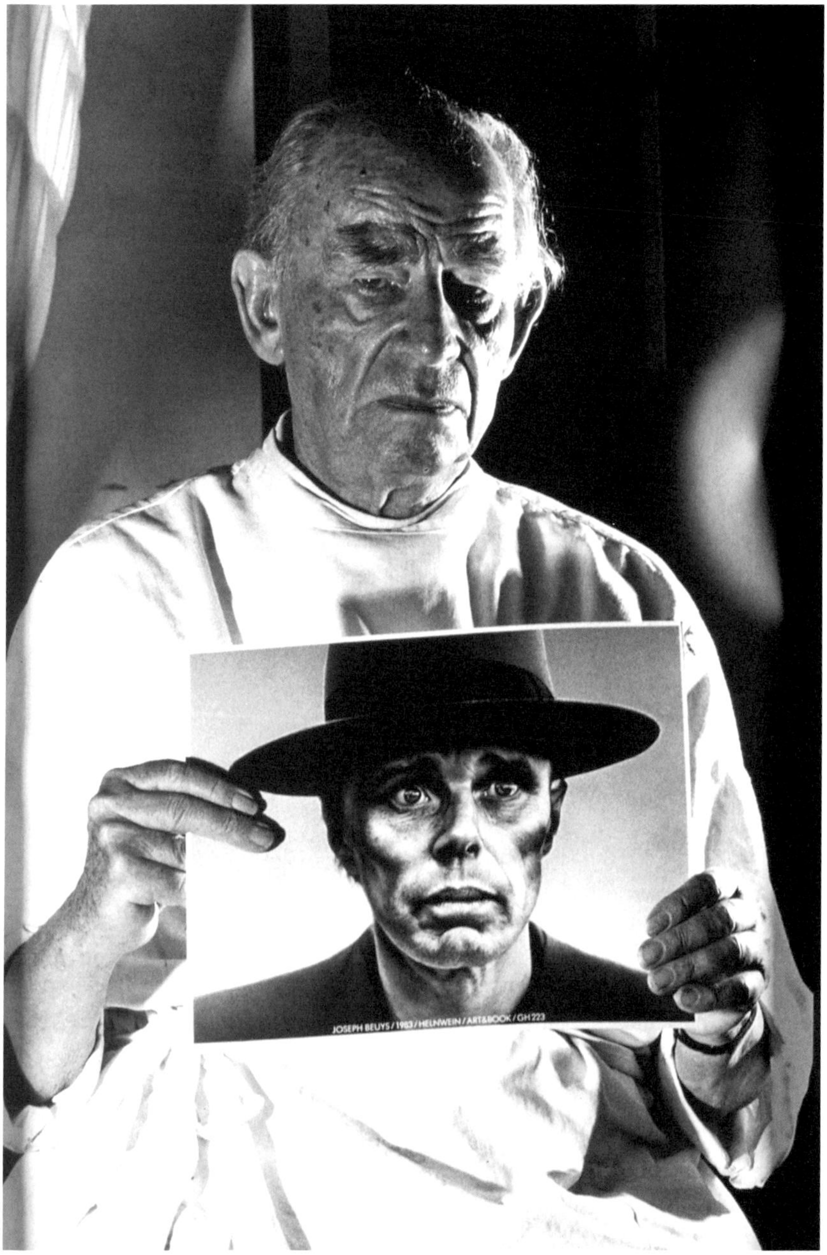

FIGURE 84. Gottfried Helnwein, *Arno Breker Holding a Picture of Joseph Beuys,* 1988, gelatin silver print, 99 × 66 cm. Museum Ludwig, Cologne. Art © 2010 Artists Rights Society (ARS), New York/VG Bild-Kunst, Bonn. Repro: Rheinisches Bildarchiv Köln.

takes off this sterile uniform when performing other social functions—such as receiving awards, attending openings, or going to the theater—Beuys practiced art itself as social theater. He costumed himself as such, in his signature many-pocketed sports vest, broad-brimmed hat, and jeans, presenting himself as a cross between a fisherman, a survivalist, a proletarian, and a clown. He was instantly recognizable and always in role.

Beuys also rejected his professor's and Breker's obsessions with muscles. He chose the bodily antipode to muscle, fat, as his preferred material metonym for the human body and metaphor for the human condition, his antidote to the Nazi "armored body." Nazi commentators interpreted the hard materials of architecture and architectural sculpture as embodying the force of the Führer's words.[9] Beuys's soft materials, often displayed low to the ground, prone rather than erect, embody their effects. Breker's sculpted figures attack, whereas Beuys wrapped himself and many of his objects in a protective layer of felt. Beuys's work literally reeks of victimhood and provoked defensive responses: laughter, anger, and resistance. Beuys claimed that he chose fat as a preferred sculptural material due to its "flexibility . . . its reactions to temperature changes. This flexibility is psychologically effective—people instinctively feel it relates to inner processes and feelings. . . . People started to laugh, get angry, or try to destroy it."[10]

One thing they did not do, according to Beuys, is cry, a reaction that would express sympathy and mourning. An installation Beuys created in 1974–75 and first shown in February 1976 features two gurneys with zinc plate containers containing fat, one including a thermometer and the other a gauze-stoppered test tube containing a bird's head.[11] A blackboard hanging above these objects, redolent of bodily diseases and decomposition, is inscribed with the piece's title: *Zeige deine Wunde* (Show your wound). Beuys's pieces, while referring to his own biography (in this case probably to a recent heart attack) also speak in the second person to the spectator, inviting direct identification with and so an empathetic, rather than sympathetic, response to their materials and messages. If, as the Beuys scholar Gene Ray has asserted, "like every German veteran of his generation," Beuys was "marked inescapably by a relation to that catastrophe"—that is, Nazi crimes against humanity—the mark he displayed was the preferred one of his generation, that of a victim.[12]

Beuys's generation was younger than that of the Nazi leaders, and, with a few notable exceptions, such as Sophie and Hans Scholl (born in 1921 and 1918, respectively), also younger than the generation of most of the Nazi resisters, but he was also born too early to enjoy what Chancellor Helmut Kohl (born in 1930) controversially referred to before the Israeli Knesset in 1984 as his own generation's supposed "mercy of a late birth" *(die Gnade der späten Geburt),* which ostensibly absolved them of responsibility for Nazi crimes. Subsequent generations of German (and non-German) artists, working with the distance that mercy would grant, began to produce works on German soil encouraging spectators' identification not *as* but *with* the victims of Nazi crimes.

Beuys was not the only German sculptor to react in the later 1950s to the legacy of Nazi sculpture and Nazi crimes. Wolf Vostell, for instance, in works such as *Auschwitz*

Searchlight 568 (1958), part of his "Black Room" cycle, confronted spectators with Dadaistic assemblages suggesting destruction and decomposition, while shining a spotlight directly into their eyes.[13] Vostell was a member of the Fluxus group, with which Beuys was also briefly associated in the early 1960s. But Beuys's individual, messianic self-presentation alienated him from this more collaborative, demythologizing group. His self-aggrandizement, though, succeeded in installing him, his objects, and especially his signature materials—fat and felt—in German public consciousness to a degree unrivalled by any other artist of the postwar period.

In his 1986 acceptance speech for the Wilhelm Lehmbruck Prize—named for the German Expressionist sculptor of gaunt, skin-and-bone figures—Beuys stated: "I was born in the lower Rhineland. During the Third Reich one was certainly surrounded by a forest of sculpture; but the type that was being made at that time didn't inspire my inner being at all."[14] Though unmoved by the aesthetics of Nazi art, Beuys admitted to being moved by the aestheticization of everyday life that Nazism encouraged, and by its celebration of Nordic myths and rituals. Many commentators have incorporated this fascination into their analyses of his work and its ritualistic tendencies.[15] But they have neglected his debt to Nazi sculpture and sculptors. Although the "forest of sculpture" surrounding Beuys during the period he grew from youth to early adulthood—from the age of twelve to twenty-five years old, and from Hitler Youth member to soldier and prisoner—may not have touched him inwardly, it influenced the outward appearance and presentation of his work and his persona, as well as their receptions.

In *Auschwitz Demonstration* (1956–64, plate 6) objects such as old sausages, blocks of fat on a hot plate, photographs, drawings, vials, and a dead rat are arranged in a vitrine resembling the remains of an experiment displayed in a natural history collection. Operating from below, Beuys's base objects undermined the pretensions and exposed the consequences of the system supporting his forebears' monuments. If the trees populating the sculptural forest in which Beuys grew up were the figures of Breker, Thorak, and other Nazi-era sculptors, he sought to reclaim the soil, ground, and natural fertilizers and remains in it from which they grew. In his 1985 speech "Talking About One's Own Country: Germany," Beuys asserted that Germans' "reanimation will allow us, through language, to recapture this soil."[16] The word he used for soil was *Boden,* which can also simply mean ground but has historical associations, especially from the Nazi period, identifying the German people, or *Volk,* as essentially united by *Blut und Boden,* blood and soil.[17] In looking down to the ground and to the soil for reanimation, he also sought to reorient German sculpture, particularly as monument. Downward orientation characterizes the spectators' gaze on vitrines like *Auschwitz Demonstration,* as it does on many of Beuys's works. In 1971 Beuys stated that his fascination with rabbits had to do with their "relationship to below, into the earth. . . . [T]hey en-grave themselves, bury their buildings."[18]

The German art and literary theorist Peter Bürger has recently interpreted Beuys's use of derelict materials as a "reaction against the ordered classicism of the Nazi era and its cult of the beautiful body."[19] Bürger formulated the influential theory that the postwar neo-avant-garde, including Beuys, reemployed the formal techniques of the interwar historical avant-garde, such as the use of found objects, the readymade, and montage, but abandoned the revolutionary goals for which they were employed by the Dadaists, Surrealists, or Soviet Constructivists: to undermine the institution of art itself and in doing so to fuse art and life.[20] The art historian Hal Foster has argued that Bürger's theory both overly valorizes the historical avant-garde's status as the absolute origin of such techniques and strategies and obscures the historically specific and often also psychologically charged meanings revealed by their repetition in the post–World War II context.[21] Both repetition, and the psychological need to repeat in order to recuperate, applies to Beuys. But as Bürger contends, Beuys's artistic education and intentions were forged by study not only of the historical avant-garde but also of its enemies. How he managed materials and formats had powerful historical and psychological resonances in the postwar period, both as art historical repetition and as historical recuperation—not only of prewar avant-garde strategies and techniques but *from* the wounds suffered during their destruction. Beuys's personal history and the persona he created as he navigated postwar artistic institutions rendered these resonances particularly dramatic, with the potential to transform, if not to dissolve, the institutions that housed and supported his work. Beuys, like the historical avant-garde, aspired to fuse art and life; not by undermining art as an institution but by opening up the institutions of art, such as museums and schools, to his conception of art as a form of participatory democracy.

Beuys often referred to homeopathy ("heal like with like") as one of his operative techniques. Among his first homeopathic patients were sculpture and the image and role of the sculptor. Beuys was keenly aware of art's and the artist's role in and as spectacle. He came of age under what the historian Peter Reichel has called the Third Reich's "beautiful illusion," its masking of violent reality under a veil of aesthetic semblances.[22] Hitler fancied himself an artist, and Nazi Germany his greatest work of art. Beuys's status as an ambiguous survivor of that state, positioned, in reality, like the majority of Germans on the side of the perpetrators (and even as a hero of Hitler's armed forces, with a charismatic story of his service to tell) but through material and metaphor imaginatively aligned with its victims, lent his persona and his work a particular friction and fascination. A German physician with only a passing interest in contemporary art but someone who, like many Germans, was acutely aware of Beuys, remarked to me over lunch one day in 1988, "Whether you liked him or hated him, he certainly struck a nerve."[23]

Beuys's construction of a biographical myth of the artist sought to make him an exemplar—not to normalize him, as Breker attempted, but to render him a living embodiment of so many historical associations that he would transcend Germany's most recent history. Not only was one to think "Beuys" when looking at his work but through his expanded concept of art, one was to contemplate numerous historical, natural historical, and philosophical referents, such as Leonardo, Rudolf Steiner, Europe's east/west divide, rabbit hutches, stag hunts, Nordic mythology, genocide, and beekeeping. Beuys emphasized the importance of these wide-ranging, cosmic, and quotidian associations to the meaning of his work, and not the more obvious visible and material ones to well-worn twentieth-century sculptural practices, especially Dadaism and Surrealism.

The history of the 1960 *Bathtub* (fig. 85), positioned as the first work in his important retrospective at the Solomon R. Guggenheim Museum in New York in 1979, illuminates the relationship of his neo-avant-garde objects to those of the historical avant-garde. Displaying a piece of plumbing as art obviously recalls Dada, and especially Duchamp's 1917 *Fountain* (fig. 86).[24] The urinal that became Duchamp's *Fountain* was made for use in a men's room, but, if one were to gender its flowing form and relationship to the male user, it would be female. *Bathtub,* as the curator and Beuys scholar Mario Kramer points out, if seen as a figure, is male, like its creator.[25] Whereas Duchamp emptied the object of any association with an affective creator by attributing it to the fictitious "R. Mutt," Beuys filled his fixture with his own affective and effective fictions. His *Bathtub,* outdated as a functional fixture at the time he refunctioned it, contrasts to Duchamp's urinal, which was state of the art in 1917. *Bathtub*'s historicism is not only functional but also personal, as Beuys claimed it as the site of his birth, connecting the object both to his and to a universal human experience. Gauze soaked in fat and bandages decorate the object with traces of bodily wounding, "the wound or trauma experienced by every person as they come into contact with hard material conditions of the world through birth . . . a kind of autobiographical key: an object from the outer world, a solid material thing invested with energy of a spiritual nature."[26] Objects, for Beuys, link individuals to history and to each other. He demonstrated this on the example of the creation of his own biographical legend, fabricated through objects. And that biographical legend, as we shall see, also resonated as a particularly German fable.

The history of these two objects is instructive. *Fountain,* after its rejection by the Society of Independent Artists in 1917, was lost. Duchamp authorized the recreation of replicas, since the idea of an original having any particular, unique significance contradicted the concept of the readymade.[27] In 1972 Beuys's *Bathtub,* then owned by the collector Lothar Schirmer, went on an exhibition tour in Germany. In November 1973 local members of the Social Democratic Party held a reception at the Leverkusen Art Museum. Having forgotten to bring along a cooler, they filled Beuys's *Bathtub* with ice and bottled beer, damaging it.[28] This led to a trial, in which the collector was ultimately granted restitution of 165,000 Deutschmarks (plus interest, for a total of about $94,000) to restore this and two other pieces to their original conditions.[29] *Bathtub*'s fat and bandages were replaced, erasing the politician's defacement, reconnecting it to Beuys's intentions, and reconstituting Beuysian meaning.

For Duchamp the rejection of the piece—not the object but its action and the actions on it—*was* the piece. Writing in the avant-garde journal *The Blind Man* in 1917 (fig. 86),

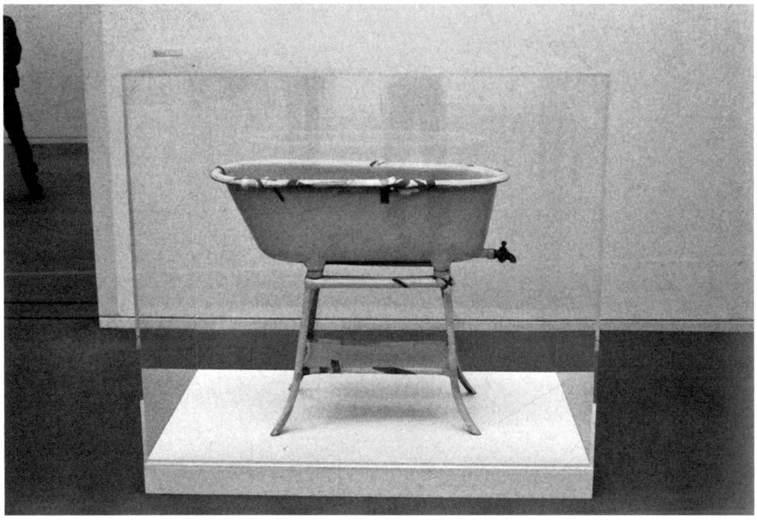

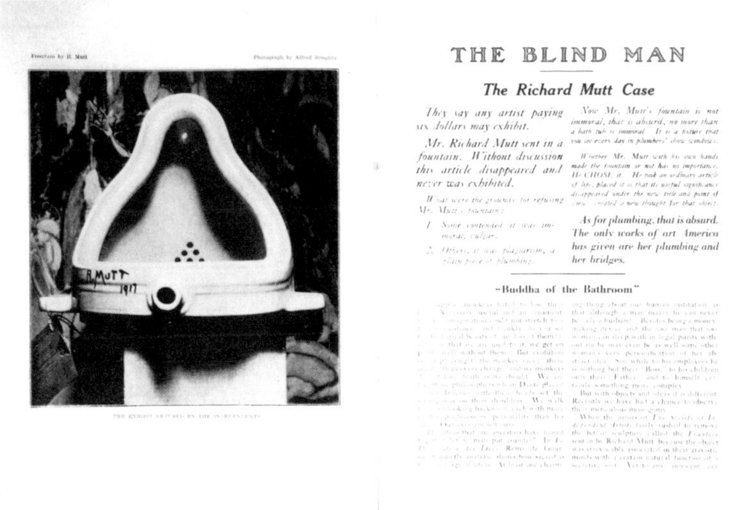

Fountain by R. Mutt

Photograph by Alfred Stieglitz

THE EXHIBIT REFUSED BY THE INDEPENDENTS

THE BLIND MAN

The Richard Mutt Case

They say any artist paying six dollars may exhibit.

Mr. Richard Mutt sent in a fountain. Without discussion this article disappeared and never was exhibited.

What were the grounds for refusing Mr. Mutt's fountain:—

1. *Some contended it was immoral, vulgar.*
2. *Others, it was plagiarism, a plain piece of plumbing.*

Now Mr. Mutt's fountain is not immoral, that is absurd, no more than a bath tub is immoral. It is a fixture that you see every day in plumbers' show windows.

Whether Mr. Mutt with his own hands made the fountain or not has no importance. He CHOSE it. He took an ordinary article of life, placed it so that its useful significance disappeared under the new title and point of view—created a new thought for that object.

As for plumbing, that is absurd. The only works of art America has given are her plumbing and her bridges.

"Buddha of the Bathroom"

FIGURE 85. Joseph Beuys, *Untitled (Bathtub),* 1960, enamel bathtub with stand, adhesive bandage, and gauze. Private collection. Art © 2010 Artists Rights Society (ARS), New York/VG Bild-Kunst, Bonn. Photo: Author. FIGURE 86. Marcel Duchamp, "The Richard Mutt Case," letter to *The Blind Man* 2 (May 1917), with Duchamp's *Fountain,* photographed by Alfred Stieglitz. Louise and Walter Arensberg Collection, Philadelphia Museum of Art. *The Blind Man* © Beatrice Wood; courtesy Beatrice Wood Center for the Arts. Duchamp art © 2010 Artists Rights Society (ARS), New York/ADAGP, Paris. Stieglitz art © Artists Rights Society (ARS), New York. Photo: Philadelphia Museum of Art/Art Resource, NY.

Duchamp asserted: "Whether Mr. Mutt with his own hands made the fountain or not has no importance. . . . He CHOSE it . . . [and] created a new thought for that object." Recreations of it simply led to new thoughts. Beuys titled a performance on German television in 1964 "Das Schweigen von Marcel Duchamp wird überbewertet" (The silence of Marcel Duchamp is overrated), by which he intended "a criticism of Duchamp's anti-art concept and equally of the cult of his later behaviour," that is, of Duchamp's withdrawal from creating artworks at all.[30] If art itself is a strategic pursuit, Duchamp's withdrawal suggested that the artist might as well pursue an activity that is pure strategy—playing chess. While Beuys would, in fact, also claim in his later years to have withdrawn from art making, this was in order to engage more actively with the world of politics, with the Green Party, and with institution building, the creation of the Free International University. For his artworks he still claimed an originary primacy linked to his own biography and unique to a particular object. Given the ever-increasing value of these works within the commercial art world, claims of ownership, or, as in the case of some factory-produced minimal and conceptual pieces, the idea behind them, is a fact of professional life for the institutionalized neo-avant-garde artist.[31]

Many American critics reacted skeptically to the Beuys retrospective at the Guggenheim in 1979. In Germany, though, it confirmed Beuys as the most prominent German artist of the day and of the postwar period. The German press service (Deutsche Presse-Agentur, or DPA) report on the exhibition appeared in dozens of German papers, with various headlines, such as "Beuys in the Guggenheim Temple in New York: with current exhibition his world renown is incontestable."[32] *Der Spiegel* put his face on its cover, under his hat and in front of one of the inscribed blackboards he used in performances. Though the cover caption asked whether the famous artist was, in fact, a charlatan, inside the magazine featured a comprehensive and admiring article that emphasized the success of the Guggenheim exhibition and the rising prices for his work, as well as an interview with an editor focusing on his political program, goals, and ambitions.[33] There was speculation that Beuys might become a member of the German parliament. In discussing his art, the article focused particularly on his uncommon sculptural materials—especially fat and felt—as had *Spiegel*'s first Beuys discussion, published in 1968.[34] Both the 1968 and 1979 articles presented his work in relation to his biography and its mythic elements, including his military service and the story of his plane crash, survival, and rescue. But, while the 1968 article reproduced the vitrine *Auschwitz Demonstration*, it captioned it generically as a "Beuys-Object Vitrine," and neither article discussed any thematic or material connections between his sculptural objects and Nazi crimes, an association that had been made several times in passing in the 1960s but that remained tangential to articulated interpretations until American responses to the Guggenheim exhibition.[35]

The Guggenheim exhibition proceeded in a series of twenty-four "stations," alluding to Christian martyrdom and pilgrimage journeys. Frank Lloyd Wright, who designed the Guggenheim Museum building, intended that exhibitions begin at the top of the museum's spiraling ramp, so that visitors could use gravity to their advantage. This worked perfectly with Beuys's installation and contributed to the feeling of being propelled through a carefully charted journey, a descent. That it was a specifically German trip was reinforced by the brilliant 1969 sculpture *The Pack* (fig. 87), featuring a real Volkswagen bus with twenty-four vintage German wooden sleds spilling out of its trunk, each bearing a role of felt, a lump of fat, and a flashlight. The Volkswagen, the "people's car," with origins in the Nazi period, had, like Beuys himself, been refunctioned in the 1960s into a countercultural icon.[36] The pack of sleds, like alpine St. Bernards, suggests a winter rescue, while the Beuysian offerings of fat, felt, and battery-generated light take the place of brandy. The art historian and critic Donald Kuspit has interpreted these sleds as Beuys's *Rosebud,* objects cathecting his resentment of bad parenting before and during the Nazi period and his "need to be rescued and healed from childhood's wounds."[37]

That Beuys's sculptural journey transported spectators through stations marked "Holocaust" was first asserted explicitly by the art critic Kim Levin in a review of the Guggenheim show published in *Arts Magazine* in April 1980. She interpreted his fat as an unambiguous allusion "to the millions of people melted down in concentration camps."[38] Presentness is not grace, but place—for Beckmann's *Departure* in New York and Berlin as for the Berlin Dadaists showing at I.B. Neumann in Berlin in 1919 or the neo-Dadaist Beuys at the Guggenheim in New York in 1979. Beuys turned down a show at New York's Museum of Modern Art in favor of one at the Guggenheim. Solomon R. Guggenheim belonged to a prominent Jewish American family of Swiss-German origins. With its Jewish name and dramatic space, a sky-lit atrium surrounding the snaking inclined plane of the exhibition ramp, the Guggenheim formed the perfect architectural base, surround, and discursive site for his work, unlike the staid, stable and conventionally lit galleries of the Museum of Modern Art, which are designed to encourage formalist presentation and interpretation. Levin went on to write that Beuys's "art mimics the symptoms, echoes the causes of the trauma; his intention is therapeutic. The effect is harder to assess."[39] One undeniable effect, though, was greatly increased public recognition for Beuys and for German art generally. As the art dealer Michael Werner asserts, "Beuys . . . thought strategically," choosing carefully where and how to display his work and himself, and he paved the way for the explosion of interest in contemporary German art in the 1980s, especially in America, and especially that dealing with the legacy of Nazism.[40]

The vitrine *Auschwitz Demonstration* was positioned at the very beginning of the Guggenheim exhibition, next to *Bathtub. Auschwitz Demonstration* consists of drawings and objects created between 1956 and 1964, including several made in 1957 for submission in spring 1958 to the international competition for a monument at Auschwitz.[41] He assembled these objects in 1968 and since 1970 the vitrine has been integrated into the "Beuys Block" in the Hessian State Museum in Darmstadt.[42] Of the nine vitrines in space 5 of the Darmstadt "Beuys Block," *Auschwitz Demonstration*

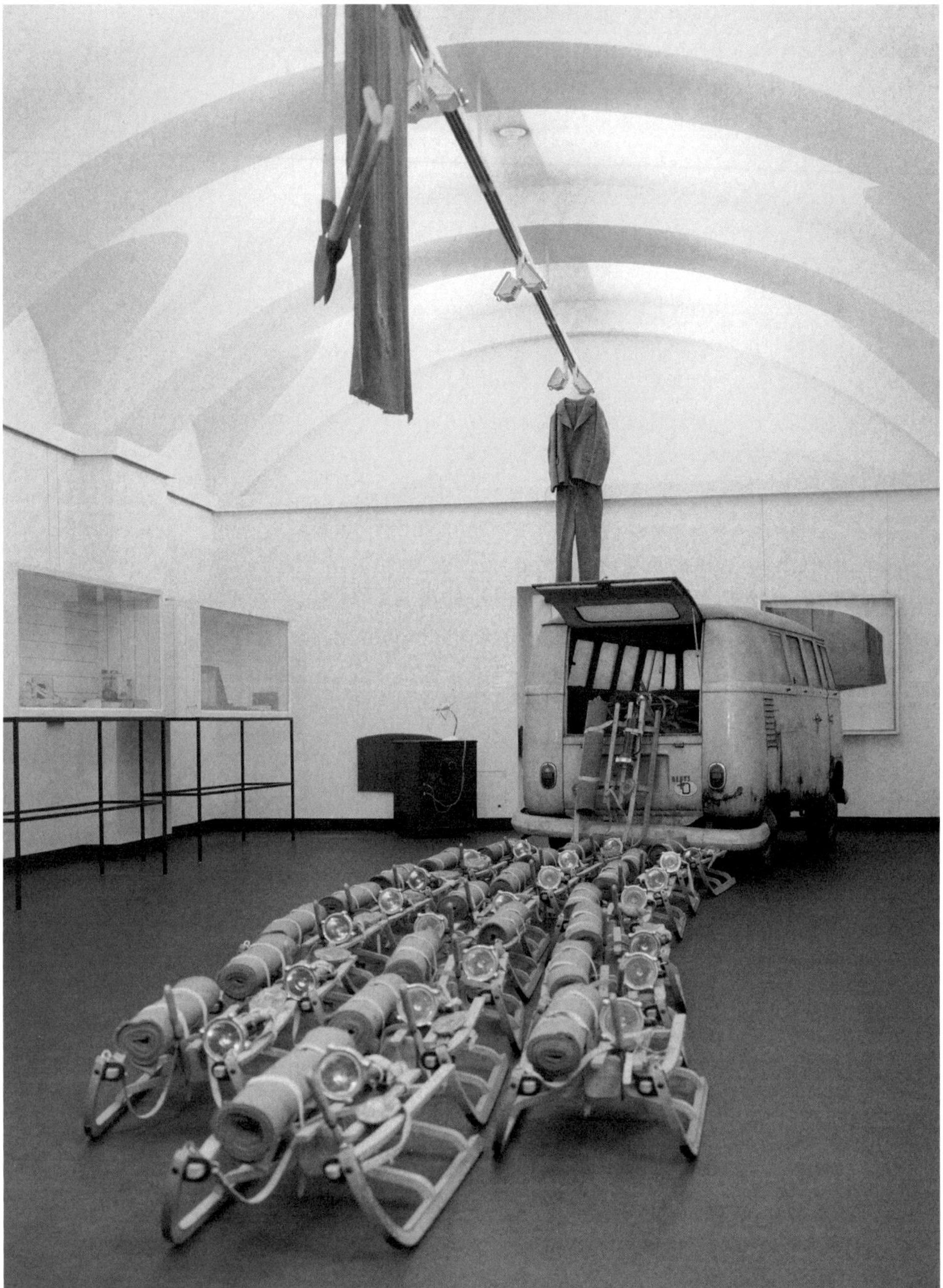

FIGURE 87. Joseph Beuys, *The Pack (Das Rudel),* 1969, 1961 Volkswagen bus, twenty-four sleds, each equipped with fat, felt blanket, braces, and flashlight, ca. 200 × 400 × 1000 cm. Neue Galerie, Museumslandschaft Hessen Kassel. Art © 2010 Artists Rights Society (ARS), New York/VG Bild-Kunst, Bonn. Photo: Bildarchiv Preussischer Kulturbesitz/Art Resource, NY.

is one of the two lowest, a sunken rather than raised monument. In the Guggenheim show catalogue Beuys commented at length on the homeopathic intentions of this vitrine, which he referred to as *Concentration Camp Essen,* a pun on the name of a German city and the German word for food:

> I do not feel that these works were made to represent catastrophe, although the experience of catastrophe has certainly contributed to my awareness. But my interest was not in illustrating it, even when I used the title *Concentration Camp Essen*. This was not a description of the events in the camp but of the content and meaning of catastrophe. That must be the starting point—like a kind of substance—something that surmounts *Concentration Camp Essen*. Similia similibus curantur: heal like with like, that is the homeopathic healing process.
>
> The human condition is Auschwitz, and the principle of Auschwitz finds its perpetuation in our understanding of science and the political systems, in the delegation of responsibility to groups of specialists and the silence of intellectuals and artists. I have found myself in permanent struggle with this condition and its roots. I find we are now experiencing Auschwitz in its contemporary character. This time bodies are outwardly preserved (cosmetic mummification) rather than exterminated, but other things are being eliminated. Ability and creativity are burnt out: a form of spiritual execution, the creation of a climate of fear perhaps even more dangerous because it is so refined.[43]

A brief look at the career of Bernard Heiliger provides perspective on Beuys's singular importance in German sculpture of the 1950s and 1960s, particularly in relationship to the monument, the memorial, the Nazi period and its aftermath, and spectatorial orientation. I have positioned Beuys as an imaginary, rebellious student of Arno Breker. Heiliger actually was Breker's student in Berlin beginning in 1938 and continuing through the war years.[44] Breker enabled Heiliger to visit Paris in 1939 and employed him at his foundry in Wriezen, where Heiliger also cast some of his own sculptures. In December 1939 Heiliger won a competition for figural sculptures for a military drill ground. The pieces, never installed, were to be called *Ehre* (honor) and *Freiheit* (freedom). Heiliger himself did military service, but Breker was able to limit the dangers to the artist he considered his most talented student. During Breker's denazification procedure in 1948, though, Heiliger was one of the very few witnesses for the prosecution, testifying about Breker's "luxurious lifestyle" in comparison to others of the time, achieved through huge state commissions that had corrupted his art, according to Heiliger.[45] In 1949 Heiliger moved into Breker's former studio on the edge of the Grunewald in Berlin-Dahlem, located today next to the Brücke Museum and headquarters of the Bernhard Heiliger Foundation (fig. 88). He declined to speak about his relationship to his former teacher and mentor.[46] Heiliger assumed the chair for sculpture at the Academy of Fine Arts in West Berlin and pursued a highly successful, accomplished, and public career to his death in 1995, developing the modernist career that Arno Breker had aborted in the 1930s.

In the 1950s Heiliger created works with affinity to Henry Moore's organic forms

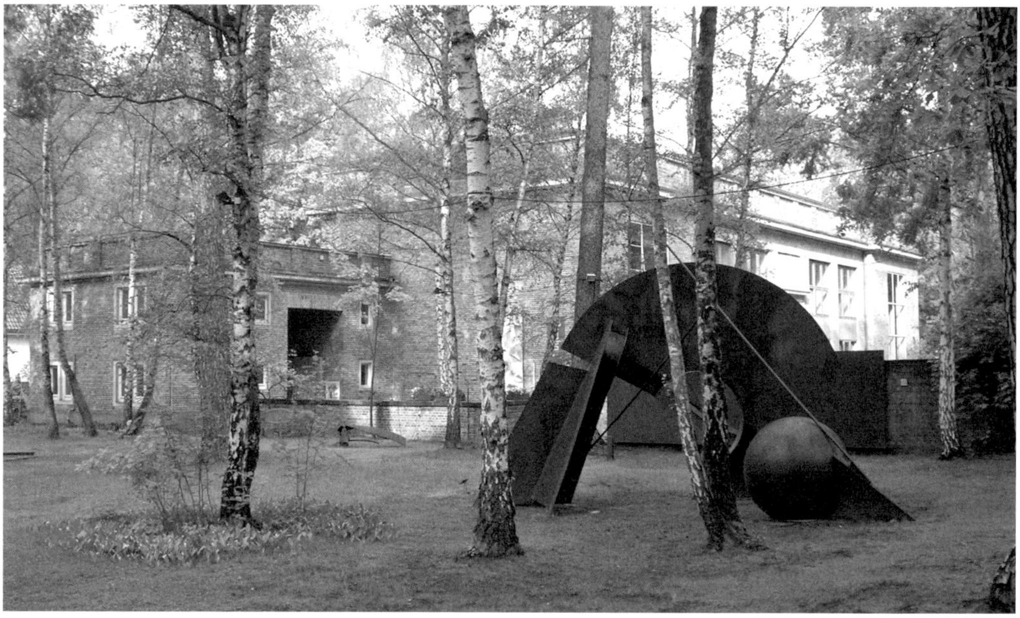

FIGURE 88. **Sculptures by Bernard Heiliger at Bernard Heiliger Foundation, Berlin. Art © 2010 Artists Rights Society (ARS), New York/VG Bild-Kunst, Bonn. Photo: Author.**

and "holed through" figures. His entry in the London Institute of Contemporary Art's competition in 1952 for a memorial for the unknown political prisoner resembles one of Herbert Ferber's welded steel caged figures.[47] Later, a relationship to Caro and to Naum Gabo's and Antoine Pevsner's versions of constructivist sculpture emerge. Heiliger created no less than sixteen monumental commissions for public sculptures in the western sector of divided Berlin, including the huge, hanging geometric abstraction *Kosmos 70*, designed in 1963 to hang in the Reichstag foyer. His welded open form *Flame* (1969) stands in front of Berlin's Technical University on Ernst Reuter Platz along the Straße des 17. Juni (Street of June 17th), which commemorates the 1953 uprising against the Communist dictatorship of the east, at the same site that Speer had planned to display Breker's massive reliefs.[48] After passing Richard Serra's 1988 *Berlin Juncture* outside the Berlin Philharmonic Hall, one encounters a Heiliger in the entry foyer. On the other side of the building, flanking the entrance to the chamber music hall, are Heiliger's Caroesque *Echo I* and *Echo II* of 1987 (fig. 89).

Heiliger was the quasi-official sculptor of the Bonn Republic and a preferred creator of modernist public monumental sculptures. Beuys, on the other hand, left his mark in the form of thousands of objects and dozens of installations in museums in Germany and abroad, and in the form of photographs of the artist performing.[49] From 1947 to 1986 he staged some seventy *Actions* and fifty installations, and he had 131 one-man exhibitions.[50] Beuys aspired to public impact and achieved it. But as a maker of sculptural objects his impact was limited almost exclusively to the public realm of museum culture,

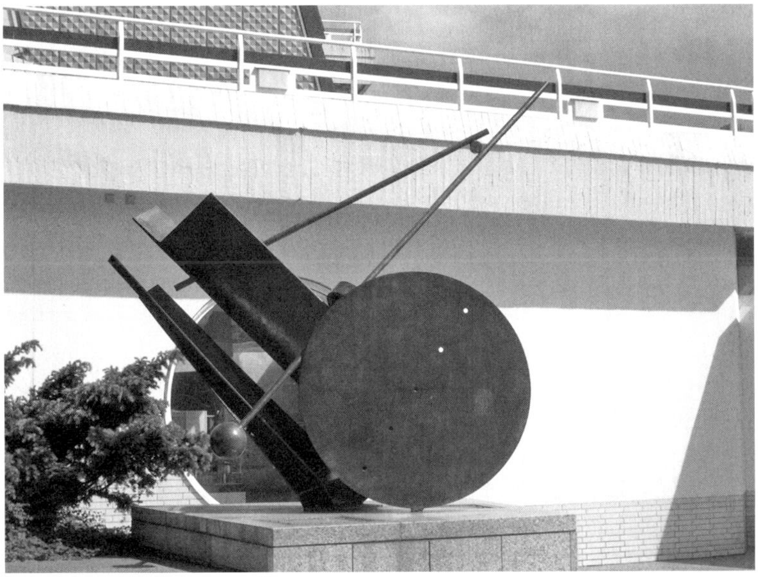

FIGURE 89. Bernhard Heiliger, *Echo II*, 1987, iron, 300 × 120 × 250 cm. Art © 2010 Artists Rights Society (ARS), New York/VG Bild-Kunst, Bonn. Photo: Author.

in which the works of Breker, the monumentalist who aspired to become a museum-worthy artist in the postwar period, generate impact only by their absence.[51] Given his prominence in public space, Heiliger, too, is underrepresented in German museums, as his works compete for space with the entire international range of related modernist sculptors from Henry Moore to sculptors of the present. His work is virtually invisible and unknown outside of Germany. Beuys grasped the changing nature of the international art world—that artistic quality would be judged by art world insiders and international art world standards, and that art would achieve its greatest impact, and ultimately in the public realm too, by impressing art experts (the villains of *Venus vor Gericht*) as opposed to other types of public officials. His impact in the art world was also mediated by particularly supportive private collectors, who bought his works en masse, lent them to museums, and then negotiated to have those loans become permanent installations. Among the most important of these collectors were the brothers Franz Joseph and Hans van der Grinten, who knew Beuys as a friend and promising local artist before he had any reputation whatsoever; they acquired their first Beuys works in 1951 and gave him his first show in 1953 (in their parent's house in Kranenburg). When Beuys died, they owned some five thousand works and one hundred thousand archival materials, which now form the heart of the Beuys museum and archive at Schloss Moyland, located about five miles from Beuys's hometown of Cleves (in German, Kleve), a small, hilly city in the northwest of North Rhine-Westphalia, near the Dutch border. The Beuys Block in Darmstadt derives from the collection of the industrialist Karl Ströher, who purchased an entire Beuys installation in Mönchengladbach in 1967; and the Beuys space in the Neue Galerie in Kassel came from the collectors Jost and Barbara Herbig, who purchased *The Pack* from Galerie René Block in 1969 and continued acquiring Beuys works until 1973, when, like Ströher in Darmstadt, they negotiated with the museum to display all the pieces together, and with the artist to install and periodically adjust the installation.[52] The Kaiser Wilhelm Museum in the industrial city of Krefeld, where Beuys was born, began integrating the Beuys collection of Walther and Helga Lauffs in 1969. Erich Marx's extensive Beuys collection forms a permanent loan exhibition in Berlin's Hamburger Bahnhof, Museum of Contemporary Art.

How did Beuys achieve such devotion, art world prominence, and broad fame? In many ways, his route was conventional, though his activities along that route were less so. His formal training took place at the Düsseldorf Kunstakademie (art academy) from 1947 to 1952. He studied first under the Aristide Maillol student Joseph Enseling, professor at the academy from 1938 to 1952.[53] Beuys transferred from Enseling's class to that of Ewald Mataré, who was dismissed by the Nazis in 1933 and reappointed to the academy immediately after the war. Beuys completed his master's degree with Mataré from 1952 to 1954. Under Mataré, best known for his elegant, semi-abstract representations of animals, Beuys received experience as a monumental sculptor, learning wood carving, metalwork, and casting. In the final years of his studies, Beuys assisted Mataré in casting a new set of doors for the Cologne cathedral, a project that made Mataré famous in Germany.

In 1955 Beuys received his only publicly commissioned work outside a museum, art school, or art fair, the Büderich *Memorial to the Victims of the World Wars* (figs. 90–91). He worked on the piece in a studio in the Cleves Kurhaus in 1957–58, and it was dedicated in 1959.[54] The work consists of a set of oak doors and a hanging carved oak and cast iron cruciform figure representing a resurrection, and it is located in a freestanding Romanesque church tower, the remains of a parish church that burned down in 1891, in the Büderich neighborhood of Meerbusch, a suburb of Düsseldorf. For a sculptor appointed in 1961 to the chair in monumental sculpture at the Düsseldorf art academy, a fifteen-minute tram ride from the Büderich tower, a sculptor whose work is widely seen to reflect upon his and his nation's wartime experiences and their aftermath, completion of this commission would seem to be a key event. But although the work has been the subject of two detailed interpretations by a specialist in architectural preservation and a theologian, it has received scant attention in the literature assessing Beuys's overall career as a sculptor.[55]

Büderich was the longtime home of Mataré, who had opposed Beuys's appointment to the Düsseldorf Art Academy in 1955; he, too, had been invited to submit plans for the memorial, along with Beuys and two other artists. It seems unlikely that the village's most famous resident, who was also the most famous sculptor in Germany at the time, known particularly for his cathedral doors, had had no hand in his student's receiving the commission for the local parish church's doors. At the very least, by not submitting

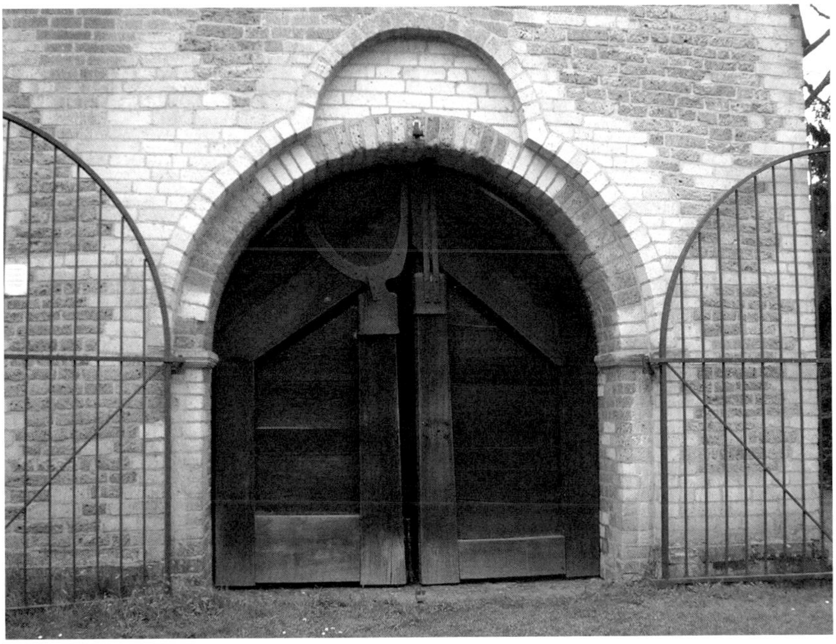

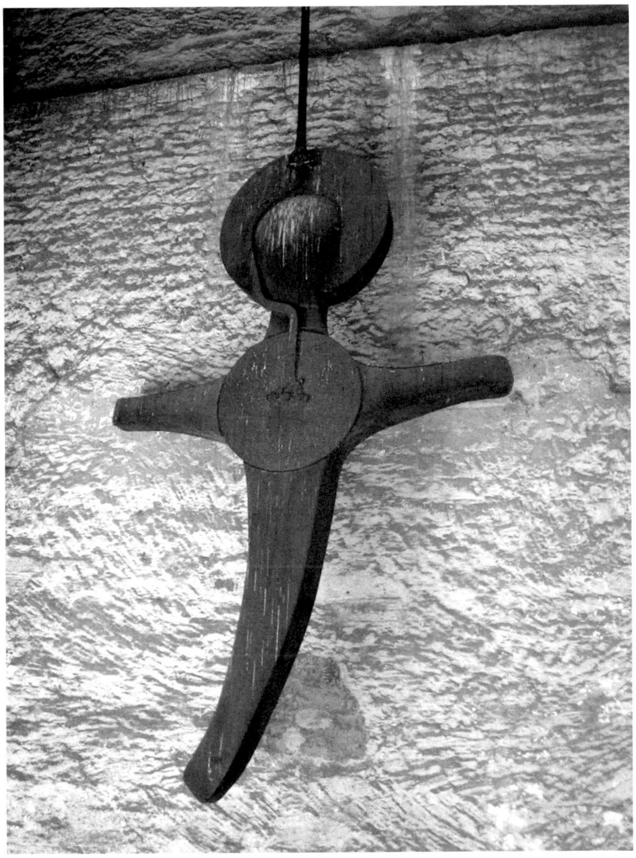

FIGURE 90. Joseph Beuys, doors for *Memorial to the Victims of the World Wars,* 1958–59, Büderich district of Meerbusch, Germany. Art © 2010 Artists Rights Society (ARS), New York/VG Bild-Kunst, Bonn. Photo: Margot Klütsch. FIGURE 91. Joseph Beuys, cruciform figure for *Memorial to the Victims of the World Wars,* 1958–59, Büderich district of Meerbusch, Germany. Art © 2010 Artists Rights Society (ARS), New York/VG Bild-Kunst, Bonn. Photo: Margot Klütsch.

to the competition, Mataré opened the door for his student to prove himself capable of completing a monumental commission.[56] At Büderich, Beuys proved his mastery of the crafts of casting, metalwork, and carving, as well as his ability to create a large-scale work, a unified sculpture orchestrating a spectatorial experience consisting of multiple elements.

Beuys crafted two great oak doors for the church in his studio, and later inscribed on the front and back of the right door panel in cuneiform-like script the names of 222 Büderich citizens killed in the two world wars (he was paid at a rate of one mark per letter).[57] The names of the World War II dead begin on the door's front and continue on the back where they are followed by World War I victims, transcribed from a 1924 memorial. While the World War I list is limited to soldiers, the list of World War II dead includes civilians. Whether these names include forced laborers in the area and deported Jews remains unclear, though it seems unlikely, as the names are typical of those of German gentiles. The broadening of those memorialized beyond soldiers, and lack of specificity as to their wartime roles and the cause of their deaths, is consistent with generalizing tendencies of German war memorials of the time.[58]

With the help of a cousin who was a blacksmith, Beuys forged two cast iron elements resembling horns and antennae for the tops of the elliptical doors.[59] For Holger Brülls, these resemble a scythe and a pike and are therefore symbols of war and peace and the transition from "swords to ploughshares." Friedhelm Mennekes interprets the pike on the inscribed right door as a male symbol, and the curved scythe form as female, together symbolizing regeneration. Through the doors one enters a twenty-meter-tall tower, empty save for the three-by-two-meter oak cruciform figure hanging not on the far but on the left wall from a long nine-section, cast iron chain tethered to a beam between two windows in the tower's ceiling. Before Beuys prepared his competition entry he requested architectural plans for the tower, which suggests that he conceived the piece spatially and in relation to the total site.[60] He constructed a model for his submission, in which the figure hangs from a shorter chain and opposite the tower doors on the far wall, which was originally the church's main entrance. The move to the left wall heightens the spectator's appreciation of the tower and its otherwise empty space. It also decreases the association of the piece with a church altar or traditional crucifixion.

The Büderich memorial is a transitional work in Beuys's career. It is the culmination of his religiously themed works of the 1950s, many of which employ crosses. In 1951, in Büderich's village cemetery, Beuys carved a slightly asymmetric cross in low relief into a small gravestone for the Niehaus family. As a class project under Mataré he designed a baptismal font in 1948–49, which led to two carved wooden figures now in the Schloss Moyland Museum, *Symbol of the Sacrifice* and *Symbol of Redemption*—the latter, with a similar gentle curvature to the figure's lower extremities, particularly resembles the Büderich figure and distinguishes it from a crucifixion (though this association is also unavoidable). This project fed into a private commission that Beuys completed simultaneously with the Büderich memorial, a grave for the van der Grinten family in Kranen-

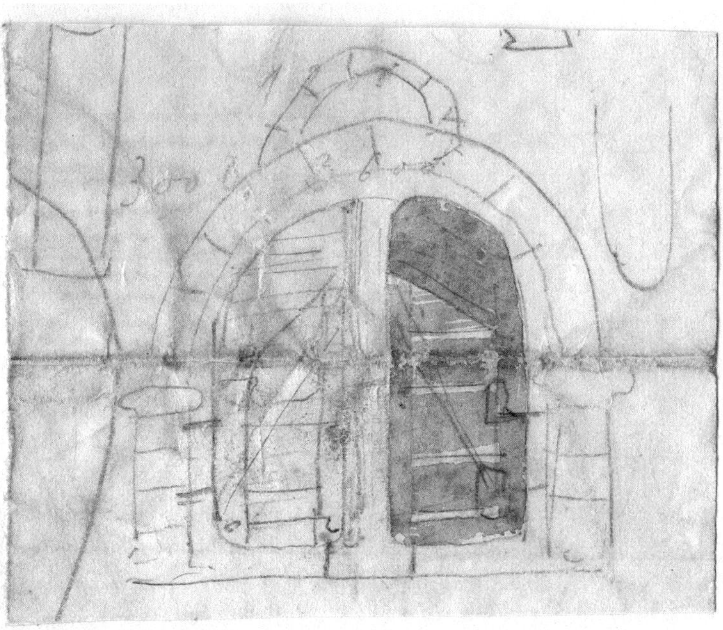

FIGURE 92. *Entwurf für ein Holztor* (Design for a wooden gate) for the Büderich memorial, 1958–59, pencil and watercolor, 6.5 × 7.8 cm. Art © 2010 Artists Rights Society (ARS), New York/VG Bild-Kunst, Bonn. Stiftung Museum Schloss Moyland/Joseph Beuys Archiv. Photo: Maurice Dorren, Stiftung Museum Schloss Moyland.

burg, commissioned in 1957 and dedicated in 1961.[61] The curvature of the bottom section of the figure lends it a zoomorphic quality, increasing the resemblance to Mataré's stylized animals, which in turn relate to Greek geometric, prehistoric, and Asian prototypes. The cross motif continued throughout Beuys's career, including those inscribed on the sausages in *Auschwitz Demonstration,* as well as those in *Crucifixion,* of 1962–63, a construction of found objects such as bottles, wire, cable, and newspaper.[62]

Like much of the artist's later practice, such as the Guggenheim installation, the Büderich memorial turns the spectator into an active performer moving through "stations." One passes through the doors like a participant in a processional. Drawings demonstrate that Beuys considered the dimensions of each element and calculated the gap between the partially opened doors, through which one already glimpses the hanging, and sometimes gently swaying, figure (fig. 92). Craft elements root it in tradition, but abstraction and visible facture lend it modernity. Beuys asserted that, contrary to the obvious formal resemblance, the Büderich figure was not a crucifix or a figure of sacrifice but a symbol of redemption—the war dead rising again in the present. In the present, it presents a warning: it is titled the Büderich *Mahnmal* (memorial warning or admonition) as opposed to *Denkmal* (memorial of remembrance).[63]

The Büderich memorial demonstrates that Beuys took a more conventional route to success than either he or most of his interpreters would have it. His self-authored "Life Course/Work Course" omits this commission and sums up the late 1950s as "1957–1960, recovery from working in the fields," which refers to his working on the van der Grinten farm to recuperate from psychological troubles. At Büderich he showed himself capable of receiving and carrying through a public commission, satisfying the demands of a commissioning committee and a community. He worked with a variety of materials, including the tower itself, which he specified should not be renovated in any way, and he orchestrated the spectator's experience spatially, materially, and viscerally. In doing so, he mobilized multiple sculptural elements to create a work designed to encourage reflection in the present on recent German history, in a vocabulary transcending the present and recent past. The Büderich memorial helped open the door to Beuys's institutional acceptance as an artist, his Düsseldorf professorship. It is also a hinge to his later and more famous practice. But, though a public piece, the work has received little attention from the art public. His subsequent challenges to traditional institutional criteria and distinctions at the academy, in the museum, and for the memorial genre enabled Beuys to emerge as a public artist and figure. Like Kaprow, he benefited from the artistic freedom of a professorship as well as from the expanding art world of the 1960s and 1970s, when artists such as Beuys and Kaprow received and created opportunities to realize often unsaleable works in a variety of environments, including factories, warehouses, fields, deserts, and swamps.[64] Not limited to museums and galleries—though still within the expanded art world—the charismatic Beuys and his unconventional objects and persona attracted an expanded audience.

In doing so, Beuys helped alter conceptions of sculpture, especially memorial monuments, as they continued to be constructed in postwar Germany. In 1950 one of the first memorial sculptures to the victims of the Nazi state was commissioned on the grounds of the crematorium in the Dachau concentration camp outside Munich. *The Unknown Prisoner* predates the gradual transformation of Dachau into a museum and memorial site sponsored by the International Dachau Committee, an organization led by former prisoners (fig. 93). According to the historian Harold Marcuse, the Bavarian government official Philipp Auerbach particularly pushed for the memorial, which was dedicated on the fifth anniversary of the camp's liberation, on April 30, 1950.[65] The commissioners apparently desired a traditional figurative monument. They gave the job to Fritz Koelle, sculptor of the Horst Wessel bust (fig. 82) and recipient of other official commissions under the Nazis, including an imperial eagle clutching a wreath that surrounds a swastika, installed above the entry to the Third Reich's postal ministry building in Berlin.[66]

Koelle's first design for the Dachau monument included two figures, one holding his starved companion from behind in an upright Pietà pose, which the historian of Holocaust memorials, Detlef Hoffmann, compares to a panel painting in the Frankfurt Städel Museum by the Master of Flémalle, in which God the Father supports his martyred son.[67] Sculpturally, the source is also Michelangelo's *Rondanini Pietà,* and, even more closely, Breker's reinterpretation of that in his *Comrades.*

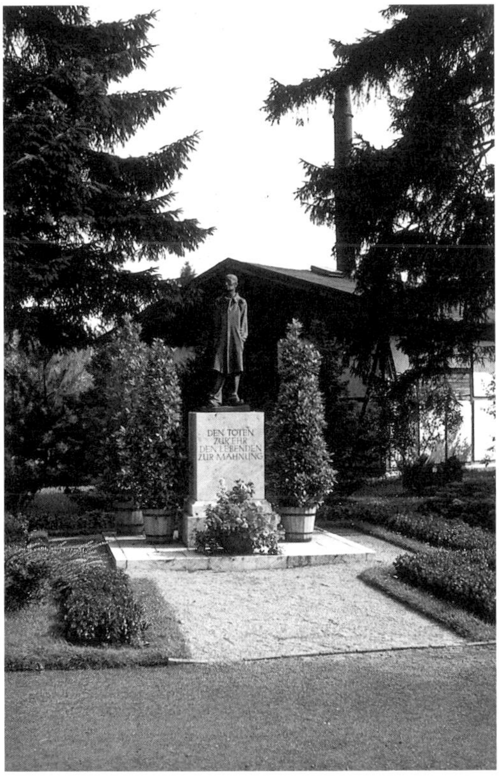

FIGURE 93. **Fritz Koelle, *The Unknown Prisoner,* 1950, bronze. Dachau Concentration Camp Memorial Site, Dachau, Germany.**

Koelle, though, derived the final version of his monument from his sculptures of workers that began in the 1920s, lending the figure a stoic dignity.[68] *The Unknown Prisoner* has become one of the visual hallmarks, reproduced on postcards and pamphlets, of a well-researched museum and memorial site devoted to documenting the infamous crimes committed at Dachau and elsewhere. *The Unknown Prisoner* generalizes victimhood—and suggests that brutal incarceration, like work, is ennobling—at a location, the first of their concentration camps, opened in March 1933, where the Nazis persecuted and killed some of their best-known opponents, among them the journalist and Nobel Peace Prize winner Carl von Ossietzky.

In the early 1960s, after the Büderich memorial and while assembling *Auschwitz Demonstration,* Beuys realized and demonstrated that art objects could gain what Stephen Greenblatt has called "resonance" if the artist manipulated the art museum setting to reference historical, anthropological, and scientific collections. He came to the realization that he could *use* the museum to orchestrate the spectator's experience and presentness in that place, as he had at the Büderich tower, even with all the constraints presented by a particular location. The tower, like a church, encourages the spectator to become immersed bodily and spiritually, and it contains only Beuys's works. Art museum spectators, on the other hand, tend to focus what the art historian Svetlana Alpers has termed their isolated "attentive looking" on many specific and discrete objects sequentially, appreciating each for its individual facture, materials, and beauty.[69] Other types of museums exploit viewers' attentiveness to different ends. At Dachau, for instance, Koelle's monument is among the weakest of memorial objects. Its tall base separates it from its context, seeking to move it into art's traditional space above and beyond the everyday. Other displays, of everyday objects at the site, are far more moving and powerful both as *Denkmal* (memorial) of the specific past and as *Mahnmal* (warning) for the present. Various objects on display in Dachau's informative historical museum shed light on a problematic aspect of Beuys's sculptural legacy: his appropriation of the aura of persecution, suffering, and survival emanating from the actual objects and residues of torture, humiliation, and death.

The Dachau *Bock zum Prügeln* (Beating rod), a battered cane displayed in a vitrine, is painfully specific (fig. 94). A visitor to this display familiar with Beuys's modification of the readymade, by which he invested everyday objects with personal, affective content, may see the beating rod as a form of readymade with historical and psychological associations, like Beuys's *Bathtub,* the place of *his* "first wounding." This association is even more explicit in relation to Beuys's 1970 multiple *Felt Suit* (created in a hundred versions—one is visible in figure 87, hanging above *The Pack*).[70] Like the Büderich piece, the suit is a hanging form, now borrowing the specific historical associations invested in the prisoner's uniform to be seen at Dachau and other concentration camp museums (fig. 95). Beuys appropriated the aura of suffering and authenticity associated with such objects and imported that aura into the art museum. At that site, historical authenticity, except that associated with Beuys, is lost, and only the aura of history remains.[71] His work participated in a blurring of distinctions, not only between types of museums but between historical memory triggered by exposure to history's actual artifacts and that triggered by simulations. Participating in the developing postmodern artistic culture, Beuys predicted the practice of artists such as Christian Boltanski, whose work explores the similarity between emotions stimulated by real memorials and those stimulated by simulations: objects, installations, and exhibitions can evoke memories to which they are connected metaphorically rather than materially.

The problematic aspect of this appropriation in Beuys's case has to do with his actual roles in the Third Reich. Beuys served the Nazi cause on a much lower and more common level than Breker, as a member first of the Hitler Youth and then as a volunteer in the Luftwaffe. Whether he killed for Hitler is unknown, but it is likely. The only life he is documented to have saved is his own. How he saved his life has become the stuff of legend, a legend Beuys himself first propagated and then distanced himself from as he noticed that it threatened to engulf all other interpretations of his work.

Beuys volunteered to serve in the German air force in 1940. He was active for the entire war, mainly in Crimea on the eastern front, but toward the end of the war also on the western front, where he ended the war as a British prisoner. Trained as a radio operator, he also took on other roles, perhaps as a pilot and certainly as a paratrooper and crew commander. On a mission in Crimea during the German retreat from the advanc-

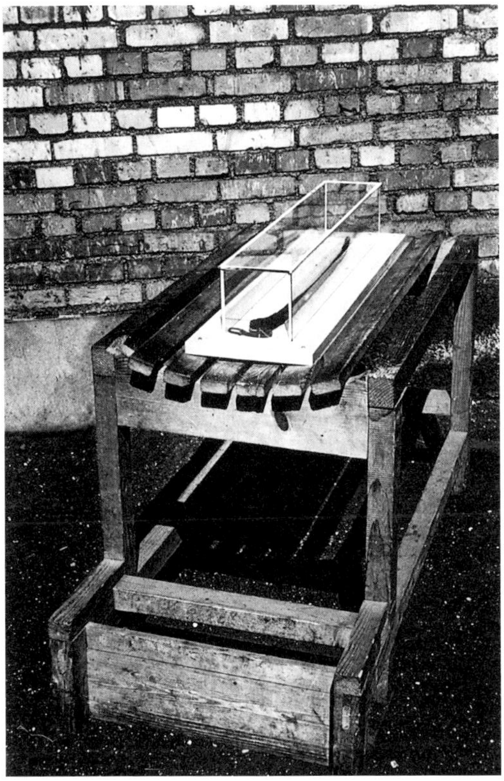

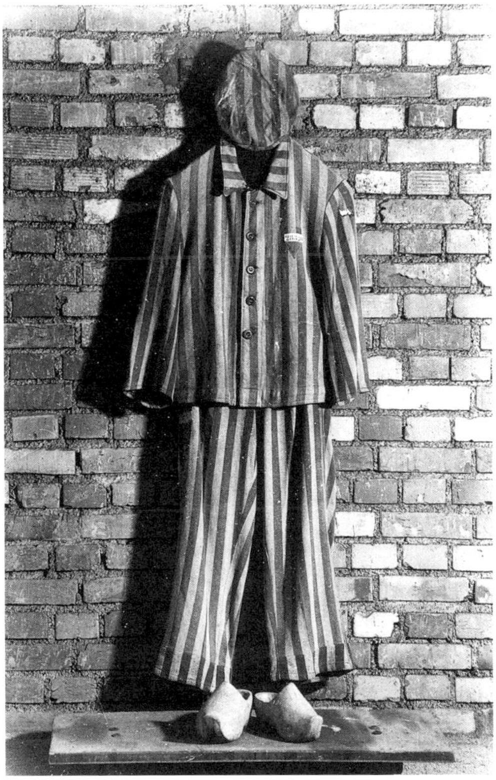

FIGURE 94. *Bock zum Prügeln* (Beating rod) at Dachau Memorial Museum, Dachau, Germany. FIGURE 95. *Kleidung eines Häftlings* (Prisoner's uniform) at Dachau Memorial Museum, Dachau, Germany.

ing Red Army, his plane took flak but managed to cross back behind German lines before crashing. Though the date of this event has often been given as 1943, military records indicate that it actually occurred on March 16, 1944.[72] According to Beuys, the other crew member in the Junkers 87 aircraft "was atomized by the impact," as he was strapped in by a seat belt, whereas Beuys, who had "always preferred free movement to safety belts," was thrown from the plane and rather miraculously survived.[73] Beuys claimed to have been found by nomadic indigenous "tribesmen," Tartars, with whom he had already had contact and who had even claimed him as one of their own. According to Beuys, they smeared his body with fat, wrapped it in felt to preserve its warmth, and nursed him back to health over the course of, according to different accounts, eight or twelve days. Beuys's artistic use of fat and felt has been widely traced back to their supposed role in his recovery. The olfactory dimension of his work, according to this interpretation, evokes his extended period of convalescence in the Tartars' felt tents, permeated by the smell of cheese and yoghurt. The journalists Gieseke's and Markart's analysis of military records, though, have revealed that Beuys was treated in a German mobile field hospital from March 17 to April 7 and so could actually have been with the Tartars for at most twenty-four hours.[74] This correction actually supports the authenticity of the famous (or infamous) photograph that Beuys produced of the (or a) crashed aircraft. It is likely that a German rescue party arriving at the scene within a day of the incident would have found the plane still in its crashed state, fuselage perpendicular to the ground, and that they photographed it. Suffering from a concussion and other wounds, the fallen flier could have had an impaired sense of time. But if, as is likely, he later ascertained the actual duration of his stay with the Tartars, he never bothered to correct the historical record.

Regardless of the authenticity of specific details, it is a compelling story, in which ancient wisdom and traditional healing techniques practiced by transnational nomads overcome wounds deriving from modern national animosities and perils. Peter Nisbet has dubbed it The Story and demonstrated that Beuys began to propagate it around 1970, in the wake of the 1968 student movement that in West Germany called for more specific reckoning with the Nazi period, with those directly involved in it, and a consequent questioning and reorganization of persistently authoritarian social structures and institutions, such as the family, schools, and universities.[75] Beuys at that time began to participate more openly in the political realm, with an assault on the hierarchical structure of the Düsseldorf Art Academy and his lead role in founding the Free International University. Later he distanced himself from The Story, feeling that the direct linkage of his work to the war and his personal war experiences threatened to limit interpretations of his use of felt and fat, for which he desired broader social, environmental, and political connotations.[76] The Story's propagation also forms the basis for the influential contemporary critic Benjamin Buchloh's famously hostile article of 1980, in which "Beuys' origin in a historic period of German fascism affirms every aspect of his work as being totally dependent on, and deriving from that period." Buchloh's critique is worth quoting at some length, as it pinpoints a particular ambivalence toward Beuys's legacy with which all subsequent commentators have had to reckon. According to Buchloh, basing interpretations of Beuys's work on The Story

> does not necessarily tell us and convince us about the transcendental impact of his artistic work (which is the manifest intention of the fable). What the myth does tell us, however, is how an artist, whose work developed in the middle and late 1950s, and whose intellectual and esthetic formation must have occurred somehow in the preceding decade, tries to come to terms with the period of history marked by German fascism and the war resulting from it, destroying and annihilating cultural memory and continuity for almost two decades and causing a rupture in history that left mental blocks and blanks and severe psychic scars on everybody living in this period and the generation following it. Beuys' individual myth is an attempt to come to terms with those blocks and scars.[77]

For Buchloh, in 1980, Beuys's work rehearsed the trauma and its repression anachronistically, and his self-mythologizing revived defunct Romantic conceptions of the artist as savior. Avant-garde strategies that were revolutionary for Dada and Surrealism became, at best, anodyne statements of false cultural continuity in their belated, neo-avant-garde form; at worst they became constituent elements subsumed into a subtly repressive and increasingly powerful culture industry, ever more able to absorb and co-opt challenges to its authority and eager to employ artists as diversions.

In 1964 Beuys first made public his "Life Course/Work Course" chronology, in which he presented his entire life as a continuous artistic career.[78] Discordant elements that would present a more conventional path to success, such as the Büderich memorial, were omitted. The objects highlighted are not memorial sculptures but memory devices, mnemonic aids for recuperating the political and the social as the personal. Beuys declared his own birth to be an exhibition: "1921 Cleves. Exhibition of a wound drawn together with plaster." By the time Beuys constructed this chronology one should not rule out the possibility that he intended it, at least in part, as self-conscious satire and clowning in what often appears a somber body of work. Numerous witnesses attest to Beuys's wit, which is communicated sculpturally in works such as *The Pack,* and in his sole American performance, the 1974 *I Like America and America Likes Me,* for which he lived with a coyote in a gallery for a week, wrapping himself in felt, his portable *Heimat,* for warmth and protection.[79]

By the time he wrote "Life Course/Work Course" Beuys was well informed about Dada activities through his exposure to its contemporary resurrection by the Fluxus movement, the American neo-Dada of Jasper Johns and Robert Rauschenberg, and the direct experience of surviving objects and individuals, among them Hannah Höch and Max Ernst, whose work from the historic Dada movement had been shown in Düsseldorf in 1958.

In 1964 Beuys participated in the Fluxus group's Festival of New Art, organized at Aachen University by Valdis Abolins and Tomás Schmit. Fully titled *Actions/Agit-Pop/De-Collage/Happening/Event/Antiart/L'Autrisme/Art Total/Reflexus,* this event coincided with the twentieth anniversary of the July 20, 1944, attempt on Hitler's life by officers of the conservative, nationalist conspiracy that hoped to stop him from leading the country further into ruin. One participant in the Festival of New Art, Bazon Brock, played Goebbels's 1943 speech at the Berlin Sportpalast over the public address system—the speech in which the propaganda minister, after Germany's defeat at the Battle of Stalingrad, had exhorted the audience to die in what was an increasingly hopeless cause, with the hectoring phrase: "Do you want total war?" Brock himself stood on his head and exhorted the audience: "Do you want total life?" Meanwhile Beuys melted fat, specifically Rama-brand margarine, on hot plates in cases.[80]

Incited by the radical artists' provocations, right-wing students stormed the stage, and Beuys was punched but continued with the performance. Heinrich Riebesehl photographed Beuys, bleeding from the nose, holding his sculpted *Crucifix Scene* in his left hand and his right arm aloft in an incantatory gesture that alluded both to blessing and to the Hitler salute (fig. 96).[81] Wounded, but a healer who "shows his wound," Beuys burst into broader public awareness as a result of this photograph. His image combined

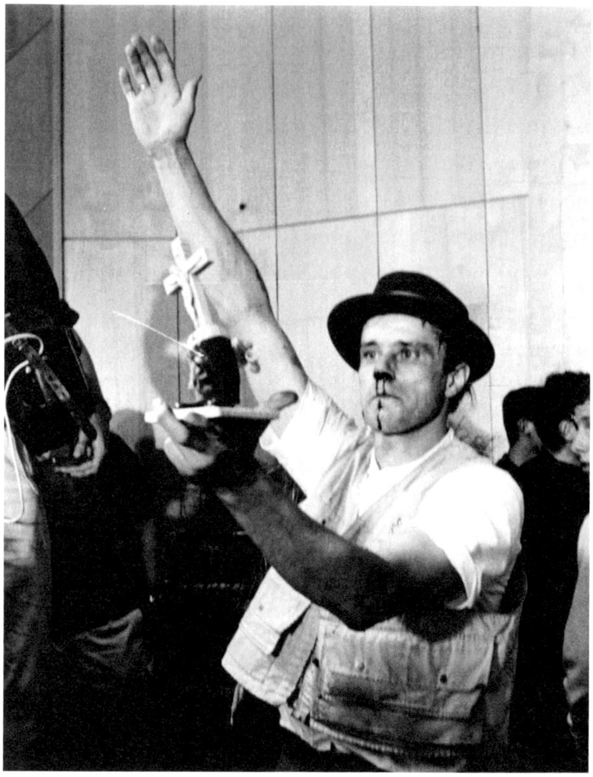

FIGURE 96. Heinrich Riebesehl, *Joseph Beuys, 1964,* photographed at "Festival of New Art," Aachen Technical University, 20 July 1964. Art © 2010 Artists Rights Society (ARS), New York/VG Bild-Kunst, Bonn. Photo: Sprengel Museum, Hannover.

"strange contemporary artist," quasi-religious figure, and German everyman—the very embodiment of esoteric aspiration and commonly felt though rarely expressed suffering and wounded survival. The liberal-intellectual newspaper *Die Zeit* reported on the event under the headline "A Professor Got Punched," casting attention not only on the rapidly changing and expanding art world but also on the emerging rough-and-tumble realities of 1960s institutional politics, where the title of professor, rather than conferring prestige and protection, could become a provocation.[82]

By incorporating his personal history into his work not only as metaphor but also as material and public, wound-baring performances, Beuys repositioned himself and his art on the side of the victims. In doing so he and his work also enacted a stage in the history of the "coming to terms" with the Nazi past in German postwar society. In 1950s West Germany, victimhood was a generalized conception, extended as readily, or even more readily, to German war veterans as to murdered Jews. As the historian Habbo Knoch points out in his study of the German reception of photographs from the Nazi period, after 1945 victimhood came "to apply to the majority of German society, from the war dead to refugees all the way to those war criminals who were supposedly unjustly convicted by the allies. . . . [B]arbed wire and shaved heads that had been associated with concentration camps even before the war ended, came to be symbols exclusively for the suffering of German prisoners of war and the struggle for the return home of German soldiers from the Soviet Union." As the pictorial evidence of Nazi crimes became better known in the 1950s, Knoch argues, the "fate of German Jews came to be interpreted as the starting point for the catastrophe of German society."[83] Beuys's work and its associations with his persona and his statements point to this generalized conception of German victimhood, making reference to the Holocaust, but not specifically limiting his works' acts of remembrance and mourning to the primary victims. It would remain for later generations to effect such historical specificity and evoke sympathy for victims rather than mere empathetic absorption of their suffering.[84]

Benjamin Buchloh has recently modified his position and averred that Beuys was perhaps "the first, if not the only, artist of the 1950s and 1960s in Germany, if not in Europe to actually have addressed the conditions of cultural production after the Holocaust."[85] The "conditions of cultural production" to which Buchloh refers is the famous dictum laid down by Theodor Adorno in 1951. "To write poetry after Auschwitz is barbaric."[86] In Ezra Pound's classic formulation the modern poet's task was to "make it new." Whatever other meanings might be latent in the text, modern poetry would renew language itself. The visual art equivalent would be high modernism as propounded by Clement Greenberg and later refined by Michael Fried—art whose originality and pure opticality, in contrast to the simulation of emotion characterizing what Greenberg called "kitsch"—would "keep culture *moving*."[87] Beuys's memorial work eschews optical effects or any attempt to "make new" the abject materials the artist recycled. They attempt to be moving emotionally rather than formally, but certainly not with the easily readable syntax of kitsch. *Auschwitz Demonstration* avoids visual poetry but also rejects a prosaic view of its subject, not attempting to narrate or depict the concentration camp, both of which attempts would risk fetishizing the minutiae of suffering endured by victims and enjoyed by sadistic perpetrators. The work relies instead on evoking a visceral reaction in the spectator, an empathetic response. Gene Ray has eloquently connected such internal feelings of revulsion and terror evoked by Beuys's work to the aesthetic category of the sublime as developed by Kant and reinterpreted by Adorno and postmodern theorists such as Slavoj Zizek.[88] Beuys's works, as one German art critic put it, "as no other artist of the postwar period embody willingness to endure suffering by finding form and symbols that otherwise would remain unspeakable, as Adorno says."[89]

Adorno did not use the term "Holocaust" in his 1950s injunction and neither did Beuys in his statements or work titles. The director of the International Research Institute at the Yad Vashem Memorial in Israel, Yehuda Bauer, offered a simple, straightforward, and useful definition of the term "Holocaust," in an address to the German parliament on January 27, 1998: "The project of the total annihilation of the Jewish people and the actual murder of all the Jews the murderers could lay their hands on."[90] This is not to diminish and certainly not to deny that the Nazi state persecuted and murdered vast numbers of non-Jews, including Sinti and Roma, Poles, Russians and other Slavs, Jehovah's Witnesses, adherents to the Confessing Church, the mentally and physically disabled, homosexuals, and Communists and other political opponents of all religions and ethnicities. The point here is not to specify the extent of the crime but to recognize the precise historical dimensions of designations of it, which are always at the same time representations and interpretations.[91] The use of the term "Holocaust," while not absolutely limited to Jewish victims, by derivation and the traditions of its usage has stressed them.

"Holocaust," according to the *Oxford English Dictionary*, derives from the Greek word *holokaustum*, "a sacrifice wholly consumed by fire; a whole burnt offering," and was used to refer to Nazi mass murders, especially of Jews, in English newspapers as early as 1942.[92] It did not enter into general German usage until the beginning of the year of Beuys's breakthrough Guggenheim exhibition. In January 1979 the four-part broadcast of the American television miniseries *Holocaust* connected the German mass audience for the first time to the Nazi mass murder of specific, Jewish individuals.[93] This melodramatic mass media narrative represented history as experienced at the local and individual level. *Holocaust* had a profound effect on popular conceptions of the Nazi period, Nazi crimes, and Nazi victims, and it added the word "Holocaust" to the German lexicon. A standard German dictionary that first appeared in 1978, like most German dictionaries to that time, does not include "Holocaust" in its third edition (1980). The fifth edition (2001), identifies as the primary definition "the annihilation of the Jews under National Socialism"; the secondary definition is genocide in general.[94]

The title for Beuys's vitrine *Auschwitz Demonstration* provides us with his only definitive naming of the crime. Auschwitz, which was situated in Poland, is the name the Germans gave to the concentration camp they established at the end of April 1940 at the site of Polish army barracks near the Silesian town of Oswiecim.[95] Auschwitz I was initially a forced-labor installation. Auschwitz II, the so-called Buna, was a center for the production of plastics. After the decision was reached to enact a "final solution" to the "Jewish question" the Polish village of Brzezinka, three miles down the road, was leveled and transformed into the industrialized death factory of Birkenau, where some 1.6 million people, 90 percent of them Jews, were murdered.

Adorno's famous injunction adopted the word "Auschwitz" as a part-for-whole designation of Nazi crimes. The Auschwitz Trials, from December 20, 1963, to August 20, 1965, in which guards from the camp were tried in Frankfurt, accelerated the adoption of "Auschwitz" as a general German term to denote the enormity of inhumanity perpetrated under Nazism.[96] This was the context of Beuys's combining elements of his 1957 competition entry along with other objects created until 1964 as a "demonstration." Later, in 1968, he assembled them together in vitrines and in 1970 they were installed in the Hessian State Museum in Darmstadt as a "block," in Auschwitz terminology, the designation for prisoners' barracks and the notorious "Block 10" in which heinous medical experiments were carried out.[97]

The Darmstadt Beuys Block consists of a series of seven rooms, designated as Spaces 1–7, arranged in a "U" configuration, with Space 1 in the top left and Space 7 in the top right, connected by a door. As at Büderich, Beuys created an immersive spectator experience. One enters and exits via Space 1, the largest room, which contains almost nothing. The visitor has the uncomfortable feeling of having accidentally stumbled into an unused area of the museum. Moving forward and crossing into Space 2, one confronts a large stack of felt topped with a metal plate, *Fond,* of 1969. Squeezing by it to the left, one passes under a *Felt Suit* hanging high on the wall above, one of the few elements necessitating an upward gaze. In the same space, after the complex installation *Stag Hunt* (dated 1961, though the newspapers in bundles bearing crosses in it are dated 1963), the felt skin of the *Infiltration-Homogen for Grand Piano* hangs on the long left wall, recalling the skin of the flayed Marsyas or Rembrandt's painting of a hanging side of beef. Turning to the right, one enters Space 3, which includes the *Chair with Fat* in a vitrine beside a "fat corner" from the performance "Das Schweigen von Marcel Duchamp wird überbewertet." Now the path turns back in the direction of Spaces 7 and 1, down a narrow corridor traversing four rather dark rooms, each filled with vitrines to the right. These rooms recall the museum's natural history collections, especially those filled with cases of stuffed birds and other zoological specimens. The *Auschwitz Demonstration* vitrine is in Space 5, one of nine display cases jammed into the room (plate 6).[98] The vitrine contains fourteen pieces dating from 1956 to 1964. Several refer directly to Auschwitz, such as a folded map of the camp—a fourfold, five-part panoramic photograph standing on its edge and therefore visible from both sides, to the left end of which Beuys appears to have added two more sections that include a plan of the camp that faces in the opposite direction from the photograph. Next to the map a viewer can read, with some effort, the beginning of a description of the photograph: "Site plan of the camp in Brzezinka, on which is visible the train tracks leading to the gas chambers and the crematorium. To the left of the tracks is the women's camp." The indication of the tracks relates to Beuys's rejected Auschwitz memorial proposal, which would have eschewed any traditional sculptural object in favor of a series of gates either over or near the railroad tracks, focusing on the transports that were essential to the organized, efficiently scheduled killing.[99] As the art historian Matthew Biro has suggested, the only possible reference to Jewish victims in the vitrine, a dead rat lying in a bed of straw in a cylindrical container (*Rat,* 1957), risks restating Nazi stereotypes of Jews as vermin *(Ungeziefer),* while the wax *Cross,* also of 1957, a crucifixion and wafer on a plate, located directly behind the blocks of fat on a hotplate used in the Aachen event of July 1964, directly connects the entire vitrine to Beuys's typical Christian, 1950s images of transubstantiation and redemption. Mario Kramer, a great admirer of Beuys's work, nonetheless finds this "irritating. . . . It claims the presence of the mystery of Golgotha in Auschwitz. An alienating idea for Christians as well as Jews."[100]

The last object the visitor passes in Space 7 is a *Pack*-like rescue sled, installed in a vitrine set at an angle to the door, funneling one back into Space 1. Emerging back into Space 1, one notices that it is not only the largest but also the brightest room: in the museum's original condition (it is currently undergoing renovation) the walls of all the galleries were covered with dark brown jute, but when Beuys designed the installation only Space 1 included sky lighting.[101] The experience of light and space now, after the journey through darker more cluttered spaces, was not discomfiting but liberating. We emerged from our journey through a natural history of Beuys and his times having survived the horror and seen the light. It is he, and not we, who has suffered, died, and left behind his relics. In a dialogue with Friedhelm Mennekes about Christ's significance, Beuys again and again intoned the importance of suffering as redemptive and healing: "One who perseveres in suffering obviously propels the world forward and, in any case, enriches the world. It would be an important question to ask who enriches the world more: the active or those who suffer? I have always decided: the suffering. . . . For it is through suffering that that the world is given Christian substance."[102] This dialogue took place in 1984, as Beuys more and more confronted his own mortality—something he claimed to be well prepared for, having already experienced death twice, after his plane crash and during his late-1950s psychological crisis. Since Beuys's death, though, his prominence has diminished rather than risen: his art's potency, its ability to arouse strong passions, seems to have required his shaman-like presence.

Gene Ray has argued persuasively that many of Beuys's objects and actions since *Auschwitz Demonstration* referred to Auschwitz in their most basic material form, through his incessant use of fat and felt, by-products of the killing centers administered productively by ruthless "specialists." Industrialized genocide was part of a broad economy of human destruction and material production. According to legend, if not fact, fat was rendered from the bodies of the murdered for use in the production of soap.[103] Hair cut from victims was shipped to factories to be made into felt. As Ray asserts, Beuys, as well as many Germans, probably learned, or were reminded, of these inhuman practices by the 1955 Alain Resnais film *Night and Fog*, translated by the poet Paul Celan from the French script by Jean Cayrol and released in 1956 in German.[104]

Night and Fog employs skillful editing to weave together the present and the past. Contemporary footage shot at Auschwitz, in color, is combined with documentary footage of Nazi rallies and camp victims in black and white. The narration intones: "This landscape: the landscape of nine million dead. Who among us will keep watch here and warn us, when the new executioners come?"[105] The film scholar Joshua Hirsch identifies it as the most important originator of what he calls "posttraumatic cinema." Even as Resnais's documentary masterpiece repressed the specific memory of the Jewish victims—(the word "Jew" is mentioned only once in the text)—through its coordinated camera movements, sound, and editing, it invented a specifically cinematic, formal, and modernist idiom by which a present haunted by this past could be evoked.[106]

Ray must be correct that Beuys would have seen, or at least read about, *Night and Fog*—which was first shown in Germany at the Berlin film festival in July 1956—around the time he prepared his submission to the Auschwitz competition of 1956–57.[107] There can be little doubt, too, that the use of fat and felt throughout his work from the early 1960s on evoked the camps, while also referring to other contexts.[108] However, it is also telling that discussion of these references did not begin until after the Guggenheim exhibition. Beuys's notorious statement, from that show's catalogue, that "we are now experiencing Auschwitz in its contemporary character" in such acts as the "delegation of responsibility to groups of specialists and the silence of intellectuals and artists," and that he had found himself "in permanent struggle with this condition and its roots," is at once insensitive to the particularity of Auschwitz and its incommensurability to his own position as a world famous artist in 1979, while at the same time a strategic attempt to activate this history in relationship to the present, a tactic similar to what Hirsch has called *Night and Fog*'s "referential fogginess."[109] His objects, in their abject states and always still in process—sausages that continue to grow mold, a rat that continues to decompose, volatile fat—pull the aura of past crimes into the present, in which they are meant to function as a continual warning. Mario Kramer quotes Beuys to conclude his exhaustive discussion of *Auschwitz Demonstration:* "For me it is a monument."[110]

While fat and felt bear a specific material relationship to the reality and legends of Auschwitz, they also have other associations. Both relate to the body's continual change: growing, shrinking, discoloring, both on the outside, as hair, and inside, as fat. Felt is one of the oldest human fabrics, made not from weaving but from pressing together fibers that can derive from many different sources, including rabbit fur. Its cultural universality, age, and ability to integrate diverse strands appealed to Beuys's transcendental ambitions.[111] Fat hardens and contracts against cold, and it expands under heat. As a soft material it was appropriate to Beuys's conception of his work as *Plastik* (modeling) as opposed to *Skulptur* (carving).[112] Fat and felt materialized Beuys's expanded concept of art.[113]

Fat also connects to Beuys's biography, both through the Tartar story and through his familial background. "After my time as a prisoner of war . . . [m]y parents would have preferred to see me—and here's something purely superficial—going into the lard factory in Cleves. Because we have in Cleves one of the largest factories for butter, margarine, and lard."[114] Numerous commentators, including his friend Nam June Paik, stressed Beuys's rootedness in the landscape and culture of the fertile Lower Rhine valley.[115] Fat, then, also affirms his connection to his native soil and its productive capabilities. As the art historian Monika Wagner points out, while fat, especially that on the hot plate burners in *Auschwitz Demonstration,* alludes to "the unspeakable connection between liquidation and transubstantiation," it also alludes to the production of a valuable commodity. In her material-based history of modern art, Wagner calls attention to the fact that fat was a carefully controlled substance in wartime Ger-

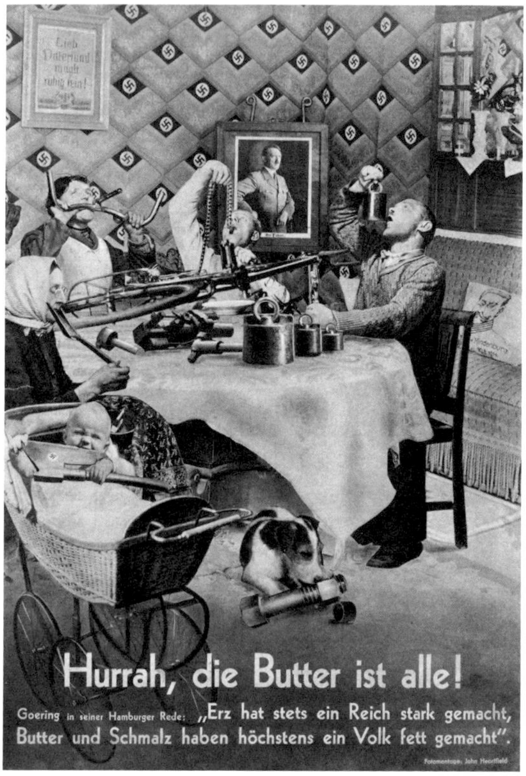

FIGURE 97. John Heartfield, *Hurrah, die Butter ist alle!* (Hurray, the butter is all gone!), photomontage in *Arbeiter Illustrierte Zeitung* (19 December 1935). Art © 2010 Artists Rights Society (ARS), New York/VG Bild-Kunst, Bonn. Photo: Art Resource, NY.

many, and that the Nazi government devised a "fat plan" for delivering this necessary source of low-cost energy to its hungry troops and population.[116] Edible fat figures prominently in German conceptions of health and happiness. It connotes both plenty and privation. To ask if everything is going smoothly in German, one can ask: "Alles in Butter?" When John Heartfield satirized Goebbels's speech praising the nation's "iron" will, he captioned his photomontage *Hurrah, die Butter ist alle!* (Hurray, the butter is all gone! fig. 97) and pictured a happy Nazi family eating metal bicycle parts. Postwar government subsidies of dairy production led to a comforting surplus referred to as the *Butterberg* (butter mountain). Butter, margarine, and fat in general have multiple associations and meanings, and "in Germany, above all," Wagner asserts, "it is a historically laden material."[117] Given the economic, historical, cultural, and psychological weight that German fat bears, and Beuys's personal involvement with it on all these levels, it is no wonder that his profligate use of this substance in the postwar period moved his spectators "to laugh, get angry, or try to destroy it," and even to punch him in the nose.

Beuys's response to the post-Auschwitz condition was specifically German and of its time. He tapped into the popular 1950s and 1960s images of everyday Germans of his generation, especially veterans, as internal opponents to and victims of the Nazi regime.[118] In what Andreas Huyssen has referred to as the "compulsive pas de deux" between mass culture and modernism, or fledgling postmodernism, if Breker's dance partner was Peter Brake in *Venus vor Gericht,* Beuys's was General Harras, the leading figure in the successful 1955 film *Des Teufels General* (The devil's general), based on a play by Carl Zuckmayer.[119] The stage version premiered in Zurich in 1946 and was performed some five thousand times on German stages prior to 1955, providing a major source for early postwar conceptions in Germany of the honorable German armed forces, its soldiers as victims, and the exceptional romance and dignity of the air force.[120] Curd Jürgens won the best actor award at the Venice film festival for his compelling performance as General Harras, an air force commander and passionate flier but no Nazi, and certainly a *Mensch.* He has Jewish friends for whom he tries in vain to intervene. Unbeknownst to him, a friend working under him, chief engineer Oderbruch, is actively involved in resistance, sabotaging planes. When he learns of his friend's treachery, rather than turn him in, Harras himself signs a confession of guilt and, in the film's conclusion, commits suicide by crashing a bomber, cockpit first, into an airfield. The image of the plane's fuselage and tail projecting into the sky is remarkably similar to that of Beuys's downed plane in the photograph of his wreck.

General Harras is an earthy, lusty, hard-drinking adventurer, who lives in a bachelor's apartment outfitted with African art and hunting trophies and wields his considerable authority with down-to-earth humor. He in no way resembles the young (or old) Joseph Beuys—just as neither he nor Oderbruch resembles most real German military men of the time. Despite, or perhaps because of, this disassociation from reality, a study of the way family histories of the Nazi era have been transmitted orally demonstrates that Harras became an important source of literal "screen memories" for Beuys's generation, Germans born in the 1920s.[121] Many of the interviewees in this study saw *The Devil's General* in their late twenties and early thirties, in the 1950s and 1960s. Aspects of the film's narrative and especially the central character constructions replaced or at least modified the actual memory of what husbands, fathers, and grandfathers—and they themselves—had felt and done in the war. *The Devil's General*'s association of crashing warplanes with internal resistance and redemption (Harras's last line is "If I was the devil's general in life, I'll be that in death, too") provides a parallel and precedent for Beuys's presentation of his personal history, which was very much in place in German public consciousness by the time he began propagating The Story.

Beuys's Story, and that of *The Devil's General* (and also that of *The Sinking of the Titanic*), testifies to specific dangers presented to human subjects by modern political, social, and technological realities, while also presenting hope for our physical and spiritual survival. The critical turn of the screw in Beuys's Story is that he survived his flight to be resurrected in the postwar era. By acknowledging and "showing our wounds," we can heal. This was already the message of the Büderich memorial. Beuys's sculptural mission was to redeem sculpture itself by employing atavistic, low-tech materials, outdated technology, and the timeless downward pull of gravity to push the sculptural object and experience beyond Breker's armored bodies and even "beyond objecthood."

Beuys realized that his institutional arena, the place that would make or break his reputation and that of his art, was the museum. As installations such as the Beuys Block demonstrate, for Beuys the art museum was the primary field of action, where he would seek to assert his authorial command over installation and interpretation, folding together display and object.[122] In a 1969 interview with the artist, writer, and curator Willoughby Sharp, Beuys stated that early on in his career he had been annoyed by the bases of sculptures, eliminated them, and only later realized their importance, after which he created some works that were nothing *but* bases. He found models for his antiaesthetic counter-monuments and for their display in historical museums, memorial sites, and natural history collections.[123] Beuys rejected aesthetic autonomy and appeal as the essence of an artwork, concepts revived in the postwar period by Baumeister, Fritz Winter, Ernst Wilhelm Nay, Julius Bissier, and other abstract painters, and by sculptors such as Brigitte Meier-Denninghoff, Norbert Kricke, and Hans Uhlmann. He also attacked the monumental vocabulary still spoken in works by artists such as Koelle or, in a modernist vernacular, by Bernhard Heiliger. In the Büderich *Mahnmal,* for instance, Beuys chose a hanging figure rather than one supported by a pedestal, or attached directly to the wall. Though it alludes to resurrection, the gravitational pull of the object itself is downwards.

Downward orientation characterizes many of Beuys's sculptures. One looks down and into the *Auschwitz Demonstration* vitrine, and down onto the triangle of fat of *Chair with Fat.* His *Fat Corners* filled the triangular intersection of floor and walls with his favorite solidified fluid, ready to ooze out into the space should it become oven-hot. The sleds in *The Pack* suggesting rescue lead one's gaze toward the floor, and at the Guggenheim installation, down the ramp. Beuys himself lay on the floor, wrapped in his protective roll of felt, in *The Chief (Fluxus Song)* of 1964 and ten years later in *I Like America and America Likes Me.* The pile of dirt on the floor as an element of the Venice Biennale piece *Tram Stop, 1961–1976—A Monument to the Future* (1976) calls attention to the floor and earth beneath it. Piles of basalt that constituted part of the *7000 Oaks* piece at the "Documenta 7" exhibition in Kassel in 1982 now reside on the floor of the Hamburger Bahnhof Museum of Contemporary Art in Berlin, titled *The End of the Twentieth Century* (1983). The elaborate installation *dernier espace avec introspecteur, 1964–1982* in the Staatsgalerie Stuttgart includes a long roll of felt on the floor, piles of plaster, and a fat chair. Like stinking preserves of wreckage, these elements contrast markedly with the clean, pristine installations in the other galleries of this landmark postmodern museum, designed by James Stirling.

In all these cases and others, Beuys's objects, installations, and actions make the spectator look down. They literalize in the body a memorial, mournful stance. This, of course, contrasts with the traditional upward-lifted and lifting position of the monument aspiring toward the sky. Downward orientation has characterized many German memorials since Beuys's reorientation. One of East Germany's most controversial art works was *Nie wieder Krieg* (Never again war), a title derived from Käthe Kollwitz, which was installed in 1982 by Anatol Erdmann, Stefan Reichmann, and Hans Scheib as part of the exhibition "Sculpture and Flowers" in Treptower Park in Berlin. In this piece and at that site, concrete clothing and bodily remains strewn on the ground contrasted with the colossal, heroic, Socialist Realist figure executed in 1949 by E. V. Vuchetich for the Soviet War Memorial for which Treptower Park is famous. Jochen and Esther Shalev Gerz's "sinking" monument—*Mahnmal gegen Faschismus, Krieg, Gewalt—Für Frieden und Menschenrechte* (also titled *Monument against Fascism, War, Violence, and for Peace and Human Rights*)—consisted of a column that gradually descended into the ground next to the Hamburg-Harburg marketplace between 1986 and 1993. The graffiti-covered shaft remains visible today, entombed in the ground, through a viewing window in a pedestrian underpass. For Jochen Gerz's Invisible Monument of 1990–93, cobblestones were surreptitiously removed, inscribed with the names of Jewish cemeteries, and returned to the plaza in front of the Saarbrücken Palace, with the inscription face down in the ground. In 1995 the Israeli artist Micha Ullman created a subterranean memorial to the book burning on Bebel Platz in Berlin in 1933, in which one looks down into the ground through a window to view empty shelves. The playwright Edward Albee has written about this mournful experience: "Even now, months later, when I remember it, I still feel like crying."[124] One looks down and mourns the past and the departed in the experience of Gunter Demnig's *Stolpersteine* (Stumbling blocks—see frontispiece), which, in a visible retort to Gerz's *Invisible Monument,* make the names and the fates of victims visible to the downward, mournful glance of passersby.[125]

In the essay "Objects Beyond Objecthood" the contemporary art critic Briony Fer adopts the term "objecthood" from Michael Fried. Analyzing the material sources for the power latent in the desublimating anthropomorphic Surrealism of Louise Bourgeois and the Postminimalism of Eva Hesse, Fer pushes beyond Fried's conception of "the literalness of the object, its mere thing-like status . . . and into a realm of excessive, bodily materiality." In the 1960s and early 1970s Hesse replaced the well-rehearsed Minimalist theater of mechanized forms with seemingly spontaneous hanging, flowing, congealing substances such as latex, rubber, string, rope, and gauze. Always in process, like Beuys's, and often oriented downward, her objects evoke fragility and transience but also resilience, with an alternatively hot and cool "draining of the body's substance. . . . The very presence of the object . . . heightens the sense of losing a portion of oneself."[126] But whereas Beuys opened up the armored male body promulgated as an ideal by Breker, slicing away the muscles and showing the wound from which fat drained down, Hesse responded viscerally and sculpturally to the floor-oriented works of Minimalists such as Carl Andre: "It does something to my insides. His metal plates were the concentration camp for me."[127]

Beuys and the German-Jewish-American Hesse probably met during her fourteen-

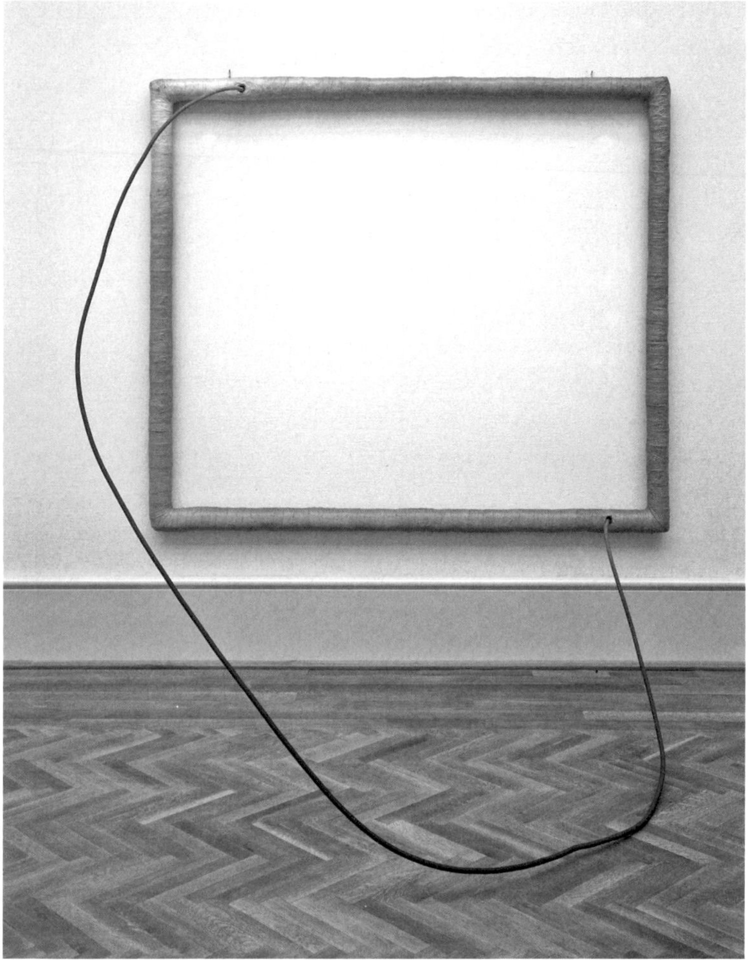

FIGURE 98. Eva Hesse, *Hang Up,* 1966, acrylic on cord and cloth, wood, and steel, 182.9 × 213.4 × 198.1 cm. The Art Institute of Chicago, through prior gifts of Arthur Keating and Mr. and Mrs. Edward Morris. Art © Estate of Eva Hesse. Reproduction: The Art Institute of Chicago.

month residence in Düsseldorf in 1964–65.[128] Their biographies and sculptural practices overlap noticeably. Each consciously linked his or her choices of materials and formats to personal history.[129] From those histories—Hesse's escape from Germany as a three-year-old in 1938 and Beuys's fateful flight as a German in early 1944; her far too early death from cancer and his also relatively early demise—arise more connections between them and more pathos associated with their very personal, historical, and materially excessive objects. But as the contemporary art and social critic Maurice Berger has asserted about Hesse, and as is also true of Beuys, their objects can move us to laughter, too.[130] Hesse said about her piece *Hang Up* (1966, fig. 98), a huge, wrapped metal frame protruding a metal rod outward and onto the gallery floor, executed just after her return from Germany in 1965, "It was the most important early statement I made. It was the first time my idea of absurdity or extreme feeling came through. . . . The frame is all cord and rope. It's all tied up like a hospital bandage. . . . It is extreme and that is why I like it and don't like it."[131] Extreme ambivalence, extreme absurdity, extreme pathos, as well as tragedy and humor characterize both artists' objects. In Beuys's case they also characterized spectators' responses to them.

Postscript in the Present: Twenty Years Ago Today

Twenty years and more after his death, Beuys's works function more as relics than as the active irritants they once were.[132] They no longer seem to inspire either the adulation or the revulsion that was so important to his reputation, and which owed much to his physical and incessantly discursive presence. In 2006 there were no major Beuys commemorations or exhibitions in Germany. The curator of a show in Vienna wrote: " 'Twenty years after his death, interest in Joseph Beuys remains meager,' ran a headline in the cultural pages of the *Süddeutsche Zeitung* at the end of January 2006, for an article commemorating the anniversary. The author noted a number of smaller exhibitions and events, but no German museum seems to have the courage to show a large-scale retrospective. It would appear that Beuys without Beuys himself can only be half as good—there is hardly another artist who managed to combine life and art as completely."[133]

In the same year a German museum did have the "courage" to attempt the first comprehensive retrospective of Arno Breker's work since 1945. The Schleswig-Holstein-Haus in Schwerin displayed some seventy Breker pieces in the summer and fall of 2006, inciting predictable controversy. Some artists and art historians called for the show's closure. The political graphic artist Klaus Staeck, who had shortly before been named president of the Academy of Fine Arts in Berlin, cancelled a planned 2007 exhibition at the museum. A leading scholar of the "degenerate art" action, Christoph Zuschlag, asserted that Breker's work should indeed be shown, but that this show provided too little historical context and so functioned as an apologia and trivialization.[134] The lack of genuine archival research and contextualization of Breker's work called to light the continuing tight control exercised by the Bodenstines and Breker's heirs, who still cling to the illusion that "objective"—that is ahistorical—viewing of the artist's objects will reveal his links to Michelangelo rather than to Hitler.

Beuys's great museum installations in Berlin, Darmstadt, Kassel, Stuttgart, and elsewhere remain on view. The Beuys Museum and Archive at Schloss Moyland devotes an entire floor of a reconstructed medieval castle, which was badly damaged in the war, mainly to his early works, displayed floor to ceiling. This setting, close to Cleves, seems particularly apt. While Beuys's works retain undeniable art historical significance, their former affective power has dissipated, like that of medieval monstrances. Today they appear to be relics of an age when some still had faith in artists' and art objects' transformative powers and in the profound, ineluctable connection between maker, object, and history. The staging of an ahistorical Breker retrospective in what would appropriately have been a "Beuys year" reflected a contemporary retreat from the real, and from critical historical consciousness, and into simulation and relativity. The reaction that ensued, though, reaffirmed the ability of historical objects to block easy escapes.

CONCLUSION

Beyond Beuys: Gerhard Richter's Choice

Max Beckmann's *Sinking of the Titanic* and Joseph Beuys's *The Pack* both evoke modern historical disasters and their creators' hopes and beliefs that their works could inspire and even rescue endangered modern mortals. For the art critic Kim Levin, Beuys was a transitional figure: "With his grandly utopian ideology, his belief in the creative and therapeutic potential of art, and his hopes for improving mankind . . . [Beuys] may have been the ultimate modern artist." But, she goes on, "in shifting the terms from progress to survival, in dredging up the horrors of history as well as the errors of art history, his work not only ceased being modern but almost ceased to be art. Of the first-generation Postmodernists with social consciousness, he was not only the most influential but the most extreme."[1]

The transition between modern and postmodern art had been foreshadowed; the two eras and outlooks intertwine. Hannah Höch's and George Grosz's Dadaist objects and actions blurred the boundaries between art and non-art. Their works continue to call attention to historical horrors and art historical exclusions. Willi Baumeister, who as a committed modernist painter and theorist espoused the autonomy of the creative act and of the artwork, was compelled in Nazi Germany to use his work to confront more directly the ideology declaring him and his art "degenerate." He responded by accepted his marginalization and his art's defamation and pushing both to an extreme, creating objects affirming his solidarity with those subject to discrimination and oppression. Simultaneously, Arno Breker moved in the opposite direction: collaborating with the murderers, providing them with objects clarifying their ideology at the time of its formulation, and embodying that ideology during its brutal realization.

Beyond Beuys, as Kim Levin observed, lies the age of postmodernism and the loss of belief in the art object as the unique and organic creation of an artist/genius able to inspire, transport, and perhaps save mankind. In his 1924 lecture "On Modern Art," Paul Klee stated that the modern artist is like a tree, rooted in the ground with his work growing and flowering toward heaven.[2] At mid-century Jackson Pollock added an exclamation point to this modern, anthropomorphic conception of the artist and his work as he rained his drips down on the canvas and declared: "I am nature!"

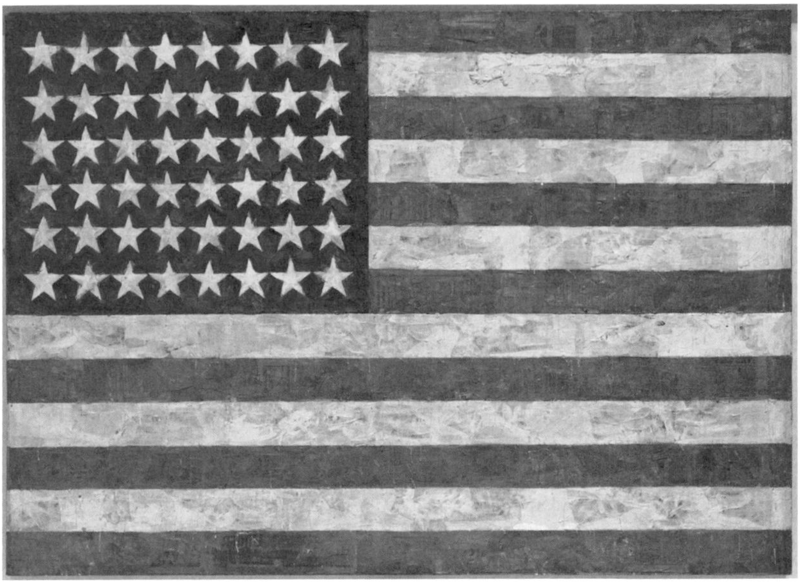

FIGURE 99. Jasper Johns, *Flag,* 1954–55, encaustic, oil, and collage on fabric mounted on plywood, 107.3 × 153.8 cm. The Museum of Modern Art, New York, gift of Philip Johnson in honor of Alred H. Barr, Jr. Art © Jasper Johns/Licensed by VAGA, New York, NY. Digital image © The Museum of Modern Art/Licensed by Scala/Art Resource, NY.

Postmodern artists have more often conceived of themselves as manipulators of preexisting signs than as godlike creators. Contradicting Abstract Expressionism's late-modernist howl, Robert Rauschenberg in the 1950s laconically erased a drawing by Willem de Kooning and assembled ramshackle constructions and collages out of the scraps of the modern city, actions and works aesthetically akin to Beuys's. But unlike Beuys, who maintained a modern and messianic commitment to art, Rauschenberg issued the paradigmatic postmodernist pronouncement: "I don't want to change the world, I just want to live in it." With the shift of the conception of the artist from natural force to cultural producer, and reproducer of existing imagery, artists such as Rauschenberg and Jasper Johns—and Beuys, too—came to conceive of themselves and their careers as cultural constructions. Beuys therefore tailored his "Life Course/Work Course" to fit his own conception of his career and its significant events and objects. Johns destroyed his early collages because they resembled too much the work of Hanover Dadaist Kurt Schwitters, and he declared his 1954–55 *Flag* to be his first work (fig. 99). Gerhard Richter has disavowed the work he produced in East Germany prior to going to the West in 1961, and he destroyed his first year's production under capitalism, which consisted of abstract, expressionistic paintings. The postmodern artist conceives of his or her career as a historical entity, and the objects he or she creates become contingent on

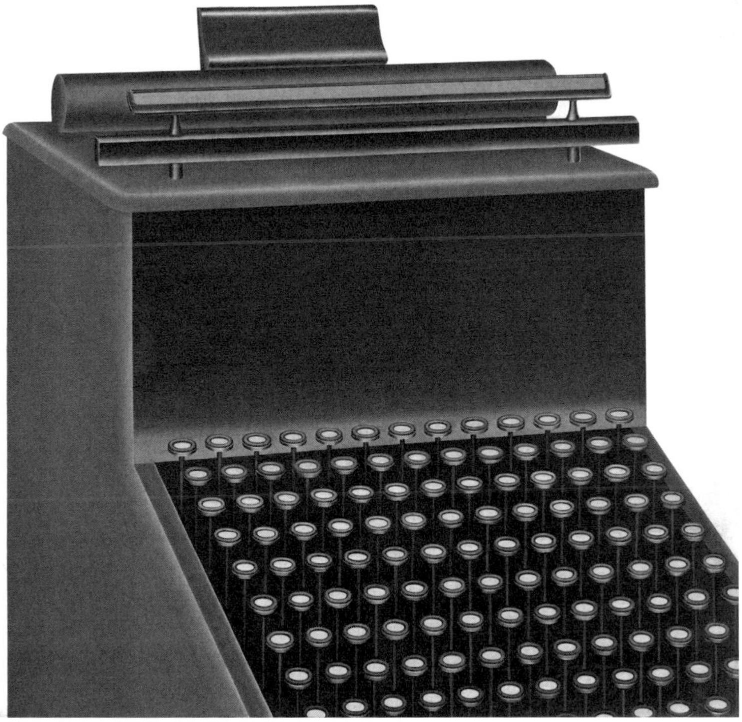

FIGURE 100. Konrad Klapheck, *The Will to Power,* 1959, oil on canvas, 90 × 100 cm. Kolumba: Kunstmuseum des Erzbistums Köln. Art © 2010 Artists Rights Society (ARS), New York/VG Bild-Kunst, Bonn. Photo © Lothar Schnepf/Kolumba Köln.

the artist's historical self-conception, as well as on ever-changing social, historical, institutional, and discursive contexts.

Postmodern painting has often been based on mechanically reproduced images, especially photographs, or, in Johns's case, standardized objects. A Johns flag calls attention to its own objecthood precisely by not being a flag and by being displayed in a museum rather than on a pole. By positing meaning's lack of stability, postmodern image production shakes spectators awake from the high modernist dream of "presentness is grace" to the morning-after reality of "presentness is place."

Johns's practice raises philosophical issues, such as the Wittgensteinian idea that things only take on their meaning through how they are used, which is often a function of where they are placed—physically, historically, and discursively. The Düsseldorf Pop painter Konrad Klapheck has repeatedly painted monumental images of typewriters that loom up like armored fortresses, which he has given titles such as *The Ideals of the Fathers,* or *The Will to Power* (fig. 100). Klapheck's objects, like Johns's, can be interpreted as philosophical gambits. But by quoting Nietzsche in the title of *Will to Power,* a painting from 1950s Germany, Klapheck—like Baumeister in his Nazi-era *Zarathustra*—also addressed substantive German historical issues. Klapheck's images of office equipment imply both bureaucratic procedures and monolithic governmental forces, suggesting not only the uses that might determine the meanings of these objects but also the Nazi misuse of philosophers' ideas and abuse of efficient functionality.

At the same time that Johns was painting flags, Gerhard Richter was doing likewise, under very different historical and personal circumstances. Born in Dresden, Richter was a child in Nazi Germany; he experienced the fire bombing of Dresden from just outside the city and came into young adulthood in the immediate postwar period. His artistic training and early career took place in the GDR. His first professional art job was with a "state-owned concern making political banners."[3] In 1957 the twenty-six-year-old Richter executed a mural in his home city that adhered to Socialist Realism in style and content (fig. 101). *Der Arbeiteraufstand (The Workers' Uprising)* adorned the wall of the first-floor meeting room of the Saxon Landtag (parliamentary) building, which dated to 1931, designed in a functional style by the architectural firm of Barthold and Tiede. From 1953 to 1990 the building served as headquarters of the GDR's ruling party, the Socialist Unity Party (SED), which commissioned the mural. The artist himself does not recall the exact title of the painting but remembers its theme as being "The Battle of the Working Class Against its Oppressors."[4]

A section of this painting was reproduced in an article in *Sonntag,* the SED cultural newspaper, in April 1958. Responding to the question of whether working on commission hampered artistic freedom, Richter answered definitively in the negative, stating: "About my latest commissioned work, a mural in the SED headquarters in Dresden, I'd like to say that I never felt that my 'artistic freedom' (what a nice word!) was limited." He went on to observe that much great art throughout history had been created on commission, and that he only regretted that though the painting was completed in November 1957 he had not yet been paid.[5]

The GDR portrayed itself as heir to the anti-fascist resistance (much of its original leadership did derive from the Communist opposition to the Nazis), nurtured after 1949 by the party into a workers' and farmers' state of real, existing, and democratic Socialism. These were themes of Richter's 1957 mural: it represented the GDR's creation struggle, and the mural's placement on a wall in the parliament building celebrated this struggle as the prehistory of the current state, the democratic and socialist GDR. The reality, as we know, was more complex and less heroic: the SED was the only functional party in the GDR, merging the Communist and Social Democratic parties and effectively eliminating the latter. In this single-party democracy, Richter was compelled to paint such paintings; similarly, he had limited choice of what to say in the article in *Sonntag.*

Like the party and the country for which it was created, Richter's Dresden SED mural no longer exists. It also plays little or no role in the Richter literature. Richter's mural exists only in photographic reproduction, a black-and-white trace even fainter than the color image of Grosz's *Germany: A Winter's Tale.* As a lost object, it has enacted the his-

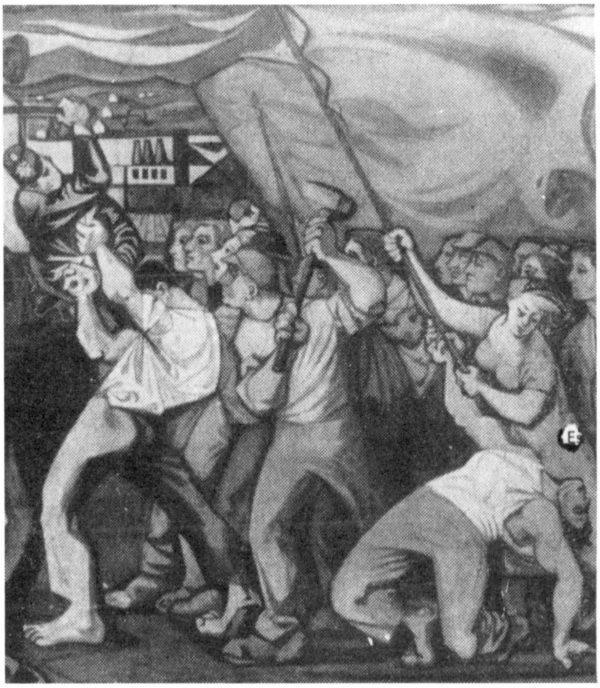

FIGURE 101. Gerhard Richter, detail from *Der Arbeiteraufstand (The Workers' Uprising),* 1957, mural, formerly in Socialist Unity Party headquarters, Dresden, now lost. From Gerd Richter, "Auseinandersetzungen halfen mir weiter," *Sonntag* 16 (20 April 1958): 12. Art © Gerhard Richter; courtesy Marian Goodman Gallery, New York/Studio Gerhard Richter.

tory of the country whose ethos it was created to represent. Richter's less political German Hygiene Museum murals, executed in Dresden in 1956, have often been reproduced and are used to stand for his work as a muralist in the GDR. The Hygiene Museum, originally designed by Arno Breker's teacher Wilhelm Kreis, was renovated in the 1990s by the same Dresden architecture firm, Atelier Peter Kulka, that renovated the Landtag building. The museum, aware of Richter's paintings, have not replastered that wall. The artist, though, demurred at the suggestion that the cover of paint might be removed and the paintings revealed.[6] Like much of the history of the GDR, Richter's Hygiene Museum murals still await direct study and analysis in the clear light of day.

In 1999, slightly more than forty years after creating the GDR murals, Richter, now one of the world's most prominent, sought-after, and highly paid painters, completed another government commission. This time, rather than depicting flag-waving crowds of workers defiantly battling with uniformed police, he executed for the entry foyer to the renovated Reichstag building in Berlin a monumental tricolor abstract painting on the theme of the West German—since 1991, all-German—flag (plate 7).[7]

Richter's remarkable forty-odd-year trajectory—from SED headquarters in Dresden to the Reichstag in Berlin—is not the span referred to in the title of the Museum of Modern Art's 2002 Richter painting retrospective, "Gerhard Richter: Forty Years of Painting." That exhibition began its survey of the artist's career with his early years in capitalist West Germany, particularly those paintings executed from photographs that began in 1962 with his "Capitalist Realism." In this respect the museum followed the artist's lead, whose authorized Web site, www.gerhardrichter.com, states: "Richter officially began painting in 1962."

Robert Storr, the organizer of the MoMA exhibition, briefly describes the Dresden commission in his catalogue essay, but he discreetly leaves out its location. The Reichstag commission goes unremarked anywhere in the catalogue, which also leaves the Dresden commission out of its "Chronology of Key Events." In fact, the Landtag and Hygiene Museum paintings, two major and prominent public and political works, are notably absent from the Richter literature in general.[8] Yet they are perfect representatives of recent German history. Richter exercises his postmodern prerogative to control his career and oeuvre and to let the unwelcome works remain out of sight. The Reichstag painting represents the absorption of postmodern art into the self-conception of the Berlin Republic at the end of the millennium, proud of its successes but circumspect about celebrating them too loudly and consciously intending to do so in a "postnational" tone. Rather than hang a huge German flag in the entry to the Reichstag, they have hung a "Richter."

Like Beuys's art world recognition, Richter's, too, has proved a stepping-stone to a broader cultural role. But whereas Beuys presented himself as a savior, and appeared as a showman and perhaps even charlatan, Richter's image is that of a subtle and circumspect thinker and conscientious craftsman in a traditional art form. With his GDR training, there is no question as to his ability to render images in paint. His work since coming to the West, though, has very much celebrated his personal artistic freedom—the freedom to choose the subject, style, and format of his work, something he did not enjoy in the East, despite his enforced avowals at the time.

Richter's story, like Beuys's, has popular appeal. Today he is rich and famous. Germany's most widely read newspaper, the tabloid *Bild-Zeitung,* in the run-up to Germany's hosting soccer's world championship tournament in the summer of 2006, trumpeted the headline "Germany Wins the World Cup in Art" over an article declaring Richter to be the world's No. 1, most highly compensated, artist.[9] At the time of his MoMA retrospective, like Beuys's 1979 Guggenheim show an important American legitimation of his significance, an admiring profile appeared in the Sunday *New York Times Magazine.* Mixing the personal and the professional, it described his third wife, Sabine Moritz, also a painter and his former student, as "a beautiful, unaffected, soft-spoken woman," with whom Richter has two children, to whom he is a dedicated father.[10] Despite Richter's personal and professional success, in his work and his statements he expresses doubt about painting's right to exist in a world whose depiction is dominated by photographic and digital depictions, and anxiety about existence itself. "I am glad to get honors and high prices. But artists are valued today in terms of money, auctions. I wish society would need art more, but it doesn't. So I feel very lonely in this culture."[11] The *New York Times* writer Michael Kimmelman asserted: "Other artists, like Jasper Johns, ask what is the meaning of a brush stroke. Richter asks what is the value of art itself—what is its use in the world." In contrast to the narcissistic excesses of Neo-Expressionists such as Anselm Kiefer, Georg Baselitz, or the late Jörg Immendorf, Richter's practice, his pronouncements, and his lifestyle bespeak an intellectually and socially appealing asceticism. He and his work have come to represent a mature, restrained, industrious, and intellectual Germany. His personal story embodies individual professional aspiration as a route to surviving and overcoming national trauma.[12]

In 1961, on his return to Dresden from Moscow, Richter's train stopped in West Berlin, where he deposited his luggage. He and his first wife, Ema Eufinger, later got a ride back to East Berlin, crossed by subway to the West, reclaimed his bags, and stayed. Richter has said that his choice not to return to East Germany was motivated less by politics than by his experience of contemporary Western art, especially seeing the audacious abstractions of Jackson Pollock and Lucio Fontana at "Documenta 2" in 1959. The "Documenta" exhibitions, which began in 1955, intended to reintroduce international modern art to Germany, link contemporary art to prewar modernism, reintegrate West Germany into the Western art world, and demonstrate the distinction between East and West Germany. In German-German relations, the exhibitions' location close to the GDR border, in the small and relatively obscure city of Kassel, made it a convenient stop for such Easterners as Richter traveling to the West, showing them the type of art they were missing at home and could enjoy if they went West.

The Richters soon did. They moved to Düsseldorf, where Gerhard enrolled at the academy, studying most importantly with the technically sophisticated *informel* abstract painter Karl Otto Götz and being at the same time appalled by Beuys's egotistical antics down the hall. For the next year Richter experimented in abstraction, in works influenced by Götz, Lucio Fontana, and Alberto Burri. "I painted through the whole history of art towards abstraction. . . . I painted like crazy." His first show in the West, in Fulda in 1962, featured some of these works—all now destroyed. "I had some success with all that, or gained some respect. But then I felt that it wasn't it, and so I burned the crap in some sort of action in the courtyard. And then I began. It was wonderful to make something and then destroy it. I was doing something and I felt very free."[13] Although a courtyard "action" immolating modernist artworks evokes dark associations in German history (even if legends of Nazis burning valuable works of art are apocryphal—for in actuality they preferred to sell them for profit), for Richter his bonfire enacted a destructive declaration of personal artistic freedom on the type of abstract, expressionistic paintings that at that very moment were most closely associated with the artistic freedom of the West versus the mandate of Socialist Realism of the East, from which he had just escaped. Feeling as constrained by the former as he had by the latter, he freed himself from ever again attempting in his art to *express* a desire for freedom stylistically or thematically. Instead he inaugurated the "forty years of painting" referred to in the title of the 2002 MoMA exhibition, in which his career was presented as a series of freely executed strategic *choices,* embracing mechanical reproduction as the basis and model for his painterly production.

"In 1962 I found my first escape hatch: by painting from photographs, I was relieved of the need to choose or construct a subject. I had to choose the photographs, of course; but I could do that in a way that avoided any commitment to the subject, by using motifs which had very little image to them and which were anachronistic."[14] These images could be either representational or abstract. They deny the possibility of abstraction as personal expression, since the abstractions do not derive from any "inner necessity," or by the logic of the pictorial surface, but are simply reproductions of existing abstract images, no less representational than those that depict faces or fields. The basic premise is not personal expression but personal choice: what the artist felt like reproducing on a given day. Richter's professed hostility to any ideological position to inform his art has also offered his critics and his admirers, as well as the general public, various choices about how to interpret his work.

Although Richter has often been portrayed as rejecting all ideology, especially the rhetoric emanating from both sides of the Cold War divide, choice was a prominent tool in Western Cold War propaganda. In July 1959 American Vice-President Richard Nixon and Soviet Premier Nikita Khrushchev toured the "American National" exhibition in Moscow. As reported by the *New York Times* on July 25, 1959, the two paused in the "gadget-filled" kitchen of a six-room, suburban-style, $14,000 model home. Here they engaged in their famous Kitchen Debate on the benefits of life under Soviet Communism versus life in the capitalist United States. Nixon concluded his points: "We do not claim to astonish the Russian people. We hope to show our diversity and our right to choose. We do not wish to have decisions made at the top by government officials who say that all homes should be built in the same way. Would it not be better to compete in the relative merits of washing machines than in the strength of rockets."

The United States and the capitalist West offered an abundance of products to choose from, and the choices could be made at the individual level. Trade shows, as the historian Robert H. Haddow has pointed out, were intended to promote the idea "that consumerism could become more than just a crass pacifier of the mob—that consumer products could be forms of artistic expression and that consumer choices could actually amount to a creative act."[15]

After burning his early abstract works, Richter began creating the works that would be included in his exhibitions of 1963 and 1964 as Capitalist Realism, which lampooned creative shopping by literalizing and regimenting it as shopping for art. Richter, Konrad Lueg (later Konrad Fischer), Manfred Kuttner, and Sigmar Polke showed under the banner of Capitalist Realism at the Laden Galerie in Düsseldorf in May 1963, and Richter and Lueg staged "Life with Pop—a Demonstration for Capitalist Realism," which was distributed throughout the multiple levels and departments of the Berges furniture store in Düsseldorf on October 11.[16] The phrase "Capitalist Realism" derives from Richter's and Polke's GDR origins and is an ironic play on the "Socialist Realism" of their youths. Describing Capitalist Realism in a 1964 catalogue essay, Manfred de la Motte claimed that Richter was painting "a reality that only exists imaginarily, our clichéd ideas of the world, people, things, as we know them from the mass media, films, TV, ads and newspapers;" however, some of Richter's photographic sources were actually family snapshots.[17]

In the department store installation, a papier-mâché mannequin of President Kennedy by Richter and Lueg recalled Berlin Dadaism's puppets and mannequins in the first International Dada Fair and, even more, the figure of Woodrow Wilson created by Grosz and Heartfield for the *Schall und Rauch* cabaret. The waiting room included thirty-nine copies of the *Frankfurter Allgemeine Zeitung*, with each chair holding an example of this conservative, business-oriented newspaper. The tea trolley in the first room included on its lower shelf the writings of Winston Churchill and copies of a home-furnishing magazine, *Schönes Heim*. The television played news and a report on the just-ended "Adenauer Era."[18] These details further intensified the association of the objects displayed in the exhibition with the political figures and commodity aesthetic that fought the Western Cold War: Churchill, who in 1946 in a Fulton, Missouri, speech coined the powerful "iron curtain" metaphor; the West German chancellor Konrad Adenauer, who had recently resigned; and products and publications that seriously presented the capitalist, consumerist ethos, ironically re-presented as readymade Capitalist Realism.[19]

Signs of socialism or Socialist Realism were conspicuously absent from "Life with Pop—a Demonstration for Capitalist Realism." The exclusion of direct confrontation with the East in fact reminds one of the propagandistic Western trade exhibitions that in the 1950s became a major Western weapon in the Cold War—such as the Moscow show of Kitchen Debate fame. Whereas Soviet propaganda attacked the United States directly, especially its economic and racial inequalities, American export-grade propaganda tended not to attack the Soviet Union but to extol itself—the products, opportunities, and, especially, choices that capitalism offered. Under this strategy, the artists' ironic substitution of "Capitalist" for "Socialist" as a modifier before "Realism" had already been earnestly predicted by the theme that became the centerpiece of the United States Information Agency's (USIA's) traveling exhibits from 1956 to the early 1960s: "People's Capitalism," a seemingly oxymoronic term coined by an advertising executive working as a consultant for the Eisenhower administration and the USIA.[20]

Sometimes, though, Richter's artistic choices have involved more direct, if ultimately ambiguous, confrontations with German history. The 1965 painting *Uncle Rudi* (fig. 102), depicting Richter's mother's brother Rudolf Schönfelder (who died at the front in 1944) in his dress *Wehrmacht* uniform around 1942, was among those works piled into the VW bus that now constitutes part of Beuys's *The Pack*, to be driven to Lidice in Moravia for a 1967 memorial exhibition. It is now part of the Czech national collection.[21] Coming from the land of the perpetrators, it is one of the first works in German postwar art to acknowledge the ordinariness of participation in the Nazi state and enactment of its policies and crimes as a part of the historical legacy of many German

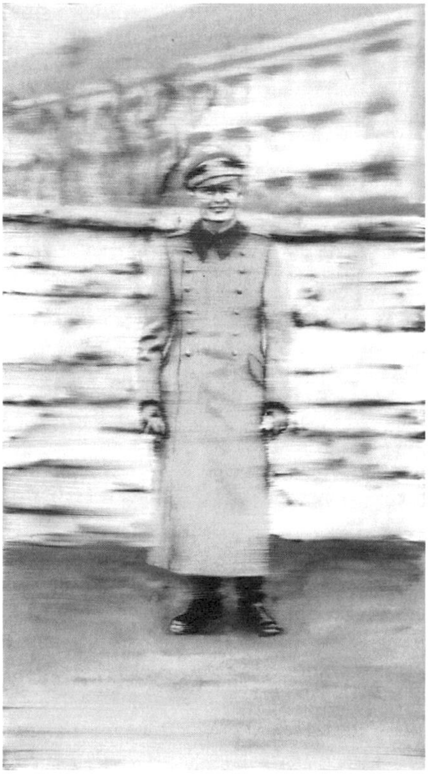

FIGURE 102. Gerhard Richter, *Uncle Rudi,* 1965, oil on canvas, 87 × 50 cm. The Czech Museum of Fine Arts, Prague, Lidice Collection. Art courtesy Marian Goodman Gallery, New York/Studio Gerhard Richter.

families. The art historian Paul Jaskot has brought the painting specifically into connection with the 1961 Adolf Eichmann Trial in Jerusalem, which Hannah Arendt reported on, coining the phrase "the banality of evil"—which could also serve as a caption to Richter's everyday image.[22]

The painting calls attention to its distinction from photography through its blurriness, as do Richter's photo-based paintings generally.[23] Their gray tones, though, evoke the morbidity latent in all photographic images, as theorized by Roland Barthes—the mortal *punctum* rupturing our disinterested historical or sociological *studium* of the photographic record. Richter chose a particular image of his uncle to paint in those gray tones. Posed in his dress uniform, gloves off, up against the wall, and shot by a photographer, Richter executed Uncle Rudi in paint.

Gray tones and gray areas of meaning characterize Richter's cycle of paintings titled *October 18, 1977,* of 1988. Based on photographs of the apprehension, death in Stuttgart Stammheim Prison, and funeral of members of the Red Army Faction, the so-called Baader-Meinhof terrorist cell, the October cycle constitutes one of the best examples of a twentieth-century German artwork functioning as a historical object around which conceptions of the past form in the ever-changing present. They have been extensively written about and variously interpreted, the subject of at least three books, the most comprehensive account in English being Robert Storr's.[24] The journalist Stefan Aust's 1985 book was Richter's major source of information on the history of the Baader-Meinhof group, whose activities in the late 1960s and early 1970s mobilized extreme governmental force to eradicate what was perceived as a left-wing threat to West German democracy, public order, and international legitimacy, causing a crackdown not only on the terrorists but on those thought to sympathize with them.[25] According to Aust, the terrorists' descent into violence and death began with the fire bombing of two Frankfurt department stores (during their closing hours) in spring 1968.[26] After their assault on these sites, emblematic of our most immediate, everyday contact with capitalism, which Richter and Company had much more gently and subtly attacked in their "Capitalist Realism" exhibition, Aust says, "there was no turning back." The terrorists essentially abdicated their freedom of choice, a freedom that artists cherish and embody, Western capitalism promises, and department store shopping represents in a thoroughly commodified form.

One of the best readings of the *October* cycle is by the art historian Lisa Saltzman, who adds to the highly influential ones by Benjamin Buchloh and Robert Storr, who both see Richter's cycle as operating dialectically and expressing both the painter's doubt and commitment to painting as an artistic medium and as a potential purveyor of historical information and interpretation.[27] Saltzman places the cycle—and this format is key to her reading—in a sacred light, as a successor to the fifteen paintings of Barnett Newman's *Stations of the Cross,* a singular modernist attempt to paint cyclically, abstractly, and mournfully, in black and white. Saltzman terms Richter's cycle a "commemorative or *memorial* painting, a pictorial practice that produces the possibility of performing the work, if not of mourning, of remembrance."[28] This concept of the performative painting, in distinction to traditional narrative history painting, is analogous to my concept of the historical object. She also calls attention to the films that preceded Richter's work, among them the anthology production *Germany in Autumn,* of 1978, which features sections by key directors such as Fassbinder, Kluge, and Schlöndorff from what is known as the New German Cinema; the title of Margarete von Trotta's *Die bleierne Zeit,* of 1981 (in English, *Marianne and Juliane*), which, in translation, means "The leaden time," also suggests the tonality of Richter's paintings.

The cycle begins with *Youth Portrait,* the one work not based on a photograph directly relating to the capture, imprisonment, and death of the urban revolutionaries. The photographic source is a frontal facial portrait of about 1970 of Ulrike Meinhof (fig. 103). As Robert Storr points out, Richter's gently stroked painting softens the photographic image and seems to reduce the age of the journalist and filmmaker, who by 1970 already had one career behind her and was entering into her anti-career as a terrorist. The portrait harkens back to an earlier moment in Meinhof's life. In his best-selling autobiography, the German Jewish literary critic and television celebrity Marcel Reich-Ranicki recalled this moment and its poignancy, to some critics' continuing irritation. In 1964 Reich-Ranicki, a survivor of the Warsaw Ghetto, was called to testify in the case of the former SS officer Karl Wolff. Reich-Ranicki described a resulting interview:

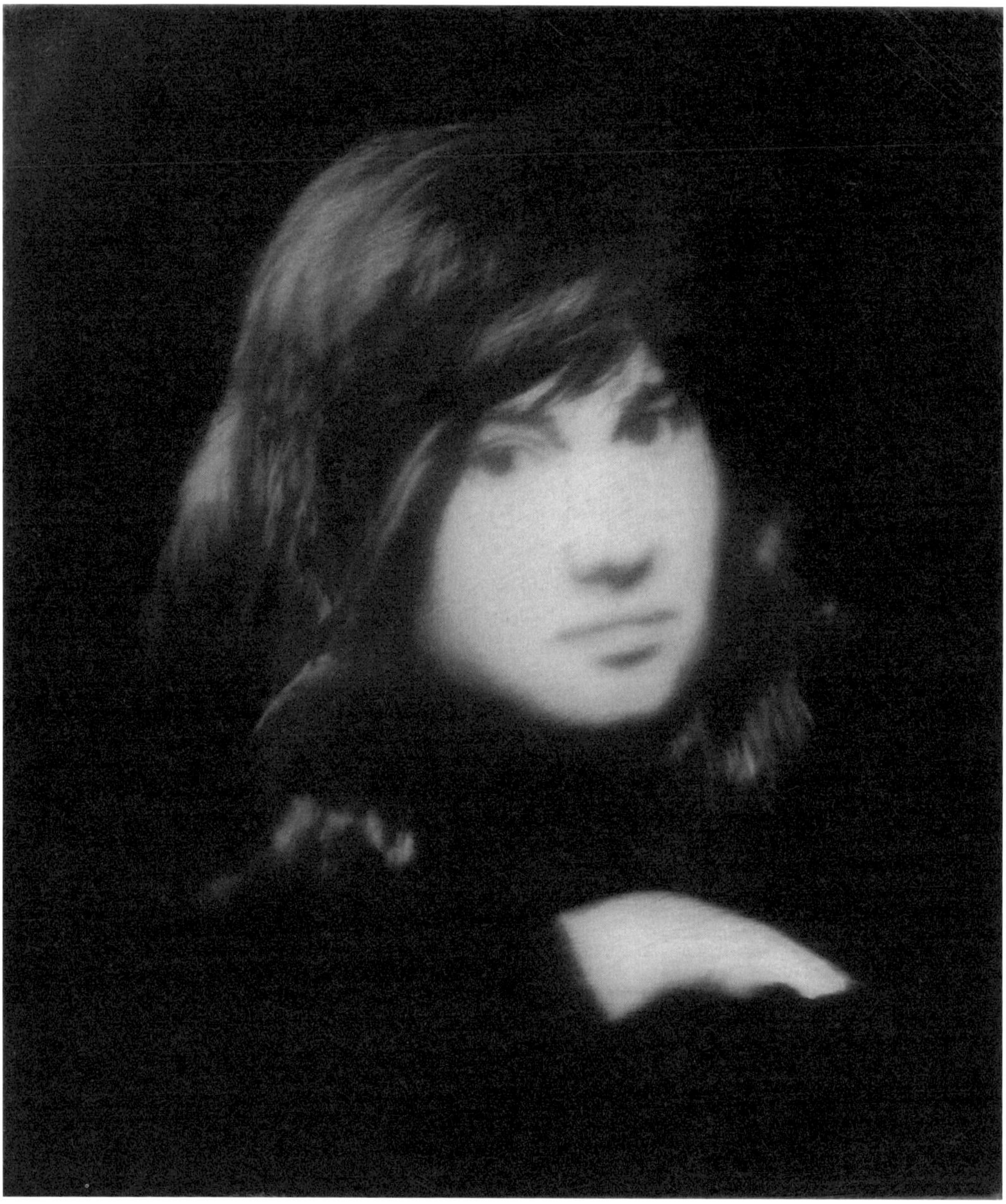

FIGURE 103. Gerhard Richter, *Jugendbildnis (Youth Portrait)*, from *October 18, 1977*, 1988, oil on canvas, 67 × 62 cm. The Museum of Modern Art, New York, the Sidney and Harriet Janis Collection, gift of Philip Johnson, and acquired through the Lillie P. Bliss Bequest (all by exchange); Enid A. Haupt Fund; Nina and Gordon Bunshaft Bequest Fund; and gift of Emily Rauh Pulitzer. Art © Gerhard Richter; courtesy Marian Goodman Gallery, New York/Studio Gerhard Richter. Digital image © Museum of Modern Art/Licensed by SCALA/Art Resource, NY.

> . . . by a female journalist, it seemed hardly thirty, not particularly pretty, but not without a certain charm, perhaps deriving from an obvious seriousness that contrasted to her youth. She wanted to record a thirty-minute conversation. Her questions were precise and intelligent and centered on a particular problem: How could it have happened? The recording went on without any break. When it was over I noticed to my astonishment that we had spoken for fifty minutes. Why did she need so much? She answered a bit evasively: Partly out of personal interest. I didn't take amiss to her inquisitiveness. But I did want to know a bit more about her. But she was in a hurry. I looked at her and saw that there were tears in her eyes. I asked her quickly, "Excuse me, but I didn't catch your name exactly—Meienberg?" "No, Meinhof, Ulrike Meinhof."
>
> How come Ulrike Meinhof stands out so in my memory? Could it be that she was the first person in the Federal Republic who so forthrightly and seriously wanted to find out about my experiences in the Warsaw Ghetto?[29]

That forthright, direct, youthful, overly conscientious, and potentially teary-eyed young woman is the very image Richter's portrait commemorates and mourns. The remainder of the *October* cycle documents the fatal results of the choices later taken by her and her companions.

In addition to the possibility of spectators performing in response to Richter's cycle, which, as Saltzman argues, has sacred forebears, the *October* paintings have also performed and enacted history, with their presentness in or absence from different places forming a part of their "reception aesthetic," the stage on which, or at least the backdrop before which, spectators perform. From the cycle's first showings in Germany in 1989, and the United States in 1990, to their acquisition by MoMA in 1995, the objects in the cycle have generated controversy about what they might mean, and how that meaning might change in a new context.[30]

The cycle was on loan to Frankfurt's Museum of Contemporary Art for a ten-year period beginning in 1989, during the middle of which MoMA purchased it from Richter for three million marks. The hometown paper, the *Frankfurt Allgemeine Zeitung*, in the person of its influential chief art critic, Eduard Beaucamp, lamented this sale as the export of a locus for the remembrance of a national trauma. In Frankfurt the work's presence had been a reminder and an irritant of an open wound. After the initial showing the Dresdner Bank withdrew support from the Frankfurt museum, claiming that Richter's paintings amounted to a monument to terrorists who had especially targeted leading German businesses and businessmen. Beaucamp, like Saltzman, used religious terms to characterize the cycle, referring to it as an "altar," dedicated to this "leaden trauma," that was now being exported to the "Vatican of modernism," where, he argued, it would become primarily an aesthetic object, like a Rothko, sheltered from the world by the walls of what had become a remote and rather provincial cloister.[31]

The Hamburg-based liberal, national paper *Die Zeit* called MoMA's purchase an act of "selling off catharsis" to the highest bidder (meaning, of course, the United States), while the liberal Munich *Süddeutsche Zeitung* called for outrage that the paintings were going to a place where people may know all about O. J. Simpson but nothing about Gudrun Enslin, Andreas Baader, or Ulrike Meinhof, stating that German remembrance deeply relies on the presence of imagery and objects as mnemonic aids.[32]

Although MoMA's impressive and expensive recent expansion indicates that the acquisition of *October 18, 1977*, and staging of a large Richter show into which the cycle was integrated in 2002, did not alienate its financial supporters, the works have also met with some critical American opposition. The neo-conservative critic Hilton Kramer charged MoMA with "glorifying terrorists." Jed Perl called them "a dictionary definition of radical chic" in a review of the MoMA retrospective that began, "Gerhard Richter is a bullshit artist masquerading as a painter."[33] Others have seen them more positively and portrayed them more creatively. The postmodern writer Don DeLillo used the gallery in which they were displayed and the images themselves as a locus for fictional anomic lost souls discovering in their presence their own potential for hopeless relationships and pointless violence.[34] What they perform may be a form of remembrance and mourning, but it has more to do with them than with the supposed subjects of the paintings. In an award-winning article Rainer Usselmann also proposed that they may have an active presence in New York, playing a potentially therapeutic role (totally lacking in DeLillo) in the post-9/11 city.[35] Since the Richter retrospective of 2002, though, this has not been possible. MoMA closed for renovation and expansion shortly thereafter, and after the museum reopened in expanded quarters in 2004 the Richter cycle has not been on view. Perhaps its consignment to storage has something to do with the post-9/11 War on Terror and the museum's temerity about inciting further attacks from the likes of Hilton Kramer. Perhaps there is simply no space for it in MoMA's already so richly endowed galleries. The fact that Robert Storr is no longer on MoMA's staff may also play a role. Whatever the reason, it is hard to imagine that any other museum of modern and contemporary art in the world would be able to acquire these paintings, widely regarded as the most significant works by one of the world's most significant contemporary painters, and not hang them as part of its permanent exhibition.

For the highly influential contemporary art historians and critics Hal Foster, Rosalind Krauss, Yves Alain Bois, and Benjamin Buchloh, in their joint textbook of twentieth-century art, *Art Since 1900*, Richter's *October* paintings present the culmination of "a long, complex succession of German artists' attempts to position painting as a critical reflection on German history."[36] That history, Richter's history, encompasses the Nazi period, the Cold War, and most recently the united Berlin Republic. The Cold War divide skewered by Capitalist Realism ended the year after Richter painted the *October* cycle. But history did not end in 1989, and much post-1988 painting continues to confront German history critically, and it continues to search through the photographic record of that history for images to interrogate. The Karlsruhe painter Rolf Zimmermann confronted his family's complicity in Nazi crimes in the cycle *In Poland 1942*

(1989–90), and in the *Asylum Applicants Waiting* series of 1992–93 he hideously transformed asylum seekers from Bosnia, Iran, Somalia, and other strife-infested locations into insect-headed vermin waiting and waiting for restoration of their humanity. The 1996 series of grisaille paintings of Nazi architectural sites by the Leipzig-born painter Ben Wilkin, or Irene von Neuendorff's stylish later 1990s paintings featuring Adolf Hitler, ask whether the still very present visual record of Nazi Germany can ever be "normalized." Richter's *October* cycle, though, may have been that artist's last critical reflection on German history. After German unification and his own ascension to the position of "World's No. 1 Artist," his work has been more affirmative than critical, nowhere more so than at the heart of unified Germany, the Reichstag.

The Reichstag reopened as the capitol building of the Berlin Republic in 1999. In the entry foyer to the building brilliantly renovated by Sir Norman Foster, visible through the colonnade, hangs Richter's huge glass triptych, *Schwarz, Rot, Gold* (Black, red, gold; plate 7). Richter's Reichstag triptych is an iconic post-Cold War, postmodern expression of German posttraditional national identity. It can be seen as the all-German flag, or, if one chooses, as a prized piece of contemporary art—a branded product of the international art market created by its best-compensated producer, a "Richter." This twenty-one-meter-tall, vertically oriented triptych, painted on six glass panels, was part of the program, budgeted at between thirty and sixty million marks, to decorate and provide a depth of meaning to the building with the works of blue-chip German and international artists. These included Sigmar Polke, Richter's old friend and fellow GDR émigré and Capitalist Realist, whose works on the theme of German legends hang opposite Richter's. Other artists represent Germany's postwar occupying powers, including Jenny Holzer representing the United States, Christian Boltanski France, Krisha Bruskin the Soviet Union, and the architect of the renovation, Norman Foster, representing Great Britain. Subsequent commissioned works by other German artists, as well as by the émigré Hans Haacke, attest to the important symbolic function granted to contemporary art in the Berlin Republic.

At MoMA, Jasper Johns's flag represents postmodern representational painting. If Richter's Reichstag flag, too, hung in a museum, it would function as a representative of his abstract, monochrome painting. Such is its function on his Web site.[37] At the Reichstag, however, the Richter proclaims both the triumph of German democracy and the triumph of postmodern German painting. The site codetermines each reading. Imagine if, instead of Jenny Holzer's LED light piece, which sends fragments of speeches delivered in the Reichstag soaring into the Berlin air, celebrating on high the free discourse of German democracy, the United States were represented at the Reichstag by Frank Stella's *Die Fahne hoch!* (fig. 104), of 1959. Like others of his "black" paintings of this time, that work consists of a series of stripes generated by the structure of the object itself. Displayed unframed, as it should be, one notices the unusually deep stretcher bars that project the painting from the wall, turning it into a relief of uniform height. The height of projection from the wall, six inches, is also the width of the painted stripes.

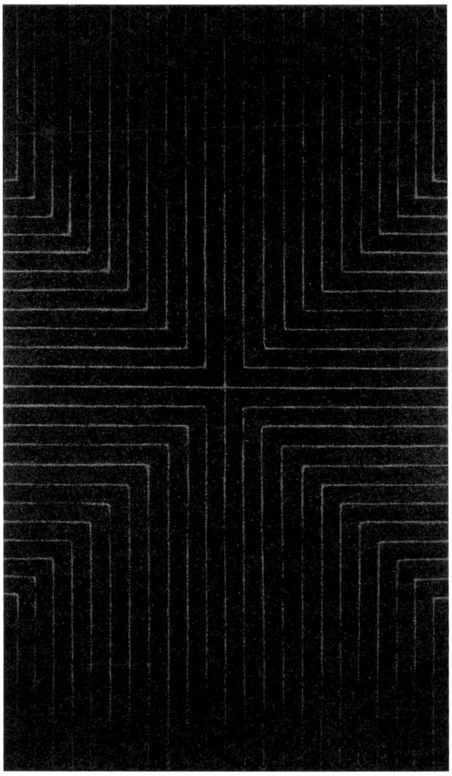

FIGURE 104. Frank Stella, *Die Fahne hoch!* 1959, enamel on canvas, 308.6 × 185.4 cm. Whitney Museum of American Art, New York. Art © 2010 Frank Stella/Artists Rights Society (ARS), New York. Photo: Whitney Museum of American Art.

This height and the object's rectangular shape generate the pattern on the object's surface and make us empirically aware that the painting "really is an object," as Stella asserted in a 1964 interview.[38] But Stella also attached to this object a rather tendentious title. The words *Die Fahne hoch!* (Raise the flag!) derive from the "Horst Wessel Song"—the marching song of the Hitler Youth, written by the young Nazi who became a martyr to the movement and one of its central icons (fig. 82). Part of the spectator's response while reading this title will depend on whether or not he or she understands the reference. In Germany the reference would be widely recognized and controversial, and would confound Stella's famous assertion from that 1964 interview: "What you see is what you see." Often, what one sees, and how it resonates, is a function of what one already thinks, what one knows, and what one thinks one knows.

Once spectators know that *Schwarz, Rot, Gold* is a Richter painting, they are more apt to notice that it departs from the flag by virtue of using vertical rather than horizontal rectangles and by its muted and slightly off-key colors. The bottom panel of yellow is also somewhat streaked. Instead of representing the flag, Richter created an image alluding to and potentially critiquing it. Continuing the tradition of Capitalist Realism, an appropriate "movement" title for Richter's Reichstag painting might be Postnational Nationalism. Most viewers will recognize Richter's painting's resemblance to the German flag. Germans will see it as resembling their flag, and, like Americans who learn in elementary school the history and meaning of the Stars and Stripes, most will know something of the history and symbolism of the colors. The black, red, and gold of the German flag has a long association with German liberalism, going back at least to the students who staged a celebration of republican, anti-aristocratic, and anti-authoritarian ideals in the southwestern town of Hambach (Baden) in May 1832. The student unions' adoption of these colors was popularly understood to derive from the gold buttons and black and red trim of soldiers' uniforms in the German wars of liberation against Napoleon. The flag pulled these colors off the uniforms, decorporealizing and immobilizing them, and creating a paradigmatic precedent for a modernist abstraction connoting both liberal republican aspirations and national pride and ambitions.

Black, red, and gold derives its meaning and legitimacy from a series of historical connections. With origins in the struggle for German self-determination, these colors also came to be associated with German liberalism and were adopted by the Weimar Republic. The Federal Republic of Germany restored the black, red, and gold and incorporated the Weimar constitution into its basic law. Identification with that banner expresses the "constitutional patriotism" that the philosopher Jürgen Habermas advocates as the expression of contemporary "post-traditional" German identity: not identified with imperial leadership or the myths of a homogeneous folk community or a classless society, the black, red, and gold have been adopted as the symbol of contemporary Germany's postnational nationalism.

Even as Richter's flag participates in a celebration of the idea that the Hambach students' republicanism should now, after more than 150 years, finally have triumphed in Germany, the painting's deviation from the official flag offers a critique of modernism's often tacit participation in nationalist movements, while its readymade imagery also critiques modernism's cult of originality. According to Norman Foster, Richter was initially reluctant to accept the Reichstag commission but was persuaded by the German president, Richard von Weiszacker, that *this* German flag was "no longer taboo."[39] By 1997 the black, red, and gold no longer had the provocative thrust of Markus Lüpertz's "dithyrambic" works displaying "German motifs," among them the triptych *Black, Red, Gold I, II, III* of 1974 (fig. 105). Lüpertz's painting was still identifying connections between the Federal Republic and its more immediate past rather than those suggested by the colors of the flag: *Black, Red, Gold* features a *Stahlhelm*, the German army's characteristic earflap steel helmet of the world wars, standing in a field atop an empty uniform like a memorial to an unmarked grave or an apotropaic scarecrow.[40]

During the World Cup Soccer championship held in Germany in June 2006, Germans waved their flag, wore it on their bodies, and flew it on their cars and homes and gardens and in public space with an unself-conscious pride that would previously have been considered dangerous (fig. 106). This new freedom to display the flag, predicted by von Weiszacker and affirmed and encouraged by Richter, was discussed in newspa-

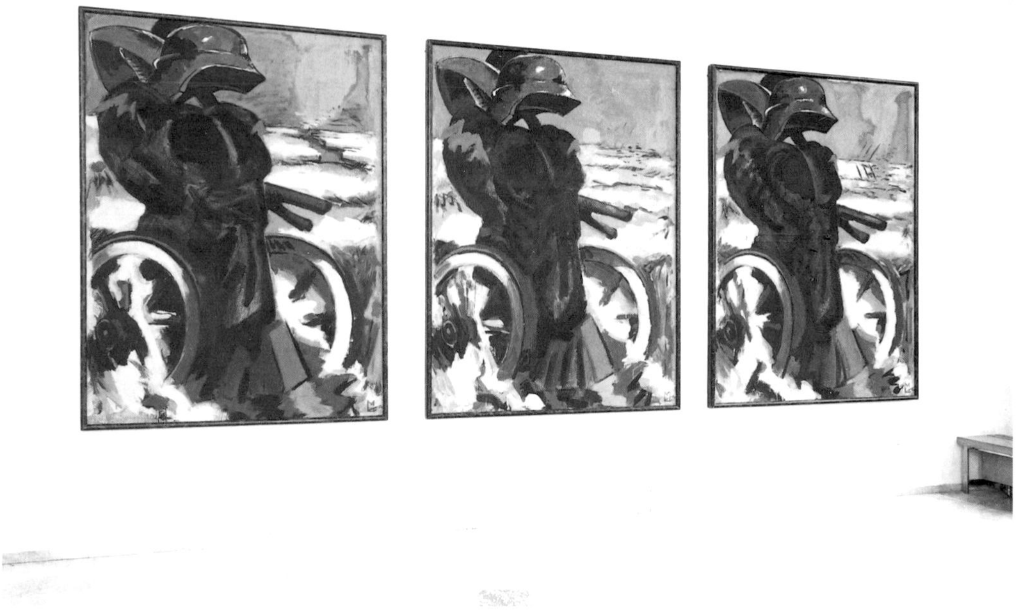

FIGURE 105. Markus Lüpertz, *Black, Red, Gold I, II, III,* 1974, distemper on canvas, 260 × 199 cm. Art © Markus Lüpertz; courtesy Galerie Michael Werner Berlin, Cologne, and New York. Photo courtesy Kunstmuseum Stuttgart.

pers, on television, and at the *Stammtisch* (regulars' table in a local pub), by politicians, pundits, and the national soccer team's youthful coach, the California resident Jürgen Klinsman, who declared that flag display is a good thing, if unaccompanied by xenophobia, excessive nationalism, or violence.[41] Understandably, many left-wing Germans, as well as many foreigners, are uncomfortable with crowds of flag-waving Germans. The specific symbolism of the black, red, and gold flag remained a mystery to most foreign commentators. It is decidedly not the swastika, not the imperial black, white, and red, and not the GDR's black, red, and gold, which from 1959 was overlaid with a wreath of grain surrounding a hammer and compass, signifying class solidarity between farm, industrial, and intellectual workers.

Most Germans today have no direct personal contact with NS-Germany. As the GDR fades into the past, its flag remains available for purchase on souvenir schnapps bottles labeled *Vergessenheitstrunk—ein Ostprodukt* (Forgetfulness drink—an Eastern product). Meanwhile, Richter's Reichstag flag (or not-flag) continues to embody the triumph of Western-style democracy in Germany, its current status as a sovereign, democratic state, and the artist's international prestige for the choices he has made in his postmodern painting practice. Should those conditions change, so too will Richter's flag, an object as history.

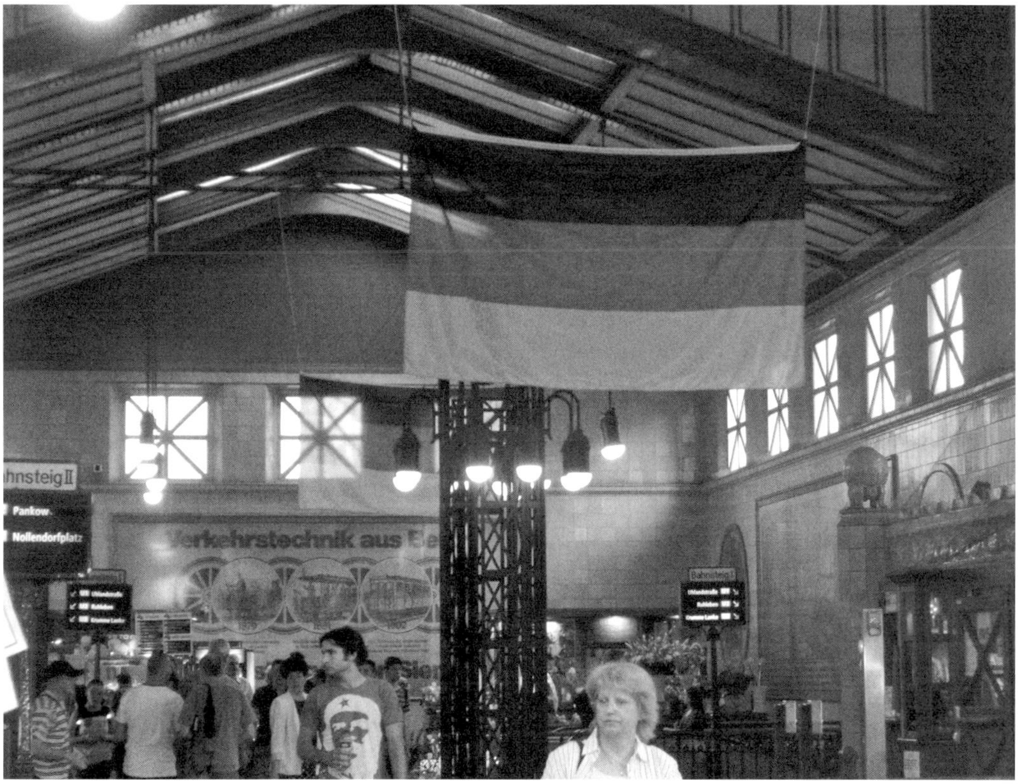

FIGURE 106. Wittenbergplatz subway station, Berlin, 2006. Photo: Author.

From Beckmann to Beuys and beyond, German art objects—large and small, public and private, surviving and lost—have enacted and embodied history. No doubt many that derive from other nations and their artists have also. In the contemporary world, as Andreas Huyssen has argued about the late twentieth- and early twenty-first-century museum boom, material objects resonate with history with an immediacy and poignancy that has not been superseded—in fact may have been enhanced—by television, film, and digital imagery. If history and its material remains have no end, neither does this function for art objects.

Notes

All translations are by the author unless otherwise noted. The following abbreviations are used for archival sources:

GGA	George Grosz Archiv, Akademie der Künste, Berlin
HHA	Hannah-Höch-Archiv, Berlinische Galerie, Berlin
JBA	Joseph Beuys Archiv, Stiftung Museum Schloss Moyland, Bedburg-Hau
WBA	Willi Baumeister Archiv, Kunstmuseum Stuttgart, Stuttgart

Introduction: Art Objects as History

1. Belting, 1998, 1, 5.
2. Fulbrook, 1999.
3. See Thomas DaCosta Kaufmann, *Toward a Geography of Art* (Chicago: University of Chicago Press, 2004); and Thomas DaCosta Kaufmann and Elizabeth Pilliod, eds., *Time and Place: The Geohistory of Art* (London: Ashgate, 2005).
4. Seuphor, in *Willi Baumeister*, 1931, 22–23.
5. Fried, 1968, 147. On the contingency of the minimal objects whose theatricality Fried deplored, as well as that of more recent object- and concept-based works, see Buskirk, 2003.
6. Fried, 1968, 126. Fried returned to Morris's idea of "strong gestalt" in a lecture in 2006 and, while conceding that in the years since "Art and Objecthood," despite his objections to it, "Minimalism wiped the floor with high Modernism," asserted that nothing that has happened in the last forty years has caused him "to soften the main point" of his 1967 essay. (Michael Fried, "Autonomy Now: Some Recent Photography," lecture at the Kunsthistorisches Institut, Freie Universität Berlin, 16 January 2006.)
7. Fried, 1968, 146.
8. Greenblatt, 1992, 42.
9. Kai-Uwe Hemken, *Gerhard Richter: 18. Oktober 1977* (Frankfurt am Main: Insel, 1998), 132–133.
10. Eduard Beaucamp, "A Break with Socialist Realism: Werner Tübke, *Reminiscences of JD Schulze III*," in Gillen, 1997, 170.

Chapter 1: *Titanic* Sinks, *Departure* Arrives

An earlier version of this chapter was published as "*Titanic* sinks, *Departure* arrives: On Beckmann, Film, and the Fall of History Painting and Rise of the Historical Object" in *Of 'Truths Impossible to Put in Words': Max Beckmann Contextualized*, ed. Rose-Carol Washton Long and Maria Makela (Bern: Peter Lang, 2009), 229–265.

1. Lecture delivered in London at the "Exhibition of 20th-Century German Art" at the New Burlington Gallery, an occasion organized in response to the Nazi "Degenerate Art" exhibition and thus an implicit, if muted, art political stage. (See Buenger, 1997, 298–307; Sean Rainbird, afterword, in Beckmann, 2003, 23–40; and Holz, 2004, 195–222.) The speech was delivered in German and simultaneously translated. The German original of the quoted section reads: "Er winkte mir freundlich zu mit einer überirdischen Väterlichkeit. Habe Vertrauen zu den Dingen—sagte er,—lasse Dich nicht schrecken von all dem Entsetzlichen der Welt" (Beckmann, 1990, 55).
2. Göpel, 1984, 134.
3. MoMA closed for renovation and expansion in 2003, and reopened in November 2004. In its new hanging, *Departure* was initially shown in a gallery along with such socially engaged, historical works as David Alfaro Siqueiros's *Echo of a Scream* (1937)

and selections from Jacob Lawrence's *Migration of the Negro* (1940–41). The only other Beckmann on display, next to *Departure,* was the small 1923 *Self-Portrait with Cigarette,* supporting, as did the wall label text between them, identification of the painting's theme with the artist's biography.

4. *Guernica* is the most famous example of a twentieth-century art object *as* history. On the history of *Guernica*'s creation, movements and reception, and use in a variety of causes beyond the Republican one of the Spanish Civil War for which it was created (among them, anti–Vietnam War protests, Basque nationalism, etc.), see Chipp, 1988; and van Hensbergen, 2004. On its use in a German army advertisement in 1990, see "Picassos *Guernica* kehrt nach Deutschland zurück," in Werckmeister, 1997, 102–144. On the draping of the United Nations General Assembly chamber's *Guernica* tapestry during Colin Powell's presentation leading up to the 2003 American bombardment of Iraq, see Maureen Dowd, "Powell Without Picasso," *New York Times,* 5 February 2003; and van Hensbergen, 2004, 1–2.

5. James Thrall Soby, "Max Beckmann," in *Beckmann* (New York: Buchholz Gallery, 1947), n.p. Not all observers shared Soby's admiration. In 1946 Clement Greenberg called *Departure* "his clumsy and callow triptych" ("Review of Exhibitions of Max Beckmann and Robert De Niro," *The Nation,* 18 May 1946; see also Greenberg, 1986, 80). The formalist champion of abstraction was no great admirer of *Guernica,* either, saying that it "reminds one of a battle scene from a pediment that has been flattened under a defective steam-roller" ("Picasso at Seventy-Five," *Arts Magazine,* October 1957, quoted here from Greenberg, 1961, 65).

6. "New Liner Titanic Hits an Iceberg; Sinking by the Bow at Midnight; Women Put Off in Life Boats; Last Wireless at 12:27 A.M. Blurred," *New York Times,* 15 April 1912; "Titanic Disaster," *London Times,* 16 April 1912.

7. Kirsten Lehman and Lydia Wiehring von Wendrin, "Mime Misu—Der Regisseur des ersten 'Titanic'-Films," an online publication of the Hochschulbibliothek, Hochschule für Film und Fernsehen "Konrad Wolf" Potsdam-Babelsberg (www.bibl.hff-potsdam.de_deutsch/hochsculebibliothek/veroeffentlichungen/mime-misu.html; viewed 17 June 2003 and 8 November 2009). On the film, see also Wedel, 1997[/98], 41–45; and on Misu, see Wedel, 2002.

8. The first *Titanic* film was apparently the American *Saved from the Titanic,* starring the actress and actual *Titanic* survivor Dorothy Gibson, released just twenty-one days after the disaster. No prints of the film survive. The Misu film, thus the oldest extant *Titanic* feature, was rediscovered in 1998 when a German collector realized that he possessed a print of it in the wake of the *Titanic* frenzy brought about by the 1997 blockbuster film directed by James Cameron. Clips from *In Nacht und Eis* (and many other *Titanic* films) can be seen in the documentary film *Beyond Titanic,* directed by Edith Becker II, Arts and Entertainment network, 1998, and were posted on youtube.com in 2008–9. See also Bottomore, 2000.

9. The opening titles of *In Nacht und Eis* read: "In Nacht und Eis"; "Seedrama"; and "Lebensgewahr gestellt nach authentischen Berichten." The film was directed by Mime Misu, with camera by Willy Hameister, Emil Schünnemann, and Viktor Zimmermann, and sets by Siegfried Wroblewsky, and starring Anton Ernst Rückert, Otto Rippert, and Waldemar Hecker.

10. Wedel, 1997[/98], 42. The film scholar Susan Felleman, with whom I viewed the film at the Deutsche Kinemathek of the Filmmuseum Berlin, feels that the relatively lush mise-en-scène, emphasizing costuming and sets, as well as the rather operatic acting (especially of the captain) is closer to early Italian cinema than to Griffith.

11. Kemp, 1998, 187.

12. Charles Darwent, "The Anatomy of Agony, with Balloons," *The Independent on Sunday,* 16 February 2003 (quoted from Bergfelder and Street, 2004, 5).

13. See Paret, 1980; and Paret, 2001.

14. "in den dürftigen Vorortbezirken des Nordostens" (Scheffler, 1913, 298).

15. *The Sinking of the Titanic* was shown at the Berlin Secession exhibition in the summer of 1913, at the Bremen Kunsthalle in 1914, and then not again until the memorial exhibition of 1951 following the artist's death. It was shown in the memorial exhibitions in 1951 in Munich and Berlin; in 1952 at the Günter Franke Gallery in Munich; in 1953–54 in Braunschweig and Bremen; and at the City Art Museum of St. Louis (now the Saint Louis Art Museum) in 1956, when it was acquired by Morton May for his collection. The painting entered the collection of the Saint Louis Art Museum in 1983 as part of the Morton May bequest.

16. Haxthausen, 1985, 6. See also Haxthausen, "Beckmann and the First World War," in Schulz-Hoffmann and Weiss, 1984, 73–74.

17. Adler, 23. In his diary Beckmann mentions working on the painting right up to its exhibition in mid-April 1913 (Buenger, 1997, 127). Beckmann's famous 1912 confrontation in the journal *Pan* with Blue Rider and Sturm artist Franz Marc over the issue of abstraction—in which Beckmann advocated representational painting—was probably a factor in the decision by *Der Sturm*'s editor, Herwarth Walden, to publish Adler's polemic against Beckmann's work. For Beckmann's and Marc's texts, see Long, 1995, 96–101.

18. Glaser, 1913, 464. Glaser, who cowrote an important monograph on the artist in 1924, was the subject a 1929 portrait by Beckmann: *Portrait of Curt Glaser* (Saint Louis Art Museum; Göpel and Göpel, no. 304). Hans Belting calls this portrait "Beckmann's programmatic declaration of his place in art history" (Belting, 1989, 27).

19. Nochlin, 1971, 184–185.

20. Glaser, 1913, 464. Heckel showed three paintings in the exhibition: *Luftbad, Sterbenden Pierrot,* and *Kanal,* nos. 196, 202, and 203; see *1913 Berlin Secession Exhibition* 26 (Spring 1913), and the exhibition checklist in Donald Gordon, *Modern Art Exhibitions 1900–1916,* vol. 2 (Munich: Prestel, 1974), 693. The listings in the same source for the 19 March–18 May Paris Indépendants exhibition, just before the Secession show, does not include any "Sinking of the Titanic"–themed work.

21. Crane's next line states, "If men could only train for them and have them occur when the men had reached pink condition, there would be less drowning at sea."

22. Peucker, 1995, 4.

23. Hansen, 1995, 365.

24. Anette Kruszynski has compared Beckmann's later triptychs to the sets in Expressionist films such as *The Cabinet of Dr. Caligari* and *Metropolis* (Kruszynski, "Beckmann and the Triptych: A Sacred Form in the Context of Modernism," in Rainbird, 2003, 111, n. 39). On the genre of history painting, see Gaehtgens and Fleckner, 1996; and on contemporary art, see Green and Seddon, 2000. More recently Olaf Peters, too, has related *Departure*'s triptych format to cinematic editing (Peters, 2005, 169–203).

25. Sean Rainbird, "Images of the Times in Beckmann's Early Work," in Rainbird, 2003, 21.

26. Selz, 1996, 16.

27. Panofsky, 2003, 71. Whereas Panofsky concentrated on motion as a formal and iconographic effect, other early film theorists, equally enthralled by the motion in these pictures, "hovered uneasily around the subject of movement, around issues of life and lifelessness, body and soul, the fantastic and the uncanny effect." (Peucker, 1995, 8.)

28. Schatz, 1981, 221–222. Feminist film criticism has rehabilitated the genre of melodrama, especially as it often dramatizes social tensions involving gender, family, race, and class (Douglas Sirk's *Imitation of Life* is the classic example). See, for instance, the special issue "Melodrama and Transgression," *Screen* 29, no. 3 (Summer 1988); and Jackie Byars, *All That Hollywood Allows: Re-Reading Gender in 1950s Melodrama* (Chapel Hill: University of North Carolina Press, 1991).

29. Kaes, 1992, 309.

30. Cf. the film *Beyond Titanic* (see note 8 above).

31. Wedel, 1997[/98], 43; and Wedel, 2004, 100. The film was, however, discussed in trade publications; at least one negative trade-press article noted the prerelease claims.

32. Several articles assessed cinema's educational potential by such devices as showing alpine landscapes three-dimensionally or botanical forms in detail. See, for example, "Wissenschaftliche Kinematographie," *Berliner Volks-Zeitung,* 27 August 1912; and Fr. Welsch, "Kulturelle und Wissenschaftliche Werte in der Kinematographie," *Vossische Zeitung,* 18 August 1912, morning edition. Concern for the (lack of) educational content in several recent hit entertainment films informed the negative notice of *In Nacht und Eis* in a film trade journal; Walter Thielemann, "Belehrung in unterhaltender Form durch den Kinematograph? Kritische Bemerkungen über einige neue Schlager," *Lichtbild-Theater* 40, no. 4 (3 October 1912): 8, excerpted in Köster and Lischeid, 1999, 98–100. On bourgeois intellectuals' skepticism about the cinema as "a plebeian counter-culture which, without invitation, had established itself beside mainstream culture," see Kaes, 1987. Wedel (2004, 100) cites a trade journal article that criticized *In Nacht und Eis* in similar terms, as indicative of "the cultural battleground on which Misu's project took place."

33. "Polizeilich zensiert" appears in bold font in two-page advertisements for the film in the Düsseldorf journal *Der Kinematograph: Fachzeitung für Kinematographie, Phonographie, Musik-Automaten*

289 (10 July 1912) and 290 (17 July 1912). Issue 288 (3 July 1912) contained a highly detailed, practically shot-by-shot description of the film.

34. Hansen, 1983, 168.

35. Kaes, 1985, 321. See also Koss, 2006, 145, which includes a photograph (fig. 6) of a diverse film audience in 1913 Berlin.

36. André Breton, "As in a Wood," in *The Shadow and Its Shadow: Surrealist Writing on the Cinema*, ed. Paul Hammond (Edinburgh: Polygon, 1991), 82.

37. Walter Benjamin, "Surrealism: The Last Snapshot of the European Intelligentsia," in Benjamin, 1978, 179.

38. Göpel, 1984, 134.

39. Walter Benjamin, "The Work of Art in the Age of Mechanical Reproduction," in Benjamin, 1969, 234.

40. Eberle, 1985, 1–3, claims that Beckmann posed as if he were struggling for survival, like the shipwreck victims. The photograph is also discussed by Gallwitz (1983), who interprets Beckmann's placement of *Titanic* as the center panel of a triptych, flanked by *Resurrection* (1908) and *Large Death Scene* (1906). Belting (1989, 17), on the contrary, claims that "Beckmann assumes the self-glorifying studio pose of the artist who interprets the world and thereby asserts his dominion over it." Gallwitz (151) mentions Pollock, referring to the famous photographs of him at work, in his description of the Beckmann photograph. As do I below, Belting (19) alludes to Duchamp's readymades as an art historical context in relationship to Beckmann's hat and coat.

41. Fred Miller Robinson, *The Man in the Bowler Hat: His History and Iconography* (Chapel Hill: University of North Carolina Press, 1993).

42. Gandelman (1978) has suggested that one source for Beckmann's triptychs was movement in the theater of the 1920s, as used by such directors as Erwin Piscator.

43. Barbara Stehlé-Akhtar, "From Obscurity to Recognition: Max Beckmann and America," in *Max Beckmann in Exile*, 1996, 44.

44. The painting *Film Studio*, part of the Saint Louis Art Museum, is no. 374 in Göpel and Göpel, 1976.

45. Peters, 2005, 194–196.

46. Peters, 2005, 189–190.

47. The term *Neue Sachlichkeit* was first used in a 1923 letter to Beckmann from the Mannheim Kunsthalle director Gustav Friedrich Hartlaub, while he was organizing the 1925–26 exhibition that popularized the term and concept; the exhibit, "Die Neue Sachlichkeit: German Painting Since Expressionism," included Beckmann and Dix among its most important and well-represented artists. (See Crockett, 1999, 151–160.)

48. See Tobia Bezzola, "Quappi in Blue," in Bezzola and Homburg, 1998, 22.

49. Hans Belting has noted that Stephan Lackner's 1938 iconographic study "The World Theater of the Painter Beckmann" soon became "the bible of Beckmann studies." (Belting, 1989, 14, 69–71). The majority of interpretations of *Departure* and of the triptychs in general have been involved with unraveling their iconography. See, for instance, Kessler, 1970; and Spieler, 1998.

50. Such thematics are least evident in his work of the 1920s. On Beckmann's use of black paint as a strategy to incorporate into his representational works the challenge of abstract painters such as Malevich, see Westheider, 1995.

51. Kessler, 1955, 213–214.

52. The dating of the painting is problematic—and Beckmann seems to have contributed to rather than solved the problem. The following information is from MoMA curatorial files: At its first showing in America at the Valentin Gallery in 1938, the painting was dated 1932–35. The MoMA catalogue of 1948 dated it 1937. A note to MoMA curator Dorothy Miller from Beckmann, dated 21 October 1948, claims that he finished it in 1935 in Berlin. A memo from Peter Selz to Alfred Barr, dated 16 March 1964, claims to have found in Beckmann's diary notes about the names of the panels and dates of their completions. The left is "Das Schloss" (The palace), begun ca. May 1932 in Frankfurt and finished 31 December 1933 in Berlin. The right is "Die Treppe" (The stairs), begun ca. May 1932 in Frankfurt and finished 4 November 1933 in Berlin. The center is "Die Heimkehr" (Return home), begun ca. May 1932 in Frankfurt and finished 15 November 1933 in Berlin. Most recent publications, including Sean Rainbird, "A Gathering Storm: Beckmann and Cultural Politics 1925–38," in Rainbird, 2003, 161, 171–172, accept the 1933 completion date. Peters (2005), on the other hand, dates the work's first assemblage into a triptych and its naming as *Departure* to 1935.

53. Carlyle Burrows, "Notes and Comment on Events in Art: Max Beckmann," *New York Herald Tribune*, 16 January 1938.

54. "On its face it is an allegory of social suffering and protest, just as many a fine German artist and writer of the age has been forced into the language of fable to express his social ideas. But the symbolism is by no means clear. . . . [I]t would seem that Beckmann does not think of this mural as a social document; but as an expression of painful, personal emotion, for which the solution is found only in the central panel; in other words, in departure or flight. Flight, of course, has been the necessity of the best contemporary German artists from a regime which ignorantly condemns all modern art." (Elisabeth McCausland, "Gallery Notes," *Parnassus* 10, no. 2 [February 1938]: 28.)

55. Jacob Kainen, "Art: 'Departure' Proves an Exciting and Revolutionary Painting," *Daily Worker*, 15 January 1938.

56. *Art in Our Time* (New York: Museum of Modern Art, 1939), 127. For the influence of this interpretation in California, see Forster-Hahn, 2007, 39–43.

57. Stehlé-Akhtar, "From Obscurity to Recognition," in *Max Beckmann in Exile*, 1996, 3.

58. C. J. Bulliet, "Around the Galleries," *Chicago Daily News*, 10 January 1942. The review begins: "Melodrama, strong and spectacular, greets the January visitor at the Arts Club, where is hanging the first comprehensive show to be staged in Chicago of the paintings of Max Beckmann."

59. The show had no catalogue. It included works by Barlach, Beckman, Kollwitz, and Nolde (checklist, MoMA curatorial files). The title of this show is the same as the explicitly political and anti-Nazi exhibition organized by exiled artists and critics in Paris in 1938 as a more pointed response to the Nazi "Degenerate Art" exhibition of 1937 than the New Burlington Gallery show in London had been. See Buenger, 1997, 300. See also, especially, Holz, 2004, 222–240; and Holz, "Free German Art (1938)," in Holz and Schopf, 2001, 148–169, both of which include the photographer Breitenbach's documentation of the exhibition. In light of the facts that Barr's working title for the summer 1942 exhibition was the clunky "Non-Nazi German Art" (according to a handwritten note on a draft of the wall label text, MoMA curatorial files) and that Breitenbach arrived in New York in the summer of 1941, questions arise as to whether Barr had contact with Breitenbach and whether he had borrowed the title of the show from the Paris event.

60. "Free German Art Acquisitions Shown by Museum of Modern Art, 24 June–24 August 1942," press release, MoMA curatorial files.

61. James Thrall Soby, *Contemporary Painters* (New York: Museum of Modern Art, 1949), 90–91, quoted from Selz, 1996, 52.

62. Kessler, 1955, 207.

63. In one source, for example, we read: "The picture quite clearly symbolized the artist's own sense of relief on departing from Germany for the Netherlands and freedom, leaving a world of sadistic memories, symbolized by the tortured and trussed figures, to find a more serene life beckoning from beyond the brilliant blue sea." (Sam Hunter, John Jacobus, and Daniel Wheeler, *Modern Art: Painting, Sculpture, Architecture*, 3rd rev. ed. [New York: Prentice-Hall and Harry N. Abrams, 2000], 129.) *Departure* is not reproduced in Foster et al., 2004, in which Beckmann receives only very brief and dismissive mention, and his triptychs none. For criticism of this book, see the review by Robert Storr, *Art Bulletin* 88, no. 2 (June 2006): 383.

64. H. W. Janson, *The History of Art* (New York: Harry N. Abrams, 1962), 519, and color plate 75. The color plate and text continued to be featured unchanged in the many subsequent editions of this text, including the 2004 sixth edition, in which the dating is changed to 1932–33. Janson's assessment is representative of the author's own position as a German exile and anti-Nazi who had left Germany for the United States in 1935; perhaps also a factor is the fact that for a short time Janson and Beckmann were colleagues at Washington University in St. Louis, where the painter taught in 1947 and 1948 and the art historian served as curator of the art collection from 1944 to 1948. See Sabine Eckmann, *Exilic Vision: H. W. Janson and the Legacy of Modern Art at Washington University* (New York: Salander O'Reilly; and St. Louis: Washington University, 2002.)

65. Eric Fischl, Leon Golub, Susan Rothenberg, and Julian Schnabel, "Expressionism Today: An Artist Symposium," interviews by Carter Ratcliff and Hayden Herrera, in *Artists, Critics, Context: Reading in and around American Art Since 1945*, ed. Paul Fabozzi (Upper Saddle River, NJ: Prentice Hall, 2002), 383; the article was originally published in *Art in America* (December 1982).

66. See Horak, 1985. On exiles in Hollywood, see Heilbut, 1983; and Lawrence Weschler, "Paradise: The Southern California Idyll of Hitler's Cultural Exiles," in Barron et al., 1997, 341–361.

67. Schatz, 1997, 466.
68. Schatz, 1988, 316.
69. Schatz, 1988, 317.
70. Leja, 1993, 203.
71. Jan-Christopher Horak, "The Other Germany in Zinnemann's *The Seventh Cross*," in Rentschler, 1986, 117–131.
72. Ibid., 118–120.
73. Minturn, 1999, 296. Minturn (1999, 278–285), as well as Leja (1993, 111), connect the image of the web or labyrinth in Pollock's drip paintings to film noir and both, in arguments that parallel mine about Beckmann, argue that the Abstract Expressionist painter becomes like a character in a film noir, embodying the culturally potent image of the existential hero (whom Leja connects to "Modern Man discourse," such as that propounded by Lewis Mumford) alone and adrift in a world gone mad.
74. Foster Hirsch, *The Dark Side of the Screen: Film Noir* (New York: Da Capo, 1983), 115; quoted from Koepnick, 2002, 166. Koepnick departs from this standard account in a very interesting and nuanced way, seeing noir as more varied in its modes and sources, and ultimately "holding up a mirror" to the film industry itself and questioning its conceptions of authorship.
75. Hans Belting's description of *The Actors* could also stand as an analysis of film noir plots and stylistics: "Beckmann succeeded here in introducing a very dense depiction precisely because the depicted situation does not allow for any simple resolution. Entrapment in the play of life permits only a fatal exit, a departure from the game" (Belting, 1984, 96).
76. Koepnick, 2002, 166.
77. While Clement Greenberg lamented Beckmann's use of "black contour lines to animate and sustain his color" he went on in his 1946 review to praise the Holland period paintings, in contrast to *Departure*, for "the power of Beckman's emotion, the tenacity with which he insists on the distortions that correspond most exactly to that emotion, the flattened, painterly vision he has of the world, and the unity this vision imposes." ("Review of Exhibitions of Max Beckmann and Robert De Niro," 80.)
78. Amelia Jones, "Dis/playing the phallus: Male artists perform their masculinities," *Art History* 17, no. 4 (December 1994): 546–584, and "'Clothes Make the Man': The Male Artist as Performative Function," *The Oxford Art Journal* 18, no. 2 (1995): 18–32. For Beckmann's self-presentation, see Selz, 1992; Döring and Lenz, 2000; Beckett, 1997; and Petra Kipphoff, "'I Am Who I Am'": Max Beckmann's Self-Portraits," *Kultur Chronik* 10/11, no. 3 (1993): 4–6.
79. The phrase "shipwreck of modernity" derives from the film director Jean Luc Godard's description of the characters in his mythic, allegorical, and modern (or postmodern) 1963 film *Contempt* (Felleman, 2006, 74–75).
80. William Boston, "Airlift for Art: Modern Painting Returns to One of Its Cradles," *New York Times*, 1 March 2004.

Chapter 2: Lost and Found Dada Objects and Subjects

1. Helen Adkins, "Erste Internationale Dada-Messe," in *Stationen der Moderne*, 1988, 157–183. See also Jentsch, 1997, 91.
2. Kristin Makholm, "Chronology," in Makela and Boswell, 1996, 185; and Dech, 2002, 13.
3. Makholm, "Chronology," 186; and *Hannah Höch: Eine Lebenscollage*, vol. 1, 1989, part 1, 101.
4. Adriani, 1971, 29. The transitional years in the orthographical history of her name seem to be 1915–16. Both Hanna and Hannah appear as spellings at that time. (*Hannah Höch: Eine Lebenscollage*, vol. 1, part 1, 1989, 76–79.) See the handwritten Hanna in her Ullstein employee ID (fig. 27), which a sharp-eyed student, Michelle Rinard, called to my attention. At this time Höch was also attending evening gatherings at the Meidners', and one wonders if the more Jewish spelling of Hannah (the name of the mother of Samuel in the Old Testament), as in the German-Jewish philosopher Hannah Arendt, could be related to Höch's exposure to this ambience. In any case, her assumption of a name is consistent with the practice of many Dadaists and their friends. It has been suggested that Kurt Schwitters suggested the spelling of her name to make it a palindrome, like the first name of his poetic heroine Anna Blume, but Höch's usage seems to predate her having met Schwitters.
5. On Höch's American reception, see Makela, "Dadadame und Urfeministen: Die Hannah-Höch Rezeption in den USA," in *Hannah Höch: Eine Lebenscollage*, vol. 3, part 1, 2001, 198–247. Reviews of Höch's seventy-fifth birthday exhibition at Galerie Nierendorf in Berlin position her, especially in paintings of the 1920s such as *Roma* and *The Bride*,

as a precursor of Pop Art, which was being shown at the Akademie der Künste at the time. See HF, "Dada wird Klassisch: Hannah Höch zum 75 Geburtstag," *Berliner Stimme,* 5 December 1964; and Jürgen Morschel, "Clownerie mit Großtadtpfiff," *Frankfurter Rundschau,* 10 December 1964. On Höch's painting until 1945, see Maurer, 1995. Maud Lavin's book (1993) included a dust jacket blurb from Kruger. Scholars such as Brett van Hoesen and Melissa Johnson have recently been working on the relationship of Höch's Weimar-era photomontages, especially the "Ethnographic Museum" series, to German colonialism and the Rhineland occupation by French colonials.

6. Flavell, 1988, 15.

7. On Grosz, Bearden, and Rosenquist at the Art Students League, see Ruth Fine, *The Art of Romare Bearden* (Washington, DC: The National Gallery of Art; New York: Harry N. Abrams, 2003), 8–9. On Grosz and Lawrence, see Romare Bearden and Harry Henderson, *A History of African-American Artists: From 1792 to the Present* (New York: Pantheon, 1993), 293.

8. Höch trained in a variety of graphic and applied arts, including jewelry and fashion design, weaving and embroidery, as well as painting, under Harold Bengen (*Hannah Höch: Eine Lebenscollage,* vol. 1, part 1, 1989, 57; and Dech, 2002, 19).

9. See Otto, 1997. Orlik grew up in the Prague Ghetto *(Stará kolkovna),* though one would be hard pressed to learn this from the art historical literature on him. See, though, the Web site of the Jewish Museum, Prague, for a summary of the 2004 exhibition "Emil Orlik (1870–1932): Portraits of Friends and Contemporaries," www.jewishmuseum.cz/en/aorlik.htm; and the exhibition review, Dita Asiedu, "Emil Orlik—Portraits of Friends and Contemporaries," www.radio.cz/en/artikel/51873; viewed 18 February 2010.

10. The facts of Höch's life are thoroughly presented in English in the excellent, archivally researched chronology by Kristin Makholm in Makela and Boswell, 1996, 185–210, which also includes a comprehensive bibliography of writings by and about Höch. The chronology in Adriani, 1993, 29–70, is also excellent. A similarly detailed chronology for Grosz is Ralph Jentsch, "George Grosz: Chronik zu Leben und Werk," in Schuster, 1995, 535–557. Overviews of Grosz's career are Hess, 1974; Hess, 1985; and Schneede, 1979. According to Makholm, Höch studied with Orlik from 1915 to 1920 and overlapped with and must have met Grosz between 1915 and 1917, although Höch later, in the 1976 interview with Suzanne Pagé, published in the 1976 Paris/Berlin retrospective exhibition catalogue *Hannah Höch: Collages, Peintres Aquarelles, Gouaches, Dessins/Collagen, Gemälde, Aquarelle, Gouachen, Zeichnungen,* claimed not to have crossed paths with him. According to Jentsch (1997, 536–537), Grosz was in the class sporadically between 1912 and 1917. If Höch's recollections are correct, Grosz's inconsistent attendance—and service and hospitalization during the war, from which he was finally released on 20 May 1917—may be the reason for their not having met.

11. See Ohff, 1968, 12, fig. 3. On Höch's creating collages with her mother, using images cut from the popular press, see Dech, 2002, 16. Makela and Makholm date her first collage to 1907 (Makela and Boswell, 1996, 59, 185).

12. On the Dada dispute over the "invention" of photomontage, Grosz and Heartfield vs. Hausmann and Höch, see Hans Richter, 1997, 114–118; Ades, 1976, 19–24; Benson, 1987, 110–116; and Bridget Doherty, "Berlin," in Dickermann, 2005, 90–99.

13. See Jörn Merkert, "Dada und das Ding," in Neuer Berliner Kunstverein, *Metamorphose des Dinges: Kunst und Antikunst 1910–1970* (Brussels: Palais des beaux-arts, 1971), 66–72.

14. Quoted in Hans Richter, 1997, 118.

15. On her technical virtuosity—sometimes seen as a deterrent to being a "true" (that is anti-artistic) Dadaist—see Maria Makela, "By Design: The Early Work of Hannah Höch in Context," in Makela and Boswell, 1996.

16. On Heartfield and Grosz's film work, in which Wieland Herzfelde also joined and which was facilitated by Harry Graf Kessler, see Jeanpaul Goergen, "'Filmisch sei der Strich, klar, einfach': George Grosz und der Film," in Schuster, 1995, 211–218. See also Herzfelde, 1986, 22–23. All sources claim the lost film to have actually been anti-propaganda-propaganda.

17. On Höch and the Ullstein Verlag, see Lavin, 1993; Makholm, "Chronology," 187; and Ohff, 1968, 12.

18. Elsaesser, 1987, 19. The relationship of Berlin Dada to film in "its ambitions to renovate the production and reception of art" is also stressed in Bridget Doherty, "Berlin," in Dickermann, 2005, 109–110.

19. Middleton, 1961, 45.

20. Richter, 1997, 9.

21. See Michael Impey, "Before and after Tzara: Romanian Contributions to Dada," in Janecek, 1998, 128–129. The significance of Tzara (born Sami Rosenstock) and Janco's Romanian Jewish origins for Dada is studied in Sandquist, 2005. The Jewish ethnicity of Dada's founders and other modern artists across Central and Eastern Europe has been noted in Mansbach, 1999, who calls Tzara's pre–World War I Romanian poems "dada *avant la lettre*" (248).

22. On the name "Dada" and Ball's and Huelsenbeck's competing claims to having coined it, see Elderfield, 1974. On Dada's infantilist "primitivism," see Christopher Middleton's "The Rise of Primitivism and its Relevance to the Poetry of Expressionism and Dada" and "Dada Versus Expressionism, or The Red King's Dream," in Middleton, 1978, 23–37, 62–77.

23. World War I caused some twenty million casualties and thirteen million dead soldiers. By contrast, in the previous major European conflict, the Franco-Prussian War (1870–71), fewer than 200,000 soldiers died (Mosse, 1990, 3–4).

24. Doherty, 1997.

25. Ben Hecht, "Berlin Has New 'Art' as Outlet for Ennui: 'Da Da Ismus' Is Latest Fantastic Fad to Soothe Nerves of German Capital," *Chicago Daily News*, 9 May 1919.

26. McCloskey, 1997, 24. See also Karl-Heinz Meißer, "Israel Ber Neumann—Kunsthändler—Verleger," in *Avantgard und Publikum*, ed. Henrike Junge (Cologne, Weimar, Vienna: Böhlau, 1992), 215–224.

27. Weinstein, 1990, 49.

28. Walter Mehring, "Dada Matineen," in Mehring, 1959, 46–52; and Mehring,1983, 164–168.

29. Hanne Bergius, "Dada Berlin and Its Aesthetic of Effect: Playing the Press," in Watts, 2004, 67.

30. These tendencies continued in the postwar period. The *Berliner Illustrirte*'s circulation reached almost two million by the mid-1920s (Eckstein, 16, 21).

31. Some of these titles are taken from Dech, 1989, 35. The word "Dada" itself, its repeated vowel sounds and open-ended meaning, may relate to advertising strategies (see Simmons, 1999, 134, n. 80). Höch's absence from this list is also mentioned in West, 2001, 122.

32. Though involved with and in love with Höch, Hausmann was married to another woman, with whom he had a child. On the relationship between Hausmann and Höch, which included Hausmann's striking Höch and her aborting pregnancies in May 1916 and January 1918, see Makela, 1996, 64; and Lavin, 1993, 106. Their rapid advance from first acquaintance to being lovers is recorded in letters and love poems from June 1915. (*Hannah Höch: Eine Lebenscollage*, vol. 1, part 1, 1989, 106–111.) Höch's witty and bitter response to the male artist who preaches revolutionary sexual liberation but is unwilling to give up his patriarchal prerogatives appears in the satiric short fable she wrote ca. 1920, "The Painter" (see the translation by Anne Halley in Lavin, 1993, 216–218). Nevertheless, Hausmann was instrumental in introducing Höch to the Berlin avant-garde and went so far as to threaten to withdraw his works if she were not allowed to show in the Dada Fair. Grosz had, in fact, opposed her participation.

33. Jula Dech, "Küchen- oder Kuchenmesser—das ist hier die Frage," in Dech, 2002, 34.

34. Bergius, 1989, 28.

35. *Hannah Höch: Eine Lebenscollage* comprises a total of six books, divided into three volumes. The materials in the archive from Höch's later years are particularly voluminous. They are cataloged, but only partially published, in volumes 2 and 3.

36. Wolfradt, 1921, fig 9; and Mynona, 1922, 86, available online through the University of Iowa's International Dada Archive, http://sdrc.lib.uiowa.edu/dada/George_Grosz; the Dada Fair satire appeared in "Bilder vom Tage," *Die Woche* 22, no 28 (17 July 1920): 732. See also Simmons, 1999, 144, fig. 20.

37. Barron, 1991, 245. His paintings in the exhibition included *The Adventurer* (1916), *Metropolis* (1916–17), *The Boxer* (c. 1920), and the Mannheim Kunsthalle version of *Portrait of Max Hermann-Neisse* (1925).

38. "Das Gemälde verschwand im Frühjahr 1933 aus meiner Wohnung, die ich nach dem Reichstagsbrand nicht mehr hatte betreten können, und ist verschollen." (Wieland Herzfelde, "Über George Grosz: Brief an die Moskauer Akademie der Künste," in Herzfelde, 1976, 477.) Ralph Jentsch writes, "It came into the possession of the Hanover gallery owner von Garvens in 1925 and has been considered as lost since 1933. Wieland Herzfelde stated that the picture was last hanging in his apartment,

which he had had to flee from in the spring of 1933, and had been missing since then. However, up to the present time this has not been confirmed. It remains to be hoped that this incunabulum of 20th-century art will one day be found again" (Jentsch, 1997, 79). A letter of 26 May 1922, from the gallery owner Herbert von Garvens to Grosz mentions that "Herr Dr. Karl, Düsseldorf, Bismarckstr. 40, owns the pretty watercolor 'Germany: A Winter's Tale.' " (GGA, sign. 216.) I have found no other records of such a watercolor or of the oil painting under consideration here actually going to the von Garvens gallery. If it did, it can only be that it was not sold but instead returned to the artist. The painting was shown in 1927 at the exhibition "Ölgemälde von George Grosz und Kongo Skulpturen" at the Galerie Alfred Flechtheim, in Berlin, 7–26 February 1927, where it was captioned *Nr. 5, Deutschland, ein Wintermärchen,* 1917/18; and, perhaps for the last time, in the jury-free section of the 1929 exhibition "10 Jahre Novembergruppe." It was not included in the show "George Grosz: Ölgemälde und Aquarelle" that Flechtheim held in his Düsseldorf gallery in 1930.

39. H. W. Janson, *The History of Art* (New York: Abrams, 1964), 525.

40. For analysis of another major lost work from the Dada Fair, see White, 2001. The most thorough interpretation of *Germany: A Winter's Tale* to date sees the work as a parody of the Last Judgment (Bergius, 2000, 257–260).

41. On the title, *Küchenmesser* (kitchen knife), and its variations, including that of *Kuchenmesser* (cake knife), see Dech, "Küchen- oder Kuchenmesser—das ist hier die Frage," in Dech, 2002, 29–42; and Dech, 1981, 48–55.

42. See Kathrin Hoffmann-Curtius, "'Wenn Blicke töten könnten' oder: Der Künstler als Lustmörder," in Lindner et al., 1989, 369–393; Hoffmann-Curtius, "Erotik im Blick des George Grosz," in Schuster, 1995, 182–188; McCloskey, 1997, 6–9; and Tatar, 1997.

43. Beth Irwin Lewis, in the preface to the 1991 edition of *George Grosz: Art and Politics in the Weimar Republic* (iv), referring to the first edition of her book, states: "I could not now ignore the misogyny in his work and the political implications of that misogyny." Flavell (1998, 43) claims that Grosz was influenced by the "fiercely misogynist writings of Schopenhauer, Nietzsche, and Otto Weininger." Lavin (1993, 17) characterizes Grosz's depictions of women—specifically prostitutes, who predominate among his female subjects—as misogynist, and juxtaposes against them Höch's more nuanced and certainly potentially positive female imagery, a position cited approvingly by McCloskey, 1997, 72, n. 63. McCloskey's study, though (8), deemphasizes Grosz's misogyny and claims to be "more skeptical than previous writers about the possibility of recovering Grosz's true self and artistic intention."

44. Recent reevaluations of significant figures in German twentieth-century cultural history considering their Jewish identity include Dirks and Simon, 2005, on Einstein; Wolfgang Brenner, *Walther Rathenau: Deutscher und Jude* (Munich: Piper, 2005), and Viola Roggenkamp; *Erika Mann: Eine jüdische Tochter* (Zurich and Hamburg: Arche Verlag, 2005).

45. See Nochlin and Garb, 1995; Soussloff, 1998, and Soussloff, 2006; and Baigell and Heyd, 2001, which last-named source includes Heyd's essay on the American Dadaist Man Ray. Literary historians have longer dealt with this theme, albeit sometimes to dismiss its significance in favor of other identities, such as class and political affiliation. See Jost Hermand, "Juden in der Kultur der Weimarer Republik," in *Juden in der Weimarer Republik,* ed. Walter Grab and Juluis H. Schoeps, 2nd rev. ed. (Darmstadt: Wissenschaftliche Buchgesellschaft, 1998), 28.

46. This neglect is changing. Sandquist, Michael White, and Elizabeth Legge are exploring Dada's Jewish elements, as are, no doubt, other scholars. A remarkable bibliography on Dada (646 pages of citations!), attesting to the wealth of scholarship on it—though likewise to the dearth of scholarship considering ethnicity in connection with it—is provided by Schäfer, 2005. A broad consideration of Jews in the Central European avant-garde, such as the Romanian-born Zurich Dada founders Tristan Tzara and Marcel Janco, is Claus Stephani, "Jüdische Künstler der Avantgarden: Gedanken am Rande einer Retrospektive in München," *David—Jüdische Kulturzeitschrift* 59 (September 2002), also available at http://david.juden.at/kulturzeitschift. See also "Präsenz des Judentums," in *Europa, Europa: Das Jahrhundert der Avantgard in Mittel- und Osteuropa,* ed. Ryszard Stanislawski and Christopher Brockhaus, 2 vols. (Stiftung Kunst und Kultur des Landes Nordrhein-Westfalen, Kunst- und Ausstellungshalle der Bundesrepublik Deutschland, 1994), 1: 214–243.

47. Lavin, 1993, 52–53, 108–109, especially the notes to those pages. White's paper on Raoul Hausmann and Salomo Friedlaender, "Berlin Dada and Jewish Identity," delivered at the 25–26 November 2005 Tate Modern symposium "Dada in Debate" in London, complements the points made here. He has uncovered fascinating evidence of Hausmann's involvement with Martin Buber and Zionist circles in Salomo Friedlaender's roman à clef, *Graue Magie* and in an unpublished Hausmann manuscript, "Josef Gnoi (matzoh maker)," in Notizbuch 4, BG-RHA 1753, which appears on a 1923 Merz Matinee program as "Die Geschichte des Josef Gnoi" (Bergius, 1989, 128). Mynona, *Graue Magie: Ein Zukunftsroman*, 1922, features a cover design by John Heartfield. The novel reappeared in 1931 as *Geheimnisse von Berlin: Ein Roman*. White's recent article, "The Grosz Case: Paranoia, Self-hatred and Anti-Semitism," in which he also claims a Jewish heritage for Hausmann (451), is the most comprehensive and provocative assessment of Berlin Dada and Jewish identity to date.

48. The page is reproduced without comment in Elderfield, 1974, 48; Hans Richter, 1997, 115; and Joan Ockman, "Reinventing Jefim Golyscheff: Lives of a Minor Modernist," *Assemblage* 11 (April 1990): 90. The page is reproduced, as a detail that includes the Hebrew, in Riha and Bergius, 1977, 63.

49. This translation from the Hebrew by Ruth Zaslansky. See *Dada Ausstellung: Dada Vorfrühling* (Cologne, 1920), catalogue of the exhibition at Brauhaus Winter, April 1920, with texts by Johannes Baargeld, Max Ernst, and Jean Arp. The catalogue is available online through the International Dada Archive at the University of Iowa (http://sdrc.lib.uiowa.edu/DADA%20vorfruhling/index/htm).

50. Jörgen Schäfer and Dirk Teuber, "Dada in Cologne," in Watts, 2004, 155, 162–163. See also Charlotte Stokes, "Rage and Liberation: Cologne Dada," in Stokes and Foster, 1997, 45, 52–54. Louise Straus earned a PhD in art history at Bonn University in 1917. Her posthumously reconstructed memoir appeared in German as *Nomadengut* (Hannover: Sprengel Museum, 2000) and in English as Louise Straus-Ernst, *The First Wife's Tale* (New York: Midmarch Press, 2004).

51. In their devotion to the sounding symbol, among them Ball's famous 1917 poem "Karawane," Dadaists also express a continued derivation from Expressionism and especially from Wassily Kandinsky's attempts to find a system of abstract visual signification that could communicate with a directness, emotionalism, and universalism equivalent to music and to his "sound poems." On Kandinsky's influence on Hugo Ball, specifically, and on Dada, generally, see Taylor, 1990, 170–183. For Ball's 1917 lecture "Kandinsky," see Long, 1995, 263–266.

52. "Wer merkt es denn noch nicht, daß 'der Meshuggas' teils zwar tobende Jugendlust, teils aber auch eine Maske ist, unter der gedeckt die Dadaisten nur verwegener ihrer satirischen Tollheit ihrer tollen Satire nachgehen?" (L. R., "*Dada-Tribüne*," newspaper clipping, source unknown, HHA, 12.52, in *Hannah Höch: Eine Lebenscollage*, vol. 1, part 2, 1989, 612.) A perhaps related article is listed in Bergius, 2004: Anonymous, "Geistesblüten der Revolution (Meschugge ist Triumph)," *Die Warnung*, 7 May 1919.

53. Hannah Höch, chronology prepared for *Hannah Höch und Dada*, Galerie Franz, Berlin, 1949. In the catalogue her text, which goes on longer than the quotation here, was shortened to "1918 dada." (GG HHC 145/179, 1949 Galerie Franz exhibition materials, HHA.)

54. In a memoir written in the 1940s Herzfelde notes that his mother was Protestant and his father, "what enlightenment figures from previous centuries called a free spirit" *(was die Aufklärer des vorigen Jahrhunderts einen Freigeist nannten)*. (Wieland Herzfelde, "Himmel und Hölle," in Herzfelde, 1996, 41.) Alice Stolzenburg and Franz Herzfeld were apprehended and institutionalized as mentally unbalanced in 1899. Herzfeld died in a sanitorium in Valdona, which could have had some effect on the young Wieland's empathy with the institutionalized (Kotowski, 2005, 114; see also Nancy Roth, "Heartfield's Collaboration," *Oxford Art Journal* 29, no. 3 [2006]: 395–418).

55. See Hellmuth Bachmann (apparently Barbara Herzfeld), "John Heartfield: Zu seinem 50. Geburtstag am 19. Juni 1942," *Argentinisches Tageblatt* (Buenos Aires), 19 June 1942; cited from Michael Krejsa and Petra Albrecht, "Biografische Dokumentation," in *John Heartfield* (Berlin: Akademie der Künste, 1991), 390. Some of this story is retold in Herzfelde, 1986, 10–12 (but without reference to Jewish ancestry). Joseph Herzfeld served as a Social Democratic Party Reichstag member from 1912 to 1916, was one of the founders of the antiwar Inde-

pendent Socialist Party in 1917, and represented the Communist Party in the Reichstag from 1920 to 1924 (Werner T. Angress, "Juden im Politischen Leben der Revolutionszeit," in *Deutsches Judentum in Krieg und Revolution, 1916–1922,* ed. Werner Mosse and Arnold Paucker [Tübingen: J. C. B. Mohr, 1971], 137–315). Herzfeld had already been a Social Democratic member of the Reichstag from 1898 to 1906 and again from 1912 to 1917 (Kotowski, 2005, 120). Given their uncle's prominence it is unthinkable that they were unaware of their heritage, and likely the Nazis were aware of it, too.

56. "As I remember it, the credit belongs to our pair of Dadaist publishers and brothers, who also financed the enterprise with the aid of an [accidental] little legacy *[Zufallserbschaft]* they had"; quoted in Hans Richter, 1997, 110, where this passage appears without the adjectival "accidental," which is in the versions in Mehring, 1959, 67–68; and Mehring, 1983, 178. Mehring was particularly good friends with Grosz, but his relationship to the Herzfelds merits further attention. Mehring's father, Sigmar, was, like Franz Held, more of a transgressive left-wing role model than a stern paternal presence against whom a son could revolt. Like Held, Mehring was brought up on charges for a poem considered dangerous to the German imperial state, in his case an 1899 lyric supporting Dreyfus. He was also among the first to publish Grosz's drawings, in *Ulk,* and, like Franz Held (who died in 1908) was also recently deceased (1915) when Mehring was most involved with the Herzfelds (see Helberg, 1983, 5).

57. Hans Richter, 1997, 110–112; Simmons, 1999, 136–138; Bridget Doherty, "Berlin," in Dickermann, 2005, 97–98; and Benson, 1987, 113–116. See also McCloskey, 1997.

58. Bergius, 2000, 288; and Bergius, 2003, 174.

59. "Max Nordau at the Second Zionist Congress of 1898 called for the creation of 'muscle Jews' as against pale-faced and thin-chested 'coffehouse Jews'" (Mosse, 1985, 42). For an iteration of Nordau's position by a leader of the Zionist sports movement "Hakoah," in Vienna, see Rudolf Philipp, *Wir Juden und der Sport* (Vienna: Union, 1921), 13. See also Todd Samuel Presner, "'Clear Heads, Solid Stomachs, and Hard Muscles': Max Nordau and the Aesthetics of the Jewish Regeneration," *Modernism/modernity* 10, no. 2 (2003): 269–296.

60. "Aus dem Tagebuch des Primaners W. H.," in Herzfelde, 1996, 110, 117–118. Daughter of a Jewish banker, Lasker-Schüler was born in Wuppertal in 1869 and died in Jerusalem in 1945.

61. Herzfelde, 1986, 17–18, 318–322.

62. Herzfelde, 1986, 16. Helmut eventually did serve in the military, but not in combat.

63. Herzfelde, 1917.

64. Lasker-Schüler, 1986, 14. Wieland Herzfelde is mentioned by name on page 62. In an East German essay late in his life, Wieland Herzfelde stressed what he saw as Lasker-Schüler's neglected political commitment and her sympathy with the Russian and German revolutions. (Wieland Herzfelde, "Else Lasker-Schüler: Begegnungen mit der Dichterin und ihrem Werk," *Sinn und Form* 21, no. 6 [1969]: 1294–1325; cited in Hallensleben, 2000, 182–183.) One of Grosz's sketchbooks from 1916 also includes a letter employing Lasker-Schüler's nicknames for artists and transcription of a poem describing Grosz that appeared in *Neue Jugend* 8 (Lauer, 1993, cat. 1916/3 [34], ca. June–July, 157). The sketchbook is now in the GGA, *G. Grosz Skizzenbuch,* HZ 2085, renumbered as 44, rather than 34 as in Nisbet.

65. Mehring, 1959, 64–66. On the biography of Carl Einstein, the son of Daniel Einstein and Sophie Lichtenstein Einstein, see www.carleinstein.uni-muenchen.de, a site developed and run by the Carl-Einstein-Gesellschaft.

66. See Hans Peter Althaus, *Chuzpe, Schmus, und Tacheles: Jiddische Wortgeschichten* (Munich: Beck, 2004), 59–60. On *meschugge,* see Althaus, *Zochen, Zoff und Zores: Jiddische Wörter im Deutschen* (Munich: Beck, 2002), 21–39.

67. This speculation is taken from Michael White's 2005 conference paper at the Tate Modern, see note 47. According to White, the Hausmann manuscript, "Josef Gnoi (matzoh maker)," probably derives from discussions at Meidner's, which according to White touched on Zionism and Martin Buber, who founded his journal *Der Jude* in 1916. See Mark H. Gelber, "1916: The First Issue of Martin Buber's German-Jewish Journal *Der Jude* Appears," in Gilman and Zipes, 1997, 343–347.

68. Richard Huelsenbeck, "Dadaistisches Manifest," in Huelsenbeck, 1920, 36–41.

69. Kurt Borddorf, "Dadas wahres Gesicht," *Deutsche Zeitung,* 26 June 1921; quoted from Bergius, 2003, 280–281.

70. For translation of the full text of the guide, which appeared after the exhibition opened, see

Long, 1995, 307–311; and Barron, 1991; the latter also includes a facsimile and translation. The Herzfelde quotation is derived from a well-known essay that he published (as Herzfeld, in April 1914, the month of his eighteenth birthday) in the Expressionist journal *Die Aktion,* "The Ethic of the Insane," a text McCloskey (1997, 19) calls "one of the classic texts of the Expressionist era." Herzfeld goes beyond interest in the art of the insane to actual identification with it and with them, perhaps reflecting on his parents' fate.

71. Peter Gay, "The Berlin Jewish-Spirit: A Dogma in Search of Some Doubts," in Gay, 1978, 172.

72. See "Die Auswüchse der Dadamesse: Ein Prozeß wegen Beleidigung der Reichswehr—Der 'Oberdada' vor Gericht," *Berliner Tagblatt,* 21 April 1921. On Grosz's three trials, in 1921, 1924, and 1928–31, see Lewis, 1991, 216–226. An entertaining contemporary English description of the 1924 trial for "wounding the moral susceptibilities of normal persons," is "A German Cartoonist Fined: The Art of Georg Grosz," *Manchester Guardian,* 1 April 1924.

73. The famous commercial fair at Leipzig could also be seen as a precursor to the *Dada-Messe:* in August 1917, as a *Kriegsmesse,* or wartime fair, it could only offer ramshackle scrap goods.

74. Mosse, 1990, 177.

75. "Jesus Christus ist euch wurst," shouted the Swabian Baader (Bergius, 1989, 153–155).

76. On Grosz's role playing, see Flavell, 1988, passim; and Frank Whitford, "The Many Faces of George Grosz," in *The Berlin of George Grosz: Drawings, Watercolours and Prints, 1912–1930* (New Haven, CT, and London: Yale University Press, 1997), 1–20. See also Wieland Herzfelde, "Ein Kaufmann aus Holland," in Herzfelde, 1996, 164–181.

77. S. Wininger, *Grosse Jüdische National-Biographie: Ein Nachschlagwerk für das jüdische Volk und dessen Freunde,* vol. 2 (Cernausi [Czernowitz]: Arta, 1927), 529. On the trial and Captain Matthäi's anti-Semitic allegations, see White, 2007, 434–435.

78. Paul Mendes-Flohr, "The Berlin Jew as Cosmopolitan," in Bilski, 1999, 17, 31, n. 9.

79. Albert Einstein, "Die Zuwanderung aus dem Osten," *Berliner Tageblatt,* 30 December 1919; quoted from Dirks and Simon, 2005, 30–31.

80. See Kuhlmann, 2003. My thanks to Katharina Sykora for alerting me to her student's dissertation. See also Jordana Mendelson, "Architecture, Photography and (Gendered) Modernities in 1930s Barcelona," *Modernism/Modernity* 10, no. 1 (2003): 141–163.

81. Information taken from Jürgen Neffe, *Einstein: A Biography,* trans. Shelley Frisch (New York: Farrar, Straus and Giroux, 2007; originally published in German by Rowohlt in 2005). See also Corey S. Powell, "Master of the Universe," *New York Times Book Review,* 20 May 2007, 16.

82. "Introduction," *The Collected Papers of Albert Einstein,* vol. 10, *The Berlin Years,* ed. Diana Kormos Buchwald et al. (Princeton, NJ: Princeton University Press, 2006): available as a sample chapter at www.pupress.princeton.edu/chapters/i8331.html (viewed 6 June 2006).

83. For a comprehensive bibliography of the press reports and transcriptions of a selection of reports, see Hanne Bergius, "Dada Berlin and Its Aesthetic of Effect: Playing the Press," in Watts, 2004, 78, 92–130. Although the sale of only 389 tickets to the Dada Fair can be documented, there was considerable press coverage of the event in Berlin, elsewhere in Germany, and even in Italy and Prague. The admission price (3.30 marks) is noted in Adolf Behne's review. See also Helen Adkins, "Erste Internationale Dada-Messe," in *Stationen der Moderne,* 1988, 179, 157, 169; and Bergius, 2000, 288, for facsimile reproductions of reviews by Behne, Ernst Cohn-Wiener and "P. F." (Paul Fechter?), who referred to it as "Bolshevism in Art" and called for the censors to step in. Kurt Tucholsky wrote about the show, under the name Peter Panter, in the *Berliner Tageblatt,* 20 July 1920; Gertrud Alexander responded critically in the Communist Party *Rote Fahne,* 25 July 1920; and Paul Westheim reviewed it sympathetically, probably capturing its spirit better than any other contemporary commentator, in the *Frankfurter Zeitung,* 17 July 1920.

84. Andreas Kleinert, "Paul Weyland, der Berliner Einstein-Töter," in *Naturwissenschaft und Technik in der Geschichte: 25 Jahre Lehrstuhl für Geschichte der Naturwissenschaft und Technik am Historischen Institut der Universität Stuttgart,* ed. Hans Albrecht (Stuttgart: Verlag für Geschichte der Naturwissenschaften und Technik, 1993), 198–232. A shortened English version of this text, first delivered as a lecture at Smith College in 1992, is available online at www.physik.uni-halle.ed/Fachgruppen/history/weyland.htm. Bergius's comprehensive bibliography, encompassing thirteen pages of citations of newspaper reports on Berlin Dada

between 1918 and 1920 (in Watts, 2004, 135–148) certainly attests to the Dadaists' impact in the press. Two articles from the *Berliner Tageblatt*, 25–26 August 1920, listed in Bergius's bibliography (Watts, 2004, 147), also refer to the attack on Einstein.

Chapter 3: Objects of Interpretation

1. The Expressionist writer Theodore Däubler may have been referring to *Germany: A Winter's Tale* when he described a particular Grosz work as "the last judgment boiling in a metropolitan cauldron." (Däubler, 1918, 153–154.)

2. Kurt Glaser, "Dada, Theater, Musik und Kunst," newspaper clipping of unknown origin, which Hannah Höch hand-dated April 1919, in *Hannah Höch: Eine Lebenscollage*, vol. 1, part 2, 1989, 564–567; the review is listed in Bergius, "Dada Berlin and Its Aesthetic of Effect: Playing the Press," in Watts, 2004, as Kurt Glaser, "Dada," *Berliner Börsen Courier*, 1 May 1919.

3. *Der Ararat, Erstes Sonderheft: George Grosz, Katalog der 59. Ausstellung der Galerie Neue Kunst, Hans Goltz* (Munich, April–May 1920), which lists Grosz's painting as *Germany: A Winter's Tale*, 1917/18, cat. no. 4 and fig. 2.

4. Alfred Salmony, "George Grosz," *Das Kunstblatt* 4, no. 4 (1920): 96–104. On Westheim and *Das Kunstblatt*, see Lutz Windhöfel, *Paul Westheim und* Das Kunstblatt: *Eine Zeitschrift und ihr Herausgeber in der Weimarer Republik* (Cologne, Weimar, and Vienna: Böhlau Verlag, 1995).

5. "Etwa Militär mit Orden, Kriegspfarrer mit Segen und Goethe-Professor mit Stock zur scheußlichen Trinität zu Füßen des Speißers vereint im Bilde 'Deutschland ein Wintermärchen' " (97).

6. The GGA contains a collection of 216 "Kitsch Post Cards," sign. 1183. See also Hoffmann-Curtius, in Lindner, 1989, 369–393. Turn-of-the-century cards, such as GGA 3/63/480 and 3/63/429, which show old city squares with montaged-in streetcars, automobiles, and flying machines and captioned, for example, "Freiwalder in the Future," also provide precedents for Dada montages. The Berlin Dadaists' use of so-called kitsch was discussed by Sherwin Simmons in his lecture "Dada and Kitsch: Cultivation of the Trivial," presented at the Tate's 2005 "Dada in Debate" symposium.

7. "Das dicke Weibsbild, Mischblut polnisch-jüdisch, macht sich zur Freude zurecht, es trägt Seidenstrumpfe und faschingssteiefletten." (Däubler, 1917, 80–82.)

8. Wolfradt, 1921, 12.

9. Jentsch, 1997, 79; and Schuster, 1995, 332.

10. "Bilder vom Tage," *Die Woche* 22, no. 17 (July 1920): 732. See Simmons, 1999, 143–144, fig. 20.

11. Curt Glaser, *Kunst und Künstler* 28 (1929–30): 76; quoted from Schuster, 1995, 332.

12. Flavell, 1988, 38. Cf. Hess, 1985, 72–73.

13. The characterization of Heine as "German Apollo" is from the French poet Théophile Gautier, shortly after Heine's arrival in Paris in the 1830s. (Frederic Ewen, "Heinrich Heine: Humanity's Soldier," in Ewen, 1948, 25.)

14. Ewen, 1948, 11.

15. Ewen, 1948, 700.

16. See Anita Bunyan, "1843: Heinrich Heine and Karl Marx meet for the first time in Paris," and Susanne Zantop, "1844: After a Self-imposed Exile in Paris, Heinrich Heine Writes *Deutschland: Ein Wintermärchen*," in Gilman and Zipes, 1997, 171–177, 178–185.

17. Fischer, 1916, 36.

18. Scholem, 1977, 99.

19. See Kaes, Jay, and Dimendberg, 1994, 743.

20. Adolf Bartels, "Der Kampf der Zeit [The Struggle of the age]," *Deutsches Schriftum* 10 (January 1920): 1–2; quoted from Kaes, Jay, and Dimendberg, 1994, 123–124.

21. Hans Heinrich von Twardowski, "Das neue Wintermärchen," *Ulk* 47, no. 51 (20 December 1918): 3. See also Simmons, 1999, 141–142, n. 124. Twardowski is best known for his 1919 portrayal of Alan in *The Cabinet of Dr. Caligari*. In exile he had an uncredited part as the German officer involved with the French woman Yvonne in *Casablanca*, and in 1943 he played Reinhard Heydrich in Fritz Lang's anti-Nazi film noir thriller *Hangmen Also Die!*

22. In addition to his remarks on the painting's title coming from Heine, I have found only one reference to Heine by Grosz. In a 15 February 1945 letter to Horkheimer, who had apparently asked Grosz to complete what the artist thought would be "propaganda work," Grosz said he was probably not the man for the job—that he was more along the lines of a Goya or Delacroix, creating "sublimated" propaganda, than like "such useful functionaries as Raemaker or Heine" (Knust, 1979, 344).

23. Michael White's excellent article highlights Grosz's ambivalence toward his country, art, him-

self, and sanity and discusses Grosz's styling himself a pathologically self-hating Jew (White, 2007).

24. Hess (1985, 73) connects this position to that of a donor in a medieval altarpiece.

25. Thanks to my colleague Elina Gertsman for this suggestion.

26. Heinrich Heine, "Germany: A Winter's Tale," translated by Aaron Kramer, in Ewen, 1948, 181; all English Heine quotes are from this translation. The original German reads: *Im traurigen Monat November wars, / Die Tage wurden trüber, / Der Wind riß von den Bäumen das Laub, / Da reist ich nach Deutschland hinüber.* (Heinrich Heine, *Atta Troll; Ein Sommernachtstraum; Deutschland; Ein Wintermärchen* [Munich: DTV, 1981], 91.)

27. Cf. Bergius, 2000, 263; and Simmons, 1999, 139, n. 125. Beneath this paper is another that reads: "Arbeiter! Soldate . . . ," which McCloskey (1997, 75) interprets as a juxtaposition of the right-wing newspaper with a left-wing call to demonstration. This might well be, but similar calls to workers and soldiers to go out and vote for right-wing candidates were also present in the conservative press at this time. For discussion of the debate on Upper Silesia's status at this time, see Bergius, 2000, 262–263.

28. "Liebknecht und Rosa Luxemburg getötet. . . . Auf der Flucht erschossen.—Von der Volksmenge umgebracht," *Berliner Lokal-Anzeiger* (evening edition), 16 January 1919. The *Berliner Lokal-Anzeiger* came under the control of the nationalist industrialist Adolf Hugenburg in 1916. It then formed a competitor to the more liberal Ullstein and Mosse newspapers published in Berlin.

29. Quoted in Bergius, 2000, 260–261. Raoul Hausmann claimed, "Red wine makes for precision. Beer makes one fat and sluggish" (Dech, 1981, 51).

30. Bergius, 2000, 257–260.

31. Herzfeld, 1996, 182. The street, created by order of the emperor and named after General Alexander August Wilhelm von Pape, connected these military service buildings to the Tempelhof training grounds; see www.berlingeschichte.de/strassen.

32. On the other side of the general's head the number "34" appears, written in script suggesting a house number. The existing sketchbook that contains studies for the words and letters in the top right includes a note referring to *"Kriegslazarett 34/V"* (military hospital 34/V), which may relate to this number's placement in the painting (Lauer, 1993, 1918/1 [39]; Nisbet, 1993, 158; and GGA, G. Grosz Skizzenbuch HZ 2091, no. 50, p. 21 [GGA]).

33. Doherty, 1997, 118–121; and Doherty, 2003, 84.

34. G. Grosz Skizzenbuch HZ 2091, no. 50 (GGA); the decal is on the inside cover of the sketchbook, and a sketch noting colors is on page 7 (Simmons, 1999, 121, n. 2).

35. G. Grosz Skizzenbuch HZ 2091, no. 50, p. 17 (GGA), is a drawing of such an advertisement, with color notations.

36. Doherty, 2003, 87.

37. The source of a sign to the cathedral's right, with an S—I inscribed in an oval, remains obscure. It is perhaps a signpost from a train or trolley station (G. Grosz Skizzenbuch HZ 2091, no. 50, p.17 [GGA]).

38. Doherty, 2003, 78.

39. Quoted from Dech, 2002, 29.

40. Dech, 2002, 29. Höch's diary entry of 16 February 1963 is quoted in full in Ralf Burmeister, "Hannah Höch's System der Erinnerung," in *Hannah Höch: Eine Lebenscollage*, vol. 3, part 1, 2001, 28. The centrality of *Cut with the Kitchen Knife Dada* to Berlin Dada montage practice has been asserted for over thirty years now. A reviewer of the 1976 Berlin National Gallery exhibition stated: "The *Cut with the Kitchen Knife Dada* . . . which brings together grandees of the defunct Empire with representatives of science, art, politics and sports with irony and formal assurance, is not only one of the most important works in the Berlin show, but of Berlin Dadaism itself." (Helmut Kotschenreuther, "Kunst in der Antikunst: Die Ausstellung Hannah Höch in Westberlins Neuer Nationalgalerie," *Stuttgarter Zeitung*, 5 April 1976.) Benjamin Buchloh calls the montage "one of the key works of 1919 . . . in which the full range of technical and strategic ambiguities that would form the project of photomontage is apparent." (Foster, Krauss, Bois, and Buchloh, 2004, 170.)

41. Dech and Maurer, 1991, 12–23.

42. This conclusion based on my research into exhibition catalogues and checklists, the secondary literature on them, Höch's own notations and correspondence, and the picture's provenance as known to the National Gallery, as kindly provided to me by Dr. Jörn Grabowski, director of the Zentralarchiv, Staatliche Museen zu Berlin. Dech (1981, 47) also noted that the "montage remained for 41 years in the artist's own possession."

43. The "Kunstausstellung Berlin 1920" exhibition was held in the Landesausstellungsgebäude

am Lehrter Bahnhof, 21 May–31 September 1920. Halls 21–29 included November Group works. Höch showed five works, nos. 1221–1225 (exhibition catalogue, 74).

44. *Führer durch die Abteilung der Novembergruppe Kunstausstellung, 1921* (Hannover: Verlag Paul Steegeman, 1921). Höch wrote in her copy of the catalogue that she showed a large watercolor titled "Italienbild" and "Rotes Zimmer" (BG HHC 13372/79, HHA).

45. "Ich kann das Wort Dada nicht mehr hören, aber die Leute wollen ja derzeit nichts anderes, also muß ich wohl darauf eingehen." (Eberhard Roters, "Bildsymbolik im Werk Hannah Höchs," in Roters, 1990, 175.)

46. There is discussion of her work, but it is mainly of a quite general nature, as in her response to Roditi's question (1959, 64) "Could you briefly describe your own development as an artist?"

47. Roditi, 1959, 63.

48. On Nielsen in *Cut with the Kitchen Knife*, and in the 1925 painting *Roma*, see Bergius, 2000, 152; and Lavin, 1993, 22, 34–35, 191–192. On Nielsen as an object—and subject—of female spectatorship in Weimar cinema, see Petro, 1989, 159–164.

49. The exhibition "výstava fotomontáží hannah höch brno 1934" was organized by František Kalivoda in Brno in March 1934.

50. See Makela and Boswell, 1996, 10–11.

51. Joseph de Gruyter, "Aquarellen en Fotomontages door Hannah Höch: Kunstzaal d'Audretch," *Het Vaderland* ('s-Gravenhage), 8 November 1935. Many thanks to John Decker for this translation.

52. See, for instance, Hannah Höch, "A Few Words on Photomontage, 1934," a text prepared in connection with the Brno exhibition and reproduced in Lavin, 1993, 219–220.

53. The exhibition "Fotomontage" was held at the Staatliche Museen, Staatliche Kunstbibliothek, Berlin, from 25 April to 31 May 1931.

54. Galerie Gerd Rosen, "Fantasten," February 1946; Hannah Höch's text, "Fotomontage von Dada bis Heute," is dated December 1946 (HHA).

55. Hannah Höch, handwritten note, Janis Gallery exhibition file, BG HHC 1914/79, HHA. A letter from Sydney Janis of 28 February 1953 thanks her "for the excellence of your selection."

56. "Dada: Dokumente einer Bewegung," organized by Karl-Heinz Hering and Ewald Rathke at the Düsseldorf Kunsthalle for the Kunstverein für die Rheinlande und Westfalen in 1958; Höch's works are listed in the catalog as nos. 402–422. Höch also traveled to the exhibition and lectured there. The show was also seen in Amsterdam. The young Düsseldorf music student, Fluxus cofounder, and video art pioneer Nam June Paik visited the show, and he and Charlotte Moorman visited Höch in Heiligensee in 1966. On this visit and Höch's influence on Fluxus, see Ralf Burmeister, "Fluxus besucht Heiligensee," in *Hannah Höch: Eine Lebenscollage*, vol. 3, part 2, 2001, 123–153. On the 1956 exhibition's decisive influence on Wulf Vostell, see Eckhart Gillen, "Wulf Vostell: German View," in Gillen, 1997, 208–213.

57. Bergius, 2000, 152.

58. F.A. Dargel, "Ich möchte die Grenzen verwischen: Hannah Höch bei Meta Nierendorf," *Telegraf*, 9 June 1961.

59. "Hannah Höch: Bilder, Collagen, Aquarelle, 1918–1961" was held at the Galerie Meta Nierendorf in Berlin, 2 May–15 June 1961. The painting *Die Treppe* (The stairs), listed as being created in the years 1923–26, dates that Höch corrected to 1924, was priced at 9,000 marks; *Maschine*, from 1921, at 7,500 marks; and *Collage mit Pfeil* (Collage with arrow) at 1,500 marks (HHA, 61.171).

60. Roters, 1968.

61. Dech, 1981.

62. Dech, 1989, 32–59.

63. Hanne Bergius, "Hannah Höch: Künstlerin im Berliner Dadaismus," in *Hannah Höch*, 1976, 33–38. For contemporary responses to this presentation that recognize the importance of the feminist interpretation, see Sabine Zurmühl, "Hannah Höch," *Courage, Berliner Frauenzeitung* (June 1976); and Katrin Sello, "Tänzerischer Geist im Männer-Club: Hannah-Höch-Retrospektive in Berlin," *Die Zeit*, 2 March 1976. Then as now (see Foster et al., 2004), an issue for reviewers was whether Höch's montage cut as deeply politically as Heartfield's (see fig. 97). For those writing from a feminist position, such as Sello, they did, whereas for a male reviewer, they did not, though she was not considered as "aesthetically compromised" a Dadaist as Schwitters (see Peter Hans Göpbert, "Attack auf die Bierbauchkultur," *Stuttgarter Nachrichten*, 5 March 1976). A reviewer for the East German party organ complained that the exhibition did not provide enough political and historical contextualization, thus trivializing the works (Claudia Strom, "Verharmlost: Hannah Höch in der Neuen Nationalgalerie," *Die Wahrheit*, 3 March 1976).

64. Heinz Ohff, "Dada als Dornröschen: Eine Gesamtausstellung von Hannah Höch bei Nierendorf," *Der Tagesspiegel,* 4 May 1961. This was a thoroughly positive review of the exhibition. Höch seems to have been pleased by it; the HHA preserves the five copies she had kept. See also "Dadas alte Dame," *Der Abend,* 4 May 1961.

65. "Freilich, sie pflegte stets ein sehr weibliches, ein fast zärtliches Dada," *Das Kunstwerk* 17, no. 11–12 (May–June 1964): 41.

66. The 1964/65 Galerie Nierendorf exhibition in Berlin was titled "Hannah Höch zum 75. Geburtstag" (see Will Grohman, "Hannah Höch," *Frankfurter Allgemeine Zeitung,* 12 December 1964). Grohmann had written about Höch's sixtieth birthday exhibition at the Galerie Franz in Berlin in 1949, and he had called for her to continue with her photomontage practice, as he thought it could have a positive effect on commercial art as well as on fine art. Grohmann simply mentioned the Höch exhibition (and Dada) in "Das Karusell der Ausstellung," *Die Neue Zeitung,* 14 December 1949, but he returned to make the comment quoted in "Maler von gestern, heute und morgen, sieben Ausstellungen," *Die Neue Zeitung,* undated clipping BG HH 1949 (HHA, Galerie Franz exhibition file).

67. Bergius, 2000, esp. 95–107, 130–159. Biro, 2009, which appeared too late to be incorporated into my analysis, includes a chapter on *Cut with the Kitchen Knife Dada.* Biro's thesis—that Berlin Dada promulgated nontraditional, hybrid identities—is compatible with my own.

68. Clark Poling, "The City and Modernity: Art in Berlin in the First World War and Its Aftermath," in *Art in Berlin, 1815–1989* (Atlanta: High Museum of Art; Seattle and London: University of Washington Press, 1989), 86.

69. See Dech, 1989, 50.

70. Dech, 1989, 36; and Bergius, 2000, 102.

71. Bergius, 2000, 159–160. A *Waghalter* is, on the one hand, the owner of a *Wagon,* or carriage (the modern term is *Fahrzeughalter,* vehicle owner). It is also, archaically, a *Wagehalter* (today, *Waagehalter*), the holder of the scales, as in the archangel of the Last Judgment (*Deutsches Wörterbuch,* ed. Jacob Grimm and Wilhelm Grimm, 16 vols. [Leipzig: S. Hirzel, 1854–1960]; also http://germazone.unit-trier/WBB/de/woerterbuch/dwb). The face to the right of Einstein, above the words "dada siegt" (dada victorious), belongs to the first Weimar prime minister, Friedrich Ebert, who also emerges just above from Einstein's head in the pose of an orator. Ebert's face, altered to have a moustache and beard, is placed on top of a female figure with arms and hands extended to the sides in a balancing position, a bodily representation of a scale of judgment or justice. Bergius (2000, 132) also claims that the oval medallion around this composite figure makes it a "dadaistic pictorial parody of a mandorla"—another parody of Christian imagery.

72. Bergius, 2000, 159, 130.

73. Bergius, 2000, 160; Dech, 1981, 94; and Lavin, 1993, 22. Höch also made dolls, including those she displayed in the Dada Fair, and had herself photographed in doll-like outfits. Impekoven's left toe rests on the head of Graf von Mirbach-Harf, the kaiser's envoy to Lenin's Soviet Union, murdered in Moscow on 6 July 1918. This figure has been one of the most problematic to identify. In 1981 Dech identified it as Walter Rathenau, the Jewish German foreign minister. In 1989, following a drawing by Höch, Dech (1981, 32, 37) changed her identification to that of the liberal politician Ulrich Graf von Brockdorf-Rantzau. Bergius definitively identified him as Mirbach, providing the source photograph from the *Berliner Illustrirte Zeitung,* 14 July 1918 (Bergius, 2000, 147, fig. IIII.19).

74. Makela and Boswell, 1996, 62.

75. She is listed as Hanna Joseph and German champion in three-meter-board *Kunstspringen,* 1919 and 1920, at www.sport-komplett.de/sport-komplett/sportarten/w/wasserspringen/hst/31.html. Höch cut their pictures out of the *Berliner Illustrirte Zeitung,* 20 July 1919, from a general article on women as divers, in which they are pictured as winners of a diving competition at the Berlin Sports Stadium. The Josephs won the open and the senior divisions of the women's diving competition on Saturday, 29 June 1919 ("Sommersportfest im Deutschen Stadion," *Berliner Volks-Zeitung,* 30 June 1919; and "Stadion-Sportfest," *Berliner Morgenpost,* 30 June, 1919; see also Dech, 1993, 39).

76. "The hybrid European—a tolerably ugly plebeian, taken all in all—absolutely requires a costume: he needs history as a storeroom of costumes. To be sure, he notices that none of the costumes fit him properly—he changes and changes. . . . I mean as concerns morals, articles of belief, artistic tastes, and religions; we are prepared as no other age has ever been for a carnival in the grand style, for the most spiritual festival-laughter and arro-

gance, for the transcendental height of supreme folly and Aristophanic ridicule of the world. Perhaps we are still discovering the domain of our *invention* just here, the domain where even we can still be original, probably as parodists of the world's history and God's Merry-Andrews,—perhaps, though nothing else of the present have a future, our *laughter* itself may have a future." Friedrich Nietzsche, *Beyond Good and Evil,* trans. Helen Zimmern, in *The Philosophy of Nietzsche* (New York: The Modern Library, 1950), §223, 525–526.

77. *Hannah Höch: Eine Lebenscollage,* vol. 1, part 2, 1989, 635. Bergius adopted this line in the title for her still fundamental 1989 study of Berlin Dada and argued that Nietzschean concepts were the most significant philosophical source for the Berlin Dadaists' worldview.

78. See Dech, 1981, 53.

79. While there is no record of her having visited the Sistine Chapel, immediately after the Dada Fair Höch went to Rome, accomplishing most of the journey on foot, like a pilgrim.

80. Dech, 1981, 48.

81. See Dech, 2002, n. 30.

82. Lavin, 1993, 29.

83. Bergius, 2000, 102.

84. Lavin seems to be the only previous scholar to discuss Jews and Jewishness explicitly in any context in connection with Höch.

85. After reading a draft of this chapter, for which I thank her immensely, the Höch scholar Maria Makela writes of the triangle, "I cannot imagine that it was anything BUT intentional and carefully planned by Höch. It is simply too precise and exact to have been accidental, at least in my opinion." (E-mail to the author of 23 November 2007.)

86. Bergius, 2000, 102.

87. Dech has also noted that an "axis runs from the dominant head of Einstein (above left) to the grouping of Dadaists including Höch (lower right)." (Dech, 1981, 97.)

88. Benjamin Buchloh asserts that images and text "are disseminated across the field of the work according to a nonhierarchical, noncompositional, and aleatory principle of distribution" (see Foster et al., 2004, 170). Another interpreter contests what he describes as iconographic readings of the montage, which identify the individuals and objects in it, arguing that it "disperses and diminishes the iconic function of the exhibited images in favor of indexical ones," so that things and people become mere "disjunctive fragments" (Federle, 1992, 120–134).

89. After the anti-Semitic murder of the Jewish foreign minister Walther Rathenau in 1922 (which Einstein had warned him about) Einstein felt threatened enough in Berlin to move permanently to Caputh, until his 1933 emigration. (Dirks and Simon, 2005, 36–37.)

90. The Byk portrait shares certain traits, especially the averted eyes and an "overall effect of luminosity" (which also emphasizes thought), with the pictorialist photographic portraits that Catherine Soussloff has linked to the emergence of a new conception of subjectivity in Viennese theory and practice of portraiture in the early twentieth century. See Soussloff, 2006, 101.

91. Chapter 7, "The Jewish Nose," in Gilman, 1991.

92. On Reinhardt and cabaret (but not Dada), see Peter Jelavich, "Performing High and Low: Jews in Modern Theater, Cabaret, Revue, and Film," in Bilski, 1999, 213–223.

93. See Jelavich, 1993, 148.

94. Walter Mehring, "Simultaneous Berlin," in Jelavich, 1993, 149.

95. *Hannah Höch: Eine Lebenscollage,* vol. 1, part 2, 1989, 655, reproduction number 13.14, *Schall und Rauch* 5 (April 1920). The next issue of *Schall und Rauch,* 6, was a reprint of *Der Dada* 3. See also Makholm, in Makela and Boswell, 1996, 188. The dolls are reproduced in color in *Hannah Höch: Eine Lebenscollage,* vol. 1, part 2, 1989, 760, and are visible in photographs of the Dada Fair, reproduction numbers 13.34 and 13.35, 678–679.

96. This predates a similar figure created by John Heartfield for the cover of Kurt Tucholsky's *Deutschland Deutschland über alles* in 1928. On the image of the Kaiser in *Cut with the Kitchen Knife Dada,* see also Doherty, in Dickermann, 2005, 107–109.

97. Deak, 1968, 244.

98. Huelsenbeck (as noted earlier, not present in *Cut with the Kitchen Knife Dada*) had already attacked Hiller's elitist Expressionism in his April 1918 speech "Dadaistisches Manifest" (Huelsenbeck, 1920, 36–41) and again in *En Avant Dada* of 1920 (Middleton, 1961, 45–47). See also Bergius, 2000, 143.

99. Kurt Hiller, *S175: Die Schmach des Jahrhunderts!* (Hannover: Paul Steegemann Verlag, 1922); see also Taylor, 2004, 62.

100. Dech, 1989, 34, 60–68, 80, n. 32. Höch commented on the monocle as Dadaist provocation in Roditi, 1959, 65. On Dix's portrait as a "physiognomic" caricature of a lesbian Jew, see Makela, 2002, 50.

101. The man is Raimond Tost, a leader of sailors' revolts that broke out at the end World War I, in a picture from the *Berliner Illustrirte Zeitung* showing him delivering a eulogy for fallen sailors. See Dech, 1989, 34; Lavin, 1993, 22; and Bergius, 2000, 146.

102. Höch told Bergius in the 1970s that she made the change about 1921. Red smudges are still visible where she removed and replaced *Weltrevolution* (Bergius, 2003, 120).

103. On Grosz as caricaturist, see Neugebauer, 1993.

104. Friedlaender, 1918, and Friedlaender, 1926. See also Taylor, 2004, 204.

105. Anson Rabinbach, "Between Apocalypse and Enlightenment: Benjamin, Bloch and Modern German-Jewish Messianism," in Rabinbach, 1997, 27–65.

106. Hiller hated Bloch, whom he called "an unholy gaseous toad with the countenance of a superior European teacher—in short, not a Christ, but a vomitive." (Rabinbach, 1997, 31, 225–226, n. 159.)

107. See *Hannah Höch: Eine Lebenscollage,* vol. 1, part 1, 1989, 154–186.

108. Eberhard Roters, "Künstlerfreunde," in *Hannah Höch: Eine Lebenscollage,* vol. 2, part 1, 176–180. See, for instance, Friedlaender's *Verzückung in Dich* (Enraptured by you), addressed to Höch and dated 1924 by her, in Adriani, 1993, 51, with lines such as "Laß doch verschmelzen uns, einander zu genießen" (Let's melt together and take mutual pleasure).

109. Kubin's description is in Roters, *Hannah Höch: Eine Lebenscollage,* vol. 2, part 1, 1995, 178, as is Ludwig Meidner's less physiognomic one, 179.

110. Gilman, 1991, 88–189.

111. "His [Friedlaender's] lifelong obsession with Nietzsche, Schopenhauer, and Kant stemmed from his search for a new basis for ethics after his childhood rejection of conventional morality under the pressure of his own libidinous drives," writes Seth Taylor (2004, 136), in a passage that could probably be applied to any number of Dadaists—certainly to Hausmann and probably to Höch.

112. "20 Hannchen Höch: Schnitt mit dem Küchenmesser Dada durch die letzte weimarer Bierbauchkulturepoche Deutschlands." Her name is rendered in diminutive form, Hannchen, or "little Hanne," and also resembles *Hähnchen*—chicken.

113. See Schaschke, 2004, 332.

114. Middleton (1978, 25) connects Gregor to the primitivist interest in regressive infantilism that also relates to Dadaist primitivism.

115. The word *Ohrwurm* (earwig), in German, also refers to a catchy, popular tune that stays in your head. Further thanks to Maria Makela for pointing this out.

116. "German Workers Party (DAP): The Twenty-five Points," in Kaes, Jay, and Dimendberg, 1994, 125.

117. Grosz, 1983, 119.

118. *Hannah Höch: Eine Lebenscollage,* vol. 1, part 2, 631.

119. Dech, 1989, 35–36. Bergius corrects the identification of the other head on the dancer's body to the French boxer Georges Carpentier (Bergius, 2003, 173–175, 338–339, n. 142).

120. *Gedenkbuch Berlins der jüdischen Opfer des Nationalsozialismus,* 1995, 592. This memorial tome requires over four double-columned pages to list the known Berlin Jews with the surname Joseph murdered by the Nazis, also a common enough non-Jewish name. While the age and address are appropriate, I have been unable to ascertain whether this Charlotte Joseph is the same woman selected by Höch for inclusion in the montage. The Nazi victim listed in the *Gedenkbuch,* according to her birth certificate, was born in Leipzig on 15 February 1897, daughter of the Kaufmann Sally Joseph. Unfortunately, the Woman's Swim Club Charlottenburg-Nixe, which still exists, has no records pertaining to Charlotte and (the two-time national champion) Johanna Joseph. The same club produced two of German swimming's stars of the next generation, Ruth Hoffmann-Halbsguth and Gisela Arendt, whom the club acknowledges in its literature and on its Web site, the lead and anchor on the silver medal winning 400-meter-freestyle relay team at the 1936 Berlin Olympics. By this time the star insignia on the club's bathing suits had changed to a large N (J. Frank, "Nixen im Hundersten," *Berliner Morgenpost,* 5 August 1993, reproduced in the club newsletter in a report on its 100th anniversary celebration, *Nixen-Echo* 7 [September 1993]: 6–7).

121. Gay, 1978, 184.

122. The street was named for the area's Jewish real estate developer. See Ladd, 2004, 401–403.

123. Niven, 2002, 212. See also Wiedmer, 1999, 103–115.

124. See Christoph Heinrich, "Places of Remembrance," in Stih and Schnock, 2005, 4–9. The author places the piece in the tradition of Joseph Beuys's "social sculpture." Pickford interprets it as a "third way" to conceive and create memorial sculpture, neither representational nor abstract, "withholding the closure afforded by figurative conciliation or transcendent sublimity," in favor of "a making legible of the implicit political sovereignty that structures the everyday life, the 'second nature' of mass society" (167). *Places of Remembrance* is also the focal point of Koss, 2004.

125. The concept of a "negative past avant-garde" derives from Jochen Gerz, in an interview with Jacqueline Lichtenstein and Gérard Wajchman, in Gerz, 1993, 8.

126. Hutton, 1993, 10. For Yates, who influenced Nora, the art of memory begins with a traumatic disaster, the collapse of a banquet hall's roof crushing the host, Scopas, and his guests beyond recognition. The briefly absent lyric poet, Simonides, however, identifies the remains by recalling each guest's location. (Yates, 1966, 1–3.)

Chapter 4: *Absender: ich*

1. Jordana Mendelson, "Introduction: Postcards from Albums to the Academy?" in Mendelson, 2001, 374. For further discussion of artistic postcards, see Hedinger, 1992; and David Prochaska and Jordana Mendelson, eds., *Postcards: Ephemeral Histories of Modernity* (University Park, PA: Penn State University Press, 2010).

2. Richter, 1997, 117; Ades, 1976, 19; and Foster et al., 2004, 170. See Dech, 1989, for a reproduction of one of these cards. As mentioned in the preceding chapter, George Grosz's archive contains a large number of so-called kitsch postcards.

3. See Craig Eliason, "Manifestos by Mail: Postcards in the Theo van Doesburg Correspondence," in Mendelson, 2001, 449–458, fig. 2.

4. Richter, 1997, 117.

5. Leslie, 2005, 140.

6. Willi Baumeister, postcard, 10 November 1918 (WBA).

7. Willi Baumeister, postcard, 3 December 1918 (WBA).

8. On the massive production of art postcards in Nazi Germany, see Frank Wagner and Gudrun Linke, "Mächtige Körper: Staatsskulptur und Herrschaftsarchitektur," in *Inszenierung der Macht*, 1987, 72. Baumeister noted in his diary in March 1944: "Called to the police station in Urach. The state secret police have taken exception to the strange postcards that I regularly receive from Franz Krause. (I've asked Krause before not to send any more of these, since they're conspicuous these days, and won't be understood by outsiders. The cards are pasted fragments in the manner of photomontages.) I told the authorities that these are harmless cards done in jest, having to do with work at the Herberts Painting Institute." (Baumeister's unpublished diary, 23 March 1944, paginated folio 471, WBA.)

9. Nazi Sicherheitsdienst (security service) report of 28 February 1940, "Verkitschung von Feldpostkarten" (Kitschification of field postcards), in *Meldungen aus dem Reich: Auswahl aus den geheimen Lageberichten des Sicherheitsdienstes der SS 1939–1944*, ed. Heinz Boberach (Neuwied and Berlin: Luchterhand, 1965), 52–53.

10. Prosser, 1998. Prosser does not discuss the cover image in the book.

11. Makholm, in Makela and Boswell, 1996, 197–198.

12. Jay Prosser, e-mail to author, 2 October 2001.

13. Bloom, 1973, 30.

14. For a summary of the uses of these images from 1989 to 2001 (but not the Prosser cover), see Chametzky, "The Post History Willi Baumeister's Anti-Nazi Postcards," in Mendelson, 2001, 459–480.

15. Baumeister was well aware of and engaged with Dadaist and also Surrealist ideas and strategies. He and Schlemmer exchanged collage letters during and after the war, and about 1919 collaboratively cut into and pasted onto a copy of the 1916 *Cabaret Voltaire* catalogue, the central document in the Zurich Dada movement. In the 1930s he had various Surrealist connections: he subscribed to Georges Bataille's dissident Surrealist magazine *Documents*, published in Paris from 1929 to 1930. He maintained his Parisian connections even during the Third Reich: in January 1939 the Parisian Surrealist Jeanne Bucher Gallery held a Baumeister exhibition in celebration of his fiftieth birthday. Baumeister traveled to Paris for it and noted in his diary visiting Miró in his studio, whose work made a somewhat gruesome but very strong impression

on him (Baumeister diary entry, 27 January 1938, 155, WBA).

16. Lutz Koepnick has criticized the exhibition in which Prosser saw these works, claiming that it reduced the complex imbrications of modernism and fascism to an "either/or" proposition, and that in doing so it "granted Hitler and Goebbels a posthumous victory as it reconstructed the past according to the Nazis's self-perceptions" ("Art and Power: Europe under the Dictators," in Koepnick, 1999, n. 1).

17. Schor, 1992, 211.

18. My first discussion of them was in Chametzky, 1989, which formed the basis for a longer treatment in chapter 8 of Chametzky, 1991. Examples of their scholarly circulation since then include: Hoffmann-Curtius, 1990, 85–88; Barron et al., 1991, 200–201; Hedinger, 1992, 202–203, plates 67–69; David Elliott, "A Life and Death Struggle: Painting and Sculpture," in Ades et al., 1995, 274; Fenton, 1996, 51; Clark, 1997, 11; Gamboni, 1997, 261–262, and Gamboni, 2002, 88–135; Julius, 2002, 153–154; and Taylor, 2004, who reproduces several, cites directly the paragraph on page 257 of my 1989 essay where I noted their exclusion from Baumeister's oeuvre, and declares them "more interesting than that," an estimation with which I can only agree and which my work emphatically supports. Leslie (2002 and 2005) has also discussed these works extensively.

19. In addition to Barthes's notion of the multiplicity of meanings made available in these and other citational texts, my 1989 article "Marginal Comments, Oppositional Work: Willi Baumeister's Confrontation with Nazi Art" employed Benjamin's essay "The Author as Producer" (in Benjamin, 1978, 220–238) to assert that the political position of these works is at core a function of their place within, or, as in this case, *outside* of, the dominant political, economic, and cultural system of their time.

20. On art in active resistance, see *Widerstand statt Anpassung*, 1980. For differentiation between resistance *(Widerstand)* and opposition, see Walther Hofer, "Diskussion zur Geschichte des Widerstands," in Schädeke and Steinbach, 1985, 1120.

21. Baumeister's postcard correspondence, and its unpoliced imagery, though, did entail certain risks (see note 8, above).

22. See Chametzky, 1989, 263–265, and Chametzky, 2001, 466–474; Hedinger, 1992, 202–203, nos. 283–286; and Gamboni, 2002, 115–116.

23. Thus the Swabian expression *herumstolzen wie ein Gockel* (prance about like a rooster). This interpretation, which I offered in 1989, has been accepted in later German publications.

24. The postcard's message is dated 26 August 1941. The message to Keller, in which Baumeister thanks him for sending a ration of real coffee, is reprinted in Hedinger, 1992, 202, no. 283. Baumeister let his alterations of the cards provide his only commentary on them.

25. Letter from Wilhelm Arntz to Willi Baumeister (WBA). Arntz refers to Hitler's attacks on modernist primitivism, especially those relating to interest in prehistoric art, such as Baumeister's.

26. The review of *Die Künstlerpostkarte* (Hedinger, 1992) reproduced *Jokkmokmädchen* over the headline "*Ein bügelechter Porno.*" The Baumeister alteration includes an iron and text about the ironing of a warm, moist wall during fresco painting. These procedures become the sexualized "ironing" of the body of Ziegler's nude. *Bügelecht* is a rather archaic term combining iron *(Bügel)* and real *(echt)* that can be applied to an article of clothing to mean "genuine" and ironable (as opposed to a cheap synthetic, wash and wear item) or colloquially to any "quality" item. Thus the headline refers to the image as a "real" or "high class" (though somewhat bourgeois) "Porno," or prostitute. (Christian Huther, "Ein bügelechter Porno: Frankfurter Schau über Künstlerpostkarte," *Südkurier* [Überlingen and Donaueschingen], 2 July 1992.) Thanks to Sabine Eckmann for help with the nuances of this phrase.

27. Derrida, 1987, 18, 41, 110.

28. www.pyb.com.au/ptcds/pcres/range.htm (last viewed 2 July 2003).

29. Chametzky, 1989, 261–263; and Chametzky, 2001, 470–471.

30. Paul Schultze-Naumburg, *Nordische Schönheit: Ihr Wunschbild im Leben und in der Kunst* (Munich and Berlin: J. F. Lehmanns, 1937), 97. See also Chametzky, 2001, 472–473.

31. Benjamin, "The Work of Art in the Age of Mechanical Reproduction," in Benjamin, 1969, 224.

32. Ibid., 238.

33. See *Willi Baumeister et la France,* 1999. Baumeister knew and was friendly with Léger and Le Corbusier from the early 1920s. In 1922 he had a two-person show with Léger at *Der Sturm* gallery in Berlin and was the subject of an article (George, 1922) in the Parisian Purist's journal. He traveled

to Paris in 1924 to meet them. He became friendly with Arp, who wrote a poem-portrait of him ("Baumeister") in the early 1930s, and he met Miró in 1939, when he was in Paris for his clandestine fiftieth birthday exhibition at the Galerie Jeanne Bucher. On all these connections and their significance, see Chametzky, 1991. For Arp's poem, the title of which became "Einem griechischen Baumeister" (To a Greek Baumeister) in later Arp anthologies, see *Willi Baumeister,* 1931, 19.

34. On Baumeister as "classic modernist," see Karin v. Maur, "Stuttgarts Beitrag zur klassischen Moderne," in Heissenbüttel, 1979, 14–71; and Bruns, 1991.

35. John Anthony Thwaites, "Report from Germany," *Arts* 30, no. 10 (July 1956): 21.

36. Grohmann, 1952, 27. I have slightly modified the English translation by Eline McKnight.

37. Grohmann, 1965, 11.

38. Haftmann, 1960, 199.

39. Baumeister was first compared with Picasso by the Picasso scholar Wilhelm Boeck (1947, 10–11). The 25 February 1948 issue of the Parisian newspaper *Opèra* called Baumeister "le Picasso allemand" in a report on an article that had appeared in the journal *Verger* by Luc Bérimont. This pleased and concerned Baumeister, who wrote to Will Grohmann: "*Opèra* writes 'le Picasso allemand.' My star is ascending to stratospheric heights and I feel an awful responsibility." (Willi Baumeister, letter to Will Grohmann, 2 April 1948, WBA.)

40. Frank Thiess, "Innere Emigration," in Heinz L. Arnold, ed., *Deutsche Literatur im Exil 1933–1945,* vol. 1, *Dokumente* (Frankfurt am Main: Athenäum Fischer, 1974), 248. This volume also includes contributions by Molo and Thomas Mann, who rejected the concept of inner emigration.

41. See Michel Seuphor's quote in the introduction (note 4), from a monograph that included short texts by Baumeister (translated from his 1929 Flechtheim Gallery catalog), Flouquet (art critic for *Le Monde*), Waldemar George, and Will Grohmann, and very short homages by Konrad Düssel, Joseph Gantner, Ernst Schoen, Christian Zervos, Seuphor, Léger, and Le Corbusier.

42. Peter-Klaus Schuster, "The 'Inner Emigration': Art for No One," in Joachimides et al., 1985, 462.

43. Baumeister, 1947; Baumeister, 1960; and Baumeister, 1988. All references here are from the 1988 edition edited by René Hirner, which includes indications of the changes from the original edition. For the Darmstadt confrontation, see Chametzky, 2001, 462–464.

44. Baumeister, 1988, 64.

45. Statement in the *New York Times,* 13 June 1943; quoted from Harrison and Wood, 1993, 562. In the best analysis of Baumeister's, Ernst Wilhelm Nay's, and other German modern artists' turn to primitivism and myth in the 1940s, which some historians, such as Jutta Held, have interpreted as tacitly allied with fascist thought, and others, such as Gudrun Inboden, have portrayed as inherently anti-Nazi, Klaus Herding (1988) sees neither specific resistance nor collaboration with Nazism. His essay links Baumeister's turn to myth with the work of many Abstract Expressionist, Surrealist, Realist, and abstract artists in Europe and America from 1942 into the postwar period, and with a widespread humanist idea advocating a "return to origins" as the basis for reconstruction of Western civilization. Cf. Held, 1981; and Gudrun Inboden, "Die Gemälde—entmythologisierend," in *Willi Baumeister, 1945–1955,* 1979, 21–24.

46. Baumeister, 1988, 152.

47. "Une troisième voie suivie par l'Américain Peter Chametzky consiste à replacer l'oeuvre et la carriére dans leur contexte historique, qu'il ait été artistique, social, institutionnel ou politique.... Cette these essentialle nous a souvent guidée, pour cette etude comme pour l'exposition." ([The American Peter Chametzky has offered a third way, consisting of placing the oeuvre and career in its historical context, whether artistic, social, institutional, or political.... This thesis has been an essential guide for us in this study and this exhibition.] Sylvie Ramond, "'Aucune trace de l'esprit germanique': Baumeister entre la France et l'Allemagne," in *Willi Baumeister et la France,* 163–164, n. 6.)

48. On the Stuttgart Üecht group, see Susanne Jakob, " 'Novembergeist' und Stuttgarter Avantgarde: Die 'Üecht-Gruppe' 1918–1924," in *Baumeister, Schlemmer und die Üechtgruppe,* 1989, 9–48; von Maur, "Stuttgarts Beitrag zur klassischen Moderne," in Heissenbüttel, 1979, 14–71; and Chametzky, 1991, 140–180. On the Klee controversy, see also Werckmeister, 1989, 215–216.

49. Jakob, *Baumeister, Schlemmer und die Üechtgruppe,* 1989, 28.

50. "Kunst und Bolschewismus," *Süddeutsche Zeitung,* 12 November 1919. Karin von Maur has identified the author as a poet named Paul Enderling.

51. Chametzky, 2002.

52. For an excellent discussion of Baumeister's sport images, comparing them to those by Moholy-Nagy and Anton Räderscheidt, see Skrypzak, 2004.

53. Cf. Mackenzie, 1999; Mackenzie, "The Athlete as Machine: A Figure of Modernity in Weimar Germany," in *Leibhaftige Moderne: Körper in Kunst und Massenmedien 1918–1933*, ed. Kai Sicks and Michael Cowan (Bielefeld: Transcript Verlag, 2005), 48–62; Mackenzie, "Maschinenmenschen, Athleten, und die Krise des Körpers in der Weimarer Republik," in *Die "Krise" der Weimarer Republik: Zur Kritik eines Deutungsmusters*, ed. Moritz Föllmer and Rudiger Graf (Frankfurt: Campus Verlag, 2005), 319–346; and Chametzky, 2002, 181–183.

54. The name changed to *die neue stadt* (the new city) in April 1932. For an extremely informative essay on this magazine, its context, and Baumeister's contribution to it (including annotated reproductions of all of Baumeister's cover designs), see Wolfgang Kermer, "Willi Baumeister und 'Das Neue Frankfurt': Ein Beitrag zu Baumeisters Frankfurter Jahren (1928–1933)," in Kermer, 1989, 212–252, 260–269, 286–288.

55. Viola Hildebrand-Schat, "Willi Baumeister—Die Frankfurter Jahre 1928–1933," in *Willi Baumeister 1889–1955: Die Frankfurter Jahre 1928–1933*, 2005, 21.

56. See Kermer, 1989, 241, n. 31–32.

57. See especially Willi Baumeister, "Das Mauerbild und einiges über die Fläche in der Malerei," *Die Baugilde* 17 (September 1925): 1186–1187. In the 1920s Baumeister also published texts in such design journals as *Pasmo, ABC, Die Form, Das Werk, Die Bauzeitung, Documents Internationaux de L'Esprit Nouveau,* and *bauhaus.*

58. René Hirner, "Anmerkungen zu Willi Baumeisters Hinwendung zum Archaischen," in *Willi Baumeister: Zeichnungen, Gouachen, Collage,* 1989, 52. The painting *Atelier III* is lost.

59. Morris, 1982, 159–160.

60. Quoted in Lane, 1968, 149.

61. Lane, 1968, 148–157; and Willett, 1979, 185.

62. "'Kunst' und Künstler in Frankfurt: Neuerwerbung des Städel," *Frankfurter Nachrichten,* 9 January 1930.

63. "Städel- oder Städtische Galerie? Oder: Der Kampf um ein schlechtes Bild mit lehrreichen Episoden," *Frankfurter Nachrichten,* 26 January 1930.

64. Ernst Benkard, "Willi Baumeister, der schwäbische Avantgardist," *Frankfurter Zeitung,* 13 February 1931.

65. Quoted from Adriani, 1971, 73.

66. Westheim, "Briefkasten," *Das Kunstblatt* 15, no. 4 (1931).

67. Westheim, "Rassenbiologische Ästhetik," in Westheim, 1985, 15.

68. Gilman, 1985, 150–162, 217–238; quotation from 236.

69. See Peter Chametzky, "Paul Westheim in Mexico: A Cosmopolitan *Man Contemplating the Heavens," Oxford Art Journal* 24, no. 1 (May 2001): 23–44.

70. Dr. W. R. [Werner Rittich?], "Vom deutschen Kunstreich jüdischer Nation," *Völkischer Beobachter* (north German edition), 25 February 1933. Westheim's name was followed by an exclamation point in the text, so that its Jewishness would not be lost on even the most obtuse of readers.

71. Baumeister diary, 30 May 1932, 42 (WBA). Chancellor Heinrich Brüning had resigned on 29 May, unable to maintain the confidence of either the military or of President von Hindenburg, which was essential to preserving order in the face of the terror tactics increasingly employed by Hitler's storm troopers.

72. Baumeister diary, 5 September 1932, 43 (WBA).

73. Baumeister diary, 15 January 1933, 49 (WBA).

74. Baumeister diary, 22 February 1933, 52 (WBA).

75. Letter from the editor of the *Frankfurter Volksblatt* to Willi Baumeister, 28 February 1933, reproduced in Kermer, 1989, 257, fig. 13 (original in WBA).

76. Baumeister diary, 27 March 1933, 53 (WBA).

77. Application of the provisional director of the Municipal School of Applied Art, Frankfurt am Main, 29 March 1933, reproduced in Kermer, 1989, 257, fig. 14.

78. Letter from the editors of the *Frankfurter Volksblatt* to Willi Baumeister, 29 March 1933 (WBA).

79. Baumeister diary, 31 March 1933, 54 (WBA).

80. Reproduced in Kermer, 1989, 259, fig. 16.

81. Baumeister diary, 7 April 1933, 54 (WBA). For detailed treatment of Baumeister's activities from 1933 to 1945, see Chametzky, 1991, chapters 6–7. Margrit refers to Baumeister's wife, Margarete (Oehm) Baumeister. They married in 1926. Their first daughter, Krista, was born in December 1928. On 26 April 1933 Margrit gave birth to their second daughter, Felicitas.

82. The exhibition "Art and Power: Europe under

the Dictators 1930–45" was at the Hayward Gallery, London, 26 October 1995–21 January 1996, and continued to Barcelona and Berlin (see Ades et al., 1995). Baumeister executed his private doodle on the reproduction on page 12 of "Die Grosse Deutsche Kunstausstellung 1941, II," *Kunst dem Volk* (Vienna) 12, no. 9 (September 1941): 1–40 (original in WBA). The other exhibitions that Fenton reviewed (Fenton, 1996) were "Berlin-Moscow 1900–1950," at the Martin-Gropius-Bau, Berlin, 3 September 1995–7 January 1996, continuing to the Pushkin Gallery, Moscow; and "Von Allen Seiten Schön," at the Altes Museum, Berlin, 31 October 1995–28 January 1996.

83. "The new north-south axis . . . was to be built up into the commercial and ideological center of the new city. . . . Monumental reliefs from the workshop of Arno Breker were to line the streets" (Brenner, 1963, 126; see also Jaskot, 1996; and Scobie, 1990, 51–52).

84. Petropoulos, 2000, 231–232. In his memoirs, Breker (1972, 295) identifies the castle's architect as Gontard and claims that he negotiated to buy it for a good price.

85. George Mosse, "Beauty without Sensuality," in Barron et al., 1991, 28. On the shifting fate of nudism in the Third Reich, its initial ban, and then resurrection under the sign of eugenics with sources in both right- and left-wing thought, see Wilfried van der Will, "The Body and the Body Politic as Symptom and Metaphor in the Transition of German Culture to National Socialism," in Taylor and van der Will, 1999, 14–52.

86. Writing about Breker's *The Avenger* (see figs. 51 and 79) a contemporary "art report" (art criticism had been banned as Jewish and, on the grounds that German art had been "cleansed," no longer necessary) stated: "A five-meter-high (half-size) version of *The Avenger* is exhibited as the second in the series of monumental reliefs, from which last year *The Comrades* was shown, for a new construction on Berlin's north-south axis. . . . As in *The Comrades,* the assured choice of a single theme to embody sweeping events is astounding. As in almost all the works of Arno Breker that have been shown in the exhibitions in the House of German Art, topical, indeed, political perspectives open up, even though the subject is depicted in a timeless, universal manner. Arno Breker has made it his task to embody symbolically in this series of reliefs the virtues and strengths of German values, so that this series of reliefs (work on which is much further advanced than the public realizes) will develop an epic both timeless and timely on the Germanic-German character." (Werner Rittich, "Neue Deutsche Plastik: Zu den Werken der Bildhauerkunst in der 'Grossen Deutschen Kunstausstellung 1941,'" *Die Kunst im Deutschen Reich* 5, nos. 8–9 [August–September 1941]: 251, 259.)

87. Wolfgang Fritz Haug, "Ästhetik der Normalität/Vor-stellung und Vorbild: Die Faschisierung des männlichen Akts bei Arno Breker," *Inszenierung der Macht,* 1987, 97.

88. Theweleit, 1980, 334.

89. A trilingual publication on Breker—by one of his apologists, but also quite comprehensive in terms of chronology and bibliography and not without merit as a source—titles the work under consideration here *Der Wächter—Le Combat contre les serpents—The Warder,* and another piece from 1940 as *The Avenger.* However, as this is how the piece was titled in the Rittich article from which Baumeister created "Altered Avenger," and how that work has now passed into the literature, I will continue referring to it as *The Avenger* (Egret, 1996, nos. 185 and 186). It was also reproduced as *Der Rächer* (The avenger) in Ulrich Christoffel, "Aus der Großen Deutschen Kunstausstellung München 1941: Gebärde und Gestalt in der Plastik," *Die Kunst für Alle* 57, no. 1 (October 1941): 13, and referred to and described as such in Ulrich Christoffel, "Die 'Grosse Deutsche Kunstausstellung 1941,'" *Die Kunst für Alle* 56 (1940–41): 270.

90. Mosse, 1985, 158–159. Homosexuals were among the persecuted groups subject to imprisonment and murder in Nazi Germany. But on the toleration of prominent and "useful" homosexuals, such as the director and actor Gustav Gründgens, see Steinweis, 1993, 130.

91. Sigmund Freud, "Medusa's Head (1922)," in *Collected Papers,* vol. 5, ed. James Strachey (London: Hogarth, 1950), 105.

92. For differentiation between the phallus as a symbol of power and exposure of the penis as a sign of vulnerability, see Jane Gallop, *The Daughter's Seduction: Feminism and Psychoanalysis* (Ithaca, NY: Cornell University Press, 1982), 37–38.

93. Clark, 1997, 11. The comparison with Tiananmen Square, however, conflates private defiance with public resistance, as Anthony Julius (2002, 171–174) points out. See also Leslie, 2002, 220–221; and Stercken (2000), who links the awkward

positioning of Breker's bodies to display panels of ideal body forms. She also compares Baumeister's "little man" to an ID photograph, which is consistent with the new interpretation I offer below (see fig. 54). For this particular work, there is no evidence that anyone beyond the artist ever saw it. The artist's daughter, Krista Baumeister, showed it to me in 1988, when it was kept in a locked safe in the Willi Baumeister Archiv; I published the first description and analysis of it in 1989.

94. Walter Benjamin, "The Author as Producer (1934)," in Benjamin, 1978, 229. See also Chametzky, 1989, 251, 267–68.

95. Hoffmann claimed to have "made millions" per month publishing *Kunst dem Volk* (Petropoulos, 2009, 123). On Hoffmann and Hitler, see the project by the German artist and art historian Rudolf Herz, *Hoffmann and Hitler: Fotografie als Medium des Führer Mythos* (Munich: Klinkhardt and Biermann, 1994).

96. My use of "transgression" throughout this chapter draws on Julius's unpacking of the origins and usages of the word and specifying of the application of the concept as an artistic strategy.

97. Julius, 2002, 172–173.

98. Author's interview with Heinz Rasch in Wuppertal, 9 January 1989. Baumeister wrote in *The Unknown in Art,* "Every work of art is a self-representation of the artist, regardless of what is actually represented" (1988, 50; this English translation is from the forthcoming edition edited and translated by Joann M. Skrypzak).

99. See *Schlemmer, Baumeister, Krause, Wuppertal 1937–1944,* 1979; and Herberts, 1989. Leslie (2005, 193–208) contrasts Baumeister and company's subversive Wuppertal activities with the collaboration of most of the German chemical industry.

100. In an undated postcard to Rasch, Baumeister stressed the importance of keeping the name of "our mutual friend" Lily H. out of their publications for Herberts. His reason was that this would jeopardize the publication, and "What good would it do L. having her name read?" (undated postcard, WBA). Lily Hildebrandt was a painter who, like Baumeister and Schlemmer, studied with Adolf Hölzel at the Stuttgart Academy. Her and her husband's papers are now at the Getty Research Institute in Los Angeles. See also *Hans Hildebrandt und sein Kreis* (Bremen: Graphisches Kabinett Kunsthandel Wolfgang Werner, 1978); and Wolfgang Venzmer, *Hölzel und sein Kreis: Der Beitrag Stuttgart zur Malerei des 20. Jahrhunderts* (Stuttgart: Württembergischer Kunstverein, 1961).

101. When Baumeister was pictured on the cover of *Der Spiegel* magazine (fig. 45) for the article "willy baumeister gross geschrieben: Buchstaben fielen vom Himmel" [willy baumeister writ large: letters fall from the sky], this commitment was emphasized in the cover caption: "Ein grosser Bühnenbildner willy baumeister schreibt sich ganz klein [willy baumeister, a great set designer, writes himself very small, or lowercase]," *Der Spiegel,* 1 November 1947.

102. Rasch, Heinz, and Bodo Rasch, eds., *Gefesselter Blick: 25 kurze Monografien und Beiträge über neue Werbegestaltung* (Stuttgart: Verlag Dr. Zaugg and Co., 1930; repr. Baden, Switzerland: Lars Müller Verlag, 2001.)

103. See Meskimmon, 1999, 199–222. Meskimmon focuses on Jeanne Mammen's illustration *The Garçonne,* for Magnus Hirschfeld's 1931 *Moral History of the Post-War Period,* an image that "gave a visual form to what Hirschfeld famously termed the 'Third Sex': the homosexual as an 'in-between' androgenous type" (199).

104. Heinz Rasch, "Aus den zwanziger Jahren," *Werk und Zeit* 9, no. 11 (November 1960): 2.

105. Skrypzak, 2004, 206.

106. Author's interview with Heinz Rasch, Wuppertal, 9 January 1989 (Willi Baumeister, *Absender: ich,* [ca. 1969]).

107. The 1892 book *Entartung* (Degeneration) by the Jewish Austro-Hungarian physician Max Nordau popularized in the German-speaking world the term and concept of biological degeneration as a cause of cultural decay manifested in criminality, mental illness, and decadent art. Nordau especially drew on the French psychiatrist B. A. Morel, "who had popularized the catchword 'degeneration' (1857) in order to describe human deviations" (George L. Mosse, "Max Nordau and His Degeneration," introduction to Nordau, 1993).

108. According to Keith Holz, "In this self-portrait retreat into subjective reflection yields to assertiveness. . . . His attentive visage is modeled by multicolored, abbreviated, and discontinuous brushstrokes—this at a moment when Hitler was railing against excesses in facture and color and when exiled leftist artists and intellectuals in Prague were asking whether they must defend ex-

pressionism merely because Hitler had defamed it." (Keith Holz, "Oskar Kokoschka in London, 1938–45," in Barron et al., 1997, 86.)

109. Lichtenstein, 2001, 138.

110. Bergius, 1989, 282. Marcel Duchamp's female alter ego Rrose Selavy (which could be read as "Eros c'est Levy," as well as "Eros c'est la vie"), which he first adopted in 1920, in a photograph by Man Ray, and after considering creating a more explicitly Jewish alter ego, provides another Dada precedent that relates male-female gender transformation and the transformation from gentile to Jew. Like Blumenfeld's and Baumeister's montages, Rrose Selavy both highlights and calls into question Jewish sexuality. See Dickerman, 2005, 15, n. 46; and Naumann, 1999, 85.

111. Gilman, 1993, 49.

112. See the chapter "Jewishness as Gender: Changing Freud's Subject," in Pellegrini, 1997, 17–37.

113. See Pellegrini, 1997. See also Sander Gilman, "Salome, Syphilis, Sarah Bernhardt and the Modern Jewess," and Carol Ockman, "When is a Jewish Star Just a Star: Interpreting Images of Sarah Bernhardt," in Nochlin and Garb, 1995, 97–120, 121–139. Gilman's essay is also in Gilman, 1998.

114. On the "Jewish nose," and its "connection" to the circumcised penis, see Sander Gilman, "The Jewish Nose: Are Jews White?" in Gilman, 1991, 169–193.

115. By the nineteenth century, the Yiddish word *judischen* (to make into a Jew), was employed for circumcision (Gilman, 1993, 49).

116. Heinz Rasch, "Rembrandts Anatomie, oder Störungen im leiblichen Bereich: Skizzen von Willi Baumeister, 1938–1954," in Baumeister, 1969, 15–18. Rasch admits to having had the procedure himself, "as a youngster."

117. And not only in Nazi Germany. See T. S. Eliot's poem "Burbank with a Baedaeker: Bleistein with a Cigar," first published in T. S. Eliot, *Poems* (New York: Knopf, 1920).

118. "Smoking Jews on the Frontier," in Gilman, 2003, 99. It might be worth noting that in order to be smoked, traditional cigars must be rather ritually cut. See also Sander L. Gilman and Zhou Xun, eds., *Smoke: A Global History of Smoking* (London: Reaktion Books, 2004), 278–285.

119. See chapter 6, "The Campaign Against Tobacco," in Proctor, 1999.

120. "Hitlers Rede zur Eröffnung der 'Großen Deutschen Kunstausstellung' 1937," in Schuster, 1987, 242, 243.

121. Gamboni, 2002, 134.

122. Quoted from Claudia Koonz, "The Competition for a Women's *Lebensraum*, 1928–1934," in Bridenthal et al., 199. On the separation of male and female realms in Nazi Germany, see the introduction to that anthology, as well as Mosse, 1985, 153–180.

123. Sigmund Freud, "Femininity," in *New Introductory Lectures on Psychoanalysis*, ed. James Strachey (New York: Norton, 1964), 114.

124. See Dech, 2002, 61–67.

125. Pellegrini, 1997, 23.

126. Lehmann-Haupt, 1973, 85–87.

127. Gilman, 1995, 111.

128. Huyssen, "Escape from Amnesia: The Museum as Mass Medium," in Huyssen, 1995, 13–35.

129. Lewis, 2003, 14–15.

130. Inka Graeve, "Internationale Ausstellung des deutschen Werkbunds Film und Foto, Stuttgart 1929," in *Stationen der Moderne*, 1988, 237.

131. Peter Guenther, "Three Days in Munich, July 1937," in Barron, 1991, 33–43. See also Etlin, "Introduction: The Perverse Logic of Nazi Thought," in Etlin, 2002, 18–19.

132. Rauterberg, available at www.zeit.de/2004/08/MOMA.

133. Andreas Huyssen, "Monument and Memory in a Postmodern Age," in Young, 1994, 12.

Chapter 5: Sculpture and Crime

1. Arie Hartog, "A Clean Tradition? Reflections on German Figurative Sculpture," in Curtis, 2002, 38.

2. Luckow (1998) provides an extremely detailed and informative study of Beuys's often unacknowledged impact on American sculpture.

3. Unfortunately, after initial agreement, Breker's dealers decided not to supply me with a photograph or permission to reproduce this work. For a reproduction, see Egret, 1996, fig. 28.

4. Krauss, 1977, 14–31; and Krauss, 1985, 151–157.

5. Krauss, 1977, 29–30. Krauss's interpretation derives from the existential phenomenology of Merleau-Ponty.

6. Werner Rittich, untitled essay in *Arno Breker*, 1944, 13. See also Probst, 1978, 13; and Egret, 1996, 55.

7. Luise Straus-Ernst, "Der Bildhauer Arno Breker," *Die Kunst für Alle* 44 (1928–29): 370–375.

8. "Alle seine Arbeiten sprechen von dem leidenschaftlichen, beinahe verbissenen Ringen um die Gestaltung und bieten sich durch diese starke, stets fühlbare Spannung in einer unerhörten Vielfältigkeit dar." (Straus-Ernst, 1928–29, 370.)

9. Werner Hager, "Der Bildhauer Arno Breker," *Die Kunst für Alle* 54, no. 1 (1938): 18–25.

10. Straus-Ernst's fate may explain why her review is passed over in writings about Breker by his contemporary supporters, who like to stress his cordial relations with Max Liebermann and that Alfred Flechtheim was his first dealer. The association of Straus-Ernst with Auschwitz—and that of Breker with Nazi crimes—seems to be one that Breker scholars want to avoid. Rolf Bothe strongly refutes Breker's self-presentation as a "friend of the Jews," especially Lieberman and his family, in an article on the circumstances under which Breker created Liebermann's death mask in 1935, "Die Totenmaske," in *Was vom Leben übrig bleibt, sind Bilder und Geschichten: Max Liebermann zum 150. Geburtstag*, ed. Herman Simon (Berlin: Stiftung "Neue Synagoge," Centrum Judaicum, 1997), 118–121.

11. See Bettina Güldner and Wolfgang Schuster, "Das Reichssportfeld," in *Skulptur und Macht*, 1983, 37–60. Breker won the silver medal in the artistic competition—the highest won by a German; the gold went to an Italian (Egret, 1996, 57). Breker's works at the Olympic Stadium site can be seen in 2004 photographs by Marc Wellmann at the extraordinary Web site and research project www.bildhauerei-in-berlin.de, which attempts to document all of Berlin's public sculpture.

12. For Hitler's speeches at the Nuremberg "Kulturtagung des Reichsparteitages" (cultural conference of the Reich's party convention), see Hinz, 1974, 139–152.

13. Petropoulos, 2000, 222–229.

14. Petropoulos, 2000, 218–253. See also his essay "From Seduction to Denial: Arno Breker's Engagement with National Socialism," in Etlin, 2002, 205–229.

15. On Breker's relationship to Parisian "middle-of-the-road and figurative" French sculptors Gustave Maillol and Charles Despiau, see Cone, 1992, 158–169.

16. "Verleger des Widerstands: Von Arno Breker gerettet, Neue Dokumente zu Peter Suhrkamp," *Frankfurther Allgemeine Zeitung*, 22 February 2005. See also Petropoulos, 2000, 238. Breker's supporters and contemporary dealers, Joe and Marco Bodenstine, have put Suhrkamp's letter of 21 August 1946 online, attesting to Breker's support in keeping the press open and personal intervention during his imprisonment. "Peter Suhrkamp: Arno Breker hat mich vor den Nazis gerettet," *Prometheus, Internet Bulletin for Art, Politics, and Science* 82 (Spring 2002), www.meaus.com/breker suhrkamp.htm (last viewed 19 December 2009).

17. Petropoulos, 2000, 242–243.

18. Wolfgang Fritz Haug, "Ästhetik der Normalität/Vor-stellung und Vorbild: Die Faschisierung des männlichen Akts bei Arno Breker," in *Inszenierung der Macht*, 1987, 97, 94.

19. Cf. Magdalena Bushart and Ulrike Müller-Hofstede, "Aktplastik," in *Skulptur und Macht*, 1983, 17–19, 29.

20. Arno Breker, "I summon the young artists to a dialogue," in Breker, 1990, 111–113; originally published in *Penthouse* 3 (German edition, 1991), 56–57.

21. Bettina Güldner and Wolfgang Schuster, "Das Reichssportfeld," *Skulptur und Macht*, 1983, 46; on Thorak's career, see Petropoulos, 2000, 262–271.

22. Güldner and Schuster, in *Skulptur und Macht*, 1983, 46, 58.

23. The studio photograph is reproduced in Egret, 1996, fig. 144. See also the 1979 interview conducted by Andre Müller with Breker, available at www.signandsight.com/features/884.html (viewed 22 March 2009). Breker always claimed that Hitler changed the titles to make the figures holding torch and sword allegories of the party and military.

24. Hitler's opening speech at the first "Great German Art" exhibition, in 1937, reproduced in Hinz, 1974, 166.

25. Breker, 1972, 90.

26. *Venus vor Gericht*, written and directed by Hans Zerlett, Bundesfilmarchiv, Berlin (see Giesen, 2003, 265).

27. Giesen first suggested that some actual works of "degenerate art" that had been seized were used in the film. My thanks to Andreas Hüneke and Christoph Zuschlag of the Forschungsstelle Entartete Kunst (Degenerate art research project) at the Art Historical Institute of the Freie Universität, Berlin, for viewing these scenes of the film with Susan Felleman and me, and identifying many of the artworks. They have since located one work shown in *Venus vor Gericht*, a painting by Wilhelm Morgner.

28. The Kleinshmidt, *Duett im Nord-Café*, 1925,

formerly in the Staatsgalerie Stuttgart, is visible in the 1937 Munich showing of "degenerate art" in Barron et al., 1991, 56, no. 15988. It is also visible in a still (fig. 76), with the caption: "The receptionist *(Empfangsdame)* in Benjamin Hecht's Salon presents 'artworks' that these days we have eliminated as 'degenerate'" (Tschauner, 1941, 410–411). The receptionist wears a monocle and a necktie, stereotyping her as a Weimar-period lesbian. The possible Grosz is also reproduced, captioned as "Das Erlebnis" (The experience; in the film it is captioned "Die Begegnung" [The meeting]), "a concoction of Jewish corruption." The Kirchner is *Das Paar,* 1923–24, acquired in 1930 by the Museum für Kunst und Gewerbe, Hamburg.

29. The censors' decision of 14 March 1934 is available at www.deutsches-filminstitut.de/filme/f035202.htm (viewed on 9 August 2007). The Kerr quote is taken from Steven Bach, *Marlene Dietrich: Life and Legend* (New York: William Morrow, 1992), 171. Scarpitta and the role of other real works of art in fictional narrative films, including *Venus vor Gericht,* is the subject of research by Susan Felleman.

30. Schulte-Sasse, 1996. For a brief discussion of *Venus vor Gericht,* see Hake, 2001, 59–60. Schulte-Sasse has also written about *Venus vor Gericht* in connection with another Nazi-era film, *Befreite Hände* (1939), in which the main figure is a woman sculptor, analyzing women's relationship to three-dimensional art in the Third Reich (Linda Schulte-Sasse, "Plastiken auf Celluloid: Frauen und Kunst im NS-Spielfilm," in Segeberg, 2004, 181–202).

31. Tschauner, 1941, 410.

32. Translation of Hitler's speech quoted from Hinz, 1974, 173.

33. Although *Venus vor Gericht* has no artists' credits, it should be mentioned that Breker did execute fragmentary torsos during the Nazi period. See *Female Torso Seated,* 1942, reproduced in Egret, 1996, no. 252. The fragmentary 1928 *Torso of the Man Seated* was shown in Breker's 1944 Potsdam exhibition, probably as evidence that he had "overcome" Rodin. Cf. the discussion of *Venus vor Gericht* in Schrödl, 2004, 51–58, where fragmentary torso representations are contrasted with the National Socialist demand for "complete" figures. It seems that in the case of pieces mimicking classical antiquity and suggesting that the completion of those fragments occurs in the present, partial figures were acceptable. Schulte-Sasse also discusses the issue of bodily wholeness and sculpture in connection with Charlotte's embodiment of a totally normal and natural ideal as a representation of the Nazi state (Schulte-Sasse, 2004, 190–191).

34. Walter Grasskamp, "The De-Nazification of Nazi Art: Arno Breker and Albert Speer Today," in Taylor and van der Will, 1999, 241.

35. A contemporary article documented Breker's work on *Prometheus* and stated that the success of his Olympic pieces led to this commission and his receiving the title of professor directly from Hitler. ("Künstler schaffen für das Dritte Reich: Der Bildhauer Arno Breker," *Die Kunst im Dritten Reich* 2, no. 1 [1938]: 94–95.) On *Readiness,* see *Skulptur und Macht,* 1983, 175; http://kunst.gymszbad.de/nationalsozialismus/plastik/kuenstler/breker/werke/breker-1939-bereitschaft.htm (last viewed 6 April 2009); and Foster et al., 2004, 283, fig. 3. In 1994 Hans Haacke recreated *Readiness* as a prop in Johan Kresnik's dance-theater piece *Ernst Jünger* (Brigitte Werneburg, "Report From Germany: The Armored Male Exposed," *Art in America* [June 1995]: 44–47).

36. Max Imdahl, "Pose und Indoktrination—Zu Werken der Plastik und Malerei im Dritten Reich," in Staeck, 1988, 87–99. Cf. Stercken, 2000, 77–78. See also Grasskamp, 1989, 241. In 1932 Breker won the Rome Prize awarded by the Prussian Ministry of Culture and spent a year at Villa Massimo. In addition to being impressed by the buildings and public monuments erected by the fascist government, as well as by Michelangelo and antiquities, he sketched the unfinished "Pieta Rondanini," from which he later executed a speculative reconstruction. See Baumgart, 1935.

37. See also Richard Etlin, "Introduction: The Perverse Logic of Nazi Thought," in Etlin, 2002, 19.

38. See B. John Zavrel, "The Guardian of the Image of Man," www.meaus.com/guardian.html (viewed 19 December 2009).

39. The first hit on a Google search for "Arno Breker," for instance, on 8 March 2006, was www.hitler.org/art/breker: "Though the return to a classical era of beauty and human potential was shattered with the collective national loss in World War 2, the vast inspiration of his art lives on."

40. See Magadalena Bushart, "Überraschende Begegung mit alten Bekannten: Arno Brekers NS-Plastik in neuer Umgebung," in *NS-Kunst: 50 Jahre danach,* 1989, 35–54.

41. Raemisch also executed eagles for the Olympic Stadium grounds. His wife was Jewish, and he emigrated to the United States in 1939. See www

.bildhauerei-in-berlin.de. For Breker's Fehrbelliner reliefs, see Probst, 1978, 50–52, figs. 60–65; and Werner, 1940, 157.

42. Petropoulos, 2000, 249.

43. The Munich historian Ernst Nolte initiated the Historians' Debate in 1987. He sought to "normalize" the Nazi dictatorship by comparing it to Stalin's Soviet Union. Many voices, most prominently that of the sociologist Jürgen Habermas, were raised in opposition to this idea, arguing that the "normalization" of violence itself did further violence to victims, that "comparative genocides" did more to obscure than to clarify the specifics of the cases under study, and that the ultimate object of such exercises was not to gain greater understanding but to assuage German guilt.

44. Ludwig's position is represented in several interviews and statements, all in Staeck, 1988, 13–15, 43–45: "Breker wird zur Seite gedrückt" (*Spiegel* interview with Ludwig of 1 September 1986); Peter Ludwig, "In der Nacht gab es viele Lichter" (Ludwig statement in the ARD-TV program "'Scholle, Schamhaar, Schützengraben': Wohin mit der Nazi-Kunst?" of 17 May 1987); and Peter Ludwig, "Pro," *Pan,* 26 December 1987.

45. Quoted from Staeck, 1988, 45.

46. Staeck, 1988, 150–153. The director of the Hamburg Kunsthalle, Werner Hofmann, did not sign the petition included in Staeck, 1988. Though he rejected the "quality" of Nazi art (stating, "There were no Pounds or Célines of the brush"), he advocated showing it along with information about the Nazi system and juxtaposed to the art that that system had banned, a dialectical presentation in the spirit of the photomontages of John Heartfield and of the Staeck anthology's editor, Klaus Staeck. (Werner Hofmann, "Plädoyer für den mündigen Bürger," in Staeck, 1988, 26–30.)

47. See the Web site of the Wilhelm-Dörpfeld-Gymnasium,www.wdg.de/websiteneu/?inhalt=wer wirsind_pallasathene (viewed 23 April 2009).

48. Walter Grasskamp, "Arno Breker ins Museum? Wider den neuen liberalen Extremismus," in Bussmann, 1988, 28.

Chapter 6: From Muscle Men to Fatty Remains

1. Joseph Beuys, introduction to Tisdall, 1979, 6.

2. Tisdall, 1979, 72.

3. Ursula Meyer, "Explain Pictures to a Dead Hare," *Art News* 68, no. 9 (January 1970): 57.

4. Although he does not enter the discussion explicitly, Beuys can be seen as one of those artists of the postwar neo-avant-garde whom Hal Foster characterizes as reworking the strategies of the historical avant-garde in the new context of a culture ever more dominated by spectacle, in a complex play of strategic deferral and recovery, refining Peter Bürger's absolute division of historical and neo-avant-garde, authentic and repetitive, significant and trivial. (Hal Foster, "Who's Afraid of the Neo-Avant-Garde," in Foster, 1996, 1–33.)

5. The figure on popular press citations is my count from indexes consulted for my first sustained study of Beuys, for a seminar report in a class titled "Alternative Art Forms" and taught by Eugene Goosen at the CUNY Graduate Center in spring 1983. The figure on his work's value at that time, forty million German marks, is from Nemeczek, 1983, an article largely devoted to Beuys's then recent abandonment of art making in favor of politics.

6. Donald Kuspit offers a suggestive interpretation of Beuys's oeuvre in connection with bad parenting—his own personal and Germany's general response to the "desperate failings of the parent state," in "Joseph Beuys: The Body of the Artist," in Kuspit, 1993, 197–204.

7. This type of image of the artist in Nazi Germany is discussed in Schrödl, 2004, 140. See also the section of artists' biographies, with photographs of some of the sculptors, in Werner, 1940, 205–213.

8. George Jappe, "Interview with Beuys about Key Experiences, September 27, 1977," trans. Peter Nisbet, in Ray, 2001, 187.

9. Troost's "Führer Building" in Munich and Speer's Reichs Chancellery in Berlin were described as "the Führer's 'words turned into stone,'" by Hermann Giesler, "Symbol des Grossdeutschen Reiches," in Eber, 1940, 10.

10. Tisdall, 1979, 72.

11. Armin Zweite, "'Zeige deine Wunde' und andere raumbezogene Arbeiten von Joseph Beuys," in Zweite, 1986, 37–58, a modified and shortened version of the same text in Beuys, 1980. The Lenbach House acquired the installation in 1976 ("Joseph Beuys—ein Grüner im Museum," *Der Spiegel,* 5 November 1979, 251).

12. Gene Ray, "Joseph Beuys and the 'After-Auschwitz' Sublime," in Ray, 2005, 36.

13. See Richard Langston, "The Art of Barbarism

and Suffering," in Barron and Eckmann, 2009, 240–255.

14. "Man muß wissen –das gehört auch zur Vorgeschichte diese Grunderlebnisses hinzu—, ich bin ja am Niederrhein geboren, und in der Zeit des Dritten Reiches war man zwar täglich von einem Wald von Skulpturen umgeben, [aber] der Art, wie sie zu dieser Zeit gemacht wurden; sie haben in mir keinerlei Erlebnis ausgelöst." (Joseph Beuys, "Dank an Wilhelm Lehmbruck," in Brockhaus, 1997, 81–82.) On his relationship to Lehmbruck, see Pamela Kort, "Rodin-Lehmbruck-Beuys," in Kort and Hollein, 2005, 64–110. Beuys claimed to have seen Lehmbruck's work in a book banned by the Nazis. One could also see a reproduction of his *Female Torso,* 1918, on p. 21 of Bruno Werner's 1940 sculpture survey, which also included works by Barlach and Käthe Kollwitz, in addition to works of sculptors the Nazis patronized.

15. For example, Michaud, 1988, 44.

16. Michaud, 1988, 44. The German original is "Wir würden durch unser eigenes Sich-Verlebendigtwerden durch Sprache den Boden mitnehmen."

17. On his use of blood and earth as sculptural materials, see Heribert Schulz, "Blut," and Uwe Claus, "Erde," in *Joseph Beuys: Die Materialien und ihre Botschaft,* 2006, 34–61.

18. Quoted from Ermen, 2007, 44.

19. Peter Bürger, "Die Avantgarde, das Material und der Tod: Annäherungen an Joseph Beuys," in *Joseph Beuys: Die Materialien und ihre Botschaft,* 14. For Bürger's earlier responses to Beuys (1987, 1997), see Mesch and Michely, 2007, 250–269. In a critique of Beuys's messianism, the Canadian artist Vera Frenkel wrote in 1981: "Beuys allows others to project on him the attributes of benign leader, a sort of counter-Führer who makes the shit visible as opposed to endorsing the pathological cleanliness of the Nazi torture and murder machine; a kind of promise of redemption through transgression of the diaper" (Mesch and Michely, 2007, 130).

20. "Neo-avant-gardist art is autonomous art in the full sense of the term, which means that it negates the avant-gardist intention of returning art to the praxis of life" (Bürger, 1984, 58).

21. Hal Foster, "Who's Afraid of the Neo-Avant-Garde," in Foster, 1996, 1–32. Foster employs the Freudian concept of *Nachträglichkeit* (deferred action) to argue that neo-avant-garde repetition constituted a belated return of the repressed traumatic blow delivered by the avant-garde to the institution of art. On this view, past, present, and future are not to be understood as distinct from each other, with the past as the origin, but to be involved in continuous exchange.

22. Reichel, 1993.

23. Statement by Herr Dr. Benz (who disliked Beuys), at one of the regular Wednesday lunches hosted by Krista Gutbrod Baumeister for her friends and anyone who happened to be doing research at the Willi Baumeister Archiv on that day.

24. Beuys stated that he first became aware of Duchamp in 1955 (interview with Willoughby Sharp, in Kuoni, 1990, 80; first published in *Artforum,* December 1969).

25. Gillen, 1997, 270.

26. Tisdall, 1979, 10.

27. See Buskirk, 2003, 63–72.

28. "Rasierter Kaktus," *Der Spiegel,* 17 March 1975, 162–164.

29. "Kunst: Richterspruch über Beuys-Badewanne," *Der Spiegel,* 19 January 1976, 105; and Tisdall, 1979, 10.

30. Tisdall, 1979. 92. The painting and collage derived from the performance is in the Joseph Beuys Museum, Schloss Moyland, Bedburg-Hau.

31. For discussion of controversies over authorship and control of increasingly valuable minimal objects and ideas, see Buskirk, 2003, 19–55.

32. Ulrich Mulert, "Beuys im Guggenheim-Tempel: Mit der jetzigen Ausstellung in New York ist sein Weltruhm unbestritten," *Hessische Allgemeine Zeitung* (Kassel), 3 November 1979; the article appeared in numerous other German newspapers (JBA).

33. The cover of *Der Spiegel,* 5 November 1979, bore the text "Künstler Beuys: Der Größte Weltruhm für einen Scharlatan?" (see fig. 83); inside was the article "Joseph Beuys—ein Grüner im Museum," 250–265, and an interview with Jürgen Hohmeyer, "Ein bisßchen Einsicht in die Seelenlage," 268–270. See also Glozer (1979), who makes the point that a big article in the *New York Times* the previous weekend had prepared the way for the American reception of Beuys.

34. "Beuys: Mythos mit Fett," *Der Spiegel,* 16 December 1968, 170–171.

35. Beuys's installations' evocations of concentration camps was mentioned in a 1964 interview in the magazine *Kunst,* in response to the Aachen Fluxus festival (cited in Angerbauer-Rau, 1998, 14–15). This association was also made in a review

of the exhibition in Mönchengladbach that would form the basis of the Beuys Block in Darmstadt, discussed below. See Peter Iden, "Moralist in Grau: Zu den Arbeiten von Joseph Beuys im Städtischen Museum Mönchengladbach," *Frankfurter Rundschau*, 6 October 1967, and the caption of a photograph of the Ströher Collection installation in the Haus der Kunst in Munich, where the installation is described as a "homemade inventory from a concentration camp torture chamber." See also Christian Enzensberger, "Versuch über den Schmutz," *Süddeutsche Zeitung*, 6–7 July 1968. None of these articles refers to the Holocaust.

36. Volkswagen buses, or "Transporters," first went into production in 1949. This particular bus had its own history as an object in and as history: it was the means of transport for the works, including Gerhard Richter's 1965 painting *Uncle Rudi* (fig. 102), sent to Prague by a group of German artists who had staged the show "Hommage à Lidice" at the René Block Gallery in Berlin in 1967, commemorating a Nazi massacre in a Bohemian village (René Block, "Not a Monument, but Rather Food for Thought," in Gillen, 1997, 214–217).

37. Kuspit, 1993, 203.

38. Kim Levin, "Joseph Beuys: The New Order," *Arts Magazine* (April 1980); cited here from Levin, 1988, 176). See also Ray, 2001, 56–57.

39. Levin, 1988, 181. On Beuys's reception in America, see Joan Rothfuss, "Joseph Beuys: Echoes in America," in Ray, 2001, 37–53.

40. Quoted in Daniel Birnbaum, "Ripening on the Rhine: The Cologne Art World of the '80s," *Artforum International* (1 March 2003); also available at www.encyclopedia.com/doc/1G1–98918660.html (viewed 2 July 2007).

41. Beuys sent his entry materials from his parents' house at Tiergarten Street 187 in Cleves on 15 March 1958, and received a receipt from the state museum in Oswiecim dated 15 April (Franz Joseph van der Grinten, "Beuys' Beitrag zum Wettbewerb für das Auschwitzmonument," in Lorenz, 1996, 199–203; see also Marie Kramer, 1997, 261–271; and Arendt, 2000, 21).

42. For detailed analyses of the individual objects and the history of their installation, see Marie Kramer, 1997, 261–27; Barbara Strieder and Sigrun Pass, "Der Block Beuys im Hessischen Landesmuseum in Darmstadt," *Blätter für Besucher* 11 (Hessisches Landesmuseum Darmstadt); Biro, 2003; Gene Ray, "Joseph Beuys and the 'After-Auschwitz' Sublime," in Ray, 2001, and Ray, 2005; Max Reithmann, "In the Rubblefield of German History," in Ray, 2001, 139–174; Matthias Bunge, "Kunst der Nachkriegszeit—Kunst nach Auschwitz," in Raab, 1998, 142–158; and Arendt, 2000.

43. Quoted from Tisdall, 1979, 21–23. A photograph of Beuys, arranging the *Auschwitz Demonstration* vitrine for a 1968 show in the Hamburg Kunstverein (which the critic found a totally inappropriate setting for these works), was captioned "Joseph Beuys in seiner Kunstküche" (Joseph Beuys in his art kitchen) (Willi Bongard, "Gebissabdruck in Talg: Gebrauchsanleitung zu Joseph Beuys," *Die Zeit*, 8 September 1968).

44. *Bernhard Heiliger, 1915–1995*, 2005, 18–22, published in connection with the exhibition "Bernhard Heiliger, 1915–1995: Kosmos eines Bildhauers."

45. *Bernhard Heiliger, 1915–1995*, 2005, 22; Petropoulos, 2000, 233; and Breker, 1972, 313–315.

46. Gabriela Walde, "Bildhauer der Bonner Republik: Heiliger-Ausstellung in Berlin," *Die Welt*, 4 January 2006 (www.welt.de/print-welt/article 188379/Bildhauer_der_Bonner_Republik.html).

47. For a reproduction of Heiliger's design for the *Denkmal des Unbekannten politschen Gefangener* (memorial for the unknown political prisoner), see Barron and Eckmann, 2009, 130.

48. See Christine Fischer-Defoy, "Artists and Art Institutions in Germany 1933–1945," in Taylor and van der Will, 1999, 109.

49. Searching for Beuys public sculptures in Berlin, for example, one finds only "Berlin Wall, 1961/64," his proposal to raise the wall's height by five centimeters to improve its proportions (www .bildhauerei-in-Berlin.de; viewed 21 December 2009).

50. Stachelhaus, 1987, 159.

51. Beuys's most notable works of public art, the "7000 Oaks" project and connected "End of the 20th Century" installation—residues of which can still be seen on the "Documenta" grounds in Kassel and outside the Dia Art Foundation in New York, Berlin's Hamburger Bahnhof Museum of Contemporary Art, and Munich's State Gallery of Modern Art—developed as part of his participation in "Documenta 7" in 1982. See Wagner, 2001, 179–184; and Fernando Groener and Rose-Maria Kendler, *7000 Eichen: Joseph Beuys* (Cologne: Walther König, 1987).

52. See Marianne Heinz, ed., *Joseph Beuys: Raum*

in der Neuen Galerie, Patrimonia 73 (Berlin and Kassel: Kulturstiftung der Länder, in association with Staatliche Museen Kassel, 1993).

53. Jappe, in Ray, 2001, 186–187.

54. Barfurth-Igel, 1992, 15–17.

55. The Meerbusch historical society, Geschichtsverein Meerbusch e.V., published the preservationist Holger Brülls's 1995 monograph. Mennekes (2005) differs from Brülls in interpreting the Büderich memorial as a crucifixion, not a resurrection. Pictures of Beuys with the piece in his studio also appear in the catalogue *Getlinger Photographiert Beuys: 1950–1963* (Kalkar: Städtisches Museum; Cologne: DuMont, 1990), where it is described in Frans Joseph van der Grinten's essay "Joseph Beuys, der Niederrhein und Fritz Getlinger" (18). In the literature on Beuys's career there are a few sentences on it in Stachelhaus (1987, 40, 41–42; and 1991, 32–33, 80). Franz Joseph van der Grinten devotes one (albeit long) sentence to it in "Joseph Beuys: Die frühen Jahre," in Bastian, 1988, 132. It is not mentioned in Schirmer (1996 and 1997), where the chronologies skip from 1953 to Beuys's appointment in Düsseldorf in 1961. The chronology in Zweite (1991, 341) notes that in 1959 Beuys married Eva Wurmbach. The creation of the Büderich Memorial is briefly described in the chronology by Claudia Schmuckli in Rosenthal, 2004, 156.

56. Brülls, 1995, 8. Beuys, Mataré, Wilhelm Hanebal, and Ivo Beucker were each offered 500 marks to submit proposals. Beuys's proposal was unanimously chosen by the committee (Barfurth-Igel, 1992, 11–15). Stachelhaus (1987, 41–42; and 1991, 33) says that Mataré blocked Beuys's appointment to the Düsseldorf Art Academy in 1955 on the grounds that, though he considered Beuys a talented artist, he would exert too much fascination on the students to be an effective teacher; and that he also opposed Beuys's receiving the Büderich commission. Barfurth-Igel (1992) repeats this supposition, giving Stachelhaus as the source. Since no documentary evidence is cited, one can only assume it derives from Stachelhaus's conversations with Beuys.

57. Barfurth-Igel, 1992, 17.

58. Many thanks to Robert Rameil, president of the Meerbusch Historical Society, for his help and hospitality. According to Brülls (1995, 8), there had been plans since the 1920s to use the Büderich tower, the remains of a thirteenth-century church, as a war memorial. Brülls also interprets the memorial as representative of generalizing tendencies in 1950s war memorials, but he sees it as also alluding to Nazi victims in institutional and concentration camps, with the iron plate on the figure's chest making reference to electroshock therapy and torture, and the spare tower alluding to the chimneys of crematoria. Mennekes (2005) stresses the tower's function since the 1920s as a power switching station, relating this to Beuys's later works dealing with electricity as a life force. He contests Brülls's interpretation of the metal plate, asserting that it derives from earlier Beuys crucifixions and connects them to electricity, referring to the Christian life force and not to torture.

59. The impressive blacksmithing also extends to two huge oval armatures attaching the doors to their hinges, as well as to the massive and unusual chain and connections attaching and suspending the figure. That Beuys put much thought into these technical and formal issues (which doubtlessly also have iconographic significance, such as those disputed by Brülls and Mennekes) is apparent in study drawings. See *Joseph Beuys: Kleine Zeichnungen*, 1995, nos. 158–161.

60. Barfurth-Igel, 1992, 12.

61. Barbara Strieder, "Ein frühes Taufbecken und das Kranenburger Grabmal," Lorenz, 1996, 190–197.

62. *Crucifixion* is in the collection of the Staatsgalerie Stuttgart. See *Kreuz + Zeichen: Religiöse Grundlagen im Werk von Joseph Beuys*, 1985, 22–25 (on Büderich); and Kotte and Milduer, 1986.

63. *Mahnmal* derives from the German word *mahnen*, to remind, warn, admonish; *Denkmal* from *denken*, to think. A *Mahnmal* is generally directed more toward vigilance in the present than retrospective contemplation of the past. On the distinction, see the sculptor Jochen Gerz's interview with Jacqueline Lichtenstein and Gérard Wajchman, in Gerz, 1993, 8.

64. On this expansion, especially in relationship to Kaprow's Happenings and to Earth Art, see the book by Philip Ursprung (2003), which argues that the 1960s and 1970s saw a shift in a basic question posed by Duchamp and the readymade—"What is art?"—to one predicated on these diverse new locations: "Where is art?" Beuys swam through a swamp near Cleves in the environmentally themed *Bog Action* of 1971; see Adams, 1992, 27.

65. Harold Marcuse, "Das ehemalige Konzentrationslager Dachau: Der mühevolle Weg zur Gedenk-

stätte, 1945–1968," *Dachauer Hefte* 6 (November 1990): 191–192, and Marcuse, 2001, 192–194. For more on Dachau as memorial site, see Barbara Distell, "Entstehung und Funktion der KZ-Gedenkstätte Dachau," in Brebeck et al., 1988, 159–168; Detlef Hoffmann, "Dachau," in Hoffmann, 1998, 38–91; and Young, 1993, 60–72.

66. It was only in labeling slides from a research trip in 1993 that included trips to Dachau and to the Bavarian Custom House repository of art from the "Great German Art" exhibitions that I realized that the same artist had executed the *Unknown Prisoner* and the Wessel bust. Detlef Hoffmann has found that Koelle's participation in exhibitions at the House of German Art was noted by the art historian Hans Eckstein in the *Süddeutsche Zeitung* of 23 September 1949, and the Wessel bust was mentioned in an article in the same newspaper, "Untersuchungen gegen Fritz Koelle," on 14 October 1949. (Hoffmann, 1998, 59, 88, n. 85–86.) For Koelle's works from before and during the early years of the Third Reich, including the postal ministry commission, see Ernst Kammerer, introduction to *Fritz Koelle* (Berlin: Rembrandt Verlag, 1939). On the *Unknown Prisoner*, see also Hoffmann-Curtius, 1998; Hoffmann, 1996; and Kramer, 2003, 179–181. The biography of Koelle available at LEMO (Lebendiges virtuelles Museum Online), a project of the German Historical Museum (DHM) in Berlin and the Haus der Geschichte der Bundesrepublik Deutschland (HdG) in Bonn, provides the information that Koelle was put under observation in the early years of the Third Reich for his images of workers, and held by the Gestapo for nine days in 1934, before he began to receive official commissions in 1936 and show in the "Great German Art" exhibition in 1937. In 1946 he was declared to have been a victim of the regime. See www.dhm.de/lemo/html/biografien/KoelleFritz/index.html (viewed 21 December 2009). His descendants have created a Web site with information about him and his work, www.koelle-online.de (viewed 21 December 2009).

67. Hoffmann, 1998, 58. This first version was included in the first installation of the permanent collection exhibition of the German Historical Museum, Berlin, which opened in early June 2006. On 7 June, when I visited the collection, the piece was unlabeled.

68. See Schirmbeck, 1984, 50–97.

69. Svetlana Alpers, "The Museum as a Way of Seeing," in *Exhibiting Cultures: The Poetics and Politics of Museum Display*, ed. Ivan Karp and Steven D. Lavine (Washington, DC, and London: Smithsonian Institution Press, 1991), 25–32.

70. Ermen, 2007, 67–70.

71. Hoffmann, 1998, 38.

72. The crash is very specifically dissected and the historical record clarified in Gieseke and Markert, 1996, 71–78. The standard Beuys biography has the crash taking place in a snowstorm in the winter of 1943 (Stachelhaus, 1987, 26). Gieseke and Markert (76) have examined military documents specifying the date as 16 March 1944. Their biography builds a detailed picture of the ideological environment in which Beuys grew up in Nazi Germany, including of the indoctrination of children in the Hitler Youth, that group's active participation in anti-Semitic actions (such as the burning of the Cleves synagogue in the night of 9–10 November 1938), school curricula in Cleves, the romance associated with the Luftwaffe, and actions that Beuys might have been party too. This is a fascinatingly detailed piece of cultural historical investigative reporting, but it yields no firm connection between Beuys's background and his later activities as either an artist or political activist.

73. Tisdall, 1979, 16–17, is the most influential telling of this story. Gieseke and Markert (1996) identify Beuys's killed colleague as Hans Laurinck.

74. Gieseke and Markert, 1996, 76.

75. Peter Nisbet, "Crash Course: Remarks on a Beuys Story," in Ray, 2001, 5–17. The earliest sighting of The Story is a 1969 article based on an interview with Beuys (Engelhard, 1969), in which the Tartars are only granted one not very explicit sentence, with no mention of fat or felt: "After several days a Tartar rescue squad dug him out of the metal wreckage." The crash, without the Tartar rescue, is mentioned as early as 1961 in an article in Beuys's hometown newspaper on his appointment to the Düsseldorf art academy ("Ehrenvolle Berufung für Klever Künstler: Bildhauer Josef Beuys wurde Professor der Staatlichen Kunstakadamie Düsseldorf," *Grenzland-Post*, 12 September 1961). Beuys Museum curator Barbara Strieder, though, told me in conversation (Bedburg-Hau, 7 July 2007) that the van der Grinten brothers swear that Beuys told them The Story as early as 1953. Meyer, 1970, also mentions the crash, but not the rescue.

76. He distanced himself specifically in a 1980 interview with Kate Horsefield (see Kuoni, 1990, 69–70).

77. Buchloh, 1980, quoted here from Ray, 2001, 203; Buchloh's article is also reprinted in Mesch and Michely, 2007, 109–126. Buchloh's conception of Beuys's origins in the Nazi period and formation in the 1940s and 1950s also forms the background for Ray's different and more affirmative interpretation and was the impetus for the symposium he organized. Some later writers have embraced the idea of Beuys's story as fable. Borer has rewritten his life story, from birth to death, as the legend of a saint (Alain Borer, "Beweinung des Joseph Beuys," in Schirmer, 1997, 13).

78. Reproduced in Tisdall, 1979, 8.

79. On Beuys's humor and costuming, see for example, Röder, 2003, 113–114.

80. Adam Oellers, "Fluxus at the Borders: Aachen, July 20, 1964," in Gillen, 1997, 200–207; Ray, 2001, 38–40; Tisdall, 1997, 90–91; Wagner, 2001, 198, 208; and Langston, 2009, 241–244. Röder (2003, 114) actually compares Beuys's own speaking style to Goebbels's, specifically referencing the latter's Sportpalast speech.

81. See Gillen, 1997, 206, for a photograph of the student punching Beuys in the nose. The student appears totally earnest, and well skilled in boxing, positioned to deliver a right hook to follow what had obviously been a solid left jab. Remarkably, while one man tries to intervene, the majority of bystanders watched the assault with what appears to be either indifference or amusement. Ray (2005, 39) attributes the violence to the fact that Beuys's melting of fat was seen as "a blunt allusion to the crematoria of the killing centers." Wagner (2001, 197–199) sees Beuys's actions (and the violent response they precipitated) as more broadly connecting to "National Socialism, war, and as memorial to the dead," specifically the execution of the failed van Stauffenberg ring of conspirators to assassinate Hitler. According to this reading, the dead beings memorialized in Beuys's work are not only Holocaust victims but victims within the German military. The photographer Heinrich Riebesehl recalls that Beuys asked the young man what he was doing on the stage, to which the man replied, "I'll show you what," before delivering several blows to the artist, who, according to another source, "removed his hat and struck back. And Joseph Beuys could really throw a punch." Ermen (2007, 53–54) claims that broader study of film documentation of the event reduces the moment of the Riebesehl photograph with its "image of the Man of Sorrows" to "a very short, ironic sequence of a few seconds. . . . Fluxus or neo-Dada quickly returns, the cross goes back in the case and the artist throws chocolate to the crowd."

82. Peter Squenz, "Ein Professor wurde geschlagen . . . und warf mit Schokolade—Eine 'etwas exceptionelle' Feier am 20. Juli in der Aachener Uni," *Die Zeit,* 31 July 1964. The article includes a photograph of Brock standing on his head.

83. Habbo Knoch, "Die Grenzen des Zeigbaren: Fotografien der NS-Verbrechen und die westdeutsche Gesellschaft 1955–1965," in Kramer, 2003, 94–95.

84. Biro (2003) argues that Anselm Kiefer's paintings of the 1980s enact a specific act of mourning for Jewish victims, making Kiefer Beuys's most important successor. For my less positive assessment of Kiefer's achievement in this regard, and for the suggestion of an alternative candidate, Rolf Zimmermann, for an artist of the generation of 1968 (when he and Kiefer were roommates) confronting the specifics of the Holocaust through his own family history, see Chametzky, 1995; Chametzky, 1997–98; and Chametzky, 2007.

85. Benjamin H. D. Buchloh, "Reconsidering Joseph Beuys, Once Again," in Ray, 2001, 78. Buchloh's more recent appraisal is the essay "1964a," in Foster et al., 2004, 480–485.

86. Theodor W. Adorno, "Cultured Criticism and Society," in Theodor W. Adorno, *Prisms,* trans. Samuel Weber and Shierry Weber Nicholson (Cambridge, MA: MIT Press, 1981), 34.

87. "Avant-Garde and Kitsch (1939)," in Greenberg, 1961, 5. The essay ends with reflections on the support for what Greenberg deemed kitsch art in Nazi Germany, Fascist Italy, and the Stalinist Soviet Union, and identified the avant-garde's historical mission to be "to keep culture *moving* in the midst of ideological confusion and violence."

88. See Ray, 2001, 58, n. 11, and Ray, 2005, 5–10.

89. Hermann Pfütze, "Von Adorno zu Beuys," *Kunstforum* 100 (April–May 1989) 243–252, quoted in Bunge, "Kunst der Nachkriegszeit," in Raab, 1998, 142.

90. Bauer, 2001, 264.

91. On the metaphorical associations of the naming of the event, see chapter 5, "Names of the Holocaust," in Young, 1988.

92. *The Oxford English Dictionary,* 2nd ed., vol. 7 (Oxford: Clarendon Press, 1989), 315.

93. Twenty million people watched the series—as Anton Kaes points out, every other adult Ger-

man. Anton Kaes, "1979: The American Television Series *Holocaust* Is Shown in West Germany," in Gilman and Zipes, 1997, 783–789. See also Knut Hicketheir, "Die Darstellung des Massenmordes an den Juden im Fernsehen der Bundesrepublik von 1960–1980," in Kramer, 2003, 129–130; Volker Zastrow, "Holocaust: Ein Wort für das Namenlose," *Frankfurter Allgemeine Zeitung*, 27 January 2005 (available online at www.faz.net); Alan Steinweis, "Der Umgang mit dem Holocaust in den USA und Deutschland," in Junger, 2001, 742–752; and Reichel, 2001. On the significance of television for German Holocaust memory, see Kansteiner, 2006.

94. "Holocaust (m; od. -s, -s; engl. –amer. Bez. für) 1. die Judenvernichtung während der Zeit des Nationalsozialismus. . . . 2. massenhafte Vernichtung menschlichen Lebens, Ausrottung eines Volkes, Völkermord" (Gerhard Wahrig, *dtv Wörterbuch der deutschen Sprache* [Munich: Deutscher Taschenbuch Verlag, 2001], 486). *Der Grosse Brockhaus* encyclopedia includes the Greek term *Holokaustum* in its 1931 fifteenth edition (p. 604); there is no entry under the term in its 1979 eighteenth edition, but there are four pages centering on the attempt to wipe out the Jews in the 1996 twentieth edition (201–204).

95. Young, 1993, 128.

96. Fulbrook, 1999, 72–75. This usage, and knowledge, may be fading. In the late 1990s, when asked "Who or what is Auschwitz," 3.5 percent of people between the ages of thirty-one and fifty answered "no idea," compared to 6.6 percent of those between the ages of eighteen and thirty-nine. In total, the authors estimated that about three million Germans over the age of fourteen would not know the answer (Silbermann and Stofters, 2000, 47, 50–51; see also Brink, 1996).

97. Biro (2003, 119) dates the piece to 1968 on the basis of its assembly in that year. Given the importance of installation to Beuys's work, I agree. For an evocative photographic documentation of the Block, see Leve, 2004.

98. For an overview of Beuys's vitrines, see Theewen, 1993.

99. See Kramer, "Joseph Beuys: Auschwitz Demonstration, 1956–1964," in Gillen 1997, 261–263. This also predicts Claude Lanzmann's focus on train tracks in the film *Shoah*, as well as the Beuys disciple Anselm Kiefer's 1990 comment, "We see train tracks somewhere, and think about Auschwitz. This will last for a long time" (quoted in Biro, 2003, 134).

100. Kramer, "Joseph Beuys: Auschwitz Demonstration," in Gillen, 1997, 266.

101. The Beuys Block closed at the end of September 2007, to accommodate the total renovation of the Hessisches Landesmuseum. The curator expects it to reopen in 2011. One would expect the layout of the Beuys Block to remain the same, though some structural aspects of the museum that could affect lighting conditions could change (Klaus-D. Pohl, e-mail to author, 1 June 2007).

102. Beuys, quoted in Mennekes, 1989, 45–47 (text given in English and German).

103. According to Lawrence Douglas (Zelizer, 2001, 289–291), despite a bar of soap having been entered as evidence in the Nuremberg Trials, "No positive evidence has ever been adduced proving that the Nazis used human fat to make soap." According to Raul Hilberg and other authorities on the Nazi death factories, though, the legend of this practice arose even during the Holocaust. Esther Leslie (2005, 184–188) cites a December 1945 article in the *New York Herald Tribune* reporting on this practice. It remains a continued area of research, hearsay, ghoulish fascination, and controversy. The lack of evidence to support the Auschwitz soap story is used as "evidence" of the fabrication of the Holocaust itself by Holocaust deniers, and of its exaggerations by "revisionists."

104. Ray, 2001, 39–40, 49. Paul Celan, "Nacht und Nebel, Kommentar zum Film von Alain Resnais," translation of Jean Cayrol's "Nuit et Brouillard, Commentaire," in Celan, 1986, 76–99. The film was edited by Chris Marker and had music by Hanns Eisler. The making of bodies into soap is mentioned on p. 95 of the German text.

105. Celan, 1986, 97.

106. See van der Knaap, 2006, 14, 41–42; and Hirsch, 2004, 31. The Web site www.imdb.com cites a 1992 interview with Resnais in which he said that *Night and Fog* was an allegory for the French intervention in Algeria. This is also mentioned in the essay on the film at www.weiterdenken.de.

107. For analysis of the film, controversies over its initial showing at the Cannes Film Festival and its considerable impact in Germany, see Knoch, 2001, 518–527; and Knaap, 2006.

108. Eva Huber has Beuys beginning to engage with fat in drawings of 1959–60, and Barbara Strieder dates his sculptural engagement with felt to around 1960 (see *Joseph Beuys: Die Materialien und ihre Botschaft*, 2006, 76, 94).

109. Hirsch, 2004, esp. x, 8–11 and chapter 2, "*Night and Fog* and the Origins of Posttraumatic Cinema," 28–62.

110. Kramer, "Joseph Beuys: Auschwitz Demonstration," in Gillen, 1997, 271.

111. As Barbara Strieder points out, these metaphoric dimensions contrast with Robert Morris's more structural interest in felt (Strieder, "Filz," *Joseph Beuys: Die Materialien und ihre Botschaft,* 2006, 94–111).

112. See Pamela Kort, "Beuys: The Profile of a Successor," in Ray, 2001, 27–28. Films of Beuys at work, such as Henning Christiansen's film of Beuys's 1969 *Eurasienstab* performance in Antwerp, show the artist carefully sculpting in fat (margarine) and delicately modeling the material with his hands and a knife while constructing a fat corner, which contrasts to the randomness associated with American process artists such as Morris or Richard Serra.

113. See Bleyl, 1989.

114. Quoted from Georg Jappe, "Interview with Beuys about key experiences, September 27, 1976," trans. and annotated by Peter Nisbet, in Ray, 2001, 197.

115. Ermen, 2007, 10–11.

116. Wagner, 2001, 197–212.

117. Wagner, 2001, 207. It is these specific, rooted, German historical associations that also cause Gieseke and Markart to criticize Beuys's (and many of his commentators') identification of the origin of his use of fat in his experience of these supposedly nomadic and transnational, ahistoricized Tartars (Gieseke and Markart, 1996, 143–150).

118. German civilian suffering under Allied bombs became a major topic in the first years of this millennium. The debate as to whether Germans had "worked through" the trauma of the wartime bombing was broken open by the novelist W. G. Sebald's *Luftkrieg und Literatur* (Munich and Vienna: Carl Hanser, 1999), originally a lecture delivered in 1997, and the subsequent novel by Günther Grass, *Im Krebsgang* (Göttingen: Steidl-Verlag, 2002; published in English translation as *Crabwalk*), and, especially, Jörg Friedrich's best-selling historical study *Der Brand: Deutschland im Bombenkrieg, 1940–1945* (Munich: Propyläen, 2002; published in English translation as *The Fire: The Bombing of Germany, 1940–45*). Nolan (2005, 21) argues that the aforementioned authors are "simply wrong to lament amnesia, condemn silence, and ask 'why only now,'" since the victimization of the German civilian population had long been a topic of private and public discourse in Germany.

119. Huyssen, 1986, 24–25. *Des Teufels General* was directed by Helmut Käutner. According to program notes on the ArtHaus DVD version, Zuckmayer wrote the play in American exile after hearing of the death and state funeral of the famous flier Ernst Udet, who he claimed was an anti-Nazi. See also Reimer and Reimer, 1992, 102–104.

120. Information on the stage version taken from www.imdb.com (viewed 3 June 2006).

121. See chapter 5, "'Des Teufels General' Film als Lebensgeschichte, oder: Wie Medien die Erinnerung formen" [*The Devil's General,* film as life history, or: How media forms memories], in Welzer, Moller, and Tschuggnall, 2002.

122. The museum director Peter Nisbet notes that "Beuys's later authority, and indeed his undoubted genius for compelling installations of his own works, have resulted in deep respect for the artist's own decisions about arrangements and layout" (Nisbet, "Crash Course," in Ray, 2001, 13–15, n. 29; see also Theewen, 1993).

123. Biro, 2003, 123. Beuys's practice also provides a precedent for and parallel to Robert Smithson's (see Reynolds, 1988).

124. Edward Albee, "Berlin: Act II," *Gourmet,* November 2003, 142.

125. On Gerz's work, see Young, 1993, 28–37 (first published in *Critical Inquiry* 18, no. 2 [Winter 1992]: 267–296); and Stephan Schmidt-Wulffen, "The Monument Vanishes: A Conversation with Esther and Jochen Gerz," in Young, 1994, 69–75. On Demnig, see the postscript to chapter 3 and my letter to the editor, "The Mute Stones Speak," *The Nation,* 5 December 2005.

126. Fer, 1999, 283, 285.

127. Eva Hesse, "An Interview with Eva Hesse," interview by Cindy Nemser, 1970, quoted in Fabozzi, 2002, 220.

128. Luckow, chapter 4, "Wesenverwandschaft und Bezüge im Werk von Eva Hesse und Beuys." See also the excerpt from Luckow's book in Mesch and Michely, 2007, 287–303.

129. Luckow, 2007, 141. See also Anne Middleton Wagner, *Three Artists (Three Women): Modernism and the Art of Hesse, Krasner and O'Keeffe* (Berkeley and Los Angeles: University of California Press, 1996), 267–273; Wagner interprets Hesse's *Hang Up,* and she cites Hesse's husband, Tom Doyle, who

later denied that Hesse had been influenced by Beuys, as well as his statement that the "artist who had the most influence on Eva was Adolf Hitler."

130. Maurice Berger, "Eva Hesse: Objects of Liberation," in Berger, 1994, 231–245.

131. Hesse, quoted in Fabozzi, 2002, 221–222. For a summary and analysis of writing, especially feminist writing, on Hesse that includes a detailed section on *Hang Up*, see Griselda Pollock, "A Very Long Engagement: Singularity and Difference in the Critical Reception on Eva Hesse," in Pollock and Corby, 2006, 23–55.

132. Scribner (2003, 645) argues that the objects in Beuys's *Economic Values* installation are not relics but souvenirs, because "his knowledge of these artifacts [of East Germany] is secondhand." Beuys's objects are, though, authentic relics of his artistic practice.

133. Wolfgang Drechsler, "Joseph Beuys in the MUMOK Collection," in *Joseph Beuys* (Nuremberg: Verlag für moderne Kunst, 2006), 10. See also Arthur Danto, foreword to Mesch and Michely, 2007.

134. Stefan Koldehoff, "Hitlers Supermännchen: Streit um den Bildhauer Arno Breker," *Süddeutsche Zeitung*, 18 July 2006; also available online at www.sueddeutsche.de/kultur/artikel/864/80784/print.html, and in English at www.signandsight.com/features/865.html. See also http://artforum.com/news/week=200632; and www.stern.de/unterhaltung/ausstellungen/:Schwerin—Breker/567209.html (viewed 1 September 2007). For a chronicle of the controversy, see Vitt and Zuschlag, 2007.

Conclusion: Beyond Beuys

1. Levin, 1988, 173.

2. Paul Klee, "On Modern Art"; quoted from Herbert, 1964, 74–91.

3. Jason Gaiger, "Post-conceptual Painting: Gerhard Richter's Extended Leave-taking," in Perry and Wood, 2004, 100.

4. This information on the title and Richter's memory of it, which is based on documents in the Dresden city archives and consultation with the artist, were kindly provided to me by Dietmar Elger of the Gerhard Richter Archive, Dresden (e-mail to author, 21 June 2006).

5. Gerd [Gerhard] Richter, "Auseinandersetzungen halfen mir weiter," *Sonntag* 16 (20 April 1958): 12.

6. The Kulka firm was unaware of the Landtag mural until informed about it by this author. Documented in the author's correspondence with Herrn Starobinski, Atelier Kulka, 2006. On the Hygiene Museum mural, see Elgar, 2010, 15–18.

7. See Chametzky and Brzyski, "Introduction," and Chametzky, "Rebuilding the Past: Norman Foster's Reichstag Renovation and Daniel Libeskind's Jewish Museum, Berlin," in Chametzky and Brzyski, 2001, 161–164, 245–264.

8. A detail of the Dresden mural, captioned "Detail from a Wall-Painting" but not discussed in the text, appears in *Gerhard Richter Bilder/Painting 1962–1985* (Cologne: DuMont, 1986), 17. The Reichstag piece is reproduced and discussed in relationship to the monochrome in Armin Zweite, "Sehen, Reflektieren, Erscheinen: Anmerkungen zum Werk von Gerhard Richter," in *Gerhard Richter*, 2005, 63.

9. "Deutschland Siegt in der Kunst-WM," *Bild Zeitung*, 28 October 2005. According to this article, thirty-one Germans were included in the list of the 100 most successful and expensive artists in the world that was compiled by the business magazine *Capital*. Sigmar Polke was in second position, Rosemarie Trockel in fourth, and Georg Baselitz in seventh. Americans Bruce Nauman, Louise Bourgeois, Cindy Sherman, Mike Kelley, and Bill Viola occupied positions 3, 5, 6, 8, and 9, respectively. The French artist Christian Boltanski came in tenth.

10. Michael Kimmelman, "An Artist Beyond Isms," *New York Times Magazine*, 27 January 2002, 22.

11. Ibid., 55.

12. Schreiber (2005) tells the story of Richter's familial trauma from the Nazi period: the probable involvement of his first father-in-law in euthanizing his aunt.

13. Quoted from Storr, 2002, 27.

14. Gerhard Richter, "Extracts from Writings and Interviews, 1962–2003," in Richter, 2003, 22.

15. Haddow, 1997, 26.

16. Storr (2002, 32) says that the department store demonstration was "partially inspired" by Claes Oldenburg's 1961 *Store*. Another inspiration was the Festum Fluxorum Fluxus that Joseph Beuys organized at the Düsseldorf Art Academy 2–3 February 1963.

17. Manfred de la Motte, "Gerd Richter oder der kapitale 'kapitalistischer Realismus,'" in Galerie René Block, *Gerd Richter: Bilder des Kapitalistischen*

Realismus, catalog to the exhibition of that name in Berlin, 18 November 1964–5 January 1965.

18. The 1949–1963 chancellorship of Konrad Adenauer, the first postwar chancellor of the Federal Republic, ended in October 1963 when the founder of the conservative Christian Democratic Union resigned as part of the compromise reached in the aftermath of the *Spiegel* scandal in which Defense Minister Franz Josef Strauss attacked the magazine and its publisher, Rudolf Augstein (and press and personal freedom), for having criticized the military's level of preparedness.

19. Lynn Boyd Hinds and Theodore Otto Windt Jr., "Churchill's 'Iron Curtain' Divides the Cold War World," in Maus, 2003, 57. Today a section of the symbol of the Cold War divide, that ultimate German object as history, the Berlin Wall, stands at Westminster College—twice made over into artwork: first as support for graffitists' markings and, second, as sculptural object entitled *Breakthrough*, carved in 1990 with figural silhouettes by Churchill's granddaughter, Edwina Sandys.

20. See Hixson, 1997, 139.

21. See Hubertus Butin, "Gerhard Richter und die Reflexion der Bildern," in Butin and Gronert, 2004, 58–60.

22. Jaskot, 2005.

23. See Koch, 1992.

24. See Butin, 1991; Hemken, 1998; Storr, 2000; Ulf-Erdmann Ziegler, "How the Soul Leaves the Body: Gerhard Richter's Cycle *18. October 18, 1977*, the Last Chapter in West German Postwar Painting," in Gillen, 1997, 374–388; and Kai-Uwe Hemken, "Suffering from Germany—Gerhard Richter's Elegy of Modernism: Philosophy of History in the Cycle *October 18, 1977*," in Gillen, 1997, 381–388.

25. Storr, 2000, 64. That similarly stringent measures had never been exercised against right-wing extremists has always been a point of controversy and consternation from the German left.

26. See section 15, "Die Brandstiftung oder: Es führt kein Weg zurück," in Aust, 1985, 58–62.

27. Saltzman, 2005. See also Buchloh, 1989; Buchloh, 1989; and Buchloh, 1996.

28. Saltzman, 2005, 35. Another strong reading is Gregg M. Horowitz, "The Tomb of Art and the Organon of Life: What Gerhard Richter Saw," in Horowitz, *Sustaining Loss: Art and Mournful Life* (Stanford, CA: Stanford University Press, 2001), 133–169. For sacred predecessors, see Elina Gertsman, ed., *Visualizing Medieval Performance: Perspectives, Histories, Contexts* (Burlington, VT, and Alderhot, UK: Ashgate, 2008).

29. Reich-Ranicki is one of Germany's best-known public intellectuals. Born in Poland in 1921, he was sent to relatives in Berlin for schooling and then expelled during the Nazi period, which he survived in the Warsaw Ghetto and in hiding with a Polish farmer at war's end (Reich-Ranicki, 2000, 459–460).

30. See Peter Chametzky, "Sieben Worte sind Genug," *Zyma—Art Today* (September–October 1990): 34–43.

31. Beaucamp, 1995, 35.

32. Schmidt, 1995, 44; V. A. "Baader-Meinhof Goes West," *Süddeutsche Zeitung*, 26 June 1995.

33. Kramer, 1995. Jed Perl, "Saint Gerhard of the Sorrows of Painting," *The New Republic Online*, www.thenewrepublic.com (post date: 29 March 2002, issue date: 1 April 2002).

34. DeLillo, 2002.

35. Usselmann, 2002. The article won the College Art Association's award for the best piece in *Art Journal* that year.

36. Foster et al., 2004, 612. Donald Kuspit, by contrast, has asserted that "Richter's intellectualized Pop art ends by endorsing the society it supposedly criticizes." (Donald Kuspit, "The Spirit of Gray," review of the Kiefer show Merkaba at the Gagosian Gallery, New York, November–December 2002, www.artnet.com/magazine/features/kuspit/kuspit12–19–02.asp; viewed 6 June 2006.)

37. Richter's Reichstag flag is number 856 in the artist's numbering system at www.gerhard-richter.com, where one can see four other examples of paintings in these colors.

38. "Questions to Stella and Judd," interview by Bruce Glaser, ed. Lucy R. Lippard, *Art News*, 65, no. 5 (September 1966): 58.

39. Norman Foster, *Rebuilding the Reichstag* (Woodstock, NY: Overlook Press, 2000), 220.

40. The scarecrow suggestion is from Hemken, 1998, 137.

41. Richard Bernstein, "World Cup and Politics, Violence and Friendship," *International Herald Tribune*, 16 June 2006.

Bibliography

Adams, David, "Joseph Beuys: Pioneer of Radical Ecology," *Art Journal* 51, no. 2 (Summer 1992): 26–34.

Ades, Dawn, *Photomontage* (London: Thames and Hudson, 1976).

———, Tim Benton, David Elliott, and Iain Boyd White, eds., *Art and Power: Europe under the Dictators 1930–45* (London: Thames and Hudson, in association with Hayward Gallery, 1995).

Adler, Joseph, "Vom andern Ufer: Der Untergang der 'Titanic' auf der Berliner Sezession," *Der Sturm* 4, nos. 158–159 (1912–13): 23.

Adriani, Götz, ed., *Willi Baumeister: Dokumente, Texte, Gemälde* (Cologne: DuMont, in association with Tübingen Kunsthalle, 1971).

———, ed., *Hannah Höch: Gotha 1889–1979* (Gotha: Museen der Stadt Gotha, 1993).

Albano, Caterina, "Displaying Lives: The Narrative of Objects in Biographical Exhibitions," *museum and society* 5, no. 1 (March 2007): 15–28; available online at www.le.ac.uk/ms/museumsociety.html.

Angerbauer-Rau, Monika, *Beuys Kompass: Ein Lexikon zu den Gesprächen von Joseph Beuys* (Cologne: DuMont, 1998).

Arendt, Jörg, "Die Thematisierung des Holocaust im Werk von Joseph Beuys. 'Verarbeitung'—Mahnung—Heilung," MA thesis, Friedrich-Wilhelm University, Bonn, 2000.

Arno Breker (Potsdam: Garnisonmuseum Lustgarten, 1944).

Aust, Stefan, *Der Baader Meinhof Komplex* (Hamburg: Hoffmann and Campe, 1985).

Baigell, Matthew, and Milly Heyd, eds., *Complex Identities: Jewish Consciousness and Modern Art* (New Brunswick, NJ: Rutgers University Press, 2001).

Barfurth-Igel, Annette, " 'Gedenkstätte Alter Kirchturm' in Meerbusch-Büderich: Ein Beispiel für religiöse Motive im Werk von Joseph Beuys," *Rheinische Heimatpflege* 29, no. 1 (January–March 1992): 10–18.

Barron, Stephanie, *Exiles and Emigres: The Flight of European Artists from Hitler* (Los Angeles: Los Angeles County Museum of Art, 1997).

———, and Sabine Eckmann, eds., *Art of Two Germanys/Cold War Cultures* (New York: Harry N. Abrams, in association with Los Angeles County Museum of Art, 2009).

———, et al., *"Degenerate Art": The Fate of the Avant-Garde in Nazi Germany* (Los Angeles: Los Angeles County Museum of Art, 1991).

Battcock, Gregory, ed., *The New Art* (New York: Dutton, 1973).

Bauer, Yehuda, *Rethinking the Holocaust* (New Haven, CT, and London: Yale University Press, 2001).

Baumeister, Schlemmer und die Üechtgruppe: Stuttgarter Avantgarde 1919 (Bonn: Landesvertretung Baden-Württemberg, in association with Böblingen Städtische Galerie, 1989).

Baumeister, Willi, *Das Unbekannte in der Kunst* (Stuttgart: Curt Schwab, 1947; Cologne: DuMont, 1960; repr. 1988).

———, *Absender: ich; 8 Hefte mit Zeichnungen aus Postkarten und Briefen*, ed. Heinz Rasch (Wuppertal: Heinz Rasch, [ca. 1969]).

Baumgart, Fritz, "Die Pieta Rondanini: Ein Beitrag zur Erkenntnis des Altersstiles Michelangelos; Mit einer Rekonstruktion von Arno Breker," *Jahrbuch der Preussischen Kunstsammlungen* 56 (1935): 44–56.

Baxandall, Michael, *Painting and Experience in*

Fifteenth-Century Italy (London, Oxford, and New York: Oxford University Press, 1972).
Beaucamp, Eduard, "Exportiertes Trauma," *Frankfurter Allgemeine Zeitung*, 8 June 1995.
Beckett, Wendy, *Max Beckmann and the Self* (Munich: Prestel Verlag, 1997).
Beckmann, Max, *Die Realität der Träume in den Bildern: Schriften und Gespräche 1911 bis 1950*, ed. Rudolf Pillep (Munich: Piper, 1990).
———, *On My Painting* (London: Tate Publishing, 2003).
Belting, Hans, *Max Beckmann: Tradition as a Problem in Modern Art*, trans. Peter Wertsman (New York: Timken, 1989); originally published in German in 1984.
———, *The Germans and Their Art: A Troublesome Relationship*, trans. Scott Kleager (New Haven, CT, and London: Yale University Press, 1998).
Benjamin, Walter, *Illuminations*, trans. Harry Zohn, ed. Hannah Arendt (New York: Schocken, 1969).
———, *Reflections: Essays, Aphorisms, Autobiographical Writings*, trans. Edmund Jephcott, ed. Peter Demetz (New York and London: Harcourt Brace Jovanovich, 1978).
Benson, Timothy, *Raoul Hausmann and Berlin Dada* (Ann Arbor, MI: UMI, 1987).
Berger, Maurice, ed., *Modern Art and Society: An Anthology of Social and Multicultural Readings* (New York: Harper Collins, 1994).
Bergfelder, Tim, and Sarah Street, eds., *The Titanic in Myth and Memory: Representations in Visual and Literary Culture* (London and New York: I. B. Tauris, 2004).
Bergius, Hanne, *Das Lachen Dadas: Die Berliner Dadaisten und ihre Aktionen* (Giessen: Anabas Verlag, 1989).
———, *Montage und Metamechanik: Dada Berlin—Artistik von Polaritäten* (Berlin: Gebr. Mann, 2000); published in English as *"Dada Triumphs!" Dada Berlin, 1917–1923, Artistry of Polarities, Montages—Mechanics—Manifestations*, trans. Brigitte Pichon, vol. 5 of *Crisis and the Arts, the History of Dada*, ed. Stephen Foster (Farmington Hills, MI: G. K. Hall, 2003).
Bernhard Heiliger, 1915–1995: Monographie und Werkverzeichnis, ed. Marc Wellman (Berlin: Bernhard-Heiliger-Stiftung, 2005).
Beuys, Joseph, *"Zeige deine Wunde"* (Munich: Schellmann and Klüser, 1980).
Bezzola, Tobia, and Cornelia Homburg, eds., *Max Beckmann and Paris: Matisse, Picasso, Braque, Leger, Rouault* (St. Louis, MO: Saint Louis Art Museum, 1998).
Bilski, Emily, ed., *Berlin Metropolis: Jews and the New Culture, 1890–1918* (New York: The Jewish Museum, 1999).
Biro, Matthew, "Representation and Event: Anselm Kiefer, Joseph Beuys, and the Memory of the Holocaust," *Yale Journal of Criticism* 16, no. 1 (2003): 113–146.
———, *The Dada Cyborg: Visions of the New Human in Weimar Berlin* (Minneapolis and London: University of Minnesota Press, 2009).
Bleyl, Matthias, ed., *Joseph Beuys: Der erweiterte Kunstbegriff* (Darmstadt: Verlag der Georg Büchner Buchhandlung, 1989).
Bloom, Harold, *The Anxiety of Influence* (London, Oxford, and New York: Oxford University Press, 1973).
Boeck, Wilhelm, *Moderne deutsche Kunst* (Tübingen: Kunstgebäude, 1947).
Boehm, Gottfried, *Willi Baumeister* (Stuttgart: Hatje, 1995).
Bottomore, Stephen, *The Titanic and Silent Cinema* (Hastings: The Projection Box, 2000).
Brebeck, Wulff, et al., eds., *Zur Arbeit in Gedenkstätten für die Opfer des Nationalsozialismus—ein internationaler Überblick* (Berlin: Aktion Sühnezeichen/Friedensdienste, Friedrich-Ebert-Stiftung, 1988).
Breker, Arno, *Im Strahlungsfeld der Ereignisse: Leben und Wirken eines Künstlers; Porträts, Begegnungen, Schicksale* (Preussisch Oldendorf: Verlag K. W. Schütz KG, 1972).
———, *The Collected Writings* (Clarence, NY: West Art, 1990).
Brenner, Hildegard, *Die Kunstpolitik des Nationalsozialismus* (Reinbek: Rowohlt, 1963).
Bridenthal, Renata, Atina Grossmann, and Marion Kaplan, eds., *When Biology Became Destiny: Women in Weimar and Nazi Germany* (New York: Monthly Review Press, 1984).
Brink, Cornelia, *Auschwitz: Geschichte, Rezeption und Wirkung* (Frankfurt: Campus, 1996).
Brockhaus, Christoph, ed., *Wilhelm Lehmbruck Preis, 1966–1996* (Ostfildern-Ruit: Cantz, 1997).
Brülls, Holger, *Kein Kreuz: Das Büdericher Mahnmal für die Toten der Weltkriege von Joseph Beuys* (Meerbusch: Geschichtsverein Meerbusch e. V., 1995).

Bruns, Jörg-Heiko, *Willi Baumeister* (Dresden: Verlag der Kunst, 1991).
Buchloh, Benjamin, "Beuys: The Twilight of the Idol," *Artforum* 18, no. 5 (January 1980): 35–43.
———, "Gerhard Richter: 18. Oktober 1977," in *Gerhard Richter 18. Oktober 1977* (Cologne: Walter König, 1989), 55–59.
———, "A Note on Gerhard Richter's October 18, 1977," *October* 48 (Spring 1989): 89–109.
———, "Divided Memory and Post-Traditional Identity: Gerhard Richter's Work of Mourning," *October* 75 (Winter 1996): 61–82.
Buenger, Barbara Copeland, *Max Beckmann: Self-Portrait in Words* (Chicago and London: University of Chicago Press, 1997).
Bürger, Peter, *Theory of the Avant-Garde*, trans. Michael Shaw (Minneapolis: University of Minnesota Press, 1984); originally published in German in 1974.
Burmeister, Ralf, *Hannah Höch: Aller Anfang ist DADA!* (Berlin: Berlinische Galerie; Hatje Cantz Verlag, 2007).
Buskirk, Martha, *The Contingent Object of Contemporary Art* (Cambridge, MA: MIT Press, 2003).
Bussmann, Georg, ed., *Arbeit in Geschichte, Geschichte in Arbeit* (Kunsthaus Hamburg, Verlag Dirk Nisen, 1988).
Butin, Hubertus, *Zu Richters Oktober-Bildern* (Cologne: Walther König, 1991).
———, and Stefan Gronert, eds., *Gerhard Richter: Editionen 1965–2004* (Ostfildern-Ruit: Hatje Cantz Verlag, 2004).
Celan, Paul, *Gesammelte Werke in fünf Bänden*, vol. 4 (Frankfurt am Main: Suhrkamp, 1986).
Chametzky, Peter, "Marginal Comments, Oppositional Work: Willi Baumeister's Confrontation with Nazi Art," in *Willi Baumeister: Zeichnungen, Gouachen, Collagen* (Stuttgart: Edition Cantz, in association with Stuttgart Staatsgalerie, 1989), 251–272.
———, "Autonomy and Authority in German Twentieth-Century Art: The Art and Career of Willi Baumeister, 1889–1955," 2 vols., PhD thesis, City University of New York, 1991.
———, "Rolf Zimmermann's Poland Paintings: A German Inheritance," *The Massachusetts Review* 36, no. 3 (Autumn 1995): 378–411; revised version of essay in *Rolf Zimmermann* (Freiburg: Morat Institut für Kunst und Kunstwissenschaft, 1992).
———, "Witnessing Tragedy, Looking at Risk: Rolf Zimmermann Revisited," *The Massachusetts Review* 38, no. 4 (Winter 1997–98): 497–511.
———, "The Post History of Willi Baumeister's Anti-Nazi Postcards," in *Postcards from Albums to the Academy?* ed. Jordana Mendelson, special issue of *Visual Resources* 17, no. 4 (2001): 459–480.
———, "From Werkbund to Entartung: Willi Baumeister's 'Wall Pictures,'" in *The Built Surface*, vol. 2 of *Architecture and the Pictorial Arts from Romanticism to the Twenty-First Century*, ed. Karen Koehler (London: Ashgate Press, 2002).
———, "Process and Politics in the Art of Rolf Zimmermann," in *Rolf Zimmermann: Asylbewerber warten/Asylum Applicants Waiting: Bilder und Zeichnungen, 1992–2003* (Karlsruhe: Internationales Begegnunszentrum; Galerie Alfred Knecht, 2007).
———, and Anna Brzyski, eds., *Modernism and Nationalism, Postmodernism and Postnationalism*, special issue of *Centropa* 1, no. 3 (September 2001).
Chipp, Herschel, *Picasso's Guernica: History, Transformations, Meanings* (Berkeley and Los Angeles: University of California Press, 1988).
Clark, Toby, *Art and Propaganda in the Twentieth Century* (New York: Harry N. Abrams, 1997).
Cone, Michèlle C., *Artists Under Vichy: A Case of Prejudice and Persecution* (Princeton, NJ: Princeton University Press, 1992).
Crockett, Dennis, *German Post-Expressionism: The Art of the Great Disorder, 1918–1924* (University Park, PA: Pennsylvania State University Press, 1999).
Curtis, Penelope, ed., *Taking Positions: Figurative Sculpture and the Third Reich* (Leeds: Henry Moore Institute, 2002).
Däubler, Theodore, "George Grosz," *Das Kunstblatt* 3 (1917): 80–82.
———, "George Grosz," *Neue Blätter für Kunst und Dichtung* 1 (November 1918): 153–154.
Deak, Istvan, *Weimar Germany's Left-Wing Intellectuals: A Political History of the Weltbühne and Its Circle* (Berkeley and Los Angeles: University of California Press, 1968).
Dech, Gertrude Jula, *Schnitt mit dem Küchenmesser DADA durch die letzte Weimarer Bierbauchkulturepoche Deutschlands: Untersuchungen zur Fotomontage bei Hannah Höch* (Münster: Lit Verlag, 1981).
———, *Hannah Höch: "Schnitt mit dem Küchenmesser Dada"—Spiegel einer Bierbauchkultur* (Frankfurt am Main: Fischer Taschenbuch Verlag, 1989).

———, *Sieben Blicke auf Hannah Höch* (Hamburg: Edition Nautilus, 2002).
———, and Ellen Maurer, *Dada Zwischen Reden: Zu Hannah Höch* (Berlin: Orlando Frauenverlag, 1991).
DeLillo, Don, "Baader-Meinhof," *New Yorker* (1 April 2002): 78–82.
Derrida, Jacques, *The Postcard: From Socrates to Freud and Beyond*, trans. Alan Bass (Chicago and London: The University of Chicago Press, 1987); originally published in 1980 as *Le carte postale: De Socrate à Freud et au-delà*.
Dickermann, Leah, ed., *Dada: Zurich, Berlin, Hannover, Cologne, New York, Paris* (Washington, DC: National Gallery of Art; D. A. P./Distributed Art Publishers, Inc., 2005).
Dietrich, Dorothea, "Allegories of Power: Markus Lüpertz's 'German Motifs,'" *Art Journal* 48, no. 2 (Summer 1989): 164–170.
Dirks, Christian, and Hermann Simon, eds., *Relativ Jüdisch: Albert Einstein—Jude, Zionist, Nonkonformist* (Berlin: Test Verlag; Centrum Judaicum, 2005).
Doherty, Brigid, "See: *We Are All Neurasthenics!*" or, The Trauma of Dada Montage," *Critical Inquiry* 24, no. 1 (Autumn 1997), 82–132.
———, "The Work of Art and the Problem of Politics in Berlin Dada," *October* 105 (Summer 2003).
Döring, Thomas, and Christian Lenz, *Max Beckmann: Selbstbildnisse* (Munich: Bayerische Staatsgemäldesammlung Neue Pinakothek, 2000).
Eber, Franz, ed., *Die Neue Reichskanzlei, Architekt Albert Speer* (Munich: Zentralverwaltung der NSDAP, 1940).
Eberle, Matthias, *World War I and the Weimar Artists: Dix, Grosz, Beckmann, Schlemmer* (New Haven, CT, and London: Yale University Press, 1985).
Eckstein, Modris, *The Limits of Reason: The German Democratic Press and the Collapse of Weimar Democracy* (London: Oxford University Press, 1975).
Egret, Dominique, *Arno Breker: Ein Leben für das Schöne, Une Vie pour le Beau, A Life for the Beautiful* (Tübingen: Edition Grabert, 1996).
Elderfield, John, "'Dada': A Code for Saints," *Artforum* 12 (February 1974): 42–48.
Elgar, Dietmar, *Gerhard Richter: A Life in Painting*, trans. Elizabeth M. Solaro (Chicago and London: University of Chicago Press, 2010); originally published in German in 2002.
Elsaesser, Thomas, "Dada/Cinema?" in *Dada and Surrealist Film*, ed. Rudolf E. Kuenzli (New York: Willis, Locker, and Owens, 1987).
Engelhard, Ernst Günter, "Der Künstler Joseph Beuys: Ein grausames Wintermärchen," *Christ und Welt* 21, no. 1 (3 January 1969): 13.
Ermen, Reinhard, *Joseph Beuys* (Reinbek: Rowohlt, 2007).
Etlin, Richard, ed., *Art, Culture and Media Under the Third Reich* (Chicago and London: University of Chicago Press, 2002).
Ewen, Frederic, ed., *The Poetry and Prose of Heinrich Heine* (New York: Citadel Press, 1948).
Fabozzi, Paul F., *Artists, Critics, Contexts: Readings in and Around American Art Since 1945* (Upper Saddle River, NJ: Prentice Hall, 2002).
Federle, Courtney, "*Küchenmesser Dada:* Hannah Höch's Cut through the Field of Vision," *Qui Parle* 5, no. 2 (Spring/Summer 1992): 120–134.
Felleman, Susan, *Art in the Cinematic Imagination* (Austin: University of Texas Press, 2006).
Fenton, James, "Subversives," *New York Review of Books* 43, no. 1 (11 January 1996): 51–54.
Fer, Briony, "Objects Beyond Objecthood," in *Art of the Twentieth Century, A Reader*, ed. Jason Gaiger and Paul Wood (New Haven, CT, and London: Yale University Press, 2003), 274–286; originally published in *Oxford Art Journal* 22, no. 2 (1999): 25–36.
Fischer, Max, *Heinrich Heine der deutsche Jude* (Stuttgart and Berlin: Cotta, 1916).
Flavell, M. Kay, *George Grosz: A Biography* (New Haven, CT, and London: Yale University Press, 1988).
Forster-Hahn, Françoise, *Max Beckmann in Kalifornien: Exil, Erinnerung und Erneuerung* (Munich and Berlin: Deutscher Kunstverlag, 2007).
Foster, Hal, *The Return of the Real* (Cambridge, MA, and London: MIT Press, 1996).
———, Rosalind Krauss, Yve-Alain Bois, and Benjamin H. D. Buchloh, *Art Since 1900: Modernism, Antimodernism, Postmodernism* (New York: Thames and Hudson, 2004).
Fried, Michael, "Art and Objecthood," in *Minimal Art: A Critical Anthology*, ed. Gregory Battcock (New York: E. P. Dutton, 1968), 116–147; first published in *Artforum* (June 1967).
Friedlaender, Salomo, *Schöpferische Indifferenz* (Munich: Müller, 1918; 2nd ed., Munich: Ernst Reinhardt, 1926).
Fulbrook, Mary, *German National Identity after the Holocaust* (Cambridge: Polity Press, 1999).

Gaehtgens, Thomas, and Uwe Fleckner, eds., *Historienmalerei* (Berlin: Reimer, 1996).
Gaiger, Jason, and Paul Wood, eds., *Art of the Twentieth Century, A Reader* (New Haven, CT, and London: Yale University Press, 2003).
Gallwitz, Klaus, "Beckmann vor Beckmann," *Max Beckmann: Die frühen Bilder* (Frankfurt: Städtische Galerie im Städelschen Kunstinstitut, 1983), 148–151.
———, Franz Joseph van der Grinten, Hans van der Grinten, Werner Hofmann, and Werner Schade, eds., *Beuys vor Beuys: Frühe Arbeiten aus der Sammlung van der Grinten; Zeichnungen, Aquarelle, Ölstudien, Collagen* (Cologne: DuMont, 1987).
Gamboni, Dario, *The Destruction of Art: Iconoclasm and Vandalism since the French Revolution* (New Haven, CT, and London, Yale University Press, 1997).
———, "Image to Destroy, Indestructible Image," in *Iconoclash: Beyond the Image Wars in Science, Religion and Art*, ed. Bruno Latour and Peter Weibel (Cambridge, MA, and London: MIT Press, 2002), 88–135.
Gandelman, Claude, "Max Beckmann's Triptychs and the Simultaneous Stage of the 20s," *Art History* 1, no. 4 (December 1978): 472–483.
Gay, Peter, *Freud, Jews and Other Germans: Masters and Victims in Modernist Culture* (New York: Oxford University Press, 1978).
Gedenkbuch Berlins der jüdischen Opfer des Nationalsozialismus (Berlin: Edition Hentrich, in association with Zentralinstitut für Sozialwissenschaftliche Forschung, Freie Universität Berlin, 1995).
George, Waldemar, "La Peinture en Allemagne: Willy Baumeister," *L'Esprit Nouveau* 15 (1922): 1790–1794.
Gerhard Richter (Düsseldorf: Kunstsammlung Nordrhein-Westfalen, 2005).
Gerz, Jochen, *2146 Steine* (Stuttgart: Gerd Hatje, 1993).
Gieseke, Frank, and Albert Markert, *Flieger, Filz, und Vaterland: Eine erweiterte Beuys-Biografie* (Berlin: Elefanten Press, 1996).
Giesen, Rolf, *Nazi Propaganda Films: A History and Filmography* (Jefferson, NC, and London: McFarland and Co., 2003).
Gillen, Eckhart, ed., *German Art from Beckmann to Richter: Images of a Divided Country* (Berlin: Martin-Gropius-Bau; Cologne: DuMont, 1997).
———, ed., *Das Kunstkombinat DDR: Zäsuren einer gescheiterten Kunstpolitik* (Cologne: DuMont, 2005).
Gilman, Sander, *Difference and Pathology: Stereotypes of Sexuality, Race, and Madness* (Ithaca, NY, and London: Cornell University Press, 1985).
———, *The Jew's Body* (New York and London: Routledge, 1991).
———, *Freud, Race, and Gender* (Princeton, NJ: Princeton University Press, 1993).
———, *Love + Marriage = Death: And Other Essays on Representing Difference* (Stanford, CA: Stanford University Press, 1998).
———, *Jewish Frontiers: Essays on Bodies, Histories, and Identities* (New York: Palgrave Macmillan, 2003).
———, and Jack Zipes, eds., *Yale Companion to Jewish Writing and Thought in German Culture, 1096–1996* (New Haven, CT, and London: Yale Press, 1997).
Glaser, Curt, "Die XXVI. Ausstellung der Berliner Secession," *Die Kunst für Alle* 28, no. 20 (15 July 1913): 457–476.
———, Julius Meier-Gräfe, Wilhelm Fraenger, and Wilhelm Hausenstein, *Max Beckmann* (Munich: R. Piper, 1924).
Glozer, Laszlo, "Beuys in New York: Das Guggenheim-Museum zeigt sein Werk in 24 Stationen," *Süddeutsche Zeitung*, 3–4 November 1979.
Goldstein, Ann, and Lisa Gabriel Mark, eds., *A Minimal Future: Art as Object, 1958–1968* (Cambridge, MA, and London: MIT Press, 2004).
Göpel, Erhard, *Max Beckmann: Berichte eines Augenzeuge* (Frankfurt am Main: Fischer Taschenbuch, 1984).
———, and Barbara Göpel, *Max Beckmann: Katalog der Gemälde*, vol. 1 (Bern: Verlag Kornfeld, 1976).
Grasskamp, Walter, *Die unbewältigte Moderne: Kunst und Öffentlichkeit* (Munich: Beck, 1989).
Green, David, and Peter Seddon, eds., *History Painting Reassessed: The Representation of History in Contemporary Art* (Manchester, UK, and New York: Manchester University Press, 2000).
Greenberg, Clement, *Art and Culture* (Boston: Beacon Press, 1961).
———, *Clement Greenberg: The Collected Essays and Criticism*, vol. 2, *Arrogant Purpose, 1945–1949*, ed. John O'Brian (Chicago and London: University of Chicago Press, 1986).
Greenblatt, Stephen, "Resonance and Wonder," in *Exhibiting Cultures: The Poetics and Politics of Mu-*

seum Display, ed. Ivan Karp and Steven Lavine (Washington DC and London: Smithsonian Institution Press, 1992), 42–55.

Grohmann, Will, *Willi Baumeister* (Stuttgart: Kohlhammer, 1952).

———, *Willi Baumeister: Life and Work*, trans. Robert Allen (New York: Harry N. Abrams, 1965); originally published in German in 1963.

Grosz, George, *George Grosz: An Autobiography*, trans. Nora Hodges (New York: MacMillan, 1983); originally published in English (from a German text) as *A Little Yes and a Big No: The Autobiography of George Grosz* (New York: Dial Press, 1946) and subsequently published in an expanded German version as *Ein kleines Ja und ein grosses Nein* in 1955.

Haddow, Robert H., *Pavilions of Plenty: Exhibiting American Culture Abroad in the 1950s* (Washington, DC, and London: Smithsonian Institution Press, 1997).

Haftmann, Werner, *Skizzenbuch zur Kultur der Gegenwart* (Munich: Piper, 1960).

———, *Verfemte Kunst: Bildende Künstler der inneren und äusseren Emigration in der Zeit des Nationalsozialismus* (Cologne: DuMont, 1986).

Hager, Werner, "Der Bildhauer Arno Breker," *Die Kunst für Alle* 54, no. 1 (1938): 18–25.

Hake, Sabine, *Popular Cinema of the Third Reich* (Austin: University of Texas Press, 2001).

Hallensleben, Markus, *Else Lasker-Schüler: Avantgardismus und Kunstinszenierung* (Tübingen and Basel: Francke Verlag, 2000).

Hannah Höch: Collages, Peintres Aquarelles, Gouaches, Dessins/Collagen, Gemälde, Aquarelle, Gouachen, Zeichnungen (Paris: Musée d'Art Moderne de la ville de Paris; Berlin: Nationalgalerie Berlin, Staatliche Museen Preußischer Kulturbesitz, 1976).

Hannah Höch: Eine Lebenscollage, vol. 1, part 1 (1889–1918) and part 2 (1919–20), ed. Cornelia Thater-Schulz (Berlin: Berlinische Galerie; Argon, 1989).

Hannah Höch: Eine Lebenscollage, vol. 2, part 1 (1921–45) and part 2, *Documents*, ed. Ralf Burmeister and Eckhard Fürlius (Berlin: Berlinische Galerie; Hatje, 1995).

Hannah Höch: Eine Lebenscollage, vol. 3 (1946–78), part 1, interpretive texts, ed. Ralf Burmeister and Karin Hoerstel, and part 2, catalogue of archival holdings, ed. Ralf Burmeister, with Eckhard Fürlius and Karin Hoerstel (Berlin: Berlinische Galerie Landesmuseum, 2001).

Hansen, Miriam, "Early Silent Cinema: Whose Public Sphere?" *New German Critique* 29 (Spring/Summer 1983): 147–184.

———, "America, Paris, the Alps: Kracauer (and Benjamin) on Cinema and Modernity," in *Cinema and the Invention of Modern Life*, ed. Leo Charney and Vanessa R. Schwartz (Berkeley, Los Angeles, and London: University of California Press, 1995).

———, "*Schindler's List* Is Not *Shoah*: Second Commandment, Popular Modernism, and Public Memory," in *Visual Culture and the Holocaust*, ed. Barbie Zelizer (New Brunswick, NJ: Rutgers University Press, 2001).

Harrison, Charles, and Fred Orton, eds., *Modernism, Criticism, Realism* (New York: Harper and Row, 1984).

———, and Paul Wood, eds., *Art in Theory 1900–1990: An Anthology of Changing Ideas* (Malden, MA: Blackwell, 1993; rev. ed., 2003, as *Art in Theory 1900–2000*).

Haxthausen, Charles, "Beckmann and the First World War," *Max Beckmann Retrospective*, ed. Carla Schulz-Hoffmann and Judith C. Weiss (St. Louis: Saint Louis Art Museum; Munich: Prestel Verlag, 1984), 73–74.

———, "Modern German Masterpieces," *Saint Louis Art Museum Bulletin* (Winter 1985): 6.

Hedinger, Bärbel, ed., *Die Künstlerpostkarte* (Munich: Prestel Verlag, in association with Altonaer Museum, Hamburg; Frankfurt am Main: Deutsches Postalmuseum, 1992).

Heilbut, Anthony, *Exiled in Paradise: German Refugee Artists and Intellectuals in America from the 1930s to the Present* (Berkeley, Los Angeles, and London: University of California Press, 1983).

Heissenbüttel, Helmut, ed., *Stuttgarter Kunst im 20. Jahrhundert* (Stuttgart: Deutsche-Verlags-Anstalt, 1979).

Helberg, Frank, *Walter Mehring: Schriftsteller zwischen Kabarett und Avantgarde* (Bonn: Bouvier, 1983).

Held, Jutta, *Kunst und Kunstpolitik in Deutschland, 1945–49* (Berlin: Elefanten Press, 1981).

Heller, Reinhold, ed., *Confronting Identities in German Art: Myths, Reactions, Reflections* (Chicago: David and Alfred Smard Museum of Art; University of Chicago Press, 2003).

Hemken, Kai-Uwe, *Gerhard Richter: 18. Oktober 1977* (Frankfurt am Main: Insel, 1998).

Hensbergen, Gijs van, *Guernica: The Biography of a*

Twentieth-Century Icon (London: Bloomsbury, 2004).
Herbert, Robert, ed., *Modern Artists on Art* (Englewood Cliffs, NJ: Prentice Hall, 1964).
Herberts, Kurt, *Modulation und Patina: Ein Dokument aus dem Wuppertaler Arbeitskreis um Willi Baumeister, Oskar Schlemmer, Franz Krause, 1937–1944* (Stuttgart: G. Hatje, 1989).
Herding, Klaus, "Humanismus und Primitivismus: Probleme früher Nachkriegskunst in Deutschland," *Jahrbuch des Zentralinstitut für Kunstgeschichte* 4 (1988): 282–310.
Herzfelde, Wieland, *Sulamith* (Berlin: Heinz Barger Verlag, 1917). Facsimile edition, Leipzig: Zentralantiquariat der DDR, 1983.
———, *Zur Sache: Geschrieben und gesprochen zwischen 18 und 80* (Berlin: Aufbau Verlag, 1976).
———, *John Heartfield: Leben und Werk* (Berlin: Verlag das Europäische Buch, 1986).
———, *Immergrün: Merkwürdige Erlebnisse und Erfahrungen eines fröhlichen Waisenknaben* (Berlin and Weimar: Aufbau Taschenbuch Verlag, 1996).
Hess, Hans, *George Grosz* (New York: Macmillan, 1974; New Haven, CT: Yale University Press, 1985).
Hinz, Berthold, *Die Malerei im deutschen Faschismus: Kunst und Konterrevolution* (Munich: Carl Hanser, 1974).
———, *Art in the Third Reich* (New York: Pantheon, 1979).
Hirsch, Joshua, *After Image: Film, Trauma, and the Holocaust* (Philadelphia, PA: Temple University Press, 2004).
Hixson, Walter, *Parting the Curtain: Propaganda, Culture, and the Cold War, 1945–1961* (New York: St. Martin's Press, 1997).
Hoffmann, Detlef, "Das Gelände der Konzentrationslager Dachau, 1945–1955, *Trierer Beiträge* (June 1996): 33–41.
———, ed., *Das Gedächtnis der Dinge: KZ-Relikte udn KZ-Denkmäler, 1945–1995* (Frankfurt and New York: Campus, 1998).
Hoffmann-Curtius, Kathrin, "Die Kampagne 'Entartete Kunst': Die Nationalsozialisten und die Moderne Kunst," in *Funk Kolleg Moderne Kunst*, Studienbegleitbrief 9 (Weinheim and Basel: Beltz, 1990).
———, "Memorials for the Dachau Concentration Camp" *Oxford Art Journal* 21, no. 2 (1998): 21–44.
Holz, Keith, *Modern German Art for Thirties Paris, Prague, and London* (Ann Arbor: University of Michigan Press, 2004).
———, and Wolfgang Schopf, *Im Auge des Exils: Josef Breitenbach und die freie deutsche Kultur in Paris, 1933–1941* (Berlin: Aufbau-Verlag, 2001).
Horak, Jan-Chistopher, *Anti-Nazi-Filme der deutschsprachigen Emigration von Hollywood 1939–1945* (Münster: Maks Publikationen, 1984).
Huelsenbeck, Richard, ed., *Dada Almanach* (Berlin: Erich Reiss Verlag, 1920).
Hutton, Patrick H., *History as an Art of Memory* (Hanover, VT, and London: University Press of New England, 1993).
Huyssen, Andreas, *After the Great Divide: Modernism, Mass Culture, Postmodernism* (Bloomington: Indiana University Press, 1986).
———, *Twilight Memories: Marking Time in the Culture of Amnesia* (New York and London: Routledge, 1995).
Inszenierung der Macht: Ästhetische Faszination im Faschismus (Berlin: Neue Gesellschaft für Bildende Kunst, 1987).
Janecek, Gerald, ed., *The Eastern Dada Orbit: Russia, Georgia, Ukraine, Central Europe and Japan,* vol. 4 of *Crisis and the Arts: The History of Dada,* ed. Stephen C. Foster (New York: G. K. Hall, 1998).
Jaskot, Paul, "Anti-Semitic Policy in Albert Speer's Plans for the Rebuilding of Berlin," *Art Bulletin* 78, no. 4 (December 1996): 622–632.
———, "Gerhard Richter and Adolf Eichmann," *Oxford Art Journal* 28, no. 3 (2005): 457–478.
Jelavich, Peter, *Berlin Cabaret* (Cambridge, MA, and London: Harvard University Press, 1993).
Jentsch, Ralph, *George Grosz: The Berlin Years* (Milan: Electa, 1997).
———, *George Grosz: Berlin—New York* (Milan: Skira, 2008).
Joachimides, Christos, et al., *German Art in the 20th Century* (Munich and London: Prestel Verlag, 1985).
Joseph Beuys: Kleine Zeichnungen aus dem Bestand der Stiftung Museum Schloss Moyland (Kranenburg: Museum Schloss Moyland, 1995).
Joseph Beuys: Die Materialien und ihre Botschaft (Bedburg-Hau: Stiftung Museum Schloss Moyland, 2006).
Julius, Anthony, *Transgressions: The Offences of Art* (London: Thames and Hudson, 2002).
Junger, Detlef, ed., *Die USA und Deutschland im Zeitalter des Kalten Krieges, 1945–1990*, vol. 1, 1945–

1968 (Stuttgart and Munich: Deutsche Verlags-Anstalt, 2001).

Kaes, Anton, "Mass Culture and Modernity: Notes Towards a Social History of Early American and German Cinema," in *America and the Germans: An Assessment of a Three-Hundred-Year History*, vol. 2, *The Relationship in the Twentieth Century*, ed. Frank Trommler and Joseph McVeigh (Philadelphia: University of Pennsylvania Press, 1985), 317–331.

———, "The Debate about Cinema: Charting a Controversy (1909–1929)," *New German Critique* 40 (Winter 1987): 7–33.

———, "History and Film: Public Memory in the Age of Electronic Dissemination," in *Framing the Past: The Historiography of German Cinema and Television*, ed. Bruce A, Murray and Christopher Wickham (Carbondale and Edwardsville: Southern Illinois University Press, 1992).

———, Martin Jay, and Edward Dimendberg, eds., *The Weimar Republic Sourcebook* (Berkeley, Los Angeles, and London: University of California Press, 1994).

Kainen, Jacob, "Art: 'Departure' Proves an Exciting and Revolutionary Painting," *Daily Worker* (15 January 1938): 7.

Kansteiner, Wulf, *In Pursuit of German Memory: Television and Politics after Auschwitz* (Athens: Ohio University Press, 2006).

Kemp, Wolfgang, "The Work of Art and Its Beholder: The Methodology of the Aesthetic of Reception," *The Subjects of Art History: Historical Objects in Contemporary Perspectives*, ed. Mark A. Cheetham, Michael Ann Holly, and Keith Moxey (New York and Cambridge: Cambridge University Press, 1998).

Kermer, Wolfgang, *Willi Baumeister: Typographie und Reklamegestaltung* (Stuttgart: Staatliche Akademie der Bildende Künste; Edition Cantz, 1989).

Kessler, Charles, "Max Beckmann's *Departure*," *Journal of Aesthetics and Art Criticism* (December 1955): 206–217.

———, *Max Beckmann's Triptychs* (Cambridge, MA: Harvard University Press, 1970).

Klonk, Charlotte, "Patterns of Attention: From Shop Windows to Gallery Rooms in Early Twentieth-Century Berlin," *Art History* 28, no. 4 (September 2005): 468–496.

Knaap, Ewout, van der, ed., *Uncovering the Holocaust: The International Reception of Night and Fog* (London and New York: Wallflower Press, 2006).

Knoch, Habbo, *Die Tat als Bild: Fotografien des Holocaust in der deutschen Erinnerungskultur* (Hamburg: Hamburger Edition, 2001).

Knust, Herbert, ed., *George Grosz, Briefe, 1913–1959* (Reinbek: Rowohlt, 1979).

Koch, Gertrud, "On the Richter-Scale of Blur," *October* 62 (Autumn 1992): 122–142.

Koepnick, Lutz, "Fascist Aesthetics Revisited," *Modernism/Modernity* 6, no. 1 (1999): 51–73.

———, *The Dark Mirror: German Cinema between Hitler and Hollywood* (Berkeley, Los Angeles, and London: University of California Press, 2002).

Kort, Pamela, and Max Hollein, *Rodin/Beuys* (Frankfurt: Schirn Kunsthalle, 2005).

Koss, Juliet, "Coming to Terms with the Present," *Grey Room* 16 (Summer 2004): 116–131.

———, "On the Limits of Empathy," *The Art Bulletin* 88, no. 1 (March 2006): 139–157.

Köster, Werner, and Thomas Lischeid, eds., *Titanic: Ein Medienmythos* (Leipzig: Reclam, 1999).

Kotowski, Elke-Vera, ed., *Juden in Berlin: Biografien* (Berlin: Henschell, 2005).

Kotte, Wouter, and Ursula Milduer, *Das Kreuz als Universalzeichen bei Joseph Beuys: Ein Requiem* (Stuttgart: Urachhaus, 1986).

Kramer, Hilton, "MoMA Helps Martyrdom of German Terrorists," *New York Observer*, 3 July 1995.

Kramer, Marie, "Joseph Beuys: Auschwitz Demonstration, 1956–1964," in *German Art from Beckmann to Richter: Images of a Divided Country*, ed. Eckhart Gillen (Berlin: Martin-Gropius-Bau; Cologne: DuMont, 1997).

Kramer, Sven, ed., *Die Shoah im Bild* (Munich: Edition text + kritik, 2003).

Krauss, Rosalind E., *Passages in Modern Sculpture* (Cambridge and London: MIT Press, 1977).

———, *The Originality of the Avant-Garde and Other Modernist Myths* (Cambridge, MA, and London: MIT Press, 1985).

Kreuz + Zeichen: Religiöse Grundlagen im Werk von Joseph Beuys (Aachen: Seermondt-Ludwig-Museum und Kunstverein, 1985).

Kuhlmann, Christiane, *Bewegte Körper—Mechanischer Apparat: Zur medialen Verschränkung von Tanz und Fotografie in den 1920er Jahren an den Beispielen von Charlotte Rudolph, Suse Byk und Lotte Jacobi* (Frankfurt am Main: Peter Lang, 2003).

Kuoni, Carin, ed., *Energy Plan for the Western Man: Joseph Beuys in America* (New York: Four Walls Eight Windows, 1990).

Kuspit, Donald, *Signs of Psyche in Modern and Postmodern Art* (Cambridge, UK, and New York: Cambridge University Press, 1993).

Ladd, Brian, *The Companion Guide to Berlin* (London: The Companion Guides, 2004).

Lane, Barbara Miller, *Architecture and Politics in Germany, 1918–1945* (Cambridge, MA, and London: Harvard University Press, 1968).

Langston, Richard, "The Art of Barbarism and Suffering," in *Art of Two Germanys/Cold War Cultures*, ed. Stephanie Barron and Sabine Eckmann (New York: Harry N. Abrams, in association with Los Angeles County Museum of Art, 2009).

Lavin, Maud, *Cut with the Kitchen Knife: The Weimar Photomontages of Hannah Höch* (New Haven, CT, and London: Yale University Press, 1993).

Lehmann-Haupt, Helmut, *Art Under a Dictatorship* (1954; repr. New York: Octagon, 1973).

Leja, Michael, *Reframing Abstract Expressionism: Subjectivity and Painting in the 1940s* (New Haven, CT, and London: Yale University Press, 1993).

Leslie, Esther, "Philistines and Art Vandals Get Upset," in *The Philistine Controversy*, ed. Dave Beech and John Roberts (London: Verso, 2002), 201–227.

———, *Synthetic Worlds: Nature, Art and the Chemical Industry* (London: Reaktion Books, 2005).

Leve, Manfred, *Leve Sieht Beuys: Block Beuys—Fotografen* (Göttingen: Steidl, 2004).

Levin, Kim, *Beyond Modernism: Essays on Art from the 70s and 80s* (New York: Harper and Row, 1988).

Lewis, Beth Irwin, *George Grosz: Art and Politics in the Weimar Republic* (Princeton, NJ: Princeton University Press, 1991; first published 1971 by University of Wisconsin Press).

———, *Art for All? The Collision of Modern Art and the Public in Late-Nineteenth Century Germany* (Princeton, NJ, and Oxford: Princeton University Press, 2003).

Lichtenstein, Therese, *Behind Closed Doors: The Art of Hans Bellmer* (Berkeley, Los Angeles, and London: University of California Press, 2001).

Lindner, Ines, et al., eds., *Blick-wechsel, Konstruktionen von Männlichkeit und Weiblichkeit in Kunst und Kunstgeschichte* (Berlin: Reimer, 1989).

Long, Rose-Carol Washton, ed., *German Expressionism: Documents from the End of the Wilhelmine Empire to the Rise of National Socialism* (Berkeley and Los Angeles: University of California Press, 1995).

———, and Maria Makela, eds., *Of 'Truths Impossible to Put in Words': Max Beckmann Contextualized* (Bern: Peter Lang, 2009).

Lorenz, Inge, ed., *Joseph Beuys Symposium Kranenburg 1995* (Bedburg-Hau: Stiftung Museum Schloss Moyland; Basel: Wiesel Verlag, 1996).

Luckow, Dirk, *Joseph Beuys und die amerikanische Anti Form-Kunst: Einfluß und Wechselwirkung zwischen Beuys und Morris, Hesse, Nauman, Serra* (Berlin: Gebr. Mann, 1998).

Mackenzie, Michael, "*Maschinenmenschen:* Images of Man as a Machine in Weimar Germany," PhD thesis, University of Chicago, 1999.

Makela, Maria, "By Design: The Early Work of Hannah Höch in Context," in Makela and Boswell, *The Photomontages of Hannah Höch* (Minneapolis: Walker Art Center, 1996).

———, "Dadadame und Urfeministen: Die Hannah-Höch Rezeption in den USA," in *Hannah Höch: Eine Lebenscollage*, vol. 3 (Berlin: Berlinisches Galerie Landesmuseum, 2001), part 1, 198–247.

———, " 'A Clear and Simple Style': Tradition and Typology in New Objectivity," in *Negotiating History: German Art and the Past*, ed. Jay A. Clarke, special issue of *Museum Studies* (Art Institute of Chicago) 28, no. 1 (2002): 39–51.

———, and Peter Boswell, *The Photomontages of Hannah Höch* (Minneapolis: Walker Art Center, 1996).

Mansbach, S. A., *Modern Art in Eastern Europe: From the Baltic to the Balkans, ca. 1890–1939* (Cambridge and New York: Cambridge University Press, 1999).

Marcuse, Harold, *Legacies of Dachau: The Uses and Abuses of a Concentration Camp, 1933–2001* (Cambridge, UK, and New York: Cambridge University Press, 2001).

Maurer, Ellen, *Hannah Höch: Jenseits fester Grenzen: Das malerische Werk bis 1945* (Berlin: Gebr. Mann, 1995).

Maus, Derek, ed., *The Cold War* (Farmington Hills, MI: Greenhaven Press, 2003).

Max Beckmann in Exile (New York: Guggenheim Museum in Soho; Abrams, 1996).

McCloskey, Barbara, *George Grosz and the Communist Party: Art and Radicalism in Crisis, 1918–1933* (Princeton, NJ: Princeton University Press, 1997).

———, foreword to *George Grosz: An Autobiography*, trans. Nora Hodges (Berkeley and London: University of California Press, 1998).

Mehring, Walter, *Berlin Dada: Eine Chronik mit Photos und Dokumentation* (Zürich: Arche, 1959).
———, *Verrufene Malerei, Berlin Dada: Erinnerungen eines Zeitgenossen und 14 Essais zur Kunst* (Düsseldorf: Classen, 1983).
Mendelson, Jordana, ed., *Postcards from Albums to the Academy?* special issue of *Visual Resources* 17, no. 4 (2001).
Mennekes, Friedhelm, *Beuys zu Christus: Eine Position im Gespräch/Beuys on Christ: A Position in Dialogue* (Stuttgart: Verlag Katholisches Bibelwerk, 1989).
———, "Memoria im Trafo-Turm, über das Büdericher Mahnmal (1958) von Joseph Beuys," *Stimmen der Zeit* 5 (April 2005): 257–273.
Mesch, Claudia, and Viola Michely, eds., *Joseph Beuys: The Reader* (Cambridge, MA: MIT Press, 2007).
Meskimmon, Marsha, *We Weren't Modern Enough: Woman Artists and the Limits of Weimar Modernism* (Berkeley and Los Angeles: University of California Press, 1999).
Meyer, Ursula, "Explain Pictures to a Dead Hare," *Art News* 68, no. 9 (January 1970): 54–57, 71.
Michaud, Éric, "The Ends of Art According to Beuys," trans. Rosalind Krauss, *October* 45 (1988): 37–46.
———, *Un Art de L'Eternité: L'image et le temps du national-socialisme* (Paris: Gallimard, 1996).
Middleton, Christopher, *Bolshevism in Art, and Other Expository Writings* (Manchester: Carcanet New Press, 1978).
Middleton, J. C., "Dada versus Expressionism, or The Red King's Dream," *German Life and Letters* 15, no. 1 (October 1961): 37–52.
Minturn, Kent, "*Peinture Noir:* Abstract Expressionism and Film Noir," in *Film Noir Reader,* vol. 2, ed. Alain Silver and James Ursini (New York: Limelight Editions, 1999), 271–309.
Morris, Warren, *The Weimar Republic and Nazi Germany* (Chicago: Nelson-Hall, 1982).
Mosse, George L., *Nationalism and Sexuality: Respectability and Abnormal Sexuality in Modern Europe* (New York: Howard Fertig, 1985).
———, *Fallen Soldiers: Reshaping the Memory of the World Wars* (New York and Oxford: Oxford University Press, 1990).
Mynona [Salomo Friedlaender], *George Grosz* (Dresden: Kammerer, 1922).
———, *Graue Magie: Ein Berliner Nachschlüsselroman,* Berliner Texte 5, ed. Detlef Bluhm (Berlin: Fannei and Walz, 1989); reprint of Mynona, *Graue Magie: Ein Zukunftsroman* (Dresden: Rudolf Kaemmerer, 1922).
Naumann, Francis, *Marcel Duchamp: The Art of Making Art in the Age of Mechanical Reproduction* (Ghent: Ludion Press; Amsterdam: Harry N. Abrams, 1999).
Nemeczek, Alfred, "Joseph Beuys: Irrweg ins Grüne?" *Art* (2 February 1983): 67–77.
Neuer Berliner Kunstverein, *Metamorphose des Dinges: Kunst und Antikunst 1910–1970* (Brussels: Palais des beaux-arts, 1971).
Neugebauer, Rosamunde, *George Grosz, Macht und Ohnmacht satirischer Kunst: Die Graphikfolgen "Gott mit Uns," Ecce Homo und Hintergrund* (Berlin: Gebr. Mann, 1993).
Nisbet, Peter, ed., *The Sketchbooks of George Grosz,* with a catalogue of the sketchbooks by Catherina Lauer (Cambridge, MA: Harvard University Art Museum, Busch-Reisinger Museum, 1993).
Niven, Bill, *Facing the Nazi Past: United Germany and the Legacy of the Third Reich* (London and New York: Routledge, 2002).
Nochlin, Linda, *Realism* (Harmondsworth: Penguin, 1971).
———, and Tamar Garb, eds., *The Jew in the Text: Modernity and the Construction of Identity* (London: Thames and Hudson, 1995).
Nolan, Mary, "Germans as Victims during the Second World War: Air Wars, Memory Wars," *Central European History* 38, no. 1 (March 2005): 7–40.
Nora, Pierre, "Between Memory and History: *Les Lieux de Mémoire,*" *Representations* 26 (Spring 1989): 7–25.
Nordau, Max, *Degeneration* (Lincoln and London: University of Nebraska Press, 1993).
NS-Kunst: 50 Jahre danach: Neue Beiträge (Marburg: Jonas, 1989).
Ohff, Heinz, *Hannah Höch* (Berlin: Deutsche Gesellschaft für Bildende Kunst; Gebr. Mann, 1968).
Otto, Eugen, ed., *Emil Orlik: Leben und Werk; 1870–1932; Prag—Wien—Berlin* (Vienna and Munich: Christian Brandstätter, 1997).
Panofsky, Erwin, "Style and Medium in the Motion Pictures," in *The Visual Turn: Classical Film Theory and Art History,* ed. Angela dalle Vacche (New Brunswick, NJ, and London: Rutgers University Press, 2003), 69–84.
Paret, Peter, *The Berlin Secession: Modernism and Its Enemies in Imperial Germany* (Cambridge, MA: Harvard University Press, 1980).

———, *German Encounters with Modernism, 1840–1945* (New York and Cambridge: Cambridge University Press, 2001).
Pellegrini, Ann, *Performance Anxieties: Staging Psychoanalysis, Staging Race* (New York: Routledge, 1997).
Perry, Gill, and Paul Wood, eds., *Themes in Contemporary Art* (New Haven, CT, and London: Yale University Press, 2004).
Peters, Olaf, *Vom schwarzen Seiltänzer: Max Beckmann zwischen Weimarer Republik und Exil* (Berlin: Dietrich Reimer, 2005).
Petro, Patrice, *Joyless Streets: Women and Melodramatic Representation in Weimar Germany* (Princeton, NJ: Princeton University Press, 1989).
Petropoulos, Jonathan, *Art as Politics in the Third Reich* (Chapel Hill and London: University of North Carolina Press, 1996).
———, *The Faustian Bargain: The Art World in Nazi Germany* (New York: Oxford University Press, 2000).
Peucker, Brigitte, *Incorporating Images: Film and the Rival Arts* (Princeton, NJ: Princeton University Press, 1995).
Pickford, Henry, "Conflict and Commemoration: Two Berlin Memorials," *Modernism/Modernity* 12, no. 1 (January 2005): 133–177.
Pollock, Griselda, and Vanessa Corby, eds., *Encountering Eva Hesse* (Munich, Berlin, London, and New York: Prestel Verlag, 2006).
Probst, Volker, *Der Bildhauer Arno Breker: Eine Untersuchung* (Bonn: Marco, 1978).
Proctor, Robert, *The Nazi War on Cancer* (Princeton, NJ: Princeton University Press, 1999).
Prosser, Jay, *Second Skins: The Body Narratives of Transsexuality* (New York: Columbia University Press, 1998).
Raab, Josef, ed., *Das 20. Jahrhundert: Nachkriegszeit* (Regensburg: Verlag Friedrich Pustet, 1998).
Rabinbach, Anson, *In the Shadow of Catastrophe: German Intellectuals between Apocalypse and Enlightenment* (Berkeley, Los Angeles, and London: University of California Press, 1997).
Rainbird, Sean, ed., *Max Beckmann* (New York: Museum of Modern Art, 2003).
Rauterberg, Hanno, "Avantgarde des Spektakels: Die Ausstellung 'Das MoMA' in Berlin soll alle Rekorde brechen—auf Kosten der Kunst," *Die Zeit,* 2 December 2004; available online at www.zeit.de/2004/08/MoMA (viewed 31 December 2009).
Ray, Gene, ed., *Joseph Beuys: Mapping the Legacy* (Sarasota, FL: John and Mable Ringling Museum of Art, 2001).
———, *Terror and the Sublime in Art and Critical Theory: From Auschwitz to Hiroshima to September 11* (New York: Palgrave Macmillan, 2005).
Reich-Ranicki, Marcel, *Mein Leben* (Munich: DTV, 2000).
Reichel, Peter, *Der schöne Schein des Dritten Reichs: Faszination und Gewalt des Faschismus* (Frankfurt: Fischer Taschenbuch Verlag, 1993).
———, *Vergangenheitsbewältigung in Deutschland: Die Auseinandersetzung mit der NS-Diktatur von 1945 bis Heute* (Munich: Beck, 2001).
Reimer, Robert C., and Carol J. Reimer, *Nazi-retro Film: How German Narrative Cinema Remembers the Past* (New York: Twayne, 1992).
Rentschler, Eric, ed., *German Film: Adaptations and Transformations* (New York: Methuen, 1986).
Reynolds, Ann, "Reproducing Nature: The Museum of Natural History as Nonsite," *October* 45 (Summer 1988): 109–127.
Richter, Gerhard, [Gerd Richter], "Auseinandersetzungen halfen mir weiter," *Sonntag* 16, 20 April 1958.
———, *The Daily Practice of Painting: Writings and Interviews 1962–1993* (London: Anthony d'Offay Gallery; Cambridge, MA: MIT Press, 1995).
———, *Atlas: The Reader* (London: Whitechapel Gallery, 2003).
Richter, Hans, *DADA: Art and Anti-Art,* trans. David Britt (London: Thames and Hudson, 1997); originally published in German in 1964.
Riha, Karl, and Hanne Bergius, *Dada Berlin: Texte, Manifeste, Aktionen* (Stuttgart: Reclam, 1977).
Röder, Andreas, *Rodin und Beuys: Über das plastische Phänomen der Linie* (Munich and Berlin: Deutsche Kunstverlag, 2003).
Roditi, Edouard, "Hannah Höch und die Berliner Dadaisten: Ein Gespräch mit der Malerin," *Der Monat* 12, no. 134 (November 1959): 60–68.
Rogoff, Irit, ed., *The Divided Heritage: Themes and Problems in German Modernism* (London: Royal Academy of Arts; Cambridge, UK: Cambridge University Press, 1990).
Rosenthal, Mark *Joseph Beuys: Actions, Vitrines, Environments* (Houston: Menil Collection, 2004).
Roters, Eberhard, "Hintergrundanalyse der Collage 'Schnitt mit dem Küchenmesser' (1920) von Hannah Höch," in *Prinzip Collage,* ed. Franz

Mon and Heinz Heidel (Neuweid and Bremen: Hermann Luchterhand, 1968), 42–44.
———, *Fabricatio nihili, oder Die Herstellung von Nichts: Dada Meditation* (Berlin: Argon, 1990).
Saltzman, Lisa, "Gerhard Richter's *Stations of the Cross:* On Martyrdom and Memory in Postwar German Art," *Oxford Art Journal* 28, no. 1 (2005): 25–44.
Sandquist, Tom, *Dada East: The Romanians of Cabaret Voltaire* (Cambridge, MA, and London: MIT Press, 2005).
Schädeke, Jürgen, and Peter Steinbach, eds., *Der Widerstand gegen den Nationalsozialismus* (Munich: Piper, 1985).
Schäfer, Jörgen, *Exquisite Dada: A Comprehensive Bibliography,* vol. 10 of *Crisis and the Arts: The History of Dada,* ed. Stephen C. Foster (Detroit and New York: G. K. Hall, 2005).
Schaschke, Bettina, *Dadaistische Verwandlungskunst: Zum Verhältnis von Kritik und Selbstbehauptung in DADA Berlin und Köln* (Berlin: Gebr. Mann, 2004).
Schatz, Thomas, *Hollywood Genres* (New York: Random House, 1981).
———, *The Genius of the System: Hollywood Filmmaking in the Studio Era* (New York: Pantheon, 1988).
———, *Boom and Bust: The American Cinema in the 1940s,* History of American Cinema 6 (New York: Charles Scribner's Sons, 1997).
Scheffler, Karl, "Max Beckmann," *Kunst und Künstler* 11, no. 2 (March 1913): 297–305.
Schieder, Martin, *Im Blick des Anderen: Die deutsch-französischen Kunstbeziehungen, 1945–1959* (Berlin: Akademie Verlag, 2005).
Schirmbeck, Peter, *Adel der Arbeit: Der Arbeiter in der Kunst der NS-Zeit* (Marburg: Jonas Verlag, 1984).
Schirmer, Lothar, ed., *Joseph Beuys: Eine Werkübersicht, Zeichnungen und Aquarelle, Drucksachen und Multiple, Skulpturen und Objekte, Räume und Aktionen, 1945–1985* (Munich: Schirmer; Mosel, 1996); subsequently published in English as Alain Borer, *The Essential Joseph Beuys,* ed. Lothar Schirmer, German trans. Anne Heritage, and with French introduction by Alain Borer, trans. Elaine Briggs (Cambridge, MA: MIT Press, 1997).
Schlemmer, Baumeister, Krause, Wuppertal 1937–1944 (Wuppertal: von der Heydt Museum, 1979).
Schlenker, Ines, *Hitler's Salon: The Grosse Deutsche Kunstausstellung at the Haus der Deutschen Kunst in Munich 1937–1944* (New York and Vienna: Peter Lang, 2008).
Schmidt, E., "Verkaufte Katharsis," *Die Zeit,* 23 June 1995.
Schneede, Uwe, *George Grosz: His Life and Work* (London: G. Fraser, 1979).
Scholem, Gerschom, *Von Berlin nach Jerusalem: Jugenderinnerungen* (Frankfurt am Main: Suhrkamp, 1977).
Schor, Naomi, "*Cartes Postales:* Representing Paris 1900," *Critical Inquiry* 18, no. 2 (Winter 1992): 188–244.
Schreiber, Jürgen, *Ein Maler aus Deutschland: Gerhard Richter, das Drama einer Familie* (Munich and Zurich: Pendo, 2005).
Schrödl, Barbara, *Das Bild des Künstlers und seiner Frauen: Beziehungen zwischen Kunstgeschichte und Populärkultur in Spielfilmen des Nationalsozialismus und der Nachkriegszeit* (Marburg: Jonas Verlag, 2004).
Schulte-Sasse, Linda, *Entertaining the Third Reich: Illusions of Wholeness in Nazi Cinema* (Durham, NC, and London: Duke University Press, 1996).
Schulz-Hoffmann, Carla, and Judith C. Weiss, eds., *Max Beckmann Retrospective* (St. Louis: Saint Louis Art Museum; Munich: Prestel Verlag, 1984).
Schuster, Peter-Klaus, ed., *Die 'Kunststadt' München: Nationalsozialismus und 'Entartete Kunst'* (Munich: Prestel Verlag, 1987).
———, ed., *George Grosz: Berlin–New York* (Berlin: Neue Nationalgalerie; Ars Nicolai, 1995).
Scobie, Alex, *Hitler's State Architecture: The Impact of Classical Antiquity,* CAA Monographs on the Fine Arts 55 (University Park and London: Pennsylvania State University Press, 1990).
Scribner, Charity, "Object, Relic, Fetish, Thing: Joseph Beuys and the Museum," *Critical Inquiry* 29 (Summer 2003): 334–649.
Segeberg, Harro, ed., *Mediale Mobilmachung I: Das Dritte Reich und der Film* (Munich: Wilhelm Fink, 2004).
Selz, Peter, *Max Beckmann: The Self-Portraits* (New York: Rizzoli, 1992).
———, *Max Beckmann* (New York, London, and Paris: Abbeville Press, 1996).
Silbermann, Alphons, and Manfred Stofters, *Auschwitz: Nie davon gehört? Erinnern und Vergessen in Deutschland* (Berlin: Rowohlt, 2000).
Simmons, Sherwin, "Grimaces on the Wall: Anti-

Bolshevist Posters and the Debate About Kitsch," *Design Issues* 14, no. 2 (Summer 1998): 16–41.

———, "Advertising Seizes Control of Life: Berlin Dada and the Power of Advertising," *Oxford Art Journal* 22, no. 1 (1999): 119–146.

Skrypzak, Joann, "Sporting Modernity: Artists and the Athletic Body in Germany, 1918–1934," in *In Sickness and in Health: Disease as Metaphor in Art and Popular Wisdom*, ed. Laurinda S. Dixon, with Gabriel Weisberg (Newark: University of Delaware Press, 2004).

Skulptur und Macht: Figurative Plastik im Deutschland der 30er und 40er Jahre (Berlin: Akademie der Künste, 1983).

Soussloff, Catherine, *Jewish Identity in Modern Art History* (Berkeley and Los Angeles: University of California Press, 1998).

———, *The Subject in Art: Portraiture and the Birth of the Modern* (Durham, NC, and London: Duke University Press, 2006).

Spieler, Reinhard, *Max Beckmann: Bildwelt und Weltbild in den Triptychen* (Cologne: DuMont, 1998).

Stachelhaus, Heiner, *Joseph Beuys* (Düsseldorf: Claasen, 1987).

———, *Joseph Beuys*, trans. David Britt (New York, London, and Paris: Abbeville, 1991).

Staeck, Klaus, ed., *Nazi Kunst ins Museum?* (Göttingen: Steidl, 1988).

Staiger, Janet, *Interpreting Films: Studies in the Historical Reception of American Cinema* (Princeton, NJ: Princeton University Press, 1992).

———, *Perverse Spectators: The Practices of Film Reception* (New York and London: New York University Press, 2000).

Stationen der Moderne: Die bedeutenden Kunstausstellungen des 20. Jahrhunderts in Deutschland (Berlin: Berlinische Galerie; Nicolai, 1988).

Steinberg, Leo, *Other Criteria: Confrontations with Twentieth-Century Art* (New York: Oxford University Press, 1972).

Steinweis, Alan, E., *Art, Ideology, and Economics in Nazi Germany* (Chapel Hill and London: University of North Carolina Press, 1993).

Stercken, Angela, "Der Rächer mit neuem Kopf: Arno Brekers Akte," in *Sprachformen des Körpers in Kunst und Wissenschaft*, ed. Gabriele Genge (Tübingen and Basel: A. Francke, 2000), 75–94.

Stih, Renata, and Frieder Schnock, *Berlin Messages* (Fort Lauderdale, FL: Fort Lauderdale Museum of Art, 2005).

Stokes, Charlottte, and Stephen C. Foster, eds., *Dada: Cologne Hanover*, vol. 3 of *Crisis and the Arts the History of Dada*, ed. Stephen C. Foster (New York: G. K. Hall and Co., 1997).

Storr, Robert, *Gerhard Richter: October 18, 1977* (New York: Museum of Modern Art, 2000).

———, *Gerhard Richter: Forty Years of Painting* (New York: MoMA, 2002).

Straus-Ernst, Luise, "Der Bildhauer Arno Breker," *Die Kunst für Alle* 44 (1928–29): 370–375.

Tatar, Maria, *Lustmord: Sexual Murder in Weimar Germany* (Princeton, NJ, and Oxford: Princeton University Press, 1997).

Taylor, Brandon, *Collage* (London: Thames and Hudson, 2004).

———, and Wilfried van der Will, eds., *The Nazification of Art: Art, Design, Music, Architecture and Film in the Third Reich* (Winchester, England: Winchester Press, 1999).

Taylor, Seth, *Left-Wing Nietzscheans: The Politics of German Expressionism, 1910–1920* (Berlin and New York: Walter de Gruyter, 1990).

Theewen, Gerhard, *Joseph Beuys: Die Vitrinen, ein Verzeichnis* (Cologne: Walther König, 1993).

Theweleit, Klaus, *Männerphantasien*, vol. 2 (Reinbek: Rowohlt, 1980).

Tisdall, Caroline, *Joseph Beuys* (New York: Solomon R. Guggenheim Museum; London: Thames and Hudson, 1979).

Tomasevski, Boris, "Literature and Biography," in *Readings in Russian Poetics: Formalist and Structuralist Views*, ed. Ladislav Matejka and Krystyna Pomorska (Cambridge, MA: MIT Press, 1971), 47–55.

Tschauner, Ellie, "Benjamin Hecht macht in 'Kunst,'" *Filmwelt: Das Film- und Foto-Magazin* (Berlin) 16 (18 April 1941): 410–411.

Ursprung, Philip, *Grenzen der Kunst: Allan Kaprow und das Happening, Robert Smithson und die Land Art* (Munich: Verlag Silke Schreiber, 2003).

Usselmann, Rainer, "18. Oktober 1977: Gerhard Richter's Work of Mourning and Its New Audience," *Art Journal* (Spring 2002): 4–25.

Vitt, Walter, and Christoph Zuschlag, eds., *Der Fall Arno Breker: Ein Kritiker-Disput zur Schweriner Ausstellung 2006* (Nördlingen: Steinmeier, 2007).

Wagner, Monika, *Das Material der Kunst: Eine andere Geschichte der Moderne* (Munich: Beck, 2001).

Watts, Harriet, ed. *Dada and the Press*, vol. 9 of *Crisis and the Arts the History of Dada*, ed. Stephen C. Foster (Farmington Hills, MI: G. K. Hall and Co., 2004).

Wedel, Michael, "Jüngst wiederaufgetaucht—damals untergegangen: Anmerkungen zur Wiederentdeckung des Titanic-Films *In Nacht und Eis* (D 1912)," *Filmblatt* 6 (Winter 1997[/98]): 41–45.
———, "Misus Mirakel: Eine transatlantische Karriere, eine transatlantische Kontroverse," *KINtopp* 10 (15 November 2002): 73–87.
———, "Early German Cinema and the Modern Media Event: Mime Misu's *Titanic—In Night and Ice* (1912)," in *The Titanic in Myth and Memory: Representations in Visual and Literary Culture*, ed. Tim Bergfelder and Sarah Street (London and New York: I. B. Tauris, 2004).
Weinstein, Joan, *The End of Expressionism: Art and the November Revolution in Germany, 1918–1919* (Chicago and London: University of Chicago Press, 1990).
Welzer, Harald, Sabine Moller, and Karoline Tschuggnall, *"Opa war kein Nazi": Nationalsozialismus und Holocaust im Familiengedächtnis* (Frankfurt: Fischer, 2002).
Werckmeister, Otto Karl, *The Making of Paul Klee's Career: 1914–1920* (Chicago and London: University of Chicago Press, 1989).
———, *Linke Ikonen: Benjamin, Eisenstein, Picasso—nach dem Fall des Kommunismus* (Munich and Vienna: Carl Hanser, 1997).
Werner, Bruno E., *Die deutsche Plastik der Gegenwart* (Berlin: Rembrandt Verlag, 1940).
West, Shearer, *The Visual Arts in Germany, 1890–1917: Utopia and Despair* (New Brunswick, NJ: Rutgers University Press, 2001).
Westheider, Ortrud, *Die Farbe Schwarz in der Malerei Max Beckmanns* (Berlin: Reimer, 1995).
Westheim, Paul, *Kunstkritik aus dem Exil* (Hanau am Main: Müller und Kiepenheuer, 1985).
White, Michael, "Johannes Baader's *Plasto-Dio-Dada-Drama:* The Mysticism of the Mass Media," *Modernism/Modernity* 8, no. 4 (2001): 583–602.
———, "The Grosz Case: Paranoia, Self-hatred and Anti-Semitism," *Oxford Art Journal* 30, no. 3 (2007): 431–453.
Widerstand statt Anpassung: Deutsche Kunst gegen den Faschismus, 1933–1945 (Berlin: Elefanten Press; Karlsruhe: Badischer Kunstverein, 1980).
Wiedmer, Caroline, *The Claims of Memory: Representations of the Holocaust in Contemporary Germany and France* (Ithaca, NY, and London: Cornell University Press, 1999).
Willett, John, *Art and Politics in the Weimar Period* (New York: Pantheon, 1979).
Willi Baumeister, Sélection Notebook 11 (Antwerp: Sélection, 1931); also issued as *Baumeister,* Masters of Modern Art (New York, Columbia University, Institute of French Studies, 1931).
Willi Baumeister, 1945–1955 (Stuttgart: Württembergischer Kunstverein, 1979).
Willi Baumeister (Berlin: Nationalgalerie Staatliche Museen Preussischer Kulturbesitz, and Stuttgart: Edition Cantz, 1989).
Willi Baumeister: Zeichnungen, Gouachen, Collagen (Stuttgart: Edition Cantz, in association with Staatsgalerie Stuttgart, 1989).
Willi Baumeister et la France (Colmar: Musée d'Unterlinden, 1999).
Willi Baumeister 1889–1955: Die Frankfurter Jahre 1928–1933 (Frankfurt am Main: Museum Giersch, 2005).
Willi Baumeister: Figuren und Zeichen (Hamburg: Bucerius Kunst Forum, 2005).
Williams, Linda, ed., *Viewing Positions: Ways of Seeing Film* (New Brunswick, NJ: Rutgers University Press, 1994).
Wolfradt, Willi, *George Grosz,* Junge Kunst 21 (Leipzig: Klinkhardt and Biermann, 1921).
Wollheim, Richard, "Minimal Art," *On Art and the Mind* (Cambridge, MA: Harvard University Press, 1974), 101–111; first published in *Arts Magazine* (January 1965): 6–32.
Yates, Frances, *The Art of Memory* (Chicago: University of Chicago Press, 1966).
Young, James E., *Writing and Rewriting the Holocaust: Narrative and the Consequences of Interpretation* (Bloomington and Indianapolis: Indiana University Press, 1988).
———, *The Texture of Memory: Holocaust Memorials and Meaning* (New Haven, CT, and London: Yale University Press, 1993).
———, ed., *The Art of Memory: Holocaust Memorials in History* (New York: The Jewish Museum; Munich: Prestel Verlag, 1994).
Zelizer, Barbie, ed., *Visual Culture and the Holocaust* (New Brunswick, NJ: Rutgers University Press, 2001).
Zuschlag, Christoph, *"Entartete Kunst": Ausstellungsstrategien im Nazi-Deutschland* (Worms: Wernersche Verlagsgesellschaft, 1995).
Zweite, Armin, *7 Vorträge zu Joseph Beuys: 1986* (Mönchengladbach: Museumsverein, 1986).
———, *Joseph Beuys: Natur, Materie, Form* (Munich: Schirmer; Mosel, 1991).

Illustrations

Index

Page numbers in italics refer to illustrations.

DESIGNER: Nola Burger
TEXT: 9.5/14 Scala
DISPLAY: Berthold Akzidenz Grotesk, Berthold Akzidenz Grotesk Condensed
INDEXER: Andrew Joron
COMPOSITOR: Integrated Composition Systems
PRINTER AND BINDER: Thomson-Shore, Inc.